Strategic Financial Management

Applications of Corporate Finance

Samuel C. Weaver

Lehigh University, Bethlehem

J. Fred Weston

University of California, Los Angeles

THOMSON
™

Australia · Brazil · Canada · Mexico · Singapore · Spain · United Kingdom · United States

THOMSON

SOUTH-WESTERN

Strategic Financial Management: Applications of Corporate Finance, First Edition
Samuel C. Weaver, J. Fred Weston

VP/Editorial Director:
Jack W. Calhoun

Editor-in-Chief:
Alex von Rosenberg

Executive Editor:
Mike Reynolds

Senior Developmental Editor:
Elizabeth Thomson

Marketing Manager:
Jason Krall

**Senior Marketing
Communications Manger:**
Jim Overly

Content Project Manager:
Patrick Cosgrove

Manager, Editorial Media:
John Barans

Senior Technology Project Manager:
Matt McKinney

Senior Manufacturing Coordinator:
Sandee Milewski

Production House:
Graphic World, Inc.

Compositor:
International Typesetting &
Composition

Printer:
Transcontinental
Louiseville-Quebec, Canada

Art Director:
Bethany Casey

Internal Designer:
C Miller Design

Cover Designer:
C Miller Design

Cover Image:
Veer, Inc.

Library of Congress Control
Number: 2006939301

For more information about
our products, contact us at:

Thomson Learning Academic
Resource Center

1-800-423-0563

Thomson Higher Education
5191 Natorp Boulevard
Mason, OH 45040
USA

brief contents

contents

CHAPTER 6
Risk, Return, and Equity Valuation   168

Perpetual Cash Flows   169
Two-Stage Supernormal Growth Model   170
Return and Risk Measures   172
Measuring Annual Returns   173
Prospective Risk and Return   174
Capital Asset Pricing Model (CAPM)   176
The Security Market Line   176
Beta Measures of Risk   177
The Market Price of Risk   179
Risk Reduction by Portfolio Diversification   180
Measurement of Equity Betas   181
Variation of Betas across Industries   182

Part 3
Financial Analysis, Planning, and Control   190

CHAPTER 7
Financial Performance Metrics   193

Comparative Basis Standards   195
Basic Financial Statement Analysis   199
Financial Ratio Analysis   201
Financial Ratios and Metrics   202
Liquidity Metrics   202
Activity Metrics   206
Leverage Metrics   208
Profitability Metrics   212
Return on Investment   213

Investment Base: Time Frame   215
Normalized Income   216
Market-Related Metrics   217
Other Ratios and Metrics   221
DuPont Ratio Analysis   221
A System of Metrics   222

Thomson One Financial Data Base   225

CHAPTER 8
Working Capital Management   243

Overview of Working Capital Management   244
The Firm's Operating and Cash Cycles   246
Cash and Marketable Securities   248
Cash Budgets   248
Overview of Cash Budgets   248

Reasons for Holding Cash   252
Marketable Securities   254

Accounts Receivable Management Policies and Practices   256
Credit Background and Assessment   256
Credit Analysis   257
Accounts Receivable Monitoring   259
Monitoring Accounts Receivable   259
Accounts Receivable Collection   259

Inventory Management   261
Controlling Investments in Inventories   262
Enterprise Resource Planning Systems   262
Inventory Management and Value Chain Reengineering   263

Short-Term Financing   264
Financing Current and Fixed Assets   264
Trade Credit   265
Short-term Financing by Commercial Banks   266
Short-term Financing Using Commercial Paper   270
Secured Short-term Financing   270

CHAPTER 9
Strategic Financial Planning (Financial Forecasting and Control)   281

Overview of Strategic Planning   282
Approaches to Strategy   282
Proven Technique   282
Strategic Planning Structure   284

Financial Planning and Control Processes   285
Basic Financial Forecasts   287
Simple Financial Model—% of Sales   288
External Funds Needed   290
Simple Integrated Financial Plan   291

Forecasting Financial Statements   293
Establishing the Financial Forecast Framework   293
Strategic Objectives and Performance Standards   294
Income Statement Objectives and Assumptions   294
Balance Sheet Objectives and Assumptions   303
Cash Flow Objectives and Assumptions   303
Calculating the Financial Statements   304

Financial Statement Summary   307
Performance Objectives   307
Alternative Scenarios   309

Corporate finance is a middle ground between economics and accounting. Corporate finance is based on theoretical, economic concepts applied to the "hard" numbers developed by accountants. It uses accounting to analyze economic events. In a phrase, finance is applied economics. While accounting is the language of business, finance provides a conceptual framework for analysis.

Financial implications are at the heart of every business decision, strategy, and transaction. Finance is not an end in and of itself. It is a tool used to monitor, communicate, and evaluate the results of business decisions. It is a tool used to assess past events as well as anticipate the consequences of future decisions. It is a tool well-suited for the board room as well as the production shop floor; from the executive suite to the distribution center; from corporate and divisional staff offices to a distant sales office. Improving financial performance is the responsibility of every member of the organization, either directly or indirectly.

In order to take on a general management role or to become the head of a business unit or functional unit, every manager must have a working knowledge of finance. They must be adaptive in improving day-to-day operations and enhancing the value of the organization. Managers must know how to make strategic investment decisions as well as operational decisions that use the many tools introduced and illustrated in this text.

Large corporations have specific staff to handle financial analysis and to help managers make business decisions. In many organizations, diverse, cross-functional project teams are formed to tackle specific objectives. These teams may include members from sales, marketing, research, production, and logistics. These teams will often include a finance professional to help lead and guide the group's efforts to financially sound decisions. It is important for each functional area to better understand the role of finance and for finance to understand the role of the other functional areas as well as the business model, its supply chain, and its strategic direction.

In smaller organizations, it is even more important for functional areas to understand finance and financial implications because often there is no dedicated financial analysis staff to assume responsibility.

The non-financial professional as well as the financial professional must be able to understand and clearly communicate financial results and objectives. A number of specific topics must be commonly understood by everyone in business. Whether you are in engineering, marketing, sales, logistics, human resources, research, legal, general management or another area, the necessary topics to be a more proactive member of any business team include:

- Reading and understanding financial statements.

- Analyzing financial statements to determine the financial health of a company and its competitors, suppliers, and customers.

- Planning the financial direction in support of the organization's mission, goals, and objectives.

- Investing in the business through new products, new facilities, and cost savings equipment.

- Financing business growth through various techniques.

- Growing the business via acquisitions and the role that all professionals need to play.

Many members of an organization have bonuses and other compensation tied to achieving certain specific financial goals as well as organization's common financial objectives. It is important to understand the drivers for attaining those goals as well as the other areas that are impacted.

For example, sales and marketing often share an objective centered on top line (sales) growth. This objective can easily be achieved with price reductions, advertising, or promotions (such as a buy one get one free), etc. Of course, all of those "solutions" have income and cash flow impacts that may negatively impact the financial health of the organization. By extending the objectives for the sales and marketing group to include sales and income targets, the situation is partially resolved. However, sales and marketing will quickly learn about extended dating on accounts receivables. That is, instead of 30 days for a customer to pay its bills, customers are given 60 or more days to pay. While there are only minimal indirect income statement impacts (i.e., lost interest income), the balance sheet implications and additional investment in working capital adds pressure to financing availability and may even result in less business reinvestment through capital expenditures.

Engineering, production, logistics, and research may want the latest equipment with the fastest capabilities and highest product output quality produced in a start-of-the-art manufacturing facility. However, the financial implications must be understood. Financing limitations may be imposed, balance sheets may be weakened, and business risk may substantially increase. Perhaps, a less expensive alternative will provide maximum shareholder value without discernibly impacting the quality of the product. Capital investment analysis determines the value enhancement attributes of any capital project while financial strategic planning anticipates the financial impact and assists in ranking alternative approaches.

Business is a series of managed conflicts. Marketing and sales want to sell an infinite variety of products while production would like to produce one product. The conflicts can be resolved through financial information and its valuation impact. It is the systematic and common approach that leads to successfully resolving these tensions. Finance provides a common focus on goal attainment and value enhancement.

The Audience

This text is targeted for the introductory corporate finance course. It is primarily directed to the MBA or Executive MBA student with limited financial background. The targeted student might only take one finance course in their MBA program. They may choose to concentrate in areas such as marketing, strategy, human resources, general management, or a variety of courses leading to a general MBA. Some executives have had no formal training in finance. With that in mind, this text centers on the critical financial topics about which every business person should be familiar.

The uniqueness of the book is the combined collaboration of Professors Weston and Weaver who believe that finance is a tool and not an end to itself. Real world examples and discussions about familiar business topics provide comforting links to finance and business for the MBA student. For example, some engineers and other professionals are familiar with capital budgeting from the technical side, but do not understand the financial aspects of the process. Through this text, that gap will be closed, and the student will appreciate the financial rationale for capital investment analysis.

Instructors who will find this text most useful include those who:

- Teach a finance foundation or core course,

- Teach in an MBA program that has a significant number of experienced business professionals,

- Teach primarily MBA students that were not undergraduate finance majors.

An instructor, who recognizes that functional silos are being replaced in Corporate America, will also be attracted to this text.

The MBA or Executive MBA student who works in the finance function and who is required to take an introductory finance course will also benefit from this text. These students may find this text helpful for:

- Solidifying key financial concepts

- Developing additional financial topics

- Discussing key concepts with non-financial professionals

- Identifying immediately applicable concepts

- Considering the role of the finance function

The financially oriented MBA or Executive MBA will see finance in a broader role and will have the required background to take more advanced finance courses. In short, the targeted audience is a professional who is taking an introductory finance course.

Additionally, due to the integrative nature of this text, this may be appropriate for the undergraduate student whose instructor wants to concentrate on the critical business aspects encountered in finance or as a supplemental text for a common basis within an advanced topics undergraduate course.

The Text

The aim of this book is to explain the procedures, practices, and policies by which accounting and financial management can contribute to the successful performance of organizations. Our emphasis is on strategies involved in the tradeoffs between risk and return in seeking to make decisions that will increase the value of the firm. Each subsequent topic is treated within this basic framework.

The central function of finance is to interact with other managers to continuously improve the performance of the organization so that value grows. Finance participates in the evaluation of alternative strategies and policies. It is equally important for the professional to be able to interact with the financial manager by understanding and speaking the same language. The subjects of this book are useful for all managers, analysts, and others seeking to understand how value is created and organization performance is improved.

This text provides a clear, practical approach to corporate finance. We follow a "matter of fact" style when presenting and discussing the material. After we build the foundation, we amplify the material with appropriate considerations and "real world" applications.

The Hershey Company is used throughout the text for illustrative purposes. Hershey is a financially sound company whose products are familiar and easy to understand. The financial and business issues that Hershey faces are faced by every company. Hershey is a highly ethical firm that never had any accounting issues. In addition, its website (Hersheys.com) provides a wealth of financial information including annual and quarterly reports, SEC filings, audio versions of earnings release conference calls, and complete investment analyst presentations. Some investment analyst presentations last more than 3 hours. The website includes the presentation slides and audio review by Hershey's senior management team. The website, also, makes available video clips of the chocolate making process which makes the capital budgeting discussion more tangible. The chapters logically develop an analysis and valuation of The Hershey Company augmented with appropriate background topical material through out the text.

The food industry provides a valuable background for comparative financial perform-ance with a "real world" presentation and feel. Other companies supplement the Hershey and food industry illustrations where appropriate, such as Dell and Wal-Mart.

The chapters logically develop an analysis and valuation of The Hershey Company aug-mented with appropriate background topical material through out the text. For example:

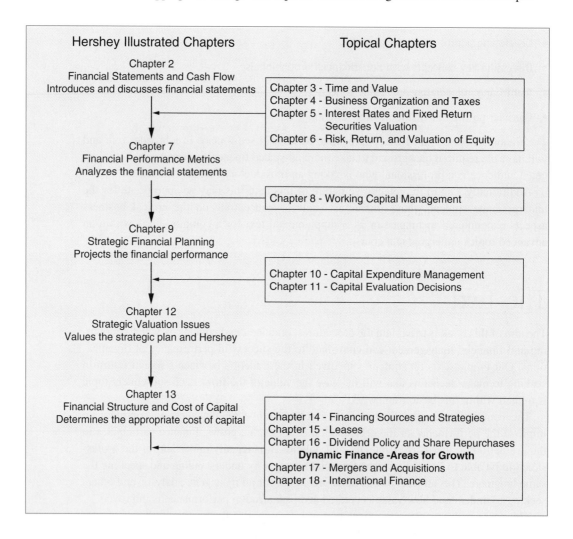

There are numerous specific examples through out the text. Three specific examples capture the distinctive essence of this text:

Financial Statement Analysis After reviewing Hershey's financial statements in Chapter 2 and building required fundamentals in Chapters 3-6, Chapter 7 begins with sim-plistic size, annual growth, and compound annual growth rates which are illustrated using graphs and compared to a self-constructed food processing industry. Then simplistic analysis follows on just Hershey itself. This demonstrates common size statements, growth, and indexed values (or common base year). After that, Hershey and Heinz are compared for 2000 and 2005 using financial performance metrics (or financial ratios). The metrics are "matter of factly" presented and interpreted. Ultimately, the DuPont approach to metrics is introduced as a method of systematically organizing any presentation or beginning any financial statement analysis.

Strategic Financial Planning and Valuation Chapter 9 briefly integrates strategy assessment into financial planning and presents simple financial planning models (e.g., external funds needed or percent of sales methods). Although these techniques are not generally used in practice, the underlying thought process of these approaches is important to understand. Based on that, we develop a more realistic approach to financial planning. This approach incorporates projected growth rates, margins, turnovers, capital investment, financing considerations, etc.

After discussing capital evaluation, Chapter 12 revisits the strategic financial plan, focuses on operating cash flows (excluding financing cash flows), estimates a cost of capital and residual value, and values Hershey based on the projections made in Chapter 9. Of course other simplistic models are also covered in Chapter 12.

Capital Investment Management Chapters 10 and 11 discuss the capital budgeting criteria such as net present value, internal rate of return, etc. as well as the development of cash flows, but we also include a discussion of the four phases of capital investment: planning, evaluation and authorization, status reporting, and post completion reviews. These terms are common to the process of capital investment and help any professional who has been involved with capital expenditures to relate to these chapters and the techniques.

In addition, the text includes "Survey of Practice" inserts. Practitioners and other students look for validation of the underlying techniques presented in a text. It helps to embellish and solidify the approaches. Consequently, where appropriate, survey summaries are included.

Organization of This Book

The text is organized into six major sections:

PART	TOPICS	CHAPTERS
1	Accounting and finance fundamentals	1, 2, 3, 4
2	Financial environment and valuation analysis	5, 6
3	Financial analysis, planning, and control	7, 8, 9,
4	Investment strategies and decisions	10, 11, 12
5	Financial policy	13, 14, 15, 16
6	Growth strategies for increasing value	17, 18

Part 1 establishes required accounting and finance fundamentals.

CHAPTER	TOPICS
1	The role of accounting and finance
2	Financial statements and cash flows
3	Time and value
4	Business organization and taxes

Chapter 1 discusses the goals of firms and the role of financial concepts in value creation. The responsibilities of effective corporate governance in achieving organization goals are set forth. Chapter 2 explains the information that can be developed from accounting and financial statements. Chapter 3 explains why time is money—it is more valuable to have cash today than to wait years to receive it. Firms make investments now in order to receive cash flows in future years. It is crucial to determine the cumulative values of past, present, and future cash flows. The foundation for valuations is thereby established. Chapter 4 describes the rules of the game under which firms are organized and operate. It discusses alternative forms of business organization that a firm may use and the important tax laws that impact financing alternatives.

Part 2 describes the financial environments within which business firms operate.

CHAPTER	TOPICS
5	Interest rates and fixed return securities valuation
6	Risk, return, and the valuation of equities

Chapter 5 summarizes the fundamental characteristics of financial markets which financial managers must understand in order to develop sound policies and decisions. Using this background, the valuation of securities with fixed returns (for example, bonds) is described. The focus of chapter 6 is an overview of equity valuation in the context of risk and reward relationships.

Part 3, Financial Performance Analysis, Planning and Control sets forth the noted topics.

CHAPTER	TOPICS
7	Financial performance metrics
8	Working capital management
9	Strategic financial planning

In Chapter 7, we describe financial performance metrics which employ financial ratios analysis and related measures. Chapter 8 discusses the management of working capital—both operating and financial working capital. Chapter 9 on strategic financial planning discusses long-term financial forecasting which can be used to set performance standards, determine management compensation goals, and anticipate future financing requirements. The strategic plan and its operating cash flows form the basis for the valuation of the firm.

Part 4 deals with investment strategies and decisions with respect to all aspects of the left hand (assets) side of the balance sheet. Its emphasis is on economizing the use of economic resources for the purpose of creating value.

CHAPTER	TOPICS
10	Capital expenditure management and alternative investment criteria
11	Capital investment decisions
12	Strategic valuation issues

Chapter 10 develops criteria for making decisions of whether to accept or reject investment proposals. Chapter 11 discusses the measurement of cash flows relevant for capital budgeting decisions. Chapter 12 discusses how the intrinsic value of an investment or enterprise can be determined. It explains the dominant approach to valuation, which is the discounted cash flow (DCF) analysis while also sensitizing the reader to the latest tool, real options. Considering optionality in capital investments stimulates decision makers to design flexibility into projects resulting in increased valuations.

Part 5 turns to the right-hand side of the balance sheet. It discusses decisions with regard to the forms and sources of financing which minimize the cost of capital.

CHAPTER	TOPICS
13	Financial structure and cost of capital
14	Financing sources and strategies
15	Leases
16	Dividend policy and share repurchase

Chapter 13 analyzes financial structure decisions with respect to the mix of equity and debt financing sources employed. Chapter 14 presents financing sources, procedures for obtaining long-term financing, and specific forms of long-term financing. Chapter 15 describes the role of leasing as a financing source. Chapter 16 discusses how dividend policy, share repurchases, and other methods of returning funds to investors may affect valuation.

Part 6 presents a financial perspective on growth strategies for increasing the firm's value.

CHAPTER	TOPICS
17	Mergers and acquisitions
18	International financial management

Chapter 17 discusses how mergers and other intercorporate relationships may increase or destroy value and applies the valuation concepts to merger decisions. Chapter 18 builds a solid theoretical background in the dynamics of international finance—exchange rates, inflation rates, interest rates.

We see central conceptual threads as well as applications running through the many topics of this text. We convey the interrelationships more fully in the individual chapters.

Financial Concepts

In this text we developed the important financial concepts that enable all managers to contribute to value creation. We summarize by chapter what we learn from finance.

Chapter 1—The Role of Accounting and Finance. Financial managers and financial decisions seek to improve the strategies and performance of organizations to create value.

Chapter 2—Financial Statements and Cash Flow. Financial statements provide a score card to mirror business reality.

Chapter 3—Time and Value. The timing of cash flows greatly impact value analysis. A dollar received today is worth more than a dollar received some time later.

Chapter 4—Business Organization and Taxes. Choices of business organization forms influence tax costs and operating effectiveness.

Chapter 5—Interest Rates and Fixed Return Securities Valuation. Debt values are influenced by the maturity patterns of debt obligations and of asset holdings.

Chapter 6—Risk, Return, and Valuation of Equities. The valuation of equity securities requires analysis of risk and return relations illustrated by the capital asset pricing model.

Chapter 7—Financial Performance Metrics. (a) Inadequate equity will cause debt ratios to be high and risky. (b) Poor management of asset resources will cause profit and valuation ratios to be low.

Chapter 8—Working Capital Management. (a) Inadequate liquidity can cause financial disruptions. (b) As sales grow, the required investments in receivables and inventories will represent long term holdings which require long term financing.

Chapter 9—Strategic Financial Planning. Strategic long term planning processes are required for sound strategies and operations.

Chapter 10—Capital Expenditure Management and Alternative Investment Criteria. Capital expenditure (CAPEX) decisions require identification of the relevant investment criteria and cash flows.

Chapter 11—Capital Investment Decisions. (a) The net present value (NPV) rule states that a project's value is determined by discounting its net cash inflows at their opportunity cost of capital. (b) The opportunity cost of capital is the expected return on assets or securities of equivalent risks.

Chapter 12—Strategic Valuation Issues. The value of a firm is the cumulative sum of the NPV investments it has made.

Chapter 13—Financial Structure and the Cost of Capital. (a) The use of debt has tax benefits, but excessive use of debt increases risks of financial distress. (b) Cost of capital minimization and firm value maximization require balancing debt to equity ratios to the operating characteristics of a firm or project including its future revenue growth patterns.

Chapter 14—Financing Sources and Strategies. The wide range of financing sources and instruments requires balancing costs, risks, and availability considerations.

Chapter 15—Leases. The leasing vs borrow-and-own decision is determined by the relative costs of capital of lessors vs lessees.

Chapter 16—Dividend Policy and Share Repurchases. Payout policy is determined by a firm's stage in its life cycle. High growth is associated with earnings retention, lower growth with maturity and requires payouts to investors.

Chapter 17—Mergers and Acquisitions. Sound mergers require analysis of premiums paid and costs of integration to the increases in revenues and cost reductions achieved by the combining entities.

Chapter 18—International Financial Management. The choice of the location of international financing is determined by a balancing of borrowing costs vs the differential between forward and spot exchange rates in domestic vs foreign markets.

Ancillary Material

Strategic Financial Planning: Applications of Corporate Finance has a series of supportive ancillary material designed to enhance the experience for both the student and the instructor. All material was directly written and developed by the authors which ensures a consistent use of terminology and presentation:

1. Solutions Manual: The comprehensive solutions manual includes answers to all end of chapter questions and problems. Many of the solutions are illustrated to help the student better understand the process involved with solving the problem. All of these illustrations can be used as PowerPoint slides.

2. PowerPoint Slides: Professional PowerPoint slides have been developed and are suitable for class room use or distribution to students as relevant chapter notes. These slides are available on the book's Web site: http://www.thomsonedu.com/finance/weaver for each chapter. The slides can be modified, deleted, or supplemented as the instructor sees fit.

3. Test Bank: The test bank offers a variety of questions and problems. Since, all questions and problems are author written, this assures consistent use of terms as well as approaches that test the student's ability to comprehend the material and perform the underlying financial work. Through the use of Thomson technology, an endless supply of problems (and answers) can be generated.

4. Excel Spreadsheets: For each chapter the authors have developed several different Excel spreadsheets that can be distributed to students or not. The spreadsheets are available on the book's Web site at: http://www.thomsonedu.com/finance/weaver

5. Thomson One—Business School Edition: The Thomson One—Business School Edition is a financial data source provided with the text. This data base is an excellent tool for students to use in order to dive into financial information for a company or group of companies. It contains information from the income statement, balance sheet, and cash flow statement as well as financial performance metrics. It is a valuable tool that the instructor can incorporate at many levels into their course and into student assignments. Illustrative problems are incorporated in the end of chapter problems for Chapters 2 and 7. They can be assigned as home work or discussed in class.

Acknowledgments

We have a number of people to thank for their efforts in making this text a reality. First thank you to our team of professionals at Thomson South-Western (Business & Economics) Publishing lead by Elizabeth R. Thomson, Senior Developmental Editor, and Michael R. Reynolds, Executive Editor—Finance.

We would also like to thank our reviewers:

H. Kent Baker
University Professor of Finance,
American University, Kogod School of Business

Maclyn L. Clouse
Professor of Finance and Director of the Reiman School of Finance
University of Denver, Daniels College of Business

Vance P. Lesseig,
Arthur G. Vieth
Assistant Professor of Finance, University of Tennessee at Chattanooga,
College of Business Administration

Stuart Michelson,
Professor of Finance
Stetson University, School of Business Administration

Emery Trahan
Professor of Finance
Northeastern University, College of Business Administration

Their advice, guidance, and suggestions helped to streamline and further shape this text.

Our efforts were also supported by many dedicated professionals and students who helped us with the manuscript along the way. A special thank you to the efforts of Juan A. Siu, Senior Research Analyst, Weston Research Institute, University of California, Los Angeles, The Anderson School. Juan provided tireless effort and support throughout this process. Kenneth Ahern, a doctoral student at UCLA, interacted on conceptual issues throughout the book.

Also, we would like to thank Celene Hadeed and Swati Mehta of Lehigh University for their attention to the details as they reviewed many areas of the manuscript and ancillary material.

Dr. Weaver thanks his colleagues at Lehigh University, College of Business and Economics, Perella Department of Finance, for direct and indirect contributions to this text. My colleagues include: Anne-Marie Anderson, Stephen G. Buell, James A. Greenleaf, Richard J. Kish, David H. Myers, Nandu Nayar, Stephen F. Thode, and Geraldo M. Vasconcellos. He also thanks his graduate and undergraduate classes for their input into the manuscript. They have successfully used much of this material over the past two years. There is no substitute for a student's reading of the material along with their willingness to make useful suggestions. We are blessed with such students who helped to refine difficult passages, improve PowerPoint slides, and detect any errors.

Dr. Weston also thanks his colleagues and students at the Anderson School at UCLA.

Errors in the Text

Despite our best, diligent efforts, there will always be errors or opportunities to improve this text and the other material. We welcome any suggestions from readers. We accept responsibility for any errors.

Conclusion

This text is the outgrowth of our never ending love affair with our chosen avocation, Corporate Finance. Finance is a discipline that moves business domestically and internationally. The material in this text is essential for anyone who wants to be involved in business. It is as important to the entrepreneur as it is to the Chief Executive Officers of the Fortune 500 companies. But the implications of finance do not stop "at the end of the day." Many of the financial principles are directly applicable to personal life as well.

This text embodies our collective years of teaching undergraduate and MBA students as well as executives. Many now lead successful firms and world class organizations. Our outstanding financial graduate students have advanced the finance profession in important directions. The text also captures the unspoiled naivety that undergraduate finance students bring to the subject. By leading extensive executive education workshops, this work also takes on a focused professional tone that is augmented with years of real world experience and consulting practice. Finally, our research ensures a book true to the latest theoretical and applied research.

We truly hope that *Strategic Financial Management: Applications of Corporate Finance* will help you and your students to appreciate the financial challenges and opportunities faced in today's business world. We know that through this text we have identified helpful and useful approaches to address those opportunities.

Samuel C. Weaver
Swartley Professor of Finance
Perella Department of Finance
Lehigh University
Rauch Business Center
621 Taylor Street
Bethlehem, PA 18015
scw0@lehigh.edu
Phone: (610) 758-5282
website: www.lehigh.edu/~incbeug/faculty/SamWeaver.htm

J. Fred Weston
Distinguished Professor of Finance, Emeritus
Recalled
University of California, Los Angeles
The Anderson School
258 Tavistock Ave.
Los Angeles, CA 90049-3229
jweston@anderson.ucla.edu
Phone: (310) 472-5110
website: www.anderson.ucla.edu/faculty/john.weston

February 2007

The Authors

Samuel C. Weaver is the Swartley Professor of Finance at Lehigh University. Prior to joining Lehigh on a full-time basis in 1998, Dr. Weaver was the Director of Financial Planning and Analysis at The Hershey Company both on a corporate level and divisional level. Dr. Weaver was on the frontline of financial analysis and was responsible for mergers and acquisition valuation, divestitures, strategic planning, industry analysis, capital budgeting, cost of capital studies, working capital recommendations, financing approaches, lease policy, dividend recommendations and other special analysis as required. While at Hershey, he worked with many senior managers and others to better understand financial concepts and approaches. This included several multiple day workshops designed for Hershey professionals.

In addition, Dr. Weaver was an adjunct instructor teaching the introductory corporate finance course at Lehigh for twelve years prior to joining the staff on a full time basis. He won the Outstanding MBA Professor of the Year in 1999 and 2002. Dr. Weaver leads many executive education workshops on accounting and finance directed at the non-financial professional. He works with senior executives on a one-on-one basis as well.

J. Fred Weston is Professor Emeritus Recalled of Managerial Economics and Finance at the John E. Anderson Graduate School of Management at UCLA. He received his Ph.D. degree from the University of Chicago in 1948. He has published 33 books, 152 journal articles, and chaired 32 doctoral dissertations. Since 1968 he has been Director of the UCLA Research Program on Takeovers and Restructuring.

Dr. Weston has served as President of the American Finance Association, President of the Western Economic Association, President of the Financial Management Association, and as a member of the American Economic Association U.S. Census Advisory Committee. In 1978, he was selected as one of five outstanding teachers on the UCLA campus. In 1994, he received the Dean's Award for Outstanding Instruction in the Anderson School at UCLA. He has been an associate editor on a number of journals. He has been selected as a Fellow of the American Finance Association, of the Financial Management Association, and of the National Association of Business Economists.

He has been a consultant to business firms and governments on financial and economic policies since the early 1950's. Professor Weston has held professional consulting assignments with many Fortune 100 corporations and numerous international financial institutions. He also is a recognized international expert in the area of Mergers and Acquisitions and conducted and continues to be involved with the UCLA Merger and Acquisition Executive

Program that attracts senior managers from the Fortune 500 companies, both domestically and internationally.

Both Dr. Weaver and Weston understand the language of business and how to effectively communicate with the non-financial professionals. Their collaboration provides an appealing bridge between theory and practice and between the classroom and practice.

Samuel C. Weaver thanks his wife Kerry for her support and patience, as well as the inspiration that his children and their families always provide: Derek and Andrea Weaver; Justin, Jennifer, and Sebastien Weaver; and John and Kristine Seasholtz.

J. Fred Weston thanks his wife Bernadine for her inspiration as well as his children and their families for their stimulation: Kenneth, Edward and Alexander; Byron; and Ellen.

Strategic
Financial
Management

part 1

Accounting and Finance Fundamentals

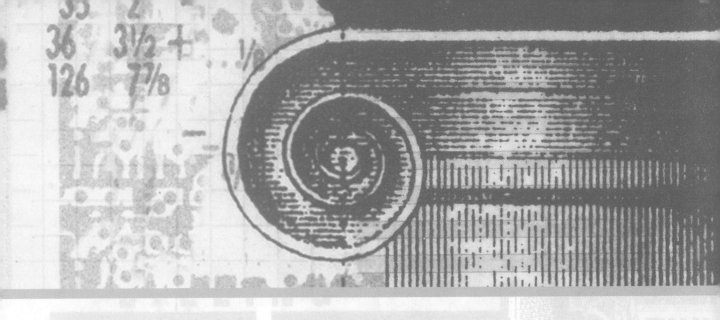

CONTENTS

CASH

CURRENCY

COIN

LIST CHECKS SINGLY

ILLING

COST OF CAPITAL

RESENT VALUE

NET DEPOSIT $

LESS CASH RECEIVED

13¾ +

7¾ + ⅛

2

3½ + ⅛

7⅞

THE UNITED

A 57928202 E

The Role of Accounting and Finance

Finance is the middle ground between theoretical economics and the accounting world of numbers. Finance is applied economics. From another view, while accounting is the language of business, finance is the literature. Financial implications are at the heart of every business transaction and decision.

Finance is not an end in and of itself. It is a tool, a most valuable tool used to communicate, judge, and monitor the results of business decisions. It is a tool well-suited for the boardroom as well as the shop floor; from the executive suite to the distribution center; from corporate and divisional staff offices to a distant sales office.

In order to rise to a general management role or to become the head of a business unit within an organization, every manager must be aware of accounting and finance. He or she must know how to make strategic investment decisions as well as operational decisions that use the many tools introduced and illustrated in this text. But the implications of finance do not stop "at the end of the day." Many of the financial principles are directly applicable to personal life as well.

Learning Outcomes

After completing this chapter, you should be able to:

1 Understand the roles and responsibilities of a financial manager

2 Discuss the financial manager's interaction with other areas of the corporation

3 Show how the financial manager is a business partner within the organization

4 Identify the value maximizing goal of the firm as the most important objective, but an objective that must be carefully balanced to meet the needs of a variety of stakeholders

5 Know the organization of this book

Integrity

With the numerous accounting scandals over the past few years and with all of the criticism faced by senior management teams, it seems fitting to begin with what we think are the most important critical elements of all of finance: honesty and integrity.

> *"If there is a hell I will be there for eternity." So reads a passage in the six-page "suicide note and confession" written by Daniel E. Marino, chief financial officer of the Bayou Group, a hedge fund firm in Stamford, Conn., that was accused by federal prosecutors on Sept. 1 of conducting a $300 million fraud."*[1]

The preceding quote is a cautionary tale. It provides a basis for the dominant theme for this book: ethical behavior. The number one requirement for a successful (financial) manager is absolute integrity. We argue more generally that integrity is necessary for personal happiness. The reason is that integrity is the right way to behave. Without integrity society does not function well. The efficient operation of market requires integrity. This is the strongest message of our book.

Finance in the Organizational Structure of the Firm

The nature of finance activities can be explained within the framework of where finance fits in the organization structure of the firm.

AN OVERVIEW

Figure 1.1 provides a picture of a general organizational structure of a firm. The board of directors represents the shareholders. The chairman of the board therefore has major responsibilities on behalf of the shareholders. The chief executive officer (CEO) is the highest ranking company employee. The CEO is involved with the strategic direction of the organization. Although the position is not shown on Figure 1.1, some corporations also have a chief operating officer (COO). The COO is responsible for the day-to-day operations. Often the title of "President" may be bestowed on either the CEO or COO, or it may not be used by the firm at all. Corporate governance authorities rate a company as having better organization when the chairman of the company and the president are separate individuals. This caused a number of companies during 2004 and 2005—Disney and Viacom, for example—to create presidential positions when formerly they had only chairman positions. Both Morningstar and Institutional Shareholder Services (ISS) publish ratings of companies on their governance. Morningstar has been publishing "stewardship grades" on its website (www.morningstar.com) since February 2005. ISS makes its corporate governance scores available on Yahoo. The firm covers 5,400 U.S. companies as well as an additional 1,700 companies in the rest of the world (*BusinessWeek*, June 13, 2005, pp. 86–87).

One of the top executives is the vice president of finance or chief financial officer (CFO), who is responsible for the formulation and implementation of major financial policies. The title may be enhanced with the title of "Senior" or "Executive Vice President." The CFO interacts with operating managers in other areas of the firm, and communicates the financial implications of alternative policies and decisions.

---

[1] The New York Times, September 17, 2005. Mr. Marino later decided not to commit suicide.

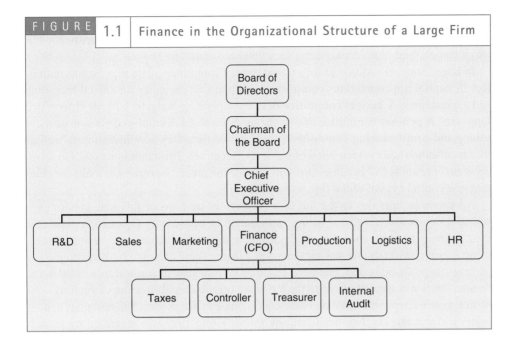

FIGURE 1.1   Finance in the Organizational Structure of a Large Firm

Some of the finance functions are performed by the controller and by the treasurer. Other functions such as the tax department and internal audit may also report to the CFO. Internal Audit may also report directly to the board of directors, chairperson, or CEO.

The **controller's** function includes accounting, reporting, and control. The controller's core function is the recording and reporting of financial information. This typically includes the preparation of financial statements and budgets. In fact, the controller is often referred to as the "Chief Accounting Officer" (CAO) of the firm. The controller may also be responsible for operational accounting functions such as accounts receivable, accounts payable, and payroll. In some firms, the controller has responsibility for internal audit.

Although the controller has the main financial accounting reporting responsibilities, the treasurer provides reports on the daily cash and working-capital position of the firm, formulates cash budgets, and generally reports on cash flow and cash conservation. The **treasurer** handles the acquisition and custody of funds. As a part of this role, the treasurer usually maintains the firm's relationships with commercial banks and investment bankers. The treasurer is also usually responsible for credit management, insurance, and pension fund management.

Some large firms include another corporate officer—the **corporate secretary**—whose activities are related to the finance function. The corporate secretary is responsible for record keeping in connection with the instruments of ownership and borrowing activities of the firm (e.g., stocks and bonds). The corporate secretary may have a legal training because the duties of that officer may also encompass legal affairs and recording of minutes of top-level committee meetings.

In addition to individual financial officers, larger enterprises use finance committees. Ideally, a committee assembles persons of different backgrounds and abilities to formulate policies and decisions. Financing decisions require a wide scope of knowledge and balanced judgments. For example, to obtain outside funds is a major decision. A difference of 0.25 or 0.50% in interest rates may represent a large amount of money in absolute terms. When such firms as IBM, Wal-Mart, or Kellogg borrow $600 million, a difference of 0.50% amounts to $3 million per year. Therefore, the judgments of senior managers with finance backgrounds are valuable in arriving at decisions with bankers on the timing and terms of a loan. Also, the finance committee, working closely with the board of directors, characteristically has major responsibility for administering the capital and operating budgets.

In larger firms, in addition to the general finance committee, there may be subcommittees. A **capital appropriations committee** is responsible primarily for capital budgeting and expenditures. A **budget committee** develops operating budgets, both short-term and long-term. A **pension committee** invests the funds involved in employee pension plans. A **salary and profit-sharing committee** is responsible for salary administration as well as the classification and compensation of top-level executives. This committee seeks to set up a system of rewards and penalties that will provide the proper incentives to make the planning and control system of the firm work effectively.

All important episodes in the life of a corporation have major financial implications: adding a new product line or reducing participation in an old one; expanding or adding a plant or changing locations; selling additional new securities; entering into leasing arrangements; paying dividends and making share repurchases. These decisions have a lasting effect on long-run profitability and, therefore, require top management consideration. Hence, the finance function is typically close to the top in the organizational structure of the firm.

In Figure 1.2, a product division basis (concentrated in like product business units or divisions) is dominant. The Hershey Company from 1976 to 1999 was organized by product

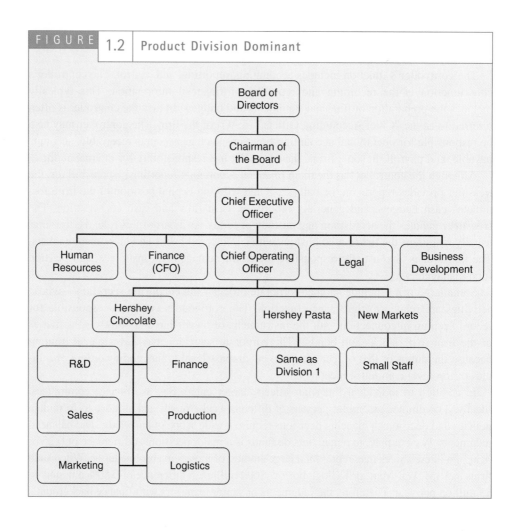

FIGURE 1.2 | Product Division Dominant

division. The CEO had a corporate staff that included the CFO's office, legal personnel, human resources, and business development. The COO also reported directly to the CEO. In this structure, the CFO's responsibilities were more strategic and less operational. The controller's office served more of a consolidating role, wherein each division's financial data were combined and consolidated with corporate items and then reported to the public.

In this structure, each division had its own vice president of finance who reported directly to the president of their division with "dotted" lines to the CFO. The division finance vice president was responsible for day-to-day transaction processing as well as advising the division's sales, marketing, production, and logistics functions.

During this period of time, Hershey had three major divisions: Hershey Chocolate, Hershey Pasta (under the brand names of San Giorgio, Ronzoni, American Beauty, and Skinner), and New Markets. Each product division had its own staff of functional vice presidents reporting to a division president. The division presidents reported to the COO. Using this framework, products can be developed and get to the market quickly. With tight budgetary control, corporate management can impose fiscal discipline. The drawback to this approach in an international market is that an individual country's product preferences may not be matched effectively.

An alternative approach is illustrated in Figure 1.3 with national organizations dominant; N.V. Philips is an example. The organization is in two major groups, corporate offices

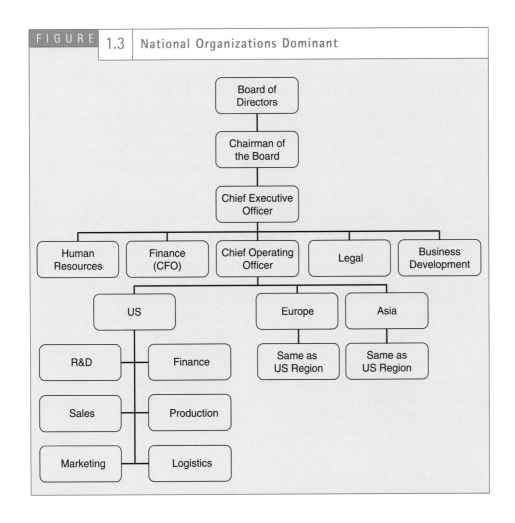

FIGURE 1.3   National Organizations Dominant

(human resources, CFO, legal, and business development) and international divisions. The geographic divisions are responsible for development, production, and global distribution so the cells below in the top three in Figure 1.1 are repeated under each geographic area. In theory, products are coordinated across national organizations. A potential problem with this organizational structure is that economies of scale may be lost by geographic dispersion of manufacturing activities; a strength is that there is greater responsiveness to individual country's preferences. However, because of the autonomy of national organizations, potentially shared products and services may not be coordinated across geographic boundaries.

A new method of organization has been developed by firms such as Dell, which are pursuing "virtual integration." Under such a system, the links of the value chain are brought together by an informal arrangement among suppliers and customers.[2] Dell establishes close ties with suppliers, enabling many of the benefits of vertical integration. Shipments of the components that Dell needs can be easily arranged through the Internet or a networked computer system. This same type of arrangement allows Dell to fully serve customers in ordering, providing services, or meeting any other needs.

Responsibilities of Financial Managers

In Figure 1.1, top-level executives are shown to be of two types. One type is based on functions (manufacturing, marketing). A second type represents more general management functions such as research, legal, and finance. Clearly, the general management functions such as finance interact with activities in the functional, product, and geographic organization groups.

INTERACTIONS WITH OTHER EXECUTIVES

These organization relationships suggest that the number one responsibility of financial managers is to interact with all other parts of the organization to help improve operating performance in all areas of the company. This significant role of finance is documented by the experience of the General Electric Company (GE) after Jack Welch became its chairman in 1981. Welch described how the finance function changed during his tenure as chairman from 1981 to 2001. During that period, the market value of GE increased from $13 billion to $400 billion or 3,077%. Welch argued that financial managers at GE had been emphasizing control and that the internal audit staff had become corporate policemen. In 1984, Welch appointed a new financial officer, Dennis Dammerman. With Welch's support, Dammerman reoriented the financial managers to see their responsibilities as performance improvement by supporting the efforts of the operating executives. Financial managers must therefore understand operating functions and how they relate to finance. Operating functions include such areas as research and development, manufacturing, marketing, production, logistics, information technology, and human resources. By interacting with all activities in a team effort, as well as understanding the firm's strategies, financial officers developed the skills of overall business leadership (Jack Welch, 2001, pp. 133–136).

Another illustration of the full-involvement concept is described at length by Lee Iacocca in his autobiography (1984). Iacocca joined the Ford Motor Company as an engineer. He switched to sales and successfully moved to product development. One of his successful products was the Ford Mustang. Some of his other ideas faced difficulties in obtaining

---

[2] The concept of a value chain lists and analyzes the steps or chains of the activities required to produce products that reduce costs and/or improve quality. It is a concept emphasized by Michael Porter (1985).

requisite investment appropriations. Iacocca wrote that the accountants and financial managers were myopic "bean counters" who failed to understand the broad strategic plans of the firm. The "bean counters" did not have sufficient involvement and participation with the design and marketing of new models to understand how they added to the market position of the automobile company as a whole.

Iacocca's disagreements with Henry Ford II forced his resignation. He was hired by Chrysler where the K car entered the market in 1980 based on design proposals that the "bean counters" had rejected at Ford. Chrysler also produced the minivan based on a concept by key executives hired from Ford. The Iacocca leadership enabled Chrysler to repay government-backed loans ahead of schedule. Iacocca left Chrysler in 1992 but in July 2005 was hired by DaimlerChrysler to promote its Employee Pricing Plus (EPP) program (with his fees going to a diabetes research foundation in memory of his wife).

So the number one responsibility of financial managers is to bring their expertise to strategic and operating decisions. Developing the relevant numbers requires a team approach. If financial managers increase their understanding of strategies, operating requirements, manufacturing, and marketing in continuing interactions with other managers, their contributions to improved company performance can be increased.

DEVELOPING INFORMATION FLOW SYSTEMS

Financial managers take responsibility for information systems capable of providing a complete and current financial picture of the firm's operations and performance related to its business model and strategies. This capability has been one of the strengths of firms such as Cisco Systems and Wal-Mart. They are able to run off a complete set of financial reports at any hour. Production performance as well as its implications are shared with workers during and after every shift of production at many plants in the Hershey manufacturing system. With command of the total financial picture of the company, the financial manager is likely to be involved in all top management policies and decisions. This kind of experience can help a financial manager become a high-level executive in a firm.

R&D AND INVESTMENT DECISIONS (CAPITAL BUDGETING)

So the first function of financial managers is to bring their expertise to all of the decision areas of the firm. A second important function is to take major responsibility for capital budgeting decisions. A successful firm is usually a growing firm, which requires the support of increased investments. Financial managers participate in establishing sales growth goals and evaluate alternative investments to support such growth. They help decide which specific investments should be made and identify the alternative sources and forms of funds for financing these investments. Decision variables include internal versus external funds, debt versus owners' funds, and long-term versus short-term financing.

FINANCING SOURCES, FORMS, AND METHODS

The financial manager links the firm to the money and capital markets in which funds are raised and in which the firm's securities are sold and traded. Financing sources are related to the life cycle of the firm. Even Dell, Google, Microsoft, Amazon, Yahoo, and Wal-Mart started as small, privately owned firms. At the earliest stages, funds come from owners plus their relatives and friends. As the firm grows, it may receive funds from "angels." Angels are wealthy individuals with experience in the industry related to the new firm. They invest seed money and help the founder test and refine his business model, recommend experienced managers, and develop business operations. As the firm grows, venture capitalists may also provide additional funds.

In 1998, the founders of Google (Brin and Page) received $100,000 initial financing from Andy Bechtolsheim, a cofounder of Sun Microsystems. Subsequently, additional financing was received from two venture capital firms—Kleiner Perkins and Sequoia. Venture capital firms are run by experienced investment professionals who receive investments ranging from individuals to pension funds. In 2004, Google's stock went public, raising $1.67 billion.

As a startup firm develops a track record, it may be able to go public by issuing securities in financial markets. Investment banking firms may contract to bring out an initial public offering (IPO). Once a firm has gone public, a wide array of debt and equity forms become available.

Financial Structure Decisions

Financing choices can be divided into two broad classes, debt and equity.

Interest payments on debt are deductible and so have tax advantages. When payments on debt are fixed per unit of time, equity holders benefit from higher returns when the sales and returns of the firm are favorable. This is called "trading on the equity." But if a firm is unable to meet its debt interest payments or repay the principal payments when they come due, the consequences may be financial distress. One of the costs of financial distress is that the equity owners of the business may lose control of the firm.

PAYOUT POLICIES

Debt forms of financing usually specify the interest payments and repayment requirements. But equity forms of financing permit greater discretion. Should the cash flow be reinvested in the business or returned to the owners? Should payouts to equity holders be cash dividends, share repurchases, or various forms of restructuring such as spin-offs to shareholders?

Corporate Governance Issues

Financial managers are directly involved in matters of corporate governance. For many years, the dominant form of corporate ownership in the United States has been limited liability ownership of the voting equity shares by a large number of individual investors. The growth of this form of ownership reflected some distinct advantages. Under limited liability, the investor could lose no more than was paid for the equity stock of the corporation. Relatively small investments could be made in a number of corporations, so the individual investor could achieve the benefits of diversification.

In theory, under widely dispersed ownership, shareholders elect the board of directors to represent their interests. This poses issues of how other stakeholders obtain representation of their views and interests. These problems have not been fully resolved. Increasingly, public expectations look to the board of directors to balance the interests of all stakeholders. Some criticize such a view as soft-headed, unrealistic "do-goodism." An alternative view is that if the needs and goals of the multiple stakeholders—shareholders, creditors, consumers, workers, government, the general public—are not addressed, then the political-economic systems will not function effectively in the long run. These are matters of great importance with respect to which the board of directors has considerable responsibility.

New Regulatory Requirements

For the period 2000 to 2002, the fraud revelations were of such magnitude and inflicted such injury to investors that some company reputations were irreparably destroyed. Stock price declines and the erosion of 401(k) values had widespread impact. The fraud and self-dealing revelations resulted in investigations by Congress, the Securities and Exchange Commission (SEC), and the State Attorney General in several jurisdictions, particularly New York. The Sarbanes-Oxley Act (SOX) was enacted into law on July 30, 2002 (for full text, see 107th Congress H.R. 3763 at www.gpoaccess.gov). Financial managers have increased responsibilities for meeting new regulatory requirements.

The combination of falling stock prices and revelations of financial fraud resulted in lawsuits and in new legislation on financial practices and on corporate governance. The purpose of such legislation is to restore the confidence of the general public in the integrity of the financial markets. Without confidence in the operations of the financial system, the efficiency of the economy would be reduced. But even stronger reasons for ethical behavior can be developed.

Business Ethics

Financial executives should help contribute to a firm's ethical reputation. Business ethics is the conduct and behavior of a firm's management toward its stockholders, employees, customers, and the community. Business ethics is measured by a firm's behavior in all aspects of its dealings with others in all areas, including product quality, treatment of employees, fair market practices, and community responsibility.

The case for ethical behavior is based on widely accepted codes of conduct. Without integrity, a person cannot be psychologically healthy. If people cannot be trusted, the social system cannot function effectively. But in addition, a reputation for ethical behavior and fairness to all stakeholders is a source of considerable organizational value. A reputation for integrity enables a firm to attract employees who believe in and behave according to ethical principles. Customers will respond favorably to business firms who treat them honestly. Such behavior contributes to the health of the community where the firm operates.

Firms should have codes of ethical behavior in writing and conduct training programs to make clear to employees the standards to which the firms seek to achieve. This is an area in which the firm's board of directors and top management must provide leadership. They must demonstrate by their actions as well as by communications their strong commitment to ethical conduct. The company's promotion and compensation systems should reward ethical behavior and punish conduct that impairs the firm's reputation for integrity.

The behavior of top executives of a firm establishes the firm's reputation. If the behavior of the firm is not consistently ethical, other stakeholders—workers, consumers, suppliers—will begin to question every action and decision of the firm. For example, the bonds and common stock of a firm with an uncertain reputation will be viewed with suspicion by the market. The securities will have to be sold at lower prices, which means that the returns to investors will have to be higher to take into account that the issuing firm may be selling a "lemon"—that is, trying to put something over on investors.

Thus, a strong case can be made that financial executives and the firm establish a reputation for unquestioned ethical behavior. The psychological health of an individual is better, the reputation of the firm is a valuable asset, and the social and economic environment is more conducive to efficient and equitable economic activity.

Goals of the Firm

Finance and accounting are important subjects as we begin the 21st century. The daily newspapers (not just the business press) as well as radio and television carry dramatic stories of growth and decline of firms, earnings surprises, corporate takeovers, and many types of corporate restructuring. To understand these developments and to participate in them effectively requires knowledge of the principles of finance. This book explains these principles and their applications in making decisions.

STAKEHOLDERS

One of the major responsibilities of senior management is to carefully balance the interests of stakeholders. A **stakeholder** is anyone who has any interest in the firm. A list of stakeholders is found below:

STAKEHOLDER
Customers
Consumers
Suppliers
Employees
Unions
Management
Government (all levels)
Local community
Banks
Other debt–holders
Stockholders

This list distinguishes Hershey's customers (e.g., Wal-Mart, Kroger, CVS) from consumers (you and me), identifies worker stakeholders, as well as the broader community and financial stakeholders.

As stated, it is a careful balance. A plant manager only wants to make one product, 24 hours a day and 7 days a week. On the other hand, marketing wants to market and sales wants to sell an infinite number of products. It is up to senior management to balance both views. Raise your prices too high and sales will decline. Underpay your employees, and talent will leave.

The number one objective as discussed below is to maximize the value of the firm by carefully balancing the interests of all stakeholders. In that way, shareholder value will be maximized.

Finance and Firm Value

A fundamental question in the study of finance is whether financial executives can increase the value of a firm. Economic and financial theorists begin with models of an idealized world where there are no taxes and no transaction costs of issuing debt or equity securities, where the managers of firms and their outside investors all have the same information about the firm's future cash flow, where there are no costs of financial distress or of resolving conflicts of interest among different stakeholders of the firm. In such a world, financial decisions do not matter.

The pure idealized models of finance are useful in that they stress the importance of investment opportunities, current and future, on the value of the firm. In the actual world, however, taxes, bankruptcy costs, transactions costs, and the information content of cash flows and dividend or share repurchase policies cause financial policies to have an influence on the value of the firm. Also of great importance is the role of finance in developing information flow so that a firm can evaluate the effectiveness of alternative strategies, policies, decisions, operations, and outcomes. The objective is to create an information flow to provide rapid feedback as a basis for the revision of strategies and decisions to enlarge the growth opportunities of firms and to improve their performance.

So there are important ways in which financial executives can contribute to the improved performance of a firm and therefore increase its value. This is the central theme of this book, which is revisited often as we demonstrate how financial concepts can contribute to increasing the value of a firm and the returns to its stakeholders, as well as to society as a whole.

VALUE MAXIMIZATION

Within the above framework, the *goal of management is to maximize the value of the firm* (for the benefit of fund suppliers), subject to the constraints of responsibilities to other stakeholders, consumers, employers, suppliers, communities, and governments. Value maximization is broader than "profit maximization." Maximizing value takes the time value of money into account. First, funds that are received this year have more value than funds that may be received 10 years from now. Second, value maximization considers the riskiness of the income stream. For example, the rate of return required on an investment starting a new business is in the range of 25 to 35%, but 10 to 15% in established firms. Third, the "quality" and timing of expected future cash flows may vary. Profit figures can vary widely depending on the accounting rules and conventions used.

Thus, value maximization is broader and more general than profit maximization and is the unifying concept used throughout this book. **Value maximization** provides criteria for pricing the use of resources such as capital investments in plant and machinery. If limited resources are not allocated by efficiency criteria, production will be inefficient. Value maximization provides a solution to these kinds of problems.

PERFORMANCE MEASUREMENT BY THE FINANCIAL MARKETS

The basic finance functions must be performed in all types of organizations and in all types of economic systems. What is unique about business organizations in a market economy is that they are directly subject to the discipline of the financial markets. These markets continuously value a business firm's securities, thereby providing measures of the firm's performance. A consequence of this continuous assessment of a firm by the capital markets is the change in valuations (stock market prices). Thus, the capital markets stimulate efficiency and provide incentives to business managers to improve their performance.

THE RISK–RETURN TRADE-OFF

Financial decisions affect the level of a firm's stock price by influencing the cash flow stream and the riskiness of the firm. These relationships are diagrammed in Figure 1.4. Policy decisions, which are subject to government constraints, affect the levels of cash flows and their risks. These two factors jointly determine the value of the firm.

The firm must first assess the international and national macroeconomic environments. Changing political and cultural factors must also be projected. The primary policy decision is made in choosing the product markets in which the firm operates. Profitability and risk

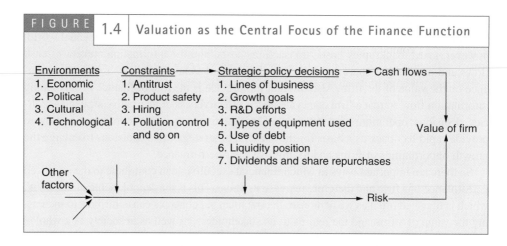

FIGURE 1.4 | Valuation as the Central Focus of the Finance Function

are further influenced by decisions relating to the size of the firm, its growth rate, the types and the methods of production and marketing, the extent to which debt is employed, the firm's liquidity position, and dividend and share repurchase policies. An increase in the cash position reduces risk; however, because cash is not an earning asset, converting other assets to cash also reduces profitability. Similarly, the use of additional debt raises the rate of return on stockholders' equity; but more debt means more risk. The financial manager seeks to strike the balance between risk and profitability that will maximize stockholder wealth. Most financial decisions involve *risk-return trade-offs*.

The Changing Economic and Financial Environments

Major changes in the economic, political, and financial environments began to explode in the 1980s. These in turn had major impacts on the practice of finance.

INTERNATIONAL COMPETITION

While the trends have been underway for decades, full recognition of the international economy took place in the 1980s, continuing to the present. In every major industry—automobile, steel, pharmaceuticals, oil, computers, other electronics products, for example—the reality of global markets had to be taken into account. In addition to competition from Western European and Japanese companies, even developing countries began to offer challenging competition in manufactured products. The pressures to reduce prices and increase profit margins presented continued challenges. Investments had to be made wisely; the importance of capital budgeting increased. To increase profit margins, efficiency had to increase.

FINANCIAL INNOVATIONS AND FINANCIAL ENGINEERING

Many financial innovations have taken place in recent years. These have been referred to as "financial engineering," representing the creation of new forms of financial products. They include debt instruments with fluctuating (floating) interest rates and various forms of rights to convert debt into equity (or vice versa), the use of higher levels of leverage and lower grade ("junk") bonds, the use of debt denominated for payment in variously designated foreign currencies, and the development of pools of funds available for investment in new firms or to take over existing firms.

INCREASED USE OF COMPUTERS

Increasingly, computers make available computational powers which in earlier decades could be obtained only from relatively large-scale systems. Thus, the ability to develop complex models and spreadsheet analysis has become widely available. It remains important, however, to have a clear understanding of the underlying principles involved. Otherwise, increased complexity will result in less clear understanding and lead to error rather than improved analysis.

MERGERS, TAKEOVERS, AND RESTRUCTURING

The increased international competition has been one of the major factors causing U.S. companies to rethink their strategies to become competitive. Mergers, takeovers, and restructuring represent, in part, responses to pressures to increase efficiency to meet increased competition resulting from the new international and technological developments.

E-COMMERCE

The e-commerce and related telecommunication developments have had a major impact on business and investments. Their significance will be similar to that of previous revolutionary innovations such as steam engines, electricity, automobiles, radio, television, and computers in all their forms. E-commerce was stimulated by the development of the Internet accompanied by transformations in computers and telecommunications.

In its initial stages, the major growth in e-commerce was seen in the business-to-consumer (B2C) market as a revolutionary distribution vehicle. Buyers could benefit from superior product selection, efficient processing, and lower prices. The business-to-business (B2B) markets have become larger than the B2C. Value will be created by streamlining the supply chain as well as improving the information chain by managing complex business information online. By the late 1990s, many traditional businesses began to awaken to the challenges and opportunities of e-commerce. The opportunities continue to be shaped.

The early e-commerce companies used their stock with high price-earnings ratios to make acquisitions to beat competitors to name recognition, critical mass, and leadership. E-commerce companies have demonstrated high volatility in their stock market prices. All firms are impacted, and financial managers must perform critical roles in the operating and financial dimensions of e-commerce activities.

Review

In review, the environments of firms have changed dynamically in recent decades. This has affected all aspects of strategic planning in all types of organizations. Since financial markets are especially sensitive and responsive to turbulence in economic environments, financial decision making has become increasingly challenging. The following chapters seek to assist financial managers in meeting these new challenges and responsibilities.

Organization of This Book

The aim of this book is to explain the procedures, practices, and policies by which accounting and financial management can contribute to the successful performance of organizations. Our emphasis is on strategies involved in the trade-offs between risk and return in seeking to make decisions that will maximize the value of the firm. Each subsequent topic is treated within this basic framework.

The central function of finance is to interact with other managers to continuously improve the performance of the organization so that value grows. Finance participates in the evaluation of alternative strategies and policies. It is equally important for you to be able to interact with the financial manager by understanding and speaking the same language. The subjects of this book are useful for all managers, analysts, and others seeking to understand how value is created and organization performance is improved.

Part 1 establishes some fundamentals. Chapter 1 discusses the goals of firms and the role of financial concepts in value creation. The responsibilities of effective corporate governance in achieving organization goals are set forth. Chapter 2 explains the information that can be developed from accounting and financial statements. Chapter 3 explains why "time is money:" It is more valuable to have cash today than to wait years to receive it. Firms make investments now in order to receive cash flow in future years. It is crucial to determine the cumulative values of past, present, and future cash flows. The foundation for valuations is thereby established. Chapter 4 describes the rules of the game under which firms are organized and operate. It discusses alternative forms of business organization that a firm may use and the important tax laws that impact financing alternatives.

Part 2 describes the financial environments within which business firms operate. Chapter 5 summarizes the fundamental characteristics of financial markets that financial managers must understand in order to develop sound policies and decisions. Using this background, the valuation of securities with fixed returns (e.g., bonds) is described. The focus of chapter 6 is an overview of equity valuation in the context of risk and reward relationships.

Part 3, Financial Performance Analysis, Planning, and Control sets forth the noted topics. In chapter 7, we describe financial performance metrics, which employ financial ratios analysis and related measures. Chapter 8 discusses the management of working capital—both operating and financial working capital. Chapter 9 on strategic financial planning discusses long-term financial forecasting, which underlies the valuation of the firm and which is used to set performance standards and management compensation goals, and to anticipate future financing requirements.

Part 4 deals with investment strategies and decisions with respect to all aspects of the left-hand (assets) side of the balance sheet. Its emphasis is on economizing on the use of economic resources for the purpose of creating value. Chapter 10 develops criteria for making decisions of whether to accept or reject investment proposals. Chapter 11 discusses the measurement of cash flows relevant for capital budgeting decisions. Chapter 12 discusses how the intrinsic value of an investment or enterprise can be determined. It explains the dominant approach to valuation, which is the discounted cash flow (DCF) analysis while also sensitizing the reader to the latest tool, real options. Considering optionality in capital investments stimulates decision makers to design flexibility into projects resulting in increased valuations.

Part 5 turns to the right-hand side of the balance sheet. It discusses decisions with regard to the forms and sources of financing that minimize the cost of capital. Chapter 13 analyzes financial structure decisions with respect to the mix of equity and debt financing sources employed. Chapter 14 discusses financing sources, procedures for obtaining long-term financing, and specific forms of long-term financing. Chapter 15 describes the role of leasing as a financing source. Chapter 16 discusses how dividend policy, share repurchases, and other methods of returning funds to investors may affect valuation.

Part 6 presents a financial perspective on growth strategies for increasing the firm's value. Chapter 17 discusses how mergers and other intercorporate relationships may increase or destroy value and applies the valuation concepts to merger decisions. Chapter 18 builds a solid theoretical background in the dynamics of international finance—exchange rates, inflation rates, interest rates.

The Hershey Company

Presentation of models, equations, and concepts can be dry and boring. Presentations of fictitious companies using contrived situations leave the professional skeptical about how things work in "the real world." Our illustrations are consistently applied to the actual financial results of The Hershey Company. While Hershey is our primary focus, other companies are also used appropriately throughout the discussion.

Hershey is "a leading snack food company and the largest North American manufacturer of quality chocolate and non-chocolate confectionery products" (Hershey website: www. hersheys.com). Its sales exceeded $4.8 billion in 2005 with well over 90% of those sales coming from North America. Hershey was founded in 1893 by Milton S. Hershey and its headquarters continue to be located in Hershey, Pennsylvania. The company's website proudly discusses Mr. Hershey's legacy and the history of The Hershey Company.

We use The Hershey Company (NYSE: HSY) as our illustrative example because Hershey's products are simple to understand. Many of us grew up understanding its product very well. Their supply chain business model (sales, marketing, production, and distribution) is straightforward. The following link demonstrates the production process through a company video (www.hersheys.com/discover/tour_video.asp). For the finance student or business professional, this video shows significant capital investments. Hershey's financial record is stellar with solid profitability and a strong balance sheet, and the website provides links to financial reports as well as investment analyst presentations. Finally, Hershey's ethical reputation is unsurpassed for quality and fair treatment of all of its stakeholders, which ties in well to the overriding theme of this text. With all of this in mind, our applications can focus on the financial aspects rather than explaining a convoluted business situation.

Hershey's practices, procedures, and issues are common throughout most organizations. We expect that you, too, will identify with the business issue discussed in this text.

summary

We develop many technical aspects of finance throughout this text. However, we need to keep in mind these very important, nontechnical aspects of financial management.

1. The number one emphasis of this book is that financial executives should interact with other executives of the firm to improve performance in individual segments and for the enterprise as a whole.

2. An important responsibility of financial managers is to participate in improving strategies by depicting the financial outcomes of alternative choices of the products and markets in which the firm operates.

3. Financial managers have important responsibilities for selecting value-increasing investments in cash, receivables, inventories, land, plants, and equipment.

4. Financial managers have the ultimate responsibility for selecting forms and sources of financing that minimize the cost of capital for projects and the firm.

5. Because financial managers make important inputs in all aspects of the firm selection of strategies, the formulation of policies and related decisions, the chief financial officer is high in the organization structure of the firm.

6. Financial officers must contribute to the fair representation of shareholders as well as other stakeholders.

7. Financial officers should contribute to the reputation of the firm for practicing high ethical behavior and taking social responsibilities in formulating policies.

8. Financial decision makers should be guided by the goal of maximizing returns to shareholders.

9. Economic, financial, cultural, and technological environments are continuously changing. Financial managers should anticipate these changes in order to make appropriate adjustments. The values of flexibility in the timing of policies and programs should be recognized.

The key concepts are revisited throughout the text.

Questions

1.1   What are the main functions of financial managers?

1.2   In a division-type of organizational structure, where each major business unit is considered its own distinct business that reports to the corporate level, to whom should the divisional vice president of finance directly report?

    a.   Discuss the pros and cons of the divisional vice president of finance directly reporting to the division president and indirectly reporting to the corporation's CFO. (This is illustrated in Figure 1.2.)

    b.   Discuss the pros and cons of the divisional vice president of finance directly reporting to the corporation's CFO and indirectly reporting to the division president.

1.3   Many corporations form cross-functional task teams for major endeavors, such as new product introductions, capital expenditure analysis, mergers and acquisitions, and so on. Why is it important to include a finance person on that task team?

1.4   Why is shareholder wealth maximization a better operating goal than profit maximization?

1.5   What is the difference between firm value maximization and shareholder wealth maximization?

1.6   What are the issues in the conflict of interest between stockholders and managers and how can they be resolved?

1.7   What are the potential conflicts of interest between shareholders and bondholders and how can they be resolved?

1.8   What role does social responsibility have in formulating business and financial goals?

1.9   What is the nature of the risk-return trade-off faced in financial decision making?

1.10   What are some of the effects of high inflation (or the threat of high inflation) on financial decisions?

1.11   What opportunities and threats are created for financial managers by increased international competition?

1.12   Please discuss the short-term and long-term impact of the following business decisions that affect the noted stakeholders:

DECISIONS	Short-Term	Long-Term
a. Increase in prices:		
Stockholders		
Customers		
Government		
b. Increase in ingredient costs:		
Stockholders		
Employees		
Bondholders		
c. Decreased demand for product:		
Stockholders		
Management		
Employees		
Suppliers		
d. Opening of a major international market:		
Stockholders		
Management		
Employees		
Suppliers		
Community		

Problems

As we stressed throughout the chapter, finance is a tool used by business people. It is not an end in itself and must be placed in the context of the business. Throughout this text, we focus on The Hershey Company.

1.1   History

Use the following website to guide you in search of specific information: www.hersheys.com/discover/history/company.asp. The history of any organization is very important. It lays the framework for future generations.

a.   When was the Hershey Company founded?

    b.   During its first 30 years, how successful was Hershey in introducing new products?

    c.   Discuss the impact of the movie "E.T."

1.2   Entrepreneurial spirit

Many major corporations of today have been forged by the entrepreneurial spirit of their founder. Go to www.hersheys.com/discover/milton/milton.asp to learn about Milton S. Hershey, the founder of The Hershey Company.

    a.   Did Mr. Hershey have immediate success in his entrepreneurial endeavors?

    b.   Discuss his "enduring legacy."

1.3   The making of chocolate candy

Capital expenditure evaluation and investment in other corporate activities is a key component of corporate finance. To better understand the production process of Hershey and to put the capital expenditure analysis into a manufacturing context, please watch the videos at www.hersheys.com/discover/tour_video.asp. Discuss the process of making a Hershey bar.

1.4   Ethical responsibility

Ethical responsibility is so important in this post-Enron business environment. Milton Hershey insisted on strong ethical dealings with all stakeholders from the very start. Go to www.thehersheycompany.com/about/conduct.asp and read its code of conduct. Answer the following questions:

    a.   What stakeholders are specifically identified in the "code of conduct?"

    b.   In what order are they placed?

    c.   Why is it important that Hershey "maintain a prudent, results-oriented approach to business that builds superior shareholder value over the long-term?"

    d.   What does the phrase "profitable real growth" mean?

1.5   Open communication

Management at The Hershey Company believes in open communication. As a result, major analyst presentations are posted on the Hershey website under investor relations. These presentations discuss the latest strategies and tactics of the Hershey business as well as new products, market share, channels of distribution, and financial information. Please look at a recent analyst presentation such as the one found at www.thehersheycompany.com/ir/presentations.asp and answer the following questions:

    a.   What is the "theme" of this presentation?

    b.   What traditional accounting and financial information is presented?

    c.   What nontraditional accounting and financial information is presented?

1.6   Investor relations

Finally, most corporations provide annual reports and Securities and Exchange Commission (SEC) filings on their website under a category often labeled as "Investor Relations." Please go to Hershey's website, investor relations, and peruse its annual reports and 10-K reports for the past few years. (For annual and quarterly reports, go to www.thehersheycompany.com/ir/reports.asp; for SEC filings, go to www.thehersheycompany.com/ir/sec16filings.asp.)

a.   What is your over all impression of the recent financial performance of The Hershey Company?

Suggested Readings

Bossidy, Larry and Ram Charan, *Execution: The Disipline of Getting Things Done*, New York: Crown Business, 2002.

Fama, Eugene F., "Agency Problems and the Theory of the Firm," *Journal of Political Economy*, 88, 1980, pp. 287–307.

Fama, Eugene F., and Michael Jensen, "Separation of Ownership and Control," *Journal of Law and Economics*, 26, 1983, pp. 301–326.

Jensen, Michael C., "Agency Costs of Free Cash Flow, Corporate Finance, And Takeovers," *American Economics Review*, 76, May 1986, pp. 323–329.

Jensen, Michael C. and William H. Meckling, "Theory of the Firm: Managerial Behavior, Agency Costs and Ownership Structure," *Journal of Financial Economics*, 3(4), 1976, 305–360.

Monks, Robert A.G. and Nell Minow, *Corporate Governance*, 3d, Malden, MA: Blackwell Publishing, 2003.

Rubin, Robert E. and Jacob Weisberg, *In an Uncertain World*, New York: Random House, 2003.

Financial Statements and Cash Flows

Financial statements report the historical performance of a company and provide a basis for assessing the firm's achievements. Along with giving general national and international economic business conditions and a strategic assessment of the company, financial statements provide a foundation for projecting the firm's future. Financial statements are guided by Generally Accepted Accounting Principles, commonly called US GAAP. For public corporations, financial statements are publicly disclosed annually, through an annual report and 10K (a Securities and Exchange Commission [SEC] requirement), and quarterly, through a more concise quarterly report and 10Q. Beyond the external reporting requirements, within most firms, financial statements are often prepared on a monthly basis to assist management. In some cases, key components of the financial statements (e.g., product sales and product costs) are available on a daily basis. The Internal Revenue Service and foreign governments (in the case of a multinational firm) have their own very specific guidelines for reporting financial data.

This chapter describes the basic financial statements, develops key accounting concepts that underlie the financial statements, demonstrates the interrelationships among the statements, and provides an overview of essential financial data contained in the accompanying notes to the financial statements. To facilitate this chapter, we use the 2005 financial statements from the annual report of The Hershey Company as well as specific statements from other companies and introduce the Thompson One Financial Data Base available with the purchase of this book.

Role of Financial Statements

We walk into a room where a friend is watching a sporting event. Whether its baseball, football, hockey, basketball, or whatever, our first question usually is "What's the score?" Financial statements provide an important measure of the firm's score. Although the firm is not meeting a competitor in a sporting event at a stadium, the firm is continuously meeting its competition head-on in the marketing arena in a battle for its customers' dollars and in the investing arena in a battle for the investors' capital.

The "score" is one measure of a team's performance. The "score" does not capture all other dimensions of the team's performance, such as the batting averages, number of first downs, shots on goal, and so on. These types of "box score" measures present additional attributes for evaluating a team's performance and individual contributions to the team's success. Although assessing the performance of a firm is more complicated because there is no simple "score," financial statements provide the scorecard for judging a company's performance.

This company assessment is extended to evaluating the performance of the management team. Management's compensation is often based on the financial information provided by financial statements. Financial statements also form the foundation upon which valuation of the firm is based. The objective for a management team is to "maximize the value of the firm." By maximizing (or enhancing) the value of the firm, the management team increases its score.

Valuation is a central theme to this book. Understanding financial statements is one of the key factors for evaluating the performance of the firm. Chapter 7, Financial Performance Metrics, builds upon the principles developed within this chapter.

A complete description of a firm's financial activities during a year consists of three basic financial statements.

1. An **income statement** shows the activities as measured by revenues (or sales) less expenses of the firm throughout the period.
2. A **balance sheet** provides a snapshot of what the firm owns and what the firm owes at a specific moment in time.
3. A **statement of cash flows** presents the underlying transactions that cause the cash balance to change between periods of time.

The accompanying notes to the financial statements, management's discussion and analysis (MD&A), the CEO's letter to shareholders, and many other inclusions in an annual report provide valuable supplementary information for assessing a firm.

Figure 2.1 presents an overview of the timing of the primary financial statements. Balance sheets are struck at a moment in time at the end of a specific period, while the

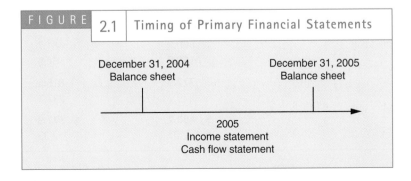

FIGURE 2.1   Timing of Primary Financial Statements

December 31, 2004
Balance sheet

December 31, 2005
Balance sheet

2005
Income statement
Cash flow statement

income statements and cash flow statements measure performance throughout a period of time. In Table 2.1, two balance sheets are prepared—one as of December 31, 2004, and one as of December 31, 2005—while the income statement and cash flow measure the activities throughout 2005.

Income Statement

The income statement records revenues and expenses to derive income over a specific period of time.

$$\text{Revenue} - \text{Expenses} = \text{Income} \qquad\qquad (2.1)$$

Table 2.1 presents the Hershey 2004 and 2005 income statements as reported in its 2005 annual report (and the 10K).

   The Hershey Company (stock symbol is HSY) is the number one chocolate and confectionery company in the United States. It is primarily a domestic company with less than 10% of its sales coming from outside the United States and even a significantly smaller portion coming from outside North America. HSY's financial statements are relatively straightforward and are used throughout this book for illustrative purposes. Selected financial data from other companies are used when appropriate.

NET SALES

The income statement begins with the revenue or net sales of the firm. In 2005, Hershey had $4,836.0 million of net sales. That represents a tremendous amount of peanut butter cups, kisses, and Hershey bars sold in 2005. The term **net sales** indicates that gross sales have been reduced for returned products, discounts taken for prompt payment of invoices, allowances for damaged products, and trade promotions or price reductions. The 2005 net sales were $406.8 million higher than in 2004, or 9.2% higher.

TABLE 2.1	Hershey Foods Corporation Consolidated Statements of Income ($ millions, except per share amounts)		
FOR THE YEARS ENDED 12/31:		2005	2004
Net sales		$4,836.0	$4,429.2
Costs and expenses			
Cost of sales		2,965.6	2,680.4
Selling, marketing, and administrative		913.0	867.1
Business realignment and asset impairment, net		96.5	—
Total costs and expense		3,975.1	3,547.5
Income before interest and income taxes		860.9	881.7
Interest expense, net		88.0	66.5
Income before income taxes		772.9	815.2
Provision for income taxes		279.7	237.3
Net income		$ 493.2	$ 577.9
Earnings per share-common stock		$ 2.07	$ 2.33

The income statement is silent about what drove the revenue growth. Further explanation must be found elsewhere in the annual report, in the MD&A, or in the CEO's letter. The 2005 net sales growth for Hershey was primarily the result of acquisitions ($145.0 million), new product introductions including limited edition brand extensions, and the base business growth.

EXPENSES

Costs and expenses include at least two lines of distinction: (1) cost of sales and (2) selling, marketing, and administrative costs.

The cost of sales captures the manufacturing expenses for the products sold. The cost of sales includes raw material (e.g., cocoa beans, milk, sugar), direct labor of the people producing the product, and factory overhead. The factory overhead includes direct and indirect overhead expenses such as electricity, property taxes, insurance, maintenance, and depreciation expense for the plant and production equipment. Also included in overhead are the salaries, employee benefits, and employment taxes of production supervisors and plant general management. The depreciation expense item deserves special attention.

US GAAP accounting is prepared using accrual-based accounting, which is in sharp contrast to a cash-based accounting. This is what drives the distinction between the income statement and statement of cash flow. Let's say that 3 years ago a piece of manufacturing equipment was purchased for $2,000 with an expected life of 10 years. A cash-based system would recognize the $2,000 purchase as an equipment expense in the year the purchase was originally made and consequently there would be no expense in the current year. An accrual-based accounting system (i.e., US GAAP) recognizes that there was cash outflow to buy the equipment 3 years ago. However, under accrual-based accounting, the expense comes from the productivity consumption over the life of the asset. In this case, $200/year ($2,000/10 years) would be recognized as depreciation expense in the current year and annually over the 10-year life of the equipment.

If the depreciating equipment was primarily used for or related to the manufacturing of product, the $200 depreciation expense would be included in cost of sales. If the depreciation was associated with corporate headquarters, that expense would be included in selling, marketing, and administrative costs. In the case of Hershey, the depreciation expense is not specifically identified on the income statement. However, a supplemental schedule in the HSY footnotes reveals a 2005 depreciation expense of $200.1 million. It is silent on the split between cost of sales and selling, marketing, and administrative expense. The majority of the depreciation would be found in the cost of sales given Hershey's business model and investment in manufacturing equipment.

Selling, marketing, and administrative expenses include the following:

1. Selling expenses, for example, salespersons' salaries, bonuses, benefits, employment taxes, automobiles, office expenses, and broker fees if the product is sold by a third party
2. Marketing expenses, for example, consumer promotions, cents-off coupons, advertising, marketing research, and salaries
3. Administrative expenses, for example, outlays for corporate and divisional staffs, executive compensation, training, consulting fees, and research and development

Selling, marketing, and administrative expense are sometimes referred to as "G&A" (general and administrative), or operating expense.

EXTRAORDINARY ITEMS

Companies incur expenses for or benefits from "one-time, nonrecurring gains or losses" that are separately listed on the income statement. Examples of these one-time events are:

- Business realignment (or restructuring charges): an accumulation of anticipated expenses associated with closing a plant, division, or other business segment, as well as the expenses incurred for a labor force reduction.

- Asset impairment: decrease in the value of purchased asset as explained below.

- Discontinued operations: current period income or loss from a business that has been identified to be discontinued through a shutdown or divestiture.

- Gains (or losses) from the disposal of businesses: a business unit, product line, or individual product was sold resulting in a gain or (loss).

- Accounting change: the cumulative impact for prior years of an implemented change in US GAAP.

- Extraordinary gains (losses): as the name implies.

These nonrecurring items may need to be adjusted to get a more accurate portrayal of the company's normal business activities.

As illustrated on Hershey's income statement, there is a 2005 one-time expense item that is separately identified as "business realignment and asset impairments, net." The 2005 business realignment and asset impairment charge ($96.5 million) was the result of expenses incurred for a voluntary work force reduction (early retirement) plan. These extraordinary expenses included early employee retirements, involuntary terminations, office closures, and a plant closure.

Over the past few years, Hershey had other extraordinary items such as a 2003 gain from the sale of specific brands of gum to Farley's & Sathers. From the MD&A, we read "the Company received cash proceeds from the sale of $20.0 million and recorded a gain of $8.3 million before or $5.7 million after tax, as a result of this transaction."[1] This gum business was acquired a few years earlier at a cost of $11.7 million, which gave rise to the reported gain. (Proceeds less cost or $20.0 million less $11.7 million resulted in a gain of $8.3 million.)

MEASURES OF INCOME

The next line, "Income before Interest and Income Taxes," or EBIT, earnings before interest and taxes, represents sales less total cost of sales, G&A expenses, and extraordinary items. Many firms also refer to this as operating income (OI). However, from a technical perspective, operating income does not include the effects of one-time extraordinary items. If a company does not have any extraordinary expenses, then operating income and EBIT are one and the same.

A variation of EBIT that has grown increasingly popular with the investment community is a measure called *earnings before interest, taxes, depreciation, and amortization* (or EBITDA). Although EBITDA is not a US GAAP measure, it is easy to compute by adding depreciation and amortization (similar to depreciation of an intangible asset) back to EBIT. For example, Hershey's EBIT was $860.9 million and adding back $218.0 million of

---

[1]Hershey Proxy Statement and 2004 Annual Report to Shareholders, page 14.

depreciation ($200.1) and amortization ($17.9), which was included in the "total cost and expenses," results in EBITDA of $1,078.9 million. The depreciation and amortization values were reported in the cash flow statement and footnotes. EBITDA represents the gross amount of cash generated by the business' operations.

"Interest expense, net," includes gross interest expense less interest income. Gross interest expense includes the cost of borrowing funds via long-term debt as part of the permanent capital structure of a firm and short-tem debt for working capital needs. Interest income represents the interest "earnings" on cash balances and marketable securities such as bank's certificates of deposit, Treasury bills, commercial paper, and so on.

Income before income taxes (IBT) or simply, pretax income, results from subtracting interest expense from EBIT. The provision for income taxes is the combined amounts that are owed to the United States, state, local, and foreign governments based on the pretax income. Subtracting taxes from IBT results in net income as shown in Table 2.1.

Net income is the famous "bottom line." Net income represents the amount left over from sales after all of the expenses have been considered. When net income is divided by the number of shares outstanding, net income per share (or earnings per share [EPS]) results.

Two additional items are worth noting although they do not appear on Hershey's 2004 or 2005 income statement.

In 2003, Hershey implemented an accounting change that recognized certain leasing transactions and required an additional one-time, pretax $12.3 million expense or $7.4 million after taxes. So, instead of directly computing net income after subtracting the provision for income taxes, Hershey reported "income before cumulative effect of accounting change." After subtracting the extraordinary charge, net income resulted as shown below:

	2005	2004	2003
Income before Income Taxes	$772.9	$815.2	$708.2
Provision for Income Taxes	279.7	237.3	258.9
Income before Cumulative Effect of Accounting Change	493.2	577.9	449.3
Cumulative effect of accounting change, net of $4.9 tax benefit	0.0	0.0	7.4
Net Income	$493.2	$577.9	$441.9

This presentation occurs whenever a company adopts a new accounting standard that cumulatively affects prior years.

The second item worth noting is "Earnings per share–Diluted" or simply diluted EPS. In 2005, Hershey adopted a new accounting pronouncement. This pronouncement estimated the expense of Hershey's outstanding executive stock option compensation. This expense was reported in G&A. However, before adoption of this new accounting regulation, Hershey did not report any expense for these options. Instead, the practice that Hershey and other companies followed converted all outstanding options into shares outstanding as if the company issued new shares of stock to cover the shares represented by the options. This process provided a conservative view on the potential number of shares outstanding and a resulting conservative EPS value. In 2003, Hershey reported earnings per share—basic of $1.75 and EPS—diluted of $1.70. This indicated that Hershey's Executive compensation program cost approximately $0.05 per share.

Income Statements of Other Companies

It is helpful to look at the income statements of other companies to see slightly different formats that management finds more useful when presenting and discussing their financial results. Remember, the basic design is revenue (or sales) less cost of goods sold and operating expenses to arrive at operating income (OI) or earnings before interest and taxes (EBIT). From EBIT, interest expense and taxes are removed to derive net income. Along the way, one-time events are also identified and considered.

Notice the 2006 income statement for Wal-Mart, the world's largest retail organization (Table 2.2). The values are listed in millions of dollars, which says that Wal-Mart's 2006 sales were $312.4 billion (with a B). Their 2006 income statement is straightforward with no one-time events. Instead of net interest, Wal-Mart provides additional details about interest right on their income statement rather than only in their footnotes.

They indicate that out of their almost $1.4 billion of interest expense, $1.2 billion came from their debt and another $0.2 billion was embedded in leases, while interest income offset more than $0.2 billion of the expense.

JOINT VENTURES

One final item of note: As part of its business activities, Wal-Mart enters into arrangements wherein they own more than 50% of the business but not the full amount. The results of those businesses are added (consolidated) into Wal-Mart's sales, cost of sales, and so on, as if Wal-Mart wholly owned the business. At the end of the income statement, the portion of the income that belongs to the minority business partners is subtracted from Wal-Mart's results.

TABLE 2.2 Wal-Mart Consolidated Statements of Income ($ millions, except per share amounts)		
FOR THE YEARS ENDED 1/31:	2006	2005
Revenue		
Net sales	$312,427	$285,222
Other income, net	3,227	2,910
Total revenue	315,654	288,132
Costs and expenses		
Cost of sales	240,391	219,793
Selling, marketing, and administrative	56,733	51,248
Operating income	18,530	17,091
Interest: debt	1,171	934
Interest: leases	249	253
Interest income	(248)	(201)
Interest expense, net	1,172	986
Income from continuing operations before tax and minority interest	17,358	16,105
Provision for income taxes	5,803	5,589
Income from continuing operations before minority interest	11,555	10,516
Minority interest	(324)	(249)
Net income	$ 11,231	$ 10,267
Earnings per share	$ 2.68	$ 2.41

Notice the line "minority interest." If Wal-Mart (or any company) owns 20 to 50 percent of a joint venture, they recognized their share of the venture's income as investment income, which is often included in other income. Finally, if Wal-Mart owns less than 20 percent of a joint venture, then they simply recognize, as income, the dividends they receive from the venture.

Balance Sheet

Balance sheets capture the financial position of a firm at a point in time. Hershey is a calendar fiscal year-end company, which means that its financial year coincides with the calendar. It begins on January 1 and ends on December 31. Table 2.3 presents the Hershey balance sheet for 2005 and 2004. For discussion purposes only, on Table 2.3, aside of the Hershey balance sheet, is a column that calculates the change (increase or decrease) from 2004 to 2005 for each line of the balance sheet.

A balance sheet is founded on the accounting identity equation:

$$\text{Assets} = \text{Liabilities} + \text{Equity} \qquad (2.2)$$

TABLE 2.3 | Hershey Foods Corporation Consolidated Balance Sheet ($ millions)

FOR THE YEARS ENDED 12/31:	2005	2004	CHANGE*
Current assets:			
Cash and cash equivalents	$ 67.2	$ 54.8	$ 12.4
Accounts receivable-trade	559.3	408.9	150.4
Inventories	610.3	557.2	53.1
Deferred income taxes	78.2	61.8	16.4
Prepaid expenses and other	93.9	115.0	(21.1)
Total current assets	1,408.9	1,197.7	211.2
Property, plant and equipment, net	1,659.1	1,682.7	(23.6)
Goodwill (Intangibles resulting from business acquisitions)	487.3	464.0	23.3
Other intangibles	142.7	125.2	17.5
Other assets	597.2	343.2	254.0
Total assets	$4,295.2	$3,812.8	$482.4
Current liabilities:			
Accounts payable	$ 167.8	$ 148.7	$ 19.1
Accrued liabilities	507.8	469.2	38.6
Accrued income taxes	23.4	42.3	(18.9)
Short-term debt	819.1	343.3	475.8
Current portion of long-term debt	0.1	279.0	(278.9)
Total current liabilities	1,518.2	1,282.5	235.7
Long-term debt	942.7	690.6	252.1
Other long-term liabilities	413.0	383.4	29.6
Deferred income taxes	400.2	319.2	81.0
Total liabilities	3,274.1	2,675.7	598.4
Total stockholders' equity	1,021.1	1,137.1	(116.0)
Total liabilities and stockholders' equity	$4,295.2	$3,812.8	$482.4

*The change column is not part of the actual balance sheet. It is provided here for later reference purposes.

Assets and liabilities are further classified as current or long-term according to how quickly they will be converted to cash (assets) or be paid off (liabilities). In general, assets with less than a year (or an operating cycle) until they are converted into cash are considered current assets, and liabilities with less than a year (or an operating cycle) until they need to be paid are considered current liabilities. Equation 2.2 can be expanded to reflect this added distinction:

$$\text{Current Assets} + \text{Long-Term Assets} = \text{Current Liabilities} + \text{Long-Term Liabilities} + \text{Equity} \qquad (2.2a)$$

By accounting conventions, many of the underlying values are based on historical costs. Equity is also referred to as the "book value" of the firm.

The common balance sheet accounts are reviewed below specifically for Hershey. Keep in mind, these captions pertain to any company.

CASH

The $67.2 million of cash and cash equivalents on Hershey's 2005 balance sheet represents cash on hand (a very minimal amount), demand deposits, and checking accounts. These cash funds are required to conduct the transactions of the firm. The cash equivalents (sometimes referred to as marketable securities) include temporary investment of "excess" (beyond the immediate needs) cash in interest income-producing investments, which can be converted into cash with relatively small risk of a decline in their stated values. Examples of such investments include certificates of deposit from banks, Treasury bills, and commercial paper.

ACCOUNTS RECEIVABLE

Accounts receivable–trade, or simply accounts receivable, reflect sales made to customers for which Hershey has not yet received payment. Accounts receivable represent the amount that customers owe to Hershey at any point in time.

INVENTORY

Inventories represent the dollar amount of raw material (e.g., cocoa beans, sugar, milk, packaging material), goods-in-process, and finished goods (at the cost of production) that Hershey has on hand. The footnotes to the financial statements detail the major components of Hershey's inventories.

There are a few alternatives available for valuing the inventory. The two most common alternatives are FIFO (first-in first-out) and LIFO (last-in first-out). FIFO records inventory as the first units in are the first units out. For example, the first candy bars made are the first candy bars sold. While FIFO is the actual inventory management practice, for "accounting" purposes, Hershey uses the LIFO inventory method. In an inflationary environment, LIFO recognizes more expensive production costs sooner, reports higher expenses and more conservative income, and results in lower income tax payments. However, LIFO implies that the last candy bars made are the first ones sold and consequently, Hershey's balance sheet indicates that they have 50-year-old candy bars in its warehouses!

OTHER CURRENT ASSETS

The remaining current assets (see Table 2.3) include current deferred income taxes (which are discussed in Chapter 4, Business Organization and Taxes) as well as prepaid expenses and other current assets, which approached $94.0 million in 2005.

PROPERTY, PLANT, AND EQUIPMENT, NET

Net property, plant, and equipment (PP&E) is a long-term asset and summarizes the company's investment in land, building, equipment, and fixtures, net, of accumulated depreciation. As discussed on the income statement, depreciation expense represents an estimate of the annual consumption of a fixed asset's value. Accumulated depreciation is the accumulation of all of the depreciation expense since the asset was first purchased. Further detail is provided in the accompanying notes of the annual report:

$ MILLIONS	2005	2004
Land	$ 81.7	$ 84.6
Building	699.9	688.6
Equipment and fixtures	2,676.8	2,596.0
Total PP & E, gross	3,458.4	3,369.2
Less: Accumulated depreciation	(1,799.3)	(1,686.5)
PP & E, net	$1,659.1	$1,682.7

PP&E, gross, is recorded at the original purchase price. Market value, economic value, replacement value, and current cost are not considered. Only historical cost is recorded in the US GAAP accounting system. This has some noteworthy implications. An 80-acre tract of land that was purchased before 1900 and currently holds Hershey's major production facilities and divisional offices, is still carried at its historical cost of $1 million instead of an appreciated value.

Another illustration, in the process of making milk chocolate, the chocolate paste needs to be "conched" for an extended period of time. (Conching is equivalent to blending and mixing.) The machines used in this process are called *conches*. The conches at Hershey are still functional, cost effective, and production efficient after 85 years of operation. Although there is significant economic value, these conches are recorded on the books at their original purchase price less their accumulated depreciation. These conches are currently on the books at a zero dollar value. In fact, these conches were fully depreciated (or written off) before any of Hershey's senior management team was born! However, there is tremendous economic value in this equipment, but due to the nature of accounting for PP&E, only historical cost less accumulated depreciation is recorded.

INTANGIBLES RESULTING FROM BUSINESS ACQUISITIONS

Also referred to as *goodwill*, the intangibles resulting from business acquisitions represent the extra amount paid for an acquisition beyond the acquired assets. To illustrate, in the 1980s, Hershey bought the Dietrich Corporation (Luden's, Fifth Avenue bar, MelloMints, etc.) for approximately $100 million. A group of accountants determined that Hershey was receiving $60 million of assets (receivables, inventory, and net PP&E) but was also assuming $20 million of liabilities (accounts payable and debt) or net assets of $40 million ($60 million assets less $20 million liabilities). The difference between what Hershey paid ($100 million) and the tangible net assets that were received ($40 million) represents $60 million of goodwill or intangibles resulting from business acquisitions.

Furthermore, this goodwill was amortized (similar to depreciated) over a 40-year horizon. The annual amortization was considered an expense. In January 2002, Hershey and many other corporations adopted Financial Accounting Standards No. 141, Business Combinations, and No. 142, Goodwill and Other Intangible Assets. The effect was that amortization of goodwill was replaced with an impairment evaluation. In the example above, there is an annual evaluation of the value of the Dietrich Corporation. As long as that value remains above $100 million, there is no impairment. On the other hand, if the evaluation ultimately shows a value of only $75 million, then the assets have been impaired and $25 million would be recognized as a one-time impairment expense and the goodwill would be decreased by a like amount.

Other intangibles primarily included trademarks and patents obtained through business acquisitions. Trademarks are held with no amortization and patents are amortized over their legal lives of approximately 17 years.

OTHER ASSETS

The final category on Hershey's assets is a catchall reporting category called *other assets*. These long-term other assets include capitalized software, long-term business investments, and long-term deferred tax assets.

In summary, Hershey reports $4.3 billion of assets at book value. Their replacement value could be higher or lower. Next we consider the liabilities—current and long-term.

Current liabilities usually contain two types: (1) operating liabilities such as payables and accruals and (2) financing liabilities such as short-term borrowings.

PAYABLES AND ACCRUALS

Hershey presents three separate accounts: accounts payable, accrued liabilities, and accrued income taxes. Other common payables include taxes payable and wages payable. Accounts payable and accrued liabilities represent the amounts owed to suppliers for purchases of goods and services. The distinguishing characteristic hinges on whether an invoice was received or not. Accounts payable have been billed by the supplier, whereas for accrued liabilities, charges for services or products have been incurred but have not yet been billed.

SHORT-TERM DEBT

Short-term debt represents interest-bearing loans. On the Hershey balance sheet, short-term borrowings are captured as short-term debt and current portion of long-term debt (long-term debt that will mature in less than a year). Other common short-term debt balance sheet line items are short-term bank borrowing and notes payable.

LONG-TERM LIABILITIES

Commonly, long-term liabilities include the three liabilities on Hershey's balance sheet. Long-term debt is interest-bearing debt. Other long-term liabilities are another catchall presentation line. However, the largest items in other long-term liabilities are pension liabilities and post-retirement benefits other than pension (PBOP). PBOP is similar to a pension liability except related to non-pension benefits such as retiree's medical premiums.

Deferred taxes represent the difference between the measure of the annual amount of tax obligations incurred by the firm during the year and the amount of taxes actually paid. It is the tax amount that a company anticipates that it will owe the government in the future. The sources of these differences are explained in the notes to the financial statements, but in general relate to differences in when certain business expenses are recognized for tax purposes and within US GAAP. Chapter 4, Business Organization and Taxes, discusses deferred taxes more fully.

STOCKHOLDERS' EQUITY

Although condensed in Table 2.3, the stockholders' equity section includes four distinct sections:

BALANCE SHEET ITEM	COMMENT
1. Preferred stock Common stock Class B common stock Additional paid in capital	In combination, these accounts represent the proceeds received when stock was originally issued.
2. Retained earnings	The accumulated net income retained (not paid as a dividend) in the corporation since inception.
3. Treasury stock	A reduction that reflects amounts paid for repurchased shares.
4. Unearned ESOP (EMPLOYEE STOCK OPTION PLANS) compensation Accumulated other	Miscellaneous impacts that directly are assigned to equity.

Once again, the current market value of the equity is not reflected in stockholder's equity. Simply put, stockholders' equity represents (1) the original proceeds from the company selling shares plus (2) the accumulated earnings that were not paid out in the form of dividends less (3) the repurchased amount of shares at the existing market prices at the time of repurchase.

The next section introduces the cash flow statement and develops a link between the three financial statements.

Analysis of Cash Flows

The income statement presents revenue, expenses, and income over a period of time. It does not detail cash flow over time due to accrual accounting. The balance sheet represents the financial picture of the firm at a point in time, what it owns and what it owes. The balance sheet includes the cash balances from one period to the next and consequently the change or total amount of cash flow for the period. From the balance sheet on Table 2.4, Hershey's cash balance increased by $12.4 million. This represents a positive cash flow for 2005. However, there are no details as to where the cash came from or where it went.

In November 1987, the Financial Accounting Standards Board (FASB) issued its Statement of Financial Accounting Standards No. 95, Statement of Cash Flows (FAS 95). FAS 95 requires a segregation of cash flow items on the cash flow statement by:

- Cash from operations

- Cash (used for) investments

- Cash from (used for) financing

In general, the cash from operations section begins with net income and adds back any non-cash expense (e.g., such as depreciation). This is followed by cash flow implications of changes in operating assets (e.g., accounts receivable, inventory) or operating liabilities (e.g., payables, accruals).

The following summarizes the cash flow implications of changes in the balance sheet:

	ASSET CHANGE	LIABILITY CHANGE
Source of cash	Decrease	Increase
Use of cash	Increase	Decrease

For example, an increase in inventory signifies that we purchased more inventory during the year. We "used" our cash to buy inventory. A decrease in accounts payable shows that we used our cash to pay off our suppliers.

Table 2.4 provides a simplified cash flow statement that categorizes each change in a balance sheet item as operating, investing, or financing cash and denotes whether the change is a source (or use). For example, from the balance sheet, Hershey's trade receivables increased by $150.4 million (as Hershey decided to finance more of their customers' purchases). This is found on Table 2.5 as a use of cash. Other noted changes in the balance

TABLE 2.4	Simplified Cash Flow 2005 Hershey Foods Corporation ($ millions)		
Cash flow from (used by) operations			
Net income		$493.2	(C)
Depreciation		200.1	(A)
Software amortization		17.9	(B)
Deferred taxes-asset		(16.4)	
Deferred taxes-liabilities		81.0	
Change in:			
Accounts receivable-trade		(150.4)	
Inventories		(53.1)	
Prepaid expenses and other		21.1	
Goodwill (intangibles resulting from business acquisitions)		(23.3)	
Other intangibles		(17.5)	
Other assets (excluding capitalized software and amortization)		(258.7)	(B)
Accounts payable		19.1	
Accrued liabilities		38.6	
Accrued income taxes		(18.9)	
Other long-term liabilities		29.6	
Net cash provided from operating activities		**$362.3**	
Cash flow from (used by) investing			
Capital expenditures		(181.1)	(A)
Other property, plant and equipment, net		4.6	(A)
Capitalized software (included in other assets)		(13.2)	(B)
Net cash used by investing activities		**(189.7)**	
Cash flow from (used by) financing			
Short-term debt		475.8	
Current portion of long-term debt		(278.9)	
Long-term debt		252.1	
Dividends		(221.2)	(C)
Share repurchases		(537.0)	(C)
Miscellaneous other stockholders' equity		149.0	(C)
Net cash used by financing activities		**(160.2)**	
Increase (decrease) in cash		$ 12.4	

sheet accounts are also easy to see on Table 2.4. However, to properly segregate changes in (1) plant, property, and equipment, net, (2) other assets, and (3) stockholders' equity, it is necessary to isolate certain key components that are detailed in the footnotes. This detail at first seems cumbersome, but it provides additional information that is worth noting before looking at Hershey's actual cash flow statement.

The annual change in PP&E, net, is usually equal to capital expenditures less depreciation. In this specific Hershey case however, there was an additional source of $4.6 million for PP&E, net. When this reclassification is considered, PP&E, net, reconciles to the balance sheet change. On Table 2.4, these three items (capital expenditures, depreciation, and capital expenditures—other) are all designated with an "A" and are found in the various cash flow areas as noted below:

CHANGE IN BALANCE SHEET ITEMS	ANNUAL CASH FLOW COMPONENT	CASH FLOW CLASSIFICATION	INCREASE (DECREASE) ($MILLIONS)
A. PP & E, net	Capital expenditures	Investing	$ 181.1 U
	Depreciation expense	Operations	(200.1) S
	Other	Investing	(4.6) S
	Balance sheet change (A)		$ (23.6) S
B. Other assets	Capitalized software	Investing	$ 13.2 U
	Software amortization	Operations	(17.9) S
	Miscellaneous other assets	Operations	258.7 U
	Balance sheet change (B)		$ 254.0 U
C. Stockholders' equity	Net income	Operations	$ 493.2 S
	Dividends	Financing	(221.2) U
	Share repurchases	Financing	(537.0) U
	Miscellaneous other	Financing	149.0 S
	Balance sheet change (C)		$(116.0) U

U—Indicates use of funds; S—Indicates source of funds.

The increase in other assets includes an investment in capitalized software offset by its amortization (which as mentioned is similar to depreciation on the company's software) as well as other, miscellaneous items. These three items are shown on Table 2.4 with a designation of "B."

Finally, the change to stockholders' equity is equal to net income, less dividends, less (plus) share repurchase (issuance), and plus or minus the miscellaneous other changes and reclassification within stockholders' equity. These four items are designated as "C" on Table 2.4.

Table 2.4 defines where cash came from and how it was used throughout 2005. Notice the result of Table 2.4 is an increase in the cash balances of $12.4 million.

Interpreting Information on the Cash Flow Statement

Reviewing Table 2.4, cash from operating activities includes two subsections. The first subsection adjusts reported net income for non-cash expenses that were deducted to arrive at net income while the second subsection captures the changes in operating assets and liabilities.

Net income is the largest source of cash, but in calculating net income some non-cash expenses were deducted. These non-cash expenses such as depreciation and amortization of capitalized software and other intangibles did not require a cash payment. Within the cash flow statement, net income is subsequently adjusted to align with cash flows by "adding back" non-cash expenses such as depreciation and amortization. In a similar fashion, an adjustment must be made for deferred taxes. The change in deferred taxes represents the difference between the tax expense on the income statement and what was actually paid to the taxing authorities. The income statement included a tax expense of $279.7 million as seen on Table 2.1. However, after filing its 2005 tax return, Hershey was obligated to pay taxes of $215.1 million. The difference from the reported expense to the actual payment represents $64.6 million of deferred taxes–assets and liabilities—and must be captured as a "source" of cash. See Chapter 4, Business Organization and Taxes, for a complete discussion of deferred taxes.

The second subsection of cash from operating activities presents the year-to-year changes in operating assets and liabilities, e.g., accounts receivable, inventories, and so on.

Cash (used for) investing details investments that the firm made. Capital expenditures, also referred to as *capital additions*, are monies that are reinvested in the business to buy new plant, property, and equipment. In 2005, Hershey spent $181.1 million in capital expenditures. Also, due to significant information technology investment, Hershey specifically highlighted capitalized software in the investing section of the cash flow and included it in other assets on the balance sheet.

The third section, cash flow from (used by) financing, includes the issuance or (repayment) of debt, dividend payments, equity, and some minor other adjustments. In 2005, Hershey borrowed $449.0 million in total, repurchased $537.0 million of its own stock, and paid a total dividend of $221.2 million to their stockholders.

Consolidated Statements of Cash Flows

The cash flow statement should be as straightforward as presented above. Table 2.4, Simplified Cash Flow, illustrates the linkage between the income statement, balance sheet, and cash flow. However, often the actual cash flow statement does not align with the changes in the balance sheet accounts, and the underlying relationship is distorted. This is the case for Hershey in 2005.

Table 2.5 presents Hershey's actual consolidated statements of cash flows. The three major categories are once again evident: operations, investments, and financing.

However, only a limited number of specific entries on this statement are consistent with the simplified cash flow statement on Table 2.4. For example, net income is the same source of $493.2 million on both tables, but some of the other values are inconsistent. On the balance sheet (see Table 2.3), accounts receivable shows an increase of $150.4 million and was reported as a use of that amount on Table 2.4. However, in Table 2.5, the actual statement of cash flow, accounts receivable are shown as a use of $149.0 million, which implies an increase of that same amount. Notice the differences in the use of cash for inventories and source from accounts payable. The impacts of acquisitions, divestitures, restructurings, discontinuance of business, and so on create this difference and blur the fundamental relationship between the balance sheet and this cash flow.

In August 2005, Hershey acquired Joseph Schmidt Confections and Scharffen Berger Chocolate Maker, Inc., for a total of $47.1 million. As a result of these acquisitions, Hershey acquired accounts receivable, inventory, property and equipment, accounts payable, etc. The actual statement of cash flows isolates the investment in acquisitions

TABLE 2.5	Hershey Foods Corporation Consolidated Statements of Cash Flows ($ millions)		
FOR THE YEARS ENDED 12/31:		**2005**	**2004**
Cash flows provided from (used by) operating activities			
Net income		$493.2	$577.9
Adjustments to reconcile net income to net cash provided from operations			
Depreciation and amortization		218.0	189.7
Stock-based compensation expense, net of tax		34.5	28.4
Deferred income taxes		71.1	(74.6)
Business realignment initiatives		74.0	–
Contributions to pension plans		(277.5)	(8.0)
Changes in assets and liabilities, net of effects from acquisitions/divestitures			
Accounts receivable		(149.0)	17.3
Inventories		(51.2)	(40.0)
Accounts payable		16.7	(11.3)
Other assets and liabilities		32.0	108.4
Net cash provided from operating activities		**461.8**	**787.8**
Cash flows provided from (used by) investing activities			
Capital additions		(181.1)	(181.7)
Capital software additions		(13.2)	(14.2)
Business acquisitions		(47.1)	(166.9)
Proceeds from divestitures		2.7	–
Net cash provided from investing activities		**(238.7)**	**(362.8)**
Cash flows provided from (used by) financing activities			
Net change in short-term borrowings		475.6	331.2
Long-term borrowings		248.3	–
Repayment of long-term debt		(278.2)	(0.9)
Cash dividends paid		(221.2)	(205.7)
Exercise of stock options, including tax impact		101.8	89.3
Repurchase of common stock		(537.0)	(698.9)
Net cash provided from financing activities		**(210.7)**	**(485.0)**
(Decrease) increase in cash and cash equivalents		**$ 12.4**	**$ (60.0)**

(or proceeds from divestitures). Consequently, the sources or uses of cash derived from the changes in receivables, inventories, and so on are related solely to the existing business, as of the beginning of the year. We can conclude that Hershey increased their base business accounts receivable by $149.0 million, but as a result of the acquisitions, Hershey added $1.4 million to the accounts receivable. So the noted change on the balance sheet was an increase of $150.4 million.

A secondary reason why there may be inconsistent values between the statements on Tables 2.4 and 2.5 relates to the level of available detail for someone inside the company versus outside the company. Each line item on the income statement and balance sheet is comprised of dozens to hundreds of lines of detailed subaccounts. Most of the changes to these subaccounts are classified as described in previous simplified cash flow statement. However, there are changes to certain specific subaccounts that do not follow the flow established in Table 2.4 for various reasons. Those changes are captured in another line item or some miscellaneous line item on the consolidated statement of cash flows.

Even with these presentation challenges, the consolidated statements of cash flow contribute additional insight into the firm. In the operating cash flow section, there is another grouping of adjustments to the income statement that addresses other non-cash expenses and extraordinary items. Examples of these items include:

LINE ITEM	RATIONALE
Stock-based compensation expense, net of tax*	The executive stock-based compensation required no cash payment, so this is a reflection of that and adds back the expense, net of taxes.
Business realignment initiatives*	Impact is included in net income, but Hershey may not have incurred any actual cash impact or if it did, those impacts were noted in other accounts.
Gain (loss) on sale of businesses	The gains were recognized and included in the net income; however, the gain is reversed here and included and presented in the "Proceeds from divestiture" line in the investing section.
Asset impairment write-downs	This is recognized as an expense for the purposes of determining income, but it did not involve any cash flow—another non-cash expense.
Cumulative effect of accounting change	This is recognized as an expense for the purposes of determining income, but it did not involve any cash flow—another non-cash expense.

*Specifically included on Table 2.6.

Additionally, the cash flows provided from (used by) investing activities section, also contains two informative lines:

LINE ITEM	RATIONALE
Business acquisitions	Acquisitions are an investment that may require the use of cash. This reflects the amount paid for acquisitions, as discussed above.
Proceeds from divestitures	This reflects the total amount received when divesting a business. It includes all proceeds, including the gain (loss) from above.

In addition to the 2005 acquisitions, Hershey acquired Mauna Loa Macadamia Nut Corporation for $127.8 million and Grupo Lorena, one of Mexico's top sugar confectionery companies, for $39.1 million in 2004. In 2005, Hershey sold a small Canadian business line for $2.7 million with no significant gain or loss.

These concepts are readily applicable to any firm.

Financial Statement Summary

Figure 2.1 presents an overview of the timing of the primary financial statements. Figure 2.2 provides the complete (albeit summarized) picture for Hershey in 2005.

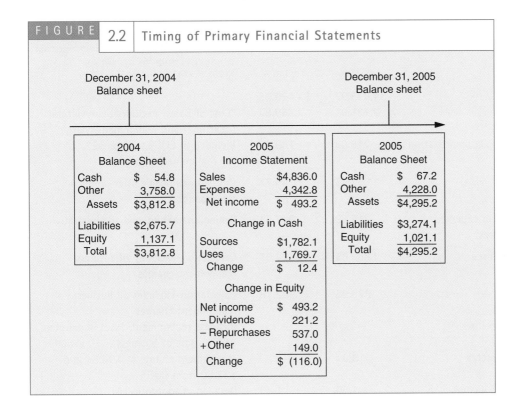

FIGURE 2.2 | Timing of Primary Financial Statements

December 31, 2004
Balance sheet

December 31, 2005
Balance sheet

2004 Balance Sheet		
Cash	$ 54.8	
Other	3,758.0	
Assets	$3,812.8	
Liabilities	$2,675.7	
Equity	1,137.1	
Total	$3,812.8	

2005 Income Statement	
Sales	$4,836.0
Expenses	4,342.8
Net income	$ 493.2

Change in Cash

Sources	$1,782.1
Uses	1,769.7
Change	$ 12.4

Change in Equity

Net income	$ 493.2
– Dividends	221.2
– Repurchases	537.0
+ Other	149.0
Change	$ (116.0)

2005 Balance Sheet		
Cash	$ 67.2	
Other	4,228.0	
Assets	$4,295.2	
Liabilities	$3,274.1	
Equity	1,021.1	
Total	$4,295.2	

Thomson One Financial Data Base

The Thomson One Financial data base provides convenient access to financial statement information. The data base provides a consistent organization of the data from one corporation to another. The next three tables compare the Thomson financial statements with those of Hershey. While Thomson provides 5 years of data, the tables only include 2 years along with a column that reconciles the statements found in Thomson One and Hershey's annual report.

Table 2.6 presents the income statement and compares/reconciles it to the actual income statement for Hershey (see Table 2.1). The Thomson data base may use some different language (e.g., cost of goods sold versus cost of sales), provide additional calculations (e.g., gross profit), require the combination of separately reported items, or detail individual lines from the company's annual report footnote information. The Extraordinary Credit–Pretax and Extraordinary Charge–Pretax are examples of Thomson's captions that are reconcilable to the reported business realignment and asset impairment expenses offset by gains (or losses) on the sale of a business. Non-Operating Interest Income, Interest Expense on Debt, and Interest Capitalized are provided in the Thomson One Financial data base from the annual report footnotes for net interest expense.

The Thomson balance sheet is presented in Table 2.7, along with its reconciliation. Once again, in some cases, the Thomson One Financial data base provides additional detail based on footnotes in Hershey's annual report, while in other cases, items reported by Hershey are combined to form a new line in Thomson One. For example, Thomson One details property, plant, and equipment–gross, which reflects the original cost of the equipment; accumulated depreciation, which is a summation of all of the depreciation

| TABLE 2.6 | Worldscope Annual Financials–Industrial Template Income Statement (Scaling Factor: Millions USD) |

ANNUAL INCOME STATEMENT	12/31/05	12/31/04	RECONCILIATION* TO HERSHEY'S INCOME STATEMENT TABLE 2.2
Sales	$4,835.97	$4,429.25	
Cost of goods sold	2,725.01	2,489.87	"Cost of Sales" excludes depreciation (next line) and realignment charge
Depreciation, depletion, & amortization	218.03	189.67	Included in COGS, except $22.50 for realignment charge
Gross Income	1,892.93	1,749.72	Calculation–Income after producing the product
Selling, general & admin expenses	912.99	847.54	Selling, marketing, and administrative
Other operating expenses	–	–	
Total operating expenses	3,856.03	3,527.07	Calculation–excludes all business realignment charges
Operating income	979.95	902.18	Calculation–excludes all business realignment charges
Extraordinary credit-pretax	–	–	Business realignment, asset impairment, gain on sale of business . . . . includes
Extraordinary charge-pretax	119.04	–	realignment charge of $96.54 and $22.50 from COGS
Non-operating interest income	1.50	1.39	Detailed in footnotes (A)
Reserves-Inc (Dec)	–	–	
Pretax equity interest earnings	–	–	
Other income/expense-net	–	–	
Earnings bef interest & taxes	862.41	903.56	Includes interest income
Interest expense on debt	89.49	70.52	Detailed in footnotes (A)
Interest capitalized	–	2.60	Detailed in footnotes (A)
Pretax income	772.93	835.64	
Income taxes	279.68	244.77	
Minority interest	–	–	
Equity interest earnings	–	–	
After tax other income/expense	–	–	
Discontinued operations	–	–	
Net income bef extraordinary items & disc ops	493.24	590.88	
Preferred dividends	–	–	
Extraordinary items & gain (Loss) sale of assets	–	–	
Net income bef preferred dividends	493.24	590.88	
Preferred dividend requirements	–	–	
Net Income available to common	$ 493.24	$ 590.88	

PER SHARE DATA	12/31/05	12/31/04	
EPS	1.99	2.30	

*Where no comments are found, the items are identical between Thomson and Hershey, as reported.
(A) Interest expense on debt less non-operating income-interest less interest capitalized equals the reported interest, net.

TABLE 2.7	Worldscope Annual Financials—Industrial Template Balance Sheet (Scaling Factor: Millions USD)

ASSETS	12/31/05	12/31/04	RECONCILIATION* TO HERSHEY'S BALANCE SHEET TABLE 2.4
Cash & equivalents	$ 67.18	$ 54.84	
Receivables net	559.29	408.93	
Inventories	610.28	557.18	
Prepaid expenses	n/a	n/a	
Other current assets	172.18	161.49	Deferred income taxes, prepaid expense, and other
Total current assets	1,408.94	1,182.44	
Long term receivables	—	—	
Investments in unconsol subsidiaries	—	—	
Other investments	—	—	
Property, plant, & equipment—Gross	3,458.42	3,369.20	Detailed in footnotes
Accumulated depreciation	1,799.28	1,686.50	Detailed in footnotes
Property, plant, & equipment—Net	1,659.14	1,682.70	
Other assets	1,227.16	932.39	Goodwill, other intangibles, and other assets
Total Assets	$4,295.24	$3,797.53	

LIAB. & SHAREHOLDERS' EQ	12/31/05	12/31/04	
Accounts payable	$ 167.81	$ 148.69	
ST Debt & current portion due LT debt	819.12	622.32	Short-term debt and current portion long-term debt
Accrued payroll	172.53	146.52	Detailed in footnotes
Income taxes payable	23.45	42.28	
Dividends payable	n/a	n/a	
Other current liabilities	335.31	325.58	Other accrued liabilities less accrued payroll
Total current liabilities	1,518.22	1,285.38	
Long term debt	942.76	690.60	
Provision for risks and charges	246.90	267.55	Detailed in footnotes—other long-term liabilities
Deferred income	n/a	n/a	
Deferred taxes	400.25	328.89	
Deferred tax liability in untaxed reserves	n/a	n/a	
Other liabilities	166.03	135.80	Other long-term liabilities less provision (above)
Total liabilities	3,274.16	2,708.23	
Non-equity reserves	n/a	—	
Minority interest	—	—	
Preferred stock	—	—	
Common equity	1,021.08	1,089.30	Total stockholder's equity
Total liabilities & shareholders' equity	$4,295.24	$3,797.53	

*Where no comments are found, the items are identical between Thomson and Hershey, as reported.

TABLE 2.8	Worldscope Annual Financials—Industrial Template Annual Cash Flow Statement
	(Scaling Factor: Millions USD)

ANNUAL CASH FLOW STMT	12/31/05	12/31/04	RECONCILIATION* HERSHTO EY'S CASH FLOW STATEMENT TABLE 2.5
Operating Activities			
Income bef extraordinary items	$493.24	$590.88	
Depreciation, depletion & amortization	218.03	189.67	
Deferred income taxes & investment tax credit	71.04	(81.93)	Stock-based compensation, business realignment, and pensions
Other cash flow	(169.02)	—	Stock-based compensation, business realignment, and pensions
Funds from operations	613.29	698.61	Subtotal
Extraordinary items	—	—	Cash extraordinary items, only
Funds from/for other operating activities	(151.53)	98.84	Change in assets and liabilities
Net cash flow from operating activities	461.76	797.45	Source of cash
Investing Activities			
Capital expenditures	181.07	181.73	Capital additions
Additions to other assets	13.24	14.16	Capitalized software additions
Net assets from acquisitions	47.07	166.86	Business acquisitions
Increase in investments	—	—	
Decrease in investments	—	—	
Disposal of fixed assets	2.71	—	Proceeds from divestitures
Other use/(source)-investing	—	—	
Net cash flow from investing activities	238.67	362.75	Use of cash
Financing Activities			
Net proceeds from sales/issue of com/prf stock	—	—	
Com/prf purchased, retired, converted, redeemed	537.00	698.91	Repurchased stock and incentive plan transactions
Long term borrowings	248.32	—	
Inc (Dec) in ST borrowings	475.58	331.25	
Reduction in long term debt	278.24	0.88	
Cash dividends paid—total	221.24	205.75	
Other source/(use)—financing	101.83	79.63	
Net cash flow from financing activities	(210.75)	(494.66)	Use of cash
Cash & cash equivalents-inc (Dec)	$ 12.35	$(59.96)	

*Where no comments are found, the items are identical between Thomson and Hershey, as reported.

expensed since the assets were first purchased; and property, plant, and equipment, net, as reported in the annual report.

Finally, Table 2.8 compares the cash flow statements with reconciling notes provided.

Notice in the investing section, capital expenditures, additions to other assets, and net assets from acquisitions are all shown as positive values, but remember they are all uses of cash.

Additional Reporting Requirements

In addition to the three primary financial statements discussed above, a company is required to report additional information that is detailed in the "notes to financial statements." Within the first note, the firm clarifies its accounting policies, which generally includes discussing its inventory, depreciation, and amortization policies; additional expense detail such as advertising and promotion expense, research and development expense; and other accounting issues such as treatment of foreign currency and financial instruments.

Additional notes discuss the firm's acquisitions and divestitures, capital stock position, short-term and long-term debt, lease commitments, income taxes, hedging activities using derivatives, retirement plans, post-retirement benefits other than pensions, incentive plans, and stock prices and dividends. These notes discuss the company's activities and/or policies related to each of the topics. A fair number of these notes have been approved by the American Medical Association as a cure against insomnia. They are long and arduous.

Additional financial statements include a reconciliation of stockholders' equity, a summary of quarterly financial data such as sales and income, line of business detail, and international diversification (geographical) data. For businesses with a substantial amount (defined as 10% or more) of its business in more than one line of business or with a substantial amount (10% or more) of its business outside of the United States, additional reporting is required for each significant line of business or geographical region:

- Net sales

- Operating income

- Identifiable assets

- Capital expenditures

- Depreciation and amortization expense

Because Hershey is primarily a domestic, single-line of business company, it does not report this supplemental information.

Table 2.9 shows the business segment and geographical financial information reported by PepsiCo, Inc. Even though the data are limited, it is clear that PepsiCo is primarily comprised of three divisions: Frito-Lay North America, PepsiCo Beverages North America, and PepsiCo International, with the Quaker Foods division being a minor piece of their total business. Each division is contributing to the organization's growth and profitability.

Despite the limited data, insights can be gleaned about the Pepsi business. PepsiCo's commitment to international expansion is clear given that its international business is the only area where capital expenditures exceeded depreciation by more than $150 million for all 3 years.

In addition to the five required data items, PepsiCo also presents "amortization of intangibles" for each business segment. At the bottom of Table 2.9, PepsiCo breaks out its revenues and long-lived assets by its four primary geographical regions.

Finally, a Summary of Key Financial Data is also provided in an annual report. The summary presents 5 to 11 years worth of data for the firm, thus providing a greater historical picture as well as fuller appreciation of underlying trends. The data are taken from the income statement, balance sheet, cash flow statement, and even selected critical pieces of data from the footnotes as management deems important. The summary may include "key" financial metrics (see Chapter 7) in addition to the financial data.

| TABLE 2.9 | Product Line Segment Information—PepsiCo, Inc. ($ Millions) |

	NET REVENUE			OPERATING PROFITS		
	2005	2004	2003	2005	2004	2003
Frito-Lay North America	$10,322	$ 9,560	$ 9,091	$ 2,529	$ 2,389	$ 2,242
Pepsico Beverages North America	9,146	8,313	7,733	2,037	1,911	1,690
Pepsico International	11,376	9,862	8,678	1,607	1,323	1,061
Quaker Foods North America	1,718	1,526	1,467	537	475	470
Total Divisions	32,562	29,261	26,969	6,710	6,098	5,463
Corporate	—	—	—	(788)	(689)	(502)
Other	—	—	2	—	(150)	(180)
Total	$32,562	$29,261	$26,971	$ 5,922	$ 5,259	$ 4,781

	CAPITAL SPENDING			DEPRECIATION		
	2005	2004	2003	2005	2004	2003
Frito-Lay North America	$ 512	$ 469	$ 426	$ 419	$ 420	$ 416
Pepsico Beverages North America	320	265	332	264	258	245
Pepsico International	667	537	521	420	382	350
Quaker Foods North America	31	33	32	34	36	36
Total divisions	1,530	1,304	1,311	1,137	1,096	1,047
Corporate	206	83	34	21	21	29
Other	—	—	—	—	—	—
Total	$ 1,736	$ 1,387	$ 1,345	$ 1,158	$ 1,117	$ 1,076

	TOTAL ASSETS			AMORTIZATION OF INTANGIBLE ASSETS		
	2005	2004	2003	2005	2004	2003
Frito-Lay North America	$ 5,948	$ 5,476	$ 5,332	$ 3	$ 3	$ 3
Pepsico Beverages North America	6,316	6,048	5,856	76	75	75
Pepsico International	9,983	8,921	8,109	71	68	66
Quaker Foods North America	989	978	995	—	1	1
Total Divisions	23,236	21,423	20,292	150	147	145
Corporate	5,331	3,569	2,384	—	—	—
Other	3,160	2,995	2,651	—	—	—
Total	$31,727	$27,987	$25,327	$ 150	$ 147	$ 145

	NET REVENUE			LONG-LIVED ASSETS		
	2005	2004	2003	2005	2004	2003
United States	$19,937	$18,329	$17,377	$10,723	$10,212	$ 9,907
Mexico	3,095	2,724	2,642	902	878	869
United Kingdom	1,821	1,692	1,510	1,715	1,896	1,724
Canada	1,509	1,309	1,147	582	548	508
All other countries	6,200	5,207	4,295	3,948	3,339	3,123
Total	$32,562	$29,261	$26,971	$17,870	$16,873	$16,131

Corporate Financial Reporting Responsibilities and Requirements

One of the important responsibilities of the chief financial officer (CFO) is to manage all financial reporting requirements both inside and outside the firm. Table 2.10 lists the numerous reporting requirements to the public, governmental agencies, and management team.

The CFO is responsible for the timely and accurate preparation of the financial statements. The board of directors has access to all reporting but may choose to remain at a consolidated and SEC level of reporting (items 1 to 4 on Table 2.10). The phrase "consolidated" means for the total corporation. These statements consolidate all operations of all the divisions, subsidiaries, strategic business units, departments, etc., into one corporate entity. Item number 5, tax books and filings, is a requirement of the Internal Revenue System for which the board of directors and senior management accept responsibility; these are discussed more in Chapter 4. From time to time, the board of directors may choose to get involved with more day-to-day details of the company (items 6 to 9).

Consolidated statements, Securities and Exchange Commission filings, as well as tax filings all require audit by a public accounting firm. The public accounting firm and its subsequent opinion letter attests that the financial reports are fairly prepared in accordance with US GAAP. Shareholders elect a board of directors who, in turn, select (1) an audit committee to oversee the external audit of the firm's accounts and to direct the preparation of an annual report to shareholders and (2) a public accounting firm to perform the audit and to approve (or disapprove) the annual report.

Congress has accepted the ultimate responsibility for the determination of accounting principles. However in the Securities Act of 1933, the authority was delegated to the Securities and Exchange Commission (SEC). Choosing not to become directly involved in the regulation of accounting principles, the SEC elected to oversee self-regulation by the accounting profession. Public accounting firms are guided by a set of generally accepted accounting principles (GAAP), which are governed by opinions, issued between 1959 and 1973, by the Accounting Principles Board (APB) and since 1973 by the Financial Accounting Standards Board (FASB).

With the financial reporting issues of the past few years as well as the outright fraud, new, sweeping legislation was enacted: the Sarbanes-Oxley Act of 2002. Sarbanes-Oxley is the most important legislation in this area since the Securities Act of 1933. Its primary impacts include:

- Establishes the Public Company Accounting Oversight Board, which is a nongovernmental panel that deals with violations

- Strengthens auditors
    - Auditors report to the Audit Committee of the company's board of directors.
    - The Audit Committee is comprised of independent board members and not management of the company and contain at least one financial expert.
    - It is now unlawful to coerce or influence auditors.
    - Auditors of the company can no longer provide other services, such as consulting, to the company.

- Establishes an Internal Control Report as part of the annual report

- Requires the CEO and CFO to sign responsibility statements for the financial statements

TABLE 2.10 | Reporting Requirements

REPORTING REQUIREMENT	CHIEF FINANCIAL OFFICER	BOARD OF DIRECTORS	PUBLIC ACCOUNTING FIRM	TARGET AUDIENCE STOCKHOLDERS	INTERNAL USE	TAX AGENCIES	SECURITIES AND EXCHANGE
1. Consolidated income statement	Required	Required	Required	Required	Required	—	—
2. Consolidated balance sheet	Required	Required	Required	Required	Required	—	—
3. Consolidated cash flow statement	Required	Required	Required	Required	Required	—	—
4. SEC reports: 10K, 10Q, other	Required	Required	Required	Required	Required	—	Required
5. Tax books and filings	Required	Required	Required	—	—	Required	—
6. Divisional financial statements	Required	Required	—	—	Required	—	—
7. Cost accounting reports	Required	Required	—	—	Required	—	—
8. Annual budgets and financial plans	Required	Required	—	—	Required	—	—
9. Project requests and reviews	Required	Required	—	—	Required	—	—

- Requires disclosure of transactions between management and principal stockholders

- Prohibits personal loans between the company and executives

The act extends widely for public company accounting reform and investor protection. Stockholders receive consolidated financial information from annual reports and quarterly reports as well as SEC filings. The SEC requires that all publicly held corporations submit a standardized annual report called a *10K*, which usually contains more information than the annual report. Firms are required to send the 10K to all stockholders that request it. In addition, there is a quarterly filing called the *10Q*. The SEC further requires that whenever a corporation wishes to issue securities to the public, it must file a registration statement that discloses the current financial data as well as such items as the purpose for issuing the securities.

Tax agencies at a federal, state, local, and international level receive their appropriate filings. As briefly discussed above and more fully explained in Chapter 4, tax reporting differs from US GAAP accounting. Tax accounting in general is more "cash oriented" than "accrual oriented."

Internal personnel focus on consolidated reports and financial reports that "drill" deeper into the organization. The internal reporting requirements are listed as items 6 through 9 on Table 2.10. The term "requirement" is strong in this case because there are no direct legal requirements to implement these tools. However, these tools are generally implemented to strengthen management decision making. For example, each division of a company usually has its own set of financial statements. These statements are not required by law but are prudent management tools. See the following discussion about internal reporting.

From time to time, additional "audiences" may require financial statements. These audiences include:

- Debt holders, debt rating agencies, and banks

- Suppliers

- Investment analysts

- Employees or potential employees

- Labor unions

- Business partners (i.e., joint venture partners)

Each of these additional audiences focus on the publicly reported consolidated financial statements and SEC filings.

Internal Financial Reporting

Table 2.10 includes four areas of reporting requirements with an internal focus: divisional financial statements, cost accounting reports, annual budgets and financial plans, and project requests and reviews. As previously stated, these activities are not requirements of law, but are financial tools and processes that facilitate the efforts of a successful management team.

Divisional financial statements provide the same financial information as consolidated financial statements and should be prepared in parallel with the organizational structure of the firm. In some companies, these divisional statements are "drilled" deeper to product lines, products, sales regions, plants, production lines, and administrative cost centers or areas such as the CFO's office. Each level may have its own full or abbreviated set of financial statements. Often an abbreviated set of financials focuses on the income statement or lines on an income statement. For example, reporting of administrative cost centers would involve detailed expense items such as salaries, travel, and training by each administrative management area such as finance, law, and human resources that total to the related administrative expense on an income statement.

Although external reporting requirements are annual or quarterly, internal reporting requirements often are monthly or shorter in order to efficiently and effectively facilitate managerial decision making and to allow for timely corrective action. The management team at a leading international pharmaceutical company has an internal financial system that provides daily information with a 1-day delay on the sales and gross profit (sales less cost of goods sold) of any of its hundreds of products from its many worldwide regions and in total worldwide.

External reporting requirements or external benchmarking and analysis are often oriented as this year versus last year wherein two historical periods are compared. A dynamic internal management style compares performance versus expectations as reflected in annual budgets and plans. A distinction is made between planning (a broader, less-detailed, longer-term direction and target setting process) and annual budgets, which provide day-to-day, detailed operational focus that ties to the plan. Most companies compare this year's financial statement performance to budgeted financial statements. Budgets embody the financial objectives and aspirations of the firm. Budgets have been already benchmarked to historical performance, and so now current performance need only be compared to the budget.

At their worst, financial plans and budgets are control tools used to keep managers in line. At their best, financial plans and budgets are wonderful management tools that:

- Facilitate communications throughout an organization

- Engage all members of the organization if implemented as a participatory exercise

- Establish a common goal and set of objectives to attain that goal

- Identify performance shortfalls from aspiration levels of performance and facilitate addressing those shortfalls without the "heat of the battle" immediately pressing

- Prioritize competing strategies

- Determine compensation targets

- Provide a barometer to gauge the progress and effectiveness of implementation.

See Chapter 9, Strategic Financial Planning, for a broader discussion of financial planning. In general, plans remain as internal standards of performance. On occasion, some annual reports discuss general objectives of the firm, such as "double-digit growth" in sales or income or profitability standards as return on assets, return on equity, and margins (see Chapter 7, Financial Performance Metrics).

Finally, project requests and reviews relate to capital investment for new equipment, new plants, new products, and acquisitions or divestitures. Often the underlying process, projecting future cash flows and discounting them at an appropriate risk-adjusted cost of capital, is extended to marketing programs, research and development, investments in information technology, and so on. This is the topic of Chapters 10 and 11.

International Reporting Requirements

Cash flow has the virtue of being tangible. It is easy to identify cash when you see it. But extracting cash flows from financial statements for the purposes of financial decision making is quite another matter and is complicated by the fact that financial reporting standards and practices differ from country to country.

In Europe, for example, a company's tax books and its annual report are generally the same. Consequently, for tax reasons, earnings are lower relative to what they would be using commonly accepted US accounting standards For example, in the United States, accelerated depreciation (which recognizes more depreciation earlier in an asset's life; see Chapter 4) is used for tax purposes but straight line depreciation is used in the annual report; thus taxable earnings are often less than reported earnings. In Europe, companies use accelerated depreciation both for their annual report and their tax books.

Furthermore in Europe, provisions (or reserves) for anticipated future costs such as pensions, reorganization, or maintenance are frequently made to the current expense. The effect is to understate current earnings. In other words, in a good year companies will "book" additional expenses by increasing their "reserves" for various expenses. In a bad year, the previously booked reserves are reversed, which is reflected as lower expenses and higher income. These reserves and the resulting "income management" are strongly frowned upon in the United States.

Until recently, European companies could, at their discretion, choose whether or not to consolidate foreign subsidiaries. If they did not consolidate, their earnings could be substantially understated.

In France, accounting standards allow for the periodic restatement of assets to replacement value. This has no cash impact on the firm except for tax implications. When assets are based on replacement value, earnings are understated relative to US GAAP-derived earnings due to higher depreciation allowances, and stockholders' equity is overstated. The amount by which the assets are written up is usually booked partly to shareholders' equity reserves and partly to deferred taxes.

It is nearly an impossible task to keep track continuously of the changing accounting standards of every country. An international accounting standards group is trying to establish international reporting standards across the world. However, it is difficult to change in-country accounting standards. Suffice it to say that one cannot readily assume that accounting numbers in one country have the same meaning as in other countries. The only certainty is that cash flow has an unambiguous meaning across borders and in most countries the accounting reports give enough information to extract cash flow information.

summary

This chapter provides an overview of the three primary financial statements of the firm: income statement, balance sheet, and cash flow statement. Hershey is used throughout as an illustrative example. Reporting requirements for external and internal audiences as well as the CFO's role in timely preparation that is consistent with US GAAP is discussed. Numerous points are made about the processes and practices of US GAAP including the complications that FASB 95 introduced to the consolidated statement of cash flow. A reconciling cash flow statement demonstrates the interrelationship of the three financial statements. This cash flow statement is then compared to the reported consolidated statements of cash flow. The Thomson One Financial data base is introduced. Finally, internal and international reporting requirements are discussed.

Questions

2.1   What are the three financial statements necessary for a description of a firm's activities during an interval of time?

2.2   Please identify the following as an expense or an asset according to US GAAP:

   a.   CFO's salary

   b.   Telephone bill

   c.   New production facility

   d.   Training

   e.   Advertising

   f.   Research and development

   g.   Computer equipment

2.3   What are the three kinds of activities associated with cash flows in the statement of cash flows required by FASB 95?

2.4   Please evaluate this statement. "It is far too confusing having financial statements that do not follow one specific format and a standard set of rules to apply for everyone. There should only be one way of keeping accounting records!" Do you agree?

2.5   At Hershey, every division depreciated personal computers over 3 years except one division. That division used a 15-year life. Why would they do that? How could they legitimately justify a 15-year life on a PC?

2.6   Please identify the following as sources or uses of cash and explain why.

   a.   Increase in accounts payable

   b.   Increase in inventories

   c.   Increase in accounts receivable

   d.   Decrease in deferred taxes

   e.   Capital expenditures

   f.   Dividends

2.7   Who are the primary external users of the firm's financial statements?

2.8   Why is it in the best interests of managers to have the financial statements of the firm audited by an independent public accounting firm?

2.9   Why is it important that financial statements be prepared more frequently than every quarter for internal management purposes?

2.10   Why do you think there is so much attention on the income statement?

2.11   Often the attainment of certain financial objectives or goals are recognized in bonus and incentive plans.

   a.   Please evaluate the following advantages and disadvantages of using the following specific data for compensation purposes:

   - Sales

   - Net income

   - Total assets

- Cash flow (change in cash)
- Cash from operations

b. What other specific financial data should be used in setting performance standards?

2.12   Why are valuation models likely to be based on cash flows rather than on net income?

Problems

2.1   Income statement relationships

Please complete the following:

	A	B	C	D	E
Sales	$8,000	$9,000	$5,000	$6,000	$4,000
Cost of goods sold	5,700		4,200		
Gross profit		1,800			
Administrative expense	1,700			1,800	400
Operating income		550	550	(400)	600
Interest expense	100				
Pre-tax income		540		(540)	
Income taxes	200		230	–	210
Net income		$ 315	$ 350	$ (540)	
Net margin (Net income/sales)		3.50%	7.00%	−9.00%	8.00%

2.2   Income statement relationships

Please complete the following:

	A	B	C	D	E
Sales	$1,000	$800	$1,500	$1,200	
Cost of goods sold	580	400	800	650	
Depreciation	120	40			145
Gross profit			520		480
Selling expense	20	50		15	
Marketing expense	30		60	95	35
Administrative expense	50	60	200	60	125
Operating income		140		310	260
Interest expense	25	5	50		10
Interest income	15		5	8	
Pre-tax income		160	115	250	260
Income taxes	75			100	
Net income		$ 90	$ 70		$160
Net margin (Net income/sales)		11.25%	4.67%		8.00%

2.3 Balance sheet relationships

Please complete the following:

	A	B	C
Total assets	$1,000	$1,200	
Liabilities	500		650
Equity		800	350

2.4 Balance sheet relationships

Please complete the following:

	A	B	C	D	E
Current assets	$2,500	$3,500	$6,000		$2,000
Long-term assets	2,500		3,000	3,000	
Total assets		$5,500	$9,000		
Current liabilities	$1,000	$3,000	$2,500		$1,500
Long-term liabilities	1,000			2,000	
Total liabilities		3,500		5,000	3,000
Equity	3,000		1,000		3,000
Total		$5,500		$8,000	

2.5 Cash flow statement

Please prepare a cash flow statement from the following:

	Year 1		Year 0	Year 1
Sales	$5,000	Cash	$ 50	$ 80
Cost of sales	3,250	Other current assets	350	420
Gross income	1,750	Long-term assets	600	650
Operating expense	1,425	Total assets	$1,000	$1,150
Operating income	325			
Interest expense	75	Current liabilities	$ 180	$ 220
Pre-tax income	250	Long-term liabilities	320	280
Income taxes	100	Stockholders' equity	500	650
Net income	$ 150	Total	$1,000	$1,150

2.6   Cash flow statement

Please prepare a cash flow statement from the following:

Year 1			Year 0	Year 1
Sales	$8,335	Cash	$ 120	$ 80
Cost of sales	5,278	Accounts receivable	240	350
Depreciation	145	Inventory	350	420
Gross income	2,912	Total current assets	710	850
Operating expense	1,997	Equipment, net	1,325	1,390
Operating income	915	Other assets	250	200
Interest income	25	Total assets	$2,285	$2,440
Pre-tax income	940			
Income taxes	380	Accounts payable	$ 289	$ 374
Net income	$ 560	Accrued liabilities	150	100
		Short-term debt	600	395
Dividends	$ 300	Total current liabilities	1,039	869
		Long-term liabilities	288	353
		Stockholders' equity	958	1,218
		Total	$2,285	$2,440

What are capital expenditures in year 1?

2.7   Accounting relationships

a. The beginning balance of net, plant, property, and equipment was $250 million. During the year, capital expenditures were $75 million and depreciation expense was $45 million. In addition, the company sold $2 million of idle equipment as scrap. What is the ending balance of net, plant, property, and equipment?

b. Stockholders' equity was $843 million at the beginning of the year. During the year, the company generated $78 million of net income and paid dividends of $33 million. If the ending stockholders' equity balance is $778 million, what dollar amount of shares were repurchased throughout the year?

2.8   Income statement preparation

The following items are listed in alphabetical order. Please prepare an income statement from this information and then answer the additional questions:

Item	2007
Administrative expense	$ 4,000
Administrative salaries	2,500
Advertising expense	5,000
Amortization of goodwill	6,000
Consulting expenses	500
Direct labor	14,000
Dividend payments	1,500
Income tax rate	40.00%

Item	2007
Interest expense	3,000
Investment in new plant	10,000
Manufacturing depreciation	7,000
Manufacturing overhead	6,000
Other administrative expense	1,000
Promotional expenses	5,000
Raw material expense	38,000
Receivables	4,500
Research and development	4,000
Sales	100,000

a. What is the gross income and gross margin (gross income/sales)?
b. What is the operating income (earnings before interest and taxes) and operating margin (operating income/sales)?
c. What items were not included on the income statement? Why were they not included?

2.9   Balance sheet preparation

The following items are listed in alphabetical order. Please prepare a balance sheet from this information and then answer the additional questions:

Item	2007
Accounts payable	$14,000
Accounts receivable	17,000
Accrued liabilities	9,000
Accumulated depreciation	(34,500)
Building	32,000
Cash	2,500
Current deferred tax asset	500
Current portion of long-term debt	1,500
Deferred taxes	13,000
Depreciation expense	7,000
Equipment	21,000
Inventory	23,500
Land	15,000
Long-term debt	5,000
Marketable securities	14,000
Net income	7,200
Office equipment	2,500
Other current assets	1,200
Other long-term liabilities	2,000
Pension liability	23,000
Stockholders' equity	25,500
Taxes payable	4,000
Wages payable	3,000

a.   What dollar amount are the following items:

Item	Amount
1. Current assets	
2. Gross plant, property, and equipment	
3. Total assets	
4. Current liabilities	
5. Total liabilities	
6. Total liabilities and equity	

b.   What items were not included on the balance sheet? Why were they not included?

2.10   Income statement and balance sheet preparation

a.   The following accounts are from the H.J. Heinz 2005 income statement and balance sheet. They are arranged alphabetically below and with three items that do not belong on either statement. Prepare an income statement and a balance sheet for the year 2005 ($000s):

Accounts payable	$1,181,652
Accrued marketing	270,147
Accumulated depreciation	1,858,781
Asset impairment charge	73,842
Buildings and leasehold improvements	844,056
Capital expenditures	240,671
Cash and equivalents	1,083,749
Cost of products sold	5,705,926
Cumulative effect of change in accounting	—
Dividends	398,869
Equipment, furniture, and other	3,111,663
Goodwill	2,138,499
Income (loss) from discontinued oper, net of tax	16,877
Income taxes payable	130,555
Interest expense	232,431
Interest income	27,776
Inventories	1,256,776
Land	67,000
Long-term debt	4,121,984
Long-term deferred income taxes	508,639
Other accrued liabilities	376,124
Other current assets	37,839
Other expense (income)	17,731
Other long-term liabilities	757,454
Other non-current assets	1,806,478
Payments on long-term debt	480,471
Portion of long-term debt due in 1 year	544,798
Prepaid expenses	174,818

Provision for income taxes	322,792
Receivables	1,092,394
Salaries and wages payable	55,321
Sales	8,912,297
Selling, general, and administrative expenses	1,851,529
Shareholders' equity	2,602,573
Short-term debt	28,471
Trademarks and other intangibles	823,227

b. Complete the following tables with values from the financial statements:

Income Statement

1. Gross profit

2. Operating profit effect of accounting change

3. Income from continuing operations before income taxes and cumulative

4. Income from continuing operations before cumulative effect of accounting change

5. Income before cumulative effect of accounting change

6. Net income

Balance Sheet

7. Total current assets

8. Total gross, plant, property, and equipment (PP&E)

9. Net, PP&E

10. Total assets

11. Total current liabilities

2.11 Interrelationship of the financial statements

The following is a consolidated balance sheet and income statement for Wal-Mart for the fiscal years ended January 31, 2005 and 2006. All dollars are in millions.

a. Compute the annual dollar change in each balance sheet line item (excluding totals and subtotals). Indicate if that change is a source or use of cash.

			BALANCE SHEET CHANGES	
	2005	2006	Source	Use
Cash and marketable securities	$ 5,488	$ 6,414	$–	$926
Accounts receivable	1,715	2,662		
Inventory	29,762	32,191		
Prepaid expenses and other	1,889	2,591		
Total current assets	38,854	43,858	–	–

	2005	2006	Source	Use
			BALANCE SHEET CHANGES	
Gross, plant, property, and equipment	84,037	97,302		
Less: accumulated depreciation	(18,637)	(21,427)		
Net, plant, property, and equipment	65,400	75,875	–	–
Net, property under capitalized lease	2,718	3,415		
Other assets and deferred charges	13,182	15,021		
Total assets	$120,154	$138,169	$–	$–
Accounts payable	$ 21,987	$ 25,373	$3,386	$–
Accrued liabilities	12,120	13,465		
Accrued income taxes	1,281	1,322		
Commercial paper	3,812	3,754		
Long-term debt due in 1 year	3,982	4,894		
Total current liabilities	43,182	48,808	–	–
Long-term debt	20,087	26,429		
Long-term debt under capital leases	3,171	3,742		
Deferred income taxes and other	4,318	6,019		
Shareholders' equity	49,396	53,171		
Total liabilities and equity	$120,154	$138,169	$–	$–

b. Table 2.2 contains the income statement for Wal-Mart. By combining that table, along with the balance sheet from above and the information noted below, construct Wal-Mart's cash flow statement for 2006.

Other Information:	2006
Common stock dividend	$2,511
Common stock repurchase and other	3,580

2.12   Interrelationship of the financial statements

The following is a consolidated balance sheet for Ruby Tuesday, Inc., for the fiscal years ended May 31, 2005, and June 1, 2004. All dollars are in thousands.

a. Compute the annual dollar change in each balance sheet line item (excluding totals and subtotals). Indicate if that change is a source or use of cash.

	2004	2005	Source	Use
			BALANCE SHEET CHANGES	
Cash and short-term investments	$19,485	$19,787	$–	$302
Accounts and notes receivable	10,089	7,627		
Inventory-merchandise	8,068	10,189		
Inventory-china, silver, and supplies	5,579	6,799		

Time and Value

Learning Outcomes

After completing this chapter, you should be able to:

1 Identify time value of money as one of the cornerstones of finance

2 Calculate the present value of a single sum of money or a recurring amount of money, called an *annuity*

3 Calculate the future value of a single sum of money or a recurring amount of money

4 Determine the interest rate earned on an investment

5 Be able to use a wide array of calculation techniques including a financial calculator

6 Construct a loan amortization schedule

K nowledge of the time value of money is fundamental and is essential to an understanding of most topics in finance. For example, capital project investment, investment in new products, project selection, lease-versus-borrow decisions, bond refunding, security valuation, acquisition valuation, financial structure decisions, and the whole question of the cost of capital are subjects that cannot be understood without knowledge of compound interest. Almost all problems involving compound interest can be handled with only a few basic concepts.

The Nature of Financial Decisions

This chapter on the time value of money (TVM) is key to the main theme of this book. Growth is a major source of value, and the analysis of expected future cash flows is the basis of the calculation of value. This theme is implemented throughout the chapters that follow. In this chapter we present the foundations for the analysis of growth and value.

Most of us are already familiar with the concept of time value of money. Many of us may share a personal childhood memory of receiving cash as a birthday or holiday present and our first encounter with the time value of money. As a small boy, the senior author remembers a birthday that didn't go quite the way he had planned. Sure there was a birthday party with memories of plenty of relatives and friends with wonderful gifts. In fact, I remember receiving enough cash so that I could buy a dump truck that I had been eyeing for weeks at the local toy store. I made arrangements with my dad that the next morning we would purchase the truck. However, my dad had another idea. Instead of heading to the toy store, we were on our way to the local bank to open a savings account.

On the way, he reassured me that the money was safe and would not be lost—which for a 5-year-old was a major concern. He also went on to explain interest. Not only would the bank keep my money safe, but they would also pay me! Unbelievable to a 5-year old! We stopped into the bank and opened the account. On the way home, my dad decided to really start me thinking and explained the concept of compound interest, "Not only do they pay you to hold onto your money, but they pay you interest on your interest!" While times have changed and business decisions may be more involved than this simple reflection, the fundamentals of time value of money endure. By the way, I finally did get that dump truck and had some extra cash for a Hershey bar.

Many of us also have numerous and various loans outstanding. Whether it's a home mortgage, home equity loan, car loan, school loan, or a credit card loan, the basics of time value of money come into play. Many of us are saving for various "life" events, such as college education, travel, weddings, or retirement. Each of these savings events requires an understanding of the time value of money.

In fact, most decisions we face in our everyday lives, as well as the decisions that confront business firms, involve a comparison of the present with the future. This involves comparing cash flows at different times—present outlays versus future benefits, or present consumption versus future payments or foregone future benefits. For example, consider an investment of $100 today that pays $110 at the end of 1 year. This returns 10% on the investment. If the cost of funds is 12%, it is not a good investment because we are not earning the cost of funds. If the funds cost 8%, we have made a net gain.

Most financial decisions require comparisons of these kinds. Because funds have earning power, $100 today is not the same as $100 received 1 year from now. If we have $100 today, we can invest it to have more than $100 in the future. Financial decisions, therefore, involve the time value of money—decisions across time. Values are determined by the timing of the future cash flows to be received. Funds received next year are worth more than the same amount of funds received in the fifth or tenth year. This chapter formalizes the concepts of time value of money and discounted cash flow analysis, which represents the fundamental technique for measuring the time value of money. Most financial decisions at both the personal and business levels must take into account the time value of money. The materials in this chapter are, therefore, key to the important topics of managerial finance.

The above is straightforward, but some important subtleties need to be drawn out. First, consider simple interest. Under a simple interest contract, the investor would receive interest of $10 for each of the years. While contracts are sometimes written to provide for simple interest, the powerful logic behind the idea of compound interest is demonstrated by Table 3.1.

If the money is invested for 3 years, and the interest earned each year is left with the financial institution, interest is earned on the interest. As shown by Column 2 in Table 3.1, the amount of interest earned under compound interest rises each year. Therefore, the value of the amount at the start of the year on which interest is earned during the year includes the interest earned in previous time periods. In year 2, an additional $1 of interest is earned on year one's interest of $10 and so on. In total, there is $30.00 of interest earned on the original $100 over this 3-year period along with $3.10 of "interest on the interest."

Notice at an interest rate of 20%, that same $100 earns a total of $72.80 in interest. Instead of doubling the $33.10 of interest earned at 10% to $66.20, at 20%, there is an extra $6.60 earned ($72.80 less $66.20). As demonstrated in Table 3.1, this is once again from the power of compounding and the fact that more interest is initially generated upon which additional interest is earned.

Second, the rate of interest applied to the interest earned is *assumed* to be the 10% provided for in the 3-year contract. However, it is possible that interest rates would be higher or lower during the 3-year period. If so, the contract could provide for adjusting the interest rate upward or downward over the life of the agreement. But the conventional practice in compound interest calculations is to assume reinvestment at the specified interest rate. Consequently, the fundamental equation of compound interest set forth in Equation 3.2 has important assumptions that should be kept in mind when compound interest rate relationships are utilized in the many individual topics of financial management.

Table 3.1 illustrates how compound interest rate relationships can be developed on a year by year basis. We could also use Equation 3.2 to calculate what the future value of $100 would be at the end of 3 years, directly, without stepping through each year individually. Any calculator with a y^x function would enable us to quickly calculate the results shown in Table 3.1.

Time Value of Money Table To round out this discussion, we illustrate how the same result of $133.10 as the future value of $100 at 10% interest can also be obtained from a time value of money table. These tables have been constructed for values of $(1 + r)^n$ for wide ranges of r and n. (See Table A.1 in Appendix A at the end of this book.)

For a given interest rate (r) and time period (n), let the future value interest factor (FVIF) equal:

$$FVIF_{r,n} = (1 + r)^n \tag{3.3}$$

We can write Equation 3.2 as $FV_{r,n} = P_0 [FVIF(r,n)]$. It is necessary only to go to an appropriate interest table to find the proper interest factor. For example, the correct interest factor for the illustration given in Table 3.1 can be found in Table A.1. A small portion of Table A.1 is reproduced in Table 3.2. Look down the period column to 3, then across this row to the appropriate number in the 10% column to find the interest factor, 1.3310. With this interest factor, the future value of $100 after 3 years is:

$$FV_{10\%, 3\,yr} = P_0 [FVIF(10\%, 3\,yr)] = \$100 [1.3310] = \$133.10 \tag{3.3a}$$

This is the same figure that was obtained by the other methods.

TABLE 3.2	Future Value Interest Factors as a Function of Interest Rates				
PERIOD	$FVIF_{r,n} = (1 + r)^n$				
n	0%	5%	10%	15%	20%
1	1.0000	1.0500	1.1000	1.1500	1.2000
2	1.0000	1.1025	1.2100	1.3225	1.4400
3	1.0000	1.1576	1.3310	1.5209	1.7280
4	1.0000	1.2155	1.4641	1.7490	2.0736
5	1.0000	1.2763	1.6105	2.0114	2.4883

The FVIF Table A.1 also demonstrates the power of compounding. Look at the last row on Table A.1, the 60-year row; see the following FVIFs at the noted rates:

r	FVIF (r, 60yr)
3%	5.8916
6%	32.9877
12%	897.5969

To put it into perspective, the items that are sold at the "dollar store" today, will sell for $5.89 in 60 years if inflation is 3%. At 6%, the store will need to change its name to the $32.99 store. Finally, at 12% inflation for 60 years, you will get change back from your thousand dollar bill when you buy an item at the $897.60 store. This is the power of compounding!

Equation 3.3 can be used to calculate how the interest factor is related to the interest rate and time, as shown numerically in Table 3.2 and graphically in Figure 3.2.

Table 3.2 and Figure 3.2 demonstrate the power of compound interest. At a 10% interest rate, our investment doubles in slightly more than 7 years. At 15%, our investment doubles in less than 5 years, and our investment has more than quadrupled in less than 10 years.

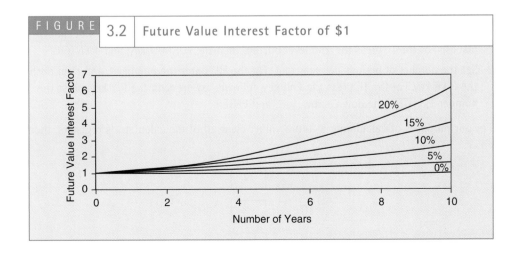

FIGURE 3.2   Future Value Interest Factor of $1

The nature of the compound interest relationships is the basis for the **rule of 72**. While this is labeled a "rule," it is really a useful mathematical relationship. If we divide 72 by the interest rate, we obtain the number of years required for an investment to double. At 6%, an investment doubles in approximately 12 years; at 9%, in about 8 years; at 24%, in roughly 3 years. Or if we have the number of years, we can use the *rule of 72* to calculate the compound interest rate required for an investment to double. If an investment doubles in 6 years, the interest rate is about 12%; in 12 years, roughly 6%; in 3 years, approximately 24%. So if we are told that a stock price will double in 12 years, that represents only a 6% return—relatively modest. If a stock price doubles in 3 years, that represents a 24% rate of return, which is good. The *rule of 72* is a handy rule of thumb.

Using a Financial Calculator   So far we have discussed the concept of future value using graphs, equations and mathematical calculations, and TVM tables. Ultimately, most finance professionals use a financial calculator to answer these questions. A good financial calculator is highly recommended and will help even the novice (let alone the student) with loans, investing, etc. Even though there are many types of financial calculators, most work in similar ways. Appendices B.1 and B.2 provide more detailed guidance on the use of the Hewlett Packard 10B (which is the predecessor of the 10BII) and Texas Instruments BAIIPlus.

In brief, a financial calculator has five important time value of money keys:

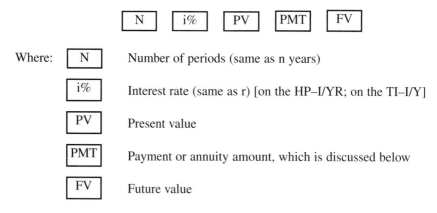

Where:	N	Number of periods (same as n years)
	i%	Interest rate (same as r) [on the HP–I/YR; on the TI–I/Y]
	PV	Present value
	PMT	Payment or annuity amount, which is discussed below
	FV	Future value

To begin, there are three steps that we must do:

1. Clear all of your calculator's registers. For the HP, push the key labeled "Clear All"; for the TI, press the 2nd level button and then CLR TVM.

2. Set the display. For the HP, push the DISP key and then the number 4 (for 4 decimal places). For the TI, press the 2nd level button, then the FORMAT key, and 4 ENTER.

3. Set the number of periods per year to 1. For the HP, enter the number 1 and then push the P/YR key. For the TI, press the 2nd key, followed by pressing the P/Y key, press the number 1, ENTER, the down arrow ↓, 1, and ENTER.

For our purposes of calculating a future value, clear all of the calculator's registers, then enter:

3   N

10   i%

−100   PV

Push 3 and then the N key; push 10 and then the i% key; and push –100 then the PV key. The present value is entered as a negative number indicating that it is an outflow. The final step is to solve for the future value. If you use a TI calculator, first push the CPT key to tell the calculator to "compute" and then press the FV key. If you use an HP calculator, simply push the FV key. In either case, the calculator displays the answer of $133.10.

Finally, spreadsheet software such as Excel includes functions to calculate the components of the time value of money equation. See Appendix C for a further discussion of the financial functions built into Excel.

Regardless how you solve for the future value (graph, equation, TVM table, financial calculator, or Excel), my $10 investment made as a 5-year-old will be worth $186.79 when I retire at age 65 assuming a 5% rate of return.

PRESENT VALUE—SINGLE SUM

We observed the power of compound interest to calculate future values. The next concept is the present-value concept, which has numerous applications in finance. The present-value concept leads directly to the **basic principle of investment decisions**, which is this: An investment is acceptable only if it earns at least its opportunity cost. The **opportunity cost** is what the funds could earn on an investment of equal risk. The *basic principle of investment decisions* may then be stated as follows: An investment is acceptable only if it earns at least the risk-adjusted market interest rate or opportunity cost of funds.

An example illustrates the relationship between future value, present value, and the basic principle of investment decisions under certainty. We have the opportunity to invest $100 today for an asset that can be sold 1 year later for $121; the applicable market rate of interest is 10%. We can analyze the decision, using the concepts of future value, present value, and rate of return.

Under future-value analysis, we could invest the $100 at the market interest rate of 10%. At the end of the year, we would have:

$$\$100(1 + 0.10) = \$110 \tag{3.3b}$$

But the asset investment would have a year 1 value of $121, which is higher than the market investment.

Alternatively, we can use the concept of present value to compare the two investments. Finding present values (*discounting*, as it is commonly called) is simply the reverse of compounding, and Equation 3.2 can readily be transformed into a present value formula by dividing both sides by the discount factor $(1 + r)^n$ and expressing P_0 as $PV_{r,n}$.

$$FV_{r,n} = P_0 (1 + r)^n$$

Solving for present value:

$$PV_{r,n} = \frac{FV_{r,n}}{(1+r)^n} = FV_{r,n}\left[\frac{1}{(1+r)^n}\right]$$

$$PV_{r,n} = FV_{r,n}[(1+r)^{-n}] = FV_{r,n}[\text{PVIF}(r,n)] \tag{3.4}$$

The subscript zero in the term P_0 indicates the present. Present-value quantities can be identified by either P_0 or $PV_{r,n}$, or more generally as PV (present value).

For our simple examples, the present value of the market investment is $100, while the present value of the asset investment is $110:

Asset investment: $P_0 = \$121/1.10 = \$110 = \$121(0.9091)$

So we should invest in the asset since its present value (at 10% on a future value of $121 in one year) is $110, whereas the market investment is worth only $100 today ($P_0$). We can calculate the present value by dividing by 1 plus the interest rate expressed as a decimal or by multiplying the future value by $1/(1 + r) = (1 + r)^{-1}$.

Finally, in this special 1-year investment case, we note that the market investment has a rate of return of 10% [(FV/PV) − 1 = ($110/$100) − 1 = 0.10 = 10%], while the asset investment has a return of 21% [(FV/PV) − 1 = ($121/$100) − 1 = 0.21 = 21%]. More is said below regarding deriving implied interest rates.

To summarize the three comparisons, we have:

	MARKET INVESTMENT	ASSET INVESTMENT
Future value	$110	$121
Present value at market rate	$100	$110
Rate of return	10%	21%

By all three methods or criteria (comparison of future values, comparison of present values, and comparison of rates of return), the asset investment is superior to an investment at the market rate. In these comparisons we have explained the concept of present value and illustrated its use.

PRESENT VALUE EQUATION—MULTIPLE YEARS

What if the asset investment paid $121, as above, but it took 2 years instead of 1? In that case, we are indifferent between a 2-year investment that pays $121 because it has a present value of $100:

$$PV_{r,n} = FV_{r,n} [(1 + r)^{-n}] = \$121/(1 + 0.10)^2 = \$100 \qquad (3.4a)$$

More generally, to obtain the present value, we divide the future value by $(1 + r)^n$ (or multiply by $(1 + r)^{-n}$).

If the asset did not pay anything for 3 years and at the end of the 3 years was worth $121, we would reject the investment because it would only have a present value of $90.91 today:

$$PV_{r,n} = FV_{r,n} [(1 + r)^{-n}] = \$121/(1 + 0.10)^3 = \$90.91 \qquad (3.4b)$$

It would be better to invest our $100 at the market investment rate of 10% and have $133.10 at the end of 3 years.

PRESENT VALUE USING TVM TABLES

Tables have been constructed for the present-value interest rate factors—$(1 + r)^{-n}$—for various rates r and time intervals n. (See Table A.2 and Table 3.3.)

For example, to determine the present value of $100 to be received 3 years from now with a discount factor of 10%, look down the 10% column in Table 3.3 (or Table A.2) to the third row. The figure shown there, 0.7513, is the present-value interest factor (PVIF) used to determine the present value of $100 payable in 3 years, discounted at 10%.

$$PV_{r,n} = P_0 = FV_{10\%,\,3\,yr.} [PVIF(10\%, 3 \text{ yr})]$$
$$= \$100 \,(0.7513) \qquad (3.4c)$$
$$= \$75.13$$

TABLE 3.3	Present Value Interest Factors as a Function of Interest Rates				
PERIOD	$PVIF_{r,n} = (1 + r)^n$				
n	0%	5%	10%	15%	20%
1	1.0000	0.9524	0.9091	0.8696	0.8333
2	1.0000	0.9070	0.8264	0.7561	0.6944
3	1.0000	0.8638	0.7513	0.6575	0.5787
4	1.0000	0.8227	0.6830	0.5718	0.4823
5	1.0000	0.7835	0.6209	0.4972	0.4019

The present value tells us what a future sum or sums would be worth to us if we had those funds today. It is obtained by discounting the future sum or sums back to the starting point, which is the present. Present-value analysis clearly involves discounting projected future cash flows back to the present. It should be understood, however, that the standard practice in finance is to call all compound interest calculations involving present values *discounted cash flow (DCF)* analysis.

Said slightly differently, Table 3.4 illustrates further the present value/future value concepts. An initial amount of $75.13 is invested at 10% earning $7.51 the first year and accumulating to $82.64. This amount is reinvested for the second year, earns 10% or $8.26, and grows to $90.91 at the end of year 2. Once again this amount is reinvested, earns $9.09 (or 10%) and becomes $100. So you can see $75.13 today is equivalent to $100 in 3 years if you can earn a 10% rate of return.

PRESENT VALUE USING A FINANCIAL CALCULATOR

A financial calculator provides an easy and effective way of calculating a present value. First clear all the registers and then enter:

3 [N]

10 [i%]

100 [FV]

As a matter of convention, the future value is entered as a positive number indicating that it is an inflow. The final step is to solve for the present value. If you use a TI calculator, first

TABLE 3.4	Compound Interest Calculations		
YEAR n	(1) AMOUNT AT START OF YEAR PV	(2) INTEREST EARNED (1) × (r)	(3) AMOUNT AT END OF YEAR (1) × (1 + r) $FV_{r,n}$
R = 10% or 0.10			
1	$75.13	$7.51	$ 82.64
2	82.64	8.26	90.91
3	90.91	9.09	100.00

push the CPT key to tell the calculator to "compute" and then press the PV key. If you use an HP calculator, simply push the PV key. In either case, the calculator displays the answer of $75.13. (Actually, the display shows –75.13, indicating a $75.13 investment.)

Finally, spreadsheets provide appropriate functions to calculate the present value of a future sum.

ANNUITIES

Thus far we have discussed the concepts of future value and present value for a single outflow or inflow. We next consider annuities.

An annuity is defined as a series of same dollar amounts of payments or receipts for a specified number of periods. The payment or receipt may occur at the end of the year or at the beginning of the year. If it occurs at the end of the year, it is called an *ordinary annuity* (or annuity paid in arrears or simply an annuity); if it occurs at the beginning of the year, it is called an *annuity due* (or an annuity paid in advance). Mortgage payments are typically made at the end of the period; lease payments are usually made at the beginning of the period. For most problems payments are received at the end of the period, so our emphasis will be on ordinary annuities.

FUTURE VALUE OF AN ANNUITY

One of the best examples of an annuity is an investment that requires the individual (or company) to invest in it on a periodic (or annual basis). Figure 3.3 illustrates 3-year investment in a 10% retirement account. Remember, as an annuity, the contract is signed today, but the first deposit does not happen until the end of the year for the next 3 years. In fact, the first investment of $100 grows for the 2 remaining years at 10%, reaching a future value of $121 at the end of 3 years. The second year investment is made at the end of year 2. Consequently, it grows for 1 year and reaches a value of $110 at the end of the 3-year period. The final cash flow of $100 is invested at the end of 3 years and has no time to accrue interest. The future value of this $100 annuity is merely the sum of the future values of the individual annual investments, as illustrated on Figure 3.3, or $331.

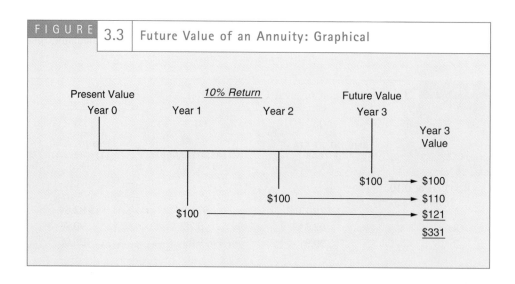

FIGURE 3.3 | Future Value of an Annuity: Graphical

FUTURE VALUE OF AN ANNUITY—EQUATION

Computationally, the sum of any general geometric series can be expressed as:

$$S_n = a \left[\frac{r^n - 1}{r - 1} \right] \qquad (3.5)$$

For calculating the future value of a periodic payment or an annuity (a) at an interest rate of r and the number of periods reflected in t, denoted by $FVA_{r,t}$, the rate of geometric growth is $1 + r$. We can write:

$$FVA_{r,t} = a \left[\frac{(1+r)^t - 1}{1 + r - 1} \right] \qquad (3.5a)$$

Solving for $FVA_{r,t}$ results in Equation 3.6, which is the formula for calculating the future value of an annuity. Again, t represents the *terminal* or final year of the annuity assuming that year 0 is the starting point.

$$FVA_{r,t} = a \left[\frac{(1+r)^t - 1}{r} \right] \qquad (3.6)$$

This can be readily solved with any standard calculator.

FUTURE VALUE OF AN ANNUITY—TVM TABLE

The interest factor in Equation 3.6 can also be written with an abbreviation in letters, as shown in Equation 3.6a.

$$FVA_{r,t} = a\ [FVIFA(r,t)] \qquad (3.6a)$$

FVIFA has been given values for various combinations of r and t. To find these, see Table 3.5 or Table A.3 for a more expansive version.

To find the answer to the 3-year, $100 annuity problem, simply refer to Table 3.5. Look down the 10% column to the row for the third year, and multiply the annuity amount of $100 by this factor of 3.3100, as shown below.

$$FVA_{r,t} = a\ [FVIFA(r,t)]$$
$$FVA_{10\%,3\ \text{yrs.}} = \$100\ [3.3100] = \$331.00$$

TABLE 3.5	Future Value of an Annuity Interest Factors as a Function of Interest Rates				
PERIOD	$FVIFA_{r,n} = (1 + r)^n$				
n	0%	5%	10%	15%	20%
1	1.0000	1.0000	1.0000	1.0000	1.0000
2	2.0000	2.0500	2.1000	2.1500	2.2000
3	3.0000	3.1525	3.3100	3.4725	3.6400
4	4.0000	4.3101	4.6410	4.9934	5.3680
5	5.0000	5.5256	6.1051	6.7424	7.4416

Notice that the *FVIFA* for the sum of an annuity is always larger than the number of years that the annuity runs. The reader should verify that the same result can be obtained with a hand calculator, using the formula in Equation 3.6.

FUTURE VALUE OF AN ANNUITY—FINANCIAL CALCULATOR

Once again, a financial calculator provides a very effective tool to calculate the future value of an annuity. Before working with TVM keys, it is important to be sure that the calculator is set for annuities occurring at the end of the period and not annuities due at the beginning of the period. Both the HP-10B and the TI-BA II Plus come preset that all annuities occur at the end of the period. The BEGIN (HP) or BGN (TI) annunciators should *not* appear in the display screen. If it does, consult Appendix B or your calculator's user guide to adjust the setting.

To calculate the future value of an annuity, clear all of the calculator's registers, then enter:

$$3 \quad \boxed{\text{N}}$$

$$10 \quad \boxed{\text{i\%}}$$

$$-100 \quad \boxed{\text{PMT}}$$

Push 3 and then the N-key; push 10 and then the i% key; and push −100 then the PMT-key. The annuity or payment amount is entered as a negative number indicating that it is an outflow. The final step is to solve for the future value. If you use a TI calculator, first push the CPT key to tell the calculator to "compute" and then press the FV key. If you use an HP calculator, simply push the FV key. In either case, the calculator displays the answer of $331.00. Be sure you cleared all of the registers!

Spreadsheet software such as Excel includes functions to calculate the components of the time value of money equation. See Appendix C for a further discussion of the financial functions built into Excel.

PRESENT VALUE OF AN ANNUITY

Many decisions in finance use the concept of the present value of an annuity. Its basic formulation is used in analyzing investment decisions in capital equipment or financial assets, in valuation calculations, and in many other applications. We start with a simple investment decision. DJK Industries is considering the purchase of a power saw; the saw will cost $200 and will generate additional cash flows of $100 per year for 3 years. The cash flows are considered available at the end of each year (ordinary annuity); the applicable discount rate is 10%. Will DJK gain from the investment? Figure 3.4 demonstrates the investment opportunity.

Clearly, by Figure 3.4, the investment is worth $248.69. The analysis is a comparison between the present value of the future cash inflows and the initial investment cash outflow. The present value of the future cash inflows is $248.69. DJK would be willing to pay up to $248.69 for the saw. The net present value (*NPV*) of the investment is the present value of benefits less the present value of costs. In our example, the *NPV* is $248.69 − $200.00 = $48.69. The investment adds value to the firm, so it should be made. (We use the *NPV* concept, which is the basis for value creation throughout the book.)

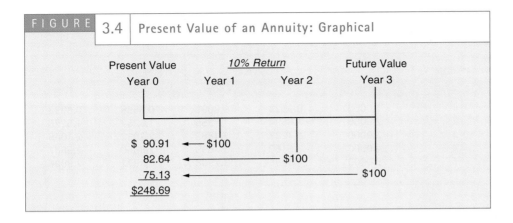

FIGURE 3.4 | Present Value of an Annuity: Graphical

PRESENT VALUE OF AN ANNUITY—EQUATION

The present value of an annuity ($PVA_{r,t}$) is expressed in Equation 3.7.

$$PVA_{r,t} = a\left[\frac{1-(1+r)^{-t}}{r}\right] \tag{3.7}$$

Equation 3.7 can also be written as below:

$$PVA_{r,t} = a\,PVIFA_{r,t} \tag{3.7a}$$

We can derive Equation 3.7 from the future-value formula:

$$PVA_{r,t} = FVA_{r,t}(1+r)^{-t}$$
$$= a\left[\frac{(1+r)^{t}-1}{r}\right](1+r)^{-t} = a\left[\frac{1-(1+r)^{-t}}{r}\right] \tag{3.7b}$$

Using $PVIFA$, the present value of an annuity interest factor, we can write $PVA_{r,t} = a\,PVIFA_{r,t}$. For our simple numerical example, we have:

$$= \$100\left[\frac{1-(1.10)^{-3}}{0.10}\right] = \$100\left[\frac{1-0.7513}{0.10}\right] = \$100[2.48685] = \$248.685 \tag{3.7c}$$

Notice that the $PVIFA$ for the present value of an annuity is always less than the number of years the annuity runs, whereas the $FVIFA$ for the sum of an annuity is larger than the number of years for which it runs.

PRESENT VALUE OF AN ANNUITY—TVM TABLE

$PVIFA$ in Equation 3.7a has been given values for various combinations of r and t. To find these, see Table 3.6 or Table A.4 for a more expansive version.

To find the answer to the 3-year, $100 annuity problem, simply refer to Table 3.6. Look down the 10% column to the row for the third year, and multiply the factor 2.4869 by $100, as shown below.

$$PVA_{r,t} = a\,PVIFA(r,t)$$
$$PVA_{10\%,\,3\,yrs.} = \$100(2.4869) = \$248.69$$

TABLE 3.6	Present Value of an Annuity Interest Factors as a Function of Interest Rates				
PERIOD	$PVIFA_{r,n} = (1 + r)^n$				
n	0%	5%	10%	15%	20%
1	1.0000	0.9524	0.9091	0.8696	0.8333
2	2.0000	1.8594	1.7355	1.6257	1.5278
3	3.0000	2.7232	2.4869	2.2832	2.1065
4	4.0000	3.5460	3.1699	2.8550	2.5887
5	5.0000	4.3295	3.7908	3.3522	2.9906

As above, this same result can be obtained with a hand calculator, using the formula in Equation 3.7.

PRESENT VALUE OF AN ANNUITY—FINANCIAL CALCULATOR

A financial calculator can easily assist in the calculation of the present value of an annuity. Remember to check that the BEGIN (HP) or BGN (TI) annunciators do *not* appear in the display screen. If it does, consult Appendix B or your calculator's user guide to adjust the setting.

To calculate the present value of an annuity, clear all of the calculator's registers, then enter:

$$3 \quad \boxed{N}$$

$$10 \quad \boxed{i\%}$$

$$100 \quad \boxed{PMT}$$

Push 3 and then the N-key; push 10 and then the i% key; and push 100 then the PMT-key. The final step is to solve for the present value. If you use a TI calculator, push the CPT key to tell the calculator to "compute" and then press the PV key. If you use an HP calculator, simply push the PV key. In either case, the calculator displays the answer of –$248.69. The negative value indicates that you should pay $248.69 for an investment that returns $100 each year for the next 3 years to earn a 10% return.

Spreadsheet software such as Excel includes functions to calculate the components of the time value of money equation. See Appendix C for a further discussion of the financial functions built into Excel.

Any of our fundamental approaches, graphs, equations, tables, financial calculators, or spreadsheets, provides the same result.

INTERRELATIONSHIPS AMONG THE TERMS

Before concluding our discussion of the fundamental TVM relationships, we need to reflect on the interrelationships and similarities when trying to find the present value or future value of a lump sum or an annuity for a given time period at a specified interest rate. For all the interest formulas, tables, or financial calculator keys, we have four basic terms, as shown by Equation 3.8.

$$\text{Value} = \text{Periodic Flow} \times \text{Interest Factor } (r,n) \qquad (3.8)$$

The interest factor is a function of both the interest rate and time. We presented some practical illustrations of how we can solve for the value. But, you should appreciate that we can solve for any fourth term when we have three of the four factors: present or future value, the periodic flow, and the interest factor components of time and rate. Keep in mind that the periodic flow can be a lump sum or an annuity.

The following section augments the fundamental approaches for determining value that we discussed above.

Additional TVM Topics

At this point, we have examined the fundamental relationships of time value of money while introducing methods to calculate present values and future values of single lump sums or of annuities. The next sections develop additional topics necessary to complete a background in TVM. Topics include unequal cash flows, perpetuities or perpetual cash flows, determining interest rates, multiple compounding periods within a year, and effective interest rates.

UNEQUAL PAYMENTS

Thus far we have used constant annual inflows to develop the basic relationships. The concepts can easily be applied to uneven payments by using the simple present-value formula. The assumed cash inflows and their present value are shown in Table 3.7. Each inflow is discounted separately and eventually summed.

This is the same as the process that a financial calculator goes through and calculates the present value of those unequal annual cash flows with the touch of a single key. More will be said about the net present value calculation in Chapter 10. Please see Appendix B for more detailed calculator instructions.

PERPETUITIES

Some securities carry no maturity date. They are perpetuities—an annuity that continues forever. The future value of a **perpetuity** is infinite because the number of periodic payments is infinite. However, the present value of an annuity can be calculated by starting with Equation 3.9.

$$PVA_{r,t} = a\left[\frac{1-(1+r)^{-n}}{r}\right]$$
(3.9)

TABLE 3.7	Present Value of Unequal Inflows		
YEAR n	CASH INFLOW	$PVIF_{10\%,n}$	PV OF EACH INFLOW
1	100.00	0.9091	$ 90.91
2	200.00	0.8264	165.29
3	300.00	0.7513	225.39
4	400.00	0.6830	273.21
5	500.00	0.6209	310.46
6	600.00	0.5645	338.68
7	700.00	0.5132	359.21
Present value of unequal inflows =			$1,763.15

Notice that the term $(1 + r)^{-n} = 1/(1 + r)^n$ is always less than 1 for positive interest rates. For example, suppose $r = 10\%$, then:

$$(1 + r)^{-1} = 0.909, (1 + r)^{-2} = 0.826, (1 + r)^{-3} = 0.751, \cdots, (1 + r)^{-100} = 0.000073 \qquad (3.9a)$$

As the number of years becomes very large (i.e., infinite), the term $(1 + r)^{-n}$ goes to zero. Consequently, if the annuity of constant payments is perpetual, we have as our final result:

$$PVA_{r,\infty} = a\left[\frac{1}{r}\right] = \frac{a}{r} \qquad (3.10)$$

So the present value of a perpetuity is the periodic flow a, divided by the discount factor. Equation 3.10 is a simple expression rich in implications. This is an easy value to calculate. You do not need a financial calculator to compute this result.

However, just to double check the result using a financial calculator and because most financial calculators do not have a "perpetuity" key, you can approximate the results by using 100,000 years as the "n," 10% as the "$i\%$," and 100 as "PMT". The resulting value is almost $1000. But as a perpetuity, the value is exactly $1000:

$$PV = \frac{\$100}{0.10} = \$1000 \qquad (3.10a)$$

Please see Table 3.8.

If r rises to 12%, PV falls to $833.33. If r falls to 8%, PV rises to $1,250. Accordingly, PV is very sensitive to the size of the discount factor. This is also generally true for investments, even if they do not have infinite lives; however, the impact is largest for a perpetuity.

PERPETUITY WITH GROWTH

A perpetuity that grows over time is a unique type of perpetuity, but not an uncommon perpetuity. For example, The Hershey Company paid a dividend of $0.93 per share in 2005. The dividends are expected to grow at 8% forever.

The value of a perpetuity with growth can be found as:

$$PVA_{r,\infty} = \frac{a_0(1+g)}{(r-g)} \qquad (3.11)$$

Where, "a_0" indicates the periodic payment in year zero and "g" denotes the underlying growth. Notice, if g is zero, Equations 3.11 and 3.10 are equivalent.

Continuing our example, let's leave "a_0" equal the current dividend or D_0 and "r" equal 10.0%. Using equation 3.11, we have:

$$PVA_{r,\infty} = \frac{\$0.93(1+0.08)}{(0.10-0.08)} = \frac{\$1.0044}{0.02} = \$50.22 \qquad (3.11a)$$

TABLE 3.8	Present Value of Annuity		
YEARS	ANNUITY AMOUNT	INTEREST RATE	PV OF ANNUITY
3	$100.00	10.0%	$ 248.69
10	100.00	10.0%	614.46
50	100.00	10.0%	991.48
100	100.00	10.0%	999.93
200	100.00	10.0%	1,000.00*
500	100.00	10.0%	1,000.00*
1000	100.00	10.0%	1,000.00*
Infinity	100.00	10.0%	1,000.00

*PV of an annuity is greater than $999.99999 but not exactly $1000.

Notice, $D_0 (1 + g)$ or [$0.93 (1.08)$] equals $1.0044 or the amount of the expected dividend during the first year:

$$D_0 (1 + g) = D_1 \qquad (3.11b)$$

So more generally, using "a_1" denotes the perpetuity amount at the end of year 1 and Equation 3.11 can be rewritten simply as:

$$PVA_{r,\infty} = \frac{a_1}{(r - g)} \qquad (3.12)$$

Using this approach, the value of Hershey's stock should be $50.22, which approximated its market value at the end of 2005.

DETERMINING INTEREST RATES

In many instances, the present values and cash flows associated with a payment stream are known, but the interest rate is not known. Suppose a bank offers to lend you $100 today if you sign a note agreeing to pay the bank $133.10 at the end of 3 years. What rate of interest would you be paying on the loan? To answer the question, we use Equation 3.2:

$$FV_{r,n} = P_0 (1 + r)^n = P_0 [FVIF(r,n)]$$

We simply solve for the *FVIF* and then look up this value in Table 3.2 along the row for the third year:

$$FVIF(r,n) = \frac{FV_{r,3yr}}{P_0} = \frac{\$133.10}{\$100} = 1.3310$$

Looking across the row for the third year, we find the value 1.3310 in the 10% column; therefore, the interest rate on the loan is 10%.

Precisely the same approach is taken to determine the interest rate implicit in an annuity. For example, suppose a bank will lend you $248.69 if you sign a note in which you agree to pay the bank $100 at the end of each of the next 3 years. What interest rate is the bank charging you? To answer the question, we solve Equation 3.7a for *PVIFA* and then look up the *PVIFA* in Table 3.6:

$$PVA_{r,t} = a\ PVIFA_{r,t}$$

$$PVIFA_{r,t} = \frac{PV_{r,3yr}}{a} = \frac{\$248.69}{\$100} = 2.4869$$

Looking across the third-year row, we find the factor 2.4869 under the 10% column; therefore, the bank is lending you money at a 10% interest rate.

A third illustration of finding interest rates involves determining the growth rates. One method is the endpoints method. We can calculate growth rates (geometric average) using the future-value formula, Equation 3.2:

$$FV_{r,n} = P_0\ (1 + r)^n$$

For Hershey's revenue stream, the 5-year compound annual growth rate (CAGR) from 2000 sales of \$3,820.4 million to 2005 sales of \$4,836.0 is 4.83%. Substituting these into the formula, we have:

$$\$4,836.0 = \$3,820.4(1+r)^5$$

$$\left(\frac{\$4,836.0}{\$3,820.4}\right)^{1/5} - 1 = r$$

$$(1.2658)^{(1/5)} - 1 = (1.0483) - 1 = r$$

$$r = 4.83\%$$

This is read as a compound annual growth rate of 4.83% or a CAGR of 4.83%.

More generally, to calculate the growth rate (*g*) or interest rate (*r*):

$$r = \left(\frac{X_n}{X_0}\right)^{1/n} - 1 = \left(\frac{FV}{PV}\right)^{1/n} - 1 \tag{3.13}$$

where:

> r = compound (geometric average) growth rate over the period
> X_n = endpoint value = FV
> X_0 = beginning value = PV
> n = number of periods of growth

A caution must be given when using the endpoints method to determine a CAGR. The caution is that the CAGR may not reflect the data patterns for the periods between the endpoints. For the 2 years between 2001 and 2003, Hershey's revenues only grew at a compound annual rate of 0.43% and 7.66% between 2003 and 2005.

USING A FINANCIAL CALCULATOR TO DETERMINE INTEREST RATES

Building upon the discussion above and recalling the five TVM keys on a financial calculator, we can easily calculate an unknown interest rate if we know the time period and any two of the three periodic flows (PV, PMT, or FV).

To illustrate the use of a financial calculator, let us review some of the examples above:

1. Bank loan of $100 today with a promise to repay $133.10 in 3 years: To calculate the interest rate when you know the present value, future value, and number of years, begin by clearing all of the calculator's registers then enter:

3	N
–100	PV
133.1	FV

The final step is to solve for the interest rate. If you use a TI calculator, push the CPT key to tell the calculator to "compute" and then press the i%-key. If you use an HP calculator, simply push the i%-key. In either case, the calculator displays the answer of 10.00%.

Notice the present value was entered as a negative number. One of the two periodic values must be entered as a negative number to indicate a cash outflow. It is generally customary to assume that the present value amount is entered as the negative value because that's when most investments occur.

2. Bank loan of $248.69 with a 3-year annuity repayment of $100: To calculate the interest rate when you know the present value, annuity amount, and number of years, begin by clearing all of the calculator's registers then enter:

3	N
248.69	PV
–100	PMT

As with a single sum, the final step is to solve for the interest rate. If you use a TI calculator, push the CPT key to tell the calculator to "compute" and then press the i%-key. If you use an HP calculator, simply push the i%-key. In either case, the calculator displays the answer of 10.00%.

3. Hershey's revenue growth from 2000 ($3,820.4) to 2005 ($4,836.0): Begin by clearing all of the calculator's registers then enter:

5	N
–3820.4	PV
4836.0	FV

Compute the CAGR by using the i%-key as above. The calculator displays the answer of 4.83%.

SEMIANNUAL AND OTHER COMPOUNDING PERIODS

In all the examples used thus far, it has been assumed that returns were received annually. For example, in the section dealing with future values, it was assumed that the funds earned 10% a year. However, suppose the earnings rate had been 10% compounded semiannually (i.e., every 6 months). What would this have meant? Consider the following example.

TABLE	3.9	Future Value with Semiannual Compounding

YEAR	PERIOD n	(1) AMOUNT AT START OF YEAR PV	(2) INTEREST EARNED (1) × (r)	(3) AMOUNT AT END OF YEAR (1) × (1 + r) $FV_{r,n}$
Year 1	1	$100.00	$5.00	$105.00
	2	105.00	5.25	110.25
Year 2	3	110.25	5.51	115.76
	4	115.76	5.79	121.55
Year 3	5	121.55	6.08	127.63
	6	127.63	6.38	134.01

Note: The interest rate (r) is a 10% APR or 5% per period.

You invest $100 in a security to receive a return of 10% compounded semiannually. How much will you have at the end of 1 year? Because semiannual compounding means that interest is actually paid every 6 months, this is shown in the tabular calculations in Table 3.9. Here the annual interest rate is divided by 2, but twice as many compounding periods are used because interest is paid twice a year. Comparing the amount on hand at the end of the second 6-month period, $110.25, with what would have been on hand under annual compounding, $110.00, shows that semiannual compounding is better for the investor. This result occurs because the saver earns interest on interest more frequently. Thus semiannual compounding results in higher effective annual rates (EAR). Notice at the end of 3 years (or six semiannual compounding periods), the $100 investment would be worth $134.01 versus a 3-year annual compounded value of $133.10.

If we required that the annual rate stays at 10% so that the value at the end of the first year is $110, then the semiannual rate would be not 10/2 = 5% but rather $(1.10)^{1/2} - 1 = 0.0488 = 4.88$ percent as illustrated in Table 3.10.

By market convention, however, the yield to maturity based on compounding at intervals of 6 months is doubled to obtain the annual yield or annual percentage rate (APR), which understates the effective annual yield. In this case, the 6-month yield to maturity is 4.88% or an APR of 9.76% (4.88% × 2).

We can extend this simple example for more frequent compounding within the year. We calculate the future sum for 1 year for multiple compounding within the year for an interest rate of 10% and an initial principal of $1, as shown in Table 3.11. We see that daily compounding increases the effective annual interest rate by 0.516%.

Equation 3.14 is a generalization of the procedure for within-the-year compounding, where q is frequency, and n is years:

$$FV_{r,n} = P_0 \left(1 + \frac{r}{q}\right)^{nq}$$

(3.14)

The four interest tables (Appendix A) can be used when compounding occurs more than once a year. Simply divide the nominal (stated) interest rate by the number of times compounding occurs per year and multiply the years by the number of compounding periods.

TABLE 3.10	Future Value with Semiannual Compounding			
YEAR	PERIOD n	(1) AMOUNT AT START OF YEAR PV	(2) INTEREST EARNED (1) × (r)	(3) AMOUNT AT END OF YEAR (1) × (1 + r) $FV_{r,n}$
Year 1	1	$100.00	$4.88	$104.88
	2	104.88	5.12	110.00
Year 2	3	110.00	5.37	115.37
	4	115.37	5.63	121.00
Year 3	5	121.00	5.91	126.91
	6	126.91	6.19	133.10

Note: The interest rate (r) is a 9.76% APR or 4.88% (r/2) per period.

For example, to find the amount to which $100 will grow after 5 years if semiannual compounding is applied to a stated 10% interest rate, divide 10% by 2 and multiply the 5 years by 2. Then look in Appendix A.1 at the end of the book under the 5% column and in the row for the tenth period, where you will find an interest factor of 1.6289. Multiplying this by the initial $100 gives a value of $162.89, the amount to which $100 will grow in 5 years at 10% compounded semiannually. This compares with $161.05 for annual compounding.

The same procedure is applied in all cases covered—compounding, discounting, single payments, and annuities. To illustrate semiannual compounding in calculating the present value of an annuity, for example, consider the case described in the section on the present value of an annuity—$100 a year for 3 years, discounted at 10%. With annual discounting or compounding, the interest factor is 2.4869, and the present value of the annuity is $248.69. For semiannual compounding, look under the 5% column and in the period 6 row of Table A.4 to find an interest factor of 5.0757. Then multiply by one-half the payment of $100, or the $50 received each 6 months, to get the present value of the annuity, or $253.78. The payments come a little more rapidly (the first $50 is paid after only 6 months), so the annuity is a little more valuable if payments are received semiannually rather than annually.

Using a financial calculator, the same logic is applied:

5	i%	10% APR/2 compounding periods
6	N	Six 6-month periods in three years
–50	PMT	Half of the $100 annual payment

This results in the same present value of $253.78 as calculated above.

CONTINUOUS COMPOUNDING AND DISCOUNTING

By letting the frequency of compounding q approach infinity, Equation 3.14 can be modified to the special case of *continuous compounding*. Continuous compounding is extremely useful in theoretical finance as well as in practical applications. Also at times computations are simplified when continuously compounded interest rates are used.

TABLE 3.11	Effective Annual Yields with Multiple Compounding within the Year			
COMPOUNDING PERIOD	CALCULATION	RESULTING VALUE OF $100	EFFECTIVE ANNUAL RETURN	COMPOUNDING PERIODS PER YEAR
Annual	$FV_{r,1} = P_0(1 + r)^q$ =	110.00	10.000%	$(q = 1)$
Semiannual	$= P_0\left(1 + \dfrac{r}{2}\right)^2$ =	110.25	10.250%	$(q = 2)$
Quarterly	$= P_0\left(1 + \dfrac{r}{4}\right)^4$ =	110.38	10.381%	$(q = 4)$
Monthly	$= P_0\left(1 + \dfrac{r}{12}\right)^{12}$ =	110.47	10.471%	$(q = 12)$
Daily	$= P_0\left(1 + \dfrac{r}{365}\right)^{365}$ =	110.52	10.516%	$(q = 365)$

When we compound continuously, the result is the equation for continuous compounding:

$$FV_{r,t} = P_0\, e^{rt} \tag{3.15}$$

where e is the constant 2.718. Letting $P_0 = 1$, we can rewrite Equation 3.15 as:

$$FV_{r,t} = e^{rt} \tag{3.15a}$$

Expressing Equation 3.15a in logarithmic form and noting that ln denotes the log to the base e, we obtain:

$$ln\, FV_{r,t} = rt\, ln\, e \tag{3.15b}$$

Because e is defined as the base of the system of natural logarithms, $ln\, e$ must equal 1.0. Therefore,

$$ln\, FV_{r,t} = rt \tag{3.15c}$$

For example, if $t = 5$ years and $r = 10\%$, the product is 0.50. To use Equation 3.15a requires a calculator with an e^x key. Both the HP-10BII and the TI-BAII+ calculators have an e^x function, so we use Equation 3.15a; enter 0.5 and push the e^x key to obtain 1.648721. If you are using a different calculator and that calculator does not have an e^x key (but has a $ln\, x$ key), use Equation 3.15c; enter the 0.5 and push INV and then the $ln\, x$ key to obtain the same result. Most calculators have some provision for performing logarithmic functions. For annual compounding, the calculation is $(1.1)^5 = 1.610510$. A $100 million investment at 10% for 5 years would be worth $3.82 million more with continuous compounding than with annual compounding.

CONTINUOUS DISCOUNTING

Equation 3.15 can be solved for P_0 (= $PV_{r,t}$) and used to determine present values under continuous compounding:

$$P_0 = PV_{r,t} = \frac{FV_{r,t}}{e^{rt}} = FV_{r,t}e^{-rt} \qquad (3.16)$$

Thus, if $164.87 is due in 5 years and if the appropriate *continuous* discount rate r is 10%, the present value of this future payment is

$$PV = \frac{\$164.87}{1.6487} = \$100$$

This is just rearranging the terms of Equation 3.15.

EFFECTIVE ANNUAL RATE

Different types of financial contracts use different compounding periods. Most bonds pay interest semiannually. Some savings accounts pay interest quarterly, but money market accounts at most financial institutions pay interest daily. Department stores, oil companies, and credit cards also specify a daily rate of interest. In addition, to obtain a home mortgage loan, the lender often uses monthly compounding. To compare the costs of different credit sources, it is necessary to calculate the effective rate of interest, or the effective annual rate (EAR), as it is generally called. The EAR is always compounded once per year.

To calculate EAR, we should recognize that we are simply making another application of Equation 3.14, where $n = 1$. Remember r represents the stated interest rate, which is also called the annual percentage rate (APR). Equation 3.14 then becomes Equation 3.17.

$$FV_{r,1} = P_0\left(1+\frac{r}{q}\right)^q \qquad (3.17)$$

The effective annual rate (EAR) of interest can be determined as follows:

$$\frac{FV_{r,1}}{P_0} = \left(1+\frac{r}{q}\right)^q = 1 + EAR$$

Solving for the *EAR*, we have:

$$EAR = \left(1+\frac{r}{q}\right)^q - 1 \qquad (3.17a)$$

Revisiting Table 3.11, we have already calculated (1 + EAR); the EAR in each of the examples was obtained by subtracting 1. For example, with a stated interest rate or annual percentage rate (APR) of 10.00%, the EAR rises from 10.25% for semiannual compounding to 10.47% for monthly compounding.

STATED RATE (APR)	INVESTMENT INSTRUMENT	EFFECTIVE ANNUAL RATE*
	TABLE 3.12 Hypothetical Bank Investment Offerings	
0.50%	Statement savings—below $1,000	0.5012%
1.00%	Statement savings—$1,000 to $10,000	1.0050%
1.75%	Statement savings—over $10,000	1.7654%
3.00%	1 to 6 month certificate of deposit	3.0453%
3.50%	6 to 12 month certificate of deposit	3.5618%
4.00%	12 to 36 month certificate of deposit	4.0808%
4.25%	37 to 60 month certificate of deposit	4.3413%
4.65%	37 to 60 month certificate of deposit—over $25,000	4.7595%

*The EAR assumes daily compounding: $(1 + APR/365)^{365} - 1$.

To help clarify the concepts, most banks offer a menu of savings options such as presented in Table 3.12. The left hand side shows the stated interest rate or the annual percentage rate (APR), while the right hand side shows the adjusted interest rate including the compounding which is the effective annual rate of return. A 4.00% (APR) certificate of deposit yields 4.0808% and so on.

Furthermore, some credit card companies list their annual percentage rate (APR) as 18.99% and then in the fine print and based on daily compounding, report the EAR as 20.91%. Applying Equation 3.17a:

$$EAR = \left(1 + \frac{0.1899}{365}\right)^{365} - 1 = 20.91\%$$

We can generalize with an application. At an interest rate of 10%, we want to know the future sum of $100 with quarterly compounding for 5 years. First we use Equation 3.12:

$$FV_{r,n} = P_0\left(1 + \frac{r}{q}\right)^{nq} = \$100\left(1 + \frac{0.10}{4}\right)^{5(4)} = \$100(1.025)^{20} = \$163.86$$

Alternatively, we can use the EAR in Table 3.11 for quarterly compounding. This is 10.381%, which we can use in Equation 3.2:

$$FV_{r,n} = P_0 (1 + EAR)^n = \$100 (1.10381)^5 = \$163.86$$

Because the results are the same, we can use either method in making calculations. In many transactions and in addition to the highly marketed APR interest rates, government regulations require that the lender provide the borrower with a written statement of the EAR in the transaction. We have described how it can be calculated.

Once again, a financial calculator can easily assist in the calculation of the future value of a single sum with multiple compounding periods. As before, remember to check that the BEGIN (HP) or BGN (TI) annunciator does *not* appear in the display screen. If it does, consult Appendix B or your calculator's user guide to adjust the setting.

To calculate the future value of a 5-year 10% investment with quarterly compounding periods, clear all of the calculator's registers, then enter:

20	N	Or: 5 years × 4 payments per year
2.5	i%	Or: 10.00% APR/4 periods for quarterly compounding
100	PV	

Solve for the future value, and the calculator displays the answer of $163.86.

Calculating Payments for Mortgages, Car Loans, and Other Amortizable Loans

The time value of money concepts are very important in business and in personal life. Many of us have home mortgages, home equity loans, car loans, or other amortizable loans. An amortizable loan is a loan where the periodic payment (monthly in these examples) includes principal repayment along with interest payments. As a new student to TVM concepts, many students confirm their understanding by reviewing their own outstanding loans. So let's say that you have a 30-year home mortgage of $100,000 at 6.00% (the stated interest rate which is also the annual percentage rate). What are the monthly payments?

Using a financial calculator, enter the information that you know and solve for the annuity (or payments). Remember to check that the BEGIN (HP) or BGN (TI) annunciator does *not* appear in the display screen. If it does, consult Appendix B or your calculator's user guide to adjust the setting. Clear all of the calculator's registers and then enter:

360	N	Or: 30 years × 12 payments per year
0.5	i%	Or: 6.00% APR/12 periods for monthly compounding
100,000	PV	

Push 360 and then the N-key; push 0.5 and then the i% key; and push 100,000 then the PV-key. The final step is to solve for the payment. If you use a TI calculator, push the CPT key to tell the calculator to "compute" and then press the PMT key. If you use an HP calculator, simply push the PMT key. In either case, the calculator displays the answer of $599.55.

The payment on a 4-year, 7.5%, $18,000 car loan can be calculated **using the procedure discussed above:**

48	N	Or: 4 years × 12 payments per year
0.625	i%	Or: 7.25% APR/12 periods for monthly compounding
18,000	PV	

The monthly payment is $435.22.

TABLE 3.13	Loan Amortization Table (5 year; $10,000; 12%)				
YEAR	BEGINNING BALANCE	PAYMENT	12.0% INTEREST	PRINCIPAL	ENDING BALANCE
1	$10,000.00	$2,774.10	$1,200.00	$1,574.10	$8,425.90
2	8,425.90	2,774.10	1,011.11	1,762.99	6,662.91
3	6,662.91	2,774.10	799.55	1,974.55	4,688.36
4	4,688.36	2,774.10	562.60	2,211.50	2,476.86
5	2,476.86	2,774.10	297.22	2,476.88	0.00

LOAN AMORTIZATION SCHEDULE

Suppose you could borrow $10,000 (PV), for 5 (n) years, at 12% (i%), as determined above; your annual payments would be $2,774.10. A portion of the payment pays for the period's interest while the remaining portion reduces principal. This is presented in Table 3.13.

In the first year, $10,000 is outstanding for the full year at a 12% interest rate for a total interest payment of $1,200. But the payment was $2,774.10! So the difference between the payment and the interest, or $1,574.10 reduces the outstanding loan balance. At the end of year 1 (or beginning of year 2), the remaining balance on the loan is $8,425.90 ($10,000 less $1,574.10), which is subject to 12% interest for that year. So the year 2 interest component is only $1,011.11 and a larger portion of the payment reduces the remaining principal amount. This process continues until the loan is paid off in year 5.

summary

A knowledge of compound interest and present-value techniques is essential to an understanding of important aspects of business finance covered in subsequent chapters: capital budgeting, financial structure, security valuation, and other topics. These are also important concepts from a personal perspective: loans, investments, retirement planning, and other topics.

The four basic equations with the notation that will be used throughout the book are:

$$FV_{r,n} = P_0 FVIF(r,n) = P_0(1 + r)^n \tag{3.2}$$

$$PV_{r,n} = FV_{r,n} PVIF(r,n) = FV_{r,n} (1 + r)^{-n} \tag{3.4}$$

$$FVA_{r,t} = aFVIFA(r,t) = a[(1 + r)^t - 1]/r \tag{3.6}$$

$$PVA_{r,t} = aPVIFA(r,t) = a[1 - (1 + r)^{-t}]/r \tag{3.7}$$

These four equations are fundamental to all TVM analysis and corporate finance.

With continuous compounding, the first two formulas become:

$$FV_{r,t} = P_0\, e^{rt} \qquad\qquad (3.15)$$

$$PV_{r,t} = FV_{r,t}\, e^{-rt} \qquad\qquad (3.16)$$

These interest formulas can be used for either an even or uneven series of receipts or payments. Some of the many applications of the basic formulas are used to find (1) the annual payments necessary to accumulate a future sum, (2) the annual receipts from a specified annuity, (3) the periodic payments necessary to amortize a loan, and (4) the interest rate implicit in a loan contract. They are the basis for all valuation formulas. The formulas can also be used with more frequent than annual compounding, including semi-annual, monthly, daily, and continuous compounding.

The general formula for within-the-year compounding is:

$$q \text{ frequency, } n \text{ years, } FV_{r,n} = P_0[1 + (r/q)]^{nq} \qquad\qquad (3.14)$$

This expression is used in determining the EAR (*effective annual rate*) implicit in a contract where the *effective interest rate* is not the same as the stated (or annual percentage rate–APR) because of the frequency of compounding. The formula for the effective annual rate is:

$$EAR = [1 + (r/q)]^q - 1 \qquad\qquad (3.17a)$$

Multiple compounding periods per year result in EARs that are greater than the stated rates (APR) and the more compounding periods per year, the higher the EAR.

A perpetuity is a special case of an annuity where the stream of cash flows goes on forever. Their present value is captured by Equation 3.11, which includes a growth component.

$$PVA_{r,\infty} = \frac{a_0(1+g)}{(r-g)} \qquad\qquad (3.11)$$

A perpetuity with no growth is simply valued as: a/r.

As discussed throughout, a financial calculator such as the HP-10BII or the TI BAII-Plus is a very effective tool to assist in these calculations.

Questions

3.1   When do financial decisions require explicit consideration of the interest factor?

3.2   Explain the relationship of discount rate levels to both present value and future value. Do the same for time to maturity.

3.3   Compound interest relationships are important for decisions other than financial ones. Why are they important to marketing managers?

3.4   Would you rather have a savings account that pays 5% interest compounded semi-annually or one that pays 5% interest compounded daily? Why?

3.5   For a given interest rate and a given number of years, is the interest factor for the sum of an annuity greater or smaller than the interest factor for the present value of the annuity?

3.6   For a single lump sum, explain the relation ship between the present value inter-est rate and the future value interest rate. What is their mathematical relationship?

3.7   Suppose you are examining two investments, A and B. Both have the same maturity, but A pays a 9% return and B yields 5%. Which investment is probably riskier? How do you know?

3.8   I have the opportunity to buy a 10-year annuity from someone who needs the cash right now. The annuity amount is certain with no risk. So the discussion is turn-ing to the appropriate discount rate. The buyer is suggesting that I should use a discount rate of 5%. Should I be arguing for a higher or lower discount rate?

3.9   The common practice in the local banking area is daily compounding. A new bank is moving to the area and is offering "nanosecond" compounding. How much of an impact does "nanosecond" compounding have for the typical savings account holder? Why do you think the bank is promoting such compounding?

3.10   A local bank is offering a promotional deal where if you open a bank account for at least $1000, they will give you a $25 gift certificate card and pay 4% interest on the account. Does this promotion result in a higher or lower return on your account? If you invest $1000, maintain the balance for 1 year, and earn 4% on the account, what is your rate of return?

Problems

3.1   Future value

Calculate the future value:

PV	%I	N	FV
$ 863	7.0%	15	
1,112	22.0%	8	
3,427	14.0%	25	
3,000	8.0%	30	

3.2   Present value

Calculate the present value:

PV	%I	N	FV
	12.0%	5	$10,000
	28.0%	28	8,436
	9.0%	15	789
	5.0%	2	12,952

3.3   Future value sensitivity

Calculate the future value as well as changes from the base:

	PV	%I	N	FV	CHANGE FROM BASE* $	%
BASE	$1,000	8.0%	12		n/a	n/a
	2,000	8.0%	12			
	1,000	16.0%	12			
	1,000	8.0%	24			

*The base is the top line ($1000 PV; 8.0%; 12N)

Doubling which variable results in the most impact to the future value? What investing lessons can be learned from this analysis?

3.4   Determining interest rates

Calculate the interest rate:

PV	%I	N	FV
$1,000		10	$ 2,000
4,351		8	11,164
3,500		35	100,000
800		5	1,600

3.5   Sum doubling

How many years does it take a single amount to double at 7%? To quadruple?

3.6   Future value of annuities

Calculate the future value of the following annuities:

Annuity	%I	N	FV
$1,200	10.0%	10	
1,460	5.0%	27	
2,312	22.0%	12	
3,000	8.0%	30	

3.7   Present value of annuities

Calculate the present value of the following annuities:

Annuity	%I	N	PV
$ 353	12.0%	10	
11,550	5.0%	22	
880	5.0%	30	
25,000	8.0%	40	

3.8 Future value sensitivity of annuities

Calculate the future value as well as the dollar and percentage changes from the base:

	Annuity	%I	N	FV	CHANGE FROM BASE*	
					$	%
BASE	$1,000	8.0%	12		n/a	n/a
	2,000	8.0%	12			
	1,000	16.0%	12			
	1,000	8.0%	24			

*The base is the top line ($1000 PV; 8.0%; 12N)

Doubling which variable results in the most impact to the future value? What investing lessons can be learned from this analysis?

3.9 Determining interest rates for annuities

Calculate the interest rate:

Annuity	%I	N	FV
$ 750		5	$ 4,812
1,325		25	511,800
3,000		33	450,000

3.10 Determining interest rates for annuities

Calculate the interest rate:

Annuity	%I	N	PV
$ 1,700		3	$ 3,526
1,000		10	7,721
10,800		30	148,660

3.11 Future value sensitivity of annuities

Calculate the future value as well as the dollar and percentage changes from the base:

	Annuity	%I	N	FV	CHANGE FROM BASE	
					$	%
BASE	$3,000	8.0%	10		n/a	n/a
	3,000	8.0%	20			
	3,000	8.0%	30			
	3,000	8.0%	35			
	3,000	8.0%	40			

What investing lessons can be learned from this analysis?

3.12   Future value with various compounding periods

Calculate the future value and the dollar amount change from question number 3.1.

PV	%I	Years	Compounding Periods Per Year	FV	Change from Question 3.1 $
$ 863	7.0%	15	Quarterly		
1,112	22.0%	8	Monthly		
3,427	14.0%	25	Daily		
3,000	8.0%	30	Monthly		

3.13   Present value with various compounding periods

Calculate the present value and the dollar amount change from question number 3.2.

PV	%I	Years	Compounding Periods Per Year	FV	Change from Question 3.2 $
	12.0%	5	Daily	$10,000	
	28.0%	28	Quarterly	8,436	
	9.0%	15	Daily	789	
	5.0%	2	Monthly	12,952	

3.14   Future value and annuities with various compounding periods.

Calculate the future value and the dollar amount change from question number 3.6.

Annuity	%I	Years	Compounding Periods Per Year	FV	Change from Question 3.6 $
$1,200	10.0%	10	Monthly		
1,460	5.0%	27	Daily		
2,312	22.0%	12	Quarterly		
3,000	8.0%	30	Monthly		

3.15   Future value and annuities with various compounding periods

Calculate the future value and the dollar amount change from the base.

	PV	%I	Years	Compounding Periods Per Year	FV	Change from Base* $
BASE	$1,500	12.0%	30	Annually		n/a
	1,500	12.0%	30	Semi-Annually		
	1,500	12.0%	30	Quarterly		
	1,500	12.0%	30	Monthly		
	1,500	12.0%	30	Daily		
	1,500	12.0%	30	Minutes*		
	1,500	12.0%	30	Continously		

*There are 525,600 minutes per year.

3.16 Measuring returns from the stock market

a. Over the past year, the S&P 500 grew at 28.68%, the NASDAQ index expanded at 50.01%, and the Russell 2000 grew at 47.25%. If I invested $10,000 in all three indexes at the beginning of the year, how much would I have at the end of the year?

b. Over the past 3 years, the S&P 500 declined at –4.05% (CAGR), and the NASDAQ index dropped at –6.75% (CAGR), while the Russell 2000 grew at 6.27% (CAGR). If I invested $10,000 in all three indexes 3 years ago, how much would I have at the end of this period?

c. Finally, on a long-term perspective, over the past 10 years, the S&P 500 expanded at 11.07% (CAGR), the NASDAQ at 9.94% (CAGR), and the Russell 2000 at 9.47% (CAGR). A $10,000 investment in all three would have grown to how much at the end of this 10-year period?

3.17 Comparison of investment values

Two investments (A and B) provided the following returns for each of the past 4 years:

	ANNUAL RETURNS	
Year	A	B
2002	20.0%	–10.0%
2003	10.0%	15.0%
2004	23.0%	10.0%
2005	–20.0%	18.0%

Which investment earned the most over this 4-year period? Assume an initial $10,000 investment in both A and B on December 31, 2001. What is the 4-year compound annual growth rate (CAGR)?

3.18 Present value of an annuity

A popular reality dating show hinted that the winner would get a $1,000,000 check. At the end of the program, in the "fine print," it was revealed that the money would be paid out in even annual dollar amounts ($25,000) over a 40-year period. If the TV broadcasting company could earn 4% on its investments, what did this prize cost the studio? If the company's cost of capital was 11%, what did this prize cost the studio?

3.19 Future value of a single sum

As you approach 50-years of age, the desire to purchase a new sports car overtakes you. You race off to your local BMW dealer and order a brand new M5 for $75,000. You plan to retire to Hilton Head in 15 years. If you did not buy that vehicle and instead saved that money in your retirement account, how much more money would you have to retire on assuming a 5% return? 8% return? 15% return?

3.20 Time to pay off a credit card invoice

a. My credit card balance is $2,377.91. If I chose to pay off the balance at the minimum monthly payment of $40 per month, how many months must I pay before the credit card balance is paid off? I pay 18.99% compounded monthly on this card.

b. If my interest rate can be reduced to 6.99% compounded monthly, at $40 per month, how many months would it take me to pay off the balance of $2,377.91?

3.21   Calculating effective annual rate (EAR)

What is the effective annual percentage rate of 15% compounded as noted below:

Compounding Periods Per Year	Effective Annual Rate (EAR)
Annual	
Semiannual	
Quarterly	
Monthly	
Daily	
Per minute*	
Continuously	

*There are 525,600 minutes per year.

3.22   Calculating and comparing present values using effective annual rates

The treasurer of Lamda Enterprises needs to borrow $10 million for 5 years and has been offered the following arrangements:

1. 12.0000% compounded annually

2. 11.4949% compounded quarterly

3. 11.3866% compounded monthly

4. 11.3346% compounded daily

What amount must be paid back for each alternative? Which alternative should be selected to provide the lowest terminal expenditure?

3.23   Future value of a retirement portfolio

a. A recent advertisement demonstrated the portfolio return of investing $3,000 per year from age 23 to age 70 (47 years). The ad stated that you would have accumulated $1,358,700. What rate of return was assumed by the advertisement?

b. Assuming that same rate of return and that you waited 1 year before starting your retirement portfolio, what is the difference in the accumulated portfolio amount?

3.24   Company performance and compound annual growth rate

Kerry Mills, Inc., had the following performance on its casual comfort sweater line and its every day blazer line:

Year	SALES ($ MILLIONS) Sweaters	Blazers
2005	$13.8	$17.6
2001	16.7	19.7
1997	12.2	22.1
1993	4.3	6.2

a.   Calculate the 2001 to 2005 compound annual growth rate (CAGR). Which line grew faster between 2001 and 2005?

b.   Calculate the 1997 to 2001 CAGRs. Which line grew faster over this time period?

c.   Calculate the CAGR 1993 to 2005. Which line grew faster?

d.   Which is the more successful line?

3.25   Perpetuity and present value

What is the present value of a $600 perpetuity at 8%? At 10%? At 12%? What general rule can you surmise from this question?

3.26   Perpetuity and return

If an investment contract costs $12,500 and promises to pay you and your heirs $1,000 per year, what is its rate of return?

3.27   Present value of unequal annual amounts

What is the present value of the following uneven annual cash flows? Assume a 12% required return or discount rate.

	CASH FLOWS	
Year	Project A	Project B
1	$225	$450
2	300	350
3	350	225
4	400	100

3.28   Present value of unequal annual amounts with a perpetuity

An investment's first year's cash flow will be $100,000 at the end of the year. The cash flows are expected to grow at the following rates for years 2, 3, and 4. Starting in year 5, the investment becomes a perpetuity.

Year	Growth	Cash Flow
2	50%	
3	40%	
4	25%	
5+	0%	

a.   Calculate the annual cash flow for years 2, 3, 4, and 5.

b.   Assuming a 7% return, what is the present value of the perpetuity in year 5?

c.   Assuming a 7% return, what is the total present value of the investment?

3.29   Present value of unequal annual amounts with a perpetuity

Often it is possible to solve the same time value of money problem from alternate perspectives.

a. Using the cash flows from problem 3.28, what is the value in year 6 of the perpetuity that starts in year 5?

b. What is the total present value of the investment?

3.30   Add-on interest

You accept the invitation of a letter, which states that you have won a valuable prize, and could collect this prize by listening to a brief overview of time-sharing vacations. Once you arrive, you are approached by a salesperson with a "great" deal, a time-sharing dream of a lifetime for only $15,000. Additionally, if you act today, you could finance the entire purchase price for 9.17% interest, which is far below what banks charge on their credit cards. Furthermore, the sales person explains that payments include "add-on" interest and would be $2,875.50 per year for 10 years. The interest was calculated as follows:

$$\text{Principal} \times \text{Interest Rate} \times \text{\# of Years} = \text{Interest}$$

$$\$15,000 \qquad 0.0917 \qquad\qquad 10 \qquad \$13,755$$

The interest is "added on" to the principal for a total of $28,755 ($13,755 + $15,000), which is payable in 10 easy annual installments of $2,875.50. What is the actual interest rate on this loan?

3.31   Add-on interest, APR, and EAR

You are interested in buying the home audio/video system of your dreams. You know that you can't afford its $15,000 price tag, but a friend tells you about his buddy at the Rent-It-All Center. Once you arrive, you are approached by a salesperson with a "great deal," the entertainment center of your dreams for only $318.75 a month (or a little over $10.00 a day). *Imagine the parties!* And if you act today, you will get to keep the system at the end of 8 years. Furthermore, the salesperson tells you about some unscrupulous merchants who rent items at exorbitant interest rates and never tell their customers. At RIAC, they always provide financing at a competitive 13%, which beats almost all credit cards. Furthermore, the sales person shows you how your low monthly payment is calculated:

$$\text{Principal} \times \text{Interest Rate} \times \text{\# of Years} = \text{Interest}$$

$$\$15,000 \qquad 0.13 \qquad\qquad 8 \qquad \$15,600$$

The interest is "added on" to the principal for a total of $30,600 ($15,000 + $15,600). Buddy also explains that since $30,600 is a large sum and since RIAC never wants members of the RIAC family to be overburdened with a huge amount of debt, RIAC will incur the administrative costs of requiring monthly payments of $318.75 ($30,600/96 months) What is the effective annual interest rate on this loan? What is the APR?

3.32   Present value of a stream of annuities

What is the present value of a 10-year stream of cash flows that includes a 3-year $300 annuity, followed by another 3-year annuity of $500, and finally a 4-year annuity of $700? Assume the investor requires a 12% rate of return.

3.33   Present value of a stream of annuities

What is the present value of a 20-year stream of cash flows that includes a 5-year $800 annuity, followed by another 5-year annuity of $1,000, and finally a 10-year annuity of $1,200? Assume the investor requires a 12% rate of return.

3.34   Present value of an annuity stream and a perpetuity

What is the present value of an 8-year annuity of $600 and $600 (in year 9) grow-ing at 3% each year thereafter? Assume that the investor requires a 15% return.

3.35   Life insurance as an investment

When you graduate, insurance sales people will be all over you to buy life insur-ance. There are two kinds of life insurance, whole life and term. Whole life pro-vides insurance if you die before age 65, and at age 65 it acts as a pension fund. At age 65, you can withdraw money from the policy for retirement. Term insur-ance only provides insurance. At age 65, there are no accumulated funds for retirement. You will be 65 years old in 35 years. Two choices face you:

Whole life: For $1,150 per year (an annuity), you can invest in the whole life policy and receive a 6% return on your money along with $100,000 of life insurance coverage.

Term insurance: You can buy $100,000 of term life insurance for $400 per year and invest the rest ($750 per year) in a mutual fund.

a.   If you buy the whole life policy, how much will you have accumulated by age 65, assuming you don't die?

b.   For the term insurance option to be comparable to the whole life (have the same amount at age 65), what rate of return would you need to earn on your $750 annual mutual fund investment?

3.36   Financing alternatives and monthly loan payments

Assume that you are negotiating financing for a new automobile. You have been given the choice between (1) a $2,000 rebate and 10% (*compounded monthly*) financing or (2) no rebate and 1.9% (*compounded monthly*) financing. Either loan would require monthly payments for a 2-year period; the cost of the vehicle is $27,000. Calculate your monthly payment under both alternatives. With which choice are you better off?

3.37   Value of a project at different required returns

You are considering an investment with the following cash flows. If your required return is 11%, what is the value of this project? If your required return is 15%, what is the value of this project?

Year	Cash Flow
1	$15,000
2	18,000
3	22,000

3.38   Project return and required savings

A new computer system costs $575,000, but will save the company $80,000 per year on processing costs for 10 years.

a.   If you require a 9% rate of return, should the investment be made?

b.   What is the current rate of return?

c.   What annual savings would you need to have to generate a 9% rate of return?

3.39   Home mortgage payments

What would your monthly payment be on a 15-year, $125,000 mortgage at 5.75% compounded monthly? What would your monthly payment be on a 30-year, $125,000 mortgage at 5.75% compounded monthly? What would your monthly payment be on a 30-year, $125,000 mortgage at 6.25% compounded monthly?

3.40   Present value of an annuity and a lump sum

What is today's value of a 20-year annuity that pays $70 per year and a $1,000 lump sum in year 20. Assume a required return of 6.4%.

3.41   Annuity rate of return

At the end of each year for the next 10 years you will receive cash flows of $80. The initial investment is $366.01. What rate of return are you expecting from this investment?

3.42   Effective annual return–inflation

A South American country has been experiencing monthly inflation of 8.2%. What is the effective annual rate of inflation if it is 8.2% each and every month for a full year?

3.43   College savings and investments

Your brother-in-law who just had a baby knows that you are taking a finance course and asks for your assistance in helping him plan for the child's college education fund. Your brother-in-law recognizes that private colleges today cost an estimated $41,500 per year. He also believes that college costs will continue rising at 6%, outpacing general inflation.

a. How much do you estimate college will cost for the child's first year (18 years from today) through the fourth year?

College Year	Child's Age	College Cost
Freshman	18	
Sophomore	19	
Junior	20	
Senior	21	

b. How much must you deposit today (Year 0) at 4% to cover all 4 years? How much must you deposit today (Year 0) at 10% to cover all 4 years?

c. As an annuity, how much must you deposit each year (for the next 17) to have enough money when your child is a senior in high school? Assume two different annuities: a 4% yielding annuity and a 10% yielding annuity.

3.44   Retirement planning

Your sister is celebrating her 32nd birthday. As the party winds down she asks you for some help. She wants to start saving for retirement at age 62. She tells you that ideally she would like to withdraw $50,000 on an annual basis for at least 20 years starting the year after she retires. She says that she would be comfortable putting aside some money each year in an annuity and believes that she should be able to earn an 8% rate of return.

a. If your sister starts making annuity payments to her savings account at the end of this year and makes her last deposit at age 62, how much must she deposit each year?

b. Your sister mentions that she already has a savings account of $25,000. If she uses that money to start the account, how much must she deposit each year until she reaches age 62.

c. She suddenly remembers that as children your parents bought both you and her a life insurance policy that matures on her 50th birthday for an amount of $50,000. If she added that to the retirement fund, along with her $25,000 (year 0) savings account, how much must she deposit each year until she reaches age 62.

3.45   Future value and investment returns

A friend of mine recently explained an investment program offered by a major insurance company. Basically, the opportunity requires an investment over a few years (see the schedule below) and provides a $1 million amount in the 40th year.

End of Year	Investment Amount
1	$12,000
2	14,000
3	16,000
4	18,000
5	20,000

For the first 5 years, the investment earns 4%. What rate of return do you earn for the remaining 35 years (Year 5 to Year 40)?

3.46   Present value of a perpetuity with growth

A perpetuity is expected to provide a year 1 cash flow of $100. The cash flow will grow at 6% per year after year 1.

a. Calculate the future value of this investment's cash flow in the following years:

	Year	Cash Flow 6.0%	PV 11.00%
Given	1	$100.00	
	2		
	3		
	4		
	5		
	10		
	50		
	100		
	200		

b. If you require a return of 11%. What is the present value (Year 0) of these projected cash flows?

c. What is the present value of this perpetuity?

3.47

In 1911, the inaugral Indianapolis 500 race was run. Prize money to the winning driver (Ray Harroun) was $14,500 in that year. The 2006 Indianapolis 500 provided the winning driver with a purse of $10 million. What growth rate is that?

3.48

a. On October 19, 1990, the Massachusettes lottery of $9,916,540 (payable in 20 annual installments of $495,827) was won. Is this a "fair" way of looking at the total lottery prize? Why or why not?

b. At a discount rate of 4%, 8%, and 12%, what is the present value of this lottery winning?

c. October 1992, the winner plead no contest to unrelated federal fraud charges. He was ordered to put up his remaining lottery winnings to immediately pay back the defrauded individuals. A financial services group offered to buy the annuity for $4.2 million. What rate of return were they offering?

Business Organization and Taxes

Learning Outcomes

After completing this chapter,
you should be able to:

1 Recognize the progressive nature of corporate income taxes

2 Cite specific corporate income tax issues related to income and expenses

3 Explain the nature of MACRS depreciation and the derivation of deferred taxes

4 Differentiate the various forms of business organizations

The federal government is often called the most important shareholder in the U.S. economy. While this is not literally true, because the government does not own corporate shares in the strict sense of the word, the government receives a significant percentage of business profits in the form of taxes. The form of business organization affects the taxes paid; income of unincorporated businesses is taxed at personal income tax rates, to a maximum rate of 35%; corporate income above $335,000 is taxed at a rate of 34%, rising to 35% on income greater than $18,333,333. Furthermore, dividends received by stockholders are subject to personal income taxes at the stockholder's individual tax rates. State and local income taxes are added to the federal taxes.

With such a large percentage of business income going to the government, it is not surprising that taxes play an important role in financial decisions. To incorporate or to conduct business as a partnership or proprietorship, to lease or to buy, to issue common stock or debt, to make or not to make a particular investment, to merge or not to merge—all these decisions are influenced by tax factors.

Tax laws are constantly changing in response to different political and public policy goals. Complex rules of taxation cannot be treated in a book of this type. Nevertheless, this chapter summarizes certain basic elements of the tax structure important for financial decisions.

Brief History of U.S. Income Tax and Recent Collections

In 1862, President Lincoln created the Commissioner of Internal Revenue and enacted an income tax to pay for the war expenses. Ten years later, the income tax was repealed. In 1894, the Congress revived the income tax, but it was found unconstitutional by the Supreme Court one year later. With the ratification of the Sixteenth Amendment in 1913, Congress was given the authority to impose a federal income tax.

The first federal income tax (1913) was at a rate of 1% for income above $3,000 to $500,000. Above $500,000, the tax rate jumped to 7%. To help finance World War I, the top income tax rate rose to 77% by 1918 and was significantly reduced after the war. Since that time, there have been major overhauls to the tax law, also called the Internal Revenue Code (IRC). In 1939, the IRC codified the federal tax provisions and included them as a separate part of Federal Statutes. In 1954, this was further refined and resequenced. The Tax Reform Act of 1986 was the most far-reaching in recent years with its much publicized goals of simplification and fairness. The IRS [Internal Revenue Service] Restructuring and Reform Act of 1998 was the most comprehensive reorganization of the IRS in almost 50 years. The 1998 legislation created four major divisions within the IRS based on the type of taxpayer.

In addition to major overhauls, tax laws are constantly revised to achieve both revenue-raising and public policy goals. The Tax Relief Reconciliation Act of 2001 and the Job Creation and Worker Assistance Act of 2002 are recent examples.

Despite the major overhauls and minor modifications, most tax issues that are important for financial decision making remain basically unchanged. In fact, there is a great deal of legislative and judicial precedent that "grandfathers" many tax structures. This provides consistency for decision makers.

The enormity of the U.S. Internal Revenue System is overwhelming. In 2005, the IRS collected $2,268.9 trillion (or $2.3 quadrillion, which is $2,268,900 billion!).

As seen on Table 4.1, more than $1.1 quadrillion (48.8% of the total) was collected through individual income taxes. With the continued improvement in the economy, corporate income taxes exhibited the highest annual growth. Longer term employment taxes

TABLE 4.1	2005 IRS Collections ($ trillions)			
	TAX AMOUNT	ANNUAL	GROWTH CAGR FROM 1973	% OF TOTAL
Income taxes				
Corporation	$ 307.1	33.2%	6.7%	13.5%
Individual	1,107.5	11.8%	7.1%	48.8%
Total	1,414.6	15.9%	7.0%	62.3%
Employment taxes	771.4	7.6%	8.8%	34.0%
Other taxes	82.9	3.1%	4.3%	3.7%
Total	$2,268.9	12.4%	7.3%	100.0%

(i.e., Federal Insurance Contributions Act, or FICA, which is commonly called *social security tax;* Federal Unemployment Tax Act, or FUTA; and Railroad Retirement fund) were the fastest growing component from 1973 at 8.8% (compound annual growth rate—CAGR). The other taxes include estate taxes ($23.6 trillion), gift taxes ($2.0 trillion), and excise taxes ($57.3 trillion).

The remainder of this chapter reviews corporate income taxes and the various forms of business organizations.

CORPORATE INCOME TAX

The following provides a brief summary of the key aspects of the tax laws and regulations that impact the financial decision maker. These aspects are used throughout the remaining chapters of this book and cover many tax issues encountered by the financial manager. However, this chapter is not intended to substitute for the need to use tax accountants and tax attorneys on real-life matters of complexity.

On the surface, the concept of the corporate income tax is simple and direct: accumulate total sales (and other income) and subtract total expenses to arrive at taxable income. Multiply the taxable income by the tax rate to determine the amount of taxes to be paid by the corporation. However simple the concept, the actual application requires a closer examination of sales, other income, and expenses.

Before considering numerous tax issues, we first discuss how taxes are actually calculated once taxable income is determined.

DETERMINING CORPORATE TAXES FROM TAXABLE INCOME

The Tax Reform Act of 1986 (effective July 1, 1987) significantly reduced the corporate tax rate structure. Immediately before this date, the highest corporate tax rate was 46%. After the Tax Reform Act (TRA), the highest corporate tax rate fell to 34%, which created a large windfall for any full tax payer such as Hershey. In 1993, the highest tax rate was raised to 35%, which is still significantly lower than pre-TRA 1986 highest tax rate of 46%. Table 4.2 presents the complete corporate tax rates. If a corporation had income of $110,000 in 2005, its tax would be calculated as follows:

> First $50,000 of income taxed at 15% ($7,500 = $50,000(0.15)).
>
> Next $25,000 of income taxed at 25% ($6,250 = $25,000(0.25)).
>
> Next $25,000 of income taxed at 34% ($8,500 = $25,000(0.34)).
>
> Remaining $10,000 is taxed at 39% ($3,900 = $10,000(0.39)).

Summing these incremental tax amount yields a total tax of $26,150 on the $110,000 of taxable income. The corporation's average tax rate is 23.8% ($26,150/$110,000).

If that same corporation had $100,000 of taxable income in 2005, its tax would have been $22,250. In this example, the 2005 incremental $10,000 increase of taxable income caused the tax amount to increase by $3,900. Said differently, this extra $10,000 caused the corporation to move to a higher tax bracket, but notice it is only this incremental $10,000 that gets taxed in the higher tax bracket. The original $100,000 is taxed at the same rate while the remaining $10,000 is taxed at an incremental tax rate of 39%! But if the top tax rate is only 35%, why is this corporation being taxed at 39%? To see the answer, let's look at another example.

TABLE 4.2	Marginal and Average Corporate Tax Rates			
TAXABLE CORPORATE INCOME (1)	MARGINAL TAX RATE (2)	INCREMENTAL TAXES PAID* (3)	TOTAL TAXES PAID* (4)	AVERAGE TAX RATE* (5)
Up to $50,000	15.000%	$ 7,500	$ 7,500	15.000%
$50,001 to $75,000	25.000%	6,250	13,750	18.333%
$75,001 to $100,000	34.000%	8,500	22,250	22.250%
$100,001 to $335,000	39.000%	91,650	113,900	34.000%
$335,0001 to $10,000,000	34.000%	3,286,100	3,400,000	34.000%
$10,000,001 to $15,000,000	35.000%	1,750,000	5,150,000	34.333%
$15,000,001 to $18,333,333	38.000%	1,266,667	6,416,667	35.000%
Over $18,333,333	35.000%	$28,583,333	$35,000,000	35.000%**

*Columns (3), (4), and (5) are based on upper limit of income range.
**The last line of the table, columns (3), (4), and (5) assumes a taxable income of $100 million.

If a second corporation had income of $500,000 in 2004, the corporation's tax on $500,000 of taxable income is computed as follows:

	INCREMENTAL TAXABLE INCOME	INCREMENTAL TAX RATE	INCREMENTAL TAX AMOUNT
	$ 50,000	15%	$ 7,500
	25,000	25%	6,250
	25,000	34%	8,500
	235,000	39%	91,650
	165,000	34%	56,100
Total	$500,000		$170,000

The corporation's tax is $170,000 for this $500,000 of taxable income. Thus, the corporation's average tax rate is $170,000/$500,000 = 34%.

The purpose of the higher tax rate (39%) between $100,001 and $335,000 is to offset the benefits of low tax rates on low levels of corporate taxable income for high-income corporations. This higher tax rate—39%—includes a 5% tax surcharge. For any corporation with taxable income greater than $335,000 (or said to be fully subject to the surtax), the marginal and average tax rates are the same, 34%, as illustrated in Table 4.2 and Figure 4.1. The effect of this "surcharge" is that all income is taxed at the 34% rate. In our example, if the first $100,000 was taxed at a 34% tax rate, the corporation would be required to pay $34,000 in taxes. However, the corporation only pays $22,250 on its first $100,000 of income. In effect, this is an $11,750 tax savings advantage provided to the small corporation. This is in line with the progressive nature of the U.S. tax system (more income gets taxed at higher rates). However, as a corporation makes significantly more than $100,000, the tax code minimizes and eventually erases this tax savings. Notice, this surcharge of 5% provides additional taxes of $11,750 on the incremental $235,000 of taxable income, thus erasing all benefits of the lower tax brackets.

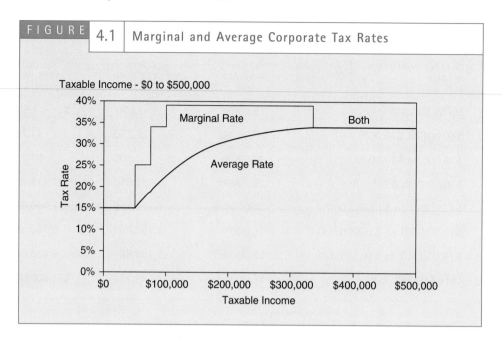

FIGURE 4.1 | Marginal and Average Corporate Tax Rates

The same logic is applied to the 3% surcharge (38% tax rate) applied between $15.0 million and $18.3 million. At $10.0 million, the corporate tax rate becomes 35%.

CORPORATE INCOME

Corporate taxable income consists of two general kinds of income: (1) ordinary income or income from the normal due course of business along with dividends, interest, rents, and royalties and (2) profits from the sale of capital assets (capital gains and losses). This income definition is very similar to the income definition in Chapter 2, Financial Statements and Cash Flows, with some noted exceptions or notable differences as discussed below.

Dividend Income Various percentages of dividends received by one corporation from another are exempt from taxation. If a corporation owns up to 20% of the stock of another, 70% of the dividends received may be excluded from taxable income. If the corporation owns at least 20% but less than 80% of another, it may exclude 80% of dividends received. If the corporation owns 80% or more of the stock of another firm, it can file a consolidated tax return. In this later situation, there are no dividends as far as the Internal Revenue Service is concerned, so there is obviously no tax on fund transfers between the two entities.

For example, Corporation H owns 40% of the stock of Corporation J and receives $100,000 in dividends from that corporation. It pays taxes on only $20,000 of the $100,000. Assuming H is in the 35% tax bracket, the tax is $7,000 or 7.0% of the dividends received. The reason for this reduced tax is that subjecting intercorporate dividends to the full corporate tax rate would be triple taxation. First, Corporation J would pay its regular taxes. Then Corporation H would pay a second tax on the dividends received from Corporation J. Finally, H's own stockholders would be subject to taxes on their individual dividend income. The dividend exclusion thus reduces the multiple taxation effect of corporate income.

Interest, Rent, Royalties, and Other Income Interest, rent, royalties, and other income are considered ordinary income and subject to income taxes. Other income consists of usually insignificant amounts and serves as a catchall for such items as partnership income and recovery of a previous year's bad debt expense.

Corporate Capital Gains and Losses Corporate taxable income consists of two kinds of profits from the sale of capital assets (capital gains and losses) and all other income (*ordinary income*). *Capital assets* (e.g., buildings or security investments) are defined as assets not bought or sold in the ordinary course of a firm's business. Gains and losses on the sale of capital assets, while technically defined as capital gains and losses, can be taxed at ordinary rates or preferential capital gains rate. Tax laws also distinguish between *long-term* versus *short-term* capital gains, based on the length of time the asset is held (currently 1 year).

For example, 5 years ago you purchased a manufacturing piece of equipment for $950,000 and incurred $50,000 of installation charges. Over the 5 years, you had depreciation totaling $776,900 (see below) and consequently a tax basis of $223,100. You can now sell the piece of equipment for $500,000. In summary:

Cost of equipment	$ 950,000
Add: installation	50,000
Depreciable basis	$1,000,000
Less: accumulated depreciation	776,900
Tax basis	$ 223,100
Sale price	$ 500,000
Less: tax basis	223,100
Capital gain (loss)	$ 276,900

These circumstances result in a long-term capital gain (technically speaking). However, this gain is taxed at ordinary rates.

While the exact handling of capital gains is beyond the scope of this review, suffice it to say that the sale of most business equipment and buildings generates a capital gain or loss that is taxed at ordinary tax rates. In this simple example, over this 5-year period, depreciation was considered an expense that reduced the corporation's ordinary income and income taxes (at a 35% tax rate). The gain effectively comes about because there was "too much" depreciation ascribed to the asset in terms of fair market value. This "excess" depreciation provided an added tax deductible expense that saved the company taxes at a rate of 35% or $96,915 ($276,900 × 0.35). To recover this "extra" tax benefit that the corporation enjoyed, the gain should be taxed at ordinary rates (35%) to fully recover the tax advantage provided by the depreciation. This process is known as *depreciation recapture*. If the gain was taxed at the favorable capital gains tax rate of 15%, the tax on the gain would only be $41,535, and the corporation's depreciation-driven tax savings would not be fully recovered by the IRS.

For our purposes, we assume throughout this text that corporate capital gains are subject to ordinary tax rates. This is typically the case for any depreciable asset or any short-term gain resulting from temporary holdings of marketable securities bought and sold on the open exchange.

Most long-term capital gains derived from the sale of a financial asset such as a share of stock is taxed at the capital gain preferential rate of 15%. For example, if the same capital gain of $276,900 occurred due to the sale of a long-term stock holding, then that gain would be subject to a 15% tax rate and $41,535 of taxes.

Deductibility of Interest and Dividend Payments Interest payments made by a corporation are a deductible expense to the firm, but dividends paid on its common stock are not. If a firm raises $100,000 (through debt) and contracts to pay the suppliers of this money 10%, or $10,000 a year, the $10,000 is deductible. It is not deductible if the $100,000 is raised by selling stock and the $10,000 is paid as dividends. This differential treatment of dividends and interest payments has an important effect on the methods by which firms raise capital.

Net Operating Losses Carryover For most businesses, net operating losses (NOLs) incurred in taxable years ending after 2003 can be carried forward for 20 years. The allowable carryback period for a net operating loss is 2 years, thereby giving firms a 22-year period in which to absorb losses against future profits or to recoup taxes paid on past profits. The purpose of permitting this "quasi-loss averaging" is to avoid penalizing firms whose incomes fluctuate widely from year to year. To illustrate, let's say: DSW Computers made $100,000 before taxes in all years except 2007, when it suffered a $500,000 operating loss (Table 4.3, panel A). DSW Computers could utilize the carryback feature to recover the taxes it paid in 2005. Because $400,000 of losses remains, the taxes paid in 2006 could also be recovered. As seen in panel B, DSW recovers $70,000 of previously paid taxes in 2007 as a result of carrybacks. The remaining $300,000 of loss (panel C) could be carried forward to reduce taxable income to zero in 2008 (thus saving $70,000 of tax expense in 2008). In 2009, $100,000 of NOL remains and is used to cut the 2009 income in half.

The Tax Reform Acts of 1976 and 1986 limited the use of a company's net operating losses in periods following a change in ownership. These rules are still in effect today. The carryover is disallowed if the following conditions exist: (1) 50% or more of the corporation's stock changes hands during a 2-year period as a result of purchase or redemption of stock, and (2) the corporation changes its trade or business. (There are other important restrictions

TABLE	4.3	Illustration of Net Operating Losses		
A. REPORTED INCOME	**2004**	**2005**	**2006**	**2007**
Taxable income	$ 100.0	$100.0	$100.0	$(500.0)
Income taxes (35%)	(35.0)	(35.0)	(35.0)	
Net income	$ 65.0	$ 65.0	65.0	
B. CARRY BACK	**2004**	**2005**	**2006**	**2007**
Taxable income	$ 100.0	$100.0	$100.0	$(500.0)
Income taxes (35%)	(35.0)	(35.0)	(35.0)	70.0
Net income	$ 65.0	$ 65.0	$ 65.0	$(430.0)
C. CARRY FORWARD	**2007**	**2008**	**2009**	**2010**
Original taxable income	$(500.0)	$200.0	$200.0	$200.0
less: carry forward	—	(200.0)	(100.0)	—
Taxable income	(500.0)	—	100.0	200.0
Income taxes (35%)	70.0	—	(35.0)	(70.0)
Net income	$(430.0)	$200.0	$165.0	$130.0

on the acquisition of a loss company, but they are too complex to be covered in this brief summary.) Net operating loss carryovers also figure prominently in the calculation of the Alternative Minimum Tax, which was strengthened by the Tax Reform Act of 1986 to ensure that all profitable corporations pay some taxes.

Depreciation **Depreciation** refers to allocating the cost of an asset over its life. Suppose a business firm buys a piece of equipment that costs $150,000 and is expected to last 5 years. The equipment will increase profits (earnings before interest, taxes, depreciation, and amortization or **EBDITA**) to $500,000 per year. Without the concept of depreciation, the entire cost of the equipment would be a business expense against the first year's income alone; this is equivalent to depreciating the asset over 1 year. The pattern of accounting net income would be as indicated below (we assume amortization and interest expense are zero to focus on depreciation):

	CASE 1: IMMEDIATE WRITE-OFF	
	YEAR 1	YEARS 2–5
EBITDA	$500,000	$500,000
Depreciation	150,000	—
Pre-tax income	350,000	500,000
Taxes (34%)	119,000	170,000
Net income	$231,000	$330,000

The cardinal assumption of depreciation is that because the equipment contributes revenues over the entire 5-year period, its cost should be allocated over the same period. If we accept this assumption, then the immediate write-off illustrated understates net income for year 1 and overstates net income for years 2 through 5.

Now assume that the firm uses straight-line depreciation, so that one-fifth of the cost of the equipment is allocated against each year's revenues, as illustrated:

	CASE 2: STRAIGHT-LINE DEPRECIATION
	YEARS 1–5
EBITDA	$500,000
Depreciation	30,000
Pre-Tax Income	470,000
Taxes (34%)	159,800
Net Income	$310,200

Accounting net income is the same for each of the 5 years.

Depreciation and Cash Flows We have illustrated the effect of depreciation on accounting earnings. However, depreciation is a special kind of tax deductible expense in that it is *not* a cash outlay. Whether we consider depreciation or not, the only cash outflow in our example occurs at the start of year 1 when the equipment is initially purchased. For Case 1, therefore, cash flows and accounting net income are the same, but for Case 2, the non-cash nature of depreciation expense causes cash flows to be different from accounting income. Now, we calculate the cash flows for Case 2:

ANNUAL CASH FLOW	CASE 2: STRAIGHT-LINE DEPRECIATION	
	YEAR 1	YEARS 2–5
Net income	$310,200	$310,200
Add: depreciation	30,000	30,000
Less: investment	(150,000)	–
Cash flow	$190,200	$340,200

Because depreciation is non-cash expense, it is added back to net income to determine cash flows. Cash flows must also be adjusted in year 1 to reflect the cash outlay that took place when the equipment was purchased.

	CASE 1: IMMEDIATE WRITE-OFF			CASE 2: 5-YR DEPRECIATION		
YEAR	NET INCOME	CASH FLOW	PV CASH FLOW	NET INCOME	CASH FLOW	PV CASH FLOW
1	$ 231,000	$ 231,000	$ 210,000	$ 310,200	$ 190,200	$72,909
2	330,000	330,000	272,727	310,200	340,200	1,157
3	330,000	330,000	247,934	310,200	340,200	5,597
4	330,000	330,000	225,394	310,200	340,200	2,361
5	330,000	330,000	204,904	310,200	340,200	1,237
	$1,551,000	$1,551,000	$1,160,960	$1,551,000	$1,551,000	$53,262

The 5-year total of net income and cash flow for both cases is $1,551,000. So what is the point of depreciation? The only effect is on the *timing of cash flows.* Assuming a 10% discount rate, we calculate the present value of the cash flows for each case as we did in Chapter 3, Time and Value. Clearly, the higher value is attained with the immediate write-off of the asset. In this example, the only difference between the two cases is when the tax benefit for the depreciation is received. The immediate write-off results in a $7,698 advantage. Firms prefer to write off assets as they are purchased, rather than depreciating them over their useful lives. This is not permitted, however, by either accounting conventions (US GAAP) or tax laws. Given that assets must be depreciated, firms generally want to depreciate them as quickly as possible.

Accelerated Depreciation There are two ways for a firm to write off assets more quickly. One is to shorten the period over which the asset is depreciated. The other is to use an accelerated depreciation method (e.g., 150% declining balance method or double declining balance method). U.S. tax laws permit firms to do both using a procedure known as the Modified Accelerated Cost Recovery System (or MACRS, pronounced "makers").

Any one who has ever purchased a new car has experienced the concepts that underlie accelerated depreciation. In that first year of use, the value of the new car drops dramatically more than in the car's tenth year! Likewise, the value of a brand new computer drops more rapidly when it is a few months old than when it is 5 years old! Accelerated depreciation systematically incorporates this feature when estimating depreciation.

TABLE 4.4	Recovery Periods for MACRS
CLASS	TYPE OF PROPERTY
3-year	Short-lived property, such as tractor units, race horses older than 2 years old, and other horses older than 12 years old
5-year	Cars and trucks, computers and peripherals, caculators, copiers and typewriters, and specific items used in research
7-year	Office furniture and fixtures, plus any asset not designated to be in another class; most industrial equipment
10-year	Vessels, barges, tugs and similar equipment related to water transportation, and single-purpose agricultural structures
15-year	Roads, shrubbery, wharves, and sewage treatment plants
20-year	Farm buildings, sewer pipe, and other long-lived equipment
27.5-year*	Residential rental real property
31.5-year*	Nonresidential real property

*Depreciated using the straight-line method.

Under MACRS, there is no need to estimate the expected useful economic life of an asset. Instead, assets are categorized into several classes, each with its own *class life* and *recovery period* over which the asset is to be depreciated. The asset classes and types of property included in each are listed in Table 4.4. Notice that most industrial manufacturing equipment is included as 7-year property. Yes, we know that equipment used to make chocolate is different than equipment used to make automobiles, which is different than equipment used to make computer chips. But rather than complicate the application of MACRS, all industrial equipment is considered to have the same 7-year tax life.

These statutory lives are generally shorter than the economic lives of the assets; furthermore, MACRS allows an accelerated depreciation method, specifically, 200% (or double-declining balance) depreciation for most classes of assets. (Fifteen-year and 20-year assets are depreciated using the 150% declining balance method, and real property must be depreciated over 27.5 or 31.5 years using the straight-line method.) The effect of MACRS is to accelerate depreciation, increasing the depreciation tax shelter, and thus increasing cash flows.

The percentages are applied to the cost of the asset, without consideration of salvage value, and use a half-year convention for the initial and final year. The half-year convention assumes that on average capital is spent mid-year of the first year. See Table 4.5.

Table 4.6, panel A, computes the MACRS depreciation and remaining tax book value for a $1 million asset with a 7-year MACRS life. Notice that the asset is fully written off after 8 years. In panel B, we reduce the earnings before depreciation by this MACRS depreciation amount to calculate taxable income less the tax payment (at 34%) to derive the company's net income according to the IRS. More is said about this when deferred taxes are discussed.

Accelerated Depreciation, Present Value, and the Impact on Capital Investment

Accelerated depreciation, such as MACRS, results in lower tax payments in the early years when compared to straight-line depreciation and thus greater cash flow in earlier years, similar to the situation above when immediate write-off was considered. Consequently, capital investment aided by MACRS depreciation is of higher value than the same investment limited by straight-line depreciation. While the total cash flows over the life of the project do not change, the timing of the cash flows does change. The project

| TABLE 4.5 | Recovery Allowance Percentages under MACRS (Half-year convention) | | | | | |

| | CLASS LIFE | | | | | |
OWNERSHIP YEAR	3-YEAR[a]	5-YEAR[a]	7-YEAR[a]	10-YEAR[a]	15-YEAR[b]	20-YEAR[b]
1	33.33%	20.00%	14.29%	10.00%	5.00%	3.750%
2	44.45	32.00	24.49	18.00	9.50	7.219
3	14.81	19.20	17.49	14.40	8.55	6.677
4	7.41	11.52*	12.49	11.52	7.70	6.177
5	100.00	11.52	8.93*	9.22	6.93	5.713
6		5.76	8.92	7.37	6.23	5.285
7		100.00	8.93	6.55*	5.90*	4.888
8			4.46	6.55	5.90	4.522
9			100.00	6.56	5.91	4.462*
10				6.55	5.90	4.461
11				3.28	5.91	4.462
12				100.00	5.90	4.461
13					5.91	4.462
14					5.90	4.461
15					5.91	4.462
16					2.95	4.461
17					100.00	4.462
18						4.461
19						4.462
20						4.461
21						2.231
						100.000

[a]Depreciated using 200% declining balance method, switch to straight-line as indicated.
[b]Depreciated using 150% declining balance method, switch to straight-line as indicated.
*Switch to straight-line depreciation.
Source: IRS Publication 534, *Depreciation*, Table 1, p. 28.

(and the depreciation approach) that delivers the cash flow more quickly is the more valuable project.

Section 179 Benefit for Small Companies   Under Section 179 of the Tax Code, companies are allowed to expense up to a total of $100,000 worth of equipment per year. For small businesses, this is equivalent to depreciating some equipment over a single year and results in an immediate tax savings for the organization.

Tax Credits   Tax credits are deductions from the tax bill itself, rather than deductions from taxable income, and thus are potentially very valuable. Today, there are only two minor tax credits detailed on Form 1120 for the corporation, credit for tax paid on undistributed capital gains and credit for federal tax on fuels. In the past, one of the major tax credits that remains in the tax code, but a 0% rate, was the investment tax credit (ITC) program.

Under the investment tax credit program, business firms could deduct from their income tax liability a specified percentage (often as high as 10%) of the dollar amount of new investment in each of certain categories of capital assets. Tax credits, like tax rates and depreciation methods, are subject to congressional changes reflecting public policy considerations. The Tax Reform Act of 1986 reduced the credit to a 0%, which effectively eliminated the investment tax credit on capital assets. However, the credit remains in the legislation and could be reinstated by simply changing the 0% credit rate.

Tax credits have also been used to stimulate other socially desirable ends, such as those for investment in targeted jobs (employers may deduct a percentage of first year wages paid to "disadvantaged" individuals), disabled access, small employer pension plan start-up costs,

TABLE	4.6	MACRS Depreciation ($1,000,000 Asset—7-Year MACRS)

PANEL A: DEPRECIATION AND BOOK VALUES

YEAR	RATE	OPENING BALANCE	DEPRECIATION	ENDING BALANCE
1	14.29%	$1,000,000	$142,900	$857,100
2	24.49%	857,100	244,900	612,200
3	17.49%	612,200	174,900	437,300
4	12.49%	437,300	124,900	312,400
5	8.93%	312,400	89,300	223,100
6	8.92%	223,100	89,200	133,900
7	8.93%	113,900	89,300	44,600
8	4.46%	44,600	44,600	—
9	0.00%	—	—	—
10	0.00%	—	—	—

PANEL B: PRE-TAX INCOME, PROVISION FOR TAXES, AND REPORTED NET INCOME

YEAR	EBIT BEFORE DEPRECIATION	DEPRECIATION	TAXABLE INCOME	INCOME TAX PAYMENT (34%)	IRS NET INCOME
1	$8,000,000	$142,900	$7,857,100	$2,671,414	$5,185,686
2	8,000,000	244,900	7,755,100	2,636,734	5,118,366
3	8,000,000	174,900	7,825,100	2,660,534	5,164,566
4	8,000,000	124,900	7,875,100	2,677,534	5,197,566
5	8,000,000	89,300	7,910,700	2,689,638	5,221,062
6	8,000,000	89,200	7,910,800	2,689,672	5,221,128
7	8,000,000	89,300	7,910,700	2,689,638	5,221,062
8	8,000,000	44,600	7,955,400	2,704,836	5,250,564
9	8,000,000	—	8,000,000	2,720,000	5,280,000
10	8,000,000	—	8,000,000	2,720,000	5,280,000

incremental R&D, alternative sources of business energy (including solar, geothermal, and ocean thermal), and low-income housing.

Payment of Tax in Installments Firms must estimate their taxable income for the current year and, if reporting on a calendar year basis, pay one-fourth of the estimated tax on April 15, June 15, September 15, and December 15 of that year. The estimated taxes must be identical to those of the previous year or at least 90% of actual tax liability for the current year, or the firm will be subject to penalties. Any differences between estimated and actual taxes are payable by March 15 of the following year. For example, if a firm expected to earn $100,000 in 2005 and to owe a tax of $22,250 on the income, then it must file an estimated income statement and pay $5,563 on the 15th of April, June, September, and December of 2005. By March 15, 2006, it must file a final income statement and pay any shortfall (or receive a refund for overages) between estimated and actual taxes.

Deferred Taxes

Deferred taxes are taxes that a company owes (liability) to the IRS that will be payable in the future or taxes that a company "prepays" (asset) to the IRS. Deferred taxes result from accounting differences between US GAAP accounting and tax accounting rules. With regard to depreciation and the book value of an asset, firms are allowed by law to keep two sets of books—one for taxes and one for reporting to investors.

For example, the use of accelerated depreciation increases cash flows (over straight-line depreciation), while reducing accounting net income. Most firms use accelerated depreciation for tax purposes but straight-line depreciation (with its higher reported net income) for stockholder reporting purposes. The use of straight-line depreciation minimizes the negative effect on accounting net income and is said to "normalize" or stabilize reported income, especially when asset purchases are inconsistent or "lumpy" from year to year.

EFFECTS OF DEPRECIATION ON TAXES AND NET INCOME

Panel A of Table 4.7 shows the US GAAP "book" balances and depreciation on a $1,000,000 piece of manufacturing equipment. The equipment is depreciated straight-line over its economic life, which is assumed to be 10 years with no assumed salvage value. Each year, $100,000 is expensed and thus the book balance of the asset is reduced by $100,000 per year until it has a zero value ("fully written off") at the end of year 10.

Table 4.7, panel B, begins with income or earnings before interest, taxes, depreciation, and amortization (EBITDA). Assuming that amortization and interest expense are zero, we can focus on the effects of depreciation. Table 4.7, panel B, continues with depreciation, pre-tax income, provision for taxes (as reported in an annual report), and reported net income. Reported pre-tax income is $7.9 million each year while reported net income is $5.214 million each year. The income is a "smoothed" and an even amount each year.

TABLE	4.7	Straight Line Depreciation ($1,000,000 Asset—10-Year Life)

PANEL A: DEPRECIATION AND BOOK VALUES

YEAR	OPENING BALANCE	DEPRECIATION	ENDING BALANCE
1	$1,000,000	$100,000	$900,000
2	900,000	100,000	800,000
3	800,000	100,000	700,000
4	700,000	100,000	600,000
5	600,000	100,000	500,000
6	500,000	100,000	400,000
7	400,000	100,000	300,000
8	300,000	100,000	200,000
9	200,000	100,000	100,000
10	100,000	100,000	—

PANEL B: PRE-TAX INCOME, PROVISION FOR TAXES (34%), AND REPORTED NET INCOME

YEAR	EBIT BEFORE DEPRECIATION	DEPRECIATION	PRE-TAX INCOME	PROVISION FOR INCOME TAX	REPORTED NET INCOME
1	$8,000,000	$100,000	$7,900,000	$2,686,000	$5,214,000
2	8,000,000	100,000	7,900,000	2,686,000	5,214,000
3	8,000,000	100,000	7,900,000	2,686,000	5,214,000
4	8,000,000	100,000	7,900,000	2,686,000	5,214,000
5	8,000,000	100,000	7,900,000	2,686,000	5,214,000
6	8,000,000	100,000	7,900,000	2,686,000	5,214,000
7	8,000,000	100,000	7,900,000	2,686,000	5,214,000
8	8,000,000	100,000	7,900,000	2,686,000	5,214,000
9	8,000,000	100,000	7,900,000	2,686,000	5,214,000
10	8,000,000	100,000	7,900,000	2,686,000	5,214,000

Panel B of Table 4.6 shows the same EBITDA, but utilizes MACRS depreciation. As a result, in year 2 taxable income is $7,755,100, taxes are $2,636,734, and net income as reported to the IRS is $5,118,366.

The following summarizes the second year from a book or reporting perspective and a tax reporting purpose (from Table 4.6 and Table 4.7):

YEAR 2			
TAX PURPOSES (TABLE 4.6)		REPORTING PURPOSES (TABLE 4.7)	
EBITDA	$8,000,000	EBITDA	$8,000,000
Depreciation	244,900	Depreciation	100,000
Taxable income	7,755,100	Pre-tax income	7,900,000
Tax payment	2,636,734	Provision for tax	2,686,000
IRS net income	$ 5,118,366	Reported net inc	$ 5,214,000

Note that in Year 2 the firm reports to the Internal Revenue Service $244,900 of depreciation and $7,755,100 of taxable income, and it pays $2,636,734 in taxes. If it uses MACRS depreciation for stockholder reporting as well, it would report net income of $5,118,366. However, more commonly, the corporation uses straight-line depreciation for stockholder reporting. It reports $100,000 in depreciation, $2,686,000 as a provision for taxes (even though its actual tax bill is only $2,636,734), and a net income of $5,214,000. The difference of $2,686,000 – $2,636,734 = $49,266 in reported versus paid taxes represents *deferred taxes*—that is, the firm has been able to defer paying these taxes until a later date because it used an accelerated depreciation method for calculating taxable income.

This effect continues throughout the 10-year life of this project. The following summarizes the ninth year from a book or reporting perspective and a tax reporting purpose (from Table 4.6 and Table 4.7):

YEAR 9			
TAX PURPOSES (TABLE 4.6)		REPORTING PURPOSES (TABLE 4.7)	
EBITDA	$8,000,000	EBITDA	$8,000,000
Depreciation	–	Depreciation	100,000
Taxable income	8,000,000	Pre-tax income	7,900,000
Tax payment	2,720,000	Provision for tax	2,686,000
IRS net income	$5,280,000	Reported net inc	$ 5,214,000

By Year 9, the asset is fully depreciated for tax purposes, but for reporting purposes, the depreciation continues. In this year, the corporation reports a provision for income taxes of $2,686,000 (the same as every year). However in the ninth year, the corporation writes a check to the government for $2,720,000. The extra $34,000 is reflected as a reduction in deferred taxes.

DEFERRED TAXES ON THE BALANCE SHEET

The cumulative deferred taxes calculated above are reported on the balance sheet under an account titled "deferred taxes." In this example, deferred taxes constitute a long-term liability (in effect, they represent an interest-free loan from the federal government). Table 4.8 reflects the account balance over our 10-year period. By the end of year 4, the account balance reaches its peak and then is whittled to a zero balance at the end of 10 years.

TABLE	4.8	Deferred Tax Balance	($1,000,000 Asset—7-Year MACRS)	
YEAR	PROVISION FOR INCOME TAXES	INCOME TAX PAYMENT	ANNUAL AMT DEFERRED	DEFERRED TAX BALANCE
1	$2,686,000	$2,671,414	$14,586	$14,586
2	2,686,000	$2,636,734	49,266	63,852
3	2,686,000	2,660,534	25,466	89,318
4	2,686,000	2,677,534	8,466	97,784
5	2,686,000	2,689,638	(3,638)	94,146
6	2,686,000	2,689,672	(3,672)	90,474
7	2,686,000	2,689,638	(3,638)	86,836
8	2,686,000	2,704,836	(18,836)	68,000
9	2,686,000	2,720,000	(34,000)	$34,000
10	$2,686,000	$2,720,000	$(34,000)	—

However, for growing firms, assets and their depreciation are growing over time, so the deferred taxes account is never reduced to zero. In this case, the total deferred tax account is likely to grow while the deferred taxes for specific individual older assets decline to zero.

DEFERRED TAX ASSETS

There are a few accounting differences between tax (IRS) accounting and US GAAP accounting. The most pronounced is the difference in depreciation as discussed above. However, some differences cause deferred tax assets. For example, say a firm currently is offering a special one-time 2-year warranty when a customer purchases its product. The firm estimates that over a 2-year period it is likely to spend a total of $200,000 in warranty repairs. The following presents the reported income for this 2-year period using US GAAP rules:

	YEAR 1	YEAR 2
Income before warranty expense	$6,000,000	$6,000,000
Warranty expense	200,000	—
Pre-tax income	5,800,000	6,000,000
Provision for income taxes (34%)	1,972,000	2,040,000
Reported net income	$3,828,000	$3,960,000

US GAAP recognizes the warranty expense when the sale (and warranty commitment) is made.

The IRS only allows a taxpayer to deduct actually paid warranty expense, not projected. Consequently, the following is reported to the IRS assuming that the warranty actually does cost $100,000 each year over this 2-year period:

	YEAR 1	YEAR 2
Income before warranty expense	$6,000,000	$6,000,000
Warranty expense	100,000	100,000
Pre-tax income	5,900,000	5,900,000
Provision for income taxes (34%)	2,006,000	2,006,000
Reported net income	$3,894,000	$3,894,000

In this example, the corporation reports a Year 1 provision for income taxes of $1,972,000, and actually paid $2,006,000 to the federal government. The difference ($34,000) is considered a deferred tax asset and is reported in the current asset portion of the balance sheet. In the second year, the corporation reports a provision for income taxes of $2,040,000, and actually pays $2,006,000 in federal income taxes. In this case, the deferred tax asset is decreased by $34,000 to a net balance of zero after this 2-year period.

Dividends Paid to Stockholders

Dividends represent payment from "earnings and profits" of a corporation, which is also considered a return of capital. For corporate income tax purposes, dividends are not a tax deductible "expense." But from your stockholders' perspective, dividends are a taxable event and individuals must pay tax on dividends. This is what gives rise to the double taxation of dividends.

From personal perspective, dividends are taxed separately from other income and at rates much lower than ordinary income. In 2005, the tax rate on dividends was 15% with a lower rate of 5% for lower income tax filers (i.e., $29,050 single and $58,100 married filing jointly).

DIVIDEND INCOME, DOUBLE TAXATION

In the discussion of dividend exclusion enjoyed by corporations, a reference is made to the triple taxation of dividends. Before this is explored further, the concept of the double taxation of dividends is introduced using the following illustration (amounts in millions):

CORPORATION A		INDIVIDUAL A	
Pre-tax income	$100	Dividend income	$65
Taxes (35%)	35	Taxes (15%)	10
Net income	$ 65	After tax income	$55
Dividends	$ 65		

Corporation A earns $100 million before taxes and is subject to a 35% tax rate. Corporation A pays a dividend of all of its income to its stockholder, Individual A, who had to report all of the dividend income as income subject to a 15% tax rate or $10 million in additional taxes. In this example, the only real income that was created was the $100 million from Corporation A. However, in total there were $45 million of taxes paid (or a 45% tax rate) on that income!

To complicate the situation further and to illustrate triple taxation, consider the following ($ millions):

CORPORATION A		CORPORATION AB		INDIVIDUAL A	
Pre-tax income	$200	Dividend income	$ 70	Dividend income	$ 65
Taxes	70	Exclusion (80%)	(56)	Taxes (15%)	10
Net income	$140	Taxable income	14	After-tax income	$ 55
Dividend	$140	Taxes (35%)	5		
		Net income	$ 65		
To AB	$ 70				
		Dividend to	$ 65		
		Individual A			

In this case, Corporation A generates $200 million of pre-tax income through its operations and after paying taxes (35%), pays dividends of half of its income to Corporation AB (which holds a 50% ownership stake in A). Corporation AB has no other income and pays $5 million of taxes after excluding 80% of the dividend amount. Corporation AB then pays a dividend of $65 million to Individual A, who again pays a 15% tax (of approximately $10 million). In this example, taxable income exists at all three entities for a total of three times or triple taxation. In total, the $100 million, AB's proportion of Corporation A's pre-tax income, generated $50 million of taxes.

Without the dividend exclusion, all $70 million of intercorporate dividends is taxed at 35% (or $24.5). The remaining net income ($45.5 million) would be dividended to Individual A, who without a preferential tax rate on dividends pays tax of $16 (or 35% on $45.5 million of dividend income). In this scenario without the dividend exclusion and preferential rates, the $100 million of A's pre-tax income would generate taxes of $75.5 million ($35.0 + $24.5 + $16.0) or a 75.5% tax rate!

Choices among Alternative Forms of Business Organization

Taxes are an important influence in choosing among alternative forms of business organization. In the following sections, the nature of the various alternatives and their advantages and disadvantages are described. Then the tax aspects are considered. From a technical and legal standpoint, there are three major forms of business organization: the sole proprietorship, the partnership, and the corporation.[1]

SOLE PROPRIETORSHIP

A **sole proprietorship** is a business owned by one individual. Going into business as a sole proprietor is simple; a person merely begins business operations. However, cities or counties may require even the smallest establishments to be licensed or registered. State licenses may also be required.

The proprietorship has key advantages for small operations. It is easily and inexpensively formed, requires no formal charter for operations, and is subject to few government regulations. Furthermore, it pays no corporate income taxes, although all earnings of the firm are subject to personal income taxes, regardless of whether the owner withdraws the funds for personal use.

The proprietorship also has important limitations. Most significant is its inability to obtain large sums of capital. Furthermore, the proprietor has unlimited personal liability for business debts; creditors can look to both business assets and personal assets to satisfy their claims. Finally, the proprietorship is limited to the life of the individual who creates it. For all these reasons, the sole proprietorship is limited primarily to small business operations. However, businesses frequently are started as proprietorships and then converted to corporations when their growth causes the disadvantages of the proprietorship form to outweigh its advantages.

---

[1]Other less common forms of organization include business trusts, joint stock companies, and cooperatives.

PARTNERSHIP

A **partnership** is the association of two or more persons to conduct a business enterprise. Partnerships can operate under different degrees of formality, ranging from an informal oral understanding to a written partnership agreement to a formal agreement filed with the state government. Like the proprietorship, the partnership has the advantages of ease and economy of formation as well as freedom from special government regulations. The partnership pays no income taxes. Instead partnership income is apportioned to the partners in proportion to the partners' claims, whether or not the income is distributed to the partner. As a result, partnership income is taxed at each partner's individual tax rate.

One of the advantages of the partnership over the proprietorship is that it makes possible a pooling of various types of resources. Some partners contribute particular skills or contacts, while others contribute funds. However, there are practical limits to the number of co-owners who can join in an enterprise without destructive conflict, so most partnership agreements provide that the individual partners cannot sell their share of the business unless all the partners agree to accept the new partner (or partners).

If a new partner comes into the business, the old partnership ceases to exist and a new one is created. The withdrawal or death of any of the partners also dissolves the partnership. To prevent disputes under such circumstances, the articles of the partnership agreement often include terms and conditions under which assets are to be distributed upon dissolution. Of course, dissolution of the partnership does not necessarily mean the end of the business; the remaining partners may simply buy out the one who left the firm. To avoid financial pressures caused by the death of one of the partners, it is a common practice for each partner to carry life insurance naming the remaining partners as beneficiaries. The proceeds of such policies can be used to buy out the investment of the deceased partner.

A number of drawbacks stemming from the characteristics of the partnership limit its use. They include impermanence, difficulty of transferring ownership, and unlimited liability (except for limited partners). Partners risk their personal assets as well as their investments in the business. Furthermore, under partnership law, the partners are jointly and separately liable for business debts. This means that if any partner is unable to meet the claims resulting from the liquidation of the partnership, the remaining partners must take over the unsatisfied claims, drawing on their personal assets if necessary.[2]

Recently, Limited Liability Partnerships (LLP) have become popular and are used by many law firms and accounting firms. An LLP allows the general partners to take an active role in the partnership without being held responsible for negligence or other acts of other partners or employees who are not under their direct control.

CORPORATION

A corporation is a legal entity created by a governmental unit—mostly states in the United States.[3] It is a separate entity, distinct from its owners and managers. This separateness gives the corporation four major advantages: (1) it has an unlimited life—changes of owners and managers do not affect its continuity; (2) it permits limited liability—stockholders are not personally liable for the debts of the firm[4]; (3) the residual risk of the owners is divided

---

[2]It is possible to limit the liabilities of some partners by establishing a limited partnership, wherein certain partners are designated general partners and others limited partners. Limited partnerships are quite common in the area of real estate and oil exploration investments.

[3]Certain types of firms (e.g., banks) are also chartered by the federal government.

[4]In the case of small corporations, the limited liability feature is often a fiction, since bankers and credit managers frequently require personal guarantees from the stockholders of small, weak businesses.

Interest Rates and Fixed Return Securities Valuation

The financial manager functions in a complex financial environment because the savings and investment functions in a modern economy are performed by different economic units. Savings surplus units (a "unit" could be a business firm or an individual), whose savings exceed their investment in real assets, own financial assets. Savings deficit units, whose current savings are less than their investment in real assets, incur financial liabilities. The transfer of funds from a savings surplus unit or the acquisition of funds by a savings deficit unit creates a financial asset and a financial liability. For example, funds deposited in a savings account in a bank represent a financial asset on the account holder's personal balance sheet but a liability account to the financial institution. Conversely, a loan from a financial institution represents a financial asset on its balance sheet but a financial liability to the borrower. A wide variety of financial claims, including promissory notes, bonds, and common stocks, are issued by savings deficit units.

This chapter overviews the U.S. financial system, reviews the impacts of fiscal and monetary policy, discusses the determination of interest rates, and applies this all to valuing fixed return securities.

Learning Outcomes

After completing this chapter, you should be able to:

1 Overview the financial system and the role of government

2 Describe the types of financial instruments and various financial market institutions

3 Understand how the market determines interest rates

4 Compare different financial instruments

5 Value bonds

6 Differentiate the impact of interest changes on short-term and long-term bonds

Financial System

The financial system links businesses that invest in physical capital to the financial sector of the economy, from which financial capital is supplied via financial institutions and financial instruments as shown in Figure 5.1. The purpose of financial markets is to allocate financial capital efficiently among alternative physical uses in the economy.

FINANCIAL MARKETS

Financial transactions involve financial assets and financial liabilities. The creation and transfer of such assets and liabilities constitute *financial markets*. The nature of financial markets can be explained by an analogy. The automobile market, for example, is defined by all transactions in automobiles, whether they occur at auto dealers' showrooms, at wholesale auctions of used cars, or at individuals' homes, because they make up the total demand and supply for autos.

Similarly, financial markets are comprised of all trades that result in the creation of financial assets and financial liabilities. Trades are made through organized institutions, such as the New York Stock Exchange or the regional stock exchanges, or through the thousands of brokers and dealers who buy and sell securities off the exchange, comprising the *over-the-counter market*. In recent years computers have facilitated systems for directly matching buyers and sellers. Individual transactions with department stores, savings banks, or other financial institutions also create financial assets and financial liabilities. Thus, financial markets are not specific physical structures remote to the average individual. Rather, everyone participates in the trading process to some degree.

Different segments of the financial markets are characterized by different maturities. When the financial claims and obligations bought and sold have maturities of less than 1 year, the transactions constitute *money markets*. If the maturities are more than 1 year, the markets are referred to as *capital markets*. Although real capital in an economy is represented by things—for example, plants, machinery, and equipment—long-term financial

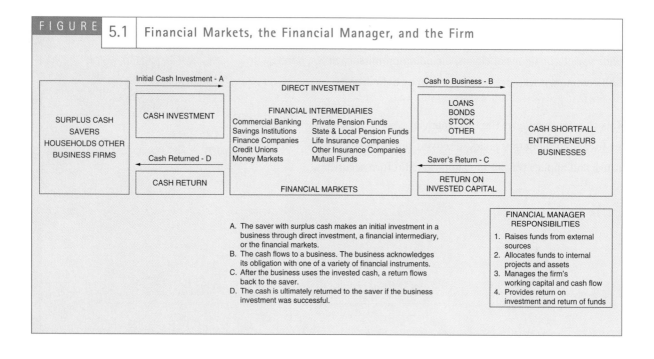

FIGURE 5.1   Financial Markets, the Financial Manager, and the Firm

TABLE 5.1	Market Share Changes for Financial Intermediaries									
	ASSETS 2003*	% OF TOTAL INTERMEDIARY ASSETS								
INTERMEDIARY	(BILLIONS OF DOLLARS)	1952	1960	1970	1980	1990	1995	2000	2003*
Commercial banking	9,324	50	39	39	37	31	28	25	27
Life insurance companies	4,351	21	19	15	12	12	13	12	12
Private pension funds	4,963	3	7	9	13	15	18	17	14
Savings institutions	1,789	14	19	19	20	12	6	5	5
State and local pension funds	2,692	2	3	5	5	7	8	9	8
Mutual funds	6,049	1	3	4	2	6	12	17	17
Finance companies	1,857	4	5	5	5	5	4	4	5
Other insurance companies	1,250	4	4	4	5	5	5	3	4
Money market funds	2,007	0	0	0	2	5	5	7	6
Credit unions	686	0	1	1	2	2	2	2	2
Total	34,968	100	100	100	100	100	100	100	100

*End of 3rd quarter 2003.

Source: Compiled from Federal Reserve Flow of Funds Accounts, Table L.109, L.114, L115, L.116, L.117, L.118, L.119, L.120, L121, L.122, L.123, L.127 www.federalreserve.gov.

instruments are regarded as ultimately representing claims on the real resources in an economy; for that reason, the markets in which these instruments are traded are referred to as *capital markets*.

FINANCIAL INTERMEDIARIES

Financial intermediation brings together, through transactions in the financial markets, the savings surplus units and the savings deficit units so that savings can be redistributed into their most productive uses. The specialized business firms whose activities include the creation of financial assets and liabilities are called **financial intermediaries**. Without these intermediaries and the processes of financial intermediation, the allocation of savings into real investment would be limited by whatever the distribution of savings happened to be. With financial intermediation, savings are transferred to economic units that have opportunities for profitable investment. In the process, real resources are allocated more effectively, and real output for the economy as a whole is increased.

The major types of financial intermediaries are briefly described in Table 5.1. Commercial banks are defined by their ability to accept demand deposits subject to transfer by depositors' checks. Such checks represent a widely accepted medium of exchange, accounting for more than 90% of the transactions that take place. Savings and loan associations traditionally received funds from passbook savings and invested them primarily in real estate mortgages that represented long-term borrowing, mostly by individuals.[1] Finance companies are business firms whose main activity is making loans to other business firms and to individuals. Life insurance companies sell protection against the loss of income from premature death or disability, and the insurance policies they sell typically have a savings element in them. Pension funds collect contributions from employees and/or employers to make periodic payments upon employees' retirement. Investment funds, also called *mutual funds*, sell shares to investors and use the proceeds to purchase existing equity securities.

---

[1]New laws by the early 1980s broadened the lending powers of savings and loan (S&L) operations so that they increasingly became department stores of finance. Lack of experience with their new areas of operations, excesses and outright fraud, and the perverse incentives provided by deposit insurance (small investments by owners taking on huge debts resulting in losses covered by the government) resulted in the multibillion-dollar S&L bailouts of the 1990s.

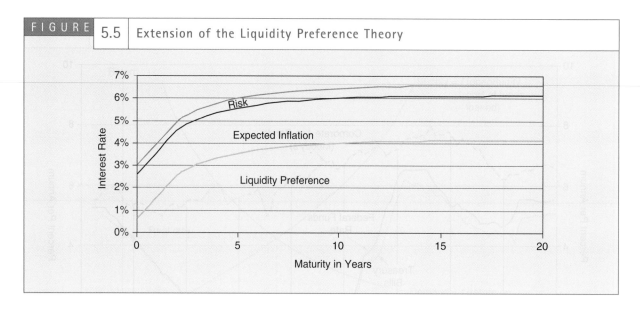

FIGURE 5.5 | Extension of the Liquidity Preference Theory

securities because they are more liquid; they can be converted to cash without losing principal. Investors prefer to be liquid, prefer to hold onto their purchasing power, and will, therefore, accept lower yields on short-term securities. Second, borrowers react exactly the opposite of investors—business borrowers generally prefer long-term debt because short-term debt subjects a firm to greater dangers of having to refund debt under adverse conditions. Accordingly, firms are willing to pay a higher rate, other things held constant, for long-term funds. This satisfies the investor's basic need of a higher return to be in a less liquid position, as illustrated in Figure 5.5.

The next component is related to expected inflation. Investors want to maintain their purchasing power and consequently want to be rewarded through a higher return for expected inflation.

The final component of the liquidity preference theory is a level of return commensurate with the underlying risk. In that regard, a risk premium is added. The higher the risk is the larger the risk premium.

Equation 5.1 shows that interest rates are a function of three components:

$$\text{Nominal rate of return} = f\,[E(\text{liquidity premium}), E(\text{inflation}),\ E(\text{risk premium})] \tag{5.1}$$

Note that each term on the right-hand side is preceded by an expectations operator, E. For example, E(inflation) is the market's estimate of expected future inflation. Investors try to estimate what inflation will be, and, consequently, the market rates of return on securities with different lives will reflect the market's expectation of inflation over the life of the asset.

MARKET SEGMENTATION HYPOTHESIS

The liquidity preference theory states that an upward bias exists—the yield curve slopes upward because investors prefer to lend short.

The *market segmentation* (also called institutional or hedging-pressure) *theory* admits the liquidity preference argument as a good description of the behavior of investors with short horizons, such as commercial banks, which regard certainty of principal as more important than certainty of income because of the nature of their deposit liabilities.

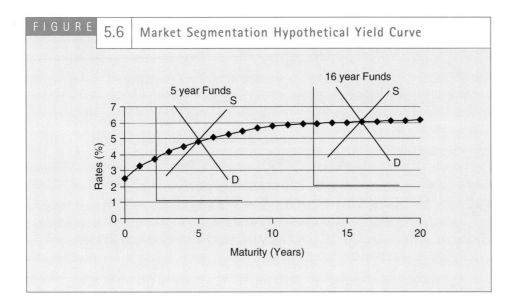

FIGURE 5.6 | Market Segmentation Hypothetical Yield Curve

However, certain other investors with long-term liabilities, such as insurance companies, might prefer to buy long-term bonds because, given the nature of their liabilities, they find certainty of income highly desirable. On the other hand, borrowers relate the maturity of their debt to the maturity of their assets. Thus, the market segmentation theory characterizes market participants as having strong maturity preferences, and then argues that interest rates are determined by supply and demand in each segmented market, with each maturity constituting a segment. In the strictest version of this theory, expectations play no role—bonds with different maturities are not substitutes for one another because of different demand preferences or the preferred habitat of both lenders and borrowers. The 5-year (intermediate) and 16-year (long-term) markets are illustrated in Figure 5.6.

EXPECTATIONS THEORY

The unbiased *expectations theory* asserts that *expected future interest rates* are equal to *forward rates* computed from observed bond prices and yields. The unbiased expectations theory attempts to explain observed forward rates by saying that expected future rates $E({}_tr_{t+1})$ will, on average, be equal to the forward rates. To illustrate, consider a cash manager who has an opportunity to invest excess cash of $100,000 for 2 years. The manager focuses on a choice between two short-term investments:

MATURITY	RATE
1–Year	4.50%
2–Years	5.00%
3–Years	5.25%
4–Years	5.45%

If the money manager decides to invest the full amount for 2 years, at the end of the 2 years $110,250 ($100,000 times $(1 + 0.050)^2$) would have accumulated. The other alternative is to invest the money for 1 year, earn 4.50% for 1 year for a total of $104,500, and "rollover" that amount for the second year at the then prevailing interest rate. If the cash manager believes

T A B L E	5.3	Implied Interest Rate Calculations
Year 1		$(1 + r_1) = (1 + {_0}f_1)$
		${_0}f_1 = r_1 = 4.50\%$
Year 2		$(1 + r_2)^2 = (1 + r_1) \times (1 + {_1}f_2)$
		$(1 + {_1}f_2) = (1 + r_2)^2/(1 + r_1)$
		$= 1.0500^2/1.0450 = 1.1025/1.0450 = 1.0550$
		${_1}f_2 = 5.50\%$
Year 3		$(1 + r_3)^3 = (1 + r_1) \times (1 + {_1}f_2) \times (1 + {_2}f_3)$
		$= (1 + r_2)^2 \times (1 + {_2}f_3)$
		$(1 + {_2}f_3) = (1 + r_3)^3/(1 + r_2)^2$
		$= 1.0525^3/1.0500^2 = 1.16591/1.1025 = 1.0575$
		${_2}f_3 = 5.75\%$
Year 4		$(1 + r_4)^4 = (1 + r_1) \times (1 + {_1}f_2) \times (1 + {_2}f_3) \times (1 + {_3}f_4)$
		$= (1 + r_3)^3 \times (1 + {_3}f_4)$
		$(1 + {_3}f_4) = (1 + r_4)^4/(1 + r_3)^3$
		$= 1.0545^4/1.05253 = 1.2365/1.16591 = 1.0605$
		${_3}f_4 = 6.05\%$

that in the second year, the 1-year interest rate will be 6.00%, then this is an appropriate strategy as the final accumulated amount would be $110,770 ($104,500 times (1 + 0.060)). On the other hand, if the money manager expected that the second year's 1-year interest rate was only going to be 5.00%, the total accumulation would be only $109,725 ($100,000 times (1 + 0.045) times (1 + 0.050)) and the 2-year investment alternative would be more attractive. With an expected 1-year interest rate 1-year from now of 5.50%, both the 2-year investment and the "rollover strategy" provide the same accumulated return. Consequently, if the money manager expected next year's 1-year interest rate to be less (more) than 5.50%, a 2-year ("rollover") investment strategy optimizes the return.

We can now generalize this simple example. Table 5.3 presents data for the relationship between yield to maturity and the related implied forward rates. We demonstrate how the implied forward rates are calculated in the material that follows.

There is a nice symmetry in the calculation procedure. For year 2, the 2-year rate is shown to be equal to the 1-year rate multiplied by the expected forward rate for period 2 observed at period 1. We know all of terms in the first equation except the $(1 + {_1}f_2)$, so we can solve for the expected forward rate.

For year 3, the yield to maturity for a 3-year financial instrument is shown in the first line. But we have already calculated the first two terms on the right hand side of the equation so that we can solve for $(1 + {_2}f_3)$. We proceed in a similar way to calculate the results shown for year 4.

The results are shown graphically in Figure 5.7. We use the data in Table 5.4 to illustrate the term structure of interest rates under the expectations theory.

The basic idea is that the expected forward rates are derived from the current spot rates. However, the actual spot rate for period 2 may not be the same as the expected spot rate measured by the observed forward rate for period 2, observed in period 1.

The future is inherently uncertain, and when uncertainty is considered, the pure expectations theory must be modified. To illustrate, let us consider a situation where future

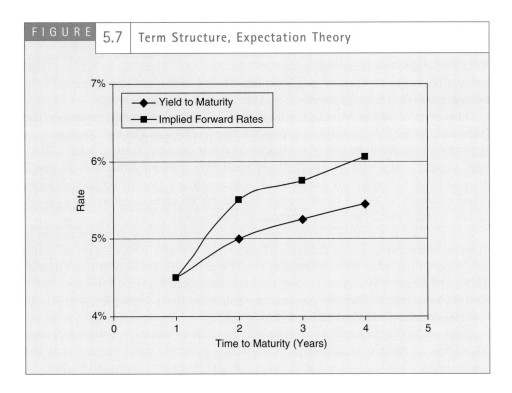

FIGURE 5.7 | Term Structure, Expectation Theory

short-term rates are expected to remain unchanged on average. In this case, the pure expectations theory suggests that short- and long-term bonds sell at equal yields. However, from the liquidity preference theory, we know there is an upward bias built into the yield cure.

EMPIRICAL EVIDENCE

Empirical studies suggest that there is some validity to each of these theories. Specifically, the evidence indicates that if lenders and borrowers have no reason for expecting a change in the general level of interest rates, the yield curve will be upward sloping because of liquidity preferences. (Under the expectations theory, the term structure of interest rates would be flat if there were no expectations of a change in the level of short-term rates.) However, it is a fact that during periods of extremely high short-term interest rates, the yield curve is downward sloping; this proves that the expectations theory also operates. At still other times, when supply and demand conditions, in particular maturity sectors, change, the term structure seems to be modified, reflecting the market segmentation theory.

TABLE 5.4 | Implied Forward Interest Rates

MATURITY (YEARS)	YIELD TO MATURITY	IMPLIED 1–YEAR FORWARD RATES
1	4.50%	4.50%
2	5.00%	5.50%
3	5.25%	5.75%
4	5.45%	6.05%

Issues of Debt and Debt Instruments

Most people have had some experience with debt. Almost everyone has a credit card that involves borrowing for short or longer periods. Many homeowners have borrowed on a mortgage with their home as security. These are all forms of *household debt*.

Other forms of debt are identified by the economic characteristics of the borrowers. The federal debt of the U.S. government is pivotal because of its size. The U.S. Treasury debt is generally regarded to be free of the risk of default at maturity. Treasury bills (T bills) have a maturity of 1 year or less. Treasury notes have maturities from 1 to 10 years. Treasury bonds (T bonds) have maturities of 10 or more years. Treasury securities have no default risk, but have the risk of interest rate fluctuations discussed in topics toward the end of this chapter. Federal government agencies also issue debt.

Individual states and cities issue debt referred to as *municipal securities,* or *municipals*. Companies that trade in bonds, dealers and brokers, also distinguish between financial and nonfinancial firms. (See www.bondsonline.com, for example.) The flow of funds data of the Federal Reserve System also recognizes this distinction. Financial firms have some special characteristics. They are government regulated to some degree, invest mainly in financial assets, and have high ratios of debt to equity.

Nonfinancial debt is issued by corporations, single proprietorships, partnerships, and other forms of business organizations. A distinction is usually made between farm and nonfarm debt. Clearly, a wide range of individuals and institutions are issuers of debt.

Debt issued by foreign governments or foreign corporations are also considered as a distinct category. The main reason is that when denominated in a foreign currency the special risk of fluctuations of the foreign currency in relation to the U.S. dollar may occur. So foreign debt carries an exchange rate risk.

The Valuation of Debt Instruments

The generally accepted methodology for the valuation of any asset (financial or physical) is the discounted cash flow (DCF) procedure. The value of a bond, common stock, equipment or buildings is *the present value of its expected future cash flows*:

$$\text{Value} = \frac{CF_1}{(1+k)} + \frac{CF_2}{(1+k)^2} + \frac{CF_3}{(1+k)^3} + \cdots + \frac{CF_n}{(1+k)^n}$$

where:

   Value = Value of any asset or financial instrument
   CF = Future cash flows
   k = Required yield or discount factor
   n = Number of periods

While the patterns of future cash flows may vary, the DCF procedure is sufficiently flexible to perform the valuation.

The valuation of a debt instrument such as a bond or note uses the concepts developed in Chapter 3, Time and Value.

   Bond Value   = Present Value of an Annuity + Present Value of a Future Sum
                = $\text{PVA}_{k,t} + \text{PV}_{k,n}$

Equivalent expressions are the following:

$$B_0 = \sum_{t=1}^{n} \frac{c_t}{(1+k_b)^t} + \frac{M}{(1+k_b)^n} \qquad (5.2)$$

where:

B_0 = Current value or price of a bond

c_t = Coupon payment = $60

k_b = Required return on the bond reflecting its risk and market condition = 6%

M = Maturity value of the bond = $1,000

t = Discounting periods running from 1, 2, 3, ..., n

n = Period at which the final coupon payment is made = 8

We can make Equation 5.2 more explicit by using an example with the data inputs given with the definitions listed above. We could then write equation 5.2 as:

$$B_0 = \frac{c_1}{(1+k_b)} + \frac{c_2}{(1+k_b)^2} + \cdots + \frac{c_n}{(1+k_b)^n} + \frac{M}{(1+k_b)^n}$$

In actual numbers we will have:

$$B_0 = \frac{\$60}{(1+.06)} + \frac{\$60}{(1+.06)^2} + \cdots + \frac{\$60}{(1+.06)^8} + \frac{\$1,000}{(1+.06)^8}$$

We could also write Equation 5.2 as 5.2a:

$$B_0 = \sum_{t=1}^{n} \frac{\$60}{(1+.06)^t} + \frac{\$1,000}{(1+.06)^8} = \$1,000 \qquad (5.2a)$$

Using the numerical inputs we have provided, we can use Equation 5.2 to determine the bond value to be $1,000. We could have obtained the same result by using time value of money tables. Additionally, a financial calculator is also a valuable, practical tool for evaluating bonds. From Chapter 3, recall that a financial calculator has five important time value of money keys:

| N | | i% | | PV | | PMT | | FV |

Where:

| N | Number of periods (same as n years)

| i% | Interest rate (same as r) [on the HP—I/YR; on the TI—I/Y]

| PV | Present value

| PMT | Payment or annuity amount, which is discussed below

| FV | Future value

For our purposes of calculating the value of this bond, clear all of the calculator's registers by "clearing all," then enter:

8	N
6	i%
60	PMT
1000	FV

Push 8 and then the N key; push 6 and then the i% key (required return); push 60 and then the PMT key (coupon interest payment); and push 1000 then the FV key. The final step is to solve for the present value. If you use a Texas Instrument calculator, you first push the CPT key to tell the calculator to "compute" and then press the PV key. If you use an HP calculator, simply push the PV key. In either case, the calculator displays the answer of $1,000. We have now established the basic valuation formula for bonds. We can now develop some of its implications.

If market conditions change causing the required return on the bond to change, the bond's value changes. Continuing this example with a drop in interest rates to 5%, push 5 and the i% key and then compute the present value as $1,064.63. If interest rates increased to 7%, push 7 and the i% key and then compute the present value as $940.29.

To this point, the coupon payments were assumed to have been made annually. Annual coupon payments represent the general convention for European countries, but in the United States, semiannual payments are used. Chapter 3 set forth a general procedure for converting annual payments to semiannual and other compounding periods. The nominal stated interest rate is divided by q (the frequency of compounding within the year), and n (the number of years) is multiplied by q. As explained in Chapter 3, this procedure is not technically correct but it is an established convention. Using the market convention for semiannual compounding we calculate the value of the bond using Equation 5.3 in which n becomes $2n$ and the discount rate k_b is divided by 2:

$$B_0 = \sum_{t=1}^{nq} \frac{c_t/q}{(1+k_b/q)^t} + \frac{M}{(1+k_b/q)^{nq}} \tag{5.3}$$

Excel provides an easy to use function to price bonds:

> PRICE (settlement date, maturity date, coupon rate, yield, redemption amount, payment frequency, basis for days)

It is detailed in the Appendix D at the end of the book. Using the Excel formula for the value of the bond, we now have:

Settlement date	1/1/2000
Maturity date	1/1/2008
Coupon rate	6.000%
Yield rate	5.000%
Redemption	$100.00
Frequency of payments	2
Basis	0
Price	$106.528

The new value expressed with respect to a $1,000 par value will be $1,065.28. This result is slightly higher than the bond value we obtained using annual compounding ($1,064.63). The reason is that the bond holder is receiving the coupon payments earlier with semiannual compounding than with annual compounding.

Of course in the above example, the required yield rate was below the coupon rate. When the reverse situation occurs, we would predict that the bond value will be lower as shown below (with semiannual compounding):

Settlement date	1/1/2000	Settlement date	1/1/2000
Maturity date	1/1/2008	Maturity date	1/1/2008
Coupon rate	6.000%	Coupon rate	6.000%
Yield rate	7.000%	Yield rate	7.000%
Redemption	$100.00	Redemption	$100.00
Frequency of payments	1	Frequency of payments	2
Basis	0	Basis	0
Price	$94.029	Price	$93.953

The reason is that the penalty effect of receiving a lower dollar coupon than the new required market yields is increased as the penalties are imposed at a faster rate.

Bond Yields

When dealing with bonds, the terms of the bond are well known (maturity, interest payments, frequency of those payments, maturity value) and often the price of the bond is also known. In this case, the question becomes, "What is the return or yield to maturity (YTM) provided by the bond?" We use annual discounting. We need to solve for k_b to understand the return. Suppose that the price for an 8-year maturity bond with an annual coupon rate of 6% was $1,064.63. The information provided enables us to calculate the YTM value. We need to solve k_b in the following equation:

$$B_0 = \$1,064.63 = \frac{\$60}{(1+k_b)} + \frac{\$60}{(1+k_b)^2} + \cdots + \frac{\$60}{(1+k_b)^8} + \frac{\$1,000}{(1+k_b)^8} \qquad (5.3a)$$

With a financial calculator, we input 8 for N, –$1,064.63 for PV, $60 for PMT, and $1000 for FV. We solve by pushing I/YR. We obtain 5.0% as the required yield to maturity.

Using Excel and the "Yield" function (also detailed in the appendix), we have the following:

Settlement date	1/1/2000
Maturity date	1/1/2008
Annual coupon rate	6.000%
Price per $100 face value	$106.463
Redemption value per $100 face value	$100.00
Frequency of payments per year	1
Day count basis:	0
Yield	5.000%

TABLE 5.5	Most Active Corporate Bonds (Tuesday, May 24, 2006)				
COMPANY (TICKER)	COUPON	MATURITY		LAST PRICE	LAST YIELD
Merrill Lynch (MER)	6.050	May 16, 2016		99.953	6.056
Goldman Sachs Group Inc (GS)	6.450	May 01, 2036		96.600	6.714
Home Depot (HD)	5.400	Mar 1, 2016		96.857	5.826
Pacific Gas and Electric (PCG)	6.050	Mar 1, 2034		95.061	6.433
Comcast Corp (CMCSA)	6.450	Mar 15, 2037		94.303	6.897
Time Warner Inc (TWX)	7.700	May 1, 2032		107.658	7.052
Target Corp (TGT)	6.350	Nov 1, 2032		103.456	6.085

Source: *The Wall Street Journal*, May 24, 2006.

Next we assume semiannual compounding. The resulting yield is 5.010%. The reason is the buyer receives his funds earlier so his realized yield has increased. In Table 5.5 we present a portion of the Wall Street Journal listing of the 40 most active fixed coupon bonds for May 23, 2006. The last column presents the yield to maturity (YTM) based on the closing price of each bond. Sufficient information is provided to verify the YTM presented.

We can use the Excel formula for calculating the yield on fixed coupon debt. For example, for the first company listed in Table 5.5, the Merrill Lynch bonds of May 16, 2016:

Settlement date	5/24/06
Maturity date	5/16/16
Coupon rate	6.050%
Price	$ 99.953
Redemption	$100.000
Frequency of payments	2
Basis	0
Yield	6.056%

We obtain, of course, the same result as presented in Table 5.5. The yield to maturity represents the expected return that the financial markets have established for an investment in the Merrill Lynch bonds made on May 24, 2006, at a price of $99.953. Implicit assumptions are that the bond is held to maturity and expectations with respect to future financial conditions and the outlook for Merrill Lynch remain unchanged. However, in reality, the calculated yield will change continuously over time because (1) expectations of the future economic and financial conditions are continuously revised and (2) expectations of the future performance of an individual company such as Merrill Lynch are also subject to change.

Another example, not on Table 5.5, is General Motors. In April 2004, a General Motors bond (July 15, 2033) traded at $111.963 to yield 7.371%. In early May 2005, Standard & Poor's downgraded GM bonds to below investment grade (junk status). On 5/5/05, the day of S&P's downgrade, the GM bonds dropped in price to $74, with the yield rising to 11.494%. S&P said that GM had relied too heavily on sales of the big SUVs, whose market dropped as oil and gasoline prices increased sharply in the spring of 2005.

Hence the reported YTM will change as expectations of the future change. This is a general characteristic of the prices and yields of financial and physical assets. The financial models developed to deal with future risks and uncertainties are discussed in later sections of this chapter and throughout the text.

In our discussion of bond prices in the previous section, we found that when the bond coupon rate equals the required market yield, a bond sells at its face value of $100 or $1000. When the coupon rate is below the required yield rate, a bond will sell at a discount from its face value and conversely at a premium. It follows that the YTM on a bond purchased at a discount is the coupon rate plus a capital gain rate. The YTM on a bond selling at a premium is the coupon rate less a capital loss rate. Because bond prices and required yields continuously change, the expected or promised yield to maturity is likely to differ from the actual or realized yields.

Current Yield

Bond price sheets in quotations from brokers and dealers may also include data on the *current yield* of the debt instrument. The current yield is simply the annual coupon interest payments divided by the current price of the debt instrument. In Table 5.5, the Time Warner bond is listed with a coupon of 7.70% and a maturity of 5/1/32. The current yield would be $7.70 divided by current price $107.658, which equals 7.15%. Note that the current yield differs from the YTM. Because the current yield does not take the time value of money into account, it is not a measure of the return from an investment.

But why is the current yield quoted if it does not measure the economic return? Investors who desire early high dollar returns from their fixed income investment may be interested in buying bonds, selling at a premium because the dollar returns would be greater than the YTM.

Interest Rate Risk

We have established that a decline in the required YTMs in relation to bond coupon rates increases bond prices and conversely. We generalize these relationships in Table 5.6 and Figure 5.8. Shorter term bonds exhibit smaller fluctuations in values or prices than longer maturities. However, the magnitude of the price increases for required YTMs below coupon rates is larger than for required YTMs above coupon rates. Table 5.6 shows the ratio of the value increase resulting from a decrease of 3.5 percentage points from the coupon rate of 7.5%, compared to the decrease in bond value due to a 3.5% increase in the YTM

TABLE 5.6	Value of 7.5% Coupon Bonds with Different Maturity Years at Different Market Yield Rates					
	VALUE OF BOND (IN DOLLARS)					
YIELD	1-YEAR BOND	5-YEAR BOND	10-YEAR BOND	20-YEAR BOND	30-YEAR BOND	100-YEAR BOND
4.0%	103.398	115.720	128.615	147.872	160.832	185.833
6.0%	101.435	106.398	111.158	117.336	120.757	124.932
7.5%	100.000	100.000	100.000	100.000	100.000	100.000
9.0%	98.595	94.070	90.244	86.199	84.521	83.335
11.0%	96.769	86.681	79.087	71.919	69.463	68.183
Ratio of value change for ±3.5 percentage points from 7.5%	3.398/3.231 ≈1.05	15.720/13.319 ≈1.18	28.615/20.913 ≈1.37	47.872/28.081 ≈1.70	60.832/30.537 ≈1.99	85.833/31.817 ≈2.70

Note: Assumes semiannual coupons and face value of $100.

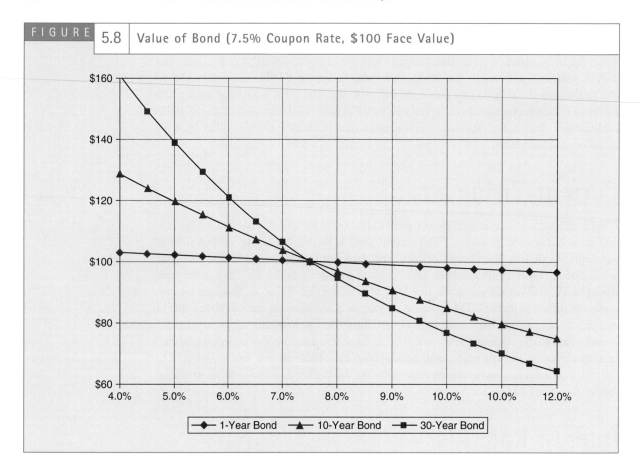

FIGURE 5.8   Value of Bond (7.5% Coupon Rate, $100 Face Value)

from 7.5% to 11%. For a 1-year bond, the increase in value from the YTM change is 3.398, whereas the decrease in value is 3.231. The increase in value is greater by a factor of 1.05. For a 30-year coupon, this ratio rises to 1.99, implying that for a negative 3.5 percentage point change in yield, the bond's value increases by double the amount that the value would have decreased had the yield increased by 3.5 percentage points instead.

Nevertheless, interest rate fluctuations represent significant interest rate risk. For business firms that raise funds selling debt instruments, the risk faced is a decline in interest rates. In practical terms, a firm with substantial debt paying interest rates higher than current market rates is at a competitive disadvantage. The firm is paying more for funds than competitors who are raising funds at the prevailing lower rate. Conversely, when a firm has debt outstanding with coupon rates lower than prevailing required market rates, their debt instruments have increased in value and their cost of funds is lower than firms currently raising funds.

For investors, the risks are reversed. Investors are hurt if they hold fixed income securities whose coupons are lower than current required yields. Investors gain if their fixed income securities have coupons higher than current required yields.

The risk faced by firms raising funds and by investors holding debt securities is not solved by always using short-term securities. When short-term interest rates are high, a firm using short-term financing is at a competitive disadvantage to firms that raise long-term funds at lower rates. Similarly, an investor earning only 1% or 2% on short-term funds as of the first half of 2004 could have earned much more had its prior investments been made in longer term securities when interest rates were higher. The risks of interest rate fluctuations are substantial.

Bond Ratings and Debt Cost

Bond ratings seek to measure the default risks of bonds. The higher the probability of default and the lower the probable recovery of the principal, the higher the required yield on a debt instrument. The three leading companies that publish debt ratings are Moody's Investors Service (Moody's), Standard & Poor's Corporation (S&P), and Fitch's Investors Service. The rating agencies are independent organizations with no ties to commercial banks, investment bankers, or other financial institutions.

The Moody's scale ranges from Aaa down to C with seven intermediate categories. The S&P scale ranges from AAA to D with eight intermediate categories. Specifically, including the intermediate steps, their comparative ratings would be as shown in Table 5.7.

IMPORTANCE OF BOND RATINGS

Bond ratings are important. The lower the bond rating, the higher the required interest rate promised on a debt instrument. Another reason why bond ratings are significant is that insurance companies, banks, and other financial institutions are not permitted by law to purchase below investment grade bonds. Bonds with a rating below BBB by S&P or Baa by Moody's do not qualify as investment grade debt. The inability to achieve investment grade will reduce the breadth of the market as well as increase the promised interest yields.

Bond ratings provide an estimate of the probability of default on the payment of interest and principal. Table 5.8 presents data on cumulative losses for the 10 years after issuance by original rating on all rated corporate bonds for the period 1971–2003 (Altman, 2004). "These losses include the difference between the purchase price and the price that the investor could have sold the bond for just after default plus the loss of one coupon payment"

TABLE 5.7 Bond Ratings

MOODY'S	S & P	DEFINITIONS
Aaa	AAA	Prime
Aa1	AA+	High Quality
Aa2	AA	
Aa3	AA–	
A1	A+	Medium Grade
A2	A	
A3	A–	
Baa1	BBB+	Marginal Grade
Baa2	BBB	
Baa3	BBB–	
Ba1	BB+	Non Investment Grade
Ba2	BB	Speculative
Ba3	BB–	
B1	B+	More Speculative
B2	B	
B3	B–	
Caa1	CCC+	
Caa2	CCC	
Caa3	CCC–	
Ca	–	Extremely Speculative
C	–	
–	D	May be in Default

TABLE 5.8	Cumulative Loss Rates by Original Rating, All Rated Corporate Bonds, 1971–2003[a]									
	YEARS AFTER ISSUANCE (%)									
	1	2	3	4	5	6	7	8	9	10
AAA	0.00	0.00	0.00	0.00	0.00	0.00	0.00	0.00	0.00	0.00
AA	0.00	0.00	0.06	0.12	0.12	0.12	0.12	0.12	0.15	0.17
A	0.00	0.04	0.05	0.09	0.11	0.17	0.19	0.23	0.31	0.31
BBB	0.28	2.81	3.93	4.83	5.45	5.80	6.24	6.38	6.48	6.75
BB	0.73	2.23	5.40	6.78	8.08	8.78	9.68	9.93	10.78	11.83
B	2.13	7.07	12.38	17.54	21.30	23.38	25.00	26.23	27.04	27.53
CCC	5.48	16.52	29.35	36.22	38.26	43.37	46.05	47.41	47.41	49.10

[a]Rated by S & P at Issuance.
Note: Based on 1,535 issues.
Source: Altman, 2004, p.19.

(Altman, 2002, p.155). The table shows that no losses were incurred on AAA issues. Losses were quite low on AA and A issues. For the below investment grade rated bonds, losses become substantial. On the BBB issues, cumulative losses jumped to 6.75% of original value by the tenth year. On BB bonds, losses are about 12%, rising on B bonds to about 28%. On CCC bonds, loss ratios rise to almost one-half their original face value. These data support the conclusion that for this large sample of 1,535 issues over a 32-year period ending in 2003, bond ratings provide useful predictions of loss ratios resulting from defaulted and distressed bonds.

summary

The financial sector of the economy, an important part of the financial manager's environment, is comprised of financial markets, financial institutions, and financial instruments. Financial markets involve the creation and transfer of financial assets and liabilities. The financial manager uses these markets to obtain needed funds for the operation and growth of the business and to employ funds temporarily not needed by the business. Funds are provided by savings surplus units to be used by savings deficit units. This transfer of funds creates a financial asset for the surplus unit and a financial liability for the deficit unit. Transfers can be made directly between a surplus and a deficit unit or can involve a financial intermediary, such as a bank. Intermediaries take on financial liabilities in order to create financial assets, typically profiting from their expertise in packaging these assets and liabilities. The operations of intermediaries, and financial markets in general, bring about a more efficient allocation of real resources.

1. The money markets involve financial assets and liabilities with maturities of less than 1 year, and the capital markets involve transfers for longer periods. Because most businesses are savings deficit units, the financial manager is concerned with the choice of financial markets, intermediaries, and instruments best suited to the financing needs of the firm and with the decision of how best to employ excess funds for short periods. Two major forms of financing are used by business firms: equity financing through common stock and various forms of debt financing.

2. The initial sale of stocks and bonds is known as the primary market. Subsequent trading takes place in the secondary market, the organized exchanges. The over-the-counter market, the third market, is a dealer market, where broker-dealers throughout the country act as market makers. Sometimes large blocks of stock are traded directly among institutional investors, constituting the fourth market.

3. A business firm invests in assets by obtaining financing from two main sources: ownership funds (equity) and funds from creditors (debt). Ultimately we are interested in calculating the costs of debt and balancing the use of debt and equity funds to minimize the costs of financing.

4. Why do we observe so many forms of debt? The answer is that the circumstances of both borrowers and lenders are widely different. This leads to different combinations of returns and risk patterns. Some of the main categories of debt include the following: short-term vs. long-term, secured vs. unsecured, sinking fund or not, options to call as well as options to put, fixed interest rates vs. floating rates vs. zero coupon bonds. Literally thousands of permutations and combinations of bond characteristics can be created based on different combinations and degrees of bond characteristics.

5. The valuation of a bond is a special case of general valuation using discounted future cash flows. The market price or valuation of a bond is determined by the discounted values of its expected future cash flows. The yields of bonds can be calculated given their current prices and expectations with regard to interest payments, maturity dates, and maturity values.

6. A major risk to financial managers is that the required yield rates (bond interest rates) will fluctuate. If required yields fluctuate, bond values would fluctuate. If required yields rise in the future, financial managers have raised money at bargain prices. But the converse is also true. Even if bonds are held to maturity, fluctuating bond costs and values have opportunity costs.

7. Another major risk is the default risk. Bond ratings provide useful estimates of default risk. AAA bonds carry a small risk of default. Bonds with ratings below BBB carry higher risk of default. Criteria used to predict bond ratings based on key financial ratios have been shown to be useful.

The main emphasis of this chapter is the importance of keeping up with financial and economic developments. The Federal Reserve System in Washington, D.C., provides a vast amount of information free of charge. See www.federalreserve.gov. See also the Federal Education website at www.federalreserveeducation.org/PFED/. Also each of the 12 Federal Reserve regional banks provide monthly data and reports obtained by writing their research departments and asking them to be put in their mailing list. The names and addresses of the 12 Federal Reserve Banks can be found at www.federalreserve.gov/fraddress.htm. Especially valuable are the publications of the Federal Reserve Bank of St. Louis, which are listed at *research.stlouisfed.org. The Wall Street Journal*, *USA Today, The New York Times*, and your own local newspaper have regular articles on economic and financial developments. A financial manager needs to keep up with this literature as a part of his job.

Questions

5.1   What happens to the real rate of interest when the demand for capital increases because technological innovations have caused the aggregate investment opportunity set to increase?

5.2   Given that the liquidity premium is positive, how can you explain a downward-sloping term structure?

5.3   There have been times when the term structure of interest rates has been such that short-term rates were higher than long-term rates. Does this necessarily imply that the best financial policy for a firm is to use all long-term debt and no short-term debt? Explain.

5.4   How would you use term structure to project inflation?

5.5   What are financial intermediaries, and what economic functions do they perform?

5.6   How could each tool of the Fed be used to slow down an expansion?

5.7   Evaluate each of the arguments in favor of today's organized securities exchanges relative to OTC markets of 100 years ago.

5.8   You are approached by salespersons from two competing mutual funds. The first fund earned an 18% rate of return last year while the second earned only 14%.

    a.   What questions do you need to ask the salespersons to determine which fund really did better?

    b.   What can be said about the expected future performance of the two funds?

5.9   Explain what is meant by the term *yield to maturity* of bonds.

5.10   Typically, the interest rates on AAA-rated debt are lower than the interest rates on AA-rated debt. Why is that?

5.11   Why is BBB-rated debt more expensive than AA-rated debt?

5.12   Since a corporation often has the right to call bonds, do you believe individuals should be able to demand repayment at any time they so desire? Explain.

5.13   Bonds are less attractive to investors during periods of inflation because a rise in the price level reduces the purchasing power of the fixed interest payments and of the principal. Discuss the advantages and disadvantages to a corporation of using a bond whose interest payments and principal would fluctuate in direct proportion to fluctuations in the price level (a floating rate bond).

5.14   A firm is seeking a term loan from a bank. Under what conditions would it want a fixed interest rate, and under what conditions would it want the rate to fluctuate with the prime rate?

Problems

5.1   Term structure of interest rates

From a recent issue of *The Wall Street Journal, Federal Reserve Bulletin,* or another convenient source:

a.   Construct a yield curve for recent monthly data for U.S. government securities, using market yields for maturities of one year or less and the capital market rates for constant maturities for the maturities from 2 to 30 years.

b.   Why does the yield curve show only U.S government security yields instead of including yields on commercial paper and corporate bonds?

5.2   Market interest rates

The quoted (nominal) interest rate on a debt security (R) can be expressed as:

$$R = r + I + D + L + M$$

where:
  r = real risk-free rate of interest
  I = a premium that reflects the average expected inflation rate over the life of the security
  D = a default risk premium that reflects on the riskiness of the security
  L = a liquidity premium
  M = a maturity risk premium which reflects the higher risk of longer term maturity bonds

a.   The 30-day T-bills are currently yielding 3.0% and you are given the following information: inflation premium = 2.5%, liquidity premium for corporate bond = 0.5%, default risk premium for A-rated corporate bond = 0.25%, and 10-year maturity risk premium = 1.75%. What is the real risk-free rate of return?

b.   Using the information in (a), what is the nominal interest rate for a 10-year, A-rated corporate bond?

5.3   Forward rates

You are given the following yield curve based on zero coupon bonds.

Year	Rate
1	3.50%
2	4.25%
3	4.60%
4	4.90%

a. The 1-year forward rate is the rate of interest that is implied by the yield rates for the period of time between the end of the year and the end of the next year. For example, investing in a 2-year zero coupon bond at a rate r_2 should give us the same outcome as investing in a 1-year zero coupon bond at a rate r_1 and reinvesting at the 1-year forward rate $_1f_2$ for the second year.

$$(1 + r_1)(1 + {}_1f_2) = (1 + r_2)^2$$

What is the implied 1-year forward rate for year 2?

b. In general, the 1-year implied forward rates can be expressed as:

$$(1 + r_{n-1})^{n-1}(1 + {}_{n-1}f_n) = (1 + r_n)^n$$

where r_n is the yield rate for the n-year investment and is the 1-year forward rate from year $n - 1$ to year n. What are the implied 1-year forward rates based on the yield curve given above?

c. If the yield to maturity for year 5 is 5.1%, what is the implied forward rate at the beginning of year 5?

5.4   Forward rates

Suppose that the following yields are observed for Treasury securities.

Maturity	Yield
1 year	4.80%
2 years	5.02%
3 years	5.18%
4 years	5.30%
5 years	5.39%

Assume that the pure expectation theory of the term structure is correct.

a. What will be the interest rate on 1-year securities 1 year from now?

b. What will be the interest rate on 3-year securities 2 years from now?

5.5   Calculation of long rates from short rates

Suppose that expected future short-term interest rates $({}_1f_2, {}_2f_3, {}_3f_4, {}_4f_5)$ have the following alternative patterns:

Year	A	B	C	D
1	4%	8%	4%	8%
2	5	7	6	7
3	6	6	15	5
4	7	5	6	7
5	8	4	4	8

a. Using a simple arithmetic average, what is the current rate on a 5-year note for each of the four patterns?

b. Using a geometric average, answer the same question as for Part (a). (Hint: Add 1 to each percentage—for example, 1.04—then multiply the five numbers, and then take their fifth root. Subtract 1 from the result. On a hand calculator, use the y^x or x^y button with 0.2, which equals 1/5. For example, for interest rate A, the product is 1.3376, and the fifth root minus 1 is 5.991 percent.)

c. Optional:

1. Calculate the current 2-, 3-, and 4-year note yields using both the arithmetic and geometric averages and then graph the resulting yield curves in four graphs of two curves each.

2. Is the height of the yield curve based on the arithmetic averages higher or lower than that based on the geometric averages?

5.6   Calculation of forward rates from spot rates of different maturities

Given below are the yields to maturity on a 5-year bond:

Years to Maturity	Yield to Maturity
1	8.0
2	9.0
3	10.0
4	10.5
5	10.8

a. What is the implied forward rate ($_2f_3$) of interest for the third year?

b. What (geometric) average annual rate of interest would you receive if you bought a bond at the beginning of the third year and sold it at the beginning of the fifth year?

5.7   Discounting cash flows using forward rates

The table below gives the yields to maturity for bonds with approximately the same risk as Project X and Project Y, for which cash flows are also given.

Year	Yield to Maturity	Cash Flows X	Cash Flows Y
0	—	−1,000	−1,000
1	14.00%	300	600
2	15.00	400	500
3	15.99	600	200

a. Find the NPV of each project using the three-year yield to maturity.

b. Find the NPV of each project using the annual forward rates to discount cash flows.

Note: To calculate a NPV (net present value), calculate the present value of each cash flow like we did in Chapter 3, add together the positive present value cash flows and subtract the investment amount.

5.8   Risks and yields

You have priced two pure discount bonds, each with 5 years to maturity and with a face value of $1,000. They pay no coupons. The first bond sells for $780.58 and the second sells for $667.43.

a. What are their yields to maturity?

b. Why does the second bond sell for less than the first?

c. If their default risk is uncorrelated with the rest of the economy, then their expected cash flows can be discounted at the riskless rate, which is 5%. If they have the same expected yield, what is the probability of default for the second bond? (Assume that if the bond defaults, you receive nothing, but if it does not default, you receive the full face value.)

5.9   Price of a bond

A corporate bond with $1000 maturity value carries a 6% coupon rate. It currently makes interest payments once a year. If the current return on similar bond is 5.0%, what is the price of this 10-year bond?

5.10   Price of a bond

A 25-year corporate bond with $1,000 maturity value carries a 7.5% coupon rate with interest payments made semi-annually. If the current return on similar bond is 8.5%, what is the price of this bond?

5.11   Bond yield

A corporate bond with $1,000 maturity value carries an 8% coupon rate. It currently makes interest payments semiannually.

a. This 18-year bond currently sells for $1,157.80. What is the rate of return on this bond?

b. If the bond sold for $834.15, what is the rate of return on this bond?

5.12   Bond prices and yields

You are looking at the following two bonds:

	Bond A	Bond B
Face value	$1,000	$1,000
Annual coupon	75	67.50
Years to maturity	20	20
Price	$927.71	???

If these bonds are identical, except for the coupons and prices, what is the price of bond B?

5.13   Bond prices and coupon comparison

Please answer the following questions about two bonds, M and X.

a. Calculate the annual return on the following bond:

Bond	M
Maturity value	$1,000
Coupon (annual—1 per year)	55
Maturity (years)	25
Bonds current selling price—value	$1,070.47
Current market interest rate	

b. Using the interest rate calculated above (Part A—Current Market Interest Rate), what is the value of the following similar bond:

Bond	X
Maturity value	$1,000
Coupon (annual—1 per year)	65
Maturity (years)	25
Current market interest rate	From Part A
Bond's current selling price—value	

c. What is the value of these bonds if one year later, market interest rates sky-rocket to 6.25%? Recalculate the values of the two bonds noted below, assumed that interest is paid once a year but that the interest rate is now 6.25%:

Bond	M	X
Maturity value	$1,000	$1,000
Coupon (annual—1 per year)	55	65
Maturity (years)	24	24
Current market interest rate	6.25%	6.25%
New value of bonds		

d. Calculate the dollar amount and percentage change in the value of these two bonds:

Bond	M	X
Change in value—$ Amount		
Change in value—XX.XX%		

e. Which bond had the more severe price reaction? What observation can you make regarding the price reaction?

5.14   Bond prices and maturity comparison

Please answer the following questions about two bonds, M and X.

a. Calculate the annual return on the following bond:

Bond	M
Maturity value	$1,000
Coupon (annual—1 per year)	80
Maturity (years)	30
Bonds current selling price—value	$1,124.09
Current market interest rate	

b. Using the interest rate calculated above (Part A—Current Market Interest Rate), what is the value of the following similar bond:

Bond	X
Maturity value	$1,000
Coupon (annual—1 per year)	80
Maturity (years)	5
Current market interest rate	From Part A
Bond's current selling price—value	

c. What is the value of these bonds if one year later, market interest rates change to 8.25%? Recalculate the values of the two bonds noted below, assumed that interest is paid once a year but that the interest rate is now 8.25%:

Bond	M	X
Maturity value	$1,000	$1,000
Coupon (annual—1 per year)	80	80
Maturity (years)	29	4
Current market interest rate	8.25%	8.25%
New value of bonds		

d. Calculate the dollar amount and percentage change in the value of these two bonds:

Bond	M	X
Change in value—$ Amount		
Change in value—XX.XX%		

e. Which bond had the more severe price reaction? What observation can you make regarding the price reaction?

5.15   Rate of return on called bonds

Three years ago, your firm issued some 18-year bonds with 10.5% coupon rates and a 10% call premium. You have called these bonds. The bonds originally sold at their face value of $1,000. (Use semiannual compounding.)

a.   Compute the realized rate of return for investors who purchased the bonds when they were issued.

b.   Given the rate of return in Part (a), did investors welcome the call? Explain.

CHAPTER 6

Risk, Return, and Equity Valuation

Learning Outcomes

After completing this chapter, you should be able to:

1 Value equity under simplified circumstances using variations of the perpetuity model

2 Measure return and risk

3 Estimate a company's risk profile vis-à-vis the market's risk

4 Apply these measures across industries

We begin this chapter with three perpetuity equations used for stock valuation. The models are simple but important. Then this chapter introduces the past 80 years of security returns as well as the underlying risk and volatility of those returns. Finally, building from this material, we summarize the modern theory of finance. It represents the contributions for which Harry Markowitz, William Sharpe, and Merton Miller shared the Nobel Prize in Financial Economics in 1990. The material is quantitative, but provides important insights for financial managers. Some basic concepts in statistics are used, but no prior work in statistics is needed to handle the material. In fact, the reader is shown how useful statistics materials are and should provide motivation for taking a statistics course. The central focus of this chapter is return and risk relationships.

Perpetual Cash Flows

In the previous chapter, we developed valuation approaches for bonds, which are securities with fixed returns that mature over a specified period of time. Stocks have neither a fixed return nor a finite period until maturity. Valuation of a share of stock is analogous to valuing a perpetual cash flow (or recurring cash flows that will last forever) as discussed in Chapter 3, Time and Value. In that chapter, we introduced two varieties of perpetuities—a zero growth model and a constant growth model.

$$\text{Zero Growth}: \quad V_{0,r,\infty} = \frac{CF_{(t+1)}}{r} \qquad\qquad (6.1)$$

$$\text{Constant Growth}: \quad V_{0,r,\infty} = \frac{CF_{(t+1)}}{(r-g)} \qquad\qquad (6.2)$$

where:

$V_{0,r,\infty}$ = Value of firm at time zero continuing perpetually
$CF_{(t+1)}$ = Cash flow at the end of year 1[1]
r = Cost of capital
g = Constant growth

These basic models are at the heart of all valuation, whether it's a project or company. From these basic models, the upcoming chapters fully expand and develop the projected cash flows, determine the cost of capital, and discuss the practical application of these two simple models.

If we assume that The Hershey Company generates about $675.0 million of cash flow per year with no growth in these operating cash flows and that investors require about an 8.2% rate of return (also called the *cost of capital*, which is the topic of Chapter 13), the value of Hershey is $8,231.7 million (or $675/0.082).

However, if we assume that Hershey will continue to grow its cash flow by 2.5% per annum due to sales growth, margin improvement, and other efficiencies, Hershey's value increases to almost $12.1 billion:

$$PVA_{r,\infty} = \frac{CF_{(0)}(1+g)}{(r-g)}$$

$$\qquad\qquad\qquad\qquad\qquad (6.2a)$$

$$= \frac{\$675(1+0.025)}{(0.082-0.025)} = \frac{\$691.9}{0.057} = \$12,138 \text{ million}$$

Much depends on the assumptions! Is Hershey grossly overvalued or severely undervalued? As seen in Table 6.1, the assumed growth rate (Panel A) and cost of capital (Panel B) are critical. The initial cash flow is also important (Panel C).

Even from this simple model, the managerial implications are evident:

1. Grow the operating cash flows of the business

   - Profitable sales growth

   - Cost reductions and margin improvements, including tax rate reduction

---

[1]Remember, the cash flow at the end of the year $(CF_{(t+1)})$ is also the same as growing this year's cash flow and can be written as $CF_{(t+1)} = CF_{(0)}(1+g)$

TABLE 6.1	Sensitivity						
A. GROWTH RATES	0.0%	1.0%	2.0%	2.5%	3.0%	4.0%	5.0%

The initial cash flow is assumed at $675 million and the cost of capital is assumed at 8.2% in all cases.

Total Company Value ($mm)	$ 8,231.7	$ 9,468.8	$11,104.8	$12,138.2 Base Case	$13,370.2	$16,714.3	$22,148.4

B. COST OF CAPITAL	10.0%	9.0%	8.5%	8.2%	8.0%	7.5%	7.0%

The initial cash flow is assumed at $675 million and the growth rate is assumed at 2.5% in all cases.

Total Company Value ($mm)	$ 9,225.0	$10,644.2	$11,531.3	$12,138.2 Base Case	$12,579.5	$13,837.5	$15,375.0

C. CASH FLOW (T)	$ 600.0	$ 625.0	$ 650.0	$ 675.0	$ 700.0	$ 725.0	$ 750.0

The assumed growth rate is 2.5% and the assumed cost of capital is 8.2% in all cases.

Total Company Value ($mm)	$10,789.5	$11,239.0	$11,688.6	$12,138.2 Base Case	$12,587.7	$13,037.3	$13,486.8

- Effective working capital management
- Fixed capital investment in buildings and equipment that add value

2. Reduce the cost of capital (or discount rate)
3. Generate more operating cash flow right away

These topics are discussed in much more detail in the upcoming chapters.

Two-Stage Supernormal Growth Model

The two-stage supernormal growth model (TSSGM) expands the perpetual model and splits the cash flows into two distinct time periods, supernormal (or abnormal) growth, which lasts a few years, and then the "normal" period, which extends into perpetuity. See Table 6.2 for an illustration and to conceptualize the TSSGM.

TABLE 6.2	Supernormal Growth Model Illustration

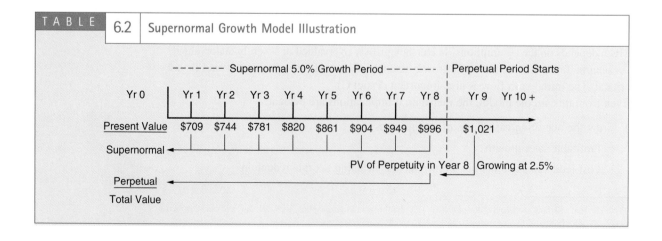

The model postulates a period during which a firm has a competitive advantage. A competitive advantage gives a firm above-average revenue growth and profitability rates. At some point in time, economic theory suggests that these advantages will begin to be eroded as the life cycles of the firm's products portfolio move toward maturity. In theory, by repeated innovations a firm could extend the period of competitive advantage. In practice, even the best firms find it difficult to maintain above-average revenue growth and profitability rates. Think of Microsoft and Cisco since 2000.

The equation is made to look more complicated by virtue of discounting the supernormal period as a series of ever-growing annuities over a limited time period while also discounting the perpetual "normal" level of activity from the end of the supernormal period to today. The concept behind the TSSGM is not complicated despite the appearance of Equation 6.3:

$$V_0 = PV \text{ (Growth Period CFs)} + PV \text{ (Perpetual Period CFs)}$$

$$V_0 = CF_0 \sum_{t=1}^{n} \frac{(1+g_s)^t}{(1+r)^t} + \frac{(CF_0(1+g_s)^n)(1+g_c)}{(r-g_c)} \cdot \frac{1}{(1+r)^n}$$

(6.3)

where: Estimates

CF_0 = Cash Flow (today – time zero) $675

g = Growth rate of cash flow

g_s = Growth rate of revenues during supernormal growth period   0.050

g_s = Growth rate of revenues during constant growth period   0.025

r = Required return (also called the cost of capital)   0.082

n = Number of years of supernormal growth   8

Using this equation with these assumptions, the value of The Hershey Company is $14,261 million as demonstrated in Table 6.3:

TABLE	6.3	Present Results of Supernormal Growth Model

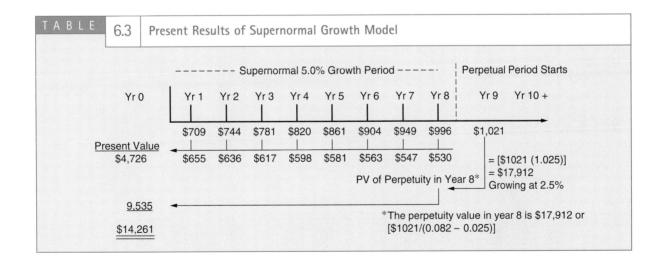

In practice, spreadsheets with a great deal of underlying analysis tend to replace our simple illustrative equations. In summary, the managerial lessons are consistent with each of these simple valuation tools:

TOOL (EQUATION)	CASH FLOW GROWTH	VALUE
Zero growth (6.1)	No growth	$ 8,232
Constant growth (6.2)	Constant growth forever	$12,138
Supernormal growth (6.3)	Supernormal growth then constant growth	$14,261

Grow the business! By increasing the growth of the firm's cash flow by 2.5%, $3,906 million value was added. With a period of 8 years of 5% growth (instead of the 2.5%), Hershey's value increases by an additional $2,123 million.

Keep these simple relationships in mind as we move forward through many important chapters that will help us drive the value of our organizations. The remainder of this chapter identifies one of the most important concepts in all of finance—return vs risk. This ultimately leads us to better understanding of the required rate of return necessary for a given level of risk.

Return and Risk Measures

The tough part of decision making under uncertainty lies in deciding how much extra return should be required to accept different levels of risk. The returns from any investment will be influenced by developments that take place during the life of the investment. Wars, international tensions, government economic policies, crop yields, and so on will all influence the future states of the world.

Figure 6.1 shows the value of $1 invested in various financial investments in December, 1925. Over this 80-year period, a $1 investment in small company stocks would now be

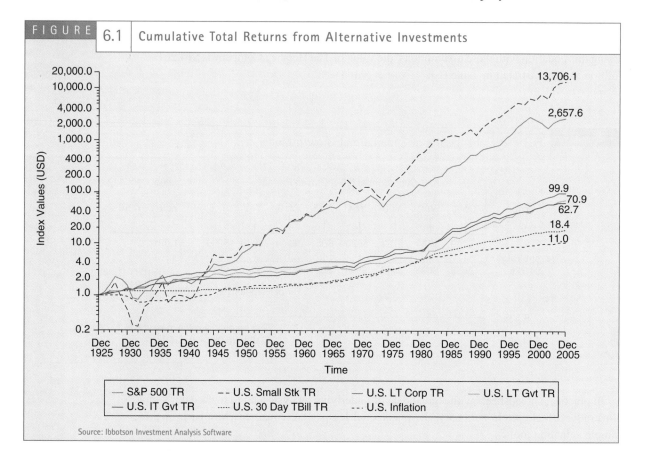

FIGURE 6.1   Cumulative Total Returns from Alternative Investments

Source: Ibbotson Investment Analysis Software

TABLE 6.4	Return Analysis (1925–2005)						
	INDEX			ANNUAL RETURNS			
U.S. INSTRUMENT	VALUE	CAGR	AVERAGE	STD DEV	MINIMUM	MAXIMUM	
Large company stocks	2,657.6	10.36%	12.30%	20.20%	−43.34%	53.99%	
Small company stocks	13,706.1	12.64	17.37	32.95	−58.01	142.87	
Long-term corporate bonds	99.9	5.92	6.24	8.51	−8.09	42.56	
Long-term U.S. bonds	70.9	5.47	5.85	9.24	−9.18	40.36	
Intermediate-term U.S. bonds	62.7	5.31	5.45	5.70	−5.14	29.10	
30-day U.S. T-Bills	18.4	3.71	3.75	3.12	−0.02	14.71	
Inflation	11.0	3.04	3.13	4.29	−10.30	18.17	

valued at $13,706.10 while an investment in U.S. Treasury bills provided a total return of $18.40. When dealing with such time-driven values, it is often better to examine the compound annual growth rate (CAGR) such as is calculated in Chapter 3. So using a financial calculator: PV = −1.00; FV = 13706.1; N = 80; compute %i. The CAGR for small company stocks is 12.64%. The CAGR returns are illustrated in Table 6.4.

Notice that over this 80-year period, inflation has been just over 3% (CAGR), which means that all returns were positive after considering inflation. As discussed in Chapter 5, there is a liquidity preference reflected in these actual returns. Compare the U.S. Treasury bill return (3.71%), the intermediate-term government bonds (5.31%), and the long-term government bonds (5.47%). Also, consider the liquidity preference model of interest rates (see Chapter 5) and notice the risk premium of 0.45% for long-term corporate bonds (5.92%) and long-term government bonds (5.47%).

Measuring Annual Returns

As presented above, the returns (CAGRs) are point-to-point returns and miss the detail of each of the 80 years of returns. So the next perspective considers the average annual returns of all 80 years as well as the volatility that underlies those returns. Here, volatility is measured as the standard deviation of those returns.

For each security above, we calculate the total annual return by assuming that the security was purchased when the markets opened on the first day of the year (P_{YB}) and was sold as the markets closed on the last day of the year (P_{YE}). This is the capital appreciation (when the price goes up) or depreciation (when the price goes down). To this we add any investment cash flows (CF_t) that we receive throughout the year, such as dividend or interest payments. This represents the dollar amount of total gain. If we divide this by our investment amount (the price that we paid on day 1 of the year), we have our annual return as follows:

$$\frac{\text{Annual}}{\text{Return}_t} = \frac{(P_{YE} - P_{YB}) + CF_t}{P_{YB}} \tag{6.4}$$

Table 6.4 lists the annual returns for all six instruments and inflation for this 80-year period. Table 6.4 provides the average annual returns for the past 80 years along with their standard deviation, minimum returns, and maximum returns.

The standard deviation is of course a statistical calculation of the riskiness or the volatility in each security's returns. Another way to appreciate the volatility is to look at the range of returns, from the minimum to the maximum. Notice that in 1 year, the small company stocks lost 58.01% (1937) and also gained 142.87% (1933).

Even the "risk-free" U.S. government investments incurred negative returns for at least 1 year due to interest rate risk, as discussed in Chapter 5. In these cases, interest rates rose throughout the year so the value of the bond fell.

A few additional points about historical risk and return can be observed from Table 6.4:

1. Small company stocks have been more volatile than large company stocks.

2. U.S. bonds have been more volatile than Treasury bills. As seen in Chapter 5, the bonds are subject to more volatility when interest rate risk is considered.

3. When compared to stocks, the returns from Treasury bonds and bills seem to have very limited variability.

4. Corporate bonds and U.S. Treasury bonds provide similar results with similar risk.

5. The short-term returns from Treasury bills are similar to but slightly higher than inflation.

The bottom line: risk and return are principles that underlie finance. Even though financial securities are used here to demonstrate this phenomenon, risk and return principles also present themselves in business operations. New products are riskier than adding capacity for an already existing product with a strong demand. But that capacity addition is riskier than a "cost savings"[2] project.

The valuation equations that begin this chapter incorporate a required rate of return that later we will come to know as the cost of capital. As risk increases, so does the required rate of return. The remaining sections of this chapter provide a conceptual framework in which to consider risk as well as application.

Prospective Risk and Return

History is often a valuable teacher for the future. While we often base our initial projections on historical performance, many alternative states may occur due to various combinations of different influences. This section illustrates through a set of calculations how to determine the required return on a project in relation to an applicable measure of risk. We then calculate the expected return and risk on the project based on our best judgment of how the project or firm will perform in the future. However, the future cannot be known with certainty, and it is unlikely that past history will be repeated exactly in the future. So we consider future prospects for the economy, our industry, our firm, the behavior of our competitors, etc., and formulate some probable patterns of returns for the future. We could formulate probabilities under alternative scenarios as well. To illustrate the methodology, we use the data inputs in Table 6.5. We consider three alternative states of the future. We formulate the probabilities of each state and the project returns and market returns under the three alternative states. We could consider more than three alternatives, but the central concepts are illustrated by the relatively simple example, so we use it to show the logical procedures involved.

Table 6.5 postulates three alternatives future states of the world with their probabilities in column 2. Column 3 presents market returns under their alternative scenarios. Columns 4 and 5 present returns for two alternative projects' investments, or securities requiring equal amount of investment outlays.

---

[2]A "cost savings" project is one that will immediately reduce the production costs of a product.

TABLE 6.5	Illustrative Data Inputs*			
(1) STATES OF NATURE (s)	(2) PROBABILITIES (p)	(3) MARKET RETURN (R_M)	(4) PROJECT 1 RETURN (R_1)	(5) PROJECT 2 RETURN (R_2)
Weak	0.20	−0.150	−0.100	0.000
Normal	0.50	0.100	0.100	0.200
Strong	0.30	0.300	0.400	0.100

*The calculations we make have been programmed so that the reader can change any of the illustrative input numbers in Table 6.5 and calculations that are in Tables 6.6 through 6.10 are performed. The implications of alternative patterns of inputs can be explored.

In Table 6.6, we calculate the average (arithmetic mean) return and measures of dispersion. Multiplying each possible return by its associated probability and adding overall future states give the expected or mean return from the investment: $E(R_1)$ equals 0.15, or 15%. In column 5, the deviation of each possible return from the average return is calculated. We are seeking a measure of the average deviation, so in column 6 we square the deviations. Finally, in column 7, each probability factor is multiplied by the associated squared deviation and is then summed over all states to obtain the variance: $Var(R_1)$ equals 0.0325.

To place the measure of dispersion in the same dimensions as the mean value, we take its square root to obtain the standard deviation, σ_1, equals 0.1803. The coefficient of variation standardizes the risk measure by dividing it by the mean value expressed in the same units, resulting in a "pure" number that can be directly compared with other pure numbers [$\sigma_j/E(R_j)$]. It gives risk per unit of return, and for our example illustrated in Table 6.6, it is calculated to be 1.2019.

We perform similar calculations for Project 2 in Table 6.7. The coefficient of variation is calculated to be 0.6008. So Project 1 has a higher expected return and higher variability measured by the variance, standard deviation, and the coefficient of variation. But Project 1 has a coefficient of variation double that of Project 2. It has an expected return 2 percentage points higher than the expected return of Project 2. We do not know whether that 2 percentage point differential is adequate compensation for the larger variability of its returns. We have no basis for determining the trade-off between return and risk. A criterion is provided by the capital asset pricing model (CAPM), which is discussed next.

TABLE 6.6	Mean, Variance, and Standard Deviation for Project 1					
(1) s	(2) p_s	(3) R_{1s}	(4) $p_s R_{1s}$	(5) $R_{1s} - \bar{R}_1$	(6) $(R_{1s} - \bar{R}_1)^2$	(7) $p_s(R_{1s} - \bar{R}_1)^2$
Weak	0.2000	−0.1000	−0.0200	−0.2500	0.0625	0.0125
Normal	0.5000	0.1000	0.0500	−0.0500	0.0025	0.0012
Strong	0.3000	0.4000	0.1200	0.2500	0.0625	0.0188
		$E(R_1) = \bar{R}_1 = 0.1500$			$Var(R_1) =$	0.0325
					Standard deviation = σ_1 =	0.1803
					Coefficient of variation = $\sigma_1/E(R_1)$ =	1.2019

T A B L E	6.7	Mean, Variance, and Standard Deviation for Project 2				
(1) s	(2) p_s	(3) R_{2s}	(4) $p_s R_{2s}$	(5) $R_{2s} - \bar{R}_2$	(6) $(R_{2s} - \bar{R}_2)^2$	(7) $p_s(R_{2s} - \bar{R}_2)^2$
Weak	0.2000	0.0000	0.0000	0.1300	0.0169	0.0034
Normal	0.5000	0.2000	0.1000	0.0700	0.0049	0.0024
Strong	0.3000	0.1000	0.0300	-0.0300	0.0009	0.0003
		$E(R_2) = \bar{R}_2 = 0.1300$			$Var(R_2) =$	0.0061
					Standard deviation $= \sigma_2 =$	0.0781
					Coefficient of variation $= \sigma_2/E(R_2) =$	0.6008

Capital Asset Pricing Model (CAPM)

CAPM has led to theoretical developments with useful applications to business finance. It is now possible to analyze rates of return, valuation, asset expansion decisions, capital structure, and other financial policies in a broader framework. CAPM provides theories of how the market prices of assets, securities, or firms are determined. These theories provide a framework to which the financial decisions of managers of individual firms must relate in order to maximize owners' wealth. With CAPM we can develop the security market line relationships discussed next.

The Security Market Line

In Table 6.8, we calculate the market parameters in the same way we calculated the mean, variance, and standard deviation for each of the two projects. We obtain an expected market return of 11% with a variance of 2.44% and a standard deviation of 15.62%.

Capital market theory guides us to calculate how the returns of individual projects covary with the market returns. This is performed in Table 6.9 and 6.10 for Projects 1 and 2, respectively. The procedure is to take the deviations of the returns in Table 6.6 column 5 for Project 1 and place them in column 3 of Table 6.9. Next we take the deviations of market returns from their means from column 5 of Table 6.8 and place them as column 4 in Table 6.9. Column 5 is the product of the project deviations with the market deviations. In column 6 we multiply the product of the deviations by the probability of each of the

T A B L E	6.8	Mean, Variance, and Standard Deviation for the Market				
(1) s	(2) p_s	(3) R_{Ms}	(4) $p_s R_{Ms}$	(5) $R_{Ms} - \bar{R}_M$	(6) $(R_{Ms} - \bar{R}_M)^2$	(7) $p_s(R_{Ms} - \bar{R}_M)^2$
Weak	0.2000	-0.1500	-0.0300	-0.2600	0.0676	0.0135
Normal	0.5000	0.1000	0.0500	-0.0100	0.0001	0.0000
Strong	0.3000	0.3000	0.0900	0.1900	0.0361	0.0109
		$E(R_M) = \bar{R}_M = 0.110$			$Var(R_M) =$	0.0244
					Standard deviation $= \sigma_M =$	0.1562

TABLE 6.9	Covariance of Project 1 with the Market				
(1) s	**(2)** p_s	**(3)** $R_{1s} - \bar{R}_1$	**(4)** $R_{Ms} - \bar{R}_M$	**(5)** $(R_{1s} - \bar{R}_1)(R_{Ms} - \bar{R}_M)$	**(6)** $p_s(R_{1s} - \bar{R}_1)(R_{Ms} - \bar{R}_M)$
Weak	0.2000	−0.2500	−0.2600	0.0650	0.0130
Normal	0.5000	−0.0500	−0.0100	0.0005	0.0003
Strong	0.3000	0.2500	0.1900	0.0475	0.0142
					$Cov(R_1, R_M) = 0.0275$

alternative future states of the world and sum these values. This gives 2.75%, which is the covariance, $Cov(R_1, R_M)$, of the returns of Project 1 with the returns on the market. In Table 6.10 we calculate the covariance of Project 2 with the market by the same procedures to obtain the result of 0.47%. We can use our measures of project covariance with the market to obtain the widely used measures of risks.

Beta Measures of Risk

The risk index can be expressed in terms of the *beta coefficient*

$$\beta_j = \frac{Cov(R_j R_m)}{\sigma_m^2} \tag{6.5}$$

$$\beta_j = \frac{Cov(R_1 R_m)}{\sigma_m^2} = \frac{0.0275}{0.0244} = 1.1270 \tag{6.5a}$$

$$\beta_2 = \frac{Cov(R_2 R_m)}{\sigma_m^2} = \frac{0.0047}{0.0244} = 0.1926 \tag{6.5b}$$

where β_j is measured by the ratio of the covariance of the returns of the individual security with market returns, divided by the variance of market returns. The security market line relationship for individual securities using betas is Equation 6.6:

$$R_j^* = R_f + [E(R_m) - R_f]\beta_j \tag{6.6}$$

TABLE 6.10	Covariance of Project 2 with the Market				
(1) s	**(2)** p_s	**(3)** $R_{2s} - \bar{R}_2$	**(4)** $R_{Ms} - \bar{R}_M$	**(5)** $(R_{2s} - \bar{R}_2)(R_{Ms} - \bar{R}_M)$	**(6)** $p_s(R_{2s} - \bar{R}_2)(R_{Ms} - \bar{R}_M)$
Weak	0.2000	−0.1300	−0.2600	0.0338	0.0068
Normal	0.5000	0.0700	−0.0100	−0.0007	−0.0004
Strong	0.3000	−0.0300	0.1900	−0.0057	−0.0017
					$Cov(R_2, R_M) = 0.0047$

We have calculated the expected return on the market to be 11%. We are using a risk-free rate of 6% for the reasons discussed below. So we can write the empirical securities market line for our data as in equation 6.7:

$$R_j^* = 6\% + [11\% - 6\%]\beta_j \qquad (6.7)$$

Equation 6.7 states that the required return on an investment or security equals the risk free rate plus a risk adjustment equal to the market price of risk, $[E(R_m) - R_f]$, multiplied by the project beta. Equations 6.7a and 6.7b calculate the required returns for Projects 1 and 2, respectively.

$$R_1^* = 6\% + 5\%(1.1270) = 11.64\% \qquad (6.7a)$$

$$R_1^* = 6\% + 5\%(0.1926) = 6.96\% \qquad (6.7b)$$

One of the values of the capital asset pricing model (CAPM) is that it conveys what lies behind the risk-adjusted returns. Both the covariance and beta concepts are helpful in explaining the source and nature of the risk adjustment factor and at the same time provide a summary of the concepts of the market model. It is useful to set forth the real world order of magnitudes of the elements in Equation 6.6.

For the economy as a whole, the risk-free rate would be related to the returns on U.S. government bonds. Because the discount factor used in valuation involves relatively long periods, the rates on relatively long-term bonds would be employed. The analysis generally gives heavy weight to interest rate levels in the current economic environment. For the United States in April 2006, the yields on long-term Treasuries (10+-year notes) had just risen above 5%. However, the meetings of the Federal Open Market Committee stated that economic conditions would require further interest rate increases. Hence we use 6%. Also, from Table 6.4, the 80-year trend on long-term government bond returns approximates 6%.

In the CAPM, the risk adjustment is the required market-determined differential between equity yields and government bonds. From Table 6.4, we see that using the CAGR of the S&P 500 versus long-term government bonds results in a risk differential of 4.89% (10.36% − 5.47%) or 5.05% using intermediate-term Treasury bonds (10.36% − 5.31%). This differential is variously referred to as the *market price of risk,* the *market equity premium,* the *equity risk premium (ERP),* or the *market risk premium (MRP).* Here we use 5% as a starting point for the market price of risk. The 5% is multiplied by the firm's beta to obtain an estimate of the risk adjustment for an individual firm. The beta of a firm is a measure of how the return on its common stock varies with returns on the market as a whole. Returns on the market as a whole have been conveniently measured by use of the S&P 500, all stocks on the New York Stock Exchange, or other broad groupings. High beta stocks exhibit higher volatility than low beta stocks in response to changes in market returns.

The beta for the market as a whole must necessarily be 1, by definition. With a risk-free rate of 6% and a market price of risk of 5%, we can write an equation for the expected return on the market:

$$\text{Return on the market} = 6\% + 5\% \ (1) = 11\%$$

From this relationship, we can generalize to individual firms with betas equal to our two projects.

$R_1^* = $ Required return on equity for firm 1 $= 6\% + 5\% \ (1.1270) = 11.64\%$
$R_2^* = $ Required return on equity for firm 2 $= 6\% + 5\% \ (0.1926) = 6.96\%$

TABLE 6.11	Expected vs Required Returns	
	PROJECT 1	PROJECT 2
Expected return = E(R)	15.00%	13.00%
Required return = R*	11.64%	6.96%
Excess return	3.36%	6.04%

With the beta of firm 1 of 1.1270, its required return will be 11.64%. With the beta of firm 2 of 0.1926, its required return will be 6.96%.

We can now analyze which project is preferred. We can do this by comparing the expected or mean return of each project with the required returns using the security market line. This is shown in Table 6.11, which compares expected versus required returns. The expected or mean returns of the two projects were 15% for Project 1 and 13% for Project 2. As shown in Table 6.11, the required returns were 11.64% for Project 1 and 6.96% for Project 2. Project 2 is preferred because it has a greater return in excess of the security market line relationship than Project 1. Figure 6.2 depicts the results graphically. Thus capital market theory provides a basis for choosing between the two projects. As observed earlier, without such a framework, we are unable to choose between the two projects.

The Market Price of Risk

For many years, based on patterns of the long-term relationships between returns on long- and short-term government bonds, on long- and short-term corporate bonds, and on equity groups such as large capitalization, small capitalization, high technology, etc., the market price of risk appeared to be in the range of 6.5% to 7.5%. But by the mid-1990s, a new paradigm for a new economy began to emerge. Analysts moved toward using 5% to 6% as the market price of risk.

A number of arguments have been offered to justify a lower market risk premium in the new economy. The U.S. economy experienced a period of sustained economic growth for

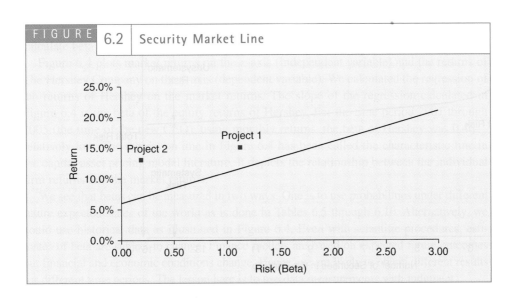

FIGURE 6.2   Security Market Line

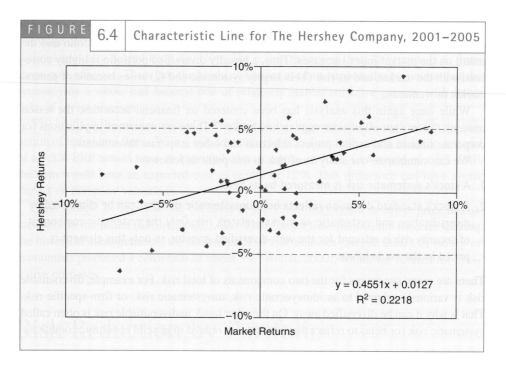

FIGURE 6.4 | Characteristic Line for The Hershey Company, 2001–2005

$$y = 0.4551x + 0.0127$$
$$R^2 = 0.2218$$

Variation of Betas across Industries

In a booming economy, market returns are high; in a recession, they are low. In an industry such as machinery, the swings of returns in relation to the market as a whole are magnified. Table 6.12 presents Value Line estimates of beta for 10 leading machinery companies. Their average beta is 1.37. This indicates that when market returns rise or fall by 10%, the returns of machinery companies rise or fall by 13.7%.

Table 6.13 presents Value Line estimates of betas for 17 food processing firms. Their average beta is 0.64. This means that when market returns rise or fall by 10%, the returns in the food industry will rise or fall by 6.4%. The reason for the difference between the two industries relates to their economic characteristics. Machinery represents durable equipment

TABLE 6.12 | Machinery Industry Betas

COMPANY	BETA
Briggs & Stratton	1.10
Brooks Automation	2.10
Caterpillar Inc.	1.20
Cummins Inc.	1.35
Deere & Co.	1.05
Dover Corp.	1.15
Flowserve Corp.	1.45
Ingersoll–Rand	1.40
Milacron, Inc.	1.45
United Rentals	1.40
Mean	1.37
Standard deviation	0.30

Source: Value Line 10/28/05

TABLE 6.13	Food Processing Betas
COMPANY	BETA
Archer Daniels Midland	0.70
Campbell Soup	0.65
ConAgra Foods	0.70
Dean Foods	0.65
Del Monte Foods	0.65
Generall Mills	0.55
Hain Celestial Group	0.90
Heinz (H.J.)	0.60
Hershey Foods	0.65
Hormel Foods	0.70
Kellogg	0.60
Kraft	0.65
McCormick & Co.	0.45
Sara Lee Corp.	0.60
Smucker (J.M.)	0.65
Tootsie Roll Ind.	0.65
Wrigley (Wm.) Jr.	0.55
Mean	0.64
Standard deviation	0.09

Source: Value Line 11/4/05

whose replacement can be postponed when their usage is reduced. For the food industry, people continue to eat even in a depressed economy.

Hence, even though beta measurements are subject to change, the results are consistent with economic reasoning and business sense. The betas and therefore the returns in the food industry are consistently below 1 so their returns fluctuate less than the market returns. Firms in the machinery industry have betas greater than 1 so their returns fluctuate to a greater degree than market returns. Also the required returns for firms in the machinery industry are likely to be higher than the required returns in the food processing industry. The systematic risks of firms in the machinery industry are higher than the systematic risks of firms in the food processing industry.

summary

The basic foundation developed in Chapter 3 is once again used to value a share of stock as a perpetuity. We consider three variations: zero growth, constant growth, and supernormal growth. The managerial lessons are clear:

1. Increase your cash flow.

2. Grow the business.

3. Reduce your required return.

Even these simplistic models lead to useful managerial observations. Much more is said about value management and valuing enhancing activities as we continue through this text. But for now, these models demonstrate value creation.

Historical returns as well as its underlying risk are important to understand. While we focused on 80 years of financial returns, the principle of risk-reward is applicable in corporate finance as well.

Before the development of modern finance theory, it was not possible to choose between projects or firms based on their expected returns in relation to expected risk. Capital market theory has demonstrated that the risk of a project or a firm is composed of systematic or market risk and idiosyncratic risk. Idiosyncratic risk can be eliminated by diversification. Systematic risk is measured by the beta coefficient. The beta coefficient is measured by the ratio of the covariance of the returns of the individual security with market returns, divided by the variance of market returns. In practical terms, the beta coefficient measures how the returns of projects or firms fluctuate in relation to returns for a market portfolio, which can be measured by using a large group of firms such as the S&P 500 or all of the stocks on the New York Stock Exchange or some other broad index.

The security market line can be plotted on a graph in which the y-axis measures the required return on a portfolio or an asset in relation to the beta measure of risk on the x-axis. The security market line has a positive slope measured by the market price of risk or the risk premium measured by the average return on the market less the risk free rate. The security market line can be used to measure the return required from an investment in relation to it estimated risk measured by its beta. When the expected return from an investment is greater than its required return as measured by the security market, it makes sense to make the investment. When this criterion is not met, the financial manager does not make the investment.

Questions

6.1   Why is the pricing of a share of stock similar to pricing a perpetuity?

6.2   Discuss how the "no growth" approach (Equation 6.1) is a variation of the "constant growth" approach (Equation 6.2).

6.3   Without creating the underlying equation, discuss what a "four-stage supernormal growth" is and how to solve it.

6.4   Using Table 6.4, what is the market risk premium between large company stocks and U.S. government bonds? What is the market risk premium between large company stocks and U.S. government T bills? What does the difference in those premiums represent?

6.5   Are U.S. government T bills good protection from inflation? Why or why not?

6.6   Answer the following:

   a.   Next year, you are planning an island vacation. In general, what type of financial instrument should you invest in? Why?

   b.   In 30 years, you are planning on retiring. In general, what type of financial instrument should you invest in at this point in time? Why?

   c.   Ten years from now, your nephew is going to start college. Your brother asks you for some investment advice. In general, what type of financial instrument should they invest in? Why?

   d.   What factors cause your answers to change?

6.7   Suppose that expected inflation causes the nominal risk-free return and the market return to rise by an equal amount. How will the market risk premium be affected?

6.8   What significance does the adage "Don't put all of your eggs in one basket" have to do with this chapter?

6.9   Reconcile the seeming differences in the following two statements:

   a.   "In financial investments, diversification is seen as a risk reduction strategy."

   b.   "Corporate investments seem to add the most value when a company sticks with what it knows best."

6.10   Why is the beta of the market portfolio equal to 1.0?

6.11   Why is total risk, as measured by the variance of returns, unrelated to the market required rate of return on a project?

6.12   Consider two firms that are alike in every way except that Firm A has fixed rate debt in its capital structure and Firm B has variable rate debt. Which firm has riskier equity? Why?

6.13   Firms X and Y have exactly the same ratio of debt to total assets. However, Firm X employs short-term debt and rolls it over each year at the existing interest rate while Firm Y has just issued fixed rate long-term debt. Which firm has riskier equity? Why?

6.14   Why do firms in the same industry tend to have similar betas?

6.15   Why is the average beta of brokerage firms high (that is, 1.55) and the beta of electric utilities low (that is, 0.84)?

Problems

6.1   Stock valuation

   Trey Corporation (TC) earned $3.50 of cash flow per share. Assume a 10% required rate of return.

   a.   If TC is expected to maintain this level of cash flow forever, what is the value of TC?

   b.   If TC is expected to maintain this level of cash flow for 100 years and then go out of business, what is the value of TC?

   c.   How much additional value per share did years 101 through eternity add to TC?

6.2   Stock valuation

RM, Inc., is expected to earn $1.90 of cash flow per share next year.

a.   If RM expects to grow cash flow by 5% per year forever, what is the value of a share of RM stock? Assume that the required return is 12.5%.

b.   If the current stock price is $23.25, what is the market's expected growth rate underlying the stock price. Assume the same discount rate and expected cash flow.

6.3   Company valuation

What is the value of a company that just generated $150 million of cash flow? Assume an 11% required return and the following growth rates forever:

a.   0%

b.   4%

c.   8%

d.   11%

e.   15%

f.   What do you observe?

6.4   Company valuation

Cumberland Retail Outlets is expected to produce $200,000 of cash flows next year. These cash flows are also expected to grow at 4% per year forever. What is the value of Cumberland Retail Outlets at the following discount rates:

a.   15%

b.   12%

c.   10%

d.   8%

e.   What general management rule can you discern?

6.5   Company valuation

The Heidelberg Group is expected to grow at 20% for the next 5 years. After that, Heidelberg will grow at 4% per annum. Heidleberg last year produced $50 million of cash flow. If the required return is 15%, what is the value of Heidleberg?

6.6   Company valuation

Hess, Inc., produced $2.00 of cash flow per share last year. Answer the following questions assuming that Hess is expected to grow at 25% for the next 4 years and then 6% per annum after that forever:

a.   What are the cash flow amounts per share for years 1 through 6?

b.   What is the value of Hess at 12% required return?

6.7   Required returns

The risk-free rate is 4%, and the market risk premium is 5%. Under consideration for investment outlays are Projects A, B, and C, with estimated betas of 0.8, 1.2, and 2.0, respectively. What will be the required rates of return on these projects based on the security market line approach?

6.8   Project evaluation

The risk-free rate of return is 6%, and the market risk premium is 5%. The beta of the project under analysis is 1.8, with expected net cash flows after taxes estimated at $600 for 5 years. The required investment outlay on the project is $1,800.

a.   What is the required risk-adjusted return on the project?

b.   Should the project be accepted?

6.9   Project evaluation

The Williams Company is considering adding another project to its portfolio of projects. It is evaluating two investment projects, A and B, for which the following information has been calculated.

	Investment A	Investment B
Investment outlay required (I)	$20,000	$20,000
Expected return [E(R)]	0.20	0.20
Standard deviation of returns (σ)	0.40	0.60
Coefficient of variation of returns (CV)	2.00	3.00
Beta of returns (β)	1.80	1.20

The vice president of finance has formulated a risk adjustment relationship based on the coefficient of variation, CV, which is defined as the standard deviation of return divided by the mean:

$$\text{Required return on a project} = \text{Risk-free return} + 0.04CV.$$

He also takes into consideration the security market line relationship using 6% as the estimate of the risk-free return and 5% as the market risk premium.

a.   What is the required return on each project, using alternative methods of calculating the risk adjustment factor?

b.   If the two projects are independent, should they both be accepted?

c.   If the projects are mutually exclusive, which one should be accepted?

6.10   Project returns

Given the data here (the investment cost of each project is $1,000), calculate:

States	Probability	R_M	Return to Project 1	Return to Project 2
1	0.1	−0.3	−0.4	−0.4
2	0.2	−0.1	−0.2	−0.2
3	0.3	0.1	0.0	0.6
4	0.4	0.3	0.7	0.0

a. The three means, the variances, the standard deviations, and the covariance of Project 1 with the market, covariance of Project 2 with the market, covariance of Project 1 with Project 2, the correlation coefficients ρ_{1M}, ρ_{2M}, and the correlation coefficient of Project 1 with Project 2.

b. If Projects 1 and 2 were to be combined into a portfolio with 40% in Project 1 and 60% in Project 2, what would be the expected return on that portfolio and its standard deviation?

c. $R_F = 0.04$. Calculate the security market line. On a graph:

(1) Plot the security market line.

(2) Plot points for Project 1 and for Project 2.

d. If you had to choose between the two projects, which would you select?

e. Express the required returns for the two projects using betas.

6.11 Required return

The Pierson Company is considering two mutually exclusive investment projects, P and Q. The risk and return estimates for these two investment projects are given here:

	Project P	Project Q
Expected return [E(R)]	0.15	0.18
Standard deviation (σ)	0.50	0.75
Beta (β)	1.80	1.40

Assume that the risk-free rate is 10% and the expected market return is 14%. What would be the firm's decision if the security market line analysis is used?

6.12 Calculation of beta

Given the facts in this table:

Year	McNichols Corporation Equity Return	Market Return
1	2%	−12%
2	13	18
3	10	5
4	5	15
5	−8	10
6	−2	12
7	6	26

a. Estimate the historical beta for the equity of McNichols Corporation.

b. If the risk-free rate is currently 10% and the expected return on the market portfolio is 18%, what is the cost of equity for the McNichols Corporation?

c. What assumption do you have to make in order to use a historical estimate of beta to compute a current cost of equity?

6.13   Division betas

The Jacquier Company has three divisions, each approximately the same size. The financial staff has estimated the rates of return for different states of nature as given.

State of World	Subjective Probability	Market Return	DIVISION RATE OF RETURN		
			Division 1	Division 2	Division 3
Great	0.25	0.35	0.40	0.60	0.20
Good	0.25	0.20	0.36	0.30	0.12
Average	0.25	0.13	0.24	0.16	0.08
Horrible	0.25	−0.08	0.00	−0.26	−0.02

a.   If the risk-free rate is 9%, what rate of return does the market require for each division?

b.   What is the beta of the entire company?

c.   If the company has 30% of its funds provided by riskless debt and the remainder by equity, what is the equity beta for the company?

d.   Which of the divisions should be kept? Which should be spun off?

e.   What will the company's beta be if the actions in Part (d) are undertaken?

6.14   Mutually exclusive projects

Projects A and B are mutually exclusive equipment replacement proposals. Both require an immediate cash outlay of $1,000, both last 1 year, and both have end-of-year revenues of $3,000 with certainty and fully collected. Cash outflows at the end of the year, however, are risky. They are given here along with the market rate of return, R_M.

State of Nature	Probability	END-OF-PERIOD OUTFLOWS		
		Project A	Project B	R_M
Great	0.333	$1,000	$1,200	30%
Average	0.333	800	800	15
Horrid	0.333	600	400	0

Because you are given the cash flows, there is no need to worry about taxes, depreciation, or salvage value. Note that the cash outflows of Project B have a higher variance than those of Project A. Which project has the higher net present value?

Financial Performance Metrics

Effective planning and control are central to enhancing enterprise value. Financial plans may take many forms, but any good plan must be related to the firm's existing strengths and weaknesses. The strengths must be understood if they are to be used to proper advantage, and the weaknesses must be recognized if corrective actions are to be taken. For example, are inventories adequate to support the projected level of sales? Does the firm have too heavy an investment in accounts receivable, and does this condition reflect a lax collection policy? For efficient operations, does the firm have too much or too little invested in plant and equipment? The financial manager can plan future financial requirements in accordance with the forecasting and budgeting procedures presented in Chapter 9, Strategic Financial Planning, but the plan must begin with the type of financial analysis developed in this chapter.

Learning Outcomes

After completing this chapter, you should be able to:

1 Develop financial analysis for a company, business unit, or industry

2 Interpret financial performance of an organization

3 Judge whether the financial performance is good or needs improvement

4 Make decisions using this information

5 Set management performance targets

6 Present a variety of financial analyses: common size analysis, base year analysis, growth analysis, and other financial ratio analysis such as liquidity, activity, leverage, profitability, and market-related relationships

7 Organize the analysis into a simplified DuPont style analysis

Quarterly Financial Report for Manufacturing Corporations: The Bureau of the Census in the U.S. Department of Commerce publishes quarterly financial data on manufacturing companies. The data include an analysis by industry groups and by asset size, and financial statements in a common size format.

Trade Associations and Professional Societies: Trade associations and professional societies often compile data related to a specific industry or a particular function, for example, treasury management functions.

Financial Services: Specialist firms that compile and publish financial data, such as Value Line, Standard & Poor's, and Moody's, develop industry composites. Brokerage firms such as Merrill Lynch, USB, Smith Barney Citigroup, E*Trade, etc., periodically publish industry studies.

Financial Press: Financial periodicals such as *Business Week, Forbes,* and *Fortune* publish quarterly or annual studies that center on financial performance metrics with companies grouped by industry.

However, a problem that may be encountered is that many diverse firms may be included in the industry category. The general industry data may be fine for a quick comparison, but most companies, investment analysts, and professionals construct their own industry groups. With the considerable diversification by firms, selected firms may be more comparable than industry groupings. This was the case at Hershey. The corporation wanted to compare itself to major, branded food processing companies. Companies were selected that, in general, were larger than Hershey (a group that Hershey was aspiring to be like, which is also called an *aspirant group*) or companies that compete more directly in the broader snack food industry, even though they may be smaller.

Figure 7.1 captures a comparative industry group of branded food companies that are appropriate in the analysis of Hershey. There are notably some companies that are not included in this industry group. M & M Mars (Masterfoods) is not included in this industry group because Mars is a private organization and not required to publicly disclose its financial information. Nestle and Unilever are also not included because both are foreign companies and are subject to different accounting practices and different reporting requirements.

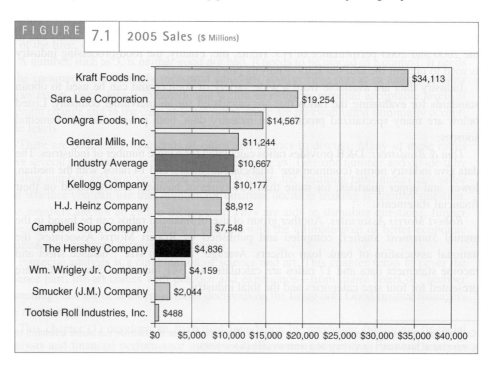

FIGURE 7.1 2005 Sales ($ Millions)

Although Tootsie Roll is about one-tenth Hershey's size, Tootsie Roll is included in this branded food processing industry because it is the only other publicly traded confectionery company in the United States.

Figure 7.1 also demonstrates a graphical technique (bar chart) to illustrate the 2005 sales of the companies in this industry group. Clearly, Kraft, Sara Lee, and ConAgra have a distinct size advantage over the other eight companies. On this absolute basis, it is no contest in that Kraft is more than 77% larger than the next closest competitor and more than seven times larger than Hershey. In fact, Kraft's 2005 net income of $2,665 million is five times larger than the sales of Tootsie Roll!

Figure 7.2 presents the 2005 annual growth in net sales and our first relative comparison metric, annual growth. This relative metric compares the performance of all 11 companies without letting size influence the result. It is commonly acknowledged that an ant is one of the strongest animals. However, that is relative to its body weight! In a similar fashion, the performance metrics that are reviewed here are generally relative metrics where size is not a determining factor.

In 2005, Hershey finished the year with growth that ranked fourth out of this industry group and exceeded both industry averages. Notice that Smucker Company is excluded due to a major acquisition (Multifoods with approximately $900 million annual sales in 2004) that propelled Smucker's growth to almost 50%, definitely, an outlier in this group.

Notice also on Figure 7.2 that there are two industry averages. The "industry average" is simply an average of all of the growth rates. That is, the average of Tootsie Roll's 16.1% annual growth, Wrigley's 14.0%, Hershey's 9.2%, and so on, but it excludes Smucker. The growth of all remaining 10 companies is treated the same, and an overall industry average is created. The second "industry average—weighted" first sums the 2005 and 2004 sales for all 11 companies and then computes the annual growth rate on these totals. Consequently, Kraft has its growth weighted the most, followed by Sara Lee, ConAgra, etc. In fact, in the

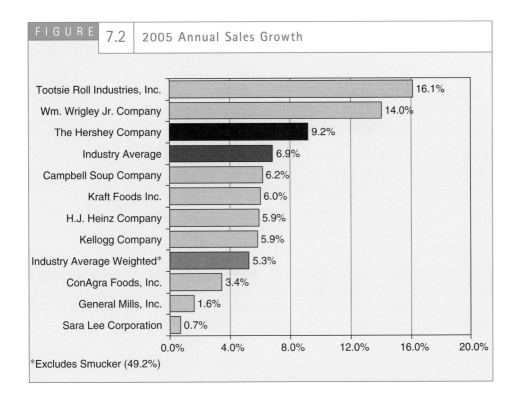

FIGURE 7.2 | 2005 Annual Sales Growth

*Excludes Smucker (49.2%)

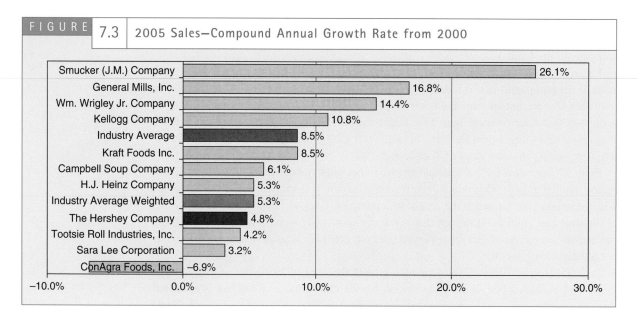

FIGURE 7.3   2005 Sales—Compound Annual Growth Rate from 2000

weighted average, the 2005 sales of Tootsie Roll are less than 1/2% of the total industry sales and consequently, its growth is "weighted" with that meager of an impact.

Figure 7.3 presents the compound annual growth rate (CAGR) over a 5-year time period from 2000 to 2005. As discussed in Chapter 3, Time and Value, the 5-year sales CAGR is calculated as:

$$(FV/PV)^{(1/n)} - 1 \qquad\qquad (7.1)$$

Specifically

$$(Sales_{2005}/Sales_{2000})^{(1/5)} - 1$$

Or ($mm)

$$(\$4,836.0/\$3,820.4)^{(0.2)} - 1 = 4.8\%$$

In addition to the arithmetic used to solve this equation, a financial calculator (please see Chapter 3) can be used as follows:

PV	=	2000 Net Sales	= –$3,820.4
FV	=	2005 Net Sales	= $4,836.0
N	=	5 Years (2000 to 2006)	= 5^2
Calculate:	**% i**		**= 4.8%**

Excel, or other spreadsheets, also facilitates this calculation. Over this period, Hershey's growth has been modest while trailing both industry averages.

Again on Figure 7.3, two industry averages are presented as discussed above. This industry group is revisited in the DuPont Analysis section.

---

[2]Notice 2000 to 2001 is 1 year; 2001 to 2002 is the second year of growth; 2002 to 2003 is the third year; 2003 to 2004 is the fourth year; and finally 2004 to 2005 is the fifth and final year of growth.

Basic Financial Statement Analysis

Basic financial statement analysis begins by examining income statements and balance sheets on a relative basis including:

- Representing line items on an income statement as a percent of sales, line items on a balance sheet as a percent of total assets, and line items on the statement of cash flows as a percent of sales (common size statement)

- Analyzing the annual growth rate of each line item

- Indexing each line item as a percentage of the first year, 2003 (common base year)

This type of analysis provides the most fundamental level of analysis. After discussing the specific calculations, a review of Hershey is conducted. Table 7.1 analyzes Hershey's income statement. Panel A provides the actual information.

On Table 7.1, the "% of Net Sales" (Panel B) is calculated as each line item on the income statement divided by net sales ($ millions):

$$\text{2005 Cost of Sales as a\% of Net Sales} = \frac{\text{Cost of Sales}}{\text{Net Sales}} = \frac{\$2,965.6}{\$4,836.0} = 61.3\%$$

Annual growth (Panel C) is calculated as:

$$\text{2005 Annual Growth in Net Sales} = \frac{\text{2005 Net Sales}}{\text{2004 Net Sales}} - 1 = \frac{\$4,836.0}{\$4,429.2} - 1 = 9.2\%$$

The CAGR, or compound annual growth rate, from 2003 to 2005 (also in Panel C) is calculated as follows:

$$\text{2005 Net Sales CAGR} = \left[\frac{\text{2005 Net Sales}}{\text{2003 Net Sales}}\right]^{0.5} - 1 = \left[\frac{\$4,836.0}{\$4,172.6}\right]^{0.5} - 1 = 7.7\%$$

Hershey's 2005 improved annual growth is of course reflected in this 2-year compound annual growth rate.

Finally, the index value (Panel D) is calculated as follows:

$$\text{2005 Index Value of Net Sales} = \frac{\text{2005 Net Sales}}{\text{2003 Net Sales}} \times 100 = \frac{\$4,836.0}{\$4,172.6} \times 100 = 115.9$$

The index value shows the accumulated growth from the base year. This is also referred to as the *common base year analysis*.

From Table 7.1, the 3 years presented (2003–2005) were a period of modest (but increasing) growth and fluctuating margins for Hershey. Both cost of sales (COS) and selling, marketing, and administrative (SM&A) expenses were managed and declined in relative terms (as a percent of sales). For example, COS increased by 0.3 percentage points as a percent of sales to an index value of 116.5 versus a 2003 index value of 100.0 (and an indexed value of 115.9 for sales). Operating income (income before interest and income taxes), pre-tax income (income before income taxes), and net income follow a similar pattern—significant growth in 2004 followed by a decline in 2005. Likewise, income as a percent of sales improved (2004) and then declined (2005). The 2005 income decline was the direct result of a one-time, extraordinary realignment charge as discussed below.

TABLE 7.1 | Income Statement Analysis (The Hershey Company 2003, 2004, and 2005 ($ Millions))

	A. INCOME STATEMENT			B. % OF NET SALES			C. ANNUAL GROWTH			D. INDEX VALUE		
	2003	2004	2005	2003	2004	2005	2004	2005	CAGR*	2003	2004	2005
Net Sales	$4,172.6	$4,429.2	$4,836.0	100.0%	100.0%	100.0%	6.1%	9.2%	7.7%	100.0	106.1	115.9
Costs and expenses												
Cost of sales	2,544.7	2,680.4	2,965.6	61.0%	60.5%	61.3%	5.3%	10.6%	8.0%	100.0	105.3	116.5
Selling, marketing, and administrative	841.1	867.1	913.0	20.2%	19.6%	18.9%	3.1%	5.3%	4.2%	100.0	103.1	108.5
Business realignment and asset impairment	23.4	—	96.5	0.6%	0.0%	2.0%	n/a	n/a	n/a	n/a	n/a	n/a
Gain on sale of business	(8.3)	—	—	−0.2%	0.0%	0.0%	n/a	n/a	n/a	n/a	n/a	n/a
Total costs and expenses	3,400.9	3,547.5	3,975.1	81.5%	80.1%	82.2%	4.3%	12.1%	8.1%	100.0	104.3	116.9
Income before interest and income taxes	771.7	881.7	860.9	18.5%	19.9%	17.8%	14.3%	−2.4%	5.6%	100.0	114.3	111.6
Interest expense, net	63.5	66.5	88.0	1.5%	1.5%	1.8%	4.7%	32.3%	17.7%	100.0	104.7	138.6
Income before income taxes	708.2	815.2	772.9	17.0%	18.4%	16.0%	15.1%	−5.2%	4.5%	100.0	115.1	109.1
Provision for income taxes	258.9	237.3	279.7	6.2%	5.4%	5.8%	−8.3%	17.9%	3.9%	100.0	91.7	108.0
Income before accounting change	449.3	577.9	493.2	10.8%	13.0%	10.2%	28.6%	−14.7%	4.8%	100.0	128.6	109.8
Cumulative effect of accounting change	7.4	—	—	0.2%	0.0%	0.0%	n/a	n/a	n/a	n/a	n/a	n/a
Net income	$ 441.9	$ 577.9	$ 493.2	10.6%	13.0%	10.2%	30.8%	−14.7%	5.6%	100.0	130.8	111.6

*CAGR, Compound annual growth rate from 2003 to 2005.

TABLE 7.2	Selected Financial Data ($ Millions, Except per Share)			
	HERSHEY		HEINZ	
	2000	2005	2000*	2005
Sales	$3,820.4	$4,836.0	$9,407.9	$8,912.3
Cost of goods sold	2,471.2	2,965.5	5,788.5	5,705.9
Administrative costs	726.6	913.0	2,350.9	1,851.5
Operating income	622.7	860.9	1,268.5	1,354.8
Interest expense	76.0	88.0	244.4	204.6
Pre-tax income	546.6	772.9	999.1	1,058.6
Net income	334.5	493.2	630.9	752.7
Earnings per share—diluted	1.21	1.99	1.75	2.13
Cash & equivalents	32.0	67.2	154.1	1,083.7
Accounts receivable	379.7	559.3	1,237.8	1,092.4
Inventory	605.2	610.3	1,599.9	1,256.8
Current assets	1,295.3	1,408.9	3,169.9	3,645.6
Net, plant, property, & equipment	1,585.4	1,659.1	2,358.8	2,163.9
Total assets	3,447.8	4,295.2	8,850.7	10,577.7
Current liabilities	766.9	1,518.2	2,126.1	2,587.1
Short-term debt	257.6	819.1	151.2	28.5
Current portion LTD	0.5	0.1	25.4	544.8
Long-term debt	877.7	942.8	3,935.8	4,122.0
Total liabilities	2,272.8	3,274.1	7,254.8	7,975.1
Stockholders' equity	1,175.0	1,021.1	1,595.9	2,602.6
Beginning of year stock price	23.72	55.54	45.06	38.08
Year-end stock price	32.19	55.25	34.00	36.87
Shares outstanding	272.6	240.5	256.8	347.7
Dividends per share	0.54	0.93	1.45	1.14

*The 2000 income measures for Heinz were adjusted to remove the one-time gain for selling Weight Watchers. Please see the discussion regarding "normalized income" later in the chapter.

This type of simple financial analysis can be applied to every member of the food processing industry and appropriate comparisons can be made. This analysis can also be applied to balance sheets and statements of cash flows. Finally, this analysis could be extended over a 5- or 10-year period to better envision underlying trends.

Financial Ratio Analysis

The basic financial statement analysis presented above, common size statement analysis, growth analysis, and common base year or indexed statements, is the most fundamental of all analyses. Although the components of the basic financial statement analysis are appropriate for comparisons between companies, the analysis was illustrated above as a way of examining a company versus itself over time.

Table 7.2 provides summary financial information. Specifically, data are provided for a comparative analysis of the past 6 years for Hershey (2000 vs 2005) and Heinz.[3] For Hershey,

[3]H.J. Heinz Company is a major, branded food processing company that serves consumers, food service, and institutional customers worldwide.

this was a period of impact for a new CEO (2001) who implemented product rationalization, new product introductions, and significant cost reduction. For Heinz, this period saw a major refocusing of the business as nonstrategic businesses were sold. The Weight Watchers division was sold in 2000.

On an analysis of the absolute financial data, the comparison of the selected financial data limits the analysis: Generally, Heinz is twice as large as Hershey. However, the next section compares and contrasts Hershey on a relative basis using financial performance metrics.

Financial Ratios and Metrics

Table 7.3 overviews financial ratio analysis and lists five broad groupings of ratios:

- *Liquidity:* How liquid is the company? These metrics measure the firm's ability to meet its maturing short-term obligations.

- *Activity:* How effectively is the company managing its assets? These metrics measure how effectively the company is using its resources.

- *Leverage:* How is the company financed? These metrics measure the extent to which the firm's assets have been financed by debt.

- *Profitability:* How profitable is the company? These metrics measure management's overall ability to generate profits in relation to its sales or investment.

- *Market:* How does the company's performance "translate" in the stock market? These metrics measure the firm's relationship to the broader stock market.

In addition, the basic financial statement analysis discussed above includes two additional categories of financial ratios:

- *Growth:* How has the company been growing? These metrics include annual growth rates and compound annual growth rates over extended time periods (see above) of key balance sheet and income statement items and measure the firm's ability to maintain its economic position in the growth of the economy and industry.

- *Cost Management:* What are the underlying cost trends relative to other measures? These metrics include measuring expenses as a percent of each sales dollar as in the common size income statement on Table 7.1.

Within each of these categories are numerous individual performance metrics. The most common of the metrics are discussed below.

LIQUIDITY METRICS

Liquidity ratios measure the firm's ability to pay off its maturing short-term obligations. The broadest view of liquidity is captured in the Current ratio.

Current ratio is calculated as current assets divided by current liabilities. Current assets include cash and marketable securities, accounts receivable, inventory, and any other line items that comprise current assets. **Current assets** are categories that will be converted to cash in the coming accounting cycle or fiscal year. Current liabilities include accounts payable, accrued liabilities, other payables and accruals, short-term debt, and current portion long-term debt. **Current liabilities** represent items that must be paid in the

TABLE 7.3	Performance Metrics			
	HERSHEY		**HEINZ**	
	2000	2005	2000	2005
Liquidity				
Current ratio	1.69	0.93	1.49	1.41
Net working capital ($ millions)	$ 528.4	$ (109.3)	$1,043.8	$ 1,058.5
Quick ratio	0.90	0.53	0.74	0.92
Cash ratio	0.04	0.04	0.07	0.42
Activity				
Total asset turnover	1.11	1.13	1.06	0.84
Fixed asset turnover	2.41	2.91	3.99	4.12
Current asset turnover	2.95	3.43	2.97	2.44
Accounts receivable turnover	10.06	8.65	7.60	8.16
Average collection period	36.3	42.2	48.0	44.7
Inventory turnover	4.08	4.86	3.62	4.54
Inventory days outstanding	89.4	75.1	100.9	80.4
Leverage				
Debt to equity	1.93	3.21	4.55	3.06
Current debt to equity	0.65	1.49	1.33	0.99
Long-term debt to equity	1.28	1.72	3.21	2.07
Financial leverage	2.93	4.21	5.55	4.06
Capitalization ratio	49.2%	63.3%	72.0%	64.3%
Long-term capitalization ratio	42.8%	48.0%	71.1%	61.3%
Interest coverage	8.19	9.78	5.19	6.62
Profitability				
Net margin	8.8%	10.2%	6.7%	8.4%
Pre-tax margin	14.3%	16.0%	10.6%	11.9%
Operating margin	16.3%	17.8%	13.5%	15.2%
Gross margin	35.3%	38.7%	38.5%	36.0%
Return on assets	9.7%	11.5%	7.1%	7.1%
Return on net assets	11.4%	13.7%	9.1%	8.8%
Return on equity	28.5%	48.3%	39.5%	28.9%
Market				
Market capitalization ($ millions)	$8,773.6	$13,287.6	$8,731.2	$12,819.7
Price/earnings	26.60	27.76	19.43	17.31
Market to book	7.47	13.01	5.47	4.93
Shareholder returns	38.0%	1.2%	−21.3%	−0.2%
Dividend yield	2.3%	1.7%	3.2%	3.0%

coming accounting cycle or fiscal year. So the current ratio is calculated by taking current liabilities or obligations that need to be paid in the coming year and dividing that into current assets or items that a company will convert into cash in the coming year. Said differently, the current ratio shows that for every dollar you owe in the coming year, you have "X" dollars to pay it off. For Hershey for 2005 ($ millions):

$$\frac{\text{Hershey's 2005}}{\text{Current Ratio}} = \frac{\text{Current Assets}}{\text{Current Liabilities}} = \frac{\$1,408.9}{\$1,518.2} = 0.93$$

For every dollar that Hershey owes over the coming year, it has $0.93 with which to pay it off.

As late as the mid-1980s, a strong current ratio had a value greater than 2. However, in the past 20 years, companies have altered their current asset structure with such processes as "just-in-time" inventory management, more aggressive management of accounts receivable, and a limiting of cash and cash equivalents. In addition, with the increased efficiencies of interest rate swaps, a number of companies have been taking advantage of lower short-term interest rates as they have made a strategy of "rolling over" short-term borrowing as a part of their permanent capital structure. Consequently, companies have systematically shed current assets while purposefully increasing their current liabilities, thus lowering the current ratio standard.

Ratios, including the current ratio, tend to have performance standards related to the industry. Restaurants or fast foods have a current ratio standard that is less than 1! Its current liabilities exceed its current assets. Think about the fast food restaurant, for example McDonald's, and the components of its current assets and current liabilities. On the current asset side, McDonald's does have cash, but only minimal accounts receivable. When was the last time that you went to McDonald's and slapped down your "Mickey D Charge Card" to charge your purchase? McDonald's has very limited franchise fee receivables. As far as inventory, again think about McDonald's business. They have no finished goods inventory or goods in process. They only have raw material inventory with limited shelf life. You can't keep hamburger "hanging around" (no pun intended). On the liability side, McDonald's has all the normal liabilities such as accounts payable, wages payable, taxes payable, accrued liabilities, short-term debt, and current portion of long-term debt. So McDonald's has all the normal liabilities but a thinner level of current assets.

Consequently, a current ratio approaching 1.00 would be a strong ratio for the fast food business. Even so, the higher the current ratio, the stronger the firm's performance. Again, anything taken to an extreme could actually show signs of an underlying weakness. For example, a current ratio of 8.00 could show:

- Hoarding of cash

- Non-collection of receivables

- Inventory build-up

- Inefficient use of "free" financing from suppliers

- Limited short-term borrowings

Industry, competitor, and self-comparisons are instrumental in determining performance strengths and weaknesses.

Table 7.3 compares the 2000 and 2005 performance of The Hershey Company along with a contrast to Heinz. For the food industry, a current ratio of approximately 1.50 times shows strength. However, this measure has weakened for Hershey over the past 6 years. In 2005, for every dollar that it owed (current liabilities) in the coming year, Hershey had only $0.93 with which to pay it off (current assets). On the surface, this is significantly weaker than Hershey in 2000 or Heinz in either year. Revisiting the "raw data" of Table 7.2 shows that Hershey has a significant amount of short-term debt and current portion of long-term debt in 2005 as a result of acquisitions and stock repurchases. Although these events were discretionary, the current ratio highlights an area that will need to remain a focal point.

A related metric, although not a comparative metric because it is expressed in absolute not relative terms, is net working capital. Net working capital is simply current assets (CA) less current liabilities (CL) and represents the amount left over after a firm pays off all of its immediate liabilities. For Hershey in 2005, working capital was $(109.3) million:

$$\begin{array}{c}\text{Hershey's 2005 Net}\\\text{Working Capital}\end{array} = \text{CA} - \text{CL} = \$1,408.9 - \$1,518.2 = \$(109.3)$$

This negative net working capital (current assets less than current liabilities) is consistent with a current ratio of less than 1.00 and suggests that Hershey may have some difficulty in meeting its short-term obligations without raising additional financing in 2006.

Quick ratio, or the acid test ratio, is similar to the current ratio except inventories are eliminated from the current assets. Why do companies go bankrupt? There are many responses to that question, but in the end it often boils down to no one wanting the company's product. There are some companies that make a highly desirable product and are successful in spite of inadequate managerial processes and leadership. There are other organizations with great management teams, but a product that no one wants. These companies are doomed to failure.

The quick ratio eliminates inventory from current assets. That is, what if you could not realize any value for your finished goods, or your goods in process, or even your raw material? The quick ratio for Hershey in 2005 was:

$$\begin{array}{c}\text{Hershey's 2005}\\\text{Quick Ratio}\end{array} = \frac{(\text{Current Assets} - \text{Inventory})}{\text{Current Liabilities}} = \frac{(\$1,408.9 - \$610.3)}{\$1,518.2} = 0.53$$

For every dollar that Hershey owes over the coming year, it has $0.53 to pay it off in current assets excluding inventories. Similar to the current ratio and also due to the impact of debt, Hershey's quick ratio has dramatically fallen and is about half of the Heinz level in 2005.

Another way of stating the quick ratio is to examine the remaining current assets that are used in the numerator. For every dollar that Hershey owes over the coming year, it has $0.53 of cash and cash equivalents, accounts receivable, and other current assets to pay it off. But what if the accounts receivable are non-collectible or partially non-collectible, what if deferred tax assets are not realizable, and what if prepaid expenses and other assets could not be readily (or fully) converted to cash. Permutations of an "adjusted" quick ratio abound for any specific situation.

Cash ratio is the most restrictive liquidity ratio and assumes that only cash and cash equivalents are available to pay off current liabilities. The cash ratio is calculated as:

$$\begin{array}{c}\text{Hershey's 2005}\\\text{Cash Ratio}\end{array} = \frac{\text{Cash and Equivalents}}{\text{Current Liabilities}} = \frac{\$67.2}{\$1,518.2} = 0.04$$

The phrase "equivalents" includes short-term investments in such things as a savings account, money market account, certificates of deposit, U.S. Treasury bills, and the like. Equivalents include any short-term, highly marketable security.

For every dollar Hershey owes, within the next year, at the end of 2005, Hershey has 4 cents of cash (and cash equivalents) with which to pay its obligations. This metric is on par as in 2000, but trails Heinz. Heinz has $0.42 in cash and marketable securities to pay off each dollar of current liabilities in 2005 ($1,083.7 million/$2,587.1 million).

In summary, the liquidity performance metrics highlight a liquidity concern for Hershey.

ACTIVITY METRICS

The activity ratios measure how effectively the company is using its resources. Throughout this section, income statement and balance sheet line items are used for comparison. In all cases, year-end balance sheet values are used. This provides the most conservative metric. These metrics could also be calculated using the beginning balance or an average of the beginning and ending balance. More elaborate averaging techniques could also be used, such as averaging the last four or five quarters of balance sheets. Unless there are some pressing business rationales or significant shifts in business, the use of balance sheet values at year-end or the beginning of the year or their average will have minimal impact on telling the story that underlies the analysis. Yes, there will be different exact, specific numbers, but the underlying trends will be consistent. For simplistic illustration, year-end balance sheet values are used is this section and throughout this chapter. The total asset turnover ratio gives the broadest and most strategically focused activity measure. Additional activity metrics target specific areas of management for closer, day-to-day scrutiny.

Total asset turnover is defined as sales divided by total assets:

$$\text{Hershey's 2005 Total Asset Turnover} = \frac{\text{Sales}}{\text{Total Assets}} = \frac{\$4,836.0}{\$4,295.2} = 1.13$$

For every dollar of assets, Hershey generates $1.13 in sales. For every dollar of assets that society has entrusted to the managers at Hershey, $1.13 worth of sales is generated. Over time, this metric has improved for Hershey as underperforming assets and plants with low capacity utilization were sold. In 2000, when comparing Hershey to Heinz, Hershey had a slightly stronger asset turnover ($1.11 of sales versus $1.06 of sales for every dollar of assets). However, Heinz asset turnover fell to only 0.84 times (or $0.84 of sales for every dollar of assets). Hershey's performance far surpasses the performance of Heinz.

The difference may be the result of Hershey's superior sales force or it may be the result of more efficient production facilities or it may be the result of factors such as asset mix, product mix, or other factors that are not related to management efficiency. The total asset turnover alerts management to overall efficiency differences. The other activity ratios make the analysis more operational by identifying key areas for management's attention.

Fixed asset turnover or the rate of fixed asset utilization is critical because investments in plant and equipment are both large and of long duration. A mistake in fixed asset investments (net, plant, property, and equipment) may be reversed, but the consequences are likely to be long lasting. To focus on plant and equipment investment, the fixed asset turnover centers on net, plant, property, and equipment and is determined as follows:

$$\text{Hershey's 2005 Fixed Asset Turnover} = \frac{\text{Sales}}{\text{Net, Plant, Property, \& Equipment}} = \frac{\$4,836.0}{\$1,659.1} = 2.91$$

Hershey's performance shows improvement over this time span. However, when compared to Heinz, Hershey trails both years. Heinz generates $1.21 more ($4.12 vs $2.91) in sales for every dollar invested in fixed assets. Although this metric points to superior managerial performance at Heinz, this difference could be due to a number of reasons, such as the age of the plants, products produced, quantity of products produced, plant production configuration, etc. The plant production configuration, that is, how many different products are produced at the same manufacturing facility, affects the plant utilization rate. Production facilities are much more efficient when producing one product rather than producing a variety of diverse products.

The age of the plants and equipment is also important. Older facilities presumably are operationally less efficient, but are represented on the books in depreciated dollar amounts based on their original purchase price. Newer facilities tend to be more efficient, cost more, and are initially underutilized. All of these aspects affect this metric.

Unfortunately, we are not able to analyze the plants of Hershey or Heinz more specifically, due to the lack of available *public* plant-specific data. However, the managerial objectives remain clear for Hershey: generate more sales and/or reduce the investment in net, plant, property, and equipment. Continuous improvement objectives can be (and are) implemented at each manufacturing facility within Hershey.

Additional activity ratios examine accounts receivable and inventory. *Accounts receivable turnover* is calculated similar to the other turnovers:

$$\text{Hershey's 2005 Accounts Receivable Turnover} = \frac{\text{Credit Sales}}{\text{Accounts Receivable}} = \frac{\$4,836.0}{\$559.3} = 8.65$$

The assumption is that all of Hershey's sales are made on credit, which is legitimate for most businesses. This measure suggests that 8.65 times a year, Hershey collects all of its accounts receivables from its customers. This performance is lower (worse) than the 2000 performance when the receivables were collected 10.06 times a year. Heinz slightly improved its performance over this 6-year period, but trails the performance of Hershey (8.16 versus 8.65).

Very closely related to the accounts receivable turnover ratio is another activity ratio called the average collection period. The **average collection period** measures the average length of time that it takes to collect from a customer. It is calculated by dividing 365 days in a year by the accounts receivable turnover:

$$\text{Hershey's 2005 Average Collection Period} = \frac{365}{\text{Accounts Receivable Turnover}} = \frac{365}{8.65} = 42.2$$

In 2005, Hershey took 42.2 days to collect from its customers. This is 5.9 days slower (worse) than in 2000. Once again, Heinz has also improved, but trails the performance of Hershey in 2005 by more than 2 days.

Usual credit terms are, "2/10 net 30," which means that if you pay in the first 10 days you get a 2% discount. If you don't pay in the first 10 days, the entire amount (no discounts) is payable in 30 days. Under these circumstances, an average collection period of 30 days or less is a standard of excellence. For a number of years, Hershey's average collection period was less than 20 days while the industry's standard was between 30 and 35 days. On the surface this was impressive, but it raised a concern. Was Hershey's accounts receivable policy too tight? Was Hershey losing sales by restricting only the best customers to being able to purchase on credit? Once again, a directionally strong metric may become a weakness if it is taken to extremes.

The final activity ratio examined in this section is the inventory turnover ratio. Inventory turnover is calculated using the cost of goods sold instead of sales to eliminate the "profit" component and more accurately reflect this metric because inventory is carried at cost, not the anticipated selling price:

$$\text{Hershey's 2005 Inventory Turnover} = \frac{\text{Cost of Goods Sold}}{\text{Inventory}} = \frac{\$2,965.6}{\$610.3} = 4.86$$

In 2005, Hershey sold off its entire inventory 4.86 times in the year. That is, it cleaned out its warehouses, sold everything off the shelves 4.86 times in 2005. This ratio has shown steady improvement at Hershey because it became an important operational objective over this time period. In 2000, the inventory "turned" only 4.08 times. In 1999, Hershey installed a new computer system that enabled the streamlining of its inventory management practices, resulting in improved inventory turns. If Hershey would have maintained the same inventory turnover as in 2000, the inventory would have been $726.8 million ($2,965.6/4.08 times). Hershey would have had almost $117 million more invested in inventory than it currently has.

A variation of the inventory turnover is to measure the number of days of inventory on hand. This is accomplished by dividing 365 days in the year by the number of turnovers per year:

$$\frac{\text{Hershey's 2005 Inventory}}{\text{Days Outstanding}} = \frac{365}{\text{Inventory Turnover}} = \frac{365}{4.86} = 75.1$$

Every 75.1 days, Hershey sells off its entire inventory, which is about a 2-week improvement over its 2000 performance and only slightly better than Heinz 2005 performance.

This metric can be applied at a lower level within a firm. This metric can be applied by business unit and by isolating inventory into raw material, goods in process, and finished goods. Standards of performance can be established for these individual inventory components.

Activity ratios provide an overview of how effectively a company is using its assets. The activity ratios listed above provide a review of the major metrics in this category. Again, this is not an exhaustive list. Turnovers can be calculated by taking any balance sheet item and dividing it into sales or cost of goods sold. Any turnover can be presented as days outstanding by dividing 365 days in a year by the turnover value. The activity ratio discussion provides an analytical framework that can be used to build other turnovers or days outstanding as specific business needs dictate.

LEVERAGE METRICS

Decisions about the use of debt must balance hoped-for higher returns against the increased risk of the consequences that firms face when they are unable to meet interest payments or maturing obligations. The use of debt has a number of implications for a firm:

- First, creditors look at equity, or owner-supplied funds, as a cushion or base for the use of debt. If owners provide only a small proportion of total financing, the risks of the enterprise are borne mainly by the creditors.

- Second, by raising funds through debt, the owners gain the benefits of increased capital while maintaining control of the firm.

- Third, the use of debt with a fixed interest rate magnifies both the gains and losses to the owners.

- Fourth, the use of debt with a fixed interest cost and a specified maturity increases the risks that the firm may not be able to meet its obligations.

Leverage metrics measure the extent to which a firm is financed by debt. The first group of leverage metrics uses the accounting identity relationship for the balance sheet:

$$\text{Assets} = \text{Liabilities} + \text{Stockholders' Equity}$$

This group of leverage metrics uses total liabilities (including accounts payable, accrued liabilities, deferred taxes, other long-term liabilities, and interest-bearing debt) synonymously with the word "debt." Another group of leverage ratios centers on balance sheet relationships, but defines debt as only interest-bearing debt. The third group of leverage metrics concentrates on income statement relationships and the ability of the firm to pay its interest expense.

Debt to equity uses the term "debt" referring to total liabilities. It is calculated as:

$$\text{Hershey's 2005 Debt to Equity Ratio} = \frac{\text{Debt (or Liabilities)}}{\text{Stockholder's Equity}} = \frac{\$3,274.1}{\$1,021.1} = 3.21$$

For every dollar of stockholders' equity, Hershey supports $3.21 worth of liabilities. A higher debt to equity ratio indicates that the firm is using more total liabilities to finance its assets. From a banker's point of view, the higher the debt to equity ratio, the weaker a company is because such a ratio indicates more risk. Said differently, a low debt to equity ratio indicates that the firm is committing a large portion of equity in financing the business. Therefore, a firm with a low debt to equity ratio is less risky and consequently stronger than a firm with a higher debt to equity. In 2000, a dollar of Hershey's equity supported $1.93 in debt and Hershey is currently in a weaker position.

Heinz has "improved" its performance, but supports $3.06 for every $1 of equity in 2005. From a banker's perspective, this is a strength of Heinz versus Hershey in 2005. Later in this chapter, we discuss that under the right circumstances and with a specific point of reference, debt can actually be a performance enhancing addition to the balance sheet.

This analysis can be extended by examining current liabilities, long-term liabilities, or any liability in relation to equity (i.e., divided by equity).

Financial leverage is closely aligned to the debt to equity ratio. **Financial leverage** measures the extent to which the shareholders' equity investment is magnified by the use of total debt (or liabilities) in financing its total assets. Financial leverage illustrates the number of dollars of assets for every 1 dollar of stockholders' equity:

$$\text{Hershey's 2005 Financial Leverage} = \frac{\text{Assets}}{\text{Stockholder's Equity}} = \frac{\$4,295.2}{\$1,021.1} = 4.21$$

At Hershey, every dollar of stockholders' equity supported $4.21 of assets. Once again, the 2005 performance of Hershey is slightly higher than 2005 Heinz (4.06).

The financial leverage can also be determined by adding "1" to the debt to equity ratio:

$$\text{Hershey's 2005 Financial Leverage} = 1 + \frac{\text{Debt (or Liabilities)}}{\text{Stockholders' Equity}} = 1 + \frac{\$3,274.1}{\$1,021.1} = 4.21$$

As an algebraic note, remember the old high school algebra "trick" that one can equal any number divided by itself (identity property). In the equation above, let 1 be equity/equity. That allows the combination of terms (Equity + Debt), which per the accounting identity equals total assets:

$$1 + \frac{\text{Debt}}{\text{Equity}} = \frac{\text{Equity}}{\text{Equity}} + \frac{\text{Debt}}{\text{Equity}} = \frac{(\text{Equity} + \text{Debt})}{\text{Equity}} = \frac{\text{Assets}}{\text{Equity}}$$

The accounting identity equation also captures this relationship:

$$\text{Assets} = \text{Liabilities} + \text{Stockholders' Equity}$$
$$\$4.21 = \$3.21 + \$1.00 \tag{7.2}$$

Additional leverage metrics can be constructed from this relationship.

These metrics look at what percentages of the assets are financed with liabilities and what percentage are financed with stockholders' equity:

$$\text{Hershey's 2005 Debt to Asset Ratio} = \frac{\text{Liabilities}}{\text{Assets}} = \frac{\$3,274.1}{\$4,295.2} = 76.2\%$$

$$\text{Hershey's 2005 Equity to Asset Ratio} = \frac{\text{Stockholder's Equity}}{\text{Assets}} = \frac{\$1,021.1}{\$4,295.2} = 23.8\%$$

These ratios must total 100%.

From the basic accounting identity relationship, we have constructed two ratios and noted some additional variations:

- Debt to equity

  - Current liabilities to equity

  - Long-term liabilities to equity

- Financial leverage (or assets to equity)

- Other

  - Debt to assets

  - Equity to assets

The underlying relationships, the trends, and the comparisons portrayed by these ratios do not change. In fact, these metrics provide redundant information. In all cases, Hershey is now more leveraged than in 2000 and uses slightly more debt (or less equity) in financing than Heinz uses. What is different among these metrics is their focus and associated discussions. How is your company's management team more comfortable in discussing leverage, in relation to percent of assets or percent of equity? That should determine how the analysis is presented.

Balance sheet line items such as accounts payable, accrued liabilities, and long-term liabilities, including deferred taxes, stem from the operations of the business. Those liabilities are some times referred to as *spontaneous operating liabilities*. The second group of leverage metrics centers on exclusively financial liabilities, interest-bearing debt, and total capital. Financial liabilities include all interest-bearing debt, which is to say all short-term debt, bank borrowings (loans), notes payable, current portion of long-term debt, and long-term debt. Total capital consists of interest-bearing debt and stockholders' equity.

Capitalization ratio calculates the percentage that the interest-bearing debt represents of the total capital pool:

$$\text{Hershey's 2005 Capitalization Ratio} = \frac{\text{Interest Bearing Debt}}{(\text{Interest Bearing Debt} + \text{Equity})} = \frac{\$1,762.0}{\$2,783.1} = 63.3\%$$

Hershey has raised over 63% of its capital with interest-bearing debt. Again, this is slightly higher than 6 years earlier (49.2%), but approximately the same as for Heinz. The value of the capitalization ratio is that we are more focused on true capital structure and do not include any operating liabilities such as accounts payable, accrued liabilities, deferred taxes, or pension liabilities. As with all of the metrics at this stage of the discussion, the values of the interest-bearing debt and equity are based on book values as found in the company's annual report. Later, a similar type of metric using the market value of the debt and equity is introduced.

Variations of the capitalization ratio differ in what is considered in the numerator. Are bank borrowings (loans), short-term debt, notes payable, and current portion long-term debt part of the permanent financial capital structure of the firm, or are they just another form of operating liabilities? If those interest-bearing debt items are merely operating liabilities, should they be excluded from the capitalization ratio? The answer lies in the motives of the corporation. Many companies have incorporated a long-term financing strategy of "rolling over" short-term debt. With the financial flexibility provided by swaps and other instruments and the relatively calm debt markets of the past few years, many firms save millions of dollars annually by taking advantage of lower short-term interest rates and finance a portion of their permanent assets with short-term borrowings. In these cases, it is clear that short-term borrowings are part of the permanent financial structure and should be included as interest-bearing debt in the capitalization ratio.

Other companies within other industries could argue that all short-term financing supports temporary working capital needs. They may choose to exclude short-term borrowings for purposes of the capitalization ratio and narrow the metric to:

$$\frac{\text{Hershey's 2005 Long}}{\text{Term Capitalization Ratio}} = \frac{\text{Long-Term Debt}}{(\text{Long-Term Debt} + \text{Equity})} = \frac{\$942.8}{\$1,963.9} = 48.0\%$$

This more narrowly focused metric centers on long-term debt as a percent of a similarly narrowed definition of capital. In this example, 48.0% of Hershey's capital pool (excluding short-term borrowings) comes from long-term debt. In 2000, Hershey derived 42.8% of its capital from long-term interest bearing debt. In this case, Heinz is significantly more leveraged (61.3%) than Hershey because they use more long-term debt in their capital structure.

Notice on Table 7.3 the difference between the capitalization ratio and the long-term capitalization ratio shows the extent to which each company used short-term interest-bearing debt. Both variations of the capitalization ratio are appropriate depending on the circumstances. It appears that the food industry incorporates short-term borrowings into their permanent capital structures. Consequently, the former version of the capitalization ratio (including short-term borrowings) would be more appropriate for the food industry.

The final type of leverage metric, **interest coverage**, centers on the income statement and examines how many times the interest could be paid off with operating income:

$$\frac{\text{Hershey's 2005}}{\text{Interest Coverage}} = \frac{\text{EBIT}}{\text{Interest Expense}} = \frac{\$860.9}{\$88.0} = 9.78$$

EBIT represents "earnings before interest and taxes" or "operating income." Simply put, for every dollar that Hershey owes for interest expense, Hershey earns $9.78 in operating income that could be used to pay the interest. From a banker's perspective, the higher this ratio, the stronger the company. Everything else the same, as leverage and interest expense increase, interest coverage declines. But notice that although Hershey is more leveraged in 2005 than in 2000, the interest coverage actually improved! This is a result of the tremendous growth in Hershey's operating income while financing its increased debt with lower cost funds. The interest coverage ratio provides an important added dimension to leverage discussions and analysis.

The next set of financial ratios centers on profitability.

PROFITABILITY METRICS

Profitability ratios measure management's overall effectiveness at generating "profits." One common set of profitability ratios examines some measure of income as a percent of sales, while another group of metrics focuses on income in relation to some measure of investment as captured by the balance sheet.

Net income margin, or simply *net margin*, is one of the most frequently cited metrics. This measure is also called the *return on sales*. Senior management often sets targets and objectives that include the net margin. Often a senior manager's bonus is tied directly or indirectly to the net margin. Simply, the net margin reflects the number of pennies of income for every dollar of sales:

$$\frac{\text{Hershey's 2005}}{\text{Net Margin}} = \frac{\text{Net Income}}{\text{Sales}} = \frac{\$493.2}{\$4,836.0} = 10.2\%$$

For every dollar of sales, Hershey generated 10.2¢ of net income, that is, income after paying all of its production costs, operating expenses, interest, and taxes. Hershey's net margin significantly improved by 1.4% (percentage points) from its 2000 level (8.8%), in part, as a result of implementing operating efficiencies and eliminating less profitable products.

For Hershey with 2005 sales of $4,836.0 million, a 0.1% improvement in the net margin enhances Hershey's profitability by over $4.8 million. Extending this further, the 1.4% net margin improvement resulted in an additional $67.7 million of income! It is easy to see why management teams pay attention to the net margin.

Generally, the higher the net margin (or any profitability metric), the better the underlying performance of the company. There are two ways to improve the net margin. One way is to reduce expenses; the other way is to increase prices. However, as mentioned before, anything taken to an extreme can become a weakness. Kellogg was the perennial leader of the food industry with net margins approaching 10% in the late 1980s when the industry average was approximately 5%. Also in the late 1980s and early 1990s, Kellogg was the number one cereal company in the United States with the largest market share. In the early 1990s, Kellogg went through a series of price increases that boosted its net margin to over 11.0%. Of course, as consumers, we were all less than thrilled to pay $4 and $5 for a box of cereal.

Companies that produced generic and store-brand cereals seized the opportunity. Competition heated up. We consumers learned that we could eat a box of cereal that didn't come in a box, but rather came in a cellophane bag. Prices fell and heavy expenses were incurred for store coupons, promotions, and advertising. Kellogg's sales declined, their number one market share eroded, and their net margin shrank to only 9.6% in 2005. Their strict adherence to raising prices for a higher net margin eventually cost them. All ratios must be carefully balanced and the industry dynamics understood to better signal when strength is becoming a weakness.

Pre-tax margin reveals how profitable the firm is before considering the effects of income taxes. It is calculated as:

$$\frac{\text{Hershey's 2005}}{\text{Pre-Tax Margin}} = \frac{\text{Pre-Tax Income}}{\text{Sales}} = \frac{\$772.9}{\$4,836.0} = 16.0\%$$

In 2005, Hershey had a pre-tax margin of 16.0%, which again sharply increased from 2000. When compared to Hershey's net margin (10.2%), the pre-tax margin shows that 5.8 cents (16.0% – 10.2%) of every dollar of Hershey's sales went to pay income taxes. In both years, Hershey remained more profitable than Heinz.

Operating margin is calculated as:

$$\frac{\text{Hershey's 2005}}{\text{Operating Margin}} = \frac{\text{Operating Income}}{\text{Sales}} = \frac{\$860.9}{\$4,836.0} = 17.8\%$$

For every dollar of sales, Hershey generated 17.8 cents of operating income or earnings before interest and tax (EBIT). This represents the profitability of the corporation before considering financing costs (interest) and income taxes. For Hershey, again, this metric has increased sharply from 2000 and is measurably stronger than that for Heinz.

The difference between operating income (EBIT) and pre-tax income is interest expense. On Table 7.2, Hershey's 2005 operating income ($860.9 million) less interest expense ($88.0 million) equals pre-tax income of $772.9 million. Similarly, the difference between the operating margin and pre-tax margin represents interest expense as a percent of sales, or in this case 1.8 cents of every sales dollar goes to pay interest expense.

Gross margin develops a profitability relationship between gross income and sales, where:

$$\text{Gross Income} = \text{Sales} - \text{Cost of Goods Sold} \qquad (7.3)$$

Gross income represents the inherent profitability of making a product. Cost of goods sold encompasses total cost of production: raw material, direct labor, plant overhead, manufacturing depreciation, and so on. After absorbing the costs of making the product, how profitable is the company? This metric is particularly interesting to manufacturing professionals.

$$\frac{\text{Hershey's 2005}}{\text{Gross Margin}} = \frac{(\text{Sales} - \text{Cost of Goods Sold})}{\text{Sales}} = \frac{(\$4,836.0 - \$2,965.6)}{\$4,836.0} = 38.7\%$$

In 2005, Hershey made 38.7 cents for every dollar of sales after considering the cost of producing their products. From the previous 6 years, Hershey significantly improved its gross margins while the gross margin at Heinz fell.

In summary, the profitability metrics presented here focus on the income statement and the relationship of various income measures to sales. Generally, the higher the income as a percent of sales, the stronger the performance of that company. Table 7.4 summarizes and highlights the profitability measures discussed so far.

RETURN ON INVESTMENT

This next series of profitability metrics looks at the amount of profitability for every dollar of investment. In these cases, profitability and investment definitions vary with the particular focus of the analysis.

TABLE 7.4	Profitability Analysis: Income Statement (% of Sales)			
	HERSHEY		HEINZ	
	2000	2005	2000	2005
Sales	100.0%	100.0%	100.0%	100.0%
Cost of goods sold	64.7%	61.3%	61.5%	64.0%
Gross margin	35.3%	38.7%	38.5%	36.0%
Selling, general administrative	19.0%	18.9%	25.0%	20.8%
Other expenses	0.0%	2.0%	0.0%	0.0%
Operating margin	16.3%	17.8%	13.5%	15.2%
Interest expense	2.0%	1.8%	2.6%	2.3%
Other expense	0.0%	0.0%	0.3%	1.0%
Pre-tax margin	14.3%	16.0%	10.6%	11.9%
Income tax provision	5.5%	5.8%	3.9%	3.5%
Net margin	8.8%	10.2%	6.7%	8.4%

Assets represent the total investment made by the corporation on behalf of its stockholders. As discussed in Chapter 2, accounting values do not represent current values, fair market values, or even replacement value of assets. In fact, a portion of the balance sheet captures only historical costs of the assets. Still other "asset" values go unacknowledged, such as the value of intellectual property, strong brands, technology, and highly knowledgeable employees. Despite these frailties, a balance sheet does reasonably capture and represent assets on a consistently measured basis among organizations.

Return on assets (ROA) measures the return (income) for every dollar of assets:

$$\frac{\text{Hershey's 2005}}{\text{Return on Assets}} = \frac{\text{Net Income}}{\text{Total Assets}} = \frac{\$493.2}{\$4,295.2} = 11.5\%$$

In 2005, Hershey generated 11.5 cents on every dollar of assets, which was substantially higher than the ROA for 2000. Once again, Hershey's profitability superiority to Heinz is evidenced as Hershey's ROA is 4.4 percentage points higher than the ROA of Heinz!

Many companies establish internal profitability metrics. Hershey called their metric *RONA (or return on net assets)*. Many companies have a similarly defined metric that goes by different acronyms and names:

- RONA, or return on net assets

- ORONA, or operating return on net assets

- RONI, or return on net investment

- ROIC, or return on invested capital

- ROCI, or return on capital invested

- ROGEC, or return on gross employed capital

While these measures may have slight variations in the definition of the denominator, we use a fairly common variety of net asset definition:

Net Assets = Total Assets − Non-Interest Bearing Current Liabilities   (7.4)

In Hershey's 2005 case, non–interest-bearing current liabilities total $699.1 million: $167.8 million accounts payable, $507.8 million accrued liabilities, and $23.5 million accrued income taxes. Net assets were:

$$\text{Net Assets} = \$4,295.2 - \$699.1 = \$3,596.1$$

Said differently, net assets represent the capital (equity, long-term debt, short-term debt, and current portion of long-term debt) and long-term operating liabilities, such as deferred taxes and other long-term liabilities. The return on net assets represents the return on total assets less spontaneous current operating liabilities:

$$\frac{\text{Hershey's 2005}}{\text{Return on Net Assets}} = \frac{\text{Net Income}}{\text{Net Assets}} = \frac{\$493.2}{\$3,596.1} = 13.7\%$$

Again, as seen with the return on assets, Hershey's 2005 RONA is significantly more than what it was in 2000 and leads Heinz, whose RONA slightly fell.

Return on equity is the final profitability metric and is the narrowest definition of a capital base used in the return metrics. Return on equity for Hershey in 2005 was 48.3%:

$$\frac{\text{Hershey's 2005}}{\text{Return on Equity}} = \frac{\text{Net Income}}{\text{Equity}} = \frac{\$493.2}{\$1,021.1} = 48.3\%$$

For every dollar of total stockholders' equity (original investment and retained earnings offset by share repurchases), Hershey generated 48.3 cents of income after paying all production costs, operating expenses, interest expense, and income taxes. Once again, a similar performance path is noted: 2005 is sharply stronger than 2000 and exceeded Heinz's 2005 performance.

Investment Base: Time Frame

When calculating any return on investment metrics as discussed above, the analyst is faced with a choice of which balance sheet values to use. In all the cases presented above, the year-end balance sheet values are used. This is a very conservative posture and assumes that management generated income throughout the year in anticipation of its total year investment. A more aggressive posture is to use the beginning balance (e.g., end of the last fiscal year) of investment. This is the same as suggesting all annual investment in the corporation occurs at the end of the year and therefore is not available throughout the year to generate any income. Another approach averages the two, the beginning and ending investment amounts. By doing this, management is more realistically charged with earning a return as investment is made in the organization. Table 7.5 illustrates.

Notice that in all ROA cases, the beginning of the year investment provides the highest return, followed by the average, and finally the most conservative end of the year values. But within a given investment timeframe, the messages are consistent. The patterns are the same; the calibrated levels are the issue. Hershey's 2005 ROA is substantially more than its 2000 ROA and almost double the 2005 Heinz ROA. The specific return numbers are at different magnitudes, but the relationships are the same.

The ROE is similar but has two noted exceptions: from Table 7.5, Hershey's 2005 ROE and Heinz's 2000 ROE. In these cases, the end of the year values were actually higher in that both companies in those years repurchased stock and drove the value of equity lower than at the beginning of the year. But the comparative trend and industry positioning remains similar.

TABLE 7.5	Investment Base ($ Millions)			
	HERSHEY		HEINZ	
	2000	2005	2000	2005
Net income	$ 334.5	$ 493.2	$ 630.9	$ 752.7
Total assets:				
Beginning of the year	3,346.7	3,812.8	8,053.6	9,877.2
Average for the year	3,397.3	4,054.0	8,452.2	10,227.5
End of the year	3,447.8	4,295.2	8,850.7	10,577.7
Stockholders' equity				
Beginning of the year	1,098.6	1,137.1	1,803.0	1,894.2
Average for the year	1,136.8	1,079.1	1,699.5	2,248.4
End of the year	1,175.0	1,021.1	1,595.9	2,602.6
Return on assets				
Beginning of the year	10.0%	12.9%	7.8%	7.6%
Average for the year	9.8%	12.2%	7.5%	7.4%
End of the year	9.7%	11.5%	7.1%	7.1%
Return on equity				
Beginning of the year	30.4%	43.4%	35.0%	39.7%
Average for the year	29.4%	45.7%	37.1%	33.5%
End of the year	28.5%	48.3%	39.5%	28.9%

As stated in the beginning of this chapter, metrics are used to compare relative performance for a company over time or versus other companies. The key is consistency and examining more than one metric for one time period.

Normalized Income

In the return measures above, we consistently used net income. However when examining a company's results or calculating any profitability metrics, it may be important to consider the concept of "normalized earnings."[4] As mentioned in Chapter 2, there are numerous transactions that represent extraordinary events for the firm, beyond the day-to-day scope of operations or simply nonrecurring, one-time events. One of the purposes of financial analysis is to develop a view about the on-going business direction. Consequently, most analysts adjust net income to reflect the after-tax implications of these one-time, non-recurring, extra-ordinary income impacts. Table 7.6 presents the normalized earnings for the Hershey Company from 1999 to 2005.

In 1999, Hershey reported its highest net income ($460.3 million) until 2004, a surge of 35% over the 1998 net income and its strongest net margin ever until 2004. However, the financial performance of 1999 was driven by a $165.0 million after-tax gain from the sale of its pasta division. When that one-time event is removed, a different picture of Hershey's performance is captured by normalized income. The normalized income (or income from

---

[4] Some analysts also call normalized income *proforma income.*

TABLE 7.6	Hershey Foods Normalized Income ($ Millions)						
	1999	2000*	2001	2002	2003	2004	2005
As reported							
Sales	$3,586.2	$3,820.4	$4,137.2	$4,120.3	$4,172.6	$4,429.2	$4,836.0
Net income	$ 460.3	$ 327.8	$ 199.3	$ 391.2	$ 441.9	$ 577.9	$ 493.2
Net income margin	12.8%	8.6%	4.8%	9.5%	10.6%	13.0%	10.2%
Net income annual growth	35.0%	−28.8%	−39.2%	96.3%	13.0%	30.8%	−14.7%
Normalized income adjustments to net income							
Net income	$ 460.3	$ 327.8	$ 199.3	$ 391.2	$ 441.9	$ 577.9	$ 493.2
Restructuring charges	–	–	171.9	21.5	15.5	–	74.0
Loss (gain) sale of business	(165.0)	–	(1.1)	–	(5.7)	–	–
Cumulative effect of accounting change	–	–	–	–	7.4	–	–
Tax settlement	–	–	–	–	–	(61.1)	–
Normalized income	$ 295.3	$ 327.8	$ 370.1	$ 412.7	$ 459.1	$ 516.8	$ 567.2
Normalized income margin	8.2%	8.6%	8.9%	10.0%	11.0%	11.7%	11.7%
Normalized income growth	−13.4%	11.0%	12.9%	11.5%	11.2%	12.6%	9.8%

*The 2000 net income is restated.

continuing operations) is only $295.3 million or the first decrease (−13.4%) in Hershey's income since the 1970s. The year 1999 was a troubled year for Hershey. That was the year of the less-than-perfect computer system (ERP) implementation, which caused the corporation to miss millions of dollars in sales during the busiest time of the year.

On the other hand, as net income is reported, the year 2001 looks like a disaster for Hershey and its new CEO. Most recently, 2004 benefited from a tax settlement while 2005 suffered from a major business realignment charge.

However, when these one-time, nonrecurring gains, losses, or expenses are eliminated and the income focus is centered on continuing operating income or normalized income, a clear picture of Hershey's improving operations is seen. Normalized income continues to expand at a double digit growth rate with solid margin improvement. Notice that the adjustments are all net of their tax implications. Often it is necessary to read the footnotes to properly understand the presented charges on an after tax basis.

As an analyst, you must employ some judgment about when to use normalized income instead of net income when calculating margins or returns as discussed earlier. When the profitability metrics are analyzed, consideration should be given to the impact of reported and "normalized" income. Often it is a good idea to present profitability metrics using net income as well as normalized income.

Market-Related Metrics

The market related metrics incorporate current stock prices into the performance metrics.

Market capitalization is the current value of a company's equity based on the stock market at any point in time. In 2005, Hershey had 240.5 million shares outstanding. Based on a year-end stock price of $55.25, Hershey had a market capitalization (or simply, a "market cap") of $13.3 billion:

$$\begin{array}{l} \text{Hershey's} \\ \text{2005 Market} \\ \text{Capitalization} \end{array} = \begin{array}{l} \text{Market} \\ \text{Price per} \\ \text{Share} \end{array} \times \begin{array}{l} \text{Shares} \\ \text{Outstanding} \end{array} = \$55.25 \times 240.5 = \$13,287.6$$

The market capitalization (or current market value) of Hershey has grown tremendously over the past 6 years. In 2005, The Hershey Company became more valuable than Heinz. Because the market capitalization is an "absolute" measure, there is little relevant direct comparison that can be made except to say "larger" or "smaller." Relative measures such as growth rates or the market-related metrics discussed below, allow comparisons of a firm's stock market–based performance.

Price/earnings (P/E) ratios compare the market price per share to earnings per share. This widely used measure is simply called the P/E ratio (or P/E multiple) and is often reported within a stock listing in a daily business newspaper such as *The Wall Street Journal*. This metric is calculated as:

$$\frac{\text{Hershey's 2005}}{\text{Price/Earnings Ratio}} = \frac{\text{Market Price Per Share}}{\text{Earnings Per Share}} = \frac{\$55.25}{\$1.99} = 27.76$$

Broadly interpreted, the P/E ratio indicates that for every $1 of Hershey's earnings, the stock market (or actually an investor) is willing to pay $27.76. This is slightly higher than it was in 2000, but notably higher than for Heinz ($17.31).

P/E ratios reflect many and sometimes offsetting influences that make their interpretations difficult. Often, the higher the growth rate of the firm, the higher the P/E ratio. All else being the same, an investor is willing to pay more for every dollar of earnings assuming that dollar will grow faster. On the other hand, some regard high rates of growth as difficult to sustain so that the risk element of high growth rates would tend to push down the P/E ratio.

In the late 1990s, P/E multiples significantly increased as did the stock market in general. In 2000, with the downturn in the stock market and the economy, P/Es moderated.

Market to book ratio measures the value that financial markets attach to the management and organization of the firm as a going concern. The ratio can be calculated two different ways based on the current market price:

$$\frac{\text{Hershey's 2005 Market}}{\text{to Book Ratio}} = \frac{\text{Market Capitalization}}{\text{Stockholders' Equity}} = \frac{\$13,287.6}{\$1,021.1} = 13.01$$

or

$$\frac{\text{Hershey's 2005 Market}}{\text{to Book Ratio}} = \frac{\text{Market Price Per Share}}{\text{Book Value Per Share}} = \frac{\$55.25}{\$4.25} = 13.01$$

Book value per share is calculated by taking stockholders' equity ($1,021.1 million) divided by the number of shares outstanding (240.5 million shares) or $4.25 per share.

Hershey's market value of equity is almost $13.3 billion. The historical "book value" of stockholders' equity is a less meaningful value due to its historical nature, as discussed in Chapter 2, Financial Statements and Cash Flow.

The market to book ratio suggests that for every dollar of Hershey's net book value (or stockholders' equity) the market is willing to pay $13.01. Because the balance sheet does not capture the value of brands, U.S. sales force and distribution system, intellectual property, proprietary processes, knowledge workers, etc., some argue that the market to book ratio reflects the relative value of these intangibles. This point is dramatically seen in extremely high market to book ratios for the "new economy" companies.

Shareholder returns have become the touchstone of much financial analysis. The theme of enhancing shareholder value is the subject of many books and articles and is highlighted in the annual reports of many individual companies. The **shareholder return** measures what shareholders actually earn over a period of time. This is a widely used measure in making comparisons between the market returns among a wide range of financial instruments.

Shareholder return (also called the *holding period return*) is defined as the sum of capital appreciation and dividends over a period of time. The period of time can be monthly, quarterly, annually, or a number of years. The shareholder return for Hershey for 2005 was:

$$\frac{\text{Hershey's 2005}}{\text{Shareholder Return}} = \frac{(\text{Stock Price}_{12/31/05} - \text{Stock Price}_{12/31/04}) + \text{Dividends}_{2005}}{\text{Stock Price}_{12/31/04}}$$

$$= \frac{(\$55.25 - \$55.54) + \$0.93}{\$55.54} = \frac{\$(0.29) + \$0.93}{\$55.54} = 1.2\%$$

In 2005, the stock of Hershey provided a slight loss of 0.5% to its stockholders. In other words, if you bought the stock on December 31, 2004, you would have paid $55.54 for that share. At year-end (whether you sell your share or not), the value of that share fell $0.29 to $55.25. The 2005 capital depreciation was –0.5% (–$0.29/$55.54). In addition, you received a dividend of $0.93 throughout 2005, which represents a dividend yield of 1.7% ($0.93/$55.54). The capital appreciation plus the dividend yield provided a total shareholder return of 1.2%.

This was worse than the 2000 shareholder return of 38.0%, when Hershey righted the computer software implementation. However, Hershey's shareholder return was stronger than Heinz's return to shareholders.

Over a longer period, from 2000 to 2005, Hershey's stock price appreciated 15.1% per year (CAGR: $23.72 on December 31, 1999, and $55.25 on December 31, 2005) along with an average dividend yield of 2.0% for an average annual shareholder return from 2000 to 2005 of 17.1%!

Dividend yield represents the dividend received over a period of time compared to the initial price of the stock. In the example above:

$$\frac{\text{Hershey's}}{\text{2005 Dividend}} = \frac{\text{Dividends}_{2005}}{\text{Stock Price}_{12/31/04}} = \frac{\$0.93}{\$55.54} = 1.7\%$$
$$\text{Yield}$$

Dividend yield measures the "current return" of owning a share of stock.

Table 7.7 summarizes the metrics discussed above, their calculation, and the general direction that indicates a stronger performance.

TABLE 7.7	Performance Metrics Summary

FINANCIAL PERFORMANCE METRIC	CALCULATION	STRENGTH
Liquidity		
Current ratio	Current assets/current liabilities	Higher
Net working capital	Current assets − current liabilities	Higher
Quick ratio	(Current assets − inventories)/current liabilities	Higher
Cash ratio	Cash/current liabilities	Higher
Activity		
Total asset turnover	Sales/total assets	Higher
Fixed asset turnover	Sales/net plant, property, and equipment	Higher
Current asset turnover	Sales/current assets	Higher
Accounts receivable turnover	Sales/accounts receivable	Higher
Average collection period	365 days/accounts receivable turnover	Lower
Inventory turnover	Cost of goods sold/inventory	Higher
Inventory days outstanding	365 days/inventory turnover	Lower
Leverage		
Debt to equity	Liabilities/equity	Lower
Current debt to equity	Current liabilities/equity	Lower
Long-term debt to equity	Long-term liabilities/equity	Lower
Financial leverage	Assets/equity	Lower
Capitalization ratio	Interest bearing debt/(interest bearing debt + equity)	Lower
Long-term capitalization ratio	Long-term interest bearing debt/ (Long-term interest bearing debt + equity)	Lower
Interest coverage	Earnings before interest and tax/ interest expense	Higher
Profitability		
Net margin	Net income/sales	Higher
Pre-tax margin	Pre-tax income/sales	Higher
Operating margin	Operating income/sales	Higher
Gross margin	(Sales − cost of goods sold)/sales	Higher
Return on assets	Net income/assets	Higher
Return on net assets	Net income/(assets − non interest bearing current liabilities)	Higher
Return on equity	Net income /equity	Higher
Market		
Market capitalization	Stock price per share × shares outstanding	Higher
Price/earnings	Stock price per share/earnings per share	Higher
Market to book	Market value/book value	Higher
Shareholder returns	(Capital appreciation + dividends)/ beginning stock price	Higher
Dividend yield	Dividend per share/beginning stock price	Higher

Other Ratios and Metrics

Two other types of ratios are important for the business professional, growth metrics and cost management metrics.

Annual growth rates and compound annual growth rates over an extended period of time are illustrated in the basic financial statement analysis section. Growth can be calculated on any income statement (see Table 7.1) or balance sheet line. Five-year and 10-year growth rates provide a long-term barometer of the firm's health and its abilities to conduct business. Chapter 3, Time and Value, discusses the tools to calculate a compound annual growth rate, or CAGR.

Cost management ratios take many forms. In the basic financial statement analysis (see Table 7.1) and the profitability analysis (see Table 7.4), we look at costs as a percent of sales. Cost management stresses that lower costs (as a percent of sales) are a sign of strength. Again, balance is key. Everything must be considered including the product's positioning and the company's product strategy. A low-cost, undifferentiated product manufacturer (i.e., a commodity business) seeks the lowest cost inputs while a high value-added, differentiated product manufacturer strives to purchase high-quality raw materials for the least amount of money.

Take the case of a vehicle seat within the auto industry. A seat serves the same purpose regardless of the quality that underlies its materials and construction. At the low end, there are (1) cloth seats, then (2) leather seats, then (3) automatic leather seats, then (4) heated automatic leather seats, then (5) heated automatic leather seats with air conditioning, until you reach the ultimate (6) heated automatic leather seats with air conditioning and massage. Obviously, the cloth seat is considerably less expensive than the heated automatic leather seat with air conditioning and massage. If Mercedes Benz wished to manage its costs, cloth seats would be installed in all new vehicles. However, the customer purchasing a $100,000 plus Mercedes would be nothing short of disappointed if the vehicle had only cloth seats. After such disappointment, sales would decline. Again, any application of the metrics taken to an extreme can turn that positive position into a negative if not fully considered in the context of the business.

Examining specific, individual expenses as a percent of sales creates additional cost management measures. That is, some expenses such as research and development, advertising, depreciation, and so on are reported in the footnotes or supplemental schedules of annual reports. Each of these expenses can be calculated as a percent of sales (e.g., R&D Expense/Sales) for a historical period and compared to other firms in the industry.

Furthermore, by using non-publicly reported, internal numbers, all of the organization's functional areas can be viewed as a percent of sales and tracked over years of experience with appropriate targets.

Finally, other relative cost management ratios can be calculated based on other statistics. One of the most common of these ratios is sales per employee. Some consider the year-to-year change in this ratio as a measure of productivity.

In summary, while there is a wide array of potential metrics, the ones discussed above provide a framework for understanding virtually any financial performance metric.

DuPont Ratio Analysis

With so many numbers and so many ratios, where do we begin our diagnosis of a company's fiscal health? The DuPont ratio analysis is a systematic approach to financial analysis that was originally developed by analysts at E.I. DuPont De Nemours & Co. It does not add to our "bag" of analytical metrics, but it does help us organize the metrics to tell a clear and concise story.

Cash and equivalents	$ 6,414	$ 5,488	$ 1,648	$ 2,245
Accounts receivable, net	2,662	1,715	5,666	5,069
Inventory	32,191	29,762	5,838	5,384
Other current assets	2,557	1,889	1,253	1,224
Total current assets	43,824	38,854	14,405	13,922
Property and equipment, net	79,290	68,118	19,038	16,860
Other noncurrent assets	15,073	13,182	1,552	1,511
Total assets	$138,187	$120,154	$34,995	$32,293
Accounts payable	$ 25,373	$ 21,987	$ 6,268	$ 5,779
Accrued liabilities	13,465	12,120	2,193	1,633
Income taxes payable	1,340	1,281	374	304
Short-term debt	8,648	7,794	753	504
Total current liabilities	48,826	43,182	9,588	8,220
Long-term debt	30,171	23,258	9,119	9,034
Deferred income taxes	4,552	2,978	851	973
Other long-term liabilities	1,467	1,340	1,232	1,037
Stockholders' equity	53,171	49,396	14,205	13,029
Total liabilities and equity	$138,187	$120,154	$34,995	$32,293

7.13

In 2005, Home Depot had current assets of $4,933 million and current liabilities of $2,857 million. In 2002, Home Depot had current assets of $4,460 million and current liabilities of $2,456 million. What was the dollar amount of change in working capital? By what amount did the current ratio change?

7.14

Using the DuPont analysis of the 2005 Food Processing Industry (Table 7.9), discuss the comparative business approaches of Tootsie Roll (the best pre-tax margin) and Sara Lee Corporation (the worst pre-tax margin). How did Sara Lee almost double its Return on Equity compared to the ROE of Tootsie Roll?

7.15

Complete the balance sheet and sales data below using the following financial data:

1. Debt/net worth = 50%
2. Acid test ratio = 1.4
3. Total asset turnover = 1.6 times
4. Days sales outstanding in receivables = 30 days
5. Gross profit margin = 25%
6. Inventory turnover = 4

Cash	Payables	
Receivables	Common stock	25,000
Inventory	Retained earnings	26,000
Net, PP&E _____	Total liabilities	
Total assets	& Equity	
Sales	Cost of goods sold	

7.16

Compute a common size income statement (using net sales =100%). Compare and contrast your results.

7.17

Compute a common size balance sheet. Compare and contrast your results.

7.18

Compute the following liquidity metrics. Compare and contrast your results.

- Current Ratio
- Net working capital ($ millions)
- Quick ratio
- Cash ratio

7.19

Compute the following activity metrics. Compare and contrast your results.

- Total asset turnover
- Fixed asset turnover
- Current asset turnover
- Accounts receivable turnover
- Average collection period
- Inventory turnover
- Inventory days outstanding

7.20

Compute the following leverage metrics. Compare and your results.

- Debt to equity
- Current debt to equity
- Long-term debt to equity
- Financial leverage
- Capitalization ratio
- Long-term capitalization ratio
- Interest coverage

7.21

Compute the following leverage metrics. Compare and contrast your results.

- Net margin
- Pre-tax margin
- Operating margin
- Gross margin
- Return on assets
- Return on net assets
- Return on equity

7.22

You have obtained the following data for Wal-Mart and Target. Combine these data with the previous data (7.16–7.21) and complete the following market metrics for 2005 and 2006 only:

| | WALMART | | | TARGET | | |
	2006	2005	2004	2006	2005	2004
Year-end:						
Price per share	$46.11	$51.39	$52.31	$54.17	$53.96	$37.93
Shares outstanding-mms	4,191	4,260	4,374	889	912	919
Earnings per share	$ 2.68	$ 2.41	$ 2.07	$ 2.71	$ 2.07	$ 1.76
Dividends per share	$ 0.60	$ 0.52	$ 0.36	$ 0.38	$ 0.31	$ 0.27
Market capitalization			n/a			n/a
Price/earnings			n/a			n/a
Market to book			n/a			n/a
Shareholder returns			n/a			n/a
Dividend yield			n/a			n/a

Discuss your results.

7.23

Use the following information to compare Costco Wholesale Corporation to Wal-Mart's total performance and its Sam's Club division:

| | SALES | | | OPERATING INCOME | | |
	2004	2005	2006	2004	2005	2006
Costco	$ 42,546	$ 48,107	$ 52,935	$ 1,157	$ 1,386	$ 1,474
Wal-Mart	256,329	285,222	312,427	15,025	17,091	18,530
Sam's Club	34,537	37,119	39,798	1,126	1,280	1,385

| | NUMBER OF STORES | | |
	2004	2005	2006
Costco	397	417	433
Wal-Mart	4,906	5,289	6,141
Sam's Club	538	551	567

a. Prepare a profitability analysis including operating margin and growth in operating income:

| | OPERATING MARGIN | | | OPERATING INCOME ANNUAL GROWTH | | |
	2004	2005	2006	2004	2005	2006
Costco				n/a		
Wal-Mart				n/a		
Sam's Club				n/a		

b.   Analyze the average sales per store and its annual growth rate:

| | SALES PER STORE | | | SALES PER STORE ANNUAL GROWTH | | |
	2004	2005	2006	2004	2005	2006
Costco				n/a		
Wal-Mart				n/a		
Sam's Club				n/a		

Discuss your results.

c.   Analyze the average operating income per store and its annual growth rate:

| | OPERATING INCOME PER STORE | | | INCOME PER STORE ANNUAL GROWTH | | |
	2004	2005	2006	2004	2005	2004
Costco						
Wal-Mart						
Sam's Club						

Discuss your results.

d.   If you were the CEO of Costco, which comparison would you find more relevant (Costco to Wal-Mart or Costco to Sam's Club)?

7.24*

Using Thomson One Business School Edition, complete the following liquidity analysis table for The Hershey Company (HSY):

% of total assets	2002	2003	2004	2005	2006
Cast & ST investments					
Receivables (Net)					
Inventories—total					
Prepaid expenses					
Other current assets					
Current assets—total					
Accounts payable					
ST debt & current portion of LT debt					
Accrued payroll					
Income taxes payable					
Dividends payable					
Other current liabilities					
Current liabilities—total					
Current ratio					
Quick ratio					

a. In general, has Hershey's liquidity improved over time or over 2006?

b. In 2006, the change in what current assets drove the change in total current assets?

c. In 2006, the change in what current liabilities drove the change in total current liabilities?

7.25*

Using Thomson One Business School Edition, complete the following liquidity analysis of The Hershey Company and H.J. Heinz, Inc. (HNZ).

	HERSHEY		HEINZ	
	2002	2006	2002	2006
Current assets—total—% of sales				
Current liabilities—total—% of sales				
Current ratio				
Quick ratio				
Cash and eqt pct current assets				

a. Has Hershey become more or less liquidity since 2002?

b. Compare Hershey and Heinz for 2006. Which company is more liquid?

c. The liquidity of which company has improved the most?

7.26*

Using Thomson One Business School Edition and with The Hershey Company (Hsy) in mind, what performance metrics would you use to measure the efficiency of Hershey?

7.27*

Using Thomson One Business School Edition, compare the financial performance of Wal-Mart (Wmt), Target (Tgt) and Costco (Cost). Complete the following table and answer the following questions for the 2006.

	Wal-Mart	Target	Costco
Gross profit margin			
Operating profit margin			
Pretax margin			
Net margin			
Asset turnover			
Inventory turnover			
Inventories days held			

a. Which retailer demonstrated the most profitability?

b. Generally, the stronger the level of profitability, the stronger the company. Is that true for these retailers? How could a high margin be a negative for these retailers?

c. Why is inventory turnover important?

7.28*

Using Thomson One Business School Edition, compare the financial performance of Home Depot (HD) and Lowe's (Low). Complete the following table and
answer the following questions for the 2006.

	Home Depot	Lowe's
Gross profit margin		
Operating profit margin		
Pretax margin		
Net margin		
Asset turnover		
Inventory turnover		
Inventories days held		

a. Which retailer demonstrated the most profitability?

b. Generally, the stronger the level of profitability, the stronger the company. Is
     that true for these retailers? How could a high margin be a negative for these
     retailers?

c. Why is inventory turnover important?

7.29*

Using Thomson One Business School Edition, compare the financial performance
of the Cheese Cake Factory (CAKE) and Darden Restaurants (DRI) for 2006.

	CAKE	DRI
Net margin		
Asset turnover		
Inventory turnover		
Inventories days held		
Common equity pct total assets		

a. Which restaurant is more profitable? What could cause the difference?

b. Which restaurant turns its asset base faster? Why could that difference exist?

c. Why are inventory turnover or inventory days held an important measure for
     restaurant's? Why would some restaurants have higher inventory days held?

d. Which company is more leveraged? Explain what "common equity pct total
     assets" means.

e. Using "common equity pct total assets," calculate each restaurant's financial
     leverage.

*Note: For problems 7.24 through 7.29, go to Thomson One Business School Edition. Go to financials, financial ratios,
Thomson ratios, annual ratios for the financial performance metrics, and go to financial statements, Thomson financials,
income statement or balance sheet, and common size statements.

7.30

Using Thomson One Business School Edition, go to financials, financial ratios, SEC database ratios, and quarterly ratios for The Hershey Company (HSY). Complete the following chart for the selected financial performance metrics using the latest data. Then answer the listed questions.

	First Quarter	Second Quarter	Third Quarter	Fourth Quarter
Gross profit margin				
Operating profit margin				
Pretax margin				
Net margin				
Asset turnover				

a. Which quarter appears to be the least profitable quarter for Hershey?

b. Why would the fourth tend to be the most profitable quarter?

c. Why does the asset turnover seem a bit off? (Note: It's a computational issue.)

Working Capital Management

I n broad terms, we have already touched on aspects of current asset management. Chapter 2, Financial Statements and Cash Flows, introduces and discusses common current assets such as cash, cash equivalents (or marketable securities), accounts receivable, inventory, and other current assets, which includes prepaid expenses, deferred income tax current assets (see Chapter 4, Business Organization and Taxes), and others. Chapter 7, Financial Performance Metrics, reviews activity metrics centered on accounts receivable and inventory turnover or days outstanding. These measures are effective metrics used to judge the management of those specific accounts from a "20,000 foot level." To be discussed are methods of forecasting current assets in a strategic financial plan (Chapter 9) and anticipating the effects of working capital in capital investment analysis (Chapters 10 and 11).

Learning Outcomes

After completing this chapter, you should be able to:

1 Rationalize why good working capital management practices are important to the firm

2 Illustrate the benefits of good working capital management

3 Detail numerous aspects of working capital management

4 Prepare a cash budget from receipts and disbursements

5 Evaluate investments in accounts receivable and inventory

6 Analyze short-term borrowing preferences

In all of these other references, we deal with working capital at an elevated level of review and management. Working capital (or current assets less current liabilities) represents the investment of hundreds of billions of dollars throughout corporate America and the world, and a critical component of most individual company's balance sheets requiring focused management attention.

This chapter deals more specifically with the management of each major type of current asset and current liabilities.

Often organizations have specific departments involved in the management of working capital. For example, the treasurer's office (at a corporate level) is responsible for cash management, marketable securities investment and short-term financing. Each division or strategic business unit may have its own accounts receivable department. Goals and objectives can be established for the organization, but implemented at a local level to be more aligned with the practices of the industry or the local country. Responsibility for inventory management is often dispersed through many departments within a strategic business unit. Often, there are separate managers for each stage of inventory (raw material, goods in process, and finished goods). As inventory moves through production, each manufacturing facility could have an inventory manager and there may be several finished goods managers assigned to manage the different finished products. Once again, management targets and objectives are established at a corporate or divisional level and it is up to the operating managers to implement the established direction.

This chapter better acquaints the reader with many of the day-to-day operational decisions and techniques used to successfully manage current assets.

We begin this chapter by discussing a very handy tool for evaluating (and contrasting) operating working capital: operating and cash cycles. We then discuss current assets (accounts receivable and inventory) and end with a discussion of current liabilities (accounts payable and short-term debt).

Overview of Working Capital Management

In Chapter 7, we introduce a number of performance measures used to judge the effective use of working capital. These metrics are appropriate as an overview of the firm's ability to manage its working capital positions. Table 8.1 presents the current assets and current liabilities, along with selected income statement details for Dell Computer and Hewlett Packard (HP).[1] Notice that HP is the larger company based on sales and net working capital (current assets less current liabilities) of approximately $4.6 billion. Although Dell's sales are about 60% to 65% the size of HP's sales, its working capital practices result in working capital that was more than $14.1 billion lower in 2004 and $5.9 billion lower in 2005 when Dell's working capital was negative.

Using two of the relative liquidity measures (current ratio and quick ratio), HP is the stronger, more liquid company. But Dell's cash ratio is stronger. Hewlett Packard and Dell's liquidity deteriorate over this 2-year period.

There is a trade-off between liquidity and effective working capital management. The following illustrates the different perspectives:

---

[1]Dell is used because it is one of the acknowledged corporate leaders in supply chain management. We also use Hewlett Packard to contrast results.

Purpose	LIQUIDITY Manage Risk	EFFECTIVENESS Increase Profitability
Current Assets	↑ Invest In	↓ Limit
Current Liabilities	↓ Avoid	↑ Use
Audience	Debt holders and Other Creditors	Stockholders and Managers

Debt holders and other creditors such as suppliers are primarily interested in receiving payment for services, products, interest, and principal. Their focus is on reducing the risk that underlies the firm by assuring that there are abundant levels of cash on hand, accounts receivable from strong (also highly liquid) customers, and highly marketable inventory. Furthermore, debt holders and other creditors want to rest assured that only a limited amount of current liabilities are used in financing. Stockholders and managers seek to maximize the firm's profitability as well as the cash flow and the underlying value of the business. In order to accomplish that, management tries to limit the amount of cash that is beyond its foreseeable business demands, collect its receivables as quickly as possible without losing profitable sales, and eliminate excess inventory that is costly to store and subject to obsolescence. In order to enhance profitability, the firm will obtain its funds from the least costly sources including suppliers, employees, and short-term debt holders, which are reflected in current liabilities.

TABLE 8.1 | Computer Industry Overview

($MILLIONS)	DESIGNATION OR CALCULATION	DELL COMPUTER 2004	2005	HEWLETT PACKARD 2004	2005
Cash and equivalents	C	$ 9,807	$ 9,058	$12,974	$ 11,429
Accounts receivable	AR	3,563	4,089	10,226	11,909
Inventory	IN	459	576	7,071	5,797
Other current assets	OCA	3,068	3,983	12,630	6,940
Total current assets	CA	$16,897	$17,706	$42,901	$36,075
Current portion of LT debt	CPLTD	$ 505	$ 504	$ —	$ —
Notes payable	NP	—	—	2,511	1,831
Accounts payable	AP	8,895	9,840	9,377	10,223
Taxes payable	TP	—	—	1,709	2,367
Other current liabilities	OCL	7,330	8,636	14,991	17,039
Total current liabilities	CL	$16,730	$18,980	$28,588	$31,460
Sales	S	$49,205	$55,908	$79,905	$86,696
Cost of sales	COS	40,190	45,958	60,621	66,224
Net working capital ($ millions)	CA − CL	$ 167	$ (1,274)	$14,313	$ 4,615
Current ratio	CA/CL	1.01	0.93	1.50	1.15
Quick ratio	(CA − IN)/CL	0.98	0.90	1.25	0.96
Cash ratio	C/CL	0.59	0.48	0.45	0.36
Accounts receivable turnover	S/AR	13.81	13.67	7.81	7.28
Accounts receivable days	365/AR Turn	26.43	26.70	46.71	50.14
Inventory turnover	COS/IN	87.56	79.79	8.57	11.42
Inventory days outstanding	365/IN Turn	4.17	4.57	42.57	31.95
Accounts payable turnover	COS/AP	4.52	4.67	6.46	6.48
Accounts payable days	365/AP Turn	80.78	78.15	56.46	56.35

The Firm's Operating and Cash Cycles

Using the days outstanding information from Table 8.1 leads to creation of Table 8.2. In 2005, Dell had 4.57 days of sales invested in inventory while HP had 31.95 days invested in inventory. For Dell, it receives its raw material and component parts, and approximately four and a half days later that inventory is shipped and becomes an account receivable. HP buys its raw material inventory and over 1 month (31.95 days) later ships the final product.

On top of it, Dell takes 26.70 days to collect its accounts receivable while HP takes 50.14. Dell's business model forces "retail" consumers (such as you and I) to buy directly from them using a credit card. On average it takes a credit card company 2 to 4 days to pay any company. For business clients, Dell extends credit, which increases the overall days outstanding.

Combining the two creates what is called the **operating cycle,** or the length of time that it takes from the time raw material is received until cash is collected from its sale. So in Dell's case, the operating cycle is about 1 month (31.27 days) while the operating cycle for HP approaches 3 months (82.09 days)!

The **cash cycle** takes the operating cycle one step further by reducing the operating cycle for the number of days that the firm takes until it pays for the inventory. The cash cycle reflects how long it takes for a firm to recoup its investment of a dollar in the operations of the firm. Figure 8.1 illustrates the cash cycle for HP.

As seen earlier, HP had an operating cycle of 82.09 days but received 56.35 days of supplier financing until HP paid its suppliers. This resulted in a cash cycle of less than 1 month. So HP has 25.74 days of operations tied up in its working capital. The cash cycle is the time that it took the company to recoup its dollar of cash outflow from its normal business transactions.

Dell (see Table 8.2) provides a stark contrast with its nonconventional cash cycle. As discussed, the Dell operating cycle is an impressive 31.27 days. Furthermore, Dell takes about two and a half months (78.15 days) to pay its suppliers and finances its day-to-day operations with its suppliers' funds. An amazing feat in this industry! Dell accomplishes

TABLE 8.2	Computer Industry: Operating and Cash Cycles				
		DELL COMPUTER		HEWLETT PACKARD	
	CALCULATION	2004	2005	2004	2005
Days outstanding:					
(1) Inventory	365/IN Turn	4.17	4.57	42.57	31.95
(2) Accounts receivable	365/AR Turn	26.43	26.70	46.71	50.14
Operating cycle	(1) + (2)	30.60	31.27	89.29	82.09
(3) Accounts payable	365/AP Turn	80.78	78.15	56.46	56.35
Cash cycle	(1) + (2) − (3)	(50.18)	(46.88)	32.83	25.74
($millions)					
1 day in receivables equals:	S/365	$134.8	$153.2	$218.9	$237.5
1 day in inventory equals:	COS/365	110.1	125.9	166.1	$181.4
1 day in payables equals:	COS/365	110.1	125.9	166.1	181.4

Note: The abbreviations used in Table 8.2 are introduced in Table 8.1.

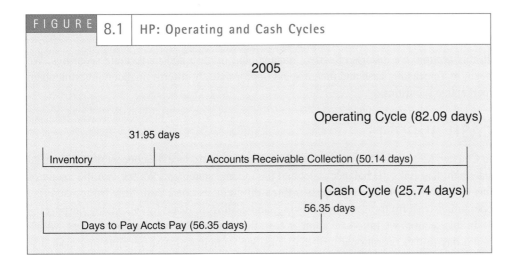

FIGURE 8.1 | HP: Operating and Cash Cycles

this with its extraordinary inventory management/production process, credit extension and collection policies, and supplier payment and relationship procedures.

Dell is extraordinary! If Dell's cash cycle paralleled HP's cash cycle, Dell would need to invest an additional $9.8 billion in the business without accounting for the extra distribution facilities necessary to house almost 1 month's worth of extra inventory (Table 8.3). When compared to HP, Dell would have an additional $3.4 billion invested in inventory. This was estimated using the number of days HP has in inventory (31.95 days, or an increase of 27.38 days) and the size (daily cost of sales) of Dell ($126 million—per Table 8.2). This procedure was applied throughout and resulted in increased investment in inventory of $3.4 billion and investment of $3.6 billion in accounts receivable with additional funding requirements of $2.8 (rounded) billion to augment for an accounts payable shortfall.

In a similar fashion, if HP could adopt the same practices, policies, and procedures as Dell, HP could withdraw $14.5 billion in working capital. Effective working capital management is just that important! While it is not possible for HP to immediately implement Dell's business approaches, HP has clear signals that it can better manage these investments.

TABLE 8.3 | Dell's Operating Investment at HP Days Outstanding

2005	DAYS OF INVESTMENT			DELL INVESTMENT ($MILLIONS)		
	DELL	HP	MORE (LESS)	ACTUAL	AT HP DAYS	MORE (LESS)
Days outstanding:						
(1) Inventory	4.57	31.95	27.38	$ 576.0	$4,022.9	$3,446.9
(2) Accounts receivable	26.70	50.14	23.44	4,089.0	7,680.1	3,591.1
Operating cycle	31.27	82.09				
Gross operating working capital investment				4,665.0	11,703.0	7,038.0
(3) Accounts payable	78.15	56.35	21.80	9,840.0	7,095.2	2,744.8
Cash cycle	(46.88)	25.74				
Net operating working capital investment				$(5,175.0)	$4,607.8	$9,782.8

Cash and Marketable Securities

In this section, we discuss effective management of cash and marketable securities. We begin by forecasting cash and then discuss appropriate short-term financial investments in marketable securities.

CASH BUDGETS

In Chapter 2, Financial Statements and Cash Flow, we introduce the concept of the financial statement that links the balance sheet and the income statement. We see that the nature of this cash flow statement encompasses three different sections: cash flow from (used for) operations, cash from (used for) investing, and cash from (used for) financing purposes.

In this section, we introduce another cash flow analysis called the **cash budget**, which is the day-to-day operational tool that considers anticipated cash receipts and cash disbursements. Will the company have excess cash above its day-to-day operating needs that can be invested in marketable securities? Or will the company be in a cash shortfall position and require short-term funds to see it through from one month to the next?

The cash budget is a projection or forecast of future cash receipts and cash disbursements over some time interval. It enables the financial executive to determine whether and when additional financing will be required and provides lead time for taking the actions necessary to provide for future financing. The cash budget also supplies information on whether and when the firm may have positive cash inflows available for a number of alternative uses.

The cash budget is similar to a personal budget. From time to time, you may prepare a personal monthly budget. This personal budget lists all of the anticipated receipts, such as the paycheck or dividend/interest income receipts. It also includes all monthly recurring disbursements, such as grocery store bills, credit card payments, home mortgage, car loans, etc., and any nonrecurring monthly payments for real estate taxes, annual life insurance payment, and so on. A personal budget lists anticipated cash receipts against cash disbursements. If it is anticipated to be a good month, you will have excess cash at the end. If it is a month of heavy cash outflow, you may need to borrow on a personal line of credit or transfer money from a savings account.

Within major corporations, the controller's office is responsible for preparing accurate financial statements that are bound by US GAAP. This includes the cash flow statement that is examined in Chapter 2. This cash flow statement conforms to all US GAAP standards and is called the indirect approach, in the sense that it results from the income statement and the balance sheet.

It is the treasurer's office, more specifically an assistant treasurer or cash manager, that is responsible for preparing a cash budget prepared directly from the organization's anticipated cash receipts and cash disbursements. Hence, this type of cash budget is referred to as a "direct" cash flow statement.

In the end, the indirect and direct cash flow statements must yield the same result, that is, the cash generated (used) over a specific time period.

OVERVIEW OF CASH BUDGETS

The cash budget we will use as an example considers the amount of cash flow for the next 6 months. It anticipates the amount of cash collected from accounts receivable and other sources as well as all cash disbursements for raw materials, labor, wages, etc. The result shows the cash manager the amount of cash that will be available for investment if there is excess cash generated in any given month, or the cash budget will highlight any cash shortfall that needs to be accommodated from a company's line of credit or other sources.

TABLE 8.4	Sales and Cash Collections								
	NOVEMBER	DECEMBER	JANUARY	FEBRUARY	MARCH	APRIL	MAY	JUNE	JULY
1. Sales	$1,200	$1,600	$ 900	$ 600	$1,000	$1,500	$1,800	$1,200	
Accounts receivable collection:									
Collections based on sales from:									
2. Current month 10.0%			90	60	100	150	180	120	
3. Prior month 60.0%			960	540	360	600	900	1,080	
4. Two months ago 30.0%			360	480	270	180	300	450	
5. Total collections from receivables			1,410	1,080	730	930	1,380	1,650	
Other collections:									
6. Sale of idle equipment				250					
7. Total collections			$1,410	$1,330	$ 730	$ 930	$1,380	$1,650	

In practice, the financial manager will create more detailed cash budgets on a weekly or even daily basis. The daily based cash budgets consider the heavier daily cash collections at the beginning of the week and the anticipated accounts payable disbursements made at the end of the week along with specific timing for payroll, loan payments, and so on.

To facilitate this illustration, we have created three separate parts to the cash budget: cash receipts (Table 8.4), cash disbursements (Table 8.5), and net cash flow including balances for cash and short-term debt (Table 8.6).

Cash Receipts As we have seen throughout, sales forecasts for product lines and for the firm as a whole are critical in every firm. The sales forecast drives the anticipated cash receipts.

In Table 8.4, we set forth a schedule of sales and cash collections. The organization sells on a 30-day basis (i.e., customers have 30 days to pay). From accounts receivable experience, the firm can estimate that, on average, 10% of the sales are collected in the month of the sale, 60% in the month following the sale, and 30% during the second month following the sales.

Row 1 in Table 8.4 presents the sales forecast. Row 2 sets forth collections made in the month of sale or 10% of January's projected sales. Row 3 lists the collections for sales from the prior month. In this example, 60% of December's sales are collected in January. In Row 4, the collections during the second month after sales would be 30% or $360 (30% of

TABLE 8.5	Purchases and Cash Disbursements								
	NOVEMBER	DECEMBER	JANUARY	FEBRUARY	MARCH	APRIL	MAY	JUNE	JULY
1. Sales			$900	$ 600	$1,000	$1,500	$1,800	$1,200	$1,000
2. Raw material purchase	40.0% of sales$_{(t+1)}$	360	240	400	600	720	480	400	
3. Raw material payment			360	240	400	600	720	480	
4. Production wages	50.0% of raw mtl purchase$_{(t)}$		120	200	300	360	240	200	
5. Administrative salaries			100	100	100	100	100	100	
6. Other operating expenses			40	40	40	40	40	40	
7. Income tax disbursement					60	120		120	
8. Capital expenditure payment					125		150		
9. Dividend payment			75			75			
10. Purchase of business line					500				
11. Debt repayment				1,200					
12 Total disbursements			$695	$1,780	$1,525	$1,295	$1,250	$ 940	

TABLE 8.6	Net Cash Flow and Account Balances					
	JANUARY	FEBRUARY	MARCH	APRIL	MAY	JUNE
1. Total collections	$1,410	$1,330	$ 730	$ 930	$1,380	$1,650
2. Total disbursements	695	1,780	1,525	1,295	1,250	940
3. Net cash flow	$ 715	$ (450)	$ (795)	$(365)	$ 130	$ 710
Account Balances						
4. Beginning balance—cash	$ 225	$ 940	$ 490	$ 50	$ 50	$ 50
5. + Net cash flow	715	(450)	(795)	(365)	130	710
6. Preliminary balance of cash	940	490	(305)	(315)	180	760
7. Required short-term borrowing	—	—	355	365	—	—
8. Payment of short-term borrowing	—	—	—	—	(130)	(590)
9. Ending balance—cash	$ 940	$ 490	$ 50	$ 50	$ 50	$ 170
10. Ending balance—short-term debt	$ —	$ —	$ 355	$ 720	$ 590	$ —

November's actual sales of $1,200). Because there were no other collections in January, total collections for January would be $1,410. The process repeats itself for each month.

Other Cash Receipts As illustrated on Table 8.4, a company can have cash receipts from other sources than just sales and the business operations of the firm. Usually, however, these other cash receipts are one-time events or arise from financing. The following is a partial list:

• Sale of idle equipment

• Sale of an operation or discontinued business

• Sale or maturing of a long-term investment

• Issuance of debt—short-term or long-term

• Issuance of equity—preferred or common

Most receipts are generated as a function of the business of the organization.

Cash Disbursements In Table 8.5, we consider the schedule of cash disbursements. Notice, the cash disbursement schedule is comprised of monthly, recurring, business-driven expenditures and other periodic disbursements that recur on a quarterly or semiannual basis as well as nonrecurring expenditures.

Monthly Recurring Disbursements Similar to the cash receipt schedule, Table 8.5 starts with the sales forecast. Purchases of raw material have to be made in anticipation of sales. Based on the firm's experience, purchases represent about 40% of next month's sales, on average. We assume further that purchases are paid for in the month after the purchase. Taking the Row 2 figures and shifting them forward 1 month gives the cash outflows for payment of raw material purchases shown in Row 3.

In January, marketing anticipates $900 of sales. In order to have enough finished goods available to satisfy this projected sales level, the company purchases raw material and completes the production in the month before the anticipated sale. Consequently, the company purchases $360 ($900 × 40%) of raw material in December (Line 2 of Table 8.5). Assuming payment terms of "net 30 days," the December raw material purchases are paid in January, as shown on Line 3. So the process continues for each month.

To convert the raw materials into final product, the company hires production employees. Due to the seasonality of the business, the company pays overtime to its full-time production team as well as augments the workforce with part-time personnel on a flexible work schedule and temporary laborers. The direct labor costs are 50% of this month's raw material purchases. We also assume that wages and other expenses are paid during the month that they are incurred. Hence Row 4, which represents cash outlays for production wages, is 50% of purchases made this month.

To illustrate further for the month of January on Table 8.5, February's sales are anticipated to be $600, which requires the support of a $240 purchase of raw materials in January. This raw material is converted to finished product at a direct labor cost of $120 (50% of $240), which is paid at the end of January to the production workers.

We assume that administrative salaries (Row 5) and other operating expenses (Row 6) remain fairly constant over this 6-month period. These expenses are more or less fixed by their very nature and are not a function of seasonal sales patterns. On the other hand, long-term company trends would certainly influence both expenses.

Lines 7 through 11 of Table 8.5 present five common other disbursements encountered by many organizations. Line 12 totals all of the monthly disbursements (lines 3 through 11).

Disbursements versus Expenses   The following three points must be remembered when comparing disbursements and expenses:

- Not all cash disbursements are expenses.

- Not all expenses are cash disbursements.

- Expenses and cash disbursements can be different dollar amounts.

These three points are discussed below.

Not all disbursements are expenses. The first five disbursements on Table 8.5 are related to the various expenses incurred by the firm. The last four line items, however, are indeed cash outflows but are not considered "expenses." The payment for capital equipment or the purchase of a line of business are reinvestments into the business and are solely reflected on the balance sheet with no immediate income statement impact. Likewise, dividend payments and debt repayments are financing transactions and represent adjustments in the capital structure of the firm.

Not all expenses are cash disbursements. When computing the company's gross margin (sales less cost of goods sold [COGS]), COGS includes expenditures for raw material, direct labor, and depreciation. There is no cash flow related to depreciation because it is a non-cash expense. The indirect cash flow statement, which is compiled from the income statement and balance sheet as in Chapter 2, began with net income and added back the non-cash expense. The direct cash flow statement, however, does not begin with net income. It only includes cash flows! Consequently, there is no need to add back depreciation.

Expenses and cash disbursements can be different dollar amounts. Some recognized expenses may have a portion that requires a cash payment and another portion that is deferred or accrued and involves no cash payment at the time of the expense. Warranty expense and income taxes are two examples wherein US GAAP requires immediate expensing of the full amount despite the actual cash payments. The cash budget only considers the cash payments.

The final section completes the discussion of the cash budget. Table 8.6 brings together the monthly cash collections and disbursements.

Net Cash Flow and Cash Requirements Lines 1 and 2 of Table 8.6 summarize the results of the previous two tables. The difference between total cash receipts and total cash expenditures is the net cash flow shown in Line 3.

For January, the company is expecting to collect $1,410 while paying out $695 for a net cash flow of $715. This amount of cash flow increases the beginning balance of cash (which is also the December ending balance of cash of $225) to a January ending balance of $940.

The January ending balance becomes the beginning cash balance for February, which is reduced by the $450 February cash shortfall. This leaves a February ending balance of $490.

For March, expenditures exceed collections by $795, which for the first time in this example creates a negative preliminary balance of cash (Line 6). Assuming that the company is required by its bank to have a $50 balance in cash at all times, leaves the company $355 short of cash. The company must arrange short-term borrowing to the tune of $355 in borrowing for the month of March (Line 7). At the end of March, the company has a cash balance of $50 (Line 9) and a short-term debt balance of $355 (Line 10).

The month of April has a cash shortfall of $365, which requires additional short-term borrowing. So the month of April ends with a cash balance of $50 and short-term borrowings of $720 ($355 opening balance plus $365 of additional borrowing in April).

During May, positive cash flows return. The cash flow is immediately applied to reduce the existing short-term debt balance to $590. In June, the company is projecting a $710 positive net cash flow, which is used to pay off the short-term debt. The company also ends June with a cash balance of $170.

As presented, the analysis did not include the impact of interest income earned on cash balances or interest expense which is paid on borrowings. The analysis could be easily expanded to include that impact. We concentrated on strictly an operating cash budget.

The cash budget facilitates banking relationships. The treasurer of this company could anticipate in January that the company would have a cash shortfall in March lasting for 3 months. In January, borrowing alternatives can be anticipated and evaluated. Short-term lines of credit can be arranged with a bank well in advance of the actual need of the line. If the shortfall appears to be nontemporary, the treasurer can evaluate intermediate or long-term financing alternatives and begin making arrangements for such financing.

REASONS FOR HOLDING CASH

Cash and marketable securities are discussed together because marketable securities can be quickly converted into cash with only small transactions costs and hence can be regarded as a form of backup cash. When we refer to cash itself, we are using cash in the broad sense of demand deposits (checking accounts) and money market accounts as well as currency holdings.

Because returns from marketable securities are generally lower returns than from operations, we are generally not advocates of cash management practices that horde amounts of cash. We believe that large cash balances should be paid to stockholders if the company has no alternative business investments. However, the 2004 list of top-30 companies that hold the largest cash balances (Table 8.7) indicates that many successful companies hold significant amounts of cash. We are the first to admit that we cannot argue with success! For example, Microsoft heads the lists with almost $60.6 billion of cash and marketable securities. This figure accounts for about 66% of Microsoft's assets, and the amount is more than 1.65 times its revenue.

Businesses and individuals have four primary motives for holding cash and cash backup in the form of marketable securities: (1) the transactions motive, (2) the precautionary motive, (3) to meet future needs, and (4) to satisfy compensating balance requirements. Each company assesses the cash requirements to satisfy these criteria:

TABLE 8.7	2004 Cash and Cash Equivalents ($millions)			
			% OF	
COMPANY NAME	CASH AND EQUIVALENTS	GICS IND GROUP	ASSETS	REVENUE
1. Microsoft Corp	$60,592	Software & Services	65.6%	164.5%
2. General Motors Corp	35,993	Automobiles & Components	7.5%	18.9%
3. Ford Motor Co	32,860	Automobiles & Components	10.8%	19.1%
4. General Electric Co	23,234	Capital Goods	3.1%	15.4%
5. Exxon Mobil Corp	23,135	Energy	11.8%	8.8%
6. Pfizer Inc	19,893	Pharmaceuticals & Biotechnology	16.1%	37.9%
7. General Motors Corp	19,803	Automobiles & Components	10.9%	12.6%
8. Ford Motor Co	19,492	Automobiles & Components	15.0%	13.2%
9. Aetna Inc	18,020	Health Care Equipment & Services	42.8%	90.5%
10. Intel Corp	17,172	Semiconductors & Semiconductor	35.7%	50.2%
11. Wellpoint Inc	15,044	Health Care Equipment & Services	37.9%	72.3%
12. Hewlett-Packard Co	12,974	Technology Hardware & Equipment	17.0%	16.2%
13. Johnson & Johnson	12,884	Pharmaceuticals & Biotechnology	24.2%	27.2%
14. Chevron Corp	10,742	Energy	11.5%	7.5%
15. Motorola Inc	10,708	Technology Hardware & Equipment	34.7%	34.2%
16. IBM Corp	10,570	Technology Hardware & Equipment	9.7%	11.0%
17. Dell Inc	9,807	Technology Hardware & Equipment	42.2%	19.9%
18. Cisco Systems Inc	8,669	Technology Hardware & Equipment	24.4%	39.3%
19. Bristol-Myers Squibb Co	7,474	Pharmaceuticals & Biotechnology	24.6%	38.6%
20. Lilly (Eli) & Co	7,464	Pharmaceuticals & Biotechnology	30.0%	53.9%
21. Merck & Co	7,090	Pharmaceuticals & Biotechnology	16.7%	30.3%
22. Coca-Cola Co	6,768	Food Beverage & Tobacco	21.6%	30.8%
23. Applied Materials Inc	6,578	Semiconductors & Semiconductor	54.4%	82.1%
24. Wyeth	6,489	Pharmaceuticals & Biotechnology	19.3%	37.4%
25. Texas Instruments Inc	6,358	Semiconductors & Semiconductor	39.0%	50.5%
26. Time Warner Inc	6,289	Media	5.1%	14.9%
27. Qualcomm Inc	5,982	Technology Hardware & Equipment	55.3%	122.6%
28. Procter & Gamble Co	5,892	Household & Personal Products	10.3%	11.5%
29. Schering-Plough	5,835	Pharmaceuticals & Biotechnology	36.7%	70.5%
30. Amgen Inc	5,808	Pharmaceuticals & Biotechnology	19.9%	55.1%

- Transactions Motive. The principal motive for holding cash is to enable the firm to conduct its ordinary business—making purchases and sales.

- Precautionary Motive. The precautionary motive for holding safety stocks of cash relates primarily to the predictability of cash inflows and outflows.

- Future Needs. The firm's cash and marketable securities accounts may rise to rather sizable levels on a temporary basis as funds are accumulated to meet specific future needs. Notice from Table 8.7, there are 10 technology firms and 8 pharmaceutical firms. These companies will invest significant amounts of money in research and development, new product introduction, and geographic expansion. Cash and marketable securities also represent a "war chest" or pool of funds from which a firm may draw quickly to meet a short-term opportunity, including acquisitions. This is sometimes referred to as the speculative motive for holding cash.

- Compensating Balance Requirements. Business firms pay for commercial banking services in part by direct fees and sometimes in part by maintaining compensating balances at the bank. Compensating balances represent the minimum levels that the firm agrees to maintain in its checking account with the bank.

The decisions with regard to holding cash and marketable securities require careful analysis in order to balance the rationales noted above with the lower returns.

MARKETABLE SECURITIES

As seen in Chapter 6, the higher the risk, the higher is the required return. Thus, in building a marketable securities portfolio, corporate treasurers must evaluate the risk-return trade-offs. To guard against uncertain and fluctuating inflows and outflows, corporate treasurers emphasize relatively short-term, highly liquid, and highly secure (limited risk) assets in constructing the marketable securities portfolio.

When evaluating an investment in marketable securities, you must consider the underlying financial risk, the interest rate risk, the purchasing power risk, the liquidity or marketability of that security, and the taxability of its returns:

- Financial Risk. The greater the degree to which the price and returns of a security fluctuate, the greater is the financial risk—the risk of default. While U.S. government securities do not carry the risk of default, securities issued by state and local governments, financial institutions, and other corporations are considered to be subject to some degree of default risk.

- Interest Rate Risk. Changes in the general level of interest rates will cause the prices of securities to fluctuate. As seen in Chapter 5, the shorter the maturity of a debt instrument, the smaller the size of fluctuations in its price.

- Purchasing Power Risk. Changes in general price levels affect the purchasing power of both the principal and the income from investments in securities. Once again, short-term securities are less impacted by inflationary considerations.

- Liquidity or Marketability Risk. The potential decline from a security's quoted market price when the security is sold is its liquidity or marketability risk. Liquidity risk is related to the breadth or thinness of the market for a security.

Taxability The tax position of a firm's marketable securities portfolio is influenced by the overall tax position of a firm. The market yields on a security will reflect the total supply and demand (Chapter 5, discussion on market segmentation), but each corporation or individual analyzes the investments return on an after-tax basis given their tax position. Consequently, tax circumstances enter into determining the supply and demand on an after tax basis. For example, let's say that the overall tax rate in the United States is 30% and taxable securities pay a 10% rate of return, a similar tax-free security will provide a return of 7.0%. That is:

$$\text{Tax-Free Return} = \text{Taxable Return} \times (1 - \text{Tax Rate})$$
$$= 10.0\% \ (1 - 30\%) = 7.0\%$$

However, the position of the individual firm may be different from the overall pattern. If a firm's tax rate is less (more) than 30%, it will prefer the 10% taxable return (the 7.0% tax-free return). For example, if a firm is expected to report a loss and thus have no taxes to pay, the 10% pre-tax rate is the same return on an after-tax basis for this firm. For a firm that pays the full marginal federal corporate tax rate (35%), a tax-free return of 7.0 is preferred to a taxable return of 10.0% less 35% taxes, or 6.5% [10.0% × (1 − 35%)] after-tax return.

Investment Alternatives The major investments meeting the objectives just set forth are listed in Table 8.8. These represent the highly liquid, short-term securities issued by the U.S. government and by the very strongest business corporations, domestic and foreign banks, and other financial institutions.

TABLE 8.8 | Marketable Securities

TYPE OF SECURITY	ISSUER	DESCRIPTION
GOVERNMENT		
Treasury bills (T bills)	U.S. Treasury	Obligations of the U.S. government. exempt from state and local income taxes.
U.S. Treasury notes and bonds	U.S. Treasury	Original maturities of more than 1 year, but maturing issues have high liquidity. Also exempt from state and local income taxes.
Federal agency issues	Federal government agencies	Notes issued by corporations and agencies created by the U.S. government.
Short-term tax exempts	State and local governments	Notes issued by states, municipalities, local housing agencies, and urban renewal agencies. Exempt from state and local taxes and from the federal income tax.
CORPORATIONS		
Commercial paper	Highest creditworthy firms	Unsecured notes issued by finance companies, bank holding companies, and industrial firms.
Bonds of domestic and foreign corporations (highest grade)	High creditworthy firms	Original maturities of more than 1 year, but issues near maturity behave similarly to short-term instruments.
BANKS AND OTHER FINANCIAL INSTITUTIONS		
Negotiable certificates of deposit (CDs)	Commercial banks	Receipts for time deposits at commercial banks that can be sold before maturity.
Bankers'acceptances	Banks	Time drafts (or orders to pay) issued by a business firm (usually an importer) that have been accepted by a bank that guarantees payment.
Eurodollars	Foreign banks	Dollar-denominated time deposits at overseas banks.
Repurchase agreements (repos)	Bank or security dealer	Sale of government securities by a bank or securities dealer with a simultaneous agreement to repurchase.
Money market mutual funds	Portfolio management company	Investment companies whose portfolios are limited to short-term money market instruments.
Money market preferred stock funds	Portfolio management company	Duration is relatively short with dividends paid at maturity. Seventy percent of dividend income can be excluded from income for tax purposes by corporations.

There are a number of conventional choices for marketable securities. There are also a number of new and engineered instruments available. The financial manager must maintain contact with developments in the markets for short- and long-term financial instruments. Your specific choice of marketable securities must keep in mind the objective of short-term investing—preserve capital and provide liquidity—not add a few basis points!

The choice of marketable securities should also match the timing determined by the monthly cash budget and more refined daily cash budget. The underlying forecasts are the key to effective cash management models.

Accounts Receivable Management Policies and Practices

While every organization has an accounts receivable function, most employees will not spend any portion of their careers in the accounts receivable department. However, professionals working in marketing, sales, treasury, and other financial areas may be involved with establishing the company's accounts receivable policies and practices. A careful operational (and even strategic) balance must be struck. Force your customers to immediately pay for everything, and sales will fall. Extend credit to all customers, and sales will flourish but bad debt expense will grow and income and cash flow will lag.

Accounts receivable management contains three interrelated phases. The first phase is establishing credit terms based on industry standards and broad economic forces as well as specific company creditworthiness. Within this phase is the need to analyze and decide to whom credit will be granted, how much will be extended, and under what terms and conditions. The second phase of accounts receivable management relates to the monitoring and tracking of customer payments and outstanding receivable balances. The third and final phase is the collection process.

CREDIT BACKGROUND AND ASSESSMENT

Credit terms specify the period for which credit is extended and the discount, if any, for early payment. For example, if a firm's credit terms to all approved customers are stated as 2/10 net 30, then a 2% discount from the stated sales price is granted if payment is made within 10 days, and the entire amount is due 30 days from the invoice date if the discount is not taken. These are very common credit terms. If the terms are stated "net 60," this indicates that no discount is offered and that the bill is due and payable 60 days after the invoice date.

The following discussion outlines five macro-level aspects of credit terms. As discussed, industry circumstances and practices play an important role in establishing a credit policy.

- Economic Nature of the Product. Commodities with high (low) sales turnover are sold on relatively short (long) credit terms. Grocery stores require immediate payment, whereas jewelry or furniture retailers may extend credit for 6 months or longer.

- Seller Circumstances. The seller's operational position, financial strength, and size all play a general role in establishing credit terms. Additionally, in many industries, variations in credit terms can be used as a sales promotion device, especially when the industry has excess capacity. In some cases, some management teams use extended credit terms as a sales stimulus. A customer who would normally buy products next month (the first month of the new fiscal year) under standard terms of 2/10 net 30, could be induced to buy those products in the last month of the current fiscal year by extending terms for 30 days to 2/40 net 60. Not only could this policy endanger sound credit management, it also endangers sound business management as the current fiscal year becomes effectively a 13-month year, and next year becomes an 11-month year unless the practice continues every year. This type of practice can be easily spotted as the company's fourth quarter accounts receivable spike.

- Buyer Circumstances. Financially sound retailers who sell on credit may, in turn, receive slightly longer terms. Some classes of retailers regarded as selling in particularly risky areas (such as clothing) receive extended credit terms but are offered large discounts to encourage early payment.

- Credit Period. Lengthening the credit period stimulates sales, but there is a cost to tying up funds in receivables. For example, if a firm changes its terms from net 30 to net 60, the average receivables for the year may rise from $100,000 to $250,000—the increase caused partly by the longer credit terms and partly by the larger volume of sales. The optimal credit period is determined by the point where marginal profits on increased sales are offset by the costs of carrying the higher amounts of accounts receivable.

- Cash Discounts. A cash discount is a reduction in price based on payment within a specified period.

From the general and macro-level to the specific company and micro-level, the next section discusses credit analysis for a specific company.

CREDIT ANALYSIS

Credit analysis seeks to determine who will receive credit and under what conditions. Two aspects of the process should be distinguished: the new customer versus continuing accounts. The second is much less difficult because experience provides considerable information. Credit analysis obviously is a tougher problem for new customers. Two main approaches are taken.

One is to determine how the prospective customer has behaved with other suppliers. This kind of information can be obtained at a price from specialized financial information agencies: Credit Interchange, a system developed by the National Association of Credit Management, and credit-reporting agencies, such as Dun & Bradstreet (D&B).

A second approach is for the firm to perform its own analysis to make its own independent decision. When trade credit is involved, the firm is both selling goods and extending credit. The two activities are intertwined. How the customer behaves may depend in part on how the sales organization has been treating the customer. In addition, the collection policies and practices of the seller may adversely affect customers. Hence a selling firm may decide not to rely completely on the experience of other selling firms. There may be an opportunity to develop a new customer relationship.

In making its own independent assessment, a firm traditionally considers the five Cs of credit: character, capacity, capital, collateral, and conditions:

- *Character* has to do with the probability that a customer will try to honor his or her obligations.

- *Capacity* describes an objective judgment of the customer's ability to pay via customer financial statement analysis (liquidity and profitability analysis) as well as physical observation of the customer's plant or store.

- *Capital* is measured by the general financial position of the firm as indicated by a financial ratio analysis, with special leverage analysis.

- *Collateral* is represented by assets the customer offers as a pledge for security of the credit extended.

- The fifth C, *conditions,* has to do with the impact of general economic trends on the firm or special developments in certain areas of the economy that may affect the customer's ability to meet the obligation.

After analysis of the customer's credit information, the seller systematically evaluates the data, ultimately leading to a "credit score" in quantitative terms. It involves a numerical measure to estimate the probability that a customer will pay on time. The better the score, the more credit is extended.

Over the past decade, many individual retail outlets abandoned their own credit cards (which were introduced to promote customer loyalty) in favor of Visa, MasterCard, and American Express. In this way, the companies no longer are in the credit scoring and granting business. Those tasks have been outsourced to the major credit card companies for fees averaging about 2% to 4% of the purchase amount.

Credit scoring can be based on relatively simple rules. For example, if a firm has a current ratio of less than one to one and if ownership equity is less than what is owed to creditors, the customer is likely to be a slow pay and therefore credit may be denied.

Most credit scoring is more involved and brings together the "five C assessment," credit reports, and customer financial analysis. A customer is objectively and subjectively graded on many individual aspects that comprise these three credit scoring dimensions to derive a credit score:

	POTENTIAL SCORE
Five C Assessment	0–100
Credit Reports	0–100
Customer Financial Analysis	0–100
Total Score	0–300

Each customer is scored. In this case, each dimension has a potential score of 100 points for a total score of up to 300 points. The customer's final score determines the specific credit granting policy.

Based on years of experience with the credit scores of other customers, a seller may set up risk categories:

Credit score:	240–300	210–240	Under 210
Terms	2/10 net 30	2/10 net 30	Cash only
Account limits	$250,000	$50,000	$0
Review period	Every 2 years	Annually	Customer request

The strongest customers (credit scores of 240 or more) will see terms of 2/10 net 30 and have an account limit of $250,000. Also, their account will be reviewed every 2 years or as conditions warrant. The third category must pay cash for a purchase. This category of customer can request a credit reevaluation when its profile becomes stronger.

After a company establishes a credit history with your firm, it is easier to monitor their payment pattern and judge their five Cs assessment. However, attention must still be paid to avoid any unpleasant surprises brought about by specific issues within your customer or the customer's industry.

ACCOUNTS RECEIVABLE MONITORING

After credit standards have been established, creditworthiness of potential customers assessed, and credit extension decisions implemented, the firm must monitor, manage, and collect from its customer. To elaborate this second phase, we discuss accounts receivable monitoring and management.

Earlier in this chapter and in Chapter 7, we discuss the general management tools of accounts receivable turnover (sales divided by accounts receivable) and days outstanding (365 divided by the accounts receivable turnover). Whereas these tools are excellent for industry comparisons, historical trend analysis, and standard setting, more refined versions of these metrics are used for day-to-day operations.

MONITORING ACCOUNTS RECEIVABLE

By its nature, credit management lends itself to the use of computer controls. Software, that is a fully integrated part of Enterprise Resource Planning (ERP) software or even stand-alone accounts receivable systems, facilitates the collection, compilation, storage, analysis, and retrieval of information. Because accurate information on fund flows is critical to good credit management, efficient information processing is important. Particular controls can be set up to monitor account delinquency or how close the account balance is to the established maximum line of credit. The software can periodically flag past-due accounts for the credit manager's attention. Based on payment activity, account balances, and predetermined credit limits, a customer's order can be accepted, rejected, or flagged for further analysis. Industry trends can also be monitored.

This information facilitates interaction with the customer and enables the credit management department to communicate promptly and effectively with other divisions in its own company as well as with general management. Thus, the effectiveness of the credit department has been greatly enhanced by making feasible computer-generated information flows that would otherwise be too expensive and time consuming to develop.

ACCOUNTS RECEIVABLE COLLECTION

In short, you want to collect your accounts receivable as quickly as possible. To minimize your collection time, you need to manage your customers' payments as well as streamline the processes surrounding cash collection. These two topics are discussed in this section.

Methods to Speed Customer Collections Typically, a customer places an order and receives the goods or services. Shortly after receipt, an invoice is issued that starts the credit collection clock. Assuming credit terms of 2/10 net 30, a customer has 30 days from the invoice date to pay their invoice. After 30 days, the account is overdue and the seller is subject to delinquent cash receipts or nonpayment.

There are common techniques used by many organizations to collect on delinquent accounts. If 30 days pass with no payment, most companies allow a 2- or 3-day grace period. At the end of that grace period, if payment is received, the account is considered "paid in full" and no further action is required, although the delay is noted in the customer's record and may ultimately lower the customer's internal credit rating. However, if after this grace period payment still is not received, a second invoice is reissued for "immediate payment." The invoice often is accompanied by a polite letter reminding the customer that the account is over due. The letter also provides contact information to call the seller's credit department to discuss payment terms. This is followed by a phone call and a more pointed

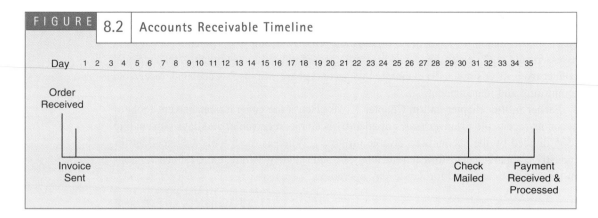

FIGURE 8.2 | Accounts Receivable Timeline

letter demanding payment and outlining the legal steps that will be taken if the seller is not contacted and arrangements made for the payment amount.

Each seller must decide how aggressive or casual to be in credit collection practices. This of course is dependent upon whether the seller or buyer holds more power. Who needs whom more—the seller or the buyer? A small company may get excellent national exposure through Wal-Mart stores and therefore may be a bit more relaxed on its credit policy when it comes to Wal-Mart. In this case, the small company needs Wal-Mart significantly more than Wal-Mart needs this supplier. Also, Wal-Mart is a very creditworthy buyer, and the small supplier knows that the credit risk is minimal.

On the other hand, this small supplier may sell to a local, one-store, "Mom and Pop" retail company, whose credit-worthiness is often under pressure. In this case, the power is somewhat neutral and the small supplier will more aggressively seek to collect its receivables from this type of customer.

Speeding Collections through Process Improvement When a customer makes a payment by check, that check needs to be mailed to the seller, the seller needs to process and deposit the check, and finally the check needs to clear the bank in order for the money to be made available to the seller. Each step along the way involves delays of 1 or 2 or more days. With each day's delay, the company is investing potentially millions of dollars needlessly.

This systematic delay is known as *float* (Figure 8.2). Specifically:

- **Mail float** is the time (number of days) that the check is "in the mail." It is the time from when the check was mailed by the customer until the check was received by the seller.

- **Processing float** is the time required by the seller to process the customer's records. It is the time from when the payment was received by the seller until it was deposited in the bank.

- **Clearing float** is the time required for the check to clear the bank system. It is the time from when the check was deposited in the seller's bank until the seller's bank makes the funds available to the seller. This step involves the process whereby the seller's bank obtains funds from the customer's account at the customer's bank.

A responsibility of the credit manager is to minimize the time spent in each of these delays.

Technology has facilitated great strides in efficient payment collection processes. In fact, electronic payments eliminate the mail float delay in its entirety. Technology enables internal process improvement, matching of payment amounts with invoices, quality of record keeping, and the overall process.

Invoice Accuracy   One of the major issues in accounts receivable management that has emerged in the past few years is related to the quality of invoices. In our simple example, a customer purchased and received $10,000 worth of product, an invoice was issued for $10,000, and payment was made for $10,000 (or $9,800 for payment within the discount period). The transaction was simple and straightforward, but far from many experiences today.

Shipping and billing errors do occur. Partial orders are shipped and products that were not ordered are shipped and invoiced. Broken or malfunctioning products may be received by the customer. Seasonal products may have arrived late in the season and be unwanted in part or in total. Customers may misunderstand pricing and promotional incentives offered by the company and may take the discount well after the discount period.

Some customers are strict about receiving their orders. They specify the day and even the hour that they expect a shipment. If a shipment is not received at that time, the customer "bills" the seller through a deduction to the invoice. At the BMW plant in South Carolina, if a supplier misses a deliver slot and the plant runs out of a part, that supplier is "charged" $10,000 for every minute the production line is shut down.

All of these circumstances give rise to discrepancies. Successful management and timely resolution of these discrepancies is a critical component of the credit manager's responsibilities and directly affects the bottom line and cash flow of every company.

Inventory Management

Manufacturing firms generally have three kinds of inventories: (1) raw materials, (2) work in process, and (3) finished goods. The level of raw materials inventories is influenced by anticipated production, seasonality of production, reliability of sources of supply, and the efficiency of scheduling purchases and production operations. Work in-process inventory is strongly influenced by the length of the production period, which is the time between placing raw material in production and completing the finished product.

The level of finished goods inventory is a matter of coordinating production and sales. Realistic sales forecast and accompanying production schedules are critical to success. Understate the sales forecast and production schedule, and shortages of the finished good may occur, leading to missed sales opportunities and "stockout" costs. A sales forecast that is too ambitious results in unsold finished goods inventory.

Our primary focus in this section is control of investment in inventories. Most firms decentralize responsibility for inventory management by the kind of inventory. For example, in the case of Hershey, raw material consisted of milk, cocoa, sugar, and hundreds of other ingredients. There is an individual person responsible for each of the three critical raw materials and someone else who has responsibility for all of the other ingredients. Additionally, plants had responsibility for the actual physical handling of the raw material. This extends to goods in process, where plant management and divisional manufacturing shoulder the responsibility of effective handling and processing. Finished product inventory often continues to be the responsibility of manufacturing (distribution center management) along with marketing.

While each business unit and organization needs to streamline its own inventory management processes, our focus is a central view and analysis of inventory. Any procedure that can reduce the investment required to generate a given sales volume will have a beneficial effect on the firm's rate of return and hence on the value of the firm, as seen at the start of this chapter where the inventory position of Dell Computer is introduced.

TABLE 8.9	Inventory Days Outstanding Retail Category		
DAYS OUTSTANDING	AVERAGE	MINIMUM	MAXIMUM
Restaurants	14.58	3.88	73.90
Food retail	34.03	6.62	90.63
Internet retail	44.21	19.47	77.65
Home improvement retail	57.13	25.26	83.72
Catalog retail	59.58	13.42	123.89
Drug retail	63.90	40.50	80.89
Computer & electronics retail	72.29	6.67	174.49
General merchandise stores	88.82	34.37	173.80
Apparel retail	90.95	28.58	260.06
Department stores	109.04	72.80	132.47
Specialty stores	123.40	15.88	434.16

CONTROLLING INVESTMENTS IN INVENTORIES

Although wide variations occur by inventory and company, inventory days outstanding are generally concentrated in the 50- to 100-day range. The major determinants of investment in inventory are (1) level of sales, (2) length and technical nature of the production processes (including the availability and complexity of raw materials), and (3) durability versus perishability (the style factors) in the end product.

Table 8.9 presents the average, minimum, and maximum days outstanding for companies within the retail industry, including restaurants. It is no surprise that the lowest number of inventory days outstanding is found in restaurants and food stores. Quality meats, fruits, and vegetables are in part determined by freshness and can only be kept on hand for limited periods. Inventories in general merchandise stores, department stores, and specialty stores are significantly longer due to the non-perishability of the stock. Also, in these cases, the customer has limited loyalty and will purchase the good where it is available. In fact, out of this group, Tiffany Jewelers has the largest days outstanding, 434.2 days. While jewelry is non-perishable, it is also a highly profitable product. Part of the added "cost" of running a successful jewelry store is carrying enough varied inventory to satisfy the customers' demands. If the product is not in the store, Tiffany's could ultimately lose the sale to a competitor.

In other industries, such as the machinery manufacturing industries, inventories are large because of the long work in-process period. However, inventories in oil and gas production are low, because raw materials and goods in process are small and finished goods are quickly sold.

ENTERPRISE RESOURCE PLANNING SYSTEMS

Enterprise Resource Planning (ERP) systems, such as SAP, Oracle, Baan, and PeopleSoft, are enabling (or perhaps demanding) the focus on working capital. These innovative technology tools are fully integrated, all-encompassing computer systems that span all processes within an organization while combining financial reporting as a natural process of the work flow. The major business processes center around the supply-side (production planning, procurement, and manufacturing) and the demand-side (new product introduction, sales, marketing, and logistics) with strong infrastructure support in the areas of accounting, finance, and human resources.

Often, the implementation of an ERP requires reengineering the organization or at least reengineering some of the major processes. One of the marked process improvements from an ERP comes in the form of enhanced communications among the various "functions" of the business. All data are shared on a consistent basis without the need for the data to be "rekeyed" into another system. All information is self-contained. For example, under some traditional processes: sales (or marketing) initiate a sales projection, which feeds to production planning (for production scheduling) and finance (for outlooks or plans). Production planning may arbitrarily reduce those projections because of the sales department's usually optimist outlook. Procurement and manufacturing, which receives the production schedule from production planning may further "tweak" the projections. Finance could also adjust the sales projections to reflect senior management's "tasking" for more aggressive sales' levels. Potentially, there could be three to five short-term, disjointed operating projections within one organization.

Within an ERP, only one sales forecast is prepared. That sales forecast is agreed to by all parties from the outset and is shared across all processes. The quality and reliability of that forecast becomes the responsibility of all parties involved in the process, and the accuracy of those short-term projections becomes fundamental to all business processes.

These short-term sales forecasts drive raw material procurement, manufacturing processes and production scheduling, and logistic efforts of the firm. It is through these enablers that inventory can be better managed and investments in working capital optimized.

INVENTORY MANAGEMENT AND VALUE CHAIN REENGINEERING

Important developments impacting the fundamental philosophy of inventory management and value chain management methods have taken place. Production methods have experienced fundamental changes. The assembly lines with long production runs for a given product have been yielding to an emphasis on flexible manufacturing systems. More intense competition to produce better products coupled with consumer desires for increased variety and product change have led to an emphasis on flexible manufacturing systems. Financial management of receivables and inventories has had to join in the effort of firms seeking to improve their competitive position.

Relationships have been forged between suppliers and customers to wring the costs out of the value chain. More information with suppliers is exchanged with greater frequency. Many manufacturing firms share production schedules with suppliers and customers. On the inbound side, raw material suppliers know when they must deliver the required amount of raw materials. On the outbound customer side, a manufacturing firm will deliver optimum quantities of inventory at the right time to help minimize the investment in inventory both for itself and for its customers. Enhanced technology (e.g., Internet, ERP systems) has facilitated such reengineering.

We emphasize that what is involved is an entire philosophic approach to manufacturing processes rather than inventory management alone. Changes in inventory methods could not have been made without rethinking the entire approach to manufacturing methods. In turn, these new approaches to manufacturing processes, including inventory planning and control methods, require a change in practices and attitudes of workers and plant supervision. Fundamental changes in the approach to human resource management are, therefore, also involved. Much new learning in management systems is required. Here is another example of our basic approach to managerial finance. Models are useful tools. But much more important is the broader philosophic approach to management systems. Financial management must be integrated with the broader aspects of operating management as well as with the broader framework of the firm's strategic planning.

Short-Term Financing

In this section we discuss the use of short-term financing for both permanent and temporary financing. We begin with a discussion of the "matching principle" in which financing sources are paired with the type of asset that is being financed. We discuss common short-term borrowing sources, understanding the advantages and disadvantages of each source, calculating the cost of such financing, and end with a discussion of secured short-term financing.

FINANCING CURRENT AND FIXED ASSETS

Figure 8.3 presents a greatly simplified view of the firm's assets. It shows a firm that is growing over time both in terms of fixed assets and current assets. But current assets are further broken out to reveal permanent current assets and temporary current assets.

The phrase "permanent current assets" seems like a contradiction in terms in that the phrase "current asset" implies an asset that is converted to cash within 1 year. Our use of the term "permanent" represents a permanent level of current assets. For example, if a company holds 30 days of inventory on hand at any one point, the specific inventory items are manufactured, stored, sold; manufactured, stored, sold; and so on. The specific inventory itself is constantly being sold and replenished. However, the firm continually has 30 days of inventory on hand. The inventory investment amount is not changing. Likewise, individual accounts receivable are collected, but the continuous operations of the firm will result in rising investments in receivables. As sales increase, the investment in receivables and inventories must grow proportionately. A steadily rising level of sales over the years will result in permanent increases in current assets.

Seasonal patterns exist for many businesses and business cycles cause asset requirements to fluctuate. Temporary seasonal fluctuations in sales would be followed by similar fluctuations in current asset requirements.

Figure 8.3 illustrates this phenomenon. There exists a level of fixed assets that is required by the business to produce product and house employees. This grows over time and in support of sales. The middle layer represents this layer of permanent current asset investment. Finally, the top portion of Figure 8.3 represents the fluctuating aspects of working capital.

The question that needs to be addressed is how to finance the asset base. That is, how much of the financing should be long-term and how much should be short-term? In this case,

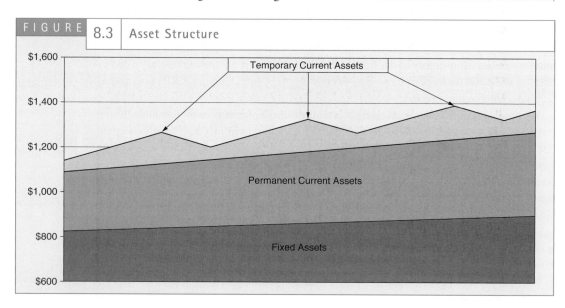

FIGURE 8.3 | Asset Structure

long-term financing includes long-term debt and stockholders' equity. In general, many companies attempt to match the type of financing with the type of asset, which is known as the "matching principle." There is no right or wrong answer. It is a matter of company policy, industry practice, and the current economic climate.

TRADE CREDIT

In the ordinary course of events, a firm buys its supplies and materials on credit from other firms, recording the liability as accounts payable. Accounts payable, or trade credit, is the largest single category of short-term credit, representing about one third of the current liabilities of nonfinancial corporations. This percentage is somewhat larger for small firms.

Trade credit is a spontaneous source of financing in that it arises from ordinary business transactions. This is the opposite side of an accounts receivable. This is a source of financing that your suppliers provide to you.

For example, suppose a firm makes average purchases of $2,000 a day on terms of net 30. On the average, it will owe 30 times $2,000, or $60,000, to its suppliers. If its sales and, consequently, its purchases double, accounts payable will also double—to $120,000. The firm will have spontaneously generated an additional $60,000 of financing. Similarly, if the terms of credit are extended from 30 to 40 days, accounts payable will expand from $60,000 to $80,000; thus, lengthening the average payment period generates additional financing.

Advantages of Trade Credit as a Source of Financing Trade credit, a customary part of doing business in most industries, is convenient and informal. A firm that does not qualify for credit from a financial institution may receive trade credit because previous experience has familiarized the seller with the creditworthiness of the customer. The seller knows the merchandising practices of the industry and is usually in a good position to judge the capacity of the customer and the risk of selling on credit. The amount of trade credit fluctuates with the buyer's purchases, subject to any established credit limits.

Trade credit is usually thought of as "free financing" in that there is no explicit interest expense associated with trade credit. However, foregoing a discount is an opportunity cost of trade credit. With terms of 2/10 net 30, when you do not pay within the first 10 days, you forego the 2% discount. The question to ask is what is the cost of foregoing this discount?

If the customer makes a $10,000 purchase with terms of 2/10 net 30, then the customer could satisfy the supplier and the customer's obligation by paying $9,800 within the first 10 days. If the customer waits until day 30 to pay, then the full amount is due and payable. From a broader perspective, the customer owes $9,800 (the discounted price). If the customer chooses not to pay within 10 days, the company requires a payment of $9,800 (discounted price) plus a $200 "fee" or interest for waiting between day 10 and day 30. In this light, there is a cost for not taking the discount offered by a supplier. In this example, the cost is $200 for passing up the discount. To determine this cost as a percentage, for a one-time skipped discount, we simplistically calculate:

$$\text{Cost of Not Taking a Discount} = (\text{Stated Rate per Period})$$
$$\times (\text{Number of Periods per Year})$$

where:

$$\text{Stated Rate per Period} = \frac{\text{Discount \%}}{(1 - \text{Discount \%})} = \frac{0.02}{(1 - .02)} = \frac{0.02}{0.98} = 0.204 \text{ or } 2.04\%$$

$$\text{Number of Periods per Year} = \frac{365 \text{ days}}{(\text{Due Data} - \text{Discount Period})} = \frac{365}{(30 - 10)} = \frac{365}{20} = 18.25$$

For the period of 20 days, which is the number of days between the discount period and the due date, the cost to borrow is 2.04% per period. However, there are 18.25 twenty-day periods in the year. Consequently, annualized cost of passing on this discount is 37.23%:

$$\text{Cost of Not Taking a Discount} = (0.0204) \times (18.25) = 37.23\%$$

So if the customer is able to borrow from another source at less than 37.23%, then the customer should do so to take advantage of the available discount. To illustrate the cost to borrow at 37.23% for 20 days:

$$
\begin{aligned}
\text{Cost to Borrow} &= \$9,800 \times (0.3723/365 \times 20) \\
&= \$9,800 \times (0.00102 \times 20) \\
&= \$9,800 \times (0.0204) \\
&= \$200
\end{aligned}
$$

Indeed, this is a very expensive way to borrow! Notice, also, if the discount was higher or if the difference between the due date and the discount period were smaller, the cost to borrow would be even higher.

The annualized cost is better represented as the effective annual rate of interest:

$$\text{EAR} = (1 + (\text{Stated Rate per Period}))^{\text{Number of Periods per Year}} - 1$$
$$\text{EAR} = (1 + (0.0204))^{18.25} - 1 = (1.0204)^{18.25} - 1 = 44.56\%$$

If the company can borrow funds at less than 44.56%, it should arrange such financing because it is less expensive than foregoing this trade discount.

Even though trade credit is "free" financing, the cost of missing discounts is high. Other financing sources should be established so that discounts are not missed.

SHORT-TERM FINANCING BY COMMERCIAL BANKS

Commercial bank borrowing, which appears on the balance sheet as notes payable, bank borrowings, or short-term debt, is second in importance to trade credit as a source of short-term financing. Banks occupy a pivotal position in the short-term and intermediate-term money markets. Their influence is greater than it appears to be from the dollar amounts they lend, because the banks provide nonspontaneous funds. As a firm's financing needs increase, it requests additional funds from banks. If the request is denied, often the alternative is to slow down the rate of growth or to cut back operations.

Characteristics of Loans from Commercial Banks In the following discussion, the main characteristics of lending patterns of commercial banks are briefly described.

- Forms of Loans. A single loan obtained from a bank by a business firm is not different in principle from a loan obtained by an individual. The loan is obtained by signing a conventional promissory note. Repayment is made in a lump sum at maturity (when the note is due) or in installments throughout the life of the loan.

A **line of credit** is an agreement between the bank and the borrower concerning the maximum loan balance the bank will allow the borrower. For example, a bank loan officer may indicate to a company's treasurer that the bank regards the firm as "good" for up to $80,000 for the forthcoming year. Subsequently, the treasurer "takes down" $15,000 of the total line of $80,000. Before repayment of the $15,000, the firm may borrow additional amounts up to the total of $80,000. The borrower may be required to pay 1/4% to 1/2% per annum for the unused line of credit.

- *Size of Customers.* Banks make loans to firms of all sizes. By dollar amount, the major proportion of loans from commercial banks is obtained by large firms. But by number of loans, small- and medium-sized firms account for more than half of bank loans. Local commercial banks are the main suppliers of most financial services used by such firms. These services include lines of credit, motor vehicle loans, equipment loans, leasing, and mortgage lending.

- *Maturity.* Commercial banks concentrate on the short-term lending market. Short-term loans make up about two thirds of bank loans by dollar amount, whereas term loans (loans with maturities longer than 1 year) make up only one third.

- *Security.* If a potential borrower is a questionable credit risk, or if the firm's financing needs exceed the amount that the loan officer of the bank considers prudent on an unsecured basis, some form of security is required. More than half the dollar value of bank loans is secured. (The forms of security are described later in this chapter.) In terms of the number of bank loans, two thirds are secured through the endorsement of a third party (such as the Small Business Administration), who guarantees the loan payment in the event the borrower defaults.

- *Compensating Balances.* Banks typically require that a regular borrower maintain an average checking account balance equal to 15% or 20% of the outstanding loan. These balances, commonly called compensating balances, are a method of raising the effective interest rate. For example, if a firm needs $80,000 to pay off outstanding obligations but must maintain a 20% compensating balance, it must borrow $100,000 in order to obtain the required $80,000. If the stated interest rate is 5%, the effective cost is actually 6.25% ($5,000 divided by $80,000).

- *Repayment of Bank Loans.* Because most bank deposits are subject to withdrawal on demand, commercial banks seek to prevent firms from using bank credit for permanent financing. A bank, therefore, may require its borrowers to "clean up" their short-term bank loans for at least 1 month each year. If a firm is unable to become free of bank debt at least part of each year, it is using bank financing for permanent needs and should develop additional sources of long-term or permanent financing.

Cost of Commercial Bank Loans   Loans from commercial banks vary in cost, with the effective rate depending on the characteristics of the firm and the level of interest rates in the economy. If the firm can qualify as a prime risk because of its size and financial strength, the rate of interest will be at the "prime" interest rate. The prime rate is a bank-set interest rate that is set above the discount rate charged by Federal Reserve banks to commercial banks. On the other hand, a small firm with below-average financial ratios may be required to provide collateral security and to pay an effective rate of interest of 2 to 3 (or more) points above the prime rate.

Determination of the effective, or true, rate of interest on a loan depends on the stated rate of interest and the lender's method of charging interest. There are three common ways to calculate interest. Each is discussed below.

- *"Regular" Interest.* If the interest is paid at the maturity of the loan, the stated rate of interest is the effective rate of interest. For example, on a $20,000 loan for 1 year at 10%, the interest is $2,000 at the end of the one year period for an effective cost of 10%.

$$\text{Regular Loan} = \frac{\text{Interest}}{\text{Borrowed Amount}} = \frac{\$2,000}{\$20,000} = 10\%$$

- *Interest with a Compensating Balance.* If there is a 20% compensating balance requirement, the effective interest rate is 12.5%.

$$\text{Compensating Balance} = \frac{\text{Interest Rate}}{(1 - \text{Compensating Balance})} = \frac{0.10}{(1 - 0.20)} = 12.5\%$$

Or to obtain $20,000, you are required to borrow $25,000 as follows:

$$\text{Amount to Borrow} = \frac{\text{Required Amount}}{(1 - \text{Compensating Balance})} = \frac{\$20,000}{(1 - 0.20)} = \frac{\$20,000}{0.80} = \$25,000$$

So the company borrows $25,000, keeps $5,000 on hand at the bank as a compensating balance, and walks away with $20,000, but it pays 10% interest on the full $25,000 ($2,500) for an effective cost of 12.5% ($2,500/$20,000).

- *Discounted Interest.* If the bank deducts the interest in advance (discounts the loan), the effective rate of interest is increased to 11.1%:

$$\text{Discounted Loan} = \frac{\text{Interest Rate}}{(1 - \text{Interest Rate})} = \frac{0.10}{(1 - 0.10)} = 11.1\%$$

To obtain $20,000 via a 10% discounted loan, the company would need to borrow $22,222.22, keep $2,222.22 at the bank as a compensating balance, walk away with the needed $20,000, and pay 11.11% ($2,222.22/$20,000.00) for its funds.

Installment Loan The loans discussed above are characterized by repayment of the loan principal at maturity. Under the installment method, principal payments are made periodically (e.g., monthly) over the term of the loan. On a 1-year loan, the borrower has the full amount of the money only during the first month and by the beginning of the last month has already paid back approximately eleven-twelfths of the loan. Thus, the effective annual rate (or EAR) of interest on an installment loan is higher than the stated rate (or the annual percentage rate [APR]).

Installment loans can be arranged in three ways. First is the standard installment loan as is considered in Chapter 3, Time and Value. In this case, the borrower secures financing at the beginning of the year and makes monthly payments that include both interest and principal. To continue the illustration from above where we borrowed $20,000 for 1 year at 10%:

1. Installment Loan—Using a financial calculator:

Amount borrowed:	$20,000	= PV
Number of payments:	12 months	= n
Stated interest rate:	10%/12 months	= 0.833333% per month = r%

Compute the monthly payment:

Monthly payment:	$1,758.32	= PMT

Also, using the equations developed in Chapter 3, we can solve for the payment amount as:

$$\text{Monthly Payment} = \$20,000 \left[\frac{1 - (1 + (r/q))^{-t}}{(r/q)} \right]$$

As in Chapter 3, "q" represents the number of periods per year. Solving, for the effective annual rate (EAR), we find an EAR of 10.47%:

$$EAR = (1 + r/q)^q - 1 = (1 + 0.10/12)^{12} - 1 = 0.1047$$

This is the pertinent cost to compare to the other costs of financing.

Table 8.10 presents a loan amortization schedule for this 12-month installment loan.

2. Add-on Interest Installment Loan. The net loan proceeds are the same as the face amount of the loan, but interest for the full term of the loan is added to the loan principal to calculate the monthly installment payments:

Amount borrowed:	$20,000
Stated interest rate:	10%
Add-on interest:	$2,000

Total loan amount:	$22,000
Monthly installment ($22,000/12):	$1,833.33

TABLE 8.10	Monthly Installment Loan				
MONTH	BEGINNING BALANCE	PAYMENT	0.833333% INTEREST	PRINCIPAL	ENDING BALANCE
January	$20,000.00	$1,758.32	$166.67	$1,591.65	$18,408.35
February	18,408.35	1,758.32	153.40	1,604.92	16,803.43
March	16,803.43	1,758.32	140.03	1,618.29	15,185.14
April	15,185.14	1,758.32	126.54	1,631.78	13,553.36
May	13,553.36	1,758.32	112.94	1,645.38	11,907.99
June	11,907.99	1,758.32	99.23	1,659.09	10,248.90
July	10,248.90	1,758.32	85.41	1,672.91	8,575.99
August	8,575.99	1,758.32	71.47	1,686.85	6,889.13
September	6,889.13	1,758.32	57.41	1,700.91	5,188.22
October	5,188.22	1,758.32	43.24	1,715.08	3,473.14
November	3,473.14	1,758.32	28.94	1,729.38	1,743.76
December	1,743.76	1,758.29	14.53	1,743.76	0.00

The computed interest rate, r_c, implicit in these terms can be found as

Amount borrowed:	$20,000	= PV
Number of payments:	12 months	= n
Monthly payment	$1,833.33	= PMT

Compute the monthly payment:

Stated interest rate: 1.4976% per month or 19.5279% per year

Solving, for the effective annual rate (EAR), we find:

$$EAR = (1 + .014976)^{12} - 1 = 0.195279$$

This is significantly more than the 10% stated rate and is the pertinent cost to compare to the other costs of financing. In this case, the cost of financing (19.5279%) is almost double the stated rate because the interest is calculated on the original amount of the loan, not on the amount actually outstanding (the declining balance).

Interest is calculated by the installment method on most consumer loans (e.g., automobile loans), but the installment method is not often used for business loans.

SHORT-TERM FINANCING USING COMMERCIAL PAPER

Commercial paper (CP) consists of unsecured promissory notes issued by only the largest, most creditworthy firms to finance short-term credit needs. CP has become an increasingly important source of short-term financing for many types of corporations, including utilities, finance companies, insurance companies, bank holding companies, and manufacturing companies. It is often sold directly to investors, including business corporations, commercial banks, insurance companies, and state and local government units. However, commercial paper dealers also function as intermediaries in the commercial paper market.

Maturities of commercial paper generally vary from 1 day to 1 year, with an average of about 5 months. The rates on prime commercial paper vary, but they are generally about half a percent below those on prime business loans.

SECURED SHORT-TERM FINANCING

Given a choice, it is ordinarily better to borrow on an unsecured basis, because the administrative costs of secured loans are often high. However, a potential borrower's credit rating may not be sufficiently strong to justify the loan. If the loan can be secured by some form of collateral to be claimed by the lender in the event of default, then the lender may extend credit to an otherwise unacceptable firm. Similarly, a firm that can borrow on an unsecured basis may elect to use security if it finds that this will induce lenders to quote a lower interest rate.

As discussed in previous chapters, real property (land and buildings) and equipment are good forms of collateral, but they are generally used as security for long-term loans. The bulk of secured short-term business borrowing involves the pledge of short-term assets—accounts receivable or inventories.

Accounts receivable financing involves either the assigning of receivables or the selling of receivables (factoring). Assigning (or pledging) or discounting of accounts receivable is characterized by the fact that the lender not only has a lien on the receivables but also has recourse to the borrower (seller of the goods); if the person or firm that bought the goods does not pay, the selling firm must take the loss. In other words, the risk of default on the accounts receivable pledged remains with the borrower.

Factoring, or selling accounts receivable, involves the purchase of accounts receivable by the lender without recourse to the borrower (seller of the goods). The buyer of the goods is notified of the transfer and makes payment directly to the lender. Because the factoring firm assumes the risk of default on bad accounts, it must do the credit checking. Accordingly, factors provide not only money but also a credit department for the borrower.

If a firm is a relatively good credit risk, the mere existence of the inventory may be a sufficient basis for receiving an unsecured loan. If the firm is a relatively poor risk, the lending institution may insist on security, which often takes the form of a blanket lien against the inventory. Alternatively, trust receipts, field warehouse financing, or collateral certificates can be used to secure loans.

The blanket inventory lien gives the lending institution a lien against all inventories of the borrower. However, the borrower is free to sell the inventories; thus, the value of the collateral can be reduced.

On the other hand, a trust receipt is an instrument acknowledging that the borrower holds the specific goods in trust for the lender and that proceeds from the sale of such goods are transmitted daily to the lender. Auto dealer financing is the best example of trust receipt financing. This may be accompanied by a field warehouse agent who acts as the controlling supervisory of this specific inventory on behalf of the lender. A collateral certificate guarantees the existence of the amount of inventory pledged as loan collateral. It is a statement issued periodically to the lender by a third party, who certifies that the inventory exists and that it will be available if needed.

summary

This chapter covers numerous topics related to working capital management. The operating cycle shows how long it takes for a firm to turn inventory into collected cash. The cash cycle shows how many days it takes the company to recover its cash after paying for the inventory. Both are effective tools to understand, manage, and assess a firm's working capital policy.

Effective cash management begins with a detailed cash budget. Monthly and even daily cash budgets are routinely prepared. These budgets are fully integrated with the operations of the firm and anticipate cash receipts and cash disbursements. Excess cash can be invested in marketable securities and any short-term borrowing needs identified well before the need arises.

In establishing a credit policy, a firm formulates its credit standards and its credit terms. Credit standards that are too strict will lose sales; credit standards that are too relaxed will result in excessive bad debt losses. To determine optimal credit standards, the firm relates the marginal costs of credit to the marginal profits on the increased sales. Credit analyses and the evaluations of prospective customers typically include assessment of the five Cs, outside credit reports, and analysis of financial ratios. Accounts receivable systems provide valuable information to credit managers, who can better assist sales and marketing in customer relations.

Inventories—raw materials, work in-process, and finished goods—are necessary in most businesses. New systems for controlling the level of inventories have been designed and enterprise resource planning (ERP) software has enabled many of the advances in this area. In addition, ERPs and the Internet facilitate closer "just-in-time" inventory relationships with suppliers and customers via the sharing of material requirements for both inbound and outbound areas.

Short-term financing considerations begin with a major policy question about the relationships among types of assets and the way these assets are financed. In our judgment, the financing of current assets should recognize that some portion bears a constant relationship to sales, so that this portion represents "permanent" investment. This calls for financing the permanent portion of current assets with the permanent portion of short-term debt (the spontaneous portion provided by accounts payable) and by long-term debt and equity financing to the extent required.

Short-term credit is debt originally scheduled for repayment within 1 year. The three major sources of short-term credit are trade credit among firms, loans from commercial banks, and commercial paper. Trade credit (accounts payable) is a spontaneous source of financing in that it arises from ordinary business transactions and the largest single category of short-term credit. Some commercial bank loans are securitized with a company's inventories and accounts receivable.

Questions

8.1   How can better methods of communication reduce the necessity for firms to hold large cash balances?

8.2   Discuss the business impact of Dell's business model on its suppliers. That is, Dell holds virtually no raw materials and takes more than 2 months to pay its suppliers. Why are suppliers eager to do business with Dell?

8.3   If you prepare a personal budget, do you prepare it in line with the cash flow statement (the cash budget) as presented in this chapter or do you prepare it similar to the cash flow statement discussed in Chapter 2? Explain.

8.4   Many Enterprise Resource Planning (ERP) systems force sales, marketing, production, logistics, and finance to use the same inventory projection. This often leads to major savings and inventory reduction. Explain why that is the case.

8.5   Give your reaction to this statement: Merely increasing the level of current asset holdings does not necessarily reduce the riskiness of the firm. Rather, the composition of the current assets, whether highly liquid or highly illiquid, is the important consideration.

8.6   Indicate whether each of the following changes will raise or lower the cost of a firm's accounts receivable financing and explain why this occurs:

   a.   The firm eases up on its credit standards in order to increase sales.

b. The firm institutes a policy of refusing to make credit sales if the amount of the purchase (invoice) is below $100. Previously, about 40% of all invoices were below $100.

c. The firm agrees to give recourse to the finance company for all defaults.

d. A firm without a recourse arrangement changes its terms of trade from net 30 to net 90.

8.7 Would a firm that manufactures specialized machinery for a few large customers be more likely to use a form of inventory financing or a form of accounts receivable financing? Why?

8.8 Many firms that find themselves with temporary surplus cash invest these funds in Treasury bills. Because Treasury bills frequently have the lowest yield of any investment security, why are they chosen as investments?

8.9 Assume that a firm sells on terms of net 30 and that its accounts are, on the average, 30 days overdue. What will its investment in receivables be if its annual credit sales are approximately $1,460,000?

8.10 Evaluate this statement: It is difficult to judge the performance of many of our employees but not that of the credit manager. If the credit manager is performing perfectly, credit losses are zero; the higher our losses (as a percent of sales), the worse is the performance.

8.11 KDWS Corporation's 2006 sales were $73.22 million. In April 2006, the accounts receivable balance was $5.35 million; by July 2006, accounts receivable had more than doubled to $11.18 million. Calculate the days' sales outstanding for each period. Did the increase necessarily represent a problem for KDWS?

8.12 What are the probable effects of the following on inventory holdings?

a. Manufacture of a part formerly purchased from an outside supplier

b. Greater use of air freight

c. Increase, from 7 to 17, in the number of styles produced

d. Large price reductions to your firm from a manufacturer of bathing suits if the suits are purchased in December and January.

8.13 Would you expect high inventory or low inventory levels (in terms of days outstanding) in the following companies or industries?

a. Tiffany's or jewelry stores

b. Iowa Beef or meat packing

c. Kroger or the grocery store business

d. Boeing or the aircraft building industry

e. Google or Internet companies

8.14 How does the seasonal nature of a firm's sales influence the decision about the amount of short-term credit in the financial structure?

8.15 What is the advantage of matching the maturities of assets and liabilities? What are the disadvantages?

8.16 It is inevitable that firms will obtain a certain amount of their financing in the form of trade credit, which is (to some extent) a free source of funds. What are some other reasons for firms to use trade credit?

Problems

8.1

Indicate the effects of the transactions listed below on each of the following: total current assets, working capital, current ratio, and net profit. Use " + " to indicate an increase, " – " to indicate a decrease, and "O" to indicate no effect. State necessary assumptions and assume an initial current ratio of more than 1 to 1.

	Total Current Assets	Working Capital	Current Ratio	Net Income
1. Cash is acquired through issuance of additional common stock.				
2. Merchandise is sold for cash.				
3. Federal income tax due for the previous year is paid.				
4. A fixed asset is sold for less than book value.				
5. A fixed asset is sold for more than book value.				
6. Merchandise is sold on credit.				
7. Payment is made to trade creditors for previous purchases.				
8. A cash dividend is declared and paid.				
9. Cash is obtained through short-term bank loans.				
10. Short-term notes receivable are sold at a discount.				
11. A profitable firm increases its fixed assets depreciation allowance account.				
12. Marketable securities are sold below cost.				
13. Uncollectible accounts are written off against the allowance account.				
14. Advances are made to employees.				
15. Current operating expenses are paid.				
16. Short-term promissory notes are issued to trade creditors for prior purchases.				
17. Ten-year notes are issued to pay off accounts payable.				
18. A wholly depreciated asset is retired.				
19. Accounts receivable are collected.				
20. A stock dividend is declared and paid.				
21. Equipment is purchased with short-term notes.				
22. The allowance for doubtful accounts is increased.				
23. Merchandise is purchased on credit.				
24. The estimated taxes payable are increased.				

8.2

You have obtained the following information for a number of retail outlets. Calculate the operating cycle, cash cycle, and the necessary components.

2006–$ millions	Wal-Mart	Target	Costco
Sales	$315,654	$52,620	$52,935
Cost of sales	240,391	34,927	46,347
Accounts receivable	2,662	5,666	400
Inventory	32,191	5,838	4,015
Accounts payable	25,373	6,268	4,214

Discuss the similarities and differences. On a relative basis, how much more does Target have invested than Costco in each component?

8.3

You have obtained the following information for Tiffany's and Whole Foods Market. Calculate the operating cycle, cash cycle, and the necessary components.

2006–$000s	Tiffany's	Whole Foods
Sales	$2,395,153	$4,701,289
Cost of sales	1,052,813	3,052,184
Accounts receivable	142,294	66,682
Inventory	1,060,164	174,848
Accounts payable	202,646	103,348

Discuss the similarities and differences. Why is there such a significant difference? What would happen if each company tried to adopt the working capital practices of the other company?

8.4

You have obtained the following information for Colgate, Johnson & Johnson, and Proctor & Gamble. Calculate the operating cycle, cash cycle, and the necessary components.

2005–$millions	Colgate	J&J	P&G
Sales	$11,397	$50,514	$56,741
Cost of sales	5,192	13,954	27,804
Accounts receivable	1,309	7,010	4,185
Inventory	856	3,959	5,006
Accounts payable	876	4,315	3,804

Discuss the similarities and differences. Discuss the paths that lead them to similar results.

8.5 to 8.8. Provide the necessary information and data to prepare a cash budget.

8.5

The Waterford Group had the following sales for October to December and projects the following monthly sales for January to June.

	($000's)
Actual Sales	
October	$100
November	250
December	400
Projected Sales	
January	250
February	300
March	400
April	500
May	600
June	600
July	450
August	400

It is estimated that 10% of sales are collected in the month of sale, 60% of sales are collected in the month after the sale, 28% are collected two months after the sale, and 2% go uncollected. Prepare a projected cash receipt schedule for January to June. In addition, Waterford receives royalty payments of $25 per month. Starting in June, the royalties increase to $40 per month.

Prepare a cash receipt schedule for January through June.

8.6

It is further estimated that raw materials are purchased two months before it is required to meet sales demand. Raw material costs 50% of anticipated sales. Payment is made in full 1 month after the raw material is purchased. So $150 of raw material for December ($300 sales) was purchased in October, and paid for in November. Production labor is incurred and paid during the month of production which is 1 month before the sales are made. Production labor is assumed to be 20% of that month's sales. For example, in November, production labor of $60 (20% of December's $300 sales) was incurred and paid.

Sales bonuses of 4% of sales are incurred and paid the month after sales have been achieved. Other marketing and administrative salaries are $45 per month.

Dividends are paid in February and May of $35, while tax payments will be made in March ($15), April ($19), and June ($19). Executive bonuses of $52 are paid in January and a debt issue is repaid in February ($32). Finally, two capital expenditure progress payments of $33 must be paid February and May.

Prepare a cash disbursement schedule for January through June.

8.7

Combine your cash recipt schedule (8.5) and cash disbursement schedule (8.6), and create a cash flow schedule for January through June.

8.8

Using the information from 8.5 through 8.7, prepare an account balance. Assume that the beginning balance of cash is $222 and a $65 minimum account balance is required. Indicate your monthly debt balances and answer the following questions:

a.   What is your maximum debt borrowing? In what month does that occur?

b.   What is your June month end cash balance?

c.   What could you do to reduce the amount of borrowing?

8.9

The Fulton Company has been reviewing its credit policies. The credit standards it has been applying have resulted in annual credit sales of $15 million. Its average collection period is 30 days, with a bad debt loss ratio of 1%. Because persistent inflation has caused deterioration in the financial position of many of its customers, Fulton is considering a reduction in its credit standards. As a result, it expects incremental credit sales of $400,000, on which the average collection period (ACP) would be 60 days and on which the bad debt loss (BDL) ratio would be 3%. The variable cost ratio (VCR) to sales for Fulton is 70%. The required return on investment in receivables is 12%. Evaluate the relaxation in credit standards that Fulton is considering.

8.10

Instead of relaxing credit standards, Fulton is considering simply lengthening credit terms from net 20 to net 50, a procedure that would increase the average collection period from 30 days to 60 days. Under the new policy, Fulton expects incremental sales to be $500,000 and the new bad debt loss ratio to rise to 2% on all sales. Assume all other returns hold. Evaluate the lengthening in credit terms that Fulton is considering.

8.11

Gulf Distributors makes all sales on a credit basis; once each year, it routinely evaluates the creditworthiness of all its customers. The evaluation procedure ranks customers from 1 to 5, in order of increasing risk. Results of the ranking are given below.

Category	% Bad Debts	Average Collection Period (Days)	Credit Decision	Annual Sales Lost through Credit Restrictions
1	None	10	Unlimited Credit	None
2	1.0%	12	Unlimited Credit	None
3	3.0%	20	Limited Credit	$1,095,000
4	9.0%	60	Limited Credit	$365,000
5	30.0%	90	No Credit	$730,000

The variable cost ratio is 75%. The opportunity cost of investment in receivables is 10%. What will be the effect on profitability of extending full credit to Category 3? To Category 4? To Category 5?

8.12

Millburn Auto Parts is considering changing its credit terms from 2/15 net 30 to 3/10 net 30 in order to speed collections. At present, 60% of Millburn's customers take the 2% discount. Under the new terms, this number is expected to rise to 70%, reducing the average collection period from 25 to 22 days. Bad debt losses are expected to rise from 1% to the 2% level. However, the more generous cash discount terms are expected to increase credit sales from $1.6 million to $2.0 million per year. Milburn's variable cost ratio is 80%, and its cost of accounts receivable is 9%. Evaluate the change.

8.13

Charles Roberts, the new credit manager of the Baskin Corporation, was alarmed to find that Baskin sells on credit terms of net 90 days, when industry-wide credit terms are net 30 days. On annual credit sales of $12.5 million, Baskin currently averages 95 days' sales in accounts receivable. Roberts estimates that tightening the credit terms to 30 days will reduce annual sales by $2,375,000 but that accounts receivable will drop to 35 days sales and the bad debt loss ratio will drop from 3% of sales to 1% of sales. Baskin's variable costs are 85% of sales. If Baskin's opportunity cost of funds is 12%, should the change be made?

8.14

Wilber Corp. is negotiating with the Citizen's Bank for a $500,000 one-year loan. Citizen has offered Wilber the following three alternatives:

- A 12% interest rate, no compensating balance, and interest due at the end of the year.

- A 10% interest rate, a 20% compensating balance, and interest due at the end of the year.

- A 10% interest rate, a 15% compensating balance, and the loan discounted.

If Wilber wishes to minimize the effective interest rate, which alternative will it choose?

8.15

Mark Industries is having difficulty paying its bills and is considering foregoing its trade discounts on $750,000 of accounts payable. As an alternative, Mark can obtain a 60-day note with an 11% annual interest rate. The note will be discounted, and the trade credit terms are 2/10 net 60.

a.   Which alternative has the lower effective cost?

b.   If Mark does not take its trade discounts, what conclusions may outsiders draw?

8.16

Best Catsup Company is considering the following two alternatives for financing next year's canning operations:

- Establishing a $2 million line of credit with a 1% interest rate on the used amount at the end of each month and a 1% per annum commitment fee rate on the unused portion (0.0833% on unused amount at the end of each month). A $300,000 compensating balance will be required at all times on the entire $2 million line.

- Using field warehousing to finance the inventory. Financing charges will be a flat fee of $1000, plus 2% of the maximum amount of credit extended, plus a 10% annual interest rate (0.833% monthly on amount outstanding at the end of each month) on all outstanding credit.

Best has $300,000 of funds available for inventory financing. All financing is done on the first of the month and is sufficient to cover the value of the expected inventory at the end of the month. Expected month-end inventory levels are given below.

Month	Amount	Month	Amount
July 2006	$300,000	January 2007	$1,200,000
August	800,000	February	900,000
September	1,200,000	March	700,000
October	1,600,000	April	450,000
November	2,000,000	May	200,000
December	1,500,000	June	0

Which financing plan has the lower cost? (Hints: Under the bank loan plan, borrowings in July are $300,000 and in December $1,500,000; under the field warehousing plan, July borrowings are zero and December borrowings are $1,200,000.)

8.17

Collins Manufacturing needs an additional $200,000. The financial manager is considering two methods of obtaining this money: a loan from a commercial bank or a factoring arrangement. The bank charges 12% per annum interest, discount basis. It also requires a 15% percent compensating balance. The factor is willing to purchase Collins's accounts receivable and to advance the invoice amount less a 3% factoring commission on the invoices purchased each month. (All sales are on 30-day terms.) A 10% annual interest rate will be charged on the total invoice price and deducted in advance. Also, under the factoring agreement, Collins can eliminate its credit department and reduce credit expenses by $2,000 per month. Bad debt losses of 10% on the factored amount can also be avoided.

a. How much should the bank loan be in order to net $200,000? How much accounts receivable should be factored to net $200,000?

b. What are the computed interest rates and the annual total dollar costs, including credit department expenses and bad debt losses, associated with each financing arrangement?

c. Discuss some considerations other than cost that may influence management's choice between factoring and a commercial bank loan.

8.18

Sunlight Sailboats estimates that due to the seasonal nature of its business, it will require an additional $200,000 of cash for the month of July. Sunlight has four options available to provide the needed funds. It can:

- Establish a 1-year line of credit for $200,000 with a commercial bank. The commitment fee will be 0.5%, and the interest charge on the used funds will be 15% per annum. The minimum time the funds can be used is 30 days.

- Forego the July trade discount of 2/10 net 40 on $200,000 of accounts payable.

- Issue $200,000 of 30-day commercial paper at a 13.8% per annum interest rate.

- Issue $200,000 of 60-day commercial paper at a 14% per annum interest rate. Since the funds are required for only 30 days, the excess funds ($200,000) can be invested in 13% per annum marketable securities for the month of August. The total transaction fee on purchasing and selling the marketable securities is 0.5% of the fair value.

  a. Which financial arrangement results in the lowest cost?

  b. Is the source with the lowest expected cost necessarily the source to select? Why or why not?

8.19

Wilkins Manufacturing needs an additional $250,000, which it plans to obtain through a factoring arrangement. The factor would purchase Wilkins's accounts receivable and advance the invoice amount, less a 2% commission, on the invoices purchased each month. (Wilkins sells on terms of net 30 days.) In addition, the factor charges 16% annual interest on the total invoice amount, to be deducted in advance.

a. What amount of accounts receivable must be factored to net $250,000?

b. If Wilkins can reduce credit expenses by $1,500 per month and avoid bad debt losses of 3% on the factored amount, what is the total dollar cost of the factoring arrangement?

8.20

Hayes Associates is short on cash and is attempting to determine whether it would be advantageous to forego the discount on this month's purchases or to borrow funds to take advantage of the discount. The discount terms are 2/10 net 45.

a. What is the maximum annual interest rate that Hayes Associates should pay on borrowed funds? Why?

b. What are some of the intangible disadvantages associated with foregoing the discount?

Strategic Financial Planning (Financial Forecasting and Control)

I t is not enough for a firm to perform well in the current quarter. The firm must always be looking ahead. Hence it must engage in long-range planning as well as operate effectively in the present. This is especially true as markets become increasingly international in scope and the economies of the world become increasingly interlinked. As a consequence, more variables affect the national economy and industries within it. The resulting increased turbulence in the economic and political environments make it necessary for business firms to engage in long-range planning.

As mentioned in Chapter 1, corporate finance does not exist as an "end" in itself. Much like a computer is a tool that is used to complete an analysis or write a report, corporate finance is a tool that helps business people maximize the value of the firm. In this chapter, we develop another important value adding dimension of corporate finance, the strategic financial plan.

This chapter first provides a brief managerial overview of strategic planning, presents simple models to approximate results of planned activities, and then develops a fully interactive and supportive financial model that includes integrated financial statements: income statement, balance sheet, and cash flow statement with financial performance metric analysis. Once again, we use a hypothetical strategic financial plan illustration for The Hershey Company.

Learning Outcomes

After completing this chapter, you should be able to:

1 Relate how a strategic financial plan fits into the strategic planning efforts of any organization

2 Anticipate the financial direction of a firm and make appropriate proactive or reactive responsive decisions to direct performance in the future

3 Build simple financial projections

4 Project a firm's income statement, balance sheet, and cash flow statement using historical performance metrics or goals and objectives of the firm

5 Determine appropriate responsibilities to achieve corporate-wide goals

6 Present alternative scenarios

CHAPTER

Overview of Strategic Planning

Strategic planning provides an organization with an opportunity for self-examination. It is an important time when senior management can step away from "fighting the fires" of running a business and reflect on the organization itself. Strategic planning is a never-ending process that develops basic business objectives and establishes (or reconfirms) business direction. The organization must come to grips with answers to a basic set of thought-provoking and discussion-provoking questions:

- What do we (the organization) want to do?

- Where do we want to do it?

- When do we want to do it?

- Who is going to do it?

- What resources do they require?

The strategic planning process:

- Facilitates communication among the senior executives of an organization

- Sets a business direction

- Prioritizes opportunities and requirements

- Establishes business performance standards and objectives

However, the strategic plan must be a living, actionable tool.

Strategy is planning for the future of the enterprise. Although the emphasis of strategy is on the long view, to be implemented properly strategy also takes into account shorter-term decisions and actions. Strategy is not static. Individual strategies, plans, or policies may be utilized in a set of formal procedures. Strategy is a way of thinking requiring diverse inputs. In these continuing interactive processes, financial management is key.

There are numerous elements, approaches, and frameworks that structure and support the strategic planning process.

APPROACHES TO STRATEGY

While diverse approaches to strategic planning are observed, Table 9.1 encompasses the critical activities involved in strategic planning. Whether these represent formal or informal procedures, they are important areas to be covered. The nature and implementation of these procedures are described at length in the literature on strategy.

PROVEN TECHNIQUE

Numerous techniques are used by many corporations and consulting firms. One self-assessment technique, Porter's Five Forces, which refers to Michael Porter's model, can be applied to each strategic business unit and/or the company as a whole. This model includes five economic dimensions. Management develops characteristics for each dimension and after considerable discussion, rates that dimension as low, medium, and high. The dimensions are as follows:

- Threat of new entrants

- Threat of substitution

TABLE	9.1	Essential Elements in the Strategic Planning Process

External Environment
1. Assessment of changes in the environments
2. Analysis of competitors, industry, domestic economy, and international economies
3. Assessment of stakeholders (e.g., shareholders, consumers, employees)

Internal Assessment
4. Evaluation of the company's capabilities and limitations
5. Formulation of the missions, goals, and policies for the master strategy
6. Formulation of long-range strategy programs

Strategic Plan
7. Formulation of mid-range and short-run plans
8. Formulation of internal organization performance measurements
9. Development of sensitivity to critical external environmental changes
10. Organization, funding, and other methods to implement the plan

Strategic Plan Implementation and Follow-Up
11. Information flow and feedback system for continued assessment of actual performance to planned performance as well as a systemic structure for revised interim forecasts at each stage
12. Review and evaluation of the above processes

- Bargaining power of suppliers

- Bargaining power of buyers

- Rivalry among competitors

Table 9.2 presents an application of Porter's Five Forces for Wal-Mart.

From Table 9.2, Wal-Mart is an organization with a low threat of new entrants directly into the retail discount store industry. Wal-Mart, Target, and Costco dominate this industry. The industry has undergone consolidation and small entrants are not likely to be able to capitalize on economies of scale. However, the threat of substitution as new distribution/retail chains (i.e., Internet) expand is a medium to high risk. Because Wal-Mart's management can anticipate and build its response to the Internet, this dimension is rated only a medium threat.

The bargaining power of a supplier to Wal-Mart is extremely low. Wal-Mart has become a substantial part of the business for any retail-oriented manufacturer. Wal-Mart represents approximately 15% of Hershey's annual sales, for instance. Suppliers are very eager to please Wal-Mart. Buyers have more power over Wal-Mart because Wal-Mart's primary customers are very price conscious and have low store loyalty. However, Wal-Mart provides a broad range of products with an every day low pricing strategy. Because customers cannot negotiate prices with store management, the only direct power that a customer has is to switch stores.

Finally, the rivalry among competitors is high. The market is mature with low overall growth. Competition mainly takes place on the battlefield of low prices for non-differentiated products.

TABLE	9.2	Porter's Five Forces Applied to Wal-Mart

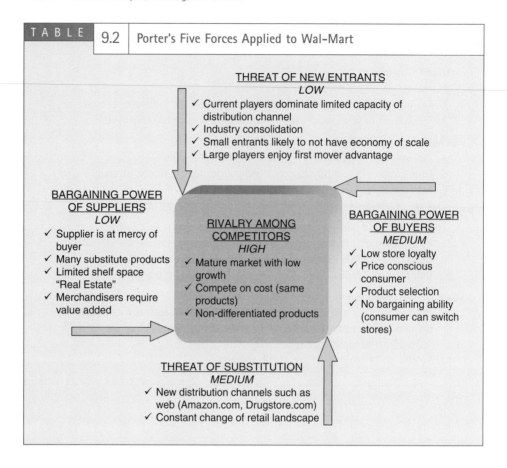

THREAT OF NEW ENTRANTS
LOW
✓ Current players dominate limited capacity of
  distribution channel
✓ Industry consolidation
✓ Small entrants likely to not have economy of scale
✓ Large players enjoy first mover advantage

BARGAINING POWER
OF SUPPLIERS
LOW
✓ Supplier is at mercy of
  buyer
✓ Many substitute products
✓ Limited shelf space
  "Real Estate"
✓ Merchandisers require
  value added

RIVALRY AMONG
COMPETITORS
HIGH
✓ Mature market with low
  growth
✓ Compete on cost (same
  products)
✓ Non-differentiated products

BARGAINING POWER
OF BUYERS
MEDIUM
✓ Low store loyalty
✓ Price conscious
  consumer
✓ Product selection
✓ No bargaining ability
  (consumer can switch
  stores)

THREAT OF SUBSTITUTION
MEDIUM
✓ New distribution channels such as
  web (Amazon.com, Drugstore.com)
✓ Constant change of retail landscape

In addition to Porter's Five Forces model, three other proven techniques stand out for stimulating corporate assessment and initiating strategic planning discussions:

TECHNIQUE	DIMENSION
Boston Consulting Group's Growth Share Matrix	Strategic Business Unit's Business Strength vs. Industry Attractiveness
General Electric's Business Screen	Strategic Business Unit's Relative Industry Position (Market Share) vs. Industry Attractiveness
SWOT Analysis	Internal Assessment: *Strengths* and *Weaknesses* External Assessment: *Opportunities* and *Threats*

Each technique goes beyond the walls of the corporation and examines the competitive economic climate.

STRATEGIC PLANNING STRUCTURE

An overall approach must be decided upon early in the strategic planning process. A tone must be set by the Chief Executive Officer. Will the strategic planning process be a "top-down" approach or a "bottom-up" approach, or even a combination of the two approaches? How much collaboration will take place in setting the firm's future direction?

The process for many corporations is a collaborative effort that begins as a "bottom-up" approach. Divisional plans are accumulated, corporate expenses are added, and projected corporate consolidated financial statements are prepared. The consolidated plan performance is compared to prior stated corporate objectives as well as the CEO's expectations. Often at a strategic planning conference, corporate and division senior management discuss the overall direction of the organization as well as address any shortfall in projected performance. Management-designed strategies eliminate performance gaps. This process is classified as a collaborative "bottom-up" initial approach that is driven to an overall corporate (top-down) level of financial performance.

At what level in the organization should the strategic plan be built? Every company has its own complex organizational structure. For many organizations, this includes the overall corporate-level with numerous divisions reporting to the corporate level. Each division has its own number of Strategic Business Units (SBUs), comprised of numerous products. Each product has a number of stockkeeping units (SKUs). For Hershey, an SKU represents a product variation such as different sizes of products, different bag weights, or different seasonal wrap. In total, Hershey has more than 1,500 SKUs. The strategic plan is prepared at the corporate and division level with some discussion of SBUs, as the situation warrants. Only on rare occasions would a strategic plan include product- or SKU-specific discussion.

Financial Planning and Control Processes

Financial planning and control processes are closely tied to strategic planning. The nature of these relations is sketched in Table 9.3, which fills in some specifics for the general framework given in Table 9.1. In Table 9.3, we begin with external factors that describe the industry, domestic macro-economic factors, and international economic factors. These external factors are blended with senior management's self-assessment through the four techniques presented above to develop the enterprise's mission statement, objectives, and strategies. In the framework of mission and objectives, business strategies are formulated.

Financial planning turns the qualitative assessment into a quantifiable plan that sets performance standards for the future. Financial planning is distinguished from budgeting in that planning is more strategic, longer duration, and less detailed than a budget. Budgets usually have a 1-year duration and are extremely explicit, including specific tactical details.

The financial plans are comprised of separate, but interlinked, plans. Each organization must decide how detailed the strategic plan needs to be. As discussed above, Hershey prepared divisional strategic financial plans that incorporate sales and production costs at an SBU level. This is in sharp contrast to the detailed annual budget that would prepare sales forecasts (by customer by region) and very detailed cost of goods sold estimates (by plant by cost component) for each of its more than 1,500 SKUs.

At this point, financial management has key responsibilities to perform, particularly in the areas of financial planning and control. Financial planning and control involve the use of projections based on standards and the development of a feedback and adjustment process to improve performance. This financial planning and control process involves forecasts and the use of several types of supporting plans. Supporting plans are developed for every significant area of the firm's activities, as shown by Table 9.3.

Key decisions involve the choice of products and markets. These decisions result in a product mix strategy complete with a schedule of new product introductions and aging

TABLE	9.3	Strategic and Financial Planning

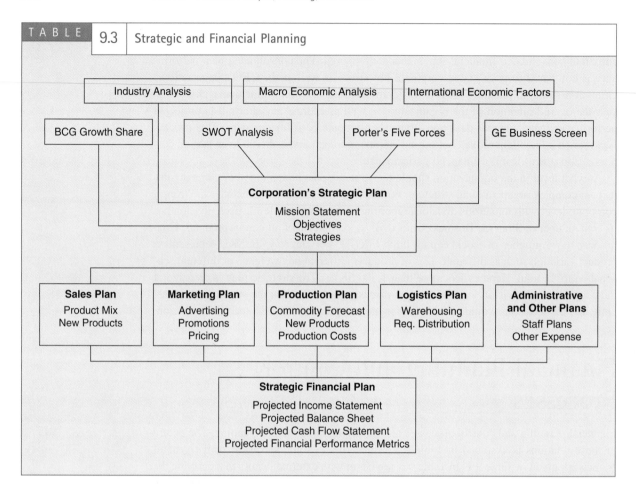

product rationalizations (or eliminations). The sales plan must also be married with the marketing plan. Sales and marketing must work closely together as they consider the marketing expenditures and emphasis in support of a particular product. This, in turn, provides a basis for long-range sales forecasts. Sales forecasts are the basis for modeling all of the other activities of the firm.

The production plan first analyzes the use of materials, parts, labor, and facilities. The production plan also reviews and incorporates increased costs of key specialty ingredients, positions in hedged commodities, labor union contract impacts, and so on. Manufacturing then completes the production plan by integrating the sales plan from sales and marketing. Any capacity shortfalls can be identified and reconciled well in advance. Supporting the production plan, each of its major elements is likely to have its own plan (or supporting schedules): a materials plan, a hedged commodity schedule, a personnel plan, and a facilities plan.

The **facilities plan** identifies any opportunities or shortfall in production capacity or new plant requirements. Because strategic planning has a long-term focus, new production lines and even new plants can be anticipated and addressed in a timely manner. This facilities plan provides the basis for the capital expenditures plan.

Likewise, logistics works with the sales and production plan to identify any changes in distribution or warehousing capacity requirements. Any shortfalls can be identified and addressed. Shortfalls in warehousing capacity can give rise to building additional warehousing space (if the shortfall appears to be permanent) or warehouse space contracts (if the shortfall appears temporary).

Administrative plans can be developed at a cost center level or for the functional area. For instance, the Senior Vice President and Chief Financial Officer may be comfortable projecting area growth, matching the rate of inflation (say, 2.0% to 3.0%) without feeling the need to have each cost center prepare a strategic plan and cost center level projections. Once again, annual budgets should be prepared for the lowest organizational unit, such as a cost center, to assist the manager of that unit in making day-to-day decisions. For a strategic plan, however, cost center detailed-budget level projections provide a false sense of accuracy and in general provide little or no value. Only when a specific functional area's plan is prepared do they provide a general sense of that area's spending to an appropriate level of detail.

Other administrative budgets are developed to cover miscellaneous administrative and executive requirements. Finally, corporate (or divisional) finance may be aware of some additional expenses that are not covered anywhere else. Interest expense is an example of this type of additional expense.

The results of projecting all these elements of cost are reflected in the projected (also called "pro forma") income statement. Anticipated sales give rise to consideration of the various types of investments in working capital that are needed to produce and sell the products. These working capital investments and the facilities/production requirements identified in the facilities plan, together with the beginning balance sheet, provide the necessary data for developing the assets side of the balance sheet.

Assets must be financed, so a cash flow analysis is needed. The cash plan integrates the income statement projections along with the projected investments in both fixed and working capital. The cash plan incorporates projected dividend payments and required debt repayment. It also reflects any planned share repurchases. The projected cash flow statement is useful in identifying any additional cash funding needs. A positive net cash flow indicates that the firm has sufficient financing. However, if an increase in the volume of operations, for example, leads to a negative cash flow, additional financing is required. The longer the lead-time in arranging for the required financing, the greater is the opportunity for assessing optimum sources of capital, developing required documentation, and working out arrangements with chosen financing sources.

Financial planning and control seek to improve profitability, avoid cash squeezes, and improve the performance of individual divisions of a company. These responsibilities involve the topics covered in this chapter.

The remainder of this chapter develops basic financial planning models as well as a comprehensive finance model that is particularly useful in strategic planning for an established organization or serves as critical financial support within a business plan for a start-up organization.

Basic Financial Forecasts

As a prelude to the comprehensive financial model, we will cover three basic models:

1. Simple financial model—% of sales

2. External funds needed

3. Simple integrated financial plan

These three basic modeling techniques are used to introduce simplified approaches to strategic financial planning. The examples presented center on forecasting Hershey's performance using the background established in Chapters 2 and 7.

SIMPLE FINANCIAL MODEL—% OF SALES

As stated above, the sales forecast is the most important value to estimate when preparing any financial model. This technique assumes that marketing and sales have combined to give us a realistic estimate of next year's sales and that we can estimate income statement and balance sheet values (as a % of sales) based on their most recent trends or averages.

Table 9.4 illustrates this approach. Panel A presents the three most recent years of Hershey's actual performance. Panel B converts all values to a percent of sales. Panel C lists the percent of sales assumption used in the projection, and Panel D creates the forecasted value from the projected sales levels and estimated percent of sales.

Notice, the financial statements have been condensed slightly from Hershey's actual statements (see Chapter 2). The income statement combines the one-time events (restructuring charges and gain on the sale of a business) into one line item called "Other expenses." Additionally, the income statement stops short of listing the cumulative effect of accounting changes in 2003. On the balance sheet, some of the accounts have been combined (e.g., deferred income taxes and prepaid expenses and other were combined to form other current assets.)

As seen in Chapter 7, Hershey has been managing its selling, marketing, and administrative costs every year. However, the cost of sales has moderated. Additionally, one-time expenses accounted for 2% of sales in 2005!

In Panel C of Table 9.4, we assume that production and operating costs (as a percent of sales) will modestly decline, there will be no other (one-time, extraordinary expenses), interest will increase to 2.0% of sales due to rising interest rates, and the one-time tax advantage realized in 2004 will not be repeated as taxes return to the 2003/2005 levels. The assumptions reflect an improving net margin of 12.2% for 2006 and beyond. The 2006 net income is estimated to be $622.2 million. The projections are found in Panel D.

It is important to remember that a 1 percentage point of sales difference impacts the forecast by $51 million in 2006 (and $57 million in 2008)! It is imperative that the plan be prepared by someone who understands the underlying business and company. Someone who has ownership and takes responsibility for achieving the sales forecast is preferred.

The individual asset accounts have generally been stable (as a percent of sales) over the past 3 years. The individual asset assumptions total to 86.0% of sales, which is comfortable given that total assets have been remarkably stable, ranging from 85.6% of sales to 88.8% over the prior 3 years.

On the liabilities side, the operating liabilities (accounts payable, accrued liabilities, and other long-term liabilities) have also been relatively stable:

| | % OF SALES | | | |
	2003	2004	2005	Assumed
Accounts payable	3.2%	3.4%	3.5%	3.5%
Accrued taxes and liabilities	10.6%	11.5%	11.0%	12.0%
Other long-term liabilities	17.9%	15.9%	16.8%	17.0%
Total operating liabilities	31.7%	30.8%	31.3%	32.5%

On the other hand, the financial liabilities (short-term debt including current portion long-term debt and long-term debt) and stockholders' equity have varied substantially throughout the past 3 years.

Given our set of assumptions for the balance sheet, we have a difference of 1.5% of sales (86.0% assets and 84.5% liabilities and equity) or $76.5 million in 2006. Clearly, there is an issue with this technique and/or the assumptions made in this exercise. We address these

TABLE 9.4   Simple Financial Model—% of Sales ($ Millions)

	A. ACTUAL VALUES ($ MILLIONS)			B. % OF SALES			C. % ASSUMED	D. PROJECTED FINANCIAL PERFORMANCE		
	2003	2004	2005	2003	2004	2005		2006	2007	2008
Sales	$4,172.6	$4,429.2	$4,836.0	100.0%	100.0%	100.0%	100.0%	$5,100.0	$5,400.0	$5,700.0
Cost of sales	2,544.7	2,680.4	2,965.5	61.0%	60.5%	61.3%	61.0%	3,111.0	3,294.0	3,477.0
Operating expense	841.1	867.1	913.0	20.2%	19.6%	18.9%	18.8%	958.8	1,015.2	1,071.6
Other expenses	15.1	—	96.6	0.4%	0.0%	2.0%	0.0%	—	—	—
EBIT	771.7	881.7	860.9	18.4%	19.9%	17.8%	20.2%	1,030.2	1,090.8	1,151.4
Interest	63.5	66.5	88.0	1.5%	1.5%	1.8%	2.0%	102.0	108.0	114.0
Pre-tax income	708.2	815.2	772.9	16.9%	18.4%	16.0%	18.2%	928.2	982.8	1,037.4
Taxes	258.9	237.3	279.7	6.1%	5.4%	5.9%	6.0%	306.0	324.0	342.0
Net income before cumulative accounting effect	$ 449.3	$ 577.9	$ 493.2	10.8%	13.0%	10.1%	12.2%	$ 622.2	$ 658.8	$ 695.4
Cash	$ 114.8	$ 54.8	$ 67.2	2.8%	1.2%	1.4%	2.0%	$ 102.0	$ 108.0	$ 114.0
Accounts receivable	407.6	408.9	559.3	9.8%	9.2%	11.6%	9.0%	459.0	486.0	513.0
Inventory	492.9	557.2	610.3	11.8%	12.6%	12.6%	12.0%	612.0	648.0	684.0
Other current assets	116.3	176.8	172.1	2.8%	4.0%	3.6%	4.0%	204.0	216.0	228.0
Current assets	1,131.6	1,197.7	1,408.9	27.1%	27.0%	29.1%	27.0%	1,377.0	1,458.0	1,539.0
Property, plant, and equipment, net	1,661.9	1,682.7	1,659.2	39.8%	38.0%	34.3%	38.0%	1,938.0	2,052.0	2,166.0
Goodwill and other assets	789.1	932.4	1,227.1	18.9%	21.1%	25.4%	21.0%	1,071.0	1,134.0	1,197.0
Total assets	$3,582.6	$3,812.8	$4,295.2	85.9%	86.1%	88.8%	86.0%	$4,386.0	$4,644.0	$4,902.0
Accounts payable	$ 132.2	$ 148.7	$ 167.8	3.2%	3.4%	3.5%	3.5%	178.5	189.0	199.5
Accrued taxes and liabilities	441.1	511.5	531.3	10.6%	11.5%	11.0%	12.0%	612.0	648.0	684.0
Short-term debt	12.5	622.3	819.1	0.3%	14.0%	16.9%	11.0%	561.0	594.0	627.0
Current liabilities	585.8	1,282.5	1,518.2	14.0%	29.0%	31.4%	26.5%	1,351.5	1,431.0	1,510.5
Long-term debt	968.5	690.6	942.8	23.2%	15.6%	19.5%	17.0%	867.0	918.0	969.0
Other long-term liab	748.4	702.6	813.1	17.9%	15.9%	16.8%	17.0%	867.0	918.0	969.0
Stockholders' equity	1,279.9	1,137.1	1,021.1	30.7%	25.7%	21.1%	24.0%	1,224.0	1,296.0	1,368.0
Total liabilities and stockholders' equity	$3,582.6	$3,812.8	$4,295.2	85.9%	86.1%	88.8%	84.5%	$4,309.5	$4,563.0	$4,816.5
Assets exceed liabilities and stockholders' equity								$ 76.5	$ 81.0	$ 85.5

issues below as we discuss other methodologies. However, this simple approach does give us an easy yet reasonable method for projecting next year's income statement, assets, and operating liabilities.

EXTERNAL FUNDS NEEDED

The external funds needed (EFN) approach is another simplistic financial forecasting tool that offers two important differences to the percent of sales model. First, EFN focuses on financial resources—cash required or cash available—beyond ordinary operations. Second, EFN incorporates a more exacting (mechanical) approach to stockholders' equity. As discussed in Chapter 2, this year's balance of stockholders' equity equals the last year's balance plus net income less dividends paid. EFN incorporates this mechanical aspect.

The EFN equation includes three components that center on sources or uses of cash: (1) cash used to acquire assets in its conduct of business, (2) sources of cash from increases in operating liabilities, and (3) sources of cash provided from retained (not paid out as a dividend) income generated by the business:

$$\begin{matrix} \text{External Funds} \\ \text{Needed (EFN)} \end{matrix} = \begin{matrix} \text{Assets Needed} \\ \text{to Support} \\ \text{Additional} \\ \text{Business} \end{matrix} - \begin{matrix} \text{Sources from} \\ \text{Additional} \\ \text{Operating} \\ \text{Liabilities} \end{matrix} - \begin{matrix} \text{Income} \\ \text{Retained by} \\ \text{the Business} \end{matrix}$$

EFN can be written as:

$$EFN = A_{(t-1)}(\Delta S_t) - L_{(t-1)}(\Delta S) - S_t M(1 - d) \tag{9.1}$$

where:

$$
\begin{aligned}
EFN &= \text{External funds needed} \\
A &= \text{Assets as a percent of sales} \\
\Delta S_t &= \text{Change in sales from Year}_{t-1} \text{ to Year}_t \\
L &= \text{Operating liabilities as a percent of sales} \\
S &= \text{Sales} \\
M &= \text{Margin} \\
d &= \text{Dividend payout} \\
\text{Year}_t &= \text{Plan year} \\
\text{Year}_{t-1} &= \text{Last year of actual results}
\end{aligned}
$$

We will continue to examine EFN using the assumptions developed in Table 9.4 for the year 2007 compared to 2006, where:

$A_{(t-1)}$ = Assets as a percent of sales		= 86.0%
ΔS_t = Change in sales from Year$_{t-1}$ to Year$_t$		= $300.0 million
$L_{(t-1)}$ = Operating liabilities as a percent of sales		= 32.5%
S_t = Sales		= $5,400.0 million
M = Margin		= 12.2%
d = Dividend payout		= 40.0%

Continuing with this example:

$$
\begin{aligned}
EFN &= [0.860\ (\$300.0)] - [0.325\ (\$300.0)] - [\$5,400.0\ (0.122)(1 - 0.400)] \\
&= [\$258.0] - [\$97.5] - [\$658.8\ (0.600)] \\
&= \$258.0 - \$97.5 - \$395.3 = -\$234.8
\end{aligned}
$$

As see on Table 9.4, 2007 assets do increase by $258 million from projected performance for 2006; operating liabilities (accounts payable, accruals, and long-term liabilities) do increase by $97.5 million; and net income is $658.8 million (12.2% net margin times sales of $5,400 million). This results in Hershey having a –$234.8 need of external funds. Or said differently, Hershey is in a cash surplus situation and can use that surplus to acquire additional capital equipment, build an additional plant, acquire another company, payoff debt, repurchase stock, or hold onto the cash.

The EFN formula allows management to broadly examine its external financing needs (or abilities). Because Hershey is a mature company, it should be no surprise that it generates "excess" cash. In a start-up or growth phase, a company is in need of external funds as a result of heavy investment.

$$EFN = A_{(t-1)}(\Delta S_t) - L_{(t-1)}(\Delta S) - S_t M(1 - d) \qquad (9.2)$$

For a growth firm:

$A_{(t-1)}$ = Assets as a percent of sales	= 150.0%
(S_t) = Change in sales from Year$_{t-1}$ to Year$_t$	= $30.0 million
$L_{(t-1)}$ = Operating liabilities as a percent of sales	= 20.0%
S_t = Sales	= $100.0 million
M = Margin	= 2.5%
d = Dividend payout	= 0.0%

Continuing with this example:

$$
\begin{aligned}
EFN &= [1.500\ (\$30.0)] - [0.250\ (\$30.0)] - [\$100.0\ (0.025)\ (1 - 0.000)] \\
&= [\$45.0] - [\$7.5] - [\$2.5\ (0.000)] \\
&= \$45.0 - \$7.5 - \$2.5 = \$35.0
\end{aligned}
$$

In this example, this growth company needs to obtain $35.0 million in sourcing to be able to fund the $45 asset expansion that it is planning!

An appreciation of the concepts behind EFN is critical. It compares expansion needs versus spontaneous sources of financing (from suppliers and the government through payables, accruals, and other long-term liabilities) and annual retained income generation. For this growth company, funds could be obtained by issuing short-term debt or long-term debt or equity. EFN highlights the shortfall and management can start planning to address this need.

However, to be most effective within the confines of EFN, the underlying relationships need to remain static or additional complexities need to be added to Equation 9.2. Instead of developing a more sophisticated version of EFN, let's consider another approach to a planning model: simple integrated financial plan.

SIMPLE INTEGRATED FINANCIAL PLAN

In Chapter 2, Table 2.7 illustrates the flow of summary statements from 2004 to 2005. Table 9.5 extends the 2005 information with an abbreviated, simplified financial strategic plan. The plan is projected for 1 year (2006) at a summary level. The 2006 projected financial statements are based on the 2005 actual statements and include the planned activity.

From assumptions 1 and 2, the 2006 income statement reflects sales growth of 5.0% and a net margin of 11.5%, resulting in net income of $584 million.

The balance sheet is also a highly summarized statement. The 2006 estimated cash account and stockholders' equity result directly from the cash flow statement and income statement, respectively. The 2005 balances in other assets (excluding cash) and liabilities

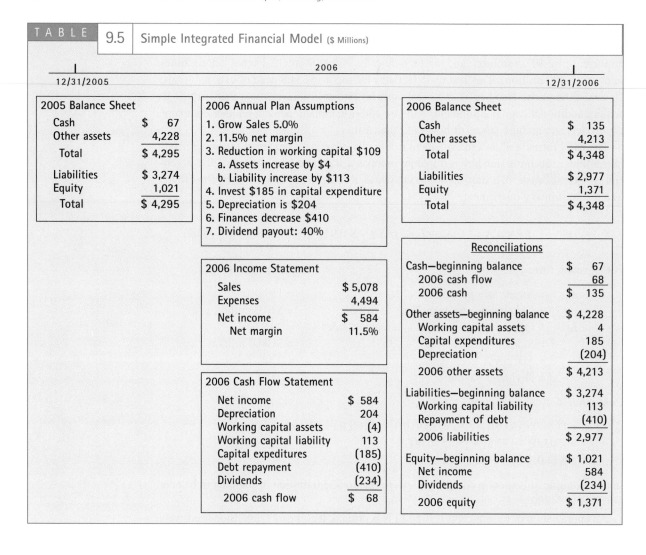

| TABLE | 9.5 | Simple Integrated Financial Model ($ Millions) |

2006

| 12/31/2005 | | 12/31/2006 |

2005 Balance Sheet

Cash	$ 67
Other assets	4,228
Total	$ 4,295
Liabilities	$ 3,274
Equity	1,021
Total	$ 4,295

2006 Annual Plan Assumptions

1. Grow Sales 5.0%
2. 11.5% net margin
3. Reduction in working capital $109
   a. Assets increase by $4
   b. Liability increase by $113
4. Invest $185 in capital expenditure
5. Depreciation is $204
6. Finances decrease $410
7. Dividend payout: 40%

2006 Income Statement

Sales	$ 5,078
Expenses	4,494
Net income	$ 584
Net margin	11.5%

2006 Cash Flow Statement

Net income	$ 584
Depreciation	204
Working capital assets	(4)
Working capital liability	113
Capital expeditures	(185)
Debt repayment	(410)
Dividends	(234)
2006 cash flow	$ 68

2006 Balance Sheet

Cash	$ 135
Other assets	4,213
Total	$ 4,348
Liabilities	$ 2,977
Equity	1,371
Total	$ 4,348

Reconciliations

Cash—beginning balance	$ 67
2006 cash flow	68
2006 cash	$ 135
Other assets—beginning balance	$ 4,228
Working capital assets	4
Capital expenditures	185
Depreciation	(204)
2006 other assets	$ 4,213
Liabilities—beginning balance	$ 3,274
Working capital liability	113
Repayment of debt	(410)
2006 liabilities	$ 2,977
Equity—beginning balance	$ 1,021
Net income	584
Dividends	(234)
2006 equity	$ 1,371

are augmented by the noted planned activities to arrive at the projected December 31, 2006, amounts. The 2006 projected balance of other assets is ($ millions):

2005 Other Assets		$4,228
Working capital investment (*Assumption 3*)	$ 4	
Capital expenditures (*Assumption 4*)	185	
Depreciation (*Assumption 5*)	(204)	
Change in other assets	($15)	
2006 Other assets		$4,213

The 2006 projected balance of liabilities is:

2005 Liabilities		$3,274
Working capital financing (*Assumption 3*)	$ 113	
Payoff of debt financing (*Assumption 6*)	(410)	
Change in liabilities	($297)	
2006 Liabilities		$2,977

The projected $113 of working capital financing includes increases in accounts payable, accrued liabilities, taxes payable, and so on.

Table 9.5 presents a grossly simplified financial strategic plan. The plan only covers 1 year at a summarized level.

This section reviews three simple approaches to strategic financial planning. While these examples are good for introducing the topic, the applied benefits are limited in scope and are often used for "quick and dirty" assignments or assignments where a "ball park" answer is required. Even though these are financial models, the additional managerial and organizational benefits are minimal because of their simplicity.

The next section builds a fully integrated strategic financial plan.

Forecasting Financial Statements

Chapter 2 discusses the basic financial statements (income statement, balance sheet, and cash flow) and numerous accounting issues surrounding those statements. Also discussed and considered are the financial statements for their "rearview mirror" qualities. Such statements show us where we were. This section uses the principles presented in Chapter 2 along with the performance metrics of Chapter 7 to develop forward-looking financial statements. We use these forward-looking financial statements to anticipate the accounting ramifications that result from successfully implementing our strategic plan. These pro forma financial statements allow us to establish additional financial performance benchmarks by which to measure first the feasibility of our aspirations and second the success of attaining those objectives.

The financial statement forecasting process has four steps that are discussed below:

1. Frame the projection detail and periods.

2. Develop appropriate assumptions.

3. Calculate the financial statement values.

4. Review the projections for reasonableness.

ESTABLISHING THE FINANCIAL FORECAST FRAMEWORK

We must first decide the level of detail to which we should create the projected financial statements. An annual budget should be extremely detailed, with every "actual" number having a corresponding "budget" value. Within a strategic plan, the level of detail is flexible. As seen in Table 9.5, financial statements can be presented at extremely aggregated levels. However, it is important to provide enough detail, at a precise-enough level to reasonably reflect anticipated performance and provide a managerial road map.

For many organizations, each division or subsidiary prepares a strategic financial plan. That is, each division prepares a strategic plan that includes an income statement, balance sheet, and cash flow statement. Corporate planning consolidates the divisions' plans along with functional corporate administrative area plans and miscellaneous corporate items (e.g., deferred taxes). The final financial statements parallel the statements as reported in the annual report.

For some organizations, partial income statements underlie each divisional plan for the major SBUs and major products sold. The partial income statements include sales projections offset by the cost of goods sold and any direct brand expenses such as advertising, trade promotions, and consumer promotions. Consolidation of these partial income statements occurs at a divisional level and forms the foundation for the division's forecasted income statement. Balance sheet projections generally are not completed at a product or SBU level, but instead are completed at a divisional level. Accounts receivable, inventory, and accounts payable policies often do not change by product because the divisional management implements working capital policies for the division and, generally, not a specific brand. Additionally, often the division's facilities or capital expenditures are aggregated at a division (not SBU) level.

The following sections depart from this divisional consolidation perspective and develop a corporate-level strategic financial plan that includes projections for the total corporation's sales, expenses, assets, liabilities, equity, and cash flows. In this case, an 8-year period is considered. Strategic plans generally tend to be anywhere from 3 to 10 years in duration. The model contains two pages of assumptions (Table 9.6A and 9.6B) and a set of final financial statements (Table 9.7A through 9.7D). The model includes 2 years of history (2004 and 2005)—as reference points, 8 years of projections (2006 to 2013), and an assumptions/comments column. Tables 9.6 and 9.7 lay out the framework of our financial model. The next section discusses the assumptions.

STRATEGIC OBJECTIVES AND PERFORMANCE STANDARDS

A financial plan is driven by the organization's strategic objectives and performance standards targeted by senior management. The objectives manifest themselves as a series of plan "assumptions." There are numerous objectives and performance standards established for each financial statement. These objectives are all interrelated and directly support the overall mission, goals, and strategies of the organization. While we use the phrase "assumption," for example, to describe a projected performance standard such as inventory turnover, the reader must keep in mind that this specific objective is part of the overall objective of the firm to reduce investment while providing high-quality customer service.

The phrase "GIGO" or "garbage in garbage out" describes the importance of using reasonable performance standards as assumptions. It is important to remember that financial plans are a series of projections. The strength of a plan revolves around the quality of the assumptions.

The phrase "GIGO" or "garbage in gospel out" also gets mistakenly applied to a plan. A false sense of precision should not be imputed for any plan. "Eight decimal" place accuracy should not be a feature of any plan.

The performance standards, corporate objectives, and ultimately the assumptions are derived from a number of sources. As depicted in Table 9.6, a strategic plan incorporates information from many external and internal sources. Senior management ultimately assumes responsibility for all assumptions and projections. Some assumptions involve direct objectives set by senior management with the concurrence of the operating managers. The finance area (treasury, tax, and accounting departments) assumes responsibility for developing minor and/or technical projections.

Tables 9.6A and 9.6B depict the assumptions and their sources used in preparing this hypothetical strategic financial plan.

INCOME STATEMENT OBJECTIVES AND ASSUMPTIONS

The basis for most important assumptions on the income statement comes directly from objectives set by senior management. These assumptions were presented in December 2005 at an investment analyst conference and made available on Hershey's website. Driving Hershey's growth rate is the realization of the first phase of Hershey's marketing strategy.

This resulted in a solid (albeit modest) 6.2% growth in 2004 and 9.2% in 2005. Recently sales growth has moderated and management's long-term targets are growth of 3% to 4% per year. Cost of goods sold (excluding depreciation) (COGS) as a percent of sales and selling, general, and administrative expense (SGA) as a percent of sales has been tasked for steady improvement over this 8-year planning period.

Technical estimates complete the income statement assumptions. Depreciation expense can be estimated in a variety of ways. In its simplest form, depreciation can be estimated as a percent of sales. While this approach is simple, it does not consider alternative levels of projected capital expenditures. Whether you anticipate capital expenditures of $100 million per year or $500 million per year, depreciation expense remains unchanged when simply expressed as a percent of sales.

A very detailed approach to estimating depreciation expense lies at the other extreme of the continuum. Depreciation is the one expense that can be estimated with certainty given the existing asset base, detailed projections of capital expenditures, and estimates of equipment or plant disposals. Each existing asset or anticipated "new" asset has its own underlying depreciation schedule. The detailed depreciation schedules of existing and planned assets can be developed and totaled to estimate a projected depreciation expense. Of course, this assumes that all projected capital expenditures have been fully detailed as to the exact property, plant, or equipment that will be acquired. While projecting a specific level of capital expenditures is a reasonable exercise, the specific equipment details are usually unavailable.

Numerous estimation techniques exist between these two extremes (percent of sales and asset-by-asset depreciation schedules). We have chosen a reasonable technique that takes into account the projected level of total capital expenditures without detailing project-by-project depreciation schedules. In fact, the depreciation estimation technique used in this model assumes that all projected capital expenditures are spent acquiring assets with average 10-year lives, with a half-year convention. This assumption can be adjusted to fit the profile for each specific company or industry.

The process (see Table 9.6B) starts with the historical depreciation schedule that represents the total depreciation on every depreciable asset held by the firm as of December 31, 2005. At the end of 2005, Hershey had property, plant, and equipment, net of $1,659.1 million. The "historical depreciation schedule" line represents the depreciation for the next 8 years of that amount. As an analyst working for the company (as an employee or consultant), this schedule is readily available from internal sources. As an external analyst, the schedule is estimated and reflects declining annual depreciation as some historical assets are fully depreciated.

Added to this base is an estimate of $9.3 million for anticipated 2006 capital expenditures of $185 million (from the cash flow assumptions), that is, straight-line depreciation assuming a 10-year life of the capital expenditure amounts. However, the half-year convention dictates that half of the depreciation be taken in the first year and the eleventh-year of the asset's life because, on average, it is assumed that the expenditures occur at mid-year. So, only $9.3 million ($185 million/10 years × 1/2) is added to the 2005 base level to derive 2006's estimated depreciation expense of $204.4 million. As seen in Table 9.6B, the process continues for 2007, when the historical depreciation schedule ($190.1 million) is augmented for a full year of depreciation on the 2006 capital expenditures ($18.5 million) and half-year of depreciation ($9.5 million) on the 2007 capital expenditures for a total depreciation of $218.1 million.

The estimated depreciation expense for 2013 is $312.6 million, assuming the projected capital expenditures. If any of the projections change in an alternative scenario, the depreciation expense needs to be recast.

TABLE 9.6A Objectives and Assumptions ($ Millions)

	ACTUAL					PROJECTED					ASSUMPTIONS
	2004	2005	2006	2007	2008	2009	2010	2011	2012	2013	
Income Statement											
Sales growth	6.2%	9.2%	5.0%	5.0%	4.5%	4.0%	4.0%	3.0%	2.5%	2.5%	Senior Management with sales dept input
Cost of goods sold (excluding depreciation)—%	56.7%	57.2%	57.0%	56.6%	56.3%	56.0%	55.7%	55.5%	55.2%	55.2%	Senior Management with manufacturing input
Depreciation	$171.2	200.1	$204.4	$218.1	$232.6	$247.6	$263.1	$279.1	$295.6	$312.6	See Table 9.6B
Spelling, general, & administrative—%	19.6%	18.99%	18.7%	18.5%	18.3%	18.1%	17.9%	17.7%	17.5%	17.5%	Senior Management
Interest rate—income	2.0%	3.0%	4.0%	4.0%	4.0%	4.0%	4.0%	4.0%	4.0%	4.0%	Economic forecast—treasury
Interest rate—expense	6.0%	6.0%	6.2%	6.2%	6.2%	6.2%	6.2%	6.2%	6.2%	6.2%	Historical & economic forecast—treasury
Tax rate	29.1%	36.2%	37.0%	37.0%	37.0%	37.0%	37.0%	37.0%	37.0%	37.0%	Tax department
Shares outstanding—year end	246.6	240.5	240.5	240.5	240.5	240.5	240.5	240.5	240.5	240.5	Prior year + (−) issuance (repurchase)
Balance Sheet											
Accounts receivable turnover	10.83	8.65	10.00	10.20	10.40	10.50	10.60	10.70	10.80	10.90	Operational objective
Inventory turnover	4.81	4.86	4.95	5.00	5.10	5.20	5.30	5.40	5.50	5.50	Operational objective
Change in other current assets	$ 45.1	$ (4.7)	$ 10.0	$ 10.0	$ 10.0	$ 10.0	$ 12.0	$ 12.0	$ 12.0	$ 12.0	Finance estimate: $ amount of change
Change in other assets	$ 68.4	$271.4	$ 30.0	$ 30.0	$ 30.0	$ 30.0	$ 40.0	$ 40.0	$ 40.0	$ 40.0	Finance estimate: $ amount of change
Accounts payable turnover	18.03	17.67	17.80	17.50	17.30	17.00	16.80	16.50	16.30	16.00	Operational objective
Accrued liabilities turnover	5.71	5.84	5.50	5.25	5.00	5.00	5.00	5.00	5.00	5.00	Operational objective
Change in accrued income taxes	$ 17.4	$ (18.8)	$ 5.0	$ 5.0	$ 5.0	$ 5.0	$ 10.0	$ 10.0	$ 10.0	$ 10.0	Finance estimate: $ amount of change
Other long-term liabilities	8.7%	8.5%	8.5%	8.5%	8.5%	8.5%	8.5%	8.5%	8.5%	8.5%	Finance Estimate: % of sales

Cash Flow Assumptions

Changed in deferred taxes	−18.2%	29.0%	8.0%	8.0%	8.0%	8.0%	8.0%	8.0%	8.0%	Tax Department: % Taxes on income stmt
Capital expenditures	$218.7	$181.7	$ 185.0	$ 190.0	$200.0	$210.0	$210.0	$220.0	$220.0	Senior management with engineering
Business acquisitions	$166.9	$ 47.1	$ —	—	$ —	$ —	$ —	$ —	$ —	Senior management
Short-term debt	$331.2	$475.6	$(410.0)	$(300.0)	$(109.1)	$ —	$ —	$ —	$ —	Debt repayment schedule-treasury
Long-term debt	(29.9)	$ (79.0)	$ (0.1)	$(190.0)	$ (0.1)	$ (0.1)	$ (0.1)	$ (0.1)	$ (0.1)	Debt Repayment Schedule-treasury
Cash dividends—payout	35.6%	44.8%	40.0%	40.0%	40.0%	40.0%	40.0%	40.0%	40.0%	Treasury estimate
Repurchase of stock	$698.9	$537.0	$ —	$ —	$ —	$ —	$ —	$ —	$ —	Senior management with treasury
Other, net financing	$ 89.3	$101.7	$ —	$ —	$ —	$ —	$ —	$ —	$ —	Treasury estimate

T A B L E 9.6B Depreciation Assumption ($ Millions)

	ACTUAL				PROJECTED							ASSUMPTIONS
	2004	2005	2006	2007	2008	2009	2010	2011	2012	2013		
Historical depreciation schedule	$171.2	$200.1	$195.1	$190.1	$185.1	$180.1	$175.1	$170.1	$165.1	$160.1		Based on 2005 Net, PP&E Schedule of Deprec
Average life (years) = 10.0												
2006 Capital expenditures $185.0	n/a	n/a	9.3	18.5	18.5	18.5	18.5	18.5	18.5	18.5		Based on 2006 expenditures, 10-year life
2007 Capital expenditures $190.0	n/a	n/a	n/a	9.5	19.0	19.0	19.0	19.0	19.0	19.0		Based on 2007 expenditures, 10-year life
2008 Capital expenditures $200.0	n/a	n/a	n/a	n/a	10.0	20.0	20.0	20.0	20.0	20.0		Based on 2008 expenditures, 10-year life
2009 Capital expenditures $200.0	n/a	n/a	n/a	n/a	n/a	10.0	20.0	20.0	20.0	20.0		Based on 2009 expenditures, 10-year life
2010 Capital expenditures $210.0	n/a	n/a	n/a	n/a	n/a	n/a	10.5	21.0	21.0	21.0		Based on 2010 expenditures, 10-year life
2011 Capital expenditures $210.0	n/a	n/a	n/a	n/a	n/a	n/a	n/a	10.5	21.0	21.0		Based on 2011 expenditures, 10-year life
2012 Capital expenditures $220.0	n/a	n/a	n/a	n/a	n/a	n/a	n/a	n/a	11.0	22.0		Based on 2012 expenditures, 10-year life
2013 Capital expenditures $220.0	n/a	n/a	n/a	n/a	n/a	n/a	n/a	n/a	n/a	11.0		Based on 2013 expenditures, 10-year life
Total depreciation	$171.2	$200.1	$204.4	$218.1	$232.6	$247.6	$263.1	$279.1	$295.6	$312.6		Calculation: Sum of all estimated depreciation.

TABLE 9.7A Income Statement ($ Millions)

	ACTUAL			PROJECTED							ASSUMPTIONS
	2004	2005	2006	2007	2008	2009	2010	2011	2012	2013	
Net sales	$4,429.2	$4,836.0	$5,077.8	$5,331.7	$5,571.6	$5,794.5	$6,026.3	$6,207.1	$6,362.3	$6,521.4	Assumed growth: Prior year $(1 + g)$
Cost of goods sold (COGS)	2,509.2	2,765.5	2,894.3	3,017.7	3,136.8	3,244.9	3,356.6	3,444.9	3,512.0	3,599.8	Assumed % of sales: sales (% COGS)
Depreciation	171.2	200.1	204.4	218.1	232.6	247.6	263.1	279.1	295.6	312.6	Assumption from depreciation schedule
Selling, general, & administrative (SGA)	867.1	913.0	949.5	986.4	1,019.6	1,048.8	1,078.7	1,098.7	1,113.4	1,141.2	Assumed % of sales: sales (% SGA)
Restructuring and other one-time	—	96.5	—	—	—	—	—	—	—	—	Assumed
Total costs	3,547.5	3,975.1	4,048.2	4,222.2	4,389.0	4,541.3	4,698.4	4,822.7	4,921.0	5,053.6	Calculation: Sum of all expenses
Earnings before interest costs and taxes (EBIT)	881.7	860.9	1,029.6	1,109.5	1,182.6	1,253.2	1,327.9	1,384.4	1,441.3	1,467.8	Calculation: sales – total
Operating margin	19.9%	17.8%	20.3%	20.8%	21.2%	21.6%	22.0%	22.3%	22.7%	22.5%	Calculation: EBIT/Sales
Interest expense	66.5	88.0	106.6	78.5	49.2	25.9	4.3	(18.8)	(43.9)	(70.5)	Calculation: See discussion in chapter
Pre-tax income (PTI)	815.2	772.9	923.0	1,031.0	1,133.4	1,227.3	1,323.6	1,403.2	1,485.2	1,538.3	Calculation: EBIT – Interest
Provision for income taxes	237.3	279.7	341.5	381.5	419.4	454.1	489.7	519.2	549.5	569.2	Calculation: Tax rate (PTI)
Net income	$ 577.9	$ 493.2	$ 581.5	$ 649.5	$ 714.0	$ 773.2	$ 833.9	$ 884.0	$ 935.7	$ 969.1	Calculation: PTI – Taxes
Net margin	13.0%	10.2%	11.5%	12.2%	12.8%	13.3%	13.8%	14.2%	14.7%	14.9%	Calculation: Net Income/Sales
Shares outstanding—average	252.8	243.6	240.5	240.5	240.5	240.5	240.5	240.5	240.5	240.5	Average of prior year and this year
Earnings per share—basic	$ 2.33	$ 2.07	$ 2.42	$ 2.70	$ 2.97	$ 3.21	$ 3.47	$ 3.68	$ 3.89	$ 4.03	Calculation: Net income/Shares Outstanding
Annual growth	35.5%	−11.2%	16.8%	11.7%	9.9%	8.3%	7.8%	6.0%	5.8%	3.6%	Calculation: (This year/prior year) – 1

TABLE 9.7B Balance Sheet ($ Millions)

	ACTUAL					PROJECTED					ASSUMPTIONS
	2004	2005	2006	2007	2008	2009	2010	2011	2012	2013	
Current assets											
Cash and cash equivalents	$54.8	$67.2	$134.1	$106.7	$518.5	$1,058.2	$1,636.0	$2,263.1	$2,928.1	$3,622.8	Beginning balance + change in cash (CF)
Accounts receivable—trade	408.9	559.3	507.8	522.7	535.7	551.9	568.5	580.1	589.1	598.3	Assumed turnover: Sales/Turnover
Inventories	557.2	610.3	626.0	647.2	660.7	671.6	683.0	689.6	692.3	711.3	Assumed turnover: COGS/Turnover
Other current assets	176.8	172.1	182.1	192.1	202.1	212.1	224.1	236.1	248.1	260.1	Assumed $ increase
Total current assets	1,197.7	1,408.9	1,450.0	1,468.7	1,917.0	2,493.8	3,111.6	3,768.9	4,457.6	5,192.5	Calculation: Sum of current assets
Plant, property, and equipment, net	1,682.7	1,659.1	1,639.7	1,611.6	1,579.0	1,531.4	1,478.3	1,409.2	1,333.6	1,241.0	Begin balance + Capital expenditures – depreciation
Intangibles from business acq	463.9	487.3	487.3	487.3	487.3	487.3	487.3	487.3	487.3	487.3	Assumed constant
Other assets	468.5	739.9	769.9	799.9	829.9	859.9	899.9	939.9	979.9	1,019.9	Assumed $ increase
Total assets	$3,812.8	$4,295.2	$4,346.9	$4,367.5	$4,813.2	$5,372.4	$5,977.1	$6,605.3	$7,258.4	$7,940.7	Calculation: Sum of assets
Current liabilities											
Accounts payable	$148.7	$167.8	$174.1	$184.9	$194.8	$205.4	$215.5	$225.7	$233.6	$244.5	Assumed turnover: COGS/Turnover
Accrued liabilities	469.2	507.8	563.4	616.3	673.9	698.5	723.9	744.8	761.5	782.5	Assumed turnover: COGS/Turnover
Accrued income taxes	42.3	23.4	28.4	33.4	38.4	43.4	53.4	63.4	73.4	83.4	Assumed $ increase
Short-term debt	343.3	819.1	409.1	109.1	—	—	—	—	—	—	Begin balance + STDebt issuance – repayment
Current portion of long-term debt (CPLTD)	279.0	0.1	190.0	0.1	0.1	0.1	0.1	0.1	0.1	—	Assumed next year LTDebt repayment
Total current liabilities	1,282.5	1,518.2	1,365.0	943.8	907.2	947.4	992.9	1,034.0	1,068.6	1,110.4	Calculation: sum of current liabilities
Long-term debt	690.6	942.8	752.8	752.7	752.6	752.5	752.4	752.3	752.2	752.2	Begin balance + LTDebt issuance – CPLTD
Other long-term liabilities	383.4	412.9	431.6	453.2	473.6	492.5	512.2	527.6	540.8	554.3	Assumed % of sales
Deferred income taxes	319.2	400.2	427.5	458.0	491.6	527.9	567.1	608.6	652.6	698.1	Begin balance + assumed % of tax expense
Stockholders' equity	1,137.1	1,021.1	1,370.0	1,759.8	2,188.2	2,652.1	3,152.5	3,682.8	4,244.2	4,825.7	Begin Balance + Net Income – Dividends
Total liabilities and stockholders' equity	$3,812.8	$4,295.2	$4,346.9	$4,367.5	$4,813.2	$5,372.4	$5,977.1	$6,605.3	$7,258.4	$7,940.7	Calculation: Sum of Liabilities and equity

TABLE 9.7C   Cash Flow Statement ($ Millions)

	ACTUAL				PROJECTED						ASSUMPTIONS
	2004	2005	2006	2007	2008	2009	2010	2011	2012	2013	
Net income	$577.9	$493.2	$581.5	$649.5	$714.0	$773.2	$833.9	$884.0	$935.7	$969.1	From income statement
Depreciation	171.2	200.1	204.4	218.1	232.6	247.6	263.1	279.1	295.6	312.6	From income statement
Deferred income taxes— long term Liability	n/a	n/a	27.3	30.5	33.6	36.3	39.2	41.5	44.0	45.5	Calculation from balance sheet
Change in:											
Accounts receivable–trade	17.3	(149.0)	51.5	(14.9)	(13.0)	(16.2)	(16.6)	(11.6)	(9.0)	(9.2)	Calculation from balance sheet
Inventory	(40.0)	(51.2)	(15.7)	(21.2)	(13.5)	(10.9)	(11.4)	(6.6)	(2.7)	(19.0)	Calculation from balance sheet
Accounts payable	(11.3)	16.7	6.3	10.8	9.9	10.6	10.1	10.2	7.9	10.9	Calculation from balance sheet
Other assets and liabilities	108.4	32.0	n/a	n/a	n/a	n/a	n/a	n/a	n/a	n/a	Used only from the actual financials
Other current assets	n/a	n/a	(10.0)	(10.0)	(10.0)	(10.0)	(12.0)	(12.0)	(12.0)	(12.0)	Calculation from balance sheet
Other assets	n/a	n/a	(30.0)	(30.0)	(30.0)	(30.0)	(40.0)	(40.0)	(40.0)	(40.0)	Calculation from balance sheet
Accrued liabilities	n/a	n/a	55.6	52.9	57.6	24.6	25.4	20.9	16.7	21.0	Calculation from balance sheet
Accrued income taxes	n/a	n/a	5.0	5.0	5.0	5.0	10.0	10.0	10.0	10.0	Calculation from balance sheet
Other long-term liabilities	n/a	n/a	18.7	21.6	20.4	18.9	19.7	15.4	13.2	13.5	Calculation from balance sheet
Other, net	(35.8)	(80.0)	n/a	n/a	n/a	n/a	n/a	n/a	n/a	n/a	Used only from the actual financials
Cash from operating activities	787.7	461.8	894.6	912.3	1,006.6	1,049.1	1,121.4	1,190.9	1,259.4	1,302.4	Calculation: Sum of operating sources (uses)
Investment activities											
Capital expenditures	(181.7)	(181.1)	(185.0)	(190.0)	(200.0)	(200.0)	(210.0)	(210.0)	(220.0)	(220.0)	Assumption
Business acquisitions	(166.9)	(47.1)	–	–	–	–	–	–	–	–	Assumption
Other, net	(14.1)	(10.5)	–	–	–	–	–	–	–	–	Assumption
Cash (used for) investing	(362.7)	(238.7)	(185.0)	(190.0)	(200.0)	(200.0)	(210.0)	(210.0)	(220.0)	(220.0)	Calculation: Sum of investing sources (uses)
Financing activities											
Change in short term borrowings	331.2	475.6	(410.0)	(300.0)	(109.1)	–	–	–	–	–	Assumption
Long term borrowings	(29.9)	(79.0)	(0.1)	(190.0)	(0.1)	(0.1)	(0.1)	(0.1)	(0.1)	(0.1)	Assumption
Cash dividends	(205.7)	(221.2)	(232.6)	(259.8)	(285.6)	(309.3)	(333.5)	(353.6)	(374.3)	(387.6)	Assumed payout % of net income
Repurchase of stock	(698.9)	(537.0)	–	–	–	–	–	–	–	–	Assumption
Other	89.3	101.7	–	–	–	–	–	–	–	–	Assumption
Cash (used for) financing	(514.0)	(259.9)	(642.7)	(749.8)	(394.8)	(309.4)	(333.6)	(353.7)	(374.4)	(387.7)	Calculation: Sum of financing sources (uses)
Change in cash	$ (89.0)	$ (36.8)	$ 66.9	$ (27.5)	$ 411.8	$ 539.7	$ 577.8	$ 627.2	$ 665.0	$ 694.7	Calculation: Sum of all cash sources (uses)

TABLE 9.7D Summary ($ Millions)

	ACTUAL				PROJECTED						GROWTH RATES	
	2004	2005	2006	2007	2008	2009	2010	2011	2012	2013	05–06	05–13
Net Sales	$4,429.2	$4,836.0	$5,077.8	$5,331.7	$5,571.6	$5,794.5	$6,026.3	$6,207.1	$6,362.3	$6,521.4	5.0%	3.8%
Annual growth	6.2%	9.2%	5.0%	5.0%	4.5%	4.0%	4.0%	3.0%	2.5%	2.5%		
Operating income (EBIT)	$ 881.7	$ 860.9	$ 1,029.6	$ 1,109.5	$ 1,182.6	$ 1,253.2	$ 1,327.9	$ 1,384.4	$ 1,441.3	$ 1,467.8	$19.6%	6.9%
Operating margin	19.9%	17.8%	20.3%	20.8%	21.2%	21.6%	22.0%	22.3%	22.7%	22.5%		
Annual growth	14.3%	−2.4%	19.6%	7.8%	6.6%	6.0%	6.0%	4.3%	4.1%	1.8%		
Net income	$ 577.9	$ 493.2	$ 581.5	$ 649.5	$ 714.0	$ 773.2	$ 833.9	$ 884.0	$ 935.7	$ 969.1	$17.9%	8.8%
Net margin	13.0%	10.2%	11.5%	12.2%	12.8%	13.3%	13.8%	14.2%	14.7%	14.9%		
Annual growth	30.8%	−14.7%	17.9%	11.7%	9.9%	8.3%	7.8%	6.0%	5.8%	3.6%		
Earnings per share	$ 2.33	$ 2.07	$ 2.42	$ 2.70	$ 2.97	$ 3.21	$ 3.47	$ 3.68	$ 3.89	$ 4.03	$16.8%	8.7%
Annual growth	35.5%	−11.2%	16.8%	11.7%	9.9%	8.3%	7.8%	6.0%	5.8%	3.6%		
Cash and cash equivalents	$ 54.8	$ 67.2	$ 134.1	$ 106.7	$ 518.5	$ 1,058.2	$ 1,636.0	$ 2,263.1	$ 2,928.1	$ 3,622.8	$99.6%	64.6%
Short-term debt	343.3	819.1	409.1	109.1	—	—	—	—	—	—	n/a	n/a
Long-term debt	279.0	0.1	190.0	0.1	0.1	0.1	0.1	0.1	0.1	—	n/a	n/a
Current portion of long-term debt	690.6	942.8	752.8	752.7	752.6	752.5	752.4	752.3	752.2	752.2	−20.2%	−2.8%
Stockholders' equity	1,137.1	1,021.1	1,370.0	1,759.8	2,188.2	2,652.1	3,152.5	3,682.8	4,244.2	4,825.7	34.2%	21.4%
Total assets	$3,812.8	$4,295.2	$4,346.9	$4,367.5	$4,813.2	$5,372.4	$5,977.1	$6,605.3	$7,258.4	$7,940.7	1.2%	8.0%
Cash from operations	$ 787.7	$ 461.8	$ 894.6	$ 912.3	$ 1,006.6	$ 1,049.1	$ 1,121.4	$ 1,190.9	$ 1,259.4	$ 1,302.4	93.7%	13.8%
Cash used for investing	(362.7)	(238.7)	(185.0)	(190.0)	(200.0)	(200.0)	(210.0)	(210.0)	(220.0)	(220.0)	−22.5%	−1.0%
Cash used for financing	(514.0)	(259.9)	(642.7)	(749.8)	(394.8)	(309.4)	(333.6)	(353.7)	(374.4)	(387.7)	147.3%	5.1%
Cash flow	$ (89.0)	$ (36.8)	$ 66.9	$ (27.5)	$ 411.8	$ 539.7	$ 577.8	$ 627.2	$ 665.0	$ 694.7	n/a	n/a
Dividends	$ 205.7	$ 221.2	$ 232.6	$ 259.8	$ 285.6	$ 309.3	$ 333.5	$ 353.6	$ 374.3	$ 387.6	5.2%	7.3%
Pre-tax margin	18.41%	15.98%	18.18%	19.34%	20.34%	21.18%	21.96%	22.61%	23.34%	23.59%		
(1 − Tax Rate)	0.709	0.638	0.630	0.630	0.630	0.630	0.630	0.630	0.630	0.630		
Net margin	13.05%	10.20%	11.45%	12.18%	12.82%	13.34%	13.84%	14.24%	14.71%	14.86%		
Total asset turnover	1.162	1.126	1.168	1.221	1.158	1.079	1.008	0.940	0.877	0.821		
Return on assets	15.16%	11.48%	13.38%	14.87%	14.83%	14.39%	13.95%	13.38%	12.89%	12.20%		
Financial leverage	3.353	4.206	3.173	2.482	2.200	2.026	1.896	1.794	1.710	1.646		
Return on equity	50.82%	48.30%	42.45%	36.91%	32.63%	29.15%	26.45%	24.00%	22.05%	20.08%		

Interest rates and income tax rates are examples of external assumptions from the finance area. The Treasurer has responsibilities for providing interest rate forecasts. Once again, specific interest rates for every existing debt instrument can be detailed, or as in this case, the interest expense rate can reflect a "blended" weighted average of existing debt instruments and anticipated borrowing rates. Also, this model's approach distinguishes between the borrowing interest rate (expense) and interest rates (income) earned on any corporate savings in cash and equivalents. The interest income rate considers the high-quality, high-liquidity, short-term nature of marketable securities, which results in a significantly lower interest rate.

The tax rate is an all-inclusive income tax rate that is projected by the tax department. The rate includes the income tax impact from all governments: federal government, foreign taxing authorities, state revenue departments, and local municipalities.

Finally, the year-end shares outstanding represent shares outstanding from the previous year increased (decreased) by the number of shares issued (repurchased).

BALANCE SHEET OBJECTIVES AND ASSUMPTIONS

Balance sheet assumptions come from two sources: operational objectives and finance/accounting estimates.

The operational objectives include performance standards for accounts receivable, inventory, accounts payable, and accrued liabilities. The objectives are listed as end-of-the-year-turnovers, but they could also be expressed as days outstanding by dividing 365 days in a year by the turnover objective. See Chapter 7 for more information about turnovers and days outstanding. In all cases, the objectives represent improving efficiency, effectiveness, and performance. That is, the turnover of assets is increasing, which represents relatively less investment in working capital. Lower turnover in liabilities increases the use of suppliers' cash for investments; once again, less investment in working capital. These objectives are often tied to a specific area's compensation objectives (e.g., receivables director held responsible for receivables turnover).

Assumptions related to miscellaneous assets and liabilities complete the balance sheet and are generally less significant. Numerous refinements can be used to estimate the values or year-to-year changes (dollars or percent) for these miscellaneous items. In this example, current deferred tax assets, prepaid expenses, other assets, and accrued income taxes are projected by estimating the annual dollar change and adding that change to the previous year's balance. Other long-term liabilities are estimated as a percent of sales. The values and the minimal annual changes remain immaterial throughout.

CASH FLOW OBJECTIVES AND ASSUMPTIONS

The cash flow statement objectives and assumptions consist of investment objectives, financing (including dividends) objectives and requirements, and remaining technical accounting assumptions. These values come directly from senior management or finance.

The remaining technical accounting item, deferred taxes, represent the differences between the reported provision for income taxes in the annual report's income statement and the tax payments to the federal government, as discussed in Chapters 2 and 4. There are many ways to potentially estimate deferred taxes or the change in deferred taxes. For the past number of years (with the exception of 2004), the change in deferred tax liability approximated 8.0% of the reported provision for income taxes. Another way of looking at this is that 92% of the reported tax provision is actually paid; the remaining 8% is deferred for future payments (and becomes an addition to deferred taxes—long-term liabilities). This same relationship can be assumed to hold throughout the 8-year projection period.

The capital expenditure plan often begins with engineering, which accumulates antici-pated capital expenditures for new products, new plants, other capacity expansion, cost reduction, and so on. The senior management team manages the capital investment process and may limit the amount of capital investment. This is called "soft rationing" of capital in contrast to "hard" capital rationing, which is imposed by financial markets. In our example, the level of estimated capital expenditures is growing to $220 million per annum over this 8-year period. In this base scenario, no business acquisitions have been included. If an organization anticipated acquiring or divesting of businesses, the estimated expenditures or proceeds should be captured in this section as well.

Finally, in conjunction with senior management, treasury supplies assumptions about debt issuance or repayment, cash dividends, and any stock repurchases. The debt repay-ment may include scheduled (or required) debt repayment and additional repayment. Dividends are estimated as a percent of net income (dividend payout) or 40% in this exam-ple. Consequently, dividends will grow at the same rate as net income. In the base scenario, stock repurchases are assumed to be zero. If there is excess cash or management wants to recapitalize, outstanding shares can be repurchased.

Once the modeling approach is developed (framework and structure) and management objectives translated to a series of assumptions, the next step is to calculate the financial statements using the framework and the objectives, performance standards, and assumptions.

CALCULATING THE FINANCIAL STATEMENTS

Tables 9.7A through 9.7C present the statements with calculations noted item by item. Discussed below are four basic calculation approaches using the noted assumptions as well as a lengthier discussion about interest expense and income.

Basic Calculations

1. Growth: On the income statement, net sales are estimated as the prior year's sales increased by the assumed growth rate. For example:

$$\text{Sales}_t = \text{Sales}_{(t-1)} \times (1 + \text{Growth}_t)$$

   or

$$\text{Sales}_{2006} = \text{Sales}_{2005} \times (1 + \text{Growth}_{2006})$$
$$= \$4,836.0 \times (1 + 0.050) = \$5,077.8$$

2. Percent of Sales: Cost of goods sold (COGS) and selling, general, and administrative (SGA) expenses as well as other long-term liabilities are projected based upon sales and the assumed relationship as a percent of sales:

$$\text{COGS}_t = \text{Sales}_t \times (\% \text{ of Sales Assumption}_t)$$

   or

$$\text{COGS}_{2006} = \text{Sales}_{2006} \times (\% \text{ of Sales}_{2006})$$
$$= \$5,077.8 \times (0.570) = \$2,894.3$$

Likewise, selling, general, and administrative expense and other long-term liabilities are estimated using their relationship with sales and the projected sales.

3. Turnovers: Receivables, inventory, payables, and accrued liabilities are all expressed in management terms as turnovers based on sales (receivables) or cost of sales:

$$\text{Receivables}_t = \text{Sales}_t/(\text{Receivables Turnover Assumption}_t)$$

or

$$\text{Receivables}_{2006} = \text{Sales}_{2006}/(\text{Turnover}_{2006})$$
$$= \$5{,}077.8/10.00 = \$507.8$$

Inventory, payables, and accruals would be calculated in a similar fashion except cost of sales would be used in place of sales.

4. "Changes in:" There are two approaches that highlight the integrative nature of the balance sheet and cash flow statement. One approach, such as with accounts receivable, projects the balance sheet item and then reflects the change in the balance sheet item on the cash flow statement. Chapter 2 discusses the interrelationship of the financial statements, the impact of the income statement, and the balance sheet reflected on the cash flow statement. The following summarizes the cash flow implications of changes in the balance sheet:

	ASSET CHANGE	LIABILITY CHANGE
Source of cash	Decrease	Increase
Use of cash	Increase	Decrease

A decrease (increase) in an asset (liability) produces a source of cash.

The other approach is based off of an assumption such as change in other current assets (OCA). That assumption is directly reflected on the cash flow statement and then added to the account on the balance sheet:

$$\text{OCA}_t = \text{OCA}_{(t-1)} + (\text{Change in OCA}_t)$$

or

$$\text{OCA}_{2006} = \text{OCA}_{2005} + (\text{Change in OCA}_{2006})$$
$$= \$172.1 + \$10.0 = \$182.1$$

Either approach works fine as long as it is coordinated between the balance sheet and cash flow.

5. Accounting relationships: There are two additional accounting relationships that are important when projecting the balances of (1) plant, property, and equipment, net (PP&E, net) and (2) stockholders' equity, as discussed in Chapter 2:

2006 PROJECTED Plant, Property, and Equipment, Net		2006 PROJECTED Stockholders' Equity	
2005 PP&E, net	$1,659.1	2005 Stockholders' equity	$1,021.1
From 2006 initial cash flow:		From 2006 initial cash flow:	
+ Capital expenditures	185.0	+ Net income	581.5
− Depreciation	(204.4)	−Dividends	(232.6)
		−Repurchases	(0.0)
Equals:	————	Equals:	————
2006 PP&E, net	$1,639.7	2006 Stockholders' equity	$1,370.0

This provides mechanical linkage between the balance sheet and the other financial statements.

6. Interest expense (income): For our example, interest expense or income is calculated based on last year's balances of interest-bearing debt and cash:

$$
\begin{aligned}
\begin{matrix} \text{Interest} \\ \text{Expense}_t \\ (\text{Income}_t) \end{matrix} &= \Big(\quad \text{Interest Expense}_t \quad \Big) - \Big(\quad \text{Interest Income}_t \quad \Big) \\[2mm]
&= \begin{pmatrix} \text{Interest-} & \text{Interest} \\ \text{Bearing} & \times & \text{Rate:} \\ \text{Debt}_{(t-1)} & & \text{Expense}_t \end{pmatrix} - \begin{pmatrix} \text{Cash} & & \text{Interest} \\ \& & \times & \text{Rate:} \\ \text{Equivl}_{(t-1)} & & \text{Income}_t \end{pmatrix} \\[2mm]
\begin{matrix} \text{Interest} \\ \text{Expense}_{06} \\ (\text{Income}_{06}) \end{matrix} &= \begin{pmatrix} \text{Interest-} & \text{Interest} \\ \text{Bearing} & \times & \text{Rate:} \\ \text{Debt}_{05} & & \text{Expense}_{06} \end{pmatrix} - \begin{pmatrix} \text{Cash} & & \text{Interest} \\ \& & \times & \text{Rate:} \\ \text{Equivl}_{05} & & \text{Income}_{06} \end{pmatrix} \\[2mm]
&= (\quad \$1{,}762.0 \times 0.062 \quad) - (\quad \$67.2 \times 0.040 \quad) \\[1mm]
&= \$109.3 - \$2.7 = \$106.6
\end{aligned}
$$

For 2006, net interest expense is estimated to be $106.6 million. That is, $109.3 million of interest expense offset by $2.7 million of interest income. Note that the interest is calculated with the interest rate assumptions for the current year times the balances as of the end of the previous year (or the first day of the current year). There are numerous ways to project interest. This approach assumes that all balances are maintained throughout the period. All debt repayment (issuance) and cash flow occur on the last day of the fiscal year and consequently have no impact on the amount of interest expense (income). This is less than an accurate portrayal of actual cash flow. However, more advanced techniques require the use of iterative (or even circular) logic to zero in on a more exacting projection. For our illustrative purposes, this methodology is appropriate, but it may need to be strengthened in practice to reflect cash flow throughout the year.

The 2005 interest-bearing debt includes:

INTEREST-BEARING DEBT	2005
Short-term debt	$ 819.1
Current portion of long-term debt	0.1
Long-term debt	942.8
Total interest-bearing debt	$1,762.0

7. Other Calculations: The provision for income taxes is estimated as the amount of pre-tax income times the assumed tax rate:

$$\text{Taxes}_t = \text{PTI}_t \times (\text{Assumed Tax Rate}_t)$$

or

$$
\begin{aligned}
\text{Taxes}_{2006} &= \text{PTI}_{2006} \times (\text{Tax Rate}_{2006}) \\
&= \$923.0 \times (0.370) = \$341.5
\end{aligned}
$$

Earnings per share result from dividing net income by the average number of shares outstanding.

Margins and the EPS growth rate are calculated as in Chapter 7:

Operating margin =   EBIT/Net sales
Net margin   =   Net income/Net sales
EPS growth   = $(EPS_t - EPS_{(t-1)})/EPS_{(t-1)}$

Totals, subtotals, and other calculations are noted on Tables 9.7A through 9.7C.

Financial Statement Summary

Tables 9.7A through 9.7C include a lot of numbers and an overwhelming amount of information. To make the process more "user-friendly," a one-page summary is recommended. The summary (see Table 9.7D) overviews the financial statements and includes a projected DuPont Analysis. A summary should include all of the financial data that the organization feels is necessary and important. Margins and annual growth rates are displayed. Also, on the far right-hand side of Table 9.7D, annual growth rates for 2005 to 2006 as well as the compound annual growth rate (CAGR) for the 8-year period from 2005 to 2013 are noted.

The final section of the summary details a DuPont Analysis (see Chapter 7). The pretax margin improves due to objectives that reduce cost of goods sold, selling, general, and administrative expense, and interest expense. Because the income tax rate is projected at a constant 37.0%, the net margin is also improving.

The total asset turnover falls as Hershey becomes less efficient in the use of its assets. That is, despite the challenges of increasing the receivables and inventory turnover, decreasing the payables and accrued liabilities turnover, and implementing minimum capital expenditures, total asset turnover is declining. Notice that cash and cash equivalents exceed $3.6 billion (that's billion, with a "B") by 2013! This increase is weighing down the total asset turnover.

However, the impact of an increasing net margin is overridden by the decreasing turnover and results in a declining return on assets starting in 2009.

Once again, due to the major build-up of cash combined with modest debt repayment, the financial leverage (Assets/Equity) fades from a 2005 level of 4.206 (when every dollar of equity supported over $4.20 of assets) to a 2013 level of 1.646 (or for every dollar of equity the corporation has almost $1.65 of assets). This depresses the return on equity by over 28 percentage points from 2005 (48.3% to 20.1%).

In this hypothetical strategic plan, Hershey institutes operating objectives for meaningful growth, improving margins, and more aggressive working capital management. These heightened objectives lead to improving income and cash flow generation. However, because of the buildup in cash and stockholders' equity, turnover and financial leverage decline. This depresses return on assets and return on equity.

Fortunately, this is only a plan! Issues such as these can be addressed and adjusted. Plans can be made to seize opportunities for improving Hershey's performance from this "base" scenario.

Performance Objectives

As Table 9.8 shows, 2006 performance objectives are often assigned to various managers. The assignments become that manager's performance objectives for the year in many cases, and the manager's bonus is often tied directly to achieving those goals.

| TABLE 9.8 | Performance Monitoring—2006 Return on Assets ($ Millions) |

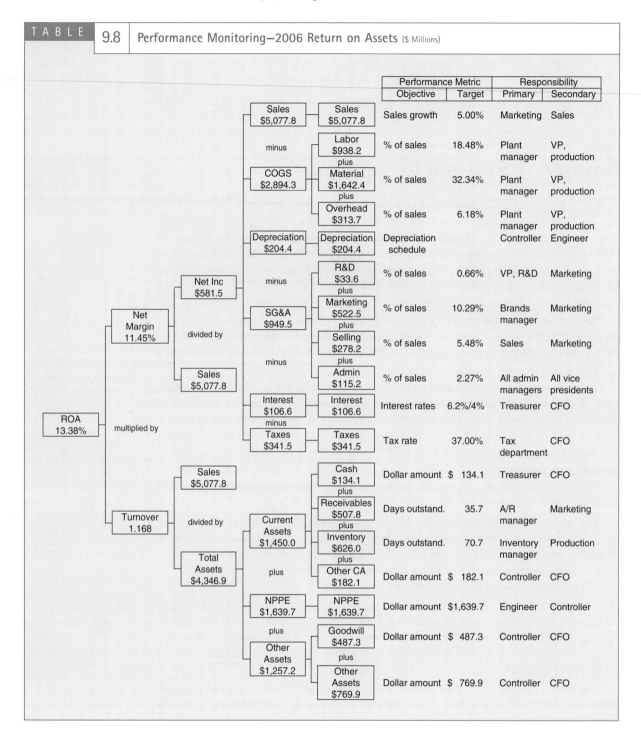

		Performance Metric		Responsibility	
		Objective	Target	Primary	Secondary
Sales $5,077.8	Sales $5,077.8	Sales growth	5.00%	Marketing	Sales
minus	Labor $938.2	% of sales	18.48%	Plant manager	VP, production
COGS $2,894.3	Material $1,642.4	% of sales	32.34%	Plant manager	VP, production
	Overhead $313.7	% of sales	6.18%	Plant manager	VP, production
Depreciation $204.4	Depreciation $204.4	Depreciation schedule		Controller	Engineer
minus	R&D $33.6	% of sales	0.66%	VP, R&D	Marketing
SG&A $949.5	Marketing $522.5	% of sales	10.29%	Brands manager	Marketing
	Selling $278.2	% of sales	5.48%	Sales	Marketing
minus	Admin $115.2	% of sales	2.27%	All admin managers	All vice presidents
Interest $106.6	Interest $106.6	Interest rates	6.2%/4%	Treasurer	CFO
Taxes $341.5	Taxes $341.5	Tax rate	37.00%	Tax department	CFO
	Cash $134.1	Dollar amount	$ 134.1	Treasurer	CFO
Current Assets $1,450.0	Receivables $507.8	Days outstand.	35.7	A/R manager	Marketing
	Inventory $626.0	Days outstand.	70.7	Inventory manager	Production
	Other CA $182.1	Dollar amount	$ 182.1	Controller	CFO
NPPE $1,639.7	NPPE $1,639.7	Dollar amount	$1,639.7	Engineer	Controller
Other Assets $1,257.2	Goodwill $487.3	Dollar amount	$ 487.3	Controller	CFO
	Other Assets $769.9	Dollar amount	$ 769.9	Controller	CFO

ROA 13.38% — Net Margin 11.45% (multiplied by) Turnover 1.168

Net Margin 11.45% = Net Inc $581.5 divided by Sales $5,077.8

Turnover 1.168 = Sales $5,077.8 divided by Total Assets $4,346.9

Attaining a sales level of $5,077.8 million is the primary responsibility of marketing and sales departments. Achieving the expense objectives is a widely held responsibility shared by many depending on the nature of the expense. Items on the balance sheet also are the responsibilities of the appropriate areas, such as the inventory manager and production jointly sharing the responsibility for limiting investment in inventory to $626.0 million.

Alternative Scenarios

From the base strategic plan, additional strategies can be explored to shore-up the declining return on assets and return on equity that is evidenced in the summary (see Table 9.7D). Should operations be challenged further? Should sales and marketing be tasked for additional sales growth? Or should the organization consider additional strategies? We call this analysis "Gap Analysis" because it helps us understand alternative approaches to closing a performance gap.

By challenging operations through tasking additional sales growth, improving margins, or enhancing working capital management, the strategic plan will produce additional income and cash flow while improving return on assets and return on equity. However, by using the cash to repurchase its own shares or by seeking growth through acquisition, the company may more productively employ its cash.

A decision for a company to repurchase its outstanding stock or acquire a company is a very complicated managerial, business, and economic event. A financial strategic plan assists in understanding the accounting ramifications of those events. First and foremost, the decision must be a good economic decision, with a positive net present value.

For our purposes, assume that the company developed the base scenario strategic financial plan discussed above. The company recognized that by the year 2013 it will have more than $3.6 billion in cash. If the following are true—(1) operations are stretched, (2) there are no viable substantial acquisition candidates, (3) the current stock price is undervalued, and (4) the cash balance is earning only 4.0% interest income (2.5% after corporate taxes)— the company should consider a share repurchase program. The economics of the transaction are validated through a self-valuation study, and a share repurchase strategy is considered. The following additional assumptions are made:

YEAR	SHARES REPURCHASED (MM)	ASSUMED PRICE PER SHARE	TOTAL REPURCHASED ($ MM)
2006	0.0	$60	—
2007	0.0	65	—
2008	5.0	70	350.0
2009	6.0	75	450.0
2010	6.0	80	480.0
2011	6.0	85	510.0
2012	7.0	90	630.0
2013	7.0	95	665.0

With the base scenario in hand, senior management (led by the recommendation of the chief financial officer) can examine a strategy of repurchasing almost $3.1 billion or 37.0 million shares over this 8-year projection period.

The results of the repurchase strategy reflect improved performance in the strategic plan. Table 9.9 compares the base scenario and the "share repurchase" augmented strategic plan. Notice that net sales (and annual growth), operating income (margin and growth), short-term and long-term debt balances, and cash used for investing do not change! These are separate projections that are unrelated to the effects of share repurchases.

Comparing scenarios, net income in 2013 decreases by $62.7 million due to reduced interest income, and the net margin drops by 0.96 percentage points (from 14.86% to 13.90%). However, earnings per share increases by $0.35 since there are fewer shares outstanding. Cash, stockholders' equity, and total assets decrease by approximately the

TABLE 9.9	Scenario Comparisons (Share Repurchase Scenario vs. Base Scenario: Year 2013 ($ Millions))		
		YEAR 2013	
	Base	Share Repurchase	Plan Difference
Net sales	$ 6,521.4	$ 6,521.4	$ —
Annual growth	2.50%	2.50%	0.00%
Operating income (EBIT)	$ 1,467.8	$ 1,467.8	$ —
Operating margin	22.51%	22.51%	0.00%
Annual growth	1.84%	1.84%	0.00%
Net income	$ 969.1	$ 906.4	$(62.7)
Net margin	14.86%	13.90%	-0.96%
Annual growth	3.57%	1.89%	-1.58%
Earnings per share	$4.03	$4.38	$0.35
Annual growth	3.57%	5.34%	1.87%
Cash and cash equivalents	$3,622.8	$ 427.4	$(3,195.4)
Short-term debt	—	—	—
Current portion of long-term debt	—	—	—
Long-term debt	752.2	752.2	—
Stockholders' equity	4,825.7	1,638.3	(3,187.4)
Total assets	7,940.7	4,745.3	(3,195.4)
Cash from operations	$1,302.4	$1,236.8	$(65.6)
Cash used for investing	(220.0)	(220.0)	—
Cash used for financing	(387.7)	(1,027.7)	(640.0)
Cash flow	$ 694.7	$ (10.9)	$ (705.6)
Dividends	$ 387.6	$ 362.6	$ (25.0)
Pretax margin	23.59%	22.06%	-1.53%
(1 − Tax rate)	0.630	0.630	0.000
Net margin	14.86%	13.90%	-0.96%
Total asset turnover	0.821	1.374	0.553
Return on assets	12.20%	19.10%	6.90%
Financial leverage	1.646	2.896	1.251
Return on equity	20.08%	55.32%	35.24%

$3.2 billion of share repurchase amount. Remember there are additional effects as a result of lost interest income, lower changes in deferred taxes (long-term liability), and as a result of fewer shares outstanding, lower dividend payments.

The DuPont analysis reveals what we anticipated. Once again, the reduced interest income depresses the pre-tax margin and with no changes in the tax rate, the reduced interest income reduces the net margin as well. However, the asset turnover shows consistent improvement and ends this 8-year projection period at 1.374 or 0.553 better than the base scenario. Despite the reduced margin, return on assets consistently improves and reaches 19.10% by 2013. Under both scenarios, financial leverage declines, but under the alternative scenario, the financial leverage is well balanced at an acceptable level of 2.896. This results in a 2013 return on equity (ROE Return of Equity) of 55.32%, above the 2005 ROE.

Working with a strong, supportive, and flexible financial model, analysts can generate multiple scenarios with multiple refinements. The modeling proves a valuable tool enabling senior management to chart the course of the corporation and build the strategies that will support the corporation's objectives leading, to a successful completion of the corporation's mission.

summary

Planning is a continuous process. The strategic review and plan usually starts in the beginning of a fiscal year. The first year of the strategic plan becomes the preliminary, targeted financial performance for the following year's budget. After consideration of many tactical alternatives by the division senior management and other operations managers, priorities are established and detailed budgets developed. The budget (compared to the strategic plan) is prepared in far more detail, at an SKU, plant, sales office, and cost center level. Tens of millions of detailed assumptions are created in the annual budgeting process. The budgeting process often starts as early as six months before the next year.

Table 9.10 presents a diagram of the complete planning cycle. Of course, developing the plan and the budget is the easy part. The hard part is successfully implementing all strategies and surpassing the objectives. This critical component, implementation, can never be overlooked. Supportive feedback systems complete the planning process,

T A B L E	9.10	Complete Planning Process

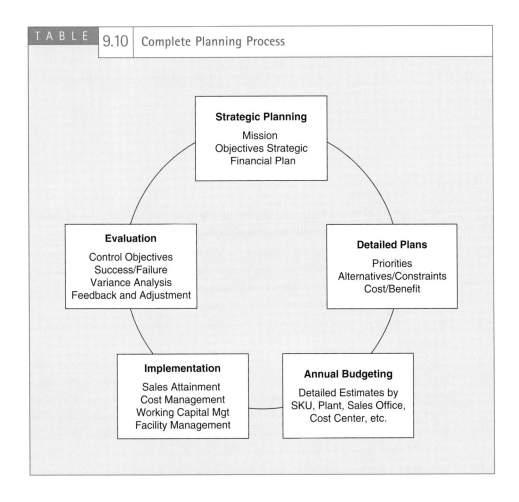

provide variance analysis, assess performance success or failure, and facilitate adjustments for incorporation during the next planning cycle.

When we complete the strategic financial plan and very detailed budgets often entailing person-decades of effort (at Fortune 500 companies), the one thing that we know with certainty is that the plan is wrong! While the strategic financial plan holds considerable value, the true value is found in the strategic planning process, which:

- Facilitates communication among the senior executives of an organization
- Sets a business direction
- Identifies, clarifies, and prioritizes opportunities and requirements
- Establishes business performance standards and objectives

Today's finance professional and business executive needs to understand the strategic planning process and the development of a strategic financial plan. Whether your company has a long-established track record or your company is a start-up organization in need of financing, an integrated, financial business plan that demonstrates the ramifications of implementing objectives and strategies is a requirement.

This chapter provides an overview of the strategic planning process and considers simple models that lead to a strategic financial planning model. The strategic financial planning model is a realistic, integrated model that is used it to quantify the strategic plan while establishing performance targets. The financial model provides a complete system of financial statements, income statement, balance sheet, and cash flow that functions as a coordinated management tool.

Questions

9.1   Please comment on the following statement: "Why bother? Why bother planning when we know the future will all change any way?"

9.2   Along with Question 1, please comment on the following statement: "OK. So we discuss where we are going, we plan for the future, but why do we bother with numbers? Why do we try to put numbers on our plans when we realize that one or two major business deals will make our numbers obsolete?"

9.3   Why do firms use multiple approaches for stimulating discussions around strategic planning?

9.4   Say you were sitting on a plane, reading your company's annual budget and your company's long-term strategic plan. The person sitting aside you is the chief operating officer from one of your major competitors. You stood up and went to use the facilities, leaving both documents on your seat. Which document would the COO be most interested in reading and why? Which document would the CEO be most interested in reading and why?

9.5   How does a strategic financial plan help the organization prioritize its directions?

9.6   A corporation has 1,000 stockkeeping units (i.e., products). Discuss why you may want to prepare a detailed annual budget by SKU. What are the advantages and the disadvantages?

9.7   For the same corporation as in Question 6, discuss why you may not want to prepare a 5-year strategic financial forecast for the 1,000 SKUs. How else could you approach it?

9.8   Annual Budget vs. Strategic Financial Planning:

   a.   During the annual budget, many large companies find themselves with more than 100 million pieces of financial data. How is that possible?

   b.   These same companies budget by each SKU (i.e., product), every ingredient, every sales region, every manufacturing facility, every distribution center, every staff cost center, every account, by month. In Fortune 200 firms, "person centuries" go into the annual budget. Why do some companies go to such extremes?

   c.   Is this level of detail appropriate for a long-term strategic financial plan?

9.9   Compare and contrast the external funds needed (EFN) approach to the percent of sales method for forecasting.

9.10   Compare and contrast the percent of sales approach to forecasting with the more detailed financial forecast.

Problems

9.1

Use the percent of sales method to forecast for the next 3 years.

   a.   Based on the last year of actual, calculate the percent of sales for each item below:

	($ millions)	% of Sales
Sales	$200	
Expenses	150	
Pre-tax income	50	
Taxes	20	
Net income	$ 30	
Cash	$ 20	
Accounts receivable	25	
Inventory	30	
Equipment, net	80	
Other assets	5	
Total assets	$160	
Accounts payable	$ 35	
Accrued liabilities	30	
Long-term debt	25	
Other liabilities	10	
Equity	60	
Total liabilities	$160	

9.10

A projected 2007 balance sheet and income statement is presented below along with the 2006 actual balance sheet. Construct the cash flow statement for 2007. What are the capital expenditures and dividends?

	2006	2007		2006	2007
Cash	$ 600	$ 550	Accounts payable	$ 2,175	$ 2,425
Accounts receivable	1,075	1,275	Notes payable	1,100	750
Inventory	1,550	1,775	Total current liabilities	3,275	3,175
Total current assets	3,225	3,600	Long-term debt	625	2,025
Net property, plant, and equipment (Net PP&E)	7,800	8,625	Common stock	3,675	3,425
Other assets	60	50	Retained earnings	3,510	3,650
Total	$11,085	$12,275	Total	$11,085	$12,275

	2007
Net sales	$4,250
Cost of goods sold (COGS)	2,750
Depreciation	900
Earnings before interest and taxes (EBIT)	600
Interest	175
Pre-tax income	425
Taxes	175
Net income	$ 250

9.11

Indicate below the impact (increase, decrease, or no effect) that the following assumption revisions have on the noted items. Assume that each revision is independent of the others.

	Sales Growth Increases from Base Scenario	Cost of Goods Sold (%) Increases	Inventory Turnover Improves
Sales			
Operating income (EBIT)			
Net income			
Cash			
Stockholders' equity			

9.12

Augusta Corporation wants to project its balance sheet for the years 2007 through 2009. Conversations with numerous members of the management team resulted in the following information:

Item	Estimation Technique	2007	2008	2009
Accounts receivable	Turnover	9.0	10.0	10.5
Inventory	Days outstanding	90	85	80
Accounts payable	Turnover	11.0	10.9	10.8
Other assets	Growth rate (%)	5%	5%	5%
Other current liabilities	Growth $	$ 3.0	$ 3.0	$ 3.0
Capital expenditures	Estimated amount	$ 25.0	$ 28.0	$ 30.0
Depreciation expense	Estimated amount	$ 15.3	$ 16.2	$ 17.5
Debt repayment	Estimated amount	$ 20.0	$ 30.0	$ 50.0
Net income	Estimated amount	$ 68.3	$ 73.2	$ 79.1
Dividend pay out (%)	% of net income	35%	38%	40%
Sales	Estimated amount	$900.0	$950.0	$1,000.0
Cost of goods sold	Estimated amount	$540.0	$570.0	$ 600.0

Use the cash account to balance the balance sheet.

Complete the following:

	ACTUAL 2006	PROJECTED 2007	2008	2009
Cash	$ 50.0			
Accounts receivable	95.0			
Inventory	148.0			
Total current assets	293.0			
Net, PP&E	350.0			
Other assets	14.0			
Total assets	$657.0			
Accounts payable	$ 45.0			
Other current liabilities	38.0			
Total current liabilities	83.0			
Long-term debt	250.0			
Stockholders' equity	324.0			
Total	$657.0			

PP&E, plant, property, and equipment.

9.13

Project the Year 1 Plan, based on the following: (Round to the nearest *whole dollar*!)

	Year 0	Projection Assumptions	Year 1 Plan
Sales	$8,000	10% growth	
Cost of goods sold (ex. Depr)	5,200	Same % of sales	
Depreciation	500	Increase by $100	
S, G, & A	1,500	Same % of sales	
EBIT	800		_____
Net, interest expense	100	See note	_____
Pre-tax income	700		
Taxes	280	40% tax rate	_____
Net income	$420		
Cash	$1,000		
Accounts receivable	833	36.5 days outstanding—sales	
Inventory	1,625	109.5 days outstanding—COGS	_____
Current assets	3,458		
Net, PP&E	3,000		
Other assets	125	Increase by $60	_____
Total assets	$6,583		
Accounts payable	$ 650	Same turnover—COGS	
Accrued liabilities	542	10% of COGS	
Short-term debt (STD)	800		
Other current liabilities	55	Decrease by $15	_____
Current liabilities	2,047		
Long-term debt (LTD)	1,200		
Stockholders' equity	3,336		_____
Total liabilities and equity	$6,583		
			Sources (Uses)
Net income	$ 420		
Depreciation	500		
Change in accounts receivable	(234)		
Change in inventory	189		
Change in other assets	(11)		
Change in accounts payable	273		
Change in accrued liabilities	(56)		
Change in other current liabilities	68		_____
Cash flow from operations	1,149		
Capital expenditures	(425)	Estimate	(550)
Change in short-term debt	50	Estimate	(650)
Change in long-term debt	50	Estimate	200
Dividends	(215)	50% dividend payout	
Cash from (used for) financing	(115)		_____
Change in cash	$ 609		

*Year 1 interest expense is calculated as 6% (the interest expense rate) times the sum of Year 0 short-term debt and Year 0 long-term debt balances, offset by 2% (the interest income rate) times the Year 0 cash balance.

9.14

Project the plan year 2008 based on the following: (Round to the nearest *whole dollar!*)

	2007	Projection Assumptions	2008 Plan
Sales	$7,500	20% growth	
Cost of goods sold (ex. Depr)	4,500	Same % of sales	
Depreciation	350	Increase by $50	
S, G, & A	1,800	Same % of sales	_____
EBIT	850		
Net, interest expense	50	See note	_____
Pre-tax income	800		
Taxes	320	40% tax rate	
Net income	$ 480		_____
Cash	$ 134		
Accounts receivable	822	Same turnover–sales	
Inventory	1,233	90 days outstanding–COGS	
Current assets	2,189		_____
Net, PP&E	2,400		
Other assets	179	Decrease by $5	
Total assets	$4,768		_____
Accounts payable	$500	Same turnover–COGS	
Accrued liabilities	348	Decrease by $18	
Short-term debt	187		
Other current liabilities	122	Increase by $8	
Current liabilities	1,157		
Long-term debt	1,423		
Stockholders' equity	2,188		
Total liabilities and equity	$4,768		_____

			Sources (Uses)
Net income	$ 480		
Depreciation	350		
Change in accounts receivable	(156)		
Change in inventory	31		
Change in other assets	(38)		
Change in accounts payable	(23)		
Change in accrued liabilities	56		
Change in other current liabilities	68		
Cash flow from operations	768		_____
Capital expenditures	(367)	Estimate	(378)
Change in short-term debt	50	Estimate	(115)
Change in long-term debt	50	Estimate	50
Dividends	(222)	60% dividend payout	
Cash from (used for) financing	(122)		_____
Change in cash	$ 279		

*2008 Interest expense is calculated as 7% (the interest expense rate) times the sum of 2007 STD and 2007 LTD balances, offset by 4% (the interest income rate) times the 2007 cash balance.
PP&E, plant, property, and equipment.

part 4

Investment Strategies and Decisions

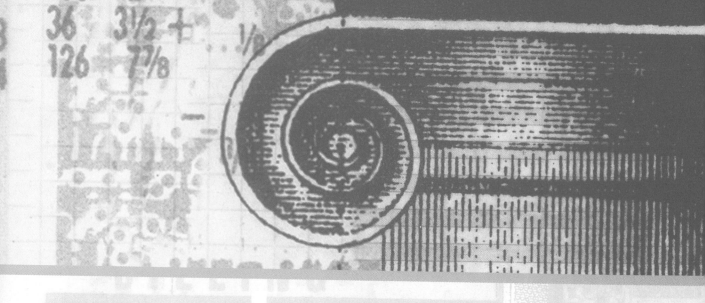

Capital Expenditure Management and Alternative Investment Criteria

The capital investment decision combines many aspects of business, economics, finance, and accounting with the organization's strategy. Chapter 2 introduced financial statements and cash flows, which provide the basic information necessary for financial evaluation. Chapter 3 provided the fundamental tool, the time value of money, which is necessary to value future cash flows. Chapters 7 and 9 discussed financial performance metrics and strategic financial planning, respectively. Building upon these topics, this chapter advances our discussion on evaluating corporate investment decisions by discussing the capital investment program and introducing evaluation techniques.

Learning Outcomes

After completing this chapter, you should be able to:

1. Identify the four phases of the capital investment process as well as other managerial aspects of a successful capital investment program

2. Apply the Time Value of Money tools learned in Chapter 3

3. Calculate multiple capital valuation techniques: *payback period* (PBP), *net present value* (NPV), *internal rate of return* (IRR), *terminal rate of return* (TRR), *discounted payback period* (DPBP), and *profitability index* (PI)

4. Recommend NPV as the superior evaluation technique

5. Appreciate the development of the underlying project cash flows

A number of business factors combine to make business investment perhaps the most important financial management decision. All departments of a firm (engineering, production, marketing, logistics, and so on) are vitally affected by investment decisions, and thus all managers (whatever their primary responsibility) must be aware of how capital investment decisions are made and how to interact effectively in the processes.

Chapter 11 continues the discussion started in this chapter, and Chapter 12 discusses a more expansive view of cash flows and investment analysis. Chapter 13 hones the required rate of return for an acceptable investment.

Overview of Investment Analysis

The broad application of the techniques presented in this chapter make these tools germane to a wide variety of corporate investment decisions. A four-phase capital investment approach, along with a successful implementation, characterizes a successful investment program. Each organization also imposes managerial directives designed to balance evaluation and control with analytical appropriateness and materiality.

Applications of Investment Analysis

The investment analysis techniques presented in this chapter are widely applicable. Each investment begins with identifying a need, clarifying the investment proposal, considering alternatives, and developing cash flow projections. Table 10.1 lists many types of investment decisions for which the application of these techniques is appropriate.

Capital expenditure analysis represents the traditional *capital investment analysis* (referred to by some as "*capital budgeting*"). Capital expenditures include investments in equipment and plants. These expenditures may reduce production costs, reduce working capital investment, speed production, expand production capacity, or enhance product quality.

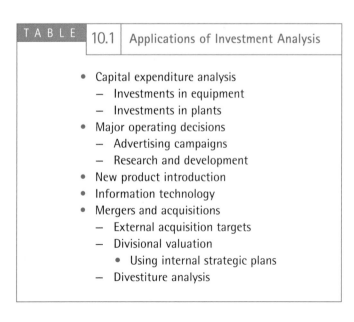

TABLE 10.1	Applications of Investment Analysis

- Capital expenditure analysis
  - Investments in equipment
  - Investments in plants
- Major operating decisions
  - Advertising campaigns
  - Research and development
- New product introduction
- Information technology
- Mergers and acquisitions
  - External acquisition targets
  - Divisional valuation
    - Using internal strategic plans
  - Divestiture analysis

Cash flow impacts correspond to the investment motive. For example, cash flows related to cost reduction (or cost avoidance) projects include savings from a reduction in incremental variable and/or fixed after-tax costs.

These reductions form the foundation necessary to evaluate the investment opportunity. In conjunction with reduced costs, some capital expenditures also reduce the amount of working capital (primarily inventory) invested in the business. The investment analysis should include all cash savings.

Capital expenditures motivated to enhance the speed of production, add required capacity, or improve the product's quality often result in increased sales along with possible cost reduction. Corresponding cash flows include the incremental sales, profits, and cash flow generated by these types of projects.

Investment analysis is not limited to capital decisions, but can also be applied to business investments that are treated as expenses, such as the investment in an advertising campaign or research and development. Thirty-second commercials in the past Super Bowls cost $2+ million each. Individual advertisement campaigns can cost tens of millions of dollars with total advertising and promotion budgets exceeding $100 million for many large companies. In 2005, Proctor & Gamble spent $3.2 billion in advertising and General Motors spent almost $3.0 billion. Some companies spend in excess of $1 billion for research and development (e.g., Pfizer spent $7.4 billion in 2005).

Although these expenditures are treated as "expenses" (*period costs*) rather than as capitalized expenditures (included on the balance sheet), these transactions involve sizeable expenditures that ultimately must be consistent with the strategy of the firm and must provide economic returns. Although the analysis is often more complicated and cash flows less certain, some companies apply the techniques to evaluate and prioritize investments in advertising and research and development.

New product introductions also require rigorous analysis. New products require investment in equipment and marketing expenses (advertising and promotion). Before embarking on a new product, an investment analysis captures the projected sales, income, and cash flow and determines the economic viability of that product.

In the "new economy," many companies heavily invest in information technology. Whether the technology is aimed at the Internet and a changing business model or the implementation of an upgraded enterprise-wide solution such as an enterprise-wide resource planning (ERP) system, companies are embracing technology and significantly investing in it. Investors and senior managers demand a return on this investment. The traditional investment analysis techniques provide a useful evaluation framework.

Finally, these analytical tools form the basis for financial evaluation of acquisition or divestiture candidates. Identification of a candidate occurs for possible acquisition or divestiture. Expected future cash flows are developed and lead to a valuation through application of the valuation tools included in this chapter.

Four Phases of a Successful Capital Program

Although nothing can guarantee the success of corporate investments, a four-phase approach increases the likelihood of success. The four phases are (1) planning, (2) project or capital evaluation, (3) status reporting, and (4) post-completion reviews. Of course, successful implementation is paramount to a successful investment.

CAPITAL EXPENDITURE PLANNING

The planning phase originates with the strategic financial plan. In the strategic financial plan, capital expenditures are estimated in total, with limited supporting details. "Major" projects might be specifically identified with minor capital expenditures estimated in total. Capacity reviews augmented with facilities reviews and merged with new product ideas identify significant future capital investment needs. Advanced identification leads to advanced planning and evaluation. Table 10.2 illustrates a planning capital expenditure summary that details the major projected capital expenditures estimated in the strategic financial plan (see Chapter 9, specifically the strategic financial plan's objectives and assumptions Table 9.6A.)

Some of these planned expenditures are "carryovers" from 2004 and 2005. If a 2004 project does not have "carryover" into the planning period, that project's expenditures are combined and reported on the "miscellaneous" line. So, for example, 2004 saw hundreds of capital projects initiated and completed. The "Production Line #1 Renovation" began in 2004, carried through 2005, and will be completed in 2006. This project is detailed. However, the other 2004 capital expenditures are accumulated and listed in total. More 2005 projects are detailed because more carry over. Note that capital expenditures are broken into four categories for planning purposes.

- *Cost savings:* Reduce the costs of production, distribution, and so on.

- *Capacity expansion:* Support corporate growth objective and strategies through increasing production capacity for existing products.

- *New products:* Support corporate growth objective and strategies through capital investment in new products.

- *Miscellaneous:* Provide necessary capital for information technology, regulatory and safety, administration, research and development, and so on.

In this example, approximately half of each year's plan is devoted to cost savings projects, which is consistent with historical trends. Capital expenditures in support of the corporation's growth objective represent approximately $70 million per year.

For cost savings, capacity expansion, and new products, capital project identification and expenditure estimates are more easily determined for the early years of the plan. That does not mean that capital will not be spent in the latter years. It does mean that at this point in time (when the strategic financial plan is prepared) longer-term capital expenditures have not been detailed. Funds are included in the strategic financial plan without all of the necessary specific project details in the outer years. Note the amount of "miscellaneous" expenditure increases throughout the planned years.

Capacity expansion, by its nature, requires detailed estimates. In this example, production lines are being added while automated warehousing robotics and a new Orlando plant are under consideration. This advanced planning facilitates communication among the members of senior management and aligns functional areas. For example, engineering and manufacturing may plan to add more production capacity for a product. Marketing, on the other hand, may see declining product sales trends and may be planning to eliminate the product. This needs to be discussed, coordinated, and resolved. A strategic plan provides this opportunity. From the strategic capital plan, more detailed annual capital expenditure budgets can be created.

Remember, plan or budget identification of a capital project generally is not authorization to proceed with the project. Good capital planning and budgeting will improve the timing of asset acquisitions and perhaps the quality of assets purchased. This result follows

TABLE 10.2 Strategic Plan: Capital Expenditure Summary ($ Millions)

	ACTUAL EXPENDITURES				PLANNED EXPENDITURES						TOTAL	
	2004	2005	2006	2007	2008	2009	2010	2011	2012	2013	Plan Only	Total
Cost savings												
Production line #1 renovation	$ 4.8	$ 15.1	$ 2.0	$ —	$ —	$ —	$ —	$ —	$ —	$ —	$ 2.0	$ 21.9
Production line #2 renovation	—	5.0	17.0	3.0	—	—	—	—	—	—	20.0	25.0
Production line #3 renovation	—	—	6.0	19.0	4.0	—	—	—	—	—	29.0	29.0
Production line #21 renovation	—	6.6	24.0	—	—	—	—	—	—	—	24.0	30.6
Production line #24 renovation	—	—	6.0	20.0	—	—	—	—	—	—	26.0	26.0
Production line #25 renovation	—	—	—	15.0	—	—	—	—	—	—	15.0	15.0
Production line #31 replacement	—	—	—	—	25.0	15.0	—	—	—	—	40.0	40.0
Production line #32 replacement	—	—	—	—	—	20.0	10.0	—	—	—	30.0	30.0
Truck fleet replacement	4.0	4.5	4.5	5.0	5.0	5.5	6.0	6.5	7.0	7.5	47.0	55.5
Miscellaneous cost savings	81.4	61.8	29.5	37.0	65.0	65.5	85.0	105.0	110.0	111.5	608.5	751.7
Total cost savings	$ 90.2	$ 93.0	$ 89.0	$ 99.0	$ 99.0	$106.0	$101.0	$111.5	$117.0	$119.0	$ 841.5	$1,024.7
Capacity expansion												
New milk handling line	$ —	$ 2.3	$ 15.0	$ —	$ —	$ —	$ —	$ —	$ —	$ —	$ 15.0	$ 17.3
New scale/packaging line	—	—	18.0	3.0	—	—	—	—	—	—	21.0	21.0
Automated warehousing robotics	—	—	—	15.0	2.0	—	—	—	—	—	17.0	17.0
Plant: Orlando location	—	—	—	—	—	5.0	40.0	—	—	—	45.0	45.0
Other capacity	23.5	29.8	11.0	6.0	6.0	2.0	6.0	12.5	12.0	8.0	63.5	116.8
Total capacity	$ 23.5	$ 32.1	$ 44.0	$ 24.0	$ 8.0	$ 7.0	$ 46.0	$ 12.5	$ 12.0	$ 8.0	$ 161.5	$ 217.1
New product												
Sweet treats	$ —	$ —	$ 20.0	$ 25.0	$ —	$ —	$ —	$ —	$ —	$ —	$ 45.0	$ 45.0
Love'O'Chocolate	—	—	—	12.0	30.0	5.0	—	—	—	—	47.0	47.0
Joy Bites	—	—	—	—	30.0	45.0	—	—	—	—	75.0	75.0
Miscellaneous new products	45.7	35.2	7.0	7.0	7.0	8.0	34.0	55.0	60.0	62.0	240.0	320.9
Total new products	$ 45.7	$ 35.2	$ 27.0	$ 44.0	$ 67.0	$ 58.0	$ 34.0	$ 55.0	$ 60.0	$ 62.0	$ 407.0	$ 487.9
Miscellaneous												
Information technology	$8.5	$5.1	$ 9.0	$ 8.0	$ 8.0	$ 10.0	$ 10.0	$ 12.0	$ 12.0	$ 12.0	$ 81.0	$ 94.6
Regulatory and safety	4.0	5.0	5.0	4.0	4.0	5.0	5.0	5.0	5.0	5.0	38.0	47.0
Administrative	3.8	2.2	3.0	3.0	4.0	4.0	4.0	4.0	4.0	4.0	30.0	36.0
Research and development	6.0	8.5	8.0	8.0	10.0	10.0	10.0	10.0	10.0	10.0	76.0	90.5
Total miscellaneous	$ 22.3	$ 20.8	$ 25.0	$ 23.0	$ 26.0	$ 29.0	$ 29.0	$ 31.0	$ 31.0	$ 31.0	$ 225.0	$ 268.1
Total capital expenditures	$181.7	$181.1	$185.0	$190.0	$200.0	$200.0	$210.0	$210.0	$220.0	$220.0	$1,635.0	$1,997.8

from the nature of capital goods and their producers. Firms often do not order capital goods until sales are beginning to press on capacity.

Such occasions occur simultaneously for many firms. When the heavy orders come in, the producers of capital goods go from a situation of idle capacity to one in which they cannot fill all orders placed. Consequently, large backlogs accumulate. Because the production of capital goods involves a relatively long *work-in-process period*, a year or more of waiting may be involved before the additional equipment is available. Furthermore, the quality of the capital goods produced on rush order may deteriorate. These factors have obvious implications for purchasing agents and plant managers.

Another reason for the importance of capital budgeting is that asset expansion typically involves substantial expenditures. Before a firm spends a large amount of money, it must make the proper plans. Large amounts of funds are not available automatically. A firm contemplating a major capital expenditure program may need to plan its financing several years in advance to be sure of having the funds required for the expansion.

CAPITAL EVALUATION AND AUTHORIZATION

Authorization (or acceptance) of a project happens during the project evaluation phase. This phase is discussed in more detail later in the chapter.

CAPITAL STATUS REPORTING

After project evaluation and management approval, a project manager is assigned to implement the project on (or below) budget and on (or before) schedule. Status reporting tracks the project investment. This process reports the total budgeted amounts, project spending, and project commitment of funds. A *commitment of funds* represents signed contracts and commitments to pay that have not been billed by the vendor. Without delivery and billing, the expenditure is not recognized. By using this report, the project manager can track the project's investment compared to the authorized approval.

Table 10.3 illustrates a hypothetical capital expenditure status report. The first section of this report incorporates actual expenditures and budget information for the current period and for the year to date. Although this is a quarterly report, it could be a monthly report if a company preferred. The report includes analysis by specific pieces of equipment. In this case, Production Line #2 Renovation has six specific pieces of equipment.

The budget for the second quarter is $4 million, with actual expenditures providing a favorable $0.5 million (12.5%) variance. The largest savings for the quarter came from the *drive shaft #3131*, which produced a $0.5-million saving by itself. For the year to date, actual expenditures totaled $6.9 million [or $0.6 (8.0%) better than the budget]. The *drive shaft #3131*'s favorable variance for the year is $0.3 million, which implies that in the first quarter there was a $0.2 unfavorable variance (perhaps a timing difference). This portion of the status report helps the project manager track spending against the budget for a specific period of time.

The second section of Table 10.3 considers the full life of the project along with the actual amounts expended over the project's life, the project's total budget, the total commitment (which includes the expenditures), and a revised outlook. The budgeted amount of $25.0 million does not change over the project's life. It represents the amount approved by management and is an unchanging performance benchmark. The revised outlook is similar to a revised budget but reflects the project manager's latest estimate for completing the project. In this example, the outlook portrays a $1.0-million (or 4.0%) favorable variance, as noted in the footnote. Unfavorable outlook variances need to be addressed by

TABLE 10.3 Hypothetical Capital Expenditure Status Report ($ 000s)

Project: Production Line #2 Renovation   Manager: _____

| | | PERIOD: SECOND QUARTER 2006 | | | | 2006 YEAR-TO-DATE: SECOND QUARTER 2006 | | | |
| | | | | Actual v. Budget | | | | Actual v. Budget | |
Asset Category	Item	Actual	Budget	$	%	Actual	Budget	$	%
Equipment	Drive shaft #3131	$1,500.0	$2,000.0	$ 500.0	25.0%	$3,700.0	$4,000.0	$300.0	7.5%
Equipment	Drive shaft #4556	—	—	—	0.0%	500.0	500.0	—	0.0%
Equipment	Piston A567	650.0	500.0	(150.0)	-30.0%	980.0	1,000.0	20.0	2.0%
Equipment	Stainless steel casing	—	—	—	0.0%	—	—	—	0.0%
Equipment	Belt drivers	500.0	500.0	—	0.0%	870.0	1,000.0	130.0	13.0%
Equipment	V-belt conveyence	850.0	1,000.0	150.0	15.0%	850.0	1,000.0	150.0	15.0%
	Total	$3,500.0	$ 4,000.0	$ 500.0	12.5%	$6,900.0	$7,500.0	$ 600.0	8.0%

| | | PROJECT LIFE (DECEMBER 2004–OCTOBER 2006) | | | | | | Uncommitted | |
| | | | | Actual v. Budget | | | | | |
Asset Category	Item	Actual	Budget	$	%	Commitment	Outlook	$	%
Equipment	Drive shaft #3131	$ 5,100	$10,000	$ 4,900.0	49.0%	$6,800	$ 9,350	$2,550.0	27.3%
Equipment	Drive shaft #4556	2,700	2,500	(200.0)	-8.0%	2,700	2,700	—	0.0%
Equipment	Piston A567	2,500	2,500	—	0.0%	2,500	2,500	—	0.0%
Equipment	Stainless steel casing	—	7,500	7,500.0	100.0%	—	7,200	7,200.0	100.0%
Equipment	Belt drivers	750	1,500	750.0	50.0%	1,350	1,400	50.0	3.6%
Equipment	V-belt conveyence	850	1,000	150.0	15.0%	850	850	—	0.0%
	Total	$ 11,900	$25,000	$13,100.0	52.4%	$14,200	$24,000	$9,800.0	40.8%

Project life outlook compared to project life budget represents a total of $1,000 (4.0%) in project savings.

the project manager and the management team. Project overruns and project supplements may need to be requested from management.

The project life "actual v. budget" comparison shows how much of the budgeted funds remain, whereas the "uncommitted" columns show (calculated as outlook less commitment) show the project manager the amount of uncommitted funds that remain against the latest outlook. Ultimately, if the project manager overcommits funds, a project cost overrun results. By using a *consolidated summary status report*, senior management can monitor the implementation progress of all projects.

POST-COMPLETION REVIEWS

Post-completion reviews are an often-overlooked phase of capital investment. Even companies that conduct post-completion reviews often consider this to be their weakest phase of the capital expenditure process. Post-completion reviews are conducted any time (one year, three years, or whenever) after the project is completed. Depending on the company, multiple post-completion reviews might be performed.

The review compares the project's original approved cash flows and economic evaluation indicators (such as NPV, IRR, and so on; discussed later in the chapter) with the cash flows and indicators based on the updated operating performance and information. That is, actual project cost or investment is compared to the projected investment estimated when the project was approved.

The first year (in the case of a one-year post-completion review) of performance is substituted for the projected first year's performance. In the case of a three-year review, three years of actual performance is substituted for the first three years of projected performance. Finally, the cash flows for the remaining years are reestimated given new information and current performance. Based on this combination of actual investment, current performance, and re-forecasted future performance, the economic evaluation indicators are recalculated and improvement or shortfalls addressed.

Post-completion reviews are excellent learning tools for the organization. However, they are time consuming, provide little "actionable" direction, and continue to incorporate projections. If a project is not performing up to the standards established in the project approval, performance shortfalls can be eradicated by painting an even rosier picture in the remaining years. Nonetheless, post-completion reporting remains a valuable learning tool from which judgments can be made about future capital evaluations, requests, and authorizations.

Many organizations provide a supportive atmosphere in which post-completion reports are used to "fix problems" and not "fix blame." Some companies prepare post-completion audits on all projects over a certain dollar threshold of investment (say, $5 or $10 million) and other organizations require the three or five largest projects each year to undergo a review. Some companies perform a post-completion review one year after the project has been implemented and in this way focus on the actual investment amount versus the projected investment and whether any major projected operating assumptions have changed.

Other organizations may also retest a major project three years into the project to compare actual performance over the first few years with the projected performance as well as to compare the assumptions for the remaining time period (current versus original projections).

At least two benefits occur with post-completion audits. In the short run, if a project has gone off track a post-completion serves as an early-alert mechanism. Corrective action or alternative uses may be employed to deal with any issue.

In the longer term, corporate senior management can learn lessons over the years from trends in post-completion reviews and better evaluate predispositions from one operating unit to another. Some operating units may display what is referred to as *"sandbagging" predispositions*, in which their post-completion reviews may indicate that this unit continually exceeds the evaluation and authorization projections. For example, if the unit's projection of sales is $70 million but a level of $60 million is enough to justify the project, that unit's management group may opt to report this more conservative estimate. Although estimate conservatism is generally a good practice, it then falls on corporate senior management to try to determine how conservative the authorization request is so as not to misallocate capital to another project.

On the other hand, another business unit may be often overly optimistic in the evaluation phase with optimistic projections that few post-completion reviews (e.g., actual performance) live up to. When funding requests come in from this business unit, the project "champions" should be more rigorously questioned and challenged by corporate senior management. The next section focuses on the second phase of a successful capital investment program, the evaluation and authorization phase.

Overview of the Investment Process

Table 10.4 summarizes the investment process. The process begins by projecting operating cash flows for a potential investment. The projected cash flows are the basis upon which capital investment techniques are applied and the investment efficacy determined. The basics of determining cash flows are introduced later in this chapter and are covered more fully in Chapter 11.

The major capital investment evaluation techniques include the following.

- PBP (payback period)

- NPV (net present value)

- IRR (internal rate of return)

- MIRR (modified internal rate of return) or TRR (terminal rate of return)

TABLE 10.4	Overview of Investment Process

- Evaluation of projected future cash flows
- Major techniques
  - Payback period
  - Net present value
  - Internal rate of return
  - Terminal rate of return
- Additional investment techniques
  - Discounted payback period
  - Profitability index
- Subject to hurdle rate
  - Risk-adjusted cost of capital

Additional techniques covered in this chapter include the following.

- DPBP (discounted pay back period)

- PI (profitability index)

These techniques are fully developed throughout this chapter. However, before discussing the appropriate approach to evaluating capital investment it is helpful to understand how *not* to make the capital investment decision.

In 1979, as part of a diversification strategy, Hershey bought Friendly Ice Cream Corporation. Friendly is primarily a northeastern restaurant chain that specializes in ice cream. In the mid 1980s, the chain's growth slowed and margins stopped improving. Many analysts and popular business press looked at Friendly as a drag on Hershey's stock price in early 1986. One major popular business publication encouraged Hershey to sell Friendly and reinvest the proceeds in the chocolate division because as they saw it the Friendly "return on investment" was only 14% (whereas the chocolate company's return was 35%). The author of the recommendation used the data for 1985 and calculated (Equation 10.1) the return on investment as the rate of return on each business segment's identifiable assets.

$$\text{Return on investment} = \frac{\text{Operating income}}{\text{Identifiable assets}}$$

$$\frac{\text{Chocolate \& confectionery}}{\text{Return on investment}} = \frac{\$212.7}{\$611.4} = 34.8\% \tag{10.1}$$

$$\frac{\text{Restaurant operations}}{\text{Return on investment}} = \frac{\$43.3}{\$310.9} = 13.9\%$$

In this case, a return-on-assets calculation (Chapter 7) was used to judge the quality of the Friendly investment. Although the financial performance metrics (in general) and return on assets (specifically) are viable metrics used to set objectives and performance standards, benchmark against other organizations, and manage the business, the financial performance metrics detailed in Chapter 7 are inappropriate measures for investment decision making.

Accounting-based performance measures (including accounting-based rates of return) differ greatly from economic rates of return. Although accounting metrics can result from future financial statement projections (as in Chapter 9), the nature of the accounting returns differ from the economic returns discussed in this chapter. The major differences are summarized:

RETURN DIFFERENCES	
Accounting Returns	Economic Returns
Single Time Periods	Multiple Time Periods
Discrete Time	Continuous Time
Accrual Income Based	Cash Flow Based
Historical Book Values	Market Values

Accounting returns are determined for discrete single time periods (month, quarter, year, and so on), whereas *economic returns* consider a continuous time frame over multiple periods. Accounting returns are income (accrual) based, whereas economic returns center on cash flows. Accounting returns can vary widely over the life of an asset (as the asset depreciates) because accounting returns use historical book values. Asset life affects accounting returns, as in the example of restaurant operations compared to chocolate and confectionery.

In 1985, the chocolate and confectionery line of business had limited reinvestment. Some of its efficient functioning assets were 70+ years old. As mentioned in Chapter 2, those assets were fully written off long ago. Said differently, those assets were included in the balance sheet at a zero-dollar book value. On the other hand, when Hershey acquired Friendly Ice Cream Corporation in 1979 Hershey "wrote up" all of Friendly's assets as part of the acquisition accounting. As a division of Hershey, one of the restaurant's growth strategies included opening additional restaurants, which required additional capital investment. Blind application of accounting-based returns leads to the divestment recommendation made by the business press but the decision is skewed due to the average age of the assets and the differences in the underlying business.

Eventually, Hershey sold Friendly Ice Cream Corporation, but not as a result of accounting returns. Hershey sold Friendly only after Hershey had an offer to sell the business to a restaurateur that exceeded the economic evaluation of Friendly's strategic plan. The following sections describe the common economic performance metrics used to evaluate investment decisions.

Major Investment Evaluation Techniques

The following sections illustrate the major investment analysis techniques: PBP, NPV, IRR, and TRR (or MIRR). The sections discuss in detail the calculation of each technique and include a review of the strengths and weaknesses of each technique.

The point of capital investment analysis (indeed, the point of all financial analysis) is to make decisions that will maximize the value of the firm. The capital budgeting process is designed to determine two things: (1) which investments among mutually exclusive[1] investments should be selected and (2) how many projects, in total, should be accepted. When comparing various capital budgeting criteria, it is useful to establish guidelines. The optimal decision rule will have the following four characteristics.

- It will consider all appropriate (incremental after-tax) cash flows.

- It will discount the cash flows at the appropriate market-determined opportunity cost of capital.

- It will select from a group of mutually exclusive projects the one that maximizes shareholders' wealth.

- It will allow managers to consider each project independently from all others. This has come to be known as the *value additivity principle.*

The value additivity principle implies that if we know the value of separate projects accepted by management the value of the firm can be calculated simply by adding their values, Vj. As Equation 10.2 calculates, if there are N projects the value of the firm will be

$$V = \sum_{j=1}^{N} V_j, \qquad \text{where:} \quad j = 1, \ldots N \qquad\qquad (10.2)$$

---

[1] A *mutually exclusive investment* is a project competing directly with another project. The selection of one project makes the other project unnecessary. For example, if Hershey were considering building a new plant in Georgia or Florida the decision of one would make the other choice no longer appropriate.

A	TABLE 10.5	Hypothetical Projects	
	A	PROJECTS	B
	$(400)	Cost (outflow year 0)	$(400)
	300	Cash inflow year 1	100
	200	Cash inflow year 2	200
	100	Cash inflow year 3	300

This is a particularly important point because it means that projects can be considered on their own merit without the necessity of looking at them in an infinite variety of combinations with other projects. We now consider alternative capital investment analysis techniques. We shall see that only one technique (the NPV method) satisfies all four of the desirable properties for capital budgeting criteria.

Table 10.5 presents the cash flows for projects A and B. They both have the same life (three years), and they require the same investment outlay ($400). These projects and their cash flows are used to discuss the capital evaluation techniques.

PAYBACK PERIOD

PBP represents the number of years required to return the original investment. As outlined in Table 10.6, project A has a 1.5-year PBP and project B has a PBP of 2.33 years. Project A costs $400, but pays back $300 cash in the first year and $200 cash in the second year. To calculate the PBP, we must include the total cash flow generated in the first year ($300). This leaves $100 outstanding until the project is paid back.

Assuming even cash flows throughout the year, it takes an additional half year (or the remaining outstanding $100 divided by the project's $200 second-year cash flow.) In total, the project pays back in 1.5 years. Project B generates $100 in the first year and $200 in the second year, for a total of $300 over the first two years. This leaves $100 until project B is paid back (one-third year; $100/$300), assuming level cash flows throughout the year for a PBP of two and one-third years.

If the projects were independent (not mutually exclusive) projects, management would need to establish some cutoff criteria for the acceptable length of payback. This criterion should correspond to the underlying business. For example, most domestic manufacturing

TABLE 10.6	Payback Period	
A	PROJECTS	B
$(400)	Cost (outflow year 0)	$(400)
300	Cash inflow year 1	100
200	Cash inflow year 2	200
100	Cash inflow year 3	300
	Accumulated cash inflow	
$ 300	Year 1	$ 100
500	Year 2	300
600	Year 3	600
1.50 Years	Payback period	2.33 years

firms use a "rule of thumb" PBP of three years or less. In this case, with a payback acceptance criterion of three years or less both of these projects would be acceptable. However, a high-tech company used PBP acceptance criteria of less than one year for some projects because if the project did not pay back in one year the technology would be obsolete and would not provide much of a return beyond the one-year period.

If management adhered strictly to the payback method with a three-year acceptance criterion, but projects A and B were mutually exclusive, project A would be preferred to project B because it has a shorter payback period. Two arguments can be given for the use of the payback method. First, it is easy to use. Second, for a company in a tight cash position it may be of great interest to know how soon it gets back the dollars it has invested. However, the PBP has the following significant drawbacks that may result in the wrong investment decision.

- The PBP does not look beyond the PBP. That is, suppose project B-1 has cash flows identical with those of project B, with the exception of the final year:

YEAR	CASH FLOW PROJECT B-1
Year 0	$ (400)
Year 1	100
Year 2	200
Year 3	3,000

- Project B-1 has a PBP of 2.03 years. Project A is still preferred and the organization misses out on the substantial third-year cash flow.

The PBP does not consider the time value of money. Consequently, an independent project such as project M has an acceptable two-year PBP but it never returns a positive contribution on the investment:

YEAR	CASH FLOW PROJECT M
Year 0	$(400)
Year 1	100
Year 2	300
Year 3	—

- In other words, yes the project pays back its investment within the three year acceptance criteria but it never provides any return on the investment. The DPBP (discussed later in the chapter) eliminates this shortcoming and is discussed later.

Nonetheless, although the PBP is not the primary investment evaluation tool many decision makers may continue to use it as a "rule of thumb."

NET PRESENT VALUE

NPV is the present value of the projected future cash flows, discounted at an appropriate cost of capital or hurdle rate less the cost of the investment. Table 10.7, graphically depicts

| TABLE 10.7 | Net Present Value: Graph |

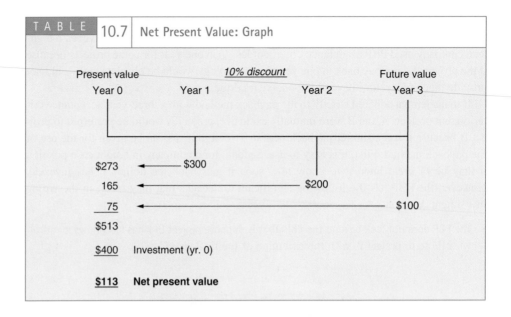

the NPV of project A. As Equation 10.3 calculates, the projected cash flows are discounted back to today (year 0) by using the time value of money tools developed in Chapter 3:

$$\frac{\text{Present}}{\text{Value}} = \frac{\text{Future Value}}{(1+r)^N} = \frac{\$300}{(1+0.10)^1} = \$273 = PV(CF_1)$$

$$= \frac{\$200}{(1+0.10)^2} = \$165 = PV(CF_2) \qquad (10.3)$$

$$= \frac{\$100}{(1+0.10)^3} = \$75 = PV(CF_3)$$

The first-year cash flow of $300 is discounted for one year at 10% for a present value of $273 and so on. This project is worth $513 (the sum of the present values), but the investment requirement is only $400. Subtracting the investment from the present value of the cash flows results in an NPV of $113.

The discount rate in this example is 10%, which approximates the organization's cost of capital. The cost of capital is the after-tax cost of all financing sources, debt, and equity. The cost of capital is often referred to as the firm's "hurdle rate," discount rate, or required return. For further definition and description of the cost of capital, see Chapter 13. More generally, NPV can be written as in Equation 10.4.

$$NPV = \frac{CF_1}{(1+k)^1} + \frac{CF_2}{(1+k)^2} + \cdots + \frac{CF_N}{(1+k)^N} - I_0$$

$$NPV = \sum_{t=1}^{N} \frac{CF_t}{(1+k)^t} - I_0 \qquad (10.4)$$

Where:

CF_t = Cash flow in period t
k = Cost of capital
t = Time period
N = Total number of periods
I_0 = Investment in time 0

TABLE	10.8	Net Present Value	

A	PROJECTS	B
$273	Present value of year 1 cash flow	$ 91
165	Present value of year 2 cash flow	165
75	Present value of year 3 cash flow	225
$513	Total present value cash flow	$481
400	Less: investment (year 0)	400
$113	Net present value (10%)	$ 81
$ 47	Net present value (20%)	$ (4)

Table 10.8 compares the NPVs for projects A and B. If these projects are independent, management should accept both projects because both have positive NPVs and add value to the organization. If the projects are mutually exclusive, rank the projects based on the size of the NPV. Project A is the investment choice under mutual exclusivity.

The NPV of the project is exactly the same as the increase in shareholders' wealth. This fact makes it the correct decision rule for capital budgeting purposes. The NPV rule also meets the other three general principles required for an optimal capital budgeting criterion. It takes all cash flows into account. All cash flows are discounted at the appropriate market-determined *opportunity cost of capital* in order to determine their present values. In addition, the NPV rule obeys the value additivity principle. The NPV of a project is exactly the same as the increase in shareholders' wealth. To see why, start by assuming a project has zero NPV. In this case, the project returns enough cash flow to do three things:

- To pay off all interest payments to debt holders who have provided debt financing

- To pay all expected returns (dividends and capital gains) to shareholders who have put up equity for the project

- To pay off the original principal (I_0) invested in the project.

Thus, a zero-NPV project is one that earns a fair return to compensate both debt holders and equity holders, each according to the returns they expect for the risk they take. A positive NPV project earns more than the required rate of return, and equity holders receive all excess cash flows because debt holders have a fixed claim on the firm. Consequently, equity holders' wealth increases by exactly the NPV of the project. It is this direct link between shareholders' wealth and the NPV definition that makes the NPV criterion so important in decision making.

For our analysis of project A, let's further assume that there are 113 shares outstanding. If the benefits and impact of this project could be effectively communicated to the stock market, and the market believed the project could be implemented as presented, the stock price should reflect an immediate $1-per-share increase ($113/113 shares).

Note in Table 10.8 that at a 20% cost of capital the NPV of both projects decreases. Project B's NPV turns negative and consequently indicates that project B is not a good investment. With a 20% cost of capital, project B should be rejected and only project A accepted regardless of whether these are mutually exclusive projects or independent projects.

INTERNAL RATE OF RETURN

The IRR is the interest rate that equates the present value of projected future cash flows to the investment expenditure. As Equation 10.5 indicates, it is the discount rate where the NPV equals $0.

$$NPV = \frac{CF_1}{(1+IRR)^1} + \frac{CF_2}{(1+IRR)^2} + \cdots + \frac{CF_N}{(1+IRR)^N} - I_0$$

$$NPV = \sum_{t=1}^{N} \frac{CF_t}{(1+IRR)^t} - I_0 = \$0$$

(10.5)

Note that the IRR formula (Equation 10.5) is simply the NPV formula (Equation 10.4) solved for that particular value of k that causes the NPV to equal zero. In other words, the same basic equation is used for both methods, but in the NPV method the discount rate (k) is specified as the market-determined opportunity cost of capital. In the IRR method, the NPV is set equal to zero and the value of IRR that forces the NPV to equal zero is found. Table 10.9 illustrates the IRR for project A and arrives at an IRR of 28.9%. Note that at 28.9% the NPV equals $0.

Financial calculators (such as the Hewlett-Packard HP-10B or Texas Instruments BA-II-Plus) or personal computers with spreadsheet software are briefly discussed in the next section. However, with an ordinary calculator the IRR can be found by trial and error. First, compute the present value of the cash flows from an investment using an arbitrarily selected interest rate (e.g., 10%). Then compare the present value so obtained with the investment's cost. If the present value is higher than the cost figure, try a higher interest rate and go through the procedure again.

TABLE 10.9	Internal Rate of Return: Graph

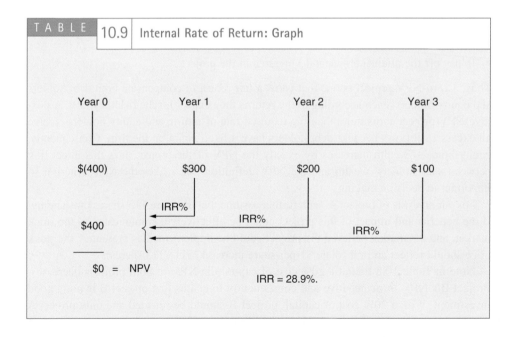

TABLE 10.10	Calculating IRR: Project A							
				DISCOUNTED CASH FLOW VALUE				
	PROJECT A CASH FLOW	Trial 1 10.0%	Trial 2 20.0%	Trial 3 30.0%	Trial 4 25.0%	Trial 5 28.0%	Trial 6 29.0%	Trial 7 28.9%
Cash inflows								
Year 1	$300	$273	$250	$231	$240	$234	$233	$233
Year 2	200	165	139	118	128	122	120	120
Year 3	100	75	58	46	51	48	47	47
Total present value		$513	$447	$395	$419	$404	$399	$400
Investment		400	400	400	400	400	400	400
Net present value		$113	$ 47	$ (5)	$ 19	$ 4	$ (1)	$ (0)

IRR is 28.9%!

Conversely, if the present value is lower than the cost lower the interest rate and repeat the process. Continue until the present value of the flows from the investment is approximately equal to its cost. The interest rate that brings about this equality is defined as the IRR. Table 10.10 outlines computations for the IRR of project A. As mentioned previously, the computations involve trial and error, as well as guessing discount rates and using those discount rates to test if the NPV is zero. From the NPV calculation, we saw that a discount rate of 10% yields a positive $113 NPV and is consequently too low. Likewise at 20%, A's NPV is $47, so we try 30% with a $(5) NPV. At 25% the NPV is $19, so trying 28% the NPV is $4 and 29% resulted in an NPV of $(1). A guess of 28.9% yielded approximately a $0 NPV on the seventh try.

Table 10.11 outlines the IRR for projects A and B. Project B has an IRR of 19.4%. If the projects are independent projects, the IRR should be compared to the cost of capital or to a hurdle rate. If the IRR exceeds this *risk-adjusted cost of capital*, the project should be accepted. If the project's IRR is less than the risk-adjusted cost of capital, the project should be rejected. If the projects are mutually exclusive and exceed the hurdle rate, in general choose the one with the larger IRR. In this example, choose project A!

TABLE 10.11	Internal Rate of Return	
A	PROJECTS	B
28.9%	Internal rate of return	19.4%
	Net present value at the internal rate of return	
$233	Present value of year 1 cash flow	$ 84
120	Present value of year 2 cash flow	140
47	Present value of year 3 cash flow	176
$400	Total present value cash flow	$400
400	Less: investment (year 0)	400
$ –	Net present value (10%)	$ –

Financial Calculator and Spreadsheet Calculations

Although the student of finance and the business professional understand the calculation of the NPV and IRR, most actual calculations can be easily facilitated with a financial calculator or spreadsheet software. In Chapter 3 we focused on two popular financial calculators: the Hewlett-Packard HP-10B and Texas Instruments BA-II-Plus. End of book Appendix B provides specific instructions on the use of both calculators. In general, both calculators function the same way, as follows:

1. Clear the calculator.
2. Input the cash flow values using the applicable cash flow keys.
3. Supply the discount rate in the case of the NPV.
4. Calculate NPV and IRR.

For example, using the Hewlett-Packard HP-10B to calculate the NPV and IRR of project A arrives at the following.

Enter value	Push key
−400	CFj
300	CFj
200	CFj
100	CFj
10	I/YR

Using the CFj key, the cash flows are entered into the calculator and the annual interest rate (10%) is also entered. The following steps complete the calculations.

Push key	Answer
NPV	113
IRR/YR	28.9

The Texas Instruments TI-BA-II-Plus is also simple to use (see end of book Appendix B for the exact keystrokes). Spreadsheet software such as Excel enables simplified calculations of NPV, IRR, and MIRR. These functions are discussed in Appendix E at the end of the book.

Modified Internal Rate of Return

The IRR implicitly assumes reinvestment of the intermediate cash flows at the IRR. Although Equation 10.5 does not specifically address reinvestment, fundamentally reinvestment at the IRR is assumed. For projects A and B, what if you cannot reinvest at their internal rates of return? Management would enjoy having 28.9% returning projects (such as project A) just sitting around waiting for funding. What if other 28.9% return opportunities do not exist? What if the best the company can do is reinvest (at 10%) their cost of capital? The MIRR explicitly addresses the reinvestment assumption.

MIRR or TRR is the interest rate that equates the cost of the investment with the accumulated future value of the intermediate cash flows assumed to be reinvested at an appropriate risk-adjusted cost of capital.

Table 10.12 represents calculation of MIRR for project A. The calculation is a two-step process.

The first step explicitly reinvests the intermediate cash flows at 10%, the cost of capital. For example, the first-year cash flow is invested for two years, between the end of the first and third years. The first-year cash flow of $300 accumulates to $363 by the end of year 3 [i.e., $300 (1 + 0.10)^2]. The second-year cash flow of $200 grows to $220 with reinvestment for one year at 10%, and the third-year cash flow of $100 remains $100 because it lacks time to grow. In total, the accumulated future value (or *terminal value*) of the intermediate cash flows assumed to be reinvested at 10% (the cost of capital) is $683.

Step 2 compares the investment to the accumulated future value of the projected and reinvested cash flows. Computed per Equation 10.6, this final step is represented in the lower portion of Table 10.12.

$$\text{MIRR}_{\text{Project A}} = \left[\frac{FV - \text{Accumulated}}{PV - \text{Investment}}\right]^{(1/n)} - 1 = \left[\frac{\$683}{\$400}\right]^{(1/3)} - 1 = 19.5\% \quad (10.6)$$

This is the same equation as that used in Chapter 3 to solve for the *compound annual growth rate (CAGR)* when you have two lump sums (*present value* and *future value*). For project A, the MIRR of return is 19.5% and reflects the interest rate that equates the cost

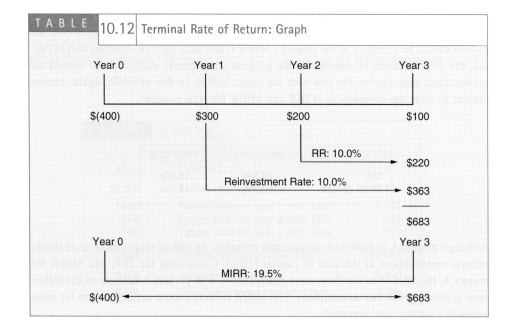

TABLE 10.12 Terminal Rate of Return: Graph

Investment Technique: Conflict Resolution

The only apparent structural difference between the NPV and IRR methods lies in the discount rates used in the two equations. That is, all values in the equations are identical except for IRR and k. Further, we can see that if IRR > k, then NPV > $0. Accordingly, it would appear that the two methods give the same accept/reject decisions for specific projects. Therefore, if a project is acceptable under the NPV criterion it is also acceptable if the IRR method is used. However, the following example illustrates that this statement is incorrect.

Consider the pattern of cash flows in Table 10.16, which contains information about two mutually exclusive projects (C and D). Both projects cost $700 and have varying (and *inverted*) *cash flows*. Although these numbers were contrived to illustrate a point, this conflict is evident in evaluating investment opportunities that stretch over 10 to 12 years. These numbers were contrived to fit within a three-year window.

Using NPV, which project would you prefer at a 10% cost of capital? The one with the higher NPV, project C ($409 NPV versus project D's NPV of $329), should be accepted. At 15%, both projects have the same NPV and thus the choice should be made for "strategic" or other reasons. At a 20% cost of capital, project D is preferable.

But why should life be so difficult? Project D's IRR is almost double the IRR of project C (55.0 versus 29.7%, respectively). Choose project D using the IRR! This is the correct decision provided you can reinvest at 55.0%. But what if the appropriate cost of capital for this type of project is substantially lower and consequently you cannot reinvest at 55.0%?

TABLE 10.16	Method Conflicts	
C	PROJECTS	D
$ 700	Investment year 0	$ 700
50	Cash inflow year 1	1,000
150	Cash inflow year 2	100
1,250	Cash inflow year 3	50
$ 409	Net present value at 10%	$ 329
278	Net present value at 15%	278
169	Net present value at 20%	232
29.7%	Internal rate of return	55.0%
28.2%	Terminal rate of return 10%	25.1%
28.6%	Terminal rate of return 15%	28.6%
29.0%	Terminal rate of return 20%	32.0%

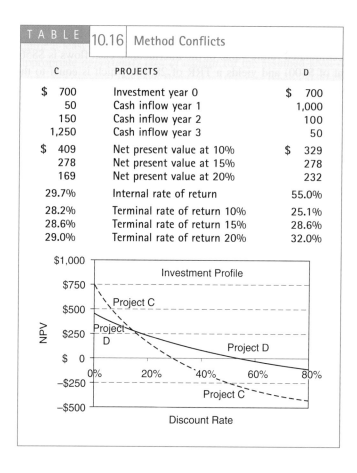

Using the MIRR with a 10% "reinvestment rate," choose project C. With a 15% "reinvestment rate," strategic rationales and other criteria need to be considered because the MIRRs are identical (at 28.6%). At a "reinvestment rate" of 20%, choose project D. Note that with the same investment amount NPV and MIRR give consistent accept/reject decisions and project rankings. MIRR provides a more realistic view of the rate of return provided by both projects, but especially project D.

Project Profiles

The lower portion of Table 10.16 graphs the project profiles for projects C and D. Project C is the dashed line, the X axis lists the discount rate, and the Y axis denotes the NPV. The project profile illustrates the NPV for the cash flows in Table 10.16 for different discount rates.

A few points need to be established. At a zero discount rate (i.e., no discounting of the cash flows), the NPV is simply the sum of the cash inflows less the investment amount. For project C, the sum of the cash inflows is $1,450 ($50 + $150 + $1,250) less the $700 investment (or an NPV of $750 without discounting). Project D's cash inflows total $1,150 less the $700 investment, which provides an NPV of $450 (at 0%). These two points are plotted on the Y axis of the profile, which corresponds to a 0% discount rate.

The IRR, by definition, is the interest rate (discount rate) that equates the present value of projected cash flows to the investment amount (i.e., the IRR is the interest rate where the NPV is zero). For project C, the IRR is 29.7%, and for project D the IRR is 55.0%. These points are plotted on the X axis representing a zero NPV.

The points between the X axis and Y axis reflect the NPV for a given discount rate. Each of the NPV and discount rate combinations from Table 10.16 is plotted on this profile. The plot includes the 15% discount rate calculation where both projects enjoy a $278 NPV. Note that with a cost of capital (discount rate) to the left (0 to 15%) of this "crossover point" project C provides a higher NPV. To the right (15 to 55%), project D is preferred. Beyond 55%, neither project is acceptable because both projects have negative NPVs. If your cost of capital is less than 15%, choose project C. If it is greater than 15%, choose project D.

The 15% *crossover rate*, where both projects have the same NPV, can be calculated by taking the difference between the projects' cash flows and calculating the IRR on these differences. For example, consider the annual differences in cash flow (project C minus project D): year 0 ($0), year 1 [$(950)], year 2 [$50], and year 3 [$1,200]. The resulting IRR is 15% (the crossover rate).

Additional IRR Issues

In addition to the reinvestment rate issue, the IRR is an inferior capital budgeting criterion because (1) it violates the value additivity principle and (2) it can result in multiple IRRs for the same project. The value additivity principle demands that managers be able to consider one project independently of all others. To demonstrate that the IRR criterion can violate the value additivity principle, consider the three projects whose cash flows are given in Table 10.17. Projects R and S are mutually exclusive, and project T is independent of them. If the value additivity principle holds, we should be able to choose the better of the two mutually exclusive projects without having to consider the independent project.

The NPVs of the three projects (as well as their IRRs) are also given in Table 10.17. If we use the IRR rule to choose between projects R and S, we would select project R.

TABLE 10.19	Additional Capital Evaluation Technique: Discounted Payback Period

A	PROJECTS	B
$(400)	Investment (year 0)	$(400)
300	Cash inflow year 1	100
200	Cash inflow year 2	200
100	Cash inflow year 3	300
	Cash flows discounted @ 10%	
$ 273	Present value of year 1 cash flow	$ 91
165	Present value of year 2 cash flow	165
75	Present value of year 3 cash flow	225
	Accumulated discounted cash inflow	
$ 273	Year 1	$ 91
438	Year 2	256
513	Year 3	481
1.77 yrs.	Discounted payback period (10%)	2.64 yrs.
1 + (127/165)		2 + (144/225)

This approach improves upon the PBP by considering the time value of money. To extend the illustration from earlier in the chapter, using the DPBP (as follows) the company would correctly reject project M (from the earlier example).

YEAR	CASH FLOW PROJECT M	DISCOUNTED CF @ 10%
Year 0	$(400)	$(400)
Year 1	100	91
Year 2	300	248
Year 3	0	0

Project M never pays back at any discount rate. At 10% (from above), the project has a negative NPV (–$61) and should correctly be rejected. However, strict adherence to this technique still does not look beyond the PBP. As presented earlier in this chapter, project B-1 has cash flows identical with those of project B, with the exception of the final year:

YEAR	CASH FLOW PROJECT B-1	DISCOUNTED CF @ 10%
Year 0	$(400)	$(400)
Year 1	100	91
Year 2	200	165
Year 3	3,000	2,254

Project B-1 has a DPBP of 2.06 years. Project A is still preferred and the organization continues to miss out on the substantial third-year cash flow.

PROFITABILITY INDEX

The PI is a variation of NPV. Per Equation 10.7, it is calculated as the present value of estimated future cash flows, discounted at an appropriate cost of capital or hurdle rate, divided by the cost of the investment.

TABLE 10.20	Additional Capital Evaluation Technique: Profitability Index	
A	PROJECTS	B
$273	Present value of year 1 cash flow	$ 91
165	Present value of year 2 cash flow	165
75	Present value of year 3 cash flow	225
$513	Total present value cash flow	$481
400	Less: investment (year 0)	400
113	Net present value (10%)	$ 81
	Profitability index	
1.28	Present value/investment	1.20
($513/$400)		($481/$400)

$$PI = \sum_{t=1}^{N} \frac{CF_t}{(1+k)^t} \div I_0 \qquad\qquad (10.7)$$

Of course, the NPV subtracts the investment amount from the present value of the cash flow. The PI suggests that for every dollar invested you receive a dollar return equal to the PI. Table 10.20 outlines the PI for projects A and B. The NPV remains as calculated in Table 10.8: $113 for project A and $81 for project B. Using the PI, project A is once again preferred. Every dollar invested in project A provides a return of $1.28 (versus a return of $1.20 for project B).

COMPARISON OF TECHNIQUES

A basic shortcoming of the PI is shared by IRR and MIRR and is illustrated by a simple example involving two projects with a significant size differential. Suppose one investment involves an outlay of $1 and returns $2.20 in one year (or a present value of $2) at 10% discount rate. Its NPV is $1, and its PI is 2.00. Another investment requires an outlay of $1 million, and at the end of one year has a return of $1.65 million (or a present value of $1.5 million) at a 10% discount rate. Its NPV is $0.5 million, and its PI is 1.50, calculated as follows.

	PROJECT R	PROJECT S
Investment (Year 0)	$1.00	$1,000,000.00
Cash Flow (Year 1)	2.20	1,650,000.00
PV of Cash Flow (10%)	2.00	1,500,000.00
Net Present Value (NPV)	$1.10	$500,000.00
Profitability Index (PI)	2.00	1.50
Internal Rate of Return (IRR)	120.0%	65.0%
Modified IRR	120.0%	65.0%

Under the NPV rule, the larger investment with the larger NPV is clearly superior. Under PI, the firm would select the smaller project (with a PI of 2.00) and enhance its value by only $1 (NPV). If the firm can finance all available investments, the PI would not provide a ranking the firm would want to follow.

Note also in this example that with such wide disparity in the size of the two competing projects the MIRR also breaks down. In this example, the smaller project has an MIRR of 120% and the larger project has an MIRR of "only" 65%. Strict adherence to the PI or

MIRR rules may lead to the wrong decision when comparing two mutually exclusive projects that widely differ in investment size.

In practice, such wide investment disparity in alternative competing projects is less than common. When are you faced with a personal purchase decision that accomplishes exactly the same end, but one alternative costs $1.00 and the other alternative costs $1.0 million? Nonetheless, the point is made that due to size difference an incorrect selection could take place if the organization centered its decision on IRR, MIRR, or PI. NPV leads to enhanced shareholder value.

Ask yourself this question: If this were my investment, would I prefer a 120% IRR or a 65% IRR? If this were my investment, would I prefer a 120% MIRR or a 65% MIRR? If this were my investment, would I prefer a PI of 2.00 or 1.50? Finally, if this were my investment would I prefer to earn $1 or $500,000? Quickly the pecentages give way to actual hard cash preferences—personally (because that is what we spend at the grocery store) and in business. NPV is the preferred investment metric.

Projects with Different Lives

We have established that the NPV rule is the correct economic criterion for ranking investment projects. It avoids the deficiencies of the alternative methods. It discounts cash flows at the appropriate opportunity cost of funds. It obeys the value additivity principle.

Following the NPV rule maximizes the value of the firm. Indeed, the value of the firm is the sum of the NPVs of the total portfolio of projects represented by the firm's assets. From the basic NPV expression, general and valid valuation measures can be derived. Thus, the NPV rule is consistent with fundamental valuation principles.

Although NPV is the preferred investment valuation technique, one application caveat should be pointed out when comparing projects with different lives. If a company evaluates two alternatives with differing project lives, the projects must be compared on common ground by assuming project replication until common life is obtained.

SAMPLE PROJECTS

The following lists the cash flows for two mutually exclusive projects, which both cost $100. Project K has a four-year life and an $11 NPV (10% discount), whereas project L has only a two-year life and a $7 NPV. Applying the NPV rule would lead us to accept project K and reject project L. However, the projects are not comparable because project L covers only a two-year period and project K covers four years. Assuming that project L can be replicated for another two years, the last two columns indicate the cash flows and resulting NPV of replicating project L to cover the same four-year period as project K. Under the project L replication cash flow, the second-year cash flow amount of $(38) is the second investment of $(100) offset by the positive $62 of cash flow from the first investment in project L.

	CASH FLOWS		NET PRESENT VALUE		PROJECT L REPLICATION	
	K	L	K	L	Cash Flow	NPV
Year 0	$(100)	$(100)	$(100)	$(100)	$(100)	$(100)
Year 1	35	62	32	56	62	56
Year 2	35	62	29	51	(38)	(31)
Year 3	35	0	26	0	62	47
Year 4	35	0	24	0	62	42
Total	N/A	N/A	$ 11	$ 7	N/A	$ 14

The replication of project L provides the higher NPV and project L should be accepted. Project K should be rejected.

EQUIVALENT ANNUAL ANNUITY

Another approach when considering the "unequal" life problem is a technique called the *equivalent annual annuity technique*. Each project's (K and L) NPV could be thought of as the NPV of an annuity.

- Project K: Four-year annuity with a present value of $11

- Project L: Two-year annuity with a present value of $7

Using the Chapter 3 techniques, an $11 four-year project has an equivalent annual annuity (N = 4, i% = 10, PV = 11) of $3.50 and project L's equivalent annuity is $4.03. Project L would once again be preferred.

Determining Cash Flow: The Basics

To this point, we assumed the determination of cash flows. Before leaving this chapter, let's examine a basic investment cash flow model. Chapter 11 considers more intermediate and advanced topics related to cash flow.

The development of cash flows for project B is framed in Table 10.21, which begins with an operating income statement and ends with the development of a complete project cash flow statement. The income statement starts with sales less cost of goods sold, distribution expense, sales and marketing expenses, administrative expenses, and so on. In this example, all costs are added together (with the noted exception of depreciation, which is isolated on a separate line).

Pre-tax income results when total expenses (including depreciation) are subtracted from sales. Subtracting tax expense from pre-tax income concludes the income statement with after-tax operating income. After-tax operating income starts the cash flow statement along with the "add-back" of any non-cash expense, such as depreciation, amortization of goodwill,

TABLE 10.21	Analysis and Computation of Project Cash Flow: Project B		
	YEAR 1	YEAR 2	YEAR 3
Project income:			
Sales	$1,000	$1,300	$1,300
Expenses (excluding depreciation)	850	1,050	1,050
Depreciation	133	133	134
Pre-tax income/operating income	17	117	116
Taxes	7	47	46
After-tax operating income	$ 10	$ 70	$ 70
Project cash flow:			
After-tax operating income	$ 10	$ 70	$ 70
Depreciation	133	133	134
Additional working capital	(43)	(3)	46
After-tax salvage value	—	—	50
Total cash flow	$ 100	$ 200	$ 300

deferred income taxes, and so on. Any additional working capital investment (primarily investment in inventory and accounts receivable offset by additional spontaneous financing through accounts payable) is taken into consideration. This includes the *working capital recovery* in the final year, when it is assumed that all project inventories are sold, all related receivables are collected, and all related payables are paid.

Some projects are significant enough that additional investment in subsequent capital is planned. Any related *incremental cash flow* must be considered in determining the project's cash flow. In the case of project B, no additional *fixed capital investment* is projected. However, an after-tax salvage (sale of the equipment) of $50 is included in the final year of cash flows.

Note that no financing costs or financing cash flows are included in the cash flow projection. That is, no interest expense (or income), no debt service, no dividends, and no other financing-related cash flows are considered. Financing costs and cash flows are considered in the cost of capital calculation (Chapter 13). We evaluate cash flow projections based solely on operating cash flows.

Cash flows can be determined for almost any situation using this framework. The cash flows for project B are $100, $200, and $300 for each of the three years, respectively. The following section raises additional managerial issues a successful organization must address to satisfy its particular needs within its capital investment program.

Additional Managerial Issues

Within the four phases of the capital investment process, each corporation must resolve a number of other issues related to the capital investment process. For example, at planning time how much detail is necessary to facilitate a strategic plan and how much detail is necessary within the annual budget? During the evaluation process, which techniques should be reported and what happens when there is a conflict? When a project has been approved and is in the implementation phase, what is the correct balance between detailed status reporting (i.e., micromanagement by senior management) and staying informed? Finally, how and when should an approved and implemented project have a post-completion audit performed?

The management team needs to determine what approaches work best for their organization and their needs. Management must also resolve issues related to other attributes of their capital investment program, as discussed in the following.

PROJECT CATEGORIES

Most companies categorize projects by the nature of their expenditures. In this way, management can broadly monitor where their capital is being invested. The categories relate to the underlying rationale of the expenditure. For example, in Table 10.2 we categorized projects (as follows) by their nature.

- Cost Savings
- Capacity Expansion
- New Products
- Information Technology
- Regulatory and Safety

- Administrative

- Research and Development

These categories are similar to the categories used at Hershey and many companies. Although these are common categories, each company can develop its own group of projects. In a separate survey, one company used 26 different categories, including five varieties of new products.

BUDGET IDENTIFICATION AND SPENDING

In the strategic planning phase, every organization struggles with the proper level of detail. If the requirements are too detailed, productivity is lost. If the requirements are on a summary level only, an opportunity to discuss future capital needs is minimized. Each organization must find its own careful balance for detailed requirements during the planning phase.

Within the annual budget, projects anticipated for the coming year are specifically identified. Most organizations will spend about 100% of the budgeted capital expenditures in total. However, only half are spent on identified projects. The other half is spent on unidentified projects that result from changing priorities, market conditions, and so on. Management must balance the organization's need for flexibility and the stringent demands of a budget.

BUDGET AUTHORIZATION

For most companies, the annual capital budget process is separate from expenditure authorization. Just because a project is identified at budget time does not mean it is authorized. Each project must undergo its own rigorous evaluation and authorization.

PROJECT EVALUATION THRESHOLD

As previously mentioned, the economic evaluation techniques are appropriate for most (if not all) expenditures. However, if a project analysis were required every time someone needed a calculator many person-hours of effort would be wasted. On the other hand, manufacturing should not be given carte blanche for investments in new production facilities costing several hundreds of millions of dollars. A careful balance must be struck to attain a certain comfort level for management and costs incurred in performing the analysis.

Until the early 1990s, Hershey had a project evaluation level of $10,000. Management felt they needed to stay involved with investment decisions. As the management team grew more comfortable, the evaluation level was increased to $100,000. This eliminated the evaluation of more than 450 projects each year, which represented less than 10% ($15 million) of the total capital spent by Hershey. Increasing the evaluation threshold eliminated person-years of time spent in project development and management review on projects costing between $10,000 and $100,000. It also focused management's time on more substantial capital project reviews.

AUTHORIZATION LEVELS

Each company must decide how deeply capital authorization should be granted within the organization and at what dollar level. For example, should a senior engineer be allowed to authorize capital expenditures? If they should, how much should they be allowed to authorize? Table 10.22 outlines authorization levels.

TABLE 10.22	Project Evaluation and Approval

- Each project undergoes its own Focused review
  - All projects > $100,000
- Approval authority
  - Director: $50,000
  - Vice president: $500,000
  - Senior vice president: $1 million
  - President: $2 million
  - CEO: $5 million
  - Board: $5 million

In this example, directors can approve up to $50,000, vice presidents up to $500,000, and so on. The CEO can approve up to $5 million with any project exceeding an estimated $5 million requiring board-level approval. Of course, out of courtesy and career preservation (even though approval authority may rest in your domain) it is always a good decision to seek your boss's concurrence on the project before you authorize the project. Each corporation must find a structure that provides enough control without hampering operations with needless bureaucracy.

Survey OF PRACTICE

Most companies no longer consider one and only one capital investment technique. When cash flows are projected, it is only a matter of calculating the specific values for any given metric. So what techniques are actually used in practice? In 2002, a survey found that Net Present Value and Internal Rate of Return are by far the most widely used investment evaluation tools. The survey also found that payback period and discounted payback are also used, but profitability index, accounting rates of return, and modified internal rates of return are rarely used.

Percent of companies who answered that they always or often use a specific technique.

Capital Evaluation Technique	Size of Annual Capital Budget ($ millions)			
	Less Than $100	$100 to $500	Greater Than $500	All Companies
Net present value	85.5	81.3	89.8	85.1
Internal rate of return	73.7	74.6	84.0	76.7
Payback period	63.7	47.9	42.5	52.6
Discounted payback	45.9	29.6	37.6	37.6
Profitability index	25.0	25.7	9.1	21.4
Accounting rate of return	13.7	14.1	18.2	14.7
Modified IRR	4.2	14.7	9.3	9.3

Source: "Capital Budgeting Practices of the Fortune 1000: How Have Things Changed?," Ryan, Patricia and Glenn P. Ryan, *Journal of Business and Management*, Volume 8, Number 4, Winter 2002.

From this you can also tell that most firms use multiple techniques.

summary

Capital investment decisions, which involve commitments for large outlays whose benefits (or drawbacks) extend well into the future, are of great significance to a firm. Decisions in these areas will therefore have a major impact on the future well-being of the firm. This chapter focused on how capital investment decisions can be made more effective in contributing to the health and growth of a firm while increasing shareholder value. The discussion stressed the development of systematic procedures and rules throughout all four phases of capital investment for preparing a list of investment proposals, for evaluating them, and for selecting a cutoff point.

The chapter emphasized that one of the most crucial phases in the process is the evaluation and authorization of a proposal. Four commonly used procedures for ranking investment proposals were discussed in the chapter: PBP, NPV, and IRR, and TRR.

PBP is defined as the number of years required to return the original investment. Although the payback method is used frequently as a simple rule of thumb, it has serious conceptual weaknesses because it ignores the fact that (1) some receipts come in beyond the PBP and (2) a dollar received today is more valuable than a dollar received in the future (the time value of money).

NPV is defined as the present value of future cash flow, discounted at the cost of capital, minus the cost of the investment. The NPV method overcomes the conceptual flaws noted in the use of the PBP method.

IRR is defined as the interest rate that equates the present value of future cash flow to the investment outlay. The IRR method, like the NPV method, discounts cash flows. However, the IRR assumes reinvestment at the IRR.

MIRR (or TRR) is the interest rate that equates the cost of the investment with the accumulated future value of the intermediate cash flows assumed to be reinvested at an appropriate risk-adjusted cost of capital. The MIRR explicitly incorporates an opportunity cost of capital as a reinvestment rate.

In most cases, the discounted cash flow methods give identical answers to questions such as the following. Which of two mutually exclusive projects should be selected? How large should the total capital budget be? However, under certain circumstances conflicts may arise. Such conflicts are caused primarily by the fact that the IRR method makes different assumptions about the rate at which cash flows may be reinvested, or the opportunity cost of cash flows. The assumption of the NPV and MIRR methods (that the opportunity cost is the cost of capital) is the correct one. Although the MIRR is an improvement on the IRR, it may lead to an incorrect choice of mutually exclusive projects if the sizes of the investment are significantly different. Accordingly, our preference is for using the NPV method to make capital investment decisions.

Questions

10.1   A firm has $100 million available for capital expenditures. Suppose project A involves purchasing $100 million of grain, shipping it overseas, and selling it within a year at a profit of $20 million. The project has an IRR of 20% and an NPV of $20 million, and it will cause earnings per share (EPS) to rise within one year. Project B calls for the use of the $100 million to develop a new process, acquire land, build a plant, and begin processing. If chosen, project B cannot be postponed, and has an NPV of $50 million and an IRR of 30%. But the fact that some of the plant costs will be written off immediately, combined with the fact that no revenues will be generated for several years, means that accepting project B will reduce short-run EPS.

   a.   Should the short-run effects on EPS influence the choice between the two projects?

   b.   How might situations such as the one described here influence a firm's decision to use payback as a screening criterion?

10.2   For many companies, the inclusion of a capital project in the firm's annual budget is not authorization for expenditure. Why do you think most firms have a separate capital authorization review process?

10.3   With three-quarters of the year already past, a project manager is showing a $500,000 favorable variance on his project. The quarterly spending details follow ($000s).

	Budget	Actual	Variance	Committed
Qtr 1	$1,000	$ 800	$200	$1,200
Qtr 2	800	600	200	1,000
Qtr 3	500	400	100	900
Year to Date	$2,300	$1,800	$500	—
Qtr 4	500	500	—	—
Year	$2,800	$2,300	$500	—

   Even though this project manager is currently showing a $500,000 favorable variance, management raised a concern. What is that concern?

10.4   With three-quarters of the year already past, a project manager proudly reports that his $2 million project currently has a $250,000 favorable variance, is on schedule, and is on budget ($2 million). The quarterly spending details follow ($000s).

	Budget	Actual	Variance	Committed
Qtr 1	$ 800	$ 700	$100	$1,200
Qtr 2	500	450	50	1,000
Qtr 3	500	400	100	900
Year to Date	$1,800	$1,550	$250	—

   Management raised a concern. What is that concern?

10.5   Are there conditions under which a firm might be better off if it chose a machine with a rapid payback rather than one with the largest rate of return?

10.6   Company X uses the payback method in evaluating investment proposals and is considering new equipment whose additional net after-tax earnings will be $150 a year. The equipment costs $500, and its expected life is 10 years (straight-line depreciation). The company uses a three-year payback as its criterion. Should the equipment be purchased under these assumptions?

10.7   What are the most critical problems that arise in calculating a rate of return for a prospective investment?

10.8   Is it beneficial for a firm to review its past capital expenditures and capital budgeting procedures? Explain.

10.9   Fiscal and monetary policies are tools used by the government to stimulate the economy. Using the analytical devices developed in this chapter, explain how each of the following might be expected to stimulate the economy by encouraging investment.

   a.   An acceleration of tax-allowable depreciation

   b.   An easing of interest rates

   c.   Passage of a new federal program giving business an investment tax credit for investing in capital equipment

Problems

10.1

Payback period (PBP): Calculate the PBP for a project with the following cash flows.

Year	Cash flow
1	$ 75
2	155
3	223
4	297
5	374

The investment amount is $952.

10.2

Net present value (NPV): Calculate the NPV for a project with the following cash flows.

Year	Cash flow
0	$(478)
1	75
2	181
3	267
4	313

Assume a 12% discount rate.

10.3

Net present value (NPV): Calculate the NPV for a project with the following cash flows using discount rates of 6, 10, and 14%.

Year	Cash flow
0	$(2,725)
1	543
2	629
3	673
4	702
5	761
6	814

10.4

Internal rate of return (IRR): Calculate the IRR for a project with the following cash flows.

Year	Cash flow
0	$(478)
1	75
2	181
3	267
4	313

10.5

Internal rate of return (IRR): Calculate the IRR for a project with the following cash flows.

Year	Cash flow
0	$(3,672)
1	(110)
2	562
3	827
4	1,012
5	1,378
6	1,789

10.6

Internal rate of return (IRR): Calculate the IRR for projects with the following cash flow projections.

Year	J	K	L
0	$(1,256)	$(1,256)	$(1,256)
1	111	311	—
2	235	311	—
3	313	311	—
4	396	311	—
5	462	311	—
6	515	311	2,564

What do your results mean? Which project would you recommend? Why? (Recall the topics in Chapter 3 for annuities and single sums.)

10.7

Internal rate of return (IRR) and modified internal rate of return (MIRR): Calculate the IRR and MIRR for a project with the following cash flows.

Year	Cash flow
0	$(2,459)
1	1,925
2	1,103
3	783

Assume a reinvestment rate of 8%. Why is there a difference?

10.8

Discounted payback period (DPBP): Answer the following questions for an investment in a $17,500 project with the following cash flows.

Year	Cash flow
1	$1,531
2	2,633
3	3,891
4	5,641
5	7,379
6	8,766

a. What is the discounted PBP at a 0% discount rate?

b. Using discounted payback, if 15% is the company's cost of capital, should you accept the project?

c. Using discounted payback, if the company's cost of capital is 9%, should you accept the project? What other information do you need?

10.9

Net present value (NPV) and profitability index (PI): Answer the following questions for an investment of $20,000 in a project with the following cash flows.

Year	Cash flow
1	$4,250
2	5,320
3	6,645
4	7,890
5	9,785

a. What is the NPV of this investment, assuming an 11% cost of capital? What is the project's PI? Should you accept this project?

b. What is the NPV of this investment, assuming a 20% cost of capital? What is the project's PI? Should you accept this project?

c. What is the relationship between the project's NPV and its profitability?

10.10

Technique comparison: Assume you have a cost of capital of 15% and are evaluating the following three mutually exclusive projects.

	A	B	C
Cost	$1,000	$1,000	$1,000
Year 1	50	250	200
Year 2	50	350	750
Year 3	75	450	150
Year 4	1,800	550	100

a. Calculate the following:

	A	B	C	Using this metric, which do you pick (A, B, or C)?
Payback period (PBP)				
Discounted PBP (15%)				
Net present value (15%)				

b. Which project (A, B, or C) should you recommend? Why?

c. Should you ever recommend project C? Why or why not?

10.11

Technique comparison: Assume you have a cost of capital of 10% and are evaluating the following two mutually exclusive projects.

	A	B
Cost	$300	$500
Year 1	50	75
Year 2	70	130
Year 3	110	170
Year 4	130	225
Year 5	180	250

a. Calculate the following and show the rates of return as XX.XX%.

	A	B	Using this metric, which do you pick (A or B)?
Net present value			
Internal rate of return			
Modified internal rate of return			
Profitability index			

b. Which project (A or B) should you recommend? Why?

10.12.

Technique comparison: Assume you are evaluating the follow in mutually exclusive projects.

	A	B	C
Cost	$11,900	$11,900	$11,900
Year 1	3,570	0	6,600
Year 2	5,950	0	6,600
Year 3	11,550	22,700	6,600

a. Complete the following analyses for projects A through C. [For the last two lines (terminal values), write in the accumulated future value of the intermediate cash flows, which are assumed to be reinvested at the noted rate until the terminal period.]

	Values A	B	C
Payback period			
NPV—10%			
NPV—15%			
IRR			
TRR—10%			
TRR—15%			
Terminal value—10%			
Terminal value—15%			

b. Rank the outcomes as your first choice, second choice, or third choice.

	Rank (First, Second, Third)		
	A	B	C
Payback period			
NPV—10%			
NPV—15%			
IRR			
TRR—10%			
TRR—15%			
Terminal value—10%			
Terminal value—15%			

c. If 10% is the required return, which project is preferred? Why?

10.13

Technique comparison: Assume you are evaluating the following three mutually exclusive projects:

	A	B	C
Cost	$3,400	$3,400	$3,400
Year 1	0	1,870	1,020
Year 2	0	1,870	1,700
Year 3	6,460	1,870	3,284

a. Complete the following analyses. [For the last two lines (terminal values), write in the accumulated future value of the intermediate cash flows, which are assumed to be reinvested at the noted rate until the terminal period.]

	Values		
	A	B	C
Payback period			
NPV—10%			
NPV—15%			
IRR			
TRR—10%			
TRR—15%			
Terminal value—10%			
Terminal value—15%			

b.   Rank the outcomes as your first choice, second choice, or third choice.

	Rank (First, Second, Third)		
	A	B	C
Payback period			
NPV—10%			
NPV—15%			
IRR			
TRR—10%			
TRR—15%			
Terminal value—10%			
Terminal value—15%			

c.   Compare and explain the conflicting rankings of the NPVs and TRRs versus the IRR.

d.   Is it possible at different discount rates to obtain different rankings within the NPV calculation? Why or why not?

e.   If 10% is the required return, which project is preferred?

f.   Which is the fairer representation of these two projects, TRR or IRR? Why?

10.14

Net present value (NPV) and IRR: An investment will return $87.50 for 19 years and $1,087.50 in the twentieth year.

a.   What is the present value of this investment if the investor wants to earn 7.5%? 9.5%?

b.   If the investment sells for $977.18, what is the project's IRR?

10.15

Net present value (NPV), IRR, and perpetuities: An investment promises you and your heirs an annual cash flow amount of $500 forever.

a.   If you required a 10% rate of return and this investment currently sells for $7,500, what is the NPV of this investment?

b.   What should the investment cost in order for it to have an IRR of 10%?

c.   If the project costs $7,500 (as in question 15a), what annual cash flows will produce a 10% IRR?

10.16

Net present value (NPV), internal rate of return (IRR), and cash flow sensitivity: Quaker Foods introduced a new eating experience. It is a morning breakfast with candy bits. The product is expected to generate cash flows of $23.75 million for five years and its cost is $115 million.

a.   Will the project provide a 9.5% return?

b.   What is the IRR of the project?

c.   What must cash flows be each year to provide the 9.5% return?

10.17

Net present value (NPV), internal rate of return (IRR), and cash flow sensitivity: A project includes the following cash flows.

Year	Cash flow
1	$(3,546)
2	1,389
3	5,222
4	8,391
5	11,916
6	15,324

In addition, given the project's risk an appropriate cost of capital is 12%.

a. If this project costs $25,000, what is the NPV?

b. To generate a 12% rate of return, how much additional cash flow must be generated each year to achieve the 12% return? In year 1, this will reduce the negative outflow.

10.18

Present value of unequal annual amounts with a perpetuity. An acquisition provides the following cash flows for its first eight years. Starting in the ninth year, cash flows become a perpetuity growing at 3% per year. Assume the appropriate discount rate is 11.0%.

Year	Cash flow
1	17,837
2	93,889
3	177,711
4	335,667
5	421,124
6	489,772
7	512,432
8	524,237

a. What is the investment's NPV, assuming an initial investment of $4.8 million?

b. The acquisition's champion, the vice president of New Product Marketing, argues that this acquisition is less risky than the company's other ventures because it is an investment that utilizes the core strengths of the company. She also suggests that a more appropriate discount rate is 9.5%. What is the NPV of this project if 9.5% is used as the discount rate?

c. What is the present value of the eight explicit years of cash flow? What is today's value ascribed to the terminal (or residual) value of the perpetuity. Consider both the 11% and 9.5% discount rates.

d. Should they complete the acquisition?

10.19.

Post-completion audit: Two years ago, a new product capital project was approved for $540 million based on the following cash flows. Marketing had full responsibility for the project.

a.   Calculate the NPV for the original proposal if the required return were 12%.

Year	Original proposal
0	$(540.00)
1	48.00
2	132.00
3	180.00
4	228.00
5	270.00

b.   The post-completion audit contains a financial reevaluation of this project. The post-completion audit reflects an overrun of $30 million during the implementation of the equipment (year 0) and ongoing performance that fell $36 million short of the year-1 projection and $40 million short of the year-2 projection. Marketing assures us that the wrinkles have been worked out, and starting this year performance will improve to the level originally projected for years 3 and 4 and then surge to $330 for year 5 (a $60 improvement in year 5). Recalculate the annual cash flows and NPV.

c.   What additional questions would you want to ask Marketing regarding this new product and their forecasts for the remaining three years?

d.   What is the NPV of this product given the revised post-completion audit assumptions with an extension of this project into year 6. Marketing believes the $76 million shortfall from years 1 and 2 can be recaptured in year 6.

e.   Return to the post-completion audit assumptions in question 19b. Marketing argues that the risk of this project has now been minimized and that a hurdle rate (discount rate) of 11% is more appropriate. Recalculate the NPV. Do you agree with their position?

Capital Investment Decisions

Learning Outcomes

*After completing this chapter,
you should be able to:*

1 Determine appropriate cash flows used to value a project

2 Justify a capital investment

3 Grasp the numerous dimensions that can shape cash flows

4 Prepare a capital project evaluation, including the appropriate cash flows and using appropriate techniques (from Chapter 10)

5 Apply these techniques to a wide variety of capital investment circumstances

6 Utilize the appropriate techniques to examine the impact of assumption uncertainty

Projected cash flows form the foundation for all of the investment analysis techniques and applications. Determining cash flows is one of the most important steps in the capital investment analysis process. In practice, when evaluating investment proposals discussions about the derivation of assumptions and the resulting cash flows dominate reports and presentations. Reasonably measurable assumptions that are achieved when the project is implemented assure the organization that it will enhance shareholder value to the level of the projected net present value (NPV). Unrealistic and aggressive assumptions make the project look significantly better in the analysis phase. However, when the project is implemented and the projected level of performance is unattained destruction of shareholder value occurs.

This chapter reviews general concepts that support the development of cash flows, defines specific structures for analyzing cash flows, and develops cash flow models for traditional investment evaluation (cost savings and new products) and *nontraditional evaluations* (e.g., information technology and strategic plan evaluation). Although this chapter concentrates on developing explicit cash flows under conditions of certainty, this chapter also progressively covers the handling of uncertainty as well as implicit cash flows embedded in "real options" provided by a project.

Overview of a Capital Authorization Request

In Chapter 10 we presented the four phases of investment analysis. This chapter centers on developing cash flow projections for the second phase, capital project evaluation, which is also called the "project approval" phase.

Although serving a vitally important financial and economic function, a good investment analysis process also incorporates the managerial and organizational qualities of a good strategic planning process. Strong investment evaluation and authorization:

- Facilitates communication among the senior executives of an organization

- Sets a business direction

- Prioritizes opportunities and requirements

- Establishes business performance standards and objectives

The investment analysis must be a living, actionable tool. Significant investment analysis can involve many areas within an organization. A new product decision involves research and development, marketing, sales, engineering, production, logistics, finance, human resources, legal, corporate communications, and so on. All areas of the organization need to be involved in the decision process, albeit to varying degrees. Even in a simple equipment replacement analysis championed by manufacturing and engineering, marketing and sales must be involved to provide consistent product sales projections.

Replacing equipment for a product that marketing plans to discontinue may not be financially feasible. In fact, without marketing's input production engineering might extrapolate historical levels when the marketing plan calls for tapering of the product's sales. To facilitate the investment analysis process, a capital authorization request (CAR) consists of numerous pages of justification and analysis with several supporting sections that may include the following.

- Summary cover page

- Complete project description and link to the firm's strategy

- Decision case cash flow assumptions

- Decision case cash flow amounts

- Decision case NPV analysis

- Sensitivity and/or scenario analysis

- Investment components, potential vendor, and cost basis

- Quarterly expenditure budget

Table 11.1 outlines a summary cover page. Many firms refer to this as a CAR. The interesting thing about this page is that it supports the collaborative nature of capital investment analysis by providing numerous areas for capturing all of the appropriate signatures: project originator, project sponsor, analyst/engineer who completes the CAR, and of course management. Not all of the signatures are necessary for every project. The form includes administrative header and identification information, an abbreviated project description, budget information, project anticipated expenditure summary, numerous financial indicators, and of course the signatures.

TABLE	11.1	Capital Authorization Request Summary

Division/Department	Cost Center	Date Prepared	Prepared By	Project Number
Project Title		Starting Date	Closing Date	Internal Reference

Project Description	[ ] Budgeted ($000's)$_____ [ ] Not Budgeted	Summary of Project Expenditures

	($000s)
New Fixed Assets	$ —
Transferred Fixed Assets	—
Capitalized Expense	—
Prior Approvals	—
Total Capital Requested	$ —
Operating Expenses	$ —
Working Capital	—
Other	—
Total Other Requested	$ —
Total Project Amount	$ —

Financial Indicators	Project Analysis Signatures
Net Present Value @_____%	Cost Estimates By
Terminal Rate of Return @_____%	
Internal Rate of Return	Technical Development By
Pay Back Period—Years	
Maximum Cash Exposure	Financial Data By
Project Life—Years	

Management Signatures	
Board of Directors	Chief Executive Officer
Chief Operating Officer	Division President
Chief Financial Officer	Vice President
Vice President	Vice President
Vice President	Vice President
Vice President	Vice President
Request Originator	Sponsor

The *base case (or decision case) assumptions*, cash flow amounts, and NPV analysis will be more fully developed throughout this chapter (along with sensitivity and scenario analysis). The project description includes a full and complete write-up of the project, its rationale, justification of the key assumptions, alternatives considered and rejected, "fit" with strategic objectives, details of budget inclusion, and key technical/engineering data if appropriate. *Sensitivity and scenario analysis* examines the degree to which changes in key assumptions effect the NPV. A detailed list of equipment components and potential vendors are provided for technical (operational) consideration. The cost basis is provided to understand if the expenditure estimate is a vendor quote (little volatility) or an estimate with maybe significant volatility. For detailed budgeting, the final schedule of the CAR documents anticipated expenditures by quarter.

CASH FLOW IDENTIFICATION

Identifying appropriate cash flows is the challenge of capital investment analysis. We want to isolate incremental after-tax cash flows that occur solely as a result of the project's implementation. Cash flows for some projects are easy to identify, but for most projects isolating the cash flow is more difficult.

For a cost savings project, engineering studies can validate productivity (labor) savings. The life of the project can be determined through engineering studies and experience with similar types of equipment. These cash flows may be easier to determine. But what about cash flows from a new product, a new process, or information technology? What about cash flows that result from years of research and development investment or advertising investment to build brand awareness? These cash flows become more tentative and more difficult to quantify. Nonetheless, a reasonable cash flow or a range of reasonable cash flows must be identified to assure sound financial management. The next few sections provide added terminology before we explore project development.

FUNDS AVAILABILITY

On the dimension of funds availability, there are two extremes: unlimited funds and capital rationing. *Unlimited funds* are a financial situation in which a firm is able to accept all independent projects that provide an acceptable rate of return. The authors know of no such organization. Every organization has funding limitations.

At the other end of the funds availability continuum lies capital rationing. *Capital rationing* has two forms: *hard capital rationing* forced on the organization by the financial markets and *soft capital rationing*, which is imposed by management. Unfortunately, at some point in the lives of some organizations the financial capital markets say "enough is enough—you can have no more capital." This is referred to as "hard capital" rationing and leads to either dramatic turnaround or bankruptcy. Management may impose soft capital rationing (internally imposed) for a variety of reasons. Soft rationing may be due to other impediments that confine the firm's ability to execute all potential projects. These impediments include limitations in the number of employees available to perform the implementation, limitations in management's ability to handle a number of major simultaneous projects, the physical constraints of facilities, concerns over debt covenant violation, restrictions imposed by the customer and the overall market, and so on. Sometimes, managers will postpone or delay the amount of capital investment to enhance short-term accounting performance metrics (i.e., return on assets).

CAPITAL DECISIONS

As we saw in Chapter 10, the first issue addressed by capital investment analysis is to accept or reject investment in a project. When two competing mutually exclusive projects have acceptable returns (actually, NPVs), the decision becomes one of ranking the projects. Capital authorization initially facilitates the accept/reject decision and then project ranking.

CASH FLOW PATTERNS

A conventional capital project has an initial period of project investment (or cash outflows), followed by years of positive cash flow. A non-conventional pattern of cash flows is one that starts with investment, followed by positive cash flows, followed by a period or two of negative cash flows, and then maybe back to positive cash flow. This non-conventional pattern often results when added investment is required to refurbish or overhaul the original investment. Although the refurbishment or overhaul decision can be made at a later time, if it is anticipated and is integral to the project the refurbishment or overhaul should be considered in the initial project stage.

SUNK COSTS

A *sunk cost* is a cost (or cash outlay) that has already been made. There is nothing to do to change the fact that cash was expended during some previous time period. Sunk costs have no relevance to the immediate decision and should not be considered part of the investment.

As an example, often when Hershey introduced a new product a year-long test market preceded that introduction. That test market often cost millions of dollars, depending on the size and duration of the test. After a successful test, a product's investment was "scaled up" to accommodate the projected sales level suggested by the test. Resulting operating cash flows were projected, and the project's NPV determined.

As in Chapter 10, a positive NPV indicates a solid and acceptable investment. For example, let's say after a favorable test market ($5 million expenditure) engineering determined that a new production line for $50 million was the proper scale and size for this new product. Furthermore, after-tax cash flows were estimated at $8.5 million each year over the project's 10-year life. At a 10% cost of capital (discount rate), the project is acceptable (with a positive $2.2 million NPV).

With a positive NPV, management should have accepted the project. However, years ago at Hershey that project might have been rejected. The "sunk cost" of the test market was imposed in the investment analysis. The investment was considered $55 million (the $50 to purchase the new production line and $5 million spent the previous year for the test market). In this example, the new product introduction would have been rejected because the $55 million investment would have exceeded the present value of the operating cash flows, resulting in a negative NPV of $(2.8).

Identifying a sunk cost is easy when you are not a part of the analysis. However, at that time (and this was changed in the early 1990s) management argued that the $5 million test market expense needed to be tracked. Someone or some project needed to be held accountable for that $5 million. Unfortunately, this was management's way of controlling, monitoring, and "accounting" for test markets.

OPPORTUNITY COSTS

Opportunity costs represent cash flows that could be realized from the best alternative use of a surplus asset that will be engaged in the proposed project. What if a project proposal includes the use of an idle asset that was once used by the business? What value should be attributed to the asset? As in many circumstances, the answer is dependent on variables and we need more additional information.

If the asset has no alternative use and the asset has no current market value or no scrap value, that asset should be included at a zero-dollar value in the analysis. On the other hand, if you can sell the asset in the open market that value should be included as part of the project's investment.

If you can sell the idle asset as only scrap value, that limited amount should be included in the investment analysis. On the summary page (Table 11.1), this value is included as a transferred fixed asset. Determining an alternative use and estimating alternative values is often confounded by the asset's book value. The book value of the idle asset has no role in the investment analysis and should not be considered when arriving at the investment amount. Book value may be necessary when transferring the asset on the accounting books (e.g., fixed asset register) of the firm for managerial control and reporting purposes.

COST SAVINGS VERSUS COST AVOIDANCE

Cost savings occur whenever a project's implementation reduces expenses from the current level of expenditures. *Cost avoidance* occurs whenever a project's implementation reduces expenses from a projected level of expenditures. This is not much of a distinction in a finance professional's mind. However, in the mind of management there is a huge difference.

Cost savings can be documented. By implementing this capital investment, we can reduce operating expenses by $10 million per year through a reduction in the labor force. We see the 200 employees and can determine that their fully loaded cost is on average $50,000 each including salary and wages, bonuses, benefits, and employer taxes.

On the other hand, cost avoidance is based more on projection. By implementing this capital investment, we can avoid hiring 200 people (at $50,000 each) and avoid $10 million of added operating expenses per year. Analytically, there is no difference in the designation of the $10 million in annual cash flow. Often, however, management teams treat these two costs as different. From a financial perspective, the difference may lie in the risk surrounding the nature of the expense. In the case of the cost savings, the savings rely on follow-through on current costs. This one-step approach is easy to trace and easy to "post-completion audit."

In the case of the cost avoidance, management must first rely on the projected expense pattern without the capital investment. Management must be convinced that without this expenditure expenses will immediately escalate by $10 million, and they must be convinced that this capital will save the estimated $10 million of projected future expense. The analysis involves a "two-step" cash flow determination process that cannot be audited. Management distinguishes more risk and less confidence and consequently sees the cash flows as distinct categories (savings versus avoidance).

Basic Cash Flow Statement

At the end of Chapter 10, a basic cash flow projection was used to illustrate the individual components of the cash flow projection. Specifically, Table 10.21 documented the operating cash flows. A cash flow projection includes three interlinked cash flow sections:

- *Initial investment:* Relevant cash outflow (or investment) at the beginning of the investment proposal

- *Operating cash flow:* Relevant after-tax incremental cash inflows or outflows from the project throughout its life

- *Terminal cash flow:* After-tax non-operating cash flow occurring in the final year of the project

Discussion of determining operating cash flows follows sections on initial investment and terminal cash flow.

INITIAL INVESTMENT

The initial investment consists of three items (as listed in Table 11.2). The first item reflects what is usually the major cash outflow: the installed cost of any new asset.

TABLE	11.2	Initial Investment

+	Installed cost of new asset
	Cost of new asset
	+ Installation costs
−	After-tax proceeds from sale of old
	Proceeds from the sale of the old assets
	± Tax on sale of old asset
±	Change in net working capital
=	Initial Investment

The *installed cost* includes the cost of new assets purchased from vendors, the *opportunity cost of equipment* absorbed by the project, and all installation costs. The installation costs include fees paid to external consultants, designers, and engineers along with capitalized in-house engineering expenses or other non-capitalized operating expenses incurred by the organization. *Capitalized in-house engineering expenses* are an accounting requirement that captures the costs of all engineer-employees (salary, bonus, benefits, and employee taxes).

Instead of expensing these costs at the time they are incurred, the costs are "capitalized" or added to the total cost of the project and depreciated over the project's life. The assumption is that if these in-house engineers were not productively employed installing this project they would be productively engaged on another project or not employed by the firm. The installed cost of the new asset is offset by any after-tax proceeds from the sale of any equipment being replaced, if in fact there is a machine replacement. To calculate the after-tax proceeds, we need the selling price, the current tax book value of the asset, and the marginal tax rate. As calculated by Equation 11.1, the current tax book value reflects the installed cost of the replaced asset less its accumulated tax depreciation.

$$\frac{\text{Tax}}{\text{Book Value}} = \frac{\text{Initial Cost of}}{\text{Replaced Asset}} - \frac{\text{Accumulated Tax}}{\text{Depreciation}} \qquad (11.1)$$

Table 11.3 illustrates the cash flow from the sale of an existing asset for three different selling prices: (1) no gain or loss (selling price = tax book value), (2) a gain (selling price > tax book value), and (3) a loss (selling price < tax book value). In this example, the asset was purchased a few years ago for $12,000. For tax purposes, using the *Modified Accelerated Cost Recovery System (MACRS)* a total of $9,000 was depreciated since the asset was purchased. This results in a tax book value of $3,000, which is constant over the three different selling price examples. In the first column (no gain or loss), the asset is sold for exactly its tax book value of $3,000. There are no tax consequences. There is no taxable gain or loss. Thus, the cash flow is equal to the selling price ($3,000).

In the second column of Table 11.3, the asset is sold for $4,000 (resulting in a gain of $1,000). Assuming a 40% tax rate, the organization would pay $400 on the gain. The cash flow is the $4,000 selling price offset by the $400 tax expense (or $3,600).

The final column illustrates a selling price of $2,000 (a loss of $1,000). Assuming that the organization can immediately offset other gains with this loss, a $400 tax savings

TABLE 11.3	Cash Proceeds from Asset Disposal		
	NO GAIN OR LOSS	GAIN	LOSS
Selling price	$3,000	$4,000	$2,000
Tax book value	3,000	3,000	3,000
Taxable gain (loss)	–	1,000	(1,000)
Taxes (40%)	–	(400)	400
After-tax gain (loss)	$ –	$ 600	$ (600)
Selling price	$3,000	$4,000	$2,000
Taxes	–	(400)	400
Cash flow	$3,000	$3,600	$2,400

offsets the loss. The cash flow is the $2,000 selling price and the $400 tax savings for a total cash flow of $2,400.

The after-tax proceeds of the sale of the old asset offset the cost of a new asset. On a personal basis, this is similar to having a trade-in when you buy a new car. Or more precisely, this is like buying a new car and selling your old car yourself. It is the net incremental cash flow (e.g., investment) we are interested in.

The final initial investment component is any additional working capital investment. When we introduce a new product, we need to invest in inventory (raw materials, goods in process, and finished goods). This ensures that we have inventory on hand to fill customers' initial orders and subsequent orders.

Customers who purchase the new products will require us to invest in accounts receivable as they continue their payment habits of 30 or so days until invoices are paid. Offsetting this is spontaneous operating financing that is enjoyed as accounts payable are automatically extended from suppliers. This *operating net working capital (NWC) investment* can be summarized as follows.

NET WORKING CAPITAL INITIAL INVESTMENT	
	Investment in inventory
+	Investment in accounts receivable
–	Accounts payable spontaneous financing
=	Net working capital investment

Note that this definition of net working capital considers only short-term operating assets and liabilities. It does not include cash and short-term debt. Each year of operations may require subsequent net working capital investment. This is further explored in regard to the development of operating cash flows, after discussion of terminal cash flow.

TERMINAL CASH FLOW

The terminal cash flow includes nonoperating cash flows that occur at the end of a project's life. These cash flows are unique and nonrecurring. To figure out the total cash flow for the

TABLE	11.4	Terminal Cash Flow

+	After-tax proceeds from sale of new
	Proceeds from the sale of the new assets
	± Tax on sale of new asset
−	After-tax proceeds from sale of old
	Proceeds from the sale of the old assets
	± Tax on sale of old asset
±	Change in net working capital
=	**Terminal cash flow**

project's final year, terminal cash flows need to be combined with the final year's operating cash flow. Table 11.4 lists the components of terminal cash flow.

The initial cash flow began by calculating the net cash outflow for the new asset. This was the installed cost of the new asset and transferred assets less after-tax proceeds from the sale of the replaced asset. In a similar fashion, the terminal cash flow begins by calculating the incremental cash generated by disposing of the new asset versus the replaced asset. Remember, we are estimating the incremental financial impact of replacing or not replacing a piece of equipment.

If we do not replace, there may be some value left in that old piece of equipment at the end of our analytical period. Often, the after-tax proceeds from the sale of the replaced equipment are considered negligible in the final year of the new asset, and thus most analysts ignore its inclusion. Once again, the cash flow from the sale of the asset is calculated on an after-tax basis, similar to the calculations in Table 11.3 and discussed previously.

The terminal cash flow includes the change in net working capital. Usually, in the final year the assumption is that all inventories are sold, all receivables collected, and all accounts payable paid in full. In other words, the full amount invested in working capital, initial investment, and all subsequent operating investment made throughout the intervening years is fully recovered. There are no tax consequences associated with *full working capital recovery*. However, the full recovery assumption can be adjusted, if necessary, to indicate only 95% (or whatever percentage) inventory recovery due to obsolescence or shrinkage and only 97% (or whatever percentage) accounts receivable collection due to bad debts of "deadbeat" customers. In these cases, additional tax savings may result from these "losses," and thus these tax savings need to be part of the terminal cash flows as well.

In rare cases, the incremental working capital could be negative. For example, if a computer technology project was partially justified on initial operating NWC savings (an initial positive inflow), the terminal period may reflect a cash outflow that signifies the previous working capital investment level.

OPERATING CASH FLOW

Many considerations of operating cash flows complete this chapter. In Chapter 10, a project's basic operating cash flow projection was presented. It is similar to the cash flow statement introduced in Chapter 2 and reconsidered in Chapter 9. As previously seen, the cash flow projection begins with a projected income statement, "adds back" any non-cash expenses, and considers all additional operating cash flow investment. In Chapter 10, we introduced different bases for project implementation and different project categories. These included the following.

- Capital expenditure analysis
  - Cost savings/avoidance
  - Capacity expansion
- New product introduction
- Major operating decisions
  - Advertising campaigns
  - Research and development
- Information technology
- Mergers and acquisitions
  - External acquisition evaluation
  - Internal self-valuation
  - Divestitures

Each project category has its own specific investment rationale, but the resulting incremental after-tax operating cash flows can generally be captured in the basic cash flow statement introduced in Table 10.21 and repeated here as Table 11.5. Although the general framework supports the analysis of many different projects, not all lines will be used for all analysis. For example, a cost savings project results only in cost or working capital reduction. The sales level is unaffected by a cost savings project. In an analysis of an advertising campaign and its subsequent incremental sales, depreciation would not be considered unless there are also incremental assets included in the project proposal.

TABLE 11.5	Analysis and Computation of Project Cash Flow: Project B		
	YEAR 1	YEAR 2	YEAR 3
Project income:			
Sales	$1,000	$1,300	$1,300
Expenses (excluding depreciation)	850	1,050	1,050
Depreciation	133	133	134
Pre-tax income/operating income	17	117	116
Taxes	7	47	46
After-tax operating income	$ 10	$ 70	$ 70
Project cash flow:			
After-tax operating income	$ 10	$ 70	$ 70
Depreciation	133	133	134
Additional working capital	(43)	(3)	46
After-tax salvage value	—	—	50
Terminal Value	$ 100	$ 200	$ 300

TABLE	11.6	Net Income Versus Cash Flow

PROFITABLE PROJECT BUT POOR INVESTMENT				UNPROFITABLE PROJECT BUT GOOD INVESTMENT		
Year 1	Year 2	Year 3		Year 1	Year 2	Year 3
			Project income			
$960	$980	$1,000	Sales	$960	$980	$1,000
(800)	(800)	(800)	Expenses (excluding depreciation)	(875)	(895)	(915)
(100)	(100)	(100)	Depreciation	(100)	(100)	(100)
60	80	100	Pre-tax income	(15)	(15)	(15)
(24)	(32)	(40)	Taxes (40%)	6	6	6
$ 36	$ 48	$ 60	After-tax operating income	$ (9)	$ (9)	$ (9)
			Project cash flow			
$ 36	$ 48	$ 60	After-tax operating income	$ (9)	$ (9)	$ (9)
100	100	100	Depreciation	100	100	100
(50)	(50)	100	Additional working capital	—	—	—
—	—	—	After-tax salvage value	—	—	200
$ 86	$ 98	$ 260	Total cash flow	$ 91	$ 91	$ 291
	$300		Initial investment		$300	
			Economic evaluation			
	$ (10)		Net present value @20%		$ 7	
	18.3%		Internal rate of return		21.3%	
	18.7%		Terminal rate of return @20%		21.0%	

Table 11.6 demonstrates that our focus is cash flow not net income. On the left-hand side of Table 11.6 there are details of a profitable project that is not a good investment. On the right-hand side of Table 11.6 there are details of an unprofitable project that is a good investment. Truth be told, these cash flows were contrived to demonstrate a point. Continual submission of unprofitable projects, will cut an otherwise successful career short. But there are practical examples of these types of good investments that are unprofitable.

First, the left-hand side of Table 11.6 shows a profitable project. In fact, this project has net income (after-tax operating income) of $36 in the first year. This grows by 33% in the second year, and by 25% the year after that. Thus, in addition to being profitable the project contains solid income growth. After-tax operating income begins the cash flow.

Add back non-cash expenses such as the depreciation and consider the working capital investment and after-tax salvage value to conclude the cash flow. In this example, additional working capital of $50 per year is invested in the first two years, with full recovery in the final (third) year. At the end of the three years, there is no additional value left in the project. The project has zero salvage value. The profitable project has cash flows of $86, $98, and $260 over its three-year life, respectively. Its NPV is negative, its IRR is 18.3% and is below the 20% cost of capital, and its TRR is 18.7% (assuming reinvestment at 20%). All three barometers lead to the rejection of the profitable project because it is a poor investment.

The unprofitable project loses $(9) each year. But when the depreciation is added to the loss this unprofitable project generates $91 of operating cash flow each year. Note that there is no additional working capital investment and the project includes an after-tax salvage value of $200. This salvage value results in a $291 final year cash flow. The NPV is positive, the IRR is 21.3%, and the TRR is 21.0%. By all indications, this unprofitable project is a viable investment opportunity.

Although there are not many projects like this (unprofitable but a good investment) in practice, this project represents the structure of many tax-motivated strategies. From a personal perspective, the cash flows of the unprofitable project represent investment in an apartment house. In these situations, often the landlord reports a loss to the federal government because depreciation is tax deductible. However, the annual cash flows remain positive. Finally, there is no working capital investment, and the landlord hopes to realize a positive after-tax salvage value. This is an unprofitable project that is also a good investment.

The key point demonstrated by Table 11.6 is that cash flow, not income, is what drives the value of a project. The next section demonstrates the development of cash flows for a basic equipment replacement decision.

Capital Evaluation: The Basic Replacement Decision

From this point forward we will use the NPV method for all capital evaluation decisions. The following replacement decision is an example of a typical problem, which illustrates the use of cash flows for capital evaluation decisions. This example emphasizes that all project cash flows must be represented as incremental or as changes in the firm's cash flows. It also demonstrates the NPV method of discounted cash flows. Although the project is totally hypothetical, it does maintain our Hershey theme.

STRAIGHT-LINE DEPRECIATION EXAMPLE

One of the tricky steps in the mass production of chocolate confection is the wrapping process. When wrapping at high rates of speed, inevitably some product gets broken (which results in scrap, as well as downtime to clean the wrapping equipment). Marketing also notes that consumer panels complain about the appearance of chocolate with "scuff marks" as a result of slightly imprecise settings on the wrapping equipment. The Hershey Company strives to incorporate consumer feedback and is considering the replacement of some wrapping equipment that was purchased four years ago at a cost of $7.0 million. The machine had an expected life of 14 years at that time, with no estimated salvage value. It is being depreciated on a straight-line basis and has a book value of $5.0 million at present and a current market value of $1.0 million.

A production engineer develops a new approach to wrapping and begins the investigative process of determining the appropriate assumptions leading to appropriate cash flows. First, a request for proposal (RFP) is circulated to a group of equipment suppliers. This will confirm the feasibility of the approach as well as provide a solid investment quote. Working with the plant manager, plant controller, and the supervisor of the wrapping department, the engineer determines that with this new design the company should be able to reduce the cost of scrap product and unproductive downtime from $9.8 million to $8.6 million.

The engineer then approaches the brand manager for her input. They discuss incremental sales as a result of a more consistent and appealing product. She believes that sales should increase by $1.0 million (or 1% of existing sales). The product has a 60% contribution margin, after considering all variable costs. The production engineer also discusses the project with members of corporate accounting, the tax department, and the Treasurer's office to obtain the following information.

- Additional working capital investment will be 10% of the incremental sales (or $0.1 million) and will be fully recoverable in the final year.

- The appropriate incremental tax rate is 40.0%.

- The cost of capital is 10.5%.

Finally, the RFPs are returned and the winning bid includes a cost of $9.3 million, with an estimate of $0.7 million installation costs. Management expects that the new equipment will have a salvage value of $1.0 million in year 10, and thus only $9.0 million of the value will be depreciated annually (resulting in a $0.9-million depreciation each year).

The decision calls for five steps: (1) estimating the initial investment attributable to the new investment, (2) determining the incremental operating cash flows, (3) projecting the terminal cash flows or expected salvage value and adding the terminal cash flows to the operating cash flows, (4) finding the present value of the total incremental cash flows, and (5) determining whether the NPV is positive. These steps are explained further in the following sections.

Step 1: Estimate Initial Investment The net initial cash outlay consists of these items: (1) payment to the manufacturer of the new equipment, (2) installation costs, and (3) after-tax proceeds from the sale of the old machine. Hershey must make a $9.3-million payment to the equipment manufacturer, and it will incur an additional installation cost (including freight) of $700,000. On the other hand, the trade-in value of the existing machine is $1.0 million, which results in tax loss of $4.0 million and a tax savings of $1.6 million (calculated as follows).

($ Thousands)	OLD MACHINE
Selling price	$ 1,000
Tax book value	5,000
Taxable gain (loss)	(4,000)
Taxes (40%)	1,600
After-tax gain (loss)	$(2,400)
Selling price	$ 1,000
Taxes savings	1,600
Cash flow	$ 2,600

A typical assumption is that any losses can be immediately used to offset gains in other parts of the business and thus there is an immediate tax benefit when a loss occurs. The after-tax proceeds from selling the old equipment reduce the initial investment in the equipment and net working capital (calculated as follows).

($ Thousands)	INITIAL INVESTMENT
Purchase price	$ 9,300
Installation costs	700
Cash flow sale of old asset	(2,600)
Net working capital investment	100
Initial investment	$ 7,500

The net initial investment is $7,500. If additional net working capital is required as a result of a capital evaluation decision, as would generally be true for sales expansion investments (as opposed to cost-reducing replacement investments), this factor must be taken into account.

Step 2: Determine Annual Incremental Operating Cash Flows

Column A in the following shows this particular product line's estimated income statement and cash flow as they would be without the new machine. Column B shows the statement as it would look if the new investment were made. Column C shows the incremental impacts.

($ Thousands)	(A) CURRENT LEVELS	(B) PROJECTED LEVELS	(C) DIFFERENCE BETTER (WORSE)
Proceeds from additional sales			
Product sales	$100,000	$101,000	$1,000
Direct cost of product (40%)	40,000	40,400	400
Contribution income	60,000	60,600	600
Operating costs	9,800	8,600	1,200
Depreciation	500	900	(400)
Operating income	49,700	51,100	1,400
Taxes (40%)	19,880	20,440	(560)
After-tax operating income	$ 29,820	$ 30,660	$840
After-tax operating income	$ 29,820	$ 30,660	$840
Depreciation	500	900	400
Additional net working capital	—	—	—
Additional fixed capital investment	—	—	—
Cash flow	$ 30,320	$ 31,560	$1,240

Although sales improve by $1.0 million (from $100 million to $101 million), contribution income grows by $0.6 million. Operating costs improve by $1.2 million, whereas depreciation expense increases by $0.4 million. In total, $1.4 million additional income is generated before tax ($840,000 after tax). When the $0.4-million incremental depreciation is added back, a favorable $1.24-million after-tax cash impact is realized.

If additional working capital investment or fixed capital investment (machinery overhaul) was expected, these incremental cash uses would need to be reflected in the foregoing calculation. We assume that Hershey will not need any additional working or fixed capital, so this is ignored in the example.

Another way of looking at the annual incremental cash flows is to isolate the after-tax cash flow impact of each item. For example, the contribution of increased sales is expected to be $600,000. This results in more taxable income upon which 40% taxes must be paid, resulting in after-tax operating income of $360,000 (which flows directly through to enhanced cash flow).

Operating expenses improve (decrease) by $1.2 million [or $720,000 after considering a 40% tax rate ($480,000 added taxes) on the savings]. The $720,000 flows directly to the projected cash flow. Finally, although depreciation is not a cash flow item it is a tax-deductible expense. The additional $0.4 million of depreciation provides a tax reduction (a tax shield) of $0.16 million. The tax shield provides an additional positive cash flow, whereas the depreciation expense has no direct impact on cash flow. In summary ($ thousands):

ITEM	($ Thousands)	CALCULATION (TAX RATE = 40%)	CASH FLOW
Additional sales—contribution		$600 × (1 – tax rate)	$ 360
Reduced operating expenses		$1,200 × (1 – tax rate)	720
Added depreciation		$400 x (tax rate)	160
		Total cash flow impact	$1,240

Either approach determines the same incremental cash flow impact ($1.24 million) for each of the 10 years of projections. However, the first approach (also shown in Table 11.7) promotes a more general framework that can provide a consistent method of examining operating cash flows for a variety of investment decisions. This is consequently a preferable approach.

Step 3: Project the Terminal Cash Flows or Expected Salvage Value and add to the final year's operating cash flow. In the initial year, $0.1 million was invested in working capital for inventory and accounts receivable was somewhat offset by accounts payable to support the incremental sales. In the final (or terminal) year, we assume that all inventory is sold, all receivables collected, and all payables paid. Thus, we assume a recovery of $0.1 million. In addition, the new machine has an estimated salvage value of $1.0 million. That is, Hershey expects to be able to sell the machine for $1.0 million after 10 years of use.

In year 10, the tax book value is also $1.0 million (the $10.0 million installed purchase price less 10 years of $0.9 million depreciation per year). Note that the salvage value is a return of capital, not taxable income, and is thus not subject to income taxes. Of course, when the new machine is actually retired 10 years from the time of the analysis it might be sold for more or less than the expected $1.0 million. Thus, either taxable income or a deductible operating loss could arise, but $1.0 million is the best current estimate of the new machine's salvage value. This results in no taxable gain or loss on the disposal of the new asset, no additional tax payments (or savings), and a cash flow impact of $1.0 million.

($ Thousands)	NEW MACHINE
Selling price	$1,000
Tax book value	1,000
Taxable gain (loss)	0
Taxes (40%)	0
After-tax gain (loss)	$ 0
Selling price	$1,000
Taxes	0
Cash flow	$1,000

The additional working capital and after-tax salvage value of the equipment are added together, representing an additional terminal value cash flow of $1.1 million (which is added to year 10's operating cash flow).

TABLE 11.7 | Replacement Decision—Straight-Line Depreciation ($000s)

	INITIAL INVESTMENT	YEAR 1	YEAR 2	YEAR 3	YEAR 4	YEAR 5	YEAR 6	YEAR 7	YEAR 8	YEAR 9	YEAR 10
Purchase price and installation	$(10,000)										
After-tax proceeds—sale of old asset	2,600										
Working capital investment	(100)										
Incremental operating cash flow											
Income from increased sales ($1000 × 60%)		$ 600	$ 600	$ 600	$600	$ 600	$ 600	$ 600	$ 600	$ 600	$ 600
Savings in operating costs		1,200	1,200	1,200	1,200	1,200	1,200	1,200	1,200	1,200	1,200
Incremental depreciation ($900 – $500)		(400)	(400)	(400)	(400)	(400)	(400)	(400)	(400)	(400)	(400)
Operating income		1,400	1,400	1,400	1,400	1,400	1,400	1,400	1,400	1,400	1,400
Taxes (40%)		(560)	(560)	(560)	(560)	(560)	(560)	(560)	(560)	(560)	(560)
After-tax operating income		$ 840	$ 840	$ 840	$840	$ 840	$ 840	$ 840	$ 840	$ 840	$ 840
After-tax operating income		$ 840	$ 840	$ 840	$840	$ 840	$ 840	$ 840	$ 840	$ 840	$ 840
Depreciation		400	400	400	400	400	400	400	400	400	400
Additional working capital (investment) recovery		—	—	—	—	—	—	—	—	—	—
Additional fixed capital (expenditures)		—	—	—	—	—	—	—	—	—	—
Incremental operating cash flow		1,240	1,240	1,240	1,240	1,240	1,240	1,240	1,240	1,240	1,240
Terminal cash flow											
Working capital recovery											100
Residual value—no gain (loss)											1,000
Total cash flow	$ (7,500)	$1,240	$1,240	$1,240	$1,240	$1,240	$1,240	$1,240	$1,240	$1,240	$2,340
Present value 10.5%	$ (7,500)	$1,122	$1,016	$ 919	$ 832	$ 753	$ 681	$ 616	$ 558	$ 505	$ 862

Gross present value (or the present value of the cash flows for years 1–10) $7,864

Net present value $ 364

Step 4: Find the Present Value of the Future Cash Flows We have explained in detail how to measure the annual benefits. The next step is to determine the present value of the *benefit stream*. This can be accomplished via Equation 11.2.

$$PV = \sum_{T=1}^{N} \frac{CF_t}{(1+k)^t} \tag{11.2}$$

Although this is a general model, the specific case in hand can be solved more straight-forwardly using a financial calculator and the NPV function (as described in Chapter 10). The present value of the estimated cash flows is $7,864,000.

Step 5: Determine the Net Present Value The project's NPV is found as the sum of the present values of the inflows (benefits) less the outflows (costs) per Equation 11.3 ($ thousands).

$$
\begin{aligned}
\text{Net Present Value} &= \text{Gross Present Value of Total Cash Flow} - \text{Initial Investment} \\
&= \$7,864 \qquad\qquad - \$7,500 \\
&= \$364
\end{aligned}
\tag{11.3}
$$

Because the NPV is positive, the project should be accepted.

CAPITAL EVALUATION WORKSHEET

Table 11.7 incorporates a worksheet for evaluating capital projects. The top section shows net cash flows at the time of investment. Because all of these flows occur immediately, no discounting is required and the interest factor is 1.0. The lower section of the table shows future cash flows [benefits from increased sales, reduced costs, depreciation, working capital recovery, and salvage (or terminal) value]. Because these flows occur over time, we must convert them to *present values*. The NPV as determined in this format [$364] agrees with the figure calculated using Equation 11.3.

Replacement Analysis with Accelerated Depreciation

We next consider the effect of MACRS depreciation on the replacement analysis. MACRS is the IRS-designated method of depreciation (Chapter 4). It groups equipment into broad classes of assets and provides accelerated (or faster) depreciation in the early years. Accelerated depreciation on both the old and the new equipment complicates the computations somewhat, but the logic is the same.

STEP 1: ESTIMATE CASH OUTLAY

The old machine had an initial cost of $7.0 million and a 14-year life. Using straight-line depreciation, its book value was $5.0 million after five years. In regard to the IRS, most manufacturing equipment is considered to have a seven-year class life under MACRS (as indicated in Table 11.8). The specific purpose of the machinery or the industry does not

TABLE	11.8	MACRS Depreciation

CLASS	EXAMPLES
3-Year	Equipment used in research
5-Year	Autos, computers
7-Year	Most industrial equipment and office furniture and fixtures

YEAR	3-YEAR	5-YEAR	7-YEAR
1	33.33%	20.00%	14.29%
2	44.44%	32.00%	24.49%
3	14.82%	19.20%	17.49%
4	7.41%	11.52%	12.49%
5		11.52%	8.93%
6		5.76%	8.93%
7			8.93%
8			4.45%
Total	100.00%	100.00%	100.00%

matter to the IRS. If the manufacturing equipment is used to make chocolate or cars or televisions, the equipment will have a life of seven years for tax purposes.

Note in Table 11.8 that the seven-year MACRS depreciation stretches over eight years assuming a half-year convention in the first and last year. The given percentages are directly applied to the purchase price of the asset without considering any anticipated salvage value. As seen in Table 11.8, after four years 68.76% of the asset has been depreciated. When this is applied to the original cost of the old machine ($7.0 million), four years of depreciation ($4,813,200) has already been depreciated, leaving a balance of $2,186,800 to be depreciated over the next four years. This is less than the book value under straight-line depreciation because MACRS results in higher depreciation earlier in the life of the asset.

The current market value of the old machine is assumed to be $1.0 million, as before. Selling the machine for $1.0 million will result in a loss of $1,186,800 (the difference between its tax book value for IRS purposes and its market value). This loss results in tax savings equal to:

$$(\text{Loss})(\text{Tax Rate}) = (\$1,186,800)(0.40) = \$474,720$$

The data given previously for the purchase of the new machine and working capital investment are unchanged from previously. However, the tax savings on the disposal of the old equipment is reduced, thus increasing the initial cash outflow:

		($ Thousands)	INITIAL INVESTMENT
Purchase price with Installation			$10,000
After-tax proceeds from selling the old asset	Selling price	$1,000	
	Tax savings	475	(1,475)
Working capital initial investment			100
Initial investment			$8,625

The initial investment increases to $8,625,000.

STEP 2: DETERMINE ANNUAL INCREMENTAL OPERATING CASH FLOWS

For capital evaluation analysis, the cash flows that are discounted are incremental after-tax operating cash flows. Income from increased sales and savings on operationg costs are unchanged. However, the incremental depreciation is different due to MACRS depreciation on both the existing asset and the new asset and because the depreciation expense is not constant from year to year under accelerated depreciation (as it is under straight-line depreciation) annual benefits will vary. The worksheet method illustrated in the footnote of Table 11.9 captures this effect of depreciation on after-tax cash flows.

STEP 3: PROJECT THE TERMINAL CASH FLOWS (EXPECTED SALVAGE VALUE)

The new machine has an estimated salvage value of $1.0 million. That is, Hershey expects to be able to sell the machine for $1.0 million after 10 years of use. The MACRS depreciation technique fully depreciates an asset over the project category's life. Consequently, a salvage value of $1.0 million results in a taxable gain of $1.0 million and an after-tax salvage value cash flow of $0.6 million:

($ Thousands)	NEW MACHINE
Selling price	$1,000
Tax book value	0
Taxable gain (loss)	1000
Taxes (40%)	(400)
After-tax gain (loss)	$ 600
Selling price	$1,000
Taxes	(400)
Cash flow salvage value	$ 600

Just as before, there is an additional working capital recovery of $0.1 million included in the terminal value for a total terminal year cash flow of $0.7 million, which is added to the operating cash flow in year 10.

STEP 4: FIND THE PRESENT VALUE OF THE FUTURE CASH FLOWS

This calculation is found in Table 11.9.

STEP 5: DETERMINE THE NET PRESENT VALUE

The project's NPV is found as the sum of the present values of the inflows (benefits) less the outflows (costs) per Equation 11.4.

$$\begin{aligned} \text{Net Present Value} &= \frac{\text{Gross Present Value}}{\text{of Total Cash Flow}} - \frac{\text{Initial}}{\text{Investment}} \\ &= \$8,898,000 - \$8,625,000 \\ &= \$273,000 \end{aligned}$$

(11.4)

TABLE 11.9   Replacement Decision—MACRS Depreciation ($000s)

	INITIAL INVESTMENT	YEAR 1	YEAR 2	YEAR 3	YEAR 4	YEAR 5	YEAR 6	YEAR 7	YEAR 8	YEAR 9	YEAR 10
Purchase Price	$(10,000)										
After-tax proceeds–sale of old asset	1,475										
Working capital investment	(100)										
Incremental operating cash flow											
Income from increased sales ($1000 × 60%)		$ 600	$ 600	$ 600	$ 600	$ 600	$ 600	$ 600	$ 600	$ 600	$ 600
Savings in operating costs		1,200	1,200	1,200	1,200	1,200	1,200	1,200	1,200	1,200	1,200
Incremental depreciation[a]		(804)	(1,824)	(1,124)	(938)	(893)	(893)	(893)	(445)	—	—
Operating income		996	(24)	676	863	907	907	907	1,355	1,800	1,800
Taxes (40%)		(398)	10	(270)	(345)	(363)	(363)	(363)	(542)	(720)	(720)
After-tax operating income		$ 598	$ (14)	$ 406	$ 518	$ 544	$ 544	$ 544	$ 813	$1,080	$1,080
After-tax operating income		$ 598	$ (14)	$ 406	$ 518	$ 544	$ 544	$ 544	$ 813	$1,080	$1,080
Depreciation		804	1,824	1,124	938	893	893	893	445	—	—
Incremental operating cash flow		1,402	1,810	1,530	1,455	1,437	1,437	1,437	1,258	1,080	1,080
Terminal cash flow											
Working capital recovery											100
Residual value–after tax											600
Total cash flow	$ (8,625)	$1,402	$1,810	$1,530	$1,455	$1,437	$1,437	$1,437	$1,258	$1,080	$1,780
Present value 10.5%	$ (8,625)	$1,268	$1,482	$1,134	$ 976	$ 872	$ 789	$ 714	$ 566	$ 440	$ 656
		$8,898	Gross present value (or the present value of the cash flows for years 1–10)								
Net present value	$ 273										
International depreciation		14.29%	24.49%	17.49%	12.49%	8.93%	8.93%	8.93%	4.45%	0.00%	0.00%
New equipment–eight-year MACRS		$1,429	$2,449	$1,749	$1,249	$ 893	$ 893	$ 893	$ 445	$ —	$ —
Old equipment–eight-year MACRS (last 4 years)		625	625	625	312	—	—	—	—	—	—
Incremental depreciation		$ 804	$1,824	$1,124	$ 938	$ 893	$ 893	$ 893	$ 445	$ —	$ —

As before, the NPV is positive, indicating that the replacement project should be accepted. Generally, MACRS depreciation should lead to a higher NPV. However, in this complicated example the NPV using MACRS is lower (by $91,000) than that using straight-line depreciation. This decrease is the net effect of three individual differences between the scenarios:

| | | PRESENT VALUE IMPACT @ 10.5% | | |
	Period	Straight Line	MACRS	Difference
Initial period:				
Cash flow impact of sale of "old" equipment	Year 0	$2,600	$1,475	$1,125
Annual incremental operating cash flows:				
Depreciation tax shield	Ongoing	962	2,143	(1,181)
Terminal period:				
After tax salvage value	Year 10	368	221	147
Total impact (straight-line case exceeds MACRS case)				$ 91

In a way, all of these considerations revolve around the difference in depreciation methods and the resulting impact. If you were not considering an equipment replacement decision but were simply trying to decide on investing in a $10-million piece of equipment, the effects of MACRS depreciation would be easier to isolate and understand.

Table 11.10 compares the seven-year MACRS depreciation versus 10-year straight-line depreciation for the full value ($10.0 million) of the new asset. Both approaches fully depreciate the equipment. However, the present value of the tax shields indicates a $438,000 advantage for MACRS depreciation. Said differently, using the MACRS depreciation schedule a project becomes more valuable (and in this case $438,000 more valuable). The following example examines cash flow development in new product capital investment projects.

T A B L E 11.10 Depreciation Method Impact ($000s)

Depreciable Amount		$10,000	$10,000
		MACRS	STRAIGHT
YEAR	Rate	Deprec	LINE
1	14.29%	$1,429	$1,000
2	24.49%	2,449	1,000
3	17.49%	1,749	1,000
4	12.49%	1,249	1,000
5	8.93%	893	1,000
6	8.93%	893	1,000
7	8.93%	893	1,000
8	4.45%	445	1,000
9	0.00%	0	1,000
10	0.00%	0	1,000
Present value @10.5%			
Depreciation		$7,110	$6,015
Tax shield—40%		2,844	2,406
MACRS tax shield benefit			438

The New Product Decision

New product growth is a strategic objective embraced by almost all organizations. New products are the lifeblood of an organization and ensure that the firm will renew itself and meet the changing needs, desires, and tastes of its customers and consumers. The following describes the process of evaluating a new product. This project and its underlying assumptions are completely hypothetical, but are illustrative of the necessary evaluation to validate the economic viability of an investment in a new product.

Once again, we continue our Hershey example, but this situation and analysis is faced by every organization. The specifics are different, but the evaluation is the same. This new product capitalizes on Hershey's knowledge of the confectionery market and its strengths in producing, selling, and distributing the product. The new product builds upon valuable relationships with customers (such as Wal-Mart, Target, Costco, Kroger, CVS, and so on) and the consumer's favorable impressions of Hershey's quality and value. The hypothetical new product is a new candy bar with swirled white chocolate and milk chocolate and macadamia nut inclusions.

The launch of a new product takes cooperative teamwork that seamlessly unites all functions within the organization. In this example, the product idea is jointly championed by sales, marketing, and research and development. A multifunctional new product task team is quickly assembled to analyze the product's viability.

Marketing develops an initial sales projection and an annual growth profile through test panels and test marketing. Originally, gross product sales were estimated at $75 million for the initial year. However, it was estimated that this new product would "cannibalize" or displace approximately $7 million of sales of other Hershey products. These cannibalized sales are relevant and constitute an incremental impact of accepting this project. Consequently, the first year's sales were estimated at $68 million. In addition, after a sophomore-year reduction in sales of −10% sales of this product would increase at 3% until the tenth year (when the product would be discontinued). The sophomore-year sales reduction occurs for a number of reasons: consumer initial trials are heaviest in the first year, the retail inventory pipeline is filled in the first year, and marketing promotional and advertising expenses are significantly reduced in the second year.

Marketing and sales also estimate that they will need $25 million ($20 million in year 1 and $5 million in year 2) for advertising, consumer coupons, and trade promotions to support the initial new product launch. This is in addition to an ongoing expenditure level of 18% of sales, which also includes hiring a brand manager and an assistant.

Engineering and manufacturing estimates the configuration and number of lines necessary to fulfill the marketing projections. In this example, engineering estimates that the corporation needs to purchase two production lines for a total installed expenditure of $50 million. They also estimate that in 10 years the assets will have a residual value of $5 million before tax considerations.

Manufacturing, with the help of research and development, estimates it will cost 59% of every sales dollar to produce this product. This pays for the raw material (cocoa, sugar, milk, nuts, and so on), direct labor, and overhead but excludes depreciation.

Accounting and finance estimate the tax rate and calculate the tax depreciation (MACRS) on the asset. Accounting and finance, with the input of the complete team, estimate that ongoing working capital needs will be 8% of next year's sales and that the initial investment (year 0) will need to include an investment of 8% ($5.44 million) to support the first year's sales. Annually, additional investment (or recovery as in year 1) is required to support the projected sales for the next year. Note that for year 2 sales are actually expected to decline, so only $4,896,000 of net working capital needs to be on hand.

Because we already have $5,440,000 of net working capital, we can recover $544,000 of working capital. In subsequent years, 8% of annual incremental sales must be invested until full recovery in year 10. Once again, the working capital investment is made in inventory (to ensure that inventory is on hand to complete sales transactions) and receivables (to finance customers' purchases)—offset by spontaneous operating financing provided by suppliers through accounts payable. Note that all of the working capital ($6,202,000) is recovered in the final year.

Finance also determines an appropriate cost of capital for this project (at 11%) and a 39% tax rate for each year. The top portion of Table 11.11 documents the key assumptions previously reviewed. The lower portion dollarizes the assumptions and evaluates them using the same five-step process discussed in regard to the evaluation of a replacement asset.

In this analysis, you can see that sales approach $78 million in the final year. In addition, the after-tax operating income displays a loss for the first two years due to the additional product launch expenses. After the third year, the product contributes positive after-tax operating income through the remainder of its life. This project produces positive cash flows throughout all years of operation. The terminal cash flows include a $3.05-million after-tax residual value along with working capital recovery of more than $6.2 million. In total, the project generates cash flows with a gross present value of $59,169,000 compared to an initial investment of $55,440,000, which results in a positive $3,729,000 NPV. The project should be accepted and the value of Hershey's stock should rise by $3.7 million.

Note that if the previously described test market sunk cost of $5 million is included in this analysis the project is unacceptable, with a negative NPV [NPV = $(1.3)]. The $5-million test market costs should not be considered in this analysis. Those costs have long been spent. Accepting or rejecting this project does not change the sunk costs for the test market. By rejecting this project, the organization foregoes $3.7 million in value. But what if our collective judgment about the assumptions is incorrect? We treated these assumptions as "certain." What if these cash flows are not certain? The following sections discuss various techniques for understanding the uncertainty underlying assumptions and their valuation impacts.

Assumption Uncertainty

To better understand the impact of uncertainty on a capital evaluation, we will use the previous new product example to examine the following.

- Sensitivity analysis

- Scenario analysis

- Probabilistic analysis

- Monte Carlo analysis

Uncertainty underlies any projection. Each organization needs to find the approach that best assists it in understanding and dealing with uncertainty in capital investment analysis.

SENSITIVITY ANALYSIS

Sensitivity analysis occurs by varying each assumption individually and observing the resulting change in the NPV. Table 11.12 tests the impact on the NPV for a reasonable conservative change in each assumption. For example, if the purchase price of the new assets escalates to $55 million from the original estimate of $50 million the NPV drops to $0.1 million (a decrease of more than $3.6 million). Table 11.12 documents the NPV reduction that results from each of the changes noted in the table.

TABLE 11.11 — New Product Decision ($000s)

	INITIAL INVESTMENT	YEAR 1	YEAR 2	YEAR 3	YEAR 4	YEAR 5	YEAR 6	YEAR 7	YEAR 8	YEAR 9	YEAR 10
Key Assumptions											
Purchase price of new equipment	$(50,000)										
Working capital (% of incremental sales)	8.0%										
Initial sales		$68,000									
Sales growth			-10.0%	3.0%	3.0%	3.0%	3.0%	3.0%	3.0%	3.0%	3.0%
Cost of sales (Excluding depreciation—% of sales)		59.0%	59.0%	59.0%	59.0%	59.0%	59.0%	59.0%	59.0%	59.0%	59.0%
Operating costs (% of sales)		18.0%	18.0%	18.0%	18.0%	18.0%	18.0%	18.0%	18.0%	18.0%	18.0%
Additional product launch expense		$20,000	$5,000	$ –	$ –	$ –	$ –	$ –	$ –	$ –	$ –
Tax rate		39.0%	39.0%	39.0%	39.0%	39.0%	39.0%	39.0%	39.0%	39.0%	39.0%
Residual value											$ 5,000
Cost of capital 11.0%											
Capital Evaluation											
Purchase price	$(50,000)										
Initial working capital	(5,440)										
Incremental operating cash flow											
Sales		$ 68,000	$ 61,200	$ 63,036	$ 64,927	$ 66,875	$ 68,881	$ 70,948	$ 73,076	$ 75,268	$ 77,526
Cost of sales		(40,120)	(36,108)	(37,191)	(38,307)	(39,456)	(40,640)	(41,859)	(43,115)	(44,408)	(45,741)
Depreciation*		(7,145)	(12,245)	(8,745)	(6,245)	(4,465)	(4,465)	(4,465)	(2,225)	–	–
Gross income		20,735	12,847	17,100	20,375	22,954	23,776	24,624	27,736	30,860	31,786
Operating expenses		(12,240)	(11,016)	(11,346)	(11,687)	(12,037)	(12,399)	(12,771)	(13,154)	(13,548)	(13,955)
Additional product launch expense		(20,000)	(5,000)	–	–	–	–	–	–	–	–
Operating income		(11,505)	(3,169)	5,753	8,688	10,916	11,378	11,853	14,582	17,312	17,831
Taxes (40%)		4,487	1,236	(2,244)	(3,388)	(4,257)	(4,437)	(4,623)	(5,687)	(6,752)	(6,954)
After-tax operating income		$ (7,018)	$ (1,933)	$3,510	$ 5,300	$ 6,659	$ 6,940	$ 7,230	$ 8,895	$ 10,560	$ 10,877
After-tax operating income		$ (7,018)	$ (1,933)	$ 3,510	$ 5,300	$ 6,659	$ 6,940	$ 7,230	$ 8,895	$ 10,560	$ 10,877
Depreciation		7,145	12,245	8,745	6,245	4,465	4,465	4,465	2,225	–	–
Additional working capital (investment)		544	(147)	(151)	(156)	(160)	(165)	(170)	(175)	(181)	–
Incremental operating cash flow		$ 671	$ 10,165	$ 12,103	$ 11,389	$ 10,963	$ 11,240	$ 11,525	$ 10,945	$ 10,379	$ 10,877
Residual value—after tax											3,050
Working capital recovery											6,202
Total cash flow	$(55,440)	$ 671	$10,165	$12,103	$11,389	$10,963	$11,240	$11,525	$10,945	$10,379	$20,129
Present value 11.0%	$(55,440)	$ 604	$ 8,250	$ 8,850	$ 7,502	$ 6,506	$ 6,009	$ 5,551	$ 4,749	$ 4,058	$ 7,089
		$59,169 Gross present value (or the present value of the cash flows for years 1 to 10)									
Net present value	$ 3,729										
*MACRS Depreciation Rate		14.29%	24.49%	17.49%	12.49%	8.93%	8.93%	8.93%	4.45%	0.00%	0.00%

TABLE 11.12	New Product: Sensitivity Analysis ($000's)			
	ORGINAL ASSUMPTION	REVISED ASSUMPTION	REVISED NPV	CHANGE IN NPV
Purchase price of new equipment	$(50,000)	$(55,000)	$ 96	$(3,633)
Working capital (% of incremental sales)	8.0%	9.0%	3,291	(438)
Initial sales	$ 68,000	$ 60,000	(2,442)	(6,171)
Sales growth	−10%/3%	−11%/2%	1,773	(1,956)
Cost of sales (excluding depreciation—% of sales)	59.0%	60.0%	1,296	(2,433)
Operating costs (% of sales)	18.0%	19.0%	1,296	(2,433)
Additional product launch expense—year 1	$ 20,000	$ 25,000	982	(2,747)
Tax rate	39.0%	40.0%	3,365	(364)
Residual value	$ 5,000	$ 2,000	3,085	(644)
Cost of capital	11.0%	12.0%	889	(2,840)

The original net present value for this new product project was $3,729.

Note that some changes in assumptions have little impact, whereas other changes in assumptions have significant consequences. The working capital support (percentage of incremental sales), tax rate, and residual value have minimal impact. Other assumptions (such as purchase price, initial sales levels, growth rates, expenses as a percent of sales, and cost of capital) have major impact.

SCENARIO ANALYSIS

Scenario analysis examines various business models or circumstances by combining adjustments to a number of assumptions simultaneously. Table 11.13 illustrates three different scenarios (business models). The original case is documented, along with a cost-cutting scenario and two growth scenarios.

TABLE 11.13	New Product: Scenario Analysis ($000's)			
	ORGINAL ASSUMPTIONS	COST CUTTING	GROWTH	AGGRESSIVE GROWTH
Purchase price of new equipment	$(50,000)	$(45,000)	$(55,000)	$(57,500)
Working capital (% of incremental sales)	8.0%	8.0%	9.0%	9.0%
Initial sales	$ 68,000	$ 55,000	72,000	78,000
Sales growth (Year 2/Year 3+)	−10%/3%	−15%/0%	−8%/5%	0%/8%
Cost of sales (exc. deprec.—% of sales)	59.0%	57.0%	59.0%	60.5%
Operating costs (% of sales)	18.0%	15.0%	20.0%	21.0%
Additional product launch expense—year 1	$ 20,000	$ 15,000	$ 22,000	$ 28,000
Tax rate	39.0%	39.0%	39.0%	39.0%
Residual value	$ 5,000	$ —	—	—
Cost of capital	11.0%	11.0%	11.0%	11.0%
Gross present value (PV − CF years 1–10)	$ 59,169	$ 51,785	$ 60,878	$ 64,665
Initial investment	55,440	49,400	61,480	63,740
Net present value	3,729	2,385	(602)	925
Change from original case	n/a	(1,344)	(4,331)	(2,804)

The cost-cutting scenario trades off reduced volumes (sales) and growth for reduced investment levels, cost of sales, and marketing expenses. In addition, there is no residual value assumed for this lower-priced equipment.

The growth scenario trades off higher sales growth for additional investment in equipment, production costs, and marketing expense. Because the equipment is utilized more heavily to produce more product, its residual value is assumed to be zero.

The aggressive growth trades off a higher initial sales level and more substantial growth for additional investment in equipment, production costs, and marketing expense. Once again, because the equipment is utilized more heavily to produce more product its residual value is assumed to be zero.

The results indicate that the original scenario was the most economically viable scenario. The original scenario resulted in an NPV $1.3 million higher than the cost-cutting scenario, $4.3 million higher than the growth scenario, and $2.8 million higher than the aggressive growth scenario. Note also from Table 11.13 that the growth scenario (as specified) results in a negative NPV. The project should not be accepted!

PROBABILISTIC ANALYSIS

Probability analysis and expected values may be an appropriate extension of the basic capital investment analysis. The company must be facing multiple capital investment decisions (not accepting the investment is always an option). The outcome of the value of the project must also be driven by events that are for the most part beyond the company's control. Events that are beyond the company's control are macroeconomic events such as the state of the economy, the level of inflation, interest rates, foreign currency, stock market performance, and so on.

Other factors (such as customer demand, price of raw material, and so on) can be more firm or project specific but ultimately still beyond the firm's control. When wide variability is a real possibility, sensitivity analysis and scenario analysis may yield results that are in a range to broad to be helpful to decision makers. In these cases, a probabilistic approach may be warranted. Table 11.14 represents this process via decision tree analysis.

TABLE 11.14	Decision Tree Analysis						
Investment (1)		Demand conditions (2)	Probability (3)	Present value of cash flows (4)	Investment (5)	Possible NPV (4) – (5) (6)	Probable NPV (3) × (6) (7)
Big plant $80.0		High	50.0%	$120.0	$80.0	$40.0	$20.0
		Medium	30.0%	$70.0	$80.0	($10.0)	($3.0)
		Low	20.0%	$25.0	$80.0	($55.0)	($11.0)
Investment decision						Expected value	$6.0
		High	50.0%	$50.0	$30.0	$20.0	$10.0
		Medium	30.0%	$40.0	$30.0	$10.0	$3.0
Small plant $30.0		Low	20.0%	$25.0	$30.0	($5.0)	($1.0)
						Expected value	$12.0

In this example, a corporation is facing the decision related to plant size. The first decision point is to build a big plant ($80 million) or a small plant ($30 million). If the new product demand is high and a large plant is built, an NPV of $40 million results. However, if a large plant is built and demand is low or medium, over-capacity leads to negative NPVs.

On the other hand, if we build a small plant at high demand levels we experience a positive but limited NPV. At low demand under the same scenario, we incur a small negative NPV of $(5) million. Ideally, if we knew the demand was going to be high we would build the larger plant and earn a $40-million NPV. On the other hand, if we knew the demand would be moderate a small plant would provide the better NPV ($10 million). Finally, if we could perfectly forecast demand (and the demand were low) we would reject building any plant. However, there is no certainty about demand in this example.

Although we can formulate the resulting investments (column 4 of Table 11.14) and cash flows (column 5) under all six scenarios, it is critical to reasonably estimate probabilities of each state of demand for the product. Considering the probabilities (column 3 multiplied by column 6) results in expected values of $6 million and $12 million for the large and small plants, respectively. *Probabilistic techniques* are applicable to the development of cash flows and capital evaluation. Monte Carlo simulation takes the probabilistic evaluation techniques a step further.

MONTE CARLO SIMULATION

Monte Carlo simulation is a statistical technique that allows the analyst the opportunity to describe a range of potential values for various and specific assumptions. For instance, returning to the new product example we can specify a range of potential values for each of the assumptions we deem appropriate. So, for example, we could include the base case's initial year sales as a range (most likely $68 million, best case $78 million, and worst case $55 million). We can also specify a range for the cost of sales (59%, with a standard deviation of 1%) and estimate working capital investment between 7 and 9% with uniform probabilities. We can continue until we define all assumptions as a range of potential outcomes.

Monte Carlo simulation is facilitated via simulation software. Using a random number generator, the software selects assumption values based on the ranges, probabilities, and probability distributions we outlined. Once the random assumptions have been selected, the spreadsheet is projected and the NPV calculated. The simulation software repeats the process hundreds or thousands of times, and describes the expected NPV with its accompanying range and statistics. Table 11.15 summarizes the significant factors and simulation process.

The Risk software provided by Palisades Corporation or Crystal Ball by Decisioneering, Inc. are very supportive and flexible Monte Carlo simulators. They are spreadsheet templates that rest on top of Excel or other spreadsheet software. The ease of use ranges from very straightforward and user friendly to extremely technical and intricate, incorporating relationships between variables. Before considering other applications of investment valuation, it is appropriate to consider a few remaining topics using the new product investment analysis.

Additional Key Concepts

Now that we have examined more comprehensive project analysis, this section reviews additional key concepts about cash flow and investment analysis.

TABLE 11.15	Monte Carlo Analysis: New Product Extension

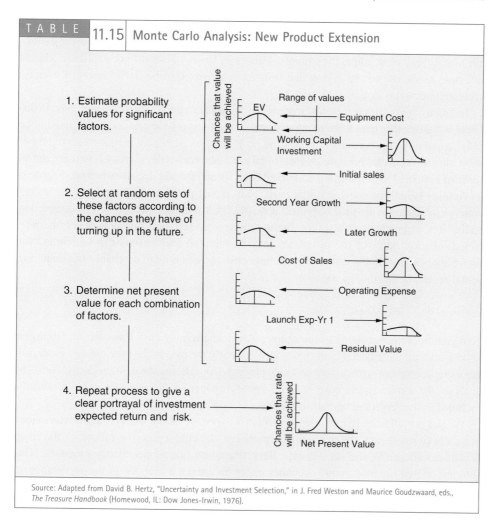

Source: Adapted from David B. Hertz, "Uncertainty and Investment Selection," in J. Fred Weston and Maurice Goudzwaard, eds., *The Treasure Handbook* (Homewood, IL: Dow Jones-Irwin, 1976).

INFLATION

Should the projected cash flows be based on *nominal estimates* (including inflation) or should the estimates be based on "real" (excluding inflation) cash flow estimates? For a number of reasons, the cash flows should be nominal and should include reasonable estimates of inflation such as the following.

- Inflation is a fact of life for most organizations.

- Deflation is also a part of life for some industries.

- Inflation affects prices and costs differently.

- Cost of capital includes a market-expected general rate of inflation.

- Comparing a nominal (including inflation) cost of capital to real (excluding inflation) cash flows can lead to the rejection of otherwise acceptable projects.

- Comparing a real cost of capital to real cash flows may lead to acceptance of an inferior project and understatement of working capital investment.

- Nominal cash flow projections provide a comparative basis for post-completion audits.

A CFO who used projections of "real" cash flows remarked, "Our Company is not in the business of forecasting inflation." This is precisely the point! Whenever cash flow projections are made, there is an implicit assumption about inflation. If we do not explicitly address inflation, implicitly we are saying that inflation is expected to be 0.0% (rarely, if ever, an accurate forecast).

Inflation affects sales prices, raw material costs, labor contracts, overhead, and so on in different ways (another reason for using nominal cash flows). These cost increases may not be fully passed on to the consumer. In addition, with inflation additional working capital investment must be increased because inventory and accounts receivables increase. By using *differentiated estimated inflation rates*, additional analysis and tactical decisions can be shaped.

Another benefit of using nominal cash flows is that performance standards are immediately established at the time of project approval. This audit trail promotes post-completion audits. Yes, circumstances are rare that the underlying inflation rate will match the projected inflation rate, but the difference may be minimal and lessons can be learned for future applications. If real cash flows are projected, there is little to no chance of comparing actual results to the anticipated cash flow.

ALLOCATED COSTS

To repeat from the beginning of the chapter, when determining cash flows we are interested in only relevant incremental cash flows. That is clearly the case in the previous two examples involving equipment replacement and new product. Considering the new-product investment analysis, the administrative costs to hire a brand manager and an assistant were specifically included in the projected operating expenses.

We did not allocate the salaries and related expenses of the marketing director, vice-president of marketing, the marketing department, the chief operating officer, or the chief executive officer. We did not allocate floor space and related occupancy expenses. The salaries, related expenses, and occupancy expenses are not a function of the acceptance or rejection of the new product. They are not incremental, and they are not relevant.

The terms *allocate*, *allocated*, and *allocation* should raise a red flag. Any allocated expenses must be reviewed and their incremental nature determined. If the expenses are not incremental, they should not be included in the analysis.

FINANCIAL COSTS AND FINANCIAL SERVICING

The two previous projects, involving equipment replacement and new product, illustrate the operational nature of the investment analysis cash flows. Related interest costs, debt repayment, dividends, stock repurchases, and so on are considered financing-related cash flows and are not directly considered in the investment cash flow development. Only operating cash flows are directly projected and considered for investment analysis. Financing implications are captured through the discount rate (the cost of capital). Consequently, if financing cash flows were to be explicitly included in the cash flow analysis and then discounted by the cost of capital the financing cash flows would have been "double counted."

Accounting Measures and Investment Analysis
In Chapter 7 we introduced and discussed a number of accounting performance metrics, and in Chapter 10 we discussed the differences between accounting measures and economic measures. Although a hypothetical example, the new-product analysis in this chapter is representative of the cash flow patterns exhibited by new retail (consumer) products.

Based on almost any accounting metric (e.g., return on assets or return on equity), this project should not be accepted because it does not generate positive returns in its first few years (even though it increases shareholder value by $3.7 million over its

10-year life). Although it is important to understand the accounting ramifications of new product introductions through strategic planning (see Chapter 9), economic measures dictate the acceptance or rejection of an investment.

Additional Applications

Aspects of three additional applications are briefly discussed in the following sections. These applications are information technology (IT) analysis, the employee identification (badge) system, and valuation of a strategic plan.

INFORMATION TECHNOLOGY APPLICATION

Table 11.16 illustrates a hypothetical software investment. In this example, we assume the following (first-level items correspond to the line items in Table 11.16).

- Total Estimated Savings:

    - Headcount reduction of 10 Human Resources (HR) support personnel at an average cost (salary, benefits, and taxes) of $35,000 for a total of $350,000 at 3% inflation

    - Elimination of costs to support the old HR system of $220,000 at 3% inflation

    - Management time savings of $1,250,000 annually

- Total Ongoing Expenditures:

    - Consultant fees of $150,000 and $100,000 in the first two years

    - Training fees of $150,000 and $100,000 in the first two years

    - Maintenance contract of $150,000 at 10% inflation

- Depreciation and amortization

    - Related expenses for direct investment (five-year MACRS schedule)

    - Total Direct Investment (Year 0):

    - New HR software ($800,000)

    - Additional expenditures to purchase servers and to equip employee kiosks ($600,000)

    - Consultant expenses, training, travel, and so on ($205,400) as part of the investment

- Other Assumptions:

    - Cost of capital (14%)

    - Tax rate (40%)

Table 11.16 modifies and expands our typical evaluation format. It begins by listing the savings offset by the added expense to derive operating income through to cash flow. As presented, this project has an NPV of almost $2.5 million.

Note that the third benefit (savings) is a managerial time savings. This one assumption dominates the NPV. Without that savings the NPV is a negative $(0.4) million. The question is: Is that savings a relevant incremental savings? If the savings are the direct result of enabling an increase in managers' and directors' span of control and result in a headcount reduction of 12 managers (at $104,000 per manager), the savings are relevant and incremental

TABLE 11.16 | Human Resource Software Investment Analysis ($000s)

	YEAR 0	YEAR 1	YEAR 2	YEAR 3	YEAR 4	YEAR 5	YEAR 6
Estimated savings							
Headcount reduction		$ 350.0	$ 360.5	$ 371.3	$ 382.4	$ 393.9	$ 405.7
Ongoing expenses of old system		220.0	226.6	233.4	240.4	247.6	255.0
Management time savings		1,250.0	1,250.0	1,250.0	1,250.0	1,250.0	1,250.0
Total savings		1,820.0	1,837.1	1,854.7	1,872.8	1,891.5	1,910.7
Ongoing expenses							
Consulting fees		150.0	100.0	—	—	—	—
Training fees		150.0	100.0	—	—	—	—
Maintenance contract		150.0	165.0	181.5	199.7	219.7	241.7
Depreciation and amortization		321.1	513.7	308.2	184.9	184.9	92.5
Total expenses		771.1	878.7	489.7	384.6	404.6	334.2
Operating income		1,048.9	958.4	1,365.0	1,488.2	1,486.9	1,576.5
Taxes (40.0%)		419.6	383.4	546.0	595.3	594.8	630.6
After tax operating income		$ 629.3	$ 575.0	$ 819.0	$ 892.9	$ 892.1	$ 945.9
After tax operating income		$ 629.3	$ 575.0	$ 819.0	$ 892.9	$ 892.1	$ 945.9
Depreciation and amortization		321.1	513.7	308.2	184.9	184.9	92.5
Working capital investment		—	—	—	—	—	—
Fixed capital investment	$ (1,605.4)	—	—	—	—	—	—
Cash flow	$(1,605.4)	$ 950.4	$1,088.7	$1,127.2	$1,077.8	$1,077.0	$1,038.4
Net present value—14%	$ 2,497.4						

and should be considered in the analysis. If the savings are calculated as a half-an-hour savings per day for all managers, as detailed in the following, the savings do not represent incremental savings.

Savings per manager per day	0.5 Hour
Days per year	250 Days
Savings per manager per year (A)	125 Hours
Number of managers (B)	200
Average manager's wage, bonus, etc.	$ 104,000 Year
Hours per year	2,080 Hours
Hourly manager's cost (C)	$ 50 Hour
Management time savings (A) × (B) × (C)	$1,250,000/Year

For this to be an actual savings, all managers must take a $6,250 (125 hours × $50 per hour) pay cut! Determining relevant incremental cash flows is extremely important in the investment analysis and authorization phase.

EMPLOYEE IDENTIFICATION (BADGE) SYSTEM

Whether we hang them around our necks or hang them from shirt pockets, employee identification systems or employee ID badges have become popular at most organizations. In evaluating these projects, after-tax cash benefits (or savings) result from a reduced number of security guards, reduced insurance premiums, and enhanced security for employee and corporate safety. The after-tax cash savings for a reduction in the number of security guards and reduced insurance costs can be easily calculated. But what is the cash flow impact of a breach in security?

At Hershey, we encountered such an investment proposal. We sharpened our pencils and resharpened our pencils to estimate the savings for security guard expenses and insurance premium reductions. For legal reasons, nothing was formally documented or considered a "cost" of a security breach. No matter how many times we reexamined the cash flows, the NPV was always negative and approximately $(50,000). (Although this is not the actual number, it is representative.) A negative NPV indicates that the project should not be accepted. However, in this case we argued that this "cost" represented a one-time premium for a 10-year additional insurance policy designed to reduce the risk of security breaches. The project was approved!

STRATEGIC PLAN VALUATION

The strategic plan (see Chapter 9) represents the most current and best available projections prepared by senior managers with the greatest insight about the organization and the responsibility to achieve the projected performance. Operating cash flows can be derived from the cash flow statement (Table 9.7C). Corporate valuation is another application of capital analysis and the determination of cash flows. Chapter 12 develops company valuation models. The tools capital evaluation tools from chapter 10 and the cash flow concepts developed in this chapter will be combined with the strategic financial plan of chapter 9 to estimate a value for The Hershey Company.

This chapter culminated our investment analysis. Using the tools developed in Chapter 10, this chapter promoted the development of cash flows through various examples of investments and the development of their underlying cash flows.

Relevant, nominal, incremental, after-tax cash flow development is the backbone of financial investment analysis. However, just as a strong strategic planning process has strong financial considerations (which also enable managerial processes) so too does a strong capital investment process and its evaluation and authorization phase. A strong evaluation and authorization phase:

- Facilitates communication among the senior executives of an organization
- Sets a business direction
- Prioritizes opportunities and requirements
- Establishes business performance standards and objectives

Within this chapter, a consistent but flexible investment analysis framework was developed and applied to a variety of projects. The framework was successfully used to value replacement projects, new product, investment in information technology, and an administrative project. After examining investment analysis with static and known cash flows, this chapter considered various alternatives for handling uncertain cash flows. The suggested approaches included the following.

- Sensitivity analysis
- Scenario analysis
- Probabilistic approaches (including decision trees)
- Monte Carlo analysis

Additional considerations for capital investment decisions are included in Chapter 12 as we determine a value for an entire organization, specifically The Hershey Company.

Questions

11.1   Why is it important to have good communications throughout the organization before, during, and after major capital investments?

11.2   Many companies' CARs includes a cover page (Table 11.1), a detailed description of the project and its business rationale, a capital investment analysis, a detailed list of equipment (with specific vendor quotes if available), an implementation schedule with anticipated expenditure timing, and sensitivity/scenario analysis. What else would you like to know if you were implementing or approving a major capital investment?

11.3   How does "costing savings" differ from "cost avoidance"?

11.4   Which of the following would you consider a sunk cost, and why?

- Research and development expenditures of the past six years on a new drug

- Promotional expense introducing an improved product

- In a computer equipment replacement decision, the book value of the replaced equipment

11.5   Which of the following are relevant incremental costs and should be included in a capital investment analysis?

- Reduction in the sales of the company's other products

- Expenditure on plant and equipment

- Cost of R&D undertaken in connection with a new product during the last three years

- Annual depreciation expense

- Dividend payments (40% of incremental income)

- Resale value of plant and equipment at the end of a project's life

- Salary and medical cost for production employees on leave

11.6   Enterprise resource planning (ERP) software (examples include SAP and Oracle) is expensive and often requires extensive process reengineering totaling a $100+ million investment. What cash flows would you want to include when justifying this type of project?

11.7   Should a roof replacement decision be required to demonstrate a positive NPV? Should administrative projects be required to have a positive NPV?

11.8   Discuss the consistency of the following two statements.

- "We need to grow the business!"

- "We need to earn adequate rates of return, so we will only accept projects that return more than 25%!"

11.9   How would you apply these techniques to estimating a return on major advertising campaigns?

Problems

11.1

Gain or loss on the sale of an asset: An asset that originally cost $45 million and was purchased six years ago can be sold for $10 million today. Answer the following questions assuming the asset was depreciated on a 10-year straight-line basis and assuming no salvage value.

a.   What is the current book value of the asset?

b.   If the asset is sold today at $10 million, what would the gain or loss be?

c.   Assuming a 38.5% tax rate, what is the after-tax gain? The tax effects from any losses can immediately be used to offset income somewhere else in the corporation.

d.   What would be the cash flow from such a sale?

11.2

Gain or loss on the sale of an asset (MACRS): Assume the same same facts as in problem 11.1 except that the asset is an industrial manufacturing piece of equipment and is subject to MACRS seven-year depreciation.

a. What is the current book value of the asset?

b. If the asset is sold today at $10 million, what would the gain or loss be?

c. Assuming a 38.5% tax rate, what is the after-tax gain? The tax effects from any losses can immediately be used to offset income somewhere else in the corporation.

d. What would be the cash flow from such a sale?

11.3

Gain or loss on the sale of an asset: A Chevrolet was purchased three years ago as a company car for $22,500. It has been depreciated using four-year straight-line depreciation assuming a $9,500 salvage value.

a. What is the current book value of the asset?

b. If the auto is sold today for $13,500, what would the gain or loss be? Assuming a 37% tax rate, what is the after-tax gain? What is the cash flow from such a sale? The tax effects from any losses can immediately be used to offset income somewhere else in the corporation.

c. If the auto is sold today for $10,000, what would the gain or loss be? Assuming a 37% tax rate, what is the after-tax gain? What is the cash flow from such a sale? The tax effects from any losses can immediately be used to offset income somewhere else in the corporation.

11.4

Gain or loss on the sale of an asset (MACRS): Assume the same same facts as in problem 11.3 except that the asset is subject to the MACRS five-year depreciation schedule.

a. What is the current book value of the asset?

b. If the auto is sold today for $13,500, what would the gain or loss be? Assuming a 37% tax rate, what is the after-tax gain? What is the cash flow from such a sale? The tax effects from any losses can immediately be used to offset income somewhere else in the corporation.

c. If the auto is sold today for $10,000, what would the gain or loss be? Assuming a 37% tax rate, what is the after-tax gain? What is the cash flow from such a sale? The tax effects from any losses can immediately be used to offset income somewhere else in the corporation.

11.5

Simple working capital and TVM: The Cut-Right LLC plans on introducing a new power saw. The project calls for a buildup in inventory of $24.6 million initially, with full recovery at the end of the project (ten years from now). If the appropriate cost of capital is 14%, what is the present value of the recovered inventory investment? What is the total impact on the project?

11.6

Working capital and TVM: Dell Computers has approximately six days outstanding in inventory. Hewlett-Packard has approximately 65 days outstanding. With competition so keen in the computer industry, if both organizations planned to introduce a new product with projected sales of $600 million and cost of goods sold of 75% what would the inventory investment be for both firms? If the new product had an expected life of three years (at which time there is a full recovery of the inventory investment), what is the total impact on the value of the project assuming a 12% cost of capital for both firms?

11.7

Determining working capital: Currently, PDA Inc. has the following investment in various components of working capital. A "black belt" task team has been studying the working capital management processes and believes PDA can make reported changes to attain the targeted working capital levels. Assuming they are successful, what is the change in working capital? What is the new level of working capital as a percentage of sales assuming sales of $1,246 million?

$ millions	Current	Projected
Receivables	$143.4	$109.2
Inventory	227.0	179.2
Payables	83.6	91.7

11.8

Determining working capital: The Bethlehem Corporation has the following working capital performance metrics. Without any adjustments in these metrics, if the corporation were to introduce a new product with expected sales of $80 million and a cost of goods sold of 62%, what would be the total investment in working capital?

	Days Outstanding	Metric Basis
Receivables	43.50	Sales
Inventory	127.20	COGS
Payables	32.70	COGS

a. Assuming 97.5% recovery in the final year of this product's projected life eight years from now, and a 9.5% cost of capital, what is the working capital impact on the NPV of this project?

11.9

Determining annual working capital and project impact: Shutters, Inc. has manufactured and sold colorful home shutters for almost 45 years. To meet a growing consumer trend for a more natural-looking shutter the company will introduce three new shutters in natural cherry, pine, and oak. Sales are expected to rise steadily throughout the first five years and level off at that point. After eight years, management expects the natural trend to fade with full recovery of all working capital investment. The following represents the expected sales from this new shutter over the next 10 years.

Year	Projected Sales ($mms)
1	$25.20
2	38.40
3	45.70
4	52.10
5	55.00
6	55.00
7	55.00
8	55.00

a. If the company typically invests 12.5% of next year's incremental sales in working capital, how much is invested in each year (including the initial year).

b. Assuming full recovery at the end of year 10, what amount is recovered?

c. If Shutters, Inc. has a cost of capital of 16%, what is the impact on the project?

d. If Shutters, Inc. could improve its working capital management process and reduce the investment to 10.0% of next year's incremental sales, how much would be invested each year? What would be the amount of recovery in year 10? What is the impact on the project at a 16-percent discount rate?

e. What business impact does this process improvement have on the company?

11.10

Working capital, perpetuities, and NPV: Parella, Inc. has sales of $800 million per year and working capital investment of 11.5% of sales. Sales have continually grown at 3.5% over the past 20 years. If the cost of capital is 12.5% and the working capital investment can be reduced to by 1% of sales, what will be the incremental increase in the value of the firm?

11.11

Incremental sales: RTT Restful Dog, Inc. currently produces and sells two types of dog beds. The first type, the Faithful Companion, is a moderately priced high-quality flannel-covered mat type of bed that sells for $15 on average (depending on the size) and costs $10.50 to produce. The second type, the Pillow Pet Bed, is a luxuriously soft pillow surrounded by short 3-inch foam walls on the sides, sells for an average $30 depending on the size, and costs $21.75 to produce. RTT Marketing wants to introduce a third type, the Pillow Dog Nest, a "soft, snuggly pillow that your pet can sink into." The PDN will sell for $22.50 and cost about $17.35 to produce. Marketing believes that PDN will sell 140,000 units annually, but the Faithful Companion line's sales will decline by 45,000 units (from 185,000 to 140,000 units) and the Pillow Pet Line will decline by 30,000 units (from 125,000 to 95,000 units). What is the incremental impact in the projected dollar amount of sales?

11.12

Incremental gross income: Given the same assumptions as in problem 11.11, what is the projected impact in gross profit (sales less cost of goods sold)?

11.13

Incremental working capital: Given the same assumptions as in problem 11.11, what is the projected impact in working capital assuming an 11% (percentage of sales) investment in working capital?

11.14

Capital investment analysis: The RTT Financial Analysis department is asked to help marketing prepare a capital authorization report (CAR) for the new product. In addition to the information learned in the prior three problems (11.11, 11.12, and 11.13), Financial Analysis also finds out that marketing is planning a $500,000 advertising campaign, with $350,000 of the total spent in the first year and $150,000 in the second year. After that, marketing is sure their existing advertising budget will suffice and they anticipate no incremental advertising expenditures. Marketing also believes that this opportunity will last only six years, at which time they will discontinue the PDN product and return to previous sales and cost levels. Manufacturing, which has been discussing the project with marketing, indicates that no incremental capital would be necessary because the PDN could be made on the existing equipment during its idle time. Financial Analysis completes a capital evaluation using a 39% tax rate and a 9.5% cost of capital. What is the project's net present value, its IRR, and the payback period?

11.15

Depreciation and investment value: MACRS depreciation was enacted to better reflect the more rapid decline in value in the first few years of most assets' useful lives. In addition, the income tax shield generated by depreciation provides a cash inflow that effectively reduces the investment and enhances the NPV of a project. Answer the following questions about an investment of $1 million in a manufacturing piece of equipment. Assume a 40.0% tax rate and a 12% cost of capital.

a.   What is the value of the tax shield if the machinery could be immediately expensed at the time of purchase? What is the net expenditure for the equipment?

b.   What is the present value of the tax shield if the machinery is depreciated using a 10-year straight-line depreciation? What is the net expenditure for the equipment?

c.   Using the seven-year MACRS tax depreciation schedule, what is the present value of the tax shield? What is the net expenditure for the equipment?

d.   Suppose the tax code would change and manufacturing equipment could be depreciated using the five-year MACRS schedule. What would be the present value of the tax shield and the net expenditure for the equipment? How could depreciation policy be used for macroeconomic policy?

11.16

Capital investment analysis: Dakota Light Company is considering the purchase of a new machine that will reduce labor costs and waste by $750,000 per year for

10 years. Assume that Dakota pays 38.5% in taxes and has a 9% cost of capital. The machine costs $3.8 million and has no salvage value.

a.   If the equipment is depreciated on a straight-line basis, what is the net present value of this project?

b.   If the equipment is depreciated using a seven-year MACRS schedule, what is the NPV of the project?

11.17

Software investment analysis: The Manna Corporation is considering the purchase of some new software for better inventory management. The software costs $500,000 and is amortized over a five-year period. By using the system, the company expects to reduce logistics cost by $200,000 each year as well as save an initial $150,000 in year 0 for a one-time working capital inventory reduction. At the end of five years, the software would be scrapped and the old processes reinstated unless there were viable alternatives designed at that time. Assuming a tax rate of 36% and a cost of capital of 11.0%, what is the net present value of this project? What is the MIRR?

11.18

Acquisition valuation: The management team at Three Tiers Corporation is interested in expanding their organization with the acquisition of Synergistic, Inc. Based on months of analysis and discussions, TTC believes that the acquisition could generate the following incremental cash flows for TTC ($ millions):

Year	Projected Cash Flow ($mms)
1	$ (5.6)
2	3.6
3	5.8
4	9.1
5	11.4
6	13.2
7	14.8
8	15.9
9	16.8
10	17.0

a.   What is the NPV of these cash flows assuming a 14% cost of capital?

b.   Assume that the year 10 cash flow of $17.0 million continues forever. What is the value of this perpetuity in year 10? What is that annuity's present value? What is the total value of the acquisition?

c.   Assume that the year 10 cash flow of $17.0 million grows at 2% forever. What is the value of this perpetuity in year 10? What is that annuity's present value? What is the total value of the acquisition?

11.19

Personal capital investment analysis: Our 15-year-old washing machine recently fell into disrepair. My wife and I have been discussing its replacement. I want to apply basic capital investment analysis in making the decision.

a. Own a washing machine or go to the laundry? My wife thinks the question is a silly one because a laundry is inconvenient and does not do a great job in getting the clothes clean. Nonetheless, she plays along. We estimate that we do five loads of wash each week. At $1.50 per load, we would save an estimated $390 each year along with mileage to and from the laundry (six miles each week at $0.36 per mile) of $112. Offsetting these savings is an estimated $6 per week expense for hot water and electricity. If the washing machine costs $459, tax of $28, and a $35 delivery charge, should I buy the washing machine or take my clothes to the laundry? Assume that a typical washing machine lasts 10 years (with no salvage value) and my required return is 6%. Since this is a personal expense, taxes and depreciation are not considered.

b. As we are shopping for a new washing machine, my attention is drawn to a "new and improved" upright washer. These washing machines will reduce the weekly electricity and water costs by 50%. Should I purchase this more expensive model, assuming a cost of $999, tax of $60, and free delivery?

c. In making this decision, there are numerous non-financial considerations. What are some of them?

11.20

Advertising investment analysis: Leap Frog Computers, Inc. is considering an enhanced advertising campaign. The marketing department, in consideration with the advertising agency, estimates that with a successful campaign the number of units should increase by 10,000 per year for the next three years. You have obtained the following information:

Units sold currently	150,000
Price per unit	$ 1,800
Variable cost per unit	$ 1,200
Fixed cost per unit	$ 300
Current selling & mkt. ex.	$1,200,000
Current G&A exp.	$ 800,000

Advertising is projected as follows:

Year	Cash Flow
0	$4,995,000
1	3,000,000
2	2,500,000
3	1,250,000
4	—

Assume a 39% tax rate, 15% cost of capital, and total fixed costs remain the same. Further assume that any negative income impacts will generate an immediate tax savings in other parts of the business. If there is a half-year delay between spending the added advertising expense and selling additional units, should the advertising campaign be implemented?

11.21

Capital investment analysis: Please answer the following questions.

a. Construct the annual cash flows and calculate the NPV and PI for a project with the given following information:

Year	Units Sold	Selling Price	Expenses*—% of Sales COGS	Expenses*—% of Sales Marketing	Admin. Expense*
1	125	$80	70.00%	24.00%	$180
2	250	$82	68.00%	22.00%	$150
3	300	$85	68.00%	20.00%	$150
4	250	$80	66.00%	15.00%	$150

*All expenses exclude depreciation.

Working capital: $600 initially (year 0); $200 (year 1); full recovery
Initial investment: $4,800
Salvage value: $500 at the end of year 4
Tax rate: 39%
Cost of capital: 10%

Assume: (1) straight-line depreciation to zero and (2) any taxable losses can be immediately used to offset taxable income somewhere else in the company.

b. You hire a brilliant marketing VP, who believes that by using a higher percentage of media advertising she can increase the number of units sold each year by 100. Recalculate the cash flows and NPV assuming this new campaign requires an additional $50 increase in administration expense and 2% (200 basis point) increase in marketing (or 26, 24, 22, and 17% in years 1 to 4, respectively) to cover the additional advertising in each of the four years to support the higher sales level. Is this a better alternative?

c. You believe that the tactic of the VP is riskier and should be discounted at a higher discount rate of 15%. Recalculate the revised project's NPV. Should you make the added investment?

11.22

Capital investment analysis: The H&N Corporation is considering the introduction of a new salty snack food, a flavored microwave popcorn thatis also "carb friendly." Based on marketing research, H&N believes it can sell the following number of units:

Year	Millions
1	42
2	45
3	48
4	50
5	32

After five years, Marketing believes that the product will have run its course and lost its appeal. Each carton sells for $8.95 and has variable production costs of $4.72.

Total fixed costs are $22.5 million per year and Marketing also needs the following advertising and promotion spending:

Year	Adv. & Prom. $mms
1	$125.0
2	100.0
3	80.0
4	50.0
5	20.0

The production equipment has an installed cost of $187.5 million and qualifies for seven-year MACRS depreciation. In five years, the equipment can be sold at 35% of its original cost. In addition, the initial year investment requires $42.0 million of working capital and additional net working capital investment of 12% of the projected sales level for the following year. Because sales are projected to decrease in year 5, there is no net working capital cash flow in year 4. If H&N pays 38.5% in income taxes and has an 11.5% cost of capital, what is this project's net present value?

11.23

Henry Frank is thinking about buying a new car, a Lexus RX. The Lexus RX330 and the Lexus RX400 are very similar five-passenger SUV vehicles. However, the RX400 costs $8,290 more than the RX330. The RX400 is a "hybrid" and delivers 27/31 miles per gallon for city and highway driving for an average of 29 miles per gallon. The traditional RX330 provides 18/24 (city/highway) miles per gallon for an average of 21 miles per gallon. With either purchase, Henry plans on owning the vehicle for five years. At that time, he plans on trading it in for a new car. Mr. Frank's opportunity cost of funds is 4%. Because this is a personal purchase, he does not need to consider tax shield from depreciation.

a. If Henry drives 15,500 miles per year and gas costs $3.00 per gallon, what does he save per year in gasoline purchases and what is the NPV of the additional expenditure for the RX400? Should he purchase the more expensive RX400 based solely on this NPV analysis?

b. If the federal government gives a $2,000 tax credit (tax reduction) in the year Henry purchases the vehicle (year 0), what is his revised NPV?

c. Referencing question 23a, without the tax credit at what price per gallon of gas will Henry have a positive NPV?

d. If Henry drives 30,000 miles per year and gas costs $3.00 per gallon, what does Henry save per year in gasoline purchases and what is the NPV of the additional expenditure for the RX400? Should Henry purchase the more expensive RX400 based solely on this NPV analysis?

e. List other quantitative factors Henry needs to consider in regard to purchasing the RX400.

f. The RX400 is the most technologically advanced vehicle Lexus has ever made. It is one of their most prestigious autos as well. It also has 45 more horsepower and is much faster than the RX330. How would Henry take these factors into consideration in regard to purchasing the vehicle?

Strategic Valuation Issues

12

We have discussed many topics. This chapter brings the previous discussion points forward and leads to valuing a company, creating shareholder value, and enhancing the value of the firm.

Valuation of a firm begins with a solid understanding of the company's strategic goals and objectives, as well as of its day-to-day business practices. To judge the financial success of the firm and to develop a reasonable value for that firm or a share of that firm's stock, it is necessary to know how to read its financial statements (Chapter 2), analyze those statements (Chapter 7), and project the firm's future performance (Chapter 9).

It also is important to consider the general economic climate (Chapter 5) while being mindful of the risk and return trade-offs (Chapter 6). In Chapter 3, we specifically developed the most funda- mental tool of finance (time value of money) and applied it to valuing equity via a *perpetual valuation model* (Chapter 6). Chapters 10 and 11 extended this "investment analysis" perspective as we considered corporate investment in new equipment, new products, software, and so on.

This chapter is organized in a manner similar to that of Chapter 9. That is, the simple perpetuity models (Chapters 3 and 6) are expanded to define cash flow using a more detailed approach. These models are embellished and consequently become a bit more applicable, although the level of complexity increases. Following this, we value the Hershey hypothetical strategic plan developed in Chapter 9.

This leads us to a general discussion of a standalone model (not requiring a full strategic plan, as in Chapter 9) that can be used to value any organization (public or private; large or small).

In this chapter we explain and illustrate the logic or theory behind each of these approaches. Although we develop the appropriate models and valuation tools, any model is only as strong as its assumptions. It remains the responsibility of the reader to develop reasonable projections for their application of this chapter to their organization.

We end the chapter with a discussion of real options, one of the latest capital investment analysis techniques. The underlying math is beyond the scope of this book, but the application concepts are important to consider whenever presenting or deciding on capital investment.

Perpetual Cash Flows

In Chapter 3 we developed the concept of *perpetual cash flows or recurring cash flows* that last forever. At that time, we introduced two types: a *zero-growth model and a constant-growth model*. We then placed these models in the context of *equity valuation* in Chapter 6. Zero growth is given by Equation 12.1, and constant growth is given by Equation. 12.2.

$$\text{Zero Growth: } V_{0,r,\infty} = \frac{CF_{(t)}}{r} \tag{12.1}$$

$$\text{Constant Growth: } V_{0,r,\infty} = \frac{CF_{(t+1)}}{(r-g)} \tag{12.2}$$

Where:
$V_{0,r,\infty}$ = Value of firm at time zero continuing perpetually
$CF_{(t+1)}$ = Cash flow at the end of year 1
r = Cost of capital
g = Constant growth

These fundamental models begin our effort at valuing an organization. Remember, the cash flow at the end of the year ($CF_{(t+1)}$) is also the same as growing this year's cash flow (derived by Equation 12.3).

$$CF_{(t+1)} = CF_{(0)} (1 + g) \tag{12.3}$$

In our example, let's assume that The Hershey Company has most recently generated $675 million of operating cash flow (operating cash flows are explored further in the next section).

We continue to use 8.2% as the required return (or cost of capital) for Hershey. (The cost of capital is fully discussed in Chapter 13.)

As we saw in Chapter 6, Hershey's value was $8,231.7 million with no growth in its operating cash flows ($675/0.082). However, if we assume that Hershey will continue to grow its cash flow by 2.5% per annum due to sales growth, margin improvement, and other efficiencies Hershey's value increases to over $12,1 billion (given by Equation 12.4).

$$PVA_{r,\infty} = \frac{CF_{(0)}(1+g)}{(r-g)} \tag{12.4}$$

$$= \frac{\$675(1+0.025)}{(0.082-0.025)} = \frac{\$692}{0.057} = \$12,140 \text{ million}$$

These were the same approaches developed and applied in Chapter 6 as a "50,000-foot" valuation framework. Our purpose here is to expand these basic equations so that they become more useful management tools. We then build on this to create a spreadsheet approach.

Constant Growth Valuation Model

Equation 12.5 enhances Equation 12.2 and develops operating cash flows. Cash flows are developed using a *percentage-of-sales method*, introduced in Chapter 9.

$$V_0 = \frac{R_0[m(1-T)+d-I_{fg}-I_w](1+g)}{(k-g)} \tag{12.5}$$

Where:
   V_0 = Value of firm as of today (year 0)
   R_0 = Revenue (or sales) of firm (can be last year of actual sales)
   m = Operating income (EBIT) margin (% of sales)
   T = Tax rate
   d = Depreciation (% of sales)
   I_{fg} = Capital expenditure, gross or fixed capital invested (% of sales)
   I_w = Working capital incremental investment (% of sales)
   g = Growth
   k = Cost of capital (previously designated r)

Before continuing, let's note some relationships by rearranging some terms:

$$R_0(1+g) = \text{Revenue (or sales) for the next (first) year } (R_1)$$
$$R_1(m) = \text{Operating income (EBIT) in year 1}$$
$$R_1(m)(1-T) = \text{After-tax operating income in year 1}$$
$$R_1(I_{fg}-d) = \text{Net capital investment}$$
$$R_1(I_{fg}-d)+I_w = \text{Investment in operating assets less operating liabilities (or net operating investment)}$$

The complete numerator represents operating cash flows, which in our previous example was $691.9.

$$V_0 = \frac{R_1[m(1-T)] - R_1[(I_{fg} + d) + I_w]}{(k-g)}$$

Or:

$$V_0 = \frac{\text{After-tax Operating Income} - \text{Net Operating Investment}}{(k-g)} \tag{12.6}$$

Assuming R_1 of $4,957 million (2005 sales of $4,836 million times 1.025, which represents our 2.5% assumed growth rate) and applying Equation 12.6 ($ millions):

$$V_0 = \frac{\$4,957[0.213](1-0.37) - \$4,957[(0.041-0.039) + (-0.0074)]}{(0.082 - 0.025)}$$
$$= (\$665 - \$10 + \$37)/0.057 = \$692/0.057 = \$12,140$$

In this example, Hershey generated $692 million of operating cash flow primarily from operating income of $665 million offset by $10 million net investment in plant property and equipment and increased due to effective working capital and other long-term liabilities management. In fact, in this case due to improving working capital management practices and the impact of other non-cash expenses such as deferred taxes and other long-term liabilities Hershey increased its operating cash flows by an additional $37 million per year.

It is estimated that Hershey will generate 13.9 cents $[m(1-T) + d - I_{fg} - I_w]$ or $[(0.213 (1.000 - 0.370) + 0.039 - 0.041 - (-0.007)]$ of operating cash flow for every dollar of revenue. The constant growth valuation model centers on the following critical value drivers of any business, and consequently any valuation.

- Revenue growth
- Operating profitability
- Tax rates
- Net fixed capital investment (capital expenditures less depreciation)
- Working capital investment, including other long-term operating assets and liabilities
- Cost of capital

Even in this simple illustration, the way to increase the value of any project or company is to increase growth and profitability while limiting investment. The value of the organization increases due to increased cash flow.

The *constant growth valuation model* determines the sources of operating cash flow by allowing the manager, analyst, entrepreneur, or other interested investor to appropriately develop each strategic performance objective or assumption. However, this approach infers that these assumptions will remain constant into perpetuity.

What if that is not the case? What if the organization is entering a high period of growth or investment? How should this type of "abnormal" activity be handled? In this case, "abnormal" means different from the long term. The next section deals with the two-stage supernormal (or abnormal) growth model, as originally presented in Chapter 6.

Two-stage Supernormal Growth Model

The *two-stage supernormal growth model (TSSGM)* is similar to the valuation model in that it derives cash flows from operations on a percentage-of-sales basis. The equation is made to look even more complicated than it did in Chapter 6. First, the process continues to discount the two stages separately (as discussed in Chapter 6). In this case, we also break cash flow into its major components. The concept behind the TSSGM is not complicated, despite the appearance of Equation 12.7.

$$V_0 = \text{PV (Growth Period CFs)} + \text{PV (Perpetual Period CFs)}$$

$$V_0 = R_0[m_s(1-T_s)-I_s]\sum_{t=1}^{n}\frac{(1+g_s)^t}{(1+k)^t}$$

$$+\frac{\left[R_0(1+g_s)^n[m_c(1-T_c)-I_c]\right](1+g_c)}{(k-g_c)}\cdot\frac{1}{(1+k)^n} \tag{12.7}$$

Where:

R_0 = Revenue (or sales) of firm (last year of actual sales)

m = After-tax operating income margin

m_s = After-tax operating income margin during supernormal growth period

m_c = After-tax operating income margin during constant growth period

T = Tax rate

T_s = Tax rate during supernormal growth period

T_c = Tax rate during constant growth period

I = Investment as a percentage of revenues (defined as the change in working capital and other long-term operating assets and liabilities plus gross capital expenditures minus depreciation)

I_s = Investment as a percentage of revenues during supernormal growth period

I_c = Investment as a percentage of revenues during constant growth period

g = Growth rate of revenues

g_s = Growth rate of revenues during supernormal growth period

g_c = Growth rate of revenues during constant growth period

k = Cost of capital

n = Number of years of supernormal growth

There are various renditions of this particular equation. Sometimes investment is broken into its three components, as detailed in Equations 12.5 and 12.6. Other times, the investment in operating assets offset by operating liabilities and depreciation is detailed. In addition, specific terms may be rearranged or appear in a different order.

Multiple-stage Models

The TSSGM is an improvement over the originally introduced *single-stage growth model* because it allows us to specifically consider different rates of growth, profitability levels, and investment amounts over two different time periods. But what if the eight-year supernormal performance period really consisted of two four-year time periods in which growth was estimated to be 6.0% over the first four years and 4.0% for years 5 through 8? What if all eight years, before the residual period, had different anticipated performance levels?

In these cases, we can develop a three-stage (or *n*-stage) equation. However, we spare the reader this. The next section discusses a very common practice of using spreadsheets to develop a valuation. Although worksheets conveniently facilitate sensitivity analysis, one of the biggest benefits is that a spreadsheet can be used as a discussion device to facilitate management's review. In addition, assumptions can be as detailed as necessary. Performance assignments (growth, margins, working capital investment, and fixed capital investment) can be made to members of the management team, which hopefully results in sounder projections and ownership of the objectives.

Valuation: Spreadsheet Models

This chapter has been consistent with the other chapters about capital evaluation (Chapters 10 and 11). To determine an asset's value, we discount its expected cash flows. In Chapter 11, we discussed and illustrated the development of those cash flows when purchasing new production equipment and introducing a new product.

As you have seen so far, valuation of a company or an organization is no different. We consistently project cash flows, and then discount those values using the required rate of return (the firm's cost of capital).

STRATEGIC FINANCIAL PLAN

This valuation approach begins with the basic framework set forth in Chapter 9, which is consistent with the organization's strategic financial plan. This requires forecasts of the broader international, national, and industrial economies in which the organization and its competitors operate. The key is in understanding the business economics of the industries and product markets in which the firm operates. This includes an analysis of the competitive forces in the industry, along with historical financial performance metrics. We start with historical data for the firm and its major rivals, as we did in Chapter 7.

In Chapter 9, we developed a detailed set of assumptions for Hershey's projected performance. You may recall that we separately estimated the cost of sales (excluding depreciation), depreciation, and SG&A expenses. Through a series of reasonable assumptions, we estimated the incremental annual cash invested in all operating assets and liabilities. For example, receivables were estimated on projected sales and a projected receivables turnover. We estimated an increasing inventory turnover due to the implementation of best demonstrated inventory management practices. We did this with each major operating assumption. As a result, the strategic financial plan in Chapter 9 provided all of the information necessary to value Hershey based on eight years of explicit operating cash flows and a terminal value.

Table 12.1 was taken from the Hershey hypothetical strategic plan in Chapter 9. It represents the collaborative efforts of all members of Hershey's senior management team. Often Hershey's (or any company's) senior managers, operating unit managers, and even functional area managers have objectives and bonuses tied directly to the strategic plan.

The detailed cash flows from Table 12.1 are identical to the cash flows of the projected cash flow statement (Table 9.7C) in every way, with the exception of two items. A focus on operating cash flows only lies at the heart of these exceptions. The valuation cash flow statement centers on *operating cash flows* (also called *free cash flows*).

First, in Table 12.1 we recast the income measure to exclude after-tax interest income and interest expense. As you see, we take operating income (EBIT) and subtract income taxes based on the income tax rate assumption (37% in this case). Second, the valuation cash flow does not consider any financial transactions, such as debt repayment, additional borrowing, equity repurchases, dividends, and so on. The operating cash flows are void of any financing cash flows. The financing cash flows are captured within the cost of capital. This leads to a value of slightly more than $5.0 billion of value as presented in these eight years. But what

TABLE 12.1　Valuation ($ Millions)

				PROJECTED					ADDITIONAL ASSUMPTIONS
	2006	2007	2008	2009	2010	2011	2012	2013	
Net sales	$5,077.8	$5,331.7	$5,571.6	$5,794.5	$6,026.3	$6,207.1	$6,362.3	$6,521.4	
Cost of sales	2,894.3	3,017.7	3,136.8	3,244.9	3,356.6	3,444.9	3,512.0	3,599.8	
Depreciation	204.4	218.1	232.6	247.6	263.1	279.1	295.6	312.6	
Selling, general, and administrative	949.5	986.4	1,019.6	1,048.8	1,078.7	1,098.7	1,113.4	1,141.2	
Total costs	4,048.2	4,222.2	4,389.0	4,541.3	4,698.4	4,822.7	4,921.0	5,053.6	
Operating Income (or earnings before interest and taxes)	1,029.6	1,109.5	1,182.6	1,253.2	1,327.9	1,384.4	1,441.3	1,467.8	
Margin	20.3%	20.8%	21.2%	21.6%	22.0%	22.3%	22.7%	22.5%	
Tax expense	381.0	410.5	437.6	463.7	491.3	512.2	533.3	543.1	Recalculated based on EBIT* tax rate
After-tax operating income	$ 648.6	$ 699.0	$ 745.0	$ 789.5	$ 836.6	$ 872.2	$ 908.0	$ 924.7	
Margin	12.8%	13.1%	13.4%	13.6%	13.9%	14.1%	14.3%	14.2%	
Depreciation	204.4	218.1	232.6	247.6	263.1	279.1	295.6	312.6	
Deferred income taxes—long-term liabilities	27.3	30.5	33.6	36.3	39.2	41.5	44.0	45.5	
Change in:									
Accounts receivable—trade	51.5	(14.9)	(13.0)	(16.2)	(16.6)	(11.6)	(9.0)	(9.2)	
Inventory	(15.7)	(21.2)	(13.5)	(10.9)	(11.4)	(6.6)	(2.7)	(19.0)	
Accounts payable	6.3	10.8	9.9	10.6	10.1	10.2	7.9	10.9	
Prepaid expenses	(10.0)	(10.0)	(10.0)	(10.0)	(12.0)	(12.0)	(12.0)	(12.0)	
Other assets	(30.0)	(30.0)	(30.0)	(30.0)	(40.0)	(40.0)	(40.0)	(40.0)	
Accrued liabilities	55.6	52.9	57.6	24.6	25.4	20.9	16.7	21.0	
Accrued income taxes	5.0	5.0	5.0	5.0	10.0	10.0	10.0	10.0	
Other long-term liabilities	18.7	21.6	20.4	18.9	19.7	15.4	13.2	13.5	
Cash from operating activities (A)	961.7	961.8	1,037.6	1,065.4	1,124.1	1,179.1	1,231.7	1,258.0	
Investment activities									
Capital expenditures	(185.0)	(190.0)	(200.0)	(200.0)	(210.0)	(210.0)	(220.0)	(220.0)	
Business acquisitions	—	—	—	—	—	—	—	—	
Other, net	—	—	—	—	—	—	—	—	
Cash (used for) investing (B)	(185.0)	(190.0)	(200.0)	(200.0)	(210.0)	(210.0)	(220.0)	(220.0)	
Free cash flow (A)+(B)	$776.7	$771.8	$837.6	$865.4	$914.1	$969.1	$1,011.7	$1,038.0	
Present value　8.2% Cost of capital	$717.8	$659.3	$661.2	$631.4	$616.4	$604.0	$582.7	$552.6	

Total present value $5,025.4 million

about beyond those eight years? As we saw in Equation 12.7, the value beyond eight years will be captured in a "terminal value." (This is explored further later in the chapter.)

As evidenced previously, the value of an organization (whether a corporation or division and whether publicly traded or privately held) can be derived from the organization's strategic financial plan. However, a more direct approach is found when building a spreadsheet centered on the major drivers of the business.

PERCENTAGE OF SALES: DIRECT VALUATION MODEL

Table 12.2 recasts the valuation cash flows as a percentage of sales. Within an organization, it is appropriate to work at a level as detailed as management requires to be comfortable (as well as at a level sufficiently detailed to be supported by projection capability). As an "outsider," we obviously do not have the same level of detail. As we prepare to value an organization, we must remind ourselves that we "have a cleaver and not a scalpel!"

The next section presents a valuation model that combines the level of detail and simplicity of the equations along with the flexibility of the strategic plan spreadsheet valuation. Table 12.2 introduces this model. Table 12.3 is derived from Table 12.2, which of course stems directly from the hypothetical strategic plan for Hershey (Table 12.1). Once again, note that the model is silent as to the terminal value. (This is discussed further later in the chapter.) Table 12.3 outlines the free cash flow during the eight specific years it covers. Ultimately, the performance of these eight years is valued at approximately $5,025 million, as we saw before.

This valuation model emulates a *multiple-stage valuation equation* (in this case, an eight-stage valuation equation). It begins with assumptions similar to those of the valuation equation, as many of the underlying assumptions are based on a percentage of sales. These assumptions include the following value drivers.

- Revenue growth

- Operating profitability

- Tax rates

- Net fixed capital investment (capital expenditures less depreciation)

- Working capital investment

- Cost of capital

Panel B of Table 12.3 lists the necessary relationships. To estimate sales, we need the initial (year 0) sales level and estimated growth. Next, we estimate after-tax operating income by subtracting the three expenses [cost of sales (COS) excluding depreciation; selling, general, and administrative (SGA); and depreciation expense]. With regard to COS and SGA, each of these expenses has been projected separately as a percentage of sales and shows annual improvement over this eight-year period.

The VP of Manufacturing has been tasked with reducing the COS, whereas the VPs of Sales, Marketing, and the other functional areas have been asked to lead cost reductions in their areas. Depreciation is a mechanical calculation detailed in Chapter 9. This leads to a projection of 2013 operating income of $1,467.8 million pre-tax, or $924.7 million after taxes. Add back in the depreciation (because it is a non-cash expense), subtract the additional capital expenditures, and consider the investment or disinvestment (in this case) in working capital and other operating assets and liabilities. This results in $1,038.0 million of cash flow in 2013. These last three items have also been estimated as a percentage of sales.

TABLE 12.2   Valuation as a Percentage of Sales ($ Millions)

	2006	2007	2008	PROJECTED (%) 2009	2010	2011	2012	2013	ADDITIONAL ASSUMPTIONS
Net sales	100.00	100.00	100.00	100.00	100.00	100.00	100.00	100.00	
Cost of sales	57.00	56.60	56.30	56.00	55.70	55.50	55.20	55.20	
Depreciation	4.03	4.09	4.17	4.27	4.37	4.50	4.65	4.79	
Selling, general, and administrative	18.70	18.50	18.30	18.10	17.90	17.70	17.50	17.50	
Total costs	79.72	79.19	78.77	78.37	77.96	77.70	77.35	77.49	
Operating Income (or earnings before interest and taxes)	20.28	20.81	21.23	21.63	22.04	22.30	22.65	22.51	Operating margin (M)
Tax expense	7.50	7.70	7.85	8.00	8.15	8.25	8.38	8.33	
After-tax operating income	12.77	13.11	13.37	13.62	13.88	14.05	14.27	14.18	
Depreciation	4.03	4.09	4.17	4.27	4.37	4.50	4.65	4.79	Depreciation (D)
Deferred income taxes—LT liability	0.54	0.57	0.60	0.63	0.65	0.67	0.69	0.70	Working capital investment (I_w)
Change in:									
Accounts receivable—trade	1.01	−0.28	−0.23	−0.28	−0.28	−0.19	−0.14	−0.14	Working capital investment (I_w)
Inventory	−0.31	−0.40	−0.24	−0.19	−0.19	−0.11	−0.04	−0.29	Working capital investment (I_w)
Accounts payable	0.12	0.20	0.18	0.18	0.17	0.16	0.12	0.17	Working capital investment (I_w)
Prepaid expenses	−0.20	−0.19	−0.18	−0.17	−0.20	−0.19	−0.19	−0.18	Working capital investment (I_w)
Other assets	−0.59	−0.56	−0.54	−0.52	−0.66	−0.64	−0.63	−0.61	Working capital investment (I_w)
Accrued liabilities	1.09	0.99	1.03	0.42	0.42	0.34	0.26	0.32	Working capital investment (I_w)
Accrued income taxes	0.10	0.09	0.09	0.09	0.17	0.16	0.16	0.15	Working capital investment (I_w)
Other long-term liabilities	0.37	0.41	0.37	0.33	0.33	0.25	0.21	0.21	Working capital investment (I_w)
Cash from operating activities	18.94	18.04	18.62	18.39	18.65	19.00	19.36	19.29	
Working capital investment (I_w)—total	2.14	0.84	1.08	0.49	0.40	0.45	0.44	0.32	Investment (I_w)
Investment activities:									
Capital expenditures	−3.64	−3.56	−3.59	−3.45	−3.48	−3.38	−3.46	−3.37	Fixed capital investment (I_{fg})
Business acquisitions	0.00	0.00	0.00	0.00	0.00	0.00	0.00	0.00	
Other, net	0.00	0.00	0.00	0.00	0.00	0.00	0.00	0.00	
Cash (used for)Investing	−3.64	−3.56	−3.59	−3.45	−3.48	−3.38	−3.46	−3.37	
Free Cash Flow—% of sales	15.30	14.48	15.03	14.93	15.17	15.61	15.90	15.92	

TABLE 12.3 Valuation Model ($ Millions)

	YEAR 1 (2006)	YEAR 2 (2007)	YEAR 3 (2008)	YEAR 4 (2009)	YEAR 5 (2010)	YEAR 6 (2011)	YEAR 7 (2012)	YEAR 8 (2013)
Panel A—Projected free cash flow								
Net Revenue	$5,077.8	$5,331.7	$5,571.6	$5,794.5	$6,026.3	$6,207.1	$6,362.3	$6,521.4
Cost of sales (excluding depreciation)	2,894.3	3,017.7	3,136.8	3,244.9	3,356.6	3,444.9	3,512.0	3,599.8
Selling, marketing, and administrative	949.5	986.4	1,019.6	1,048.8	1,078.7	1,098.7	1,113.4	1,141.2
Depreciation	204.4	218.1	232.6	247.6	263.1	279.1	295.6	312.6
Operating Income	1,029.6	1,109.5	1,182.6	1,253.2	1,327.9	1,384.4	1,441.3	1,467.8
% of sales	20.3%	20.8%	21.2%	21.6%	22.0%	22.3%	22.7%	22.5%
Taxes	381.0	410.5	437.6	463.7	491.3	512.2	533.3	543.1
After-tax operating income	648.6	699.0	745.0	789.5	836.6	872.2	908.0	924.7
% of sales	12.8%	13.1%	13.4%	13.6%	13.9%	14.1%	14.3%	14.2%
Depreciation	204.4	218.1	232.6	247.6	263.1	279.1	295.6	312.6
Working capital investment	108.7	44.7	60.0	28.3	24.4	27.8	28.1	20.7
Capital expenditures	(185.0)	(190.0)	(200.0)	(200.0)	(210.0)	(210.0)	(220.0)	(220.0)
Free Cash Flow	$ 776.7	$ 771.8	$ 837.6	$ 865.4	$ 914.1	$ 969.1	$ 1,011.7	$1,038.0
% of Sales	15.3%	14.5%	15.0%	14.9%	15.2%	15.6%	15.9%	15.9%
Present value $5,025.4 8-year total	$ 717.8	$ 659.3	$ 661.2	$ 631.4	$ 616.4	$ 604.0	$ 582.7	$ 552.6
Panel B—Valuation model assumptions								
Year 0 revenue $4,836.0								
Revenue growth	5.00%	5.00%	4.50%	4.00%	4.00%	3.00%	2.50%	2.50%
Tax rate	37.00%	37.00%	37.00%	37.00%	37.00%	37.00%	37.00%	37.00%
% of sales								
Cost of sales (excluding depreciation)	57.00%	56.60%	56.30%	56.00%	55.70%	55.50%	55.20%	55.20%
Selling, marketing, and administrative	18.70%	18.50%	18.30%	18.10%	17.90%	17.70%	17.50%	17.50%
Expenses excluding depreciation	75.70%	75.10%	74.60%	74.10%	73.60%	73.20%	72.70%	72.70%
Operating margin before depreciation	24.30%	24.90%	25.40%	25.90%	26.40%	26.80%	27.30%	27.30%
Fixed capital investment	3.64%	3.56%	3.59%	3.45%	3.48%	3.38%	3.46%	3.37%
Depreciation (% of sales)	4.03%	4.09%	4.17%	4.27%	4.37%	4.50%	4.65%	4.79%
Net, fixed investment	0.38%	0.53%	0.59%	0.82%	0.88%	1.11%	1.19%	1.42%
Working capital (Dis.) investment	-2.14%	-0.84%	-1.08%	-0.49%	-0.40%	-0.45%	-0.44%	-0.32%
Cost of capital 8.20%								

This model is less cumbersome than an eight-stage equation and is more focused (on valuation) than the complete strategic financial plan (Chapter 9). This model allows for specific assignment of performance objectives and facilitates discussions with management.

Terminal Value

As we moved through our discussion of spreadsheet valuation, we postponed the discussion of terminal value (or residual value) until this point. According to our estimates and forecasts (presented in Chapter 9 and repeated here), we expect Hershey to have a solid performance over our foreseeable horizon of eight years. As indicated previously, there is more than $5,025.4 million of value in that explicit time frame. However, after an additional eight years of successful operations does Hershey wither away or is there continuing value in the business? The continuing value is captured in the terminal value.

As of today, does management have clarity and confidence to explicitly project the next eight years (years 9 to 16) or even beyond? As of today, can management estimate that much will change about the foreseeable financial performance of the business, beyond the explicit eight-year period? As of today, does management expect unstable value drivers after this eight-year explicit time period?

If the answer is yes to any one of these questions, you should consider building a model with a longer explicit time frame. But if management feels it cannot forecast the performance of the firm beyond eight years (and even if it could, that performance will be very stable and will not vary significantly), an eight-year model is appropriate and the remaining value in the firm (years 9 through forever) can be captured using the simple one-stage valuation equation.

There are several approaches analysts use when estimating the terminal value of a firm. In principle, most approaches are based on the perpetuity models. At this junction, the mechanics behind the calculation of the terminal value and its impact on the estimated value of Hershey should be well understood. The reader should also appreciate the concept that the terminal value captures all of the anticipated cash flows from years 9, 10, 11 . . . 43, 44, 45 . . . 87, 88, 89 . . . 154, 155, 156 . . . and so on forever.

Capitalization uses the zero-growth model (Equation 12.1), in which Hershey's cash flows are assumed to remain constant into perpetuity. This is a very conservative view of the business and results in an estimated year 8 value of Hershey of $12,658.5 million and a present value of $6,738.6 million (Equation 12.8).

$$V_0 = \left[\frac{CF_8}{k} \right] / (1+k)^8 = \left[\frac{\$1,038.0}{0.082} \right] / (1+0.082)^8 \tag{12.8}$$
$$= \$12,658.5/1.8785 = \$6,738.6$$

Another approach, and the one we will use here, is to use the constant growth model (which capitalizes the year 8 cash flows into perpetuity using an estimated perpetual growth rate after year 8). Equation 12.9 may be a more realistic valuation approach.

$$V_0 = \left[\frac{CF_8(1+g_c)}{(k-g_c)} \right] / (1+k)^8 = \left[\frac{\$1,038.0(1.025)}{(0.082-0.025)} \right] / (1+0.082)^8 \tag{12.9}$$
$$= \$18,665.8/1.8785 = \$9,936.5$$

In this case, we now value Hershey at $18,665.8 million in year 8 (assuming a 2.5% terminal growth rate). In present-value terms, the terminal value adds $9,936.5 million. Some analysts also use a "comparable" (or simply a "comp") basis to estimate the terminal value. A *comp ratio* is established for the base year. The comp could be something such as price-to-sales ratio, price-to-earnings, price-to-EBITDA, and so on. In Chapter 7, we calculated Hershey's 2005 P/E multiple as 27.76. If we chose this approach, we would take the 2013 after-tax operating income ($924.7 million) times the multiple (27.76) and use that value as the terminal value ($25,669.7 million; or in present-value terms, $13,665.0 million). To summarize the results of our three techniques, consider the following table.

($ millions)	ZERO GROWTH IN PERPETUITY	CONSTANT GROWTH IN PERPETUITY	COMPARABLE P/E
Year 8—Terminal value	$12,658.5	$18,665.8	$25,669.7
Year 0—Terminal value (PV)	6,738.6	9,936.5	13,665.0

As mentioned, we prefer the constant-growth-in-perpetuity approach.

Comprehensive Valuation Model

Table 12.4 presents a comprehensive valuation model. It details the annual cash flows while incorporating the explicit eight-year period along with the residual value discussed previously. In the middle of this table, the value of the operations (or enterprise value) of Hershey is estimated at $14,961.9 million.

The comprehensive valuation model is a concise valuation model. However, it could be incorporated as part of the strategic financial planning model (as in Table 12.1). The terminal value could be added to provide a complete valuation.

Evaluating Strategies

Within the context of the strategic financial plan (Chapter 9), we observed many financial performance metrics as we tried to summarize the base scenario plan. We centered our attention on income statement values, balance sheet amounts, cash flow levels, and financial performance metrics for the first year and last year of our analysis. There were many performance indicators to keep balanced when evaluating the quality of the plan and when comparing differing scenarios. With valuation analysis, the focus is clear—the value of Hershey's business. The next section discusses valuation of the operations and of equity.

Equity Valuation

As developed previously, we value the explicit eight-year period separately and then value the terminal period. We do this by discounting the projected cash flow at the cost of capital (or 8.2%). We arrived as follows at the total value of the corporation (or the enterprise value of the operations).

TABLE 12.4 Comprehensive Valuation Model: Including Terminal Year ($ Millions)

	YEAR 1 (2006)	YEAR 2 (2007)	YEAR 3 (2008)	YEAR 4 (2009)	YEAR 5 (2010)	YEAR 6 (2011)	YEAR 7 (2012)	YEAR 8 (2013)
Panel A—Projected free cash flow								
Net Revenue	$5,077.8	$5,331.7	$5,571.6	$5,794.5	$6,026.3	$6,207.1	$6,362.3	$6,521.4
Cost of sales (excluding depreciation)	2,894.3	3,017.7	3,136.8	3,244.9	3,356.6	3,444.9	3,512.0	3,599.8
Selling, marketing, and administrative	949.5	986.4	1,019.6	1,048.8	1,078.7	1,098.7	1,113.4	1,141.2
Depreciation	204.4	218.1	232.6	247.6	263.1	279.1	295.6	312.6
Operating Income	1,029.6	1,109.5	1,182.6	1,253.2	1,327.9	1,384.4	1,441.3	1,467.8
Taxes	381.0	410.5	437.6	463.7	491.3	512.2	533.3	543.1
After-tax operating income	648.6	699.0	745.0	789.5	836.6	872.2	908.0	924.7
% of sales	12.8%	13.1%	13.4%	13.6%	13.9%	14.1%	14.3%	14.2%
Depreciation	204.4	218.1	232.6	247.6	263.1	279.1	295.6	312.6
Working capital investment	108.7	44.7	60.0	28.3	24.4	27.8	28.1	20.7
Capital expenditures	(185.0)	(190.0)	(200.0)	(200.0)	(210.0)	(210.0)	(220.0)	(220.0)
Free cash flow	$ 776.7	$ 771.8	$ 837.6	$ 865.4	$ 914.1	$ 969.1	$1,011.7	$ 1,038.0
% of sales	15.3%	14.5%	15.0%	14.9%	15.2%	15.6%	15.9%	15.9%
Terminal value								$18,665.8
Present value $ 5,025.4 8-year Total	$ 717.8	$ 659.3	$ 661.2	$ 631.4	$ 616.4	$ 604.0	$ 582.7	$ 552.6
9,936.5 Terminal value								$ 9,936.5
$14,961.9 Value of the operations								
Panel B—Valuation model assumptions								
Year 0 revenue $4,836.0								
Revenue growth	5.00%	5.00%	4.50%	4.00%	4.00%	3.00%	2.50%	2.50%
Tax rate	37.00%	37.00%	37.00%	37.00%	37.00%	37.00%	37.00%	37.00%
% of sales								
Cost of sales (excluding depreciation)	57.00%	56.60%	56.30%	56.00%	55.70%	55.50%	55.20%	55.20%
Selling, marketing, and administrative	18.70%	18.50%	18.30%	18.10%	17.90%	17.70%	17.50%	17.50%
Expenses excluding depreciation	75.70%	75.10%	74.60%	74.10%	73.60%	73.20%	72.70%	72.70%
Operating margin before depreciation	24.30%	24.90%	25.40%	25.90%	26.40%	26.80%	27.30%	27.30%
Fixed capital investment	3.64%	3.56%	3.59%	3.45%	3.48%	3.38%	3.46%	3.37%
Depreciation (% of sales)	4.03%	4.09%	4.17%	4.27%	4.37%	4.50%	4.65%	4.79%
Net, fixed investment	0.38%	0.53%	0.59%	0.82%	0.88%	1.11%	1.19%	1.42%
Working capital (Dis.) investment	-2.14%	-0.84%	-1.08%	-0.49%	-0.40%	-0.45%	-0.44%	-0.32%
Cost of capital 8.20%								

	PRESENT VALUE ($MMS)
Explicit period	$ 5,025.4
Terminal value	9,936.5
Enterprise value	$14,961.9
Value of the operations	$ 14,961.9
Add: Cash and equivalents	67.2
Less: Interest–bearing debt	(1,762.0)
Value of the equity	$ 13,267.1
Shares outstanding	240.5
Value per share	$ 55.16

To this point we valued the entire company, the enterprise value. This is also called the value of the operations, fair market value, or intrinsic value of the firm. To calculate the value of the equity and the value per share we must (1) add cash, cash equivalents, and marketable securities and (2) subtract all interest-bearing debt (short-term debt, notes payable, banking borrowings, current portion of long-term debt, and long-term debt). The result is the value of the equity! By dividing the value of the equity by the number of shares outstanding we arrive at the equity value per share.

This is the value we are willing to pay for a share of Hershey stock, given our set of assumptions. (We discuss the value of the operations and the value per share as we move forward.) If we were managers at Hershey, this would "green light" our share repurchase program because we see that the shares are fairly valued (i.e., our intrinsic estimated value of $55 versus a current price of $55 per share as of December 13, 2005). If the current stock price is less than or equal to $55, purchasing the stock is a good investment.

Strategy Formulation and Valuation

In Chapter 9, we illustrated the impact of a stock repurchase program on the base scenario strategic financial plan. That event had dramatic impact on components of the balance sheet and the financial performance metrics. Hershey's management should (and does) consider a share repurchase program. That repurchase program does not affect the value of the stock today (year 0)! It is a financing decision, not an operating decision.

Using the valuation model, it is important to test operating decisions and scenarios. Sensitivity analysis tests one item at a time. For example, if sales growth can be increased by 1% (e.g., 2006 sales growth increases from 5.0 to 5.05%) during the eight-year explicit time period, the value of the operations increases to $15,047.0 million (equity value of $55.51 per share). Table 12.5 summarizes impact on per-share values for sensitivity analysis of all assumptions. Management at Hershey has focused on cost management and on trying to raise the product's price per pound, which also will lower the expenses as a percentage of sales.

In Table 12.5, each assumption is increased by 1% of its original (base scenario) assumption in all eight years and/or the terminal period as noted. The first two columns indicate the original assumption in year 1 and how it was revised when it was increased by a factor of 1.01 (for example, to 5.05% for revenue growth). That resulted in a $0.35 increase in the stock price (or an increase of 0.641%). You can also see the direct or inverse relationship between each assumption and the underlying value of the equity. Finally, we can see that in this case expense reduction, cost of capital, and growth are Hershey's major value drivers.

TABLE 12.5	Sensitivity Analysis (1% Change in the Assumption)			
	YEAR 1 ASSUMPTION		VALUE PER SHARE IMPACT	
	Original (%)	Sensitivity 1.01 (%) Orig.	$	%
Revenue growth (explicit period only)	5.000	5.050	$0.35	0.641
Expenses (excluding depreciation)	75.700	76.457	(1.83)	−3.316
Tax rate	37.000	37.370	(0.32)	−0.587
Fixed capital investment	3.640	3.676	(0.14)	−0.246
Depreciation (% of sales)	4.030	4.070	0.07	0.126
Working capital (Dis.) investment	−2.140	−2.161	0.02	0.034
Residual period growth rate	2.500	2.525	0.19	0.348
Cost of capital	8.200	8.282	(0.65)	−1.186

Scenario analysis varies two or more variables simultaneously. What if management were discussing a more aggressive marketing campaign—one characterized as:

1. Increased spending on advertising and promotions (incremental +5.0% of sales more spending in year 2, +3.0% more in year 3, and +1.5% more in year 4),

2. Resulting in more growth (incremental +3.0% more growth in year 2, +4.0% more in year 3, +2.0% more in year 4, and +1.5% more in year 5),

3. Requiring more investment in fixed capital (incremental 1.0% of sales more spending for capital expenditures in years 1 and 2), and of course offset with depreciation (incremental 0.3% of sales more depreciation in years 3 through 8).

In Chapter 9, we would have examined the impact of this scenario on sales, income, cash flow, cash, total assets, equity, ROA, and ROE (among other financial measures). In this case, we are ultimately interested in the impact on shareholder value. Table 12.6 shows the results.

This enhanced marketing strategy increases Hershey's enterprise value by $1,130 million, and shareholder value by $4.70 per share. This alternative should be given further consideration, and should be approved if management is comfortable with the underlying improvement in assumptions.

Real Options

In Chapter 11, we discussed capital investment analysis and various techniques related to it, such as sensitivity analysis, scenario analysis, and even an advanced statistical technique called Monte Carlo analysis. Many investment decisions allow a company to modify the project if its performance is not going according to plan. We now discuss options on physical assets and investments (real options). To be a growth company, a firm must continuously develop positive net present value and new investment opportunities. These involve complex decisions with considerable uncertainties. These are strategic decisions requiring long-term perspectives. Decision makers can benefit from sequential learning. As more information is developed, the investment programs can be expanded, modified, or abandoned. This is the subject matter of real options.

A firm may acquire real options by the learning developed from embarking into new areas of activity. In the process, a firm may acquire real options through technological

TABLE 12.6 Comprehensive Valuation Model: Including Terminal Year ($ Millions)

	YEAR 1 (2006)	YEAR 2 (2007)	YEAR 3 (2008)	YEAR 4 (2009)	YEAR 5 (2010)	YEAR 6 (2011)	YEAR 7 (2012)	YEAR 8 (2013)
Panel A—Projected free cash flow								
Net Revenue	$5,077.8	$5,484.0	$5,950.1	$6,307.1	$6,654.0	$6,853.6	$7,024.9	$7,200.5
Cost of sales (excluding depreciation)	2,894.3	3,103.9	3,349.9	3,532.0	3,706.3	3,803.7	3,877.7	3,974.7
Selling, marketing, and administrative	949.5	1,288.7	1,267.4	1,236.2	1,191.1	1,213.1	1,229.4	1,260.1
Depreciation	204.4	224.3	266.3	288.4	310.5	328.7	347.5	366.5
Operating Income	1,029.6	867.1	1,066.5	1,250.5	1,446.1	1,508.1	1,570.3	1,599.2
Taxes	381.0	320.8	394.6	462.7	535.1	558.0	581.0	591.7
After-tax operating income	648.6	546.3	671.9	787.8	911.0	950.1	989.3	1,007.5
% of sales	12.8%	10.0%	11.3%	12.5%	13.7%	13.9%	14.1%	14.0%
Depreciation	204.4	224.3	266.3	288.4	310.5	328.7	347.5	366.5
Working capital investment	108.7	46.0	64.1	30.8	26.9	30.7	31.0	22.9
Capital expenditures	(235.8)	(250.3)	(213.6)	(217.7)	(231.9)	(231.9)	(242.9)	(242.9)
Free cash flow	$ 725.9	$ 566.3	$ 788.7	$ 889.3	$1,016.5	$ 1,077.6	$1,124.9	$ 1,154.0
% of sales	14.3%	10.3%	13.3%	14.1%	15.3%	15.7%	16.0%	16.0%
Terminal value								$20,751.8
Present value $ 5,045.3 8-year total	$ 670.9	$ 483.7	$ 622.6	$ 648.8	$ 685.4	$ 671.6	$ 647.9	$ 614.3
$11,047.0 Terminal value								$11,047.0
$16,092.3 Value of the operations								

Panel B—Valuation model assumptions

Year 0 revenue $4,836.0

	YEAR 1 (2006)	YEAR 2 (2007)	YEAR 3 (2008)	YEAR 4 (2009)	YEAR 5 (2010)	YEAR 6 (2011)	YEAR 7 (2012)	YEAR 8 (2013)
Revenue growth	5.00%	8.00%	8.50%	6.00%	5.50%	3.00%	2.50%	2.50%
Tax rate	37.00%	37.00%	37.00%	37.00%	37.00%	37.00%	37.00%	37.00%
% of sales								
Cost of sales (excluding depreciation)	57.00%	56.60%	56.30%	56.00%	55.70%	55.50%	55.20%	55.20%
Selling, marketing, and administrative	18.70%	23.50%	21.30%	19.60%	17.90%	17.70%	17.50%	17.50%
Expenses excluding depreciation	75.70%	80.10%	77.60%	75.60%	73.60%	73.20%	72.70%	72.70%
Operating margin before depreciation	24.30%	24.90%	25.40%	25.90%	26.40%	26.80%	27.30%	27.30%
Fixed capital investment	3.64%	4.56%	3.59%	3.45%	3.48%	3.38%	3.46%	3.37%
Depreciation (% of sales)	4.03%	4.09%	4.47%	4.57%	4.67%	4.80%	4.95%	5.09%
Net, fixed investment	−0.62%	−0.47%	0.89%	1.12%	1.18%	1.41%	1.49%	1.72%
Working capital (Dis.) investment	−2.14%	−0.84%	−1.08%	−0.49%	−0.40%	−0.45%	−0.44%	−0.32%
Cost of capital 8.20%								

advances and increased understanding of new products and markets. A firm may acquire real options through intellectual property rights such as patents and licenses. The organizational capabilities of the firm may be strengthened. Strategic alliances and joint ventures may be used to strengthen the firm's market position.

The benefits of a real-options approach to investment decisions can be substantial. A *real-options analysis* helps systematize the decision process. The analytical frameworks developed in a real-options analysis can uncover new dimensions and provide deeper insights. This type of analysis also provide a common language for communication among various managerial functions (strategy, research, production, marketing, and so on). Real-options analysis may provide insights and intuitions that may sometimes challenge conventional thinking. For example, the higher the volatility of outcomes may increase the value of the investment program.

The actual computational aspects of real options are quite advanced and well beyond this particular course. The concepts are practical in their applications. In fact, at Hershey we discussed the optionality of a few projects even before the term *real options* gained acceptance. When considering entry into the refrigerated puddings business, the project did not reach its hurdle rate. But the project's champion argued that if the puddings business would be successful Hershey could launch other refrigerated desserts. This was a form of real option.

Options on Assets

Option-pricing approaches to valuation are the best way of thinking about pricing flexibility in the modeling process. Ordinary NPV analysis tends to understate a project's value because it fails to capture adequately the benefits of operating flexibility and other strategic factors (such as follow-on investment). The following sections summarizes categories of real options and their implications to NPV analysis and investment decisions.

ABANDONMENT OPTION

The *option to abandon* (or sell) a project is equivalent to a *put option*. At numerous points in a project's life, management can decide to exit a project and realize proceeds from the sale of that project. If Hershey Foods wanted to enter another line of business, such as the restaurant business, there is an embedded option in that decision. If the industry investment were not living up to expectations, the business could be sold. This represents an abandonment option. Of course, when the original project evaluation is submitted for approval rarely does that approval include a full discussion about abandoning the project at some point.

OPTION TO EXPAND OR GROW

The *option to expand the scale* of a project's operation is equivalent to a *call option*. The "puddings" provided a real option to expand the refrigerated business into other new products, provided the "puddings" were successful. However, the "puddings" were not successful and the call option was never exercised.

As another example, in our decision tree model (Chapter 11) we reviewed the decision to build a large or small plant. We could have staged the investment in the large plant by constructing a "usable" fraction of the large plant. If demand did not materialize, stage 2 (completion of the large plant) did not need to be undertaken. If the project proved initially successful, we could add capacity and expand the business.

OPTION TO SHRINK

The *option to shrink the scale* of a project's operations is equivalent to a put option. After an engineer teams up with an accountant, cost estimates are created for building a distribution center. The initial decision could encompass the decision to build a 100,000-, 200,000-, or 300,000-square-foot facility. The cost of building the largest facility may be fractions per square foot of the cost of building the other-size facilities. In this case, management is confident of the need for the larger facility (which is accepted and built). If the actual performance does not reach the original levels anticipated, the company has the option of shrinking the project by subdividing the building and selling or leasing out that unused portion of the building.

OPTION TO DEFER DEVELOPMENT

The option to defer an investment outlay to develop a property or product is equivalent to a call option. Because the deferrable investment gives management the right, but not the obligation, to make the investment to develop a property or product a project that can be deferred is worth more than the same project without the flexibility to defer development. For a restaurant, an investment in a piece of land in a developing area without incurring the construction costs of that restaurant until the sight proves more attractive is an example of the *option to defer development*.

SWITCHING OPTION

Switching option is a general name applied to a few similar types of decisions. Restarting or shutting down options pertain to (as their name suggests) restarting or shutting down plant/line operations. The switching option also relates to flexible manufacturing equipment that may cost more initially but can produce more than one product. Manufacturing flexibility has value captured within a switching option.

Extending this thought, in an evaluation of a new product there always is concern that marketing projections will not be realized. An option is provided if the production line can be easily retrofitted to support the production of other established products.

Although the exact computational steps for real options are beyond the scope of this text, the recognition of the project's managerial flexibility leads to the consideration of multiple cash flow scenarios and analyses that span and evaluate the possible alternatives. Applying probabilities to the scenario analyses aids the management decision-making process.

summary

The topic of strategic valuation is central to the concept of this text, but more importantly it is central to business as well. The valuation process we advocate is as follows.

1. Historical financial analysis (Chapters 2, 7, and 8)

2. Review of general economic conditions (Chapters 4 through 6)

3. Forecasts of future performance (Chapter 9)

4. Valuation of projected cash flows (Chapters 3, 10, and 11)

This chapter completes the valuation process. The tools presented here are useful to management and serve various purposes, such as valuing an acquisition candidate or determining the asking price of a divestiture property. It also provides a tool for management to objectively complete its own self-valuation. The overwhelming majority of companies prepare a strategic plan, such as we saw in Chapter 9. This is a final step in valuing a business.

The most widely accepted valuation method is the *discounted cash flow (DCF) method*. The DCF methodology values the firm as the sum of projected free cash flow of the firm discounted at the appropriately weighted average cost of capital. This method can use spreadsheet projections. In addition, analysis can yield systematic relationships among revenues, cost structures, and investment requirements. These can produce estimates of the key drivers of value: revenue growth, operating income, effective tax rate, working capital, fixed investment requirements, the applicable cost of capital, and the length of time over which the firm can achieve a competitive advantage. The use of these key value drivers facilitates the use of computers in achieving effective sensitivity analysis.

Valuation is inherently a judgment. It combines science and art. The art of performing valuations is to make an initial estimate based on rational best-judgment estimates of the determinants (also called drivers) of value. Based on alternative scenarios, one then makes a sensitivity analysis of the relationship between valuations and the input value driver. The process itself can improve understanding of the firm's competitive position and lead to value enhancements.

The mantra in corporate America has been to "enhance shareholder value." This is the underlying model, which is a very appropriate and widely used technique. Yes, this is a generic model. This is not the model (30+ pages long) used at Hershey. Nor is this the model (90+ pages long[1]) used by an investment banker. Nor is this the model used by other financial advisors. However, these concepts underlie those particular models.

This approach gives you an opportunity to directly see how you can add value to the organization. Whether it is selling more product, reducing costs, or reducing the investment in both fixed and working capital, we can all create shareholder value.

More broadly, real options and the company's alternatives add to the underlying value of the organization. Financial option pricing concepts have been extended into real options analysis. The technical apparatus involved in real options analysis makes use of calls and puts and their underlying mathematical computations. Call options are used in structuring the decision to (1) expand or grow or (2) defer development.

---

[1] As an example.

Put options are involved in the analysis of abandonment (or shrinking the scale) of a project operation.

The option to switch project operations is a portfolio of options that consists of both call and put options. For example, restarting operations when a project is currently shut down is equivalent to a call option. Shutting down operations when unfavorable conditions arise is equivalent to an American put option. The cost of restarting (or shutting down) an operation may be thought of as the *exercise price of the call (or put)*. A flexible manufacturing system with the ability to produce two types of products is an example of a switching option.

Additional benefits may be generated from using real-options analysis. The analytical frameworks developed in a real-option analysis can uncover new dimensions and provide deeper insights. These also provide a common language for communication among various managerial functions.

Questions

12.1   How is the valuation of a business related to capital budgeting?

12.2   Throughout this text we have focused on the valuation of a business. We methodically performed financial analysis (Chapter 7) and projected the financial effects of business performance (Chapter 9). Why is this approach necessary?

12.3   Throughout this chapter we have listed six methods of valuation and briefly set forth the advantages and limitations of each.

Technique	Advantages	Disadvantages
Simple perpetuity methods		
Zero-growth valuation model		
Constant-growth valuation model		
More complex perpetuity methods		
Two-stage valuation model		
Multiple-stage valuation model		
Free cash flow methods		
Valuation of strategic plan		
Direct model (percentage of sales)		

12.4   When is it appropriate to use the direct model (percentage of sales)?

12.5   How does after-tax operating income differ from net income?

12.6   How are the following valuation parameters related to one another? How do they affect the general free-cash-flow valuation model?

- Revenues
- Investment
- Net operating income
- Profitability rate
- Growth rate

12.7   What is the purpose of the terminal value? Why is it necessary?

12.8   How do we adjust the value of the operations to derive the value of equity? Why do we make the adjustments?

12.9   In estimating the free cash flows using any of the models presented in this chapter, we ignored interest income, interest expense, and any other financing cash flows. Why did we ignore those important cash flows?

12.10 List the types of real options presented in this chapter.

12.11 Do real options tend to increase the NPV of a project?

12.12 A new production facility will be phased in over a five-year time span. This is an example of what type of real option?

12.13 A new product in a new market could possibly open the opportunity for line extensions. This is an example of what type of real option?

12.14 The marketing department presents a capital investment project for a new product. The project has a negative NPV of $6.3 million. The VP of marketing, an MBA, says, "This project will start us along the way of building a significant franchise in a new arena we don't compete in currently. The opportunity to grow beyond the confines of this project and our current business model is worth at least $6.3 million and more!" Discuss this comment.

12.15 If you were a member of the senior management team, would you accept the project described in question 14 (with a negative NPV)? What other analysis would you request?

12.16 Why is the equity in a levered firm considered a call option on the value of the firm's assets?

Problems

12.1

Constant growth valuation formula: A firm has free cash flows of $1,000 at time zero. Its cost of capital is 9.0%.

a.   Cash flows are expected to remain constant. What is an estimate of its present value?

b.   If cash flows were expected to grow 3.5%, what is an estimate of its present value?

c.   If cash flows were expected to grow 8.9%, what is an estimate of its present value?

d.   If cash flows were expected to grow 9.0%, what is an estimate of its present value?

e.   If cash flows were expected to grow 12.0%, what is an estimate of its present value?

12.2

A mature company had sales of $65 million this past fiscal year. It is expected that sales will continue to grow at 4% annually into perpetuity.

a.   If the operating margin is 15%, with a 40% tax rate, what are next year's projected operating income and after-tax operating income?

b. Assume that working capital investment requires additional investment equal to 3% of sales, capital expenditures are 5% of sales, and depreciation is 4% of sales. What is next year's required net investment in assets?

c. How much cash is this company expected to generate next year?

d. If the company's cost of capital is 11.5%, what is an estimate of its present value?

12.3

Valuation of a firm: Use the constant-growth valuation model developed in Equation 12.5.

a. Value a firm with the following characteristics:

Where:

R_0 = Revenue (or sales) of firm = $10,000
m = Operating income (EBIT) margin (% of sales) = 20%
T = Tax rate = 40%
d = Depreciation (% of sales) = 4%
I_{fg} = Capital expenditure, gross or fixed capital invested (% of sales) = 4%
I_w = Working capital investment (% of sales) = 6%
g = Growth = 5%
k = Cost of capital = 12%

b. Using the information cited previously, calculate the change in value for each of the following adjustments.

• Revenue is $11,000 instead of $10,000. What is the change in value?

• Return to original (problem 12.3a) assumptions. Operating margin is 22% instead of 20%. What is the change in value?

• Return to original (problem 12.3a) assumptions. Growth is 5.5% instead of 5%. What is the change in value?

• Return to original (problem 12.3a) assumptions. Tax rate is 36% instead of 40%. What is the change in value?

• Return to original (problem 12.3a) assumptions. Working capital investment is 5.4% instead of 6%. What is the change in value?

• Return to original (problem 12.3a) assumptions. Cost of capital is 10.8% instead of 12%. What is the change in value?

c. The change in which assumption had the largest impact? Which adjustment had the least impact?

12.4

The following financial information was presented by Augusta Corporation for the most recent fiscal year ($000s).

Sales	$80,000	Cash	$ 300
		Marketable securities	2,700
Cost of sales	64,000	Accounts receivable	8,800
Depreciation	4,400	Inventory	18,000
Gross income	11,600	Other current assets	440
		Total current assets	30,240

Selling expense	3,200	Gross property & equipment	80,230
General administrative	1,200	Accumulated depreciation	40,000
Other operating expense	240	Net property & equipment	40,230
Other operating income	80	Other assets	100
EBIT	7,040	Total assets	$70,570
Interest expense	860	Accounts payable	$13,500
Interest income	200	Taxes payable	440
Pre-tax income	6,380	Bank borrowings	4,375
		Current portion long-term debt	625
Provision for taxes (38%)	2,424	Total current liabilities	18,940
Net income	$3,956	Long-term debt	24,500
		Deferred taxes	12,000
Dividends	$ 970	Stockholders'equity	15,130
Capital expenditures	6,000	Total liabilities and equity	$70,570

Assume that growth for next year and into perpetuity is estimated to be 6%. Answer the following questions, using the constant growth valuation model (equation 12.6):

a. What are next year's sales, operating income (EBIT), and after tax operating income?

b. What investment will be made through gross capital expenditures and net capital expenditures (gross offset by depreciation)?

c. What investment will be made in other operating assets and liabilities?

d. Assuming a 12% cost of capital, what is the estimated value of Augusta Corporation?

12.5

The following financial information was presented by Bally Bunion, Inc. for the most recent fiscal year ($000s).

Sales	$120,000	Cash and equivalents	$ 300
		Accounts receivable	8,800
Cost of sales	54,000	Inventory	18,000
Depreciation	5,280	Deferred taxes	1,260
Gross income	60,720	Other current assets	440
		Total current assets	28,800
Selling expense	36,120	Net property & equipment	63,000
Marketing expense	12,000	Goodwill and other intangibles	40,000
Administrative expense	6,000	Other assets	100
Other operating expense	600	Total assets	$131,900
Other operating income	300		
EBIT	18,300		
		Accounts payable	$ 5,940
Interest expense	2,300	Salaries payable	480
Interest income	150	Accrued liabilities	8,910
Pre-tax income	16,150	Dividends payable	1,970
		Notes payable	355

Provision for taxes (36 %)	5,814	Short-term debt	14,375
Net income	$10,336	Current portion long-term debt	625
		Total current liabilities	32,655
		Long-term debt	27,560
		Deferred taxes	8,910
Dividends	$ 7,878	Other long-term liabilities	840
Capital expenditures	6,600	Stockholders'equity	61,935
		Total liabilities and equity	$131,900

Assume that growth for next year and into perpetuity is estimated to be 8%. Answer the following questions, using the constant growth valuation model (equation 12.6):

a. What are next year's sales, operating income (EBIT), and after tax operating income?

b. What investment will be made through gross capital expenditures and net capital expenditures (gross offset by depreciation)?

c. What investment will be made in other operating assets and liabilities?

d. Assuming a 14% cost of capital, what is the estimated value of Bally Bunion, Inc.?

12.6

The value of the operations of Turnberry Count Corporation (TCC) was estimated to be $1,439 million. TCC currently has cash of $33 million, cash equivalents of $56 million, and marketable securities of $24 million. If it also has bank borrowings of $13 million and long-term debt of $179 million, what is the value of TCC's equity? If they have 85 million shares outstanding, what is the value of one share?

12.7

Using the information in problem 12.6, Spy Glass, Inc. has just offered $18.50 per share of TCC stock.

a. What is the total value of the equity Spy Glass is willing to pay?

b. What is the total value of the operations from the Spy Glass perspective?

c. What factors would drive Spy Glass to pay a price different than the price developed in problem 12.6?

12.8

Value of unequal annual amounts with a perpetuity: An investment's first year's cash flow will be $100,000 at the end of year. The cash flows are expected to grow at the following rates for years 2, 3, and 4. Starting in year 5, the investment becomes a perpetuity.

Year	Growth	Cash Flow
2	50%	
3	40%	
4	25%	
5+	0%	

a. Calculate the annual cash flow for years 2, 3, 4, and 5.

b. Assuming a 7% return, what is the present value of the perpetuity in year 5?

c. Assuming a 7% return, what is the total present value of the investment?

12.9

In 2005, Johnson & Johnson (J&J) was pursuing the acquisition of Guidant. The following represents the expected cash flow J&J hoped to generate with this acquisition.

Year	CF ($millions)
1	$(346)
2	135
3	878
4	1,317
5	1,844
6	2,360
7	2,879
8	3,311
9	3,642
10	4,006

a. If J&J had a cost of capital of 12.5%, what is the value of these cash flows?

b. Further assume that J&J expects the cash flows after year 10 to continue into perpetuity by growing at 4.5% each year. What is the value of this perpetuity in year 10? What is its present value? What is the total value of this proposed acquisition?

Question	Answer
Value of perpetuity in year 10?	
Present value of perpetuity?	

Question	Answer
Total value of proposed acquisition	

c. J&J was outbid by Boston Scientific by $2.5 billion. If J&J decided to continue "bidding" for Guidant, by what amount would cash flows have to increase each year to justify this additional premium investment in the 10-year explicit period?

12.10

Valuation methodologies: Company A is considering the purchase of a target company T. A detailed spreadsheet analysis of the financial statements of the target has been made. On the basis of that analysis and of all aspects of the business economics of the target's industry, the acquiring firm has made the spreadsheet projections exhibited in the following table.

Spreadsheet Projections of Company T

	% OF REVENUE	YEAR 0	1	2	3	4 +
1. Revenues (R_t)	100	$1,000	$1,200	$1,440	$1,728	$1,728
2. Costs	80		960	1152	1382	1382
3. Operating income (X_t)	20		240	288	346	346
4. Taxes (T)	40		96	115	138	138
5. Operating income after taxes [$X_t(1-T)$]	12		144	173	207	207
Investment requirements						
6. Net working capital (I_w)	4		$ 48	$ 58	$ 69	$ 0
7. Net property, plant, and equipment (I_{fg})	6		72	86	104	0
8. Total (I_t)	10		120	144	173	0
9. Free cash flows [$X_t(1 - T) - I_t$]			$ 24	$ 29	$ 35	$ 207

a. Calculate the value of company T using the spreadsheet methodology.

b. Calculate the value of company T using the formula approach (Equation 12.7)

c. Compare your results.

12.11

Formula calculation: The basic DCF sales growth model is expressed as a formula (Equation 12.7) repeated here.

$$V_0 = \text{PV (Growth Period CFs)} + \text{PV (Perpetual Period CFs)}$$

$$V_0 = R_0[m_s(1-T_s) - I_s]\sum_{t=1}^{n}\frac{(1+g_s)^t}{(1+k)^t}$$

$$+ \frac{\left[R_0(1+g_s)^n[m_c(1-T_c) - I_c]\right](1+g_c)}{(k-g_c)} \cdot \frac{1}{(1+k)^n}$$

Use the data inputs following. Calculate the value beyond which you could not pay a target company with the characteristics illustrated if you as the buyer firm are to earn the applicable cost of capital for the acquisition.

Where:

R_0 = Revenue (or sales) of firm (last year of actual sales) - $mms $1,000

m = Operating income margin   20.0%

  m_s = Operating income margin during supernormal growth period

  m_c = Operating income margin during constant growth period

T = Tax rate   40.0%

  T_s = Tax rate during supernormal growth period

  T_c = Tax rate during constant growth period

I = Investment as a percentage of revenues (defined as the change in working capital and other long-term operating assets and liabilities plus gross capital expenditures minus depreciation*)   10.0%

---

*Investment is defined as the change in working capital and other long-term operating assets and liabilities plus gross capital expenditures minus depreciation.

I_s = Investment as a percentage of revenues during supernormal growth period

I_c = Investment as a percentage of revenues during constant growth period

g = Growth rate of revenues

g_s = Growth rate of revenues during supernormal growth period   20.0%

g_c = Growth rate of revenues during constant growth period   4.0%

k = Cost of capital   10.0%

n = Number of years of supernormal growth   2

12.12

Using the model presented in Tables 12.3 and 12.4, value the food service division of Starbucks coffee. Last year, the food service division had sales of $92,846 thousand.

Percentages	Year 1	Year 2	Year 3	Year 4	Year 5
Revenue growth	25.00	20.00	15.00	10.00	10.00
Tax rate	35.50	35.50	36.00	36.00	37.00
% of sales					
Cost of sales (excluding depreciation)	43.60	43.30	43.00	42.70	42.40
Selling, marketing, and administrative	27.70	27.60	27.50	27.40	27.30
Expenses excluding depreciation	71.30	70.90	70.50	70.10	69.70
Operating margin before depreciation	28.70	29.10	29.50	29.90	30.30
Fixed capital investment	9.00	8.00	7.00	6.00	5.00
Depreciation (% of sales)	4.00	4.25	4.50	4.75	5.00
Net fixed investment	5.00	3.75	2.50	1.25	0.00
Working capital investment	5.00	5.50	6.00	6.00	6.00
Cost of capital 9.30%					

a. What is the value of this explicit five-year period?

b. Assuming a 4% growth rate, what is the value of the perpetuity in year 5? The perpetuity starts in year 6.

c. What is the present value of that perpetuity today (year 0)?

d. What is the total value of the operations?

e. Assuming no cash or interest-bearing debt, what would you be willing to pay for the food service division of Starbucks?

12.13

Derek Justin is contemplating purchasing a fast-food franchise. He visited the web site and downloaded some of the following financial information. Listed below is the typical performance of a franchise unit over its first three years. The unit requires substantial support for the first year, but after the third year its performance is fairly stable. Using the model presented in Tables 12.3 and 12.4, value this franchise unit.

Percentages	Year 1	Year 2	Year 3
Revenue	$2,345		
Revenue growth		25.00	15.00
Tax rate	35.60	36.50	37.50
% of sales			
Cost of sales (excluding depreciation)	39.00	37.00	35.00
Selling, marketing, and administrative	50.00	45.00	35.00
Expenses excluding depreciation	89.00	82.00	70.00
Operating margin before depreciation	11.00	18.00	30.00
Fixed capital investment	5.00	5.00	5.00
Depreciation (% of sales)	3.00	4.00	5.00
Net fixed investment	2.00	1.00	0.00
Working capital investment	8.00	7.00	6.00
Cost of capital 15.00%			

a. What is the value of this explicit three-year period?

b. Assuming a 3% growth rate, what is the value of the perpetuity in year 3. The perpetuity starts in year 4.

c. What is the present value of that perpetuity (year 0)?

d. What is the total value of the franchise unit?

e. Assuming no cash or interest-bearing debt, what should Derek Justin be willing to pay for this franchise fast-food unit?

f. What is the value if Derek wants a 20% rate of return?

12.14

The management team is examining the Alpha Dog Corporation (ADC) for an acquisition bid. ADC had sales of $25 million last year, and the management team is comfortable with the following set of assumptions.

Percentages	Year 1	Year 2	Year 3	Year 4	Year 5	Year 6	Year 7	Year 8
Revenue ($000s) growth	50.0	40.0	35.0	25.0	15.0	10.0	8.0	6.0
Tax rate	33.0	34.0	35.0	36.0	37.0	38.0	38.0	38.0
% of sales								
Cost of sales (excluding depreciation)	52.0	51.7	51.5	51.2	51.0	50.8	50.5	50.5
Selling, marketing, and administrative	27.7	27.6	27.5	27.4	27.3	27.2	27.1	27.0
Other operating expense, net	2.0	2.0	2.0	2.0	1.0	1.0	1.0	1.0
Expenses excluding depreciation	79.7	79.3	79.0	78.6	78.3	78.0	77.6	77.5
Operating margin before depreciation	20.3	20.7	21.0	21.4	21.7	22.0	22.4	22.5
Fixed capital investment	6.0	5.0	4.0	25.0	5.0	4.0	4.0	4.0
Depreciation (% of sales)	4.0	4.0	4.0	4.3	4.5	4.5	4.0	4.0
Net fixed investment	2.0	1.0	0.0	20.8	0.5	−0.5	0.0	0.0
Working capital investment	6.5	6.0	5.5	7.0	5.0	5.0	4.0	3.0
Cost of capital 11.5%								

a.   What is the value of this explicit 8-year period?

b.   Assuming a 2% growth rate, what is the value of the perpetuity in year 8? The perpetuity starts in year 9.

c.   What is the present value of that perpetuity (year 0)?

d.   What is the total value of ADC?

e.   Assuming cash and marketable securities of $3.4 million and existing debt of $7.1 million, what should the management team be willing to pay for ADC's equity?

12.15

Purchase of a small private firm:* Highstyle, Inc. is seeking to raise $20 million to finance future growth. Industry buyers place a higher value on Highstyle than financial buyers. Synergies created by a strategic industry buyer, with managerial expertise and other capabilities, increase the value of Highstyle.

TARGET

The Target company, a rapidly growing women's sportswear company, generates more than $60 million in sales. With recent acquisitions, projected sales in the following year will exceed $80 million. The company's strengths are as follows.

- Management: Highstyle's executive management introduced a successful development strategy that has resulted in a dramatic and profitable growth.

- Growth: The creation of a strong brand name has set a strong foundation for future growth.

- Strong historical operating performance: 32% compound annual growth rate in the previous four years.

INDUSTRY

Women's apparel segment is the largest segment within the U.S. apparel market, accounting for 50%. Within the women's apparel market, women's sportswear is the largest and most influential market segment.

- Structure of the women's apparel market (fashion pyramid) is as follows.

  - Designer: Known for fashion and quality, sales are at high prices to a narrow customer base.

  - Bridge: Less expensive versions of designer styles.

  - Better: Sportswear and casual work clothes at medium price points.

  - Moderate: Emphasis on low price over style, aiming at a broad consumer base.

- Demographics: As the "baby boomer" population ages and becomes more affluent, they are the dominant consumers in women's apparel (the target audience for Highstyle's brands). Growth in the women's apparel market was a result of growth of specialty and department store segments (key distribution channels for Highstyle).

---

*This case was originally presented by Trenwith Securities, Inc. to the UCLA Anderson's Mergers & Acquisition Program. The names of participating companies have been changed to protect the confidentiality of the client. This case is used with permission of Mr. Ron E. Ainsworth, Managing Partner.

- Highstyle: Positioned in the mid to upper "better" market.

- Trends: Demand for designer styles at lower prices has resulted in a compression of the fashion pyramid. Rapid growth in the demand for Better-Bridge apparel. Increasing importance of brand names.

FINANCIALS

The buyer of Highstyle used a general five-year DCF spreadsheet valuation model. After analysis of the historical data and the future prospects of Highstyle as a part of the buyer, estimates of the operating relationships (for years $1 - n + 1$) are shown in the following table. The base year revenues of Highstyle were $60 million.

Operating Relationships

Percentages of Sates	Year 0	Year 1	Year 2	Year 3	Year 4	Year 5	Year n+1
Operating income	–	30.0	30.0	30.0	30.0	30.0	30.0
After-tax operating income	–	18.0	18.0	18.0	18.0	18.0	18.0
Depreciation	–	5.0	5.0	5.0	5.0	5.0	5.0
Change in working capital	–	4.0	4.0	4.0	4.0	4.0	0.0
Capital expenditures	–	5.0	5.0	5.0	5.0	5.0	5.0
Change in other assets net	–	0.00	0.00	0.00	0.00	0.00	0.00
Free cash flow	–	14.0	14.0	14.0	14.0	14.0	18.0

a. Why could a strategic buyer pay more than a financial buyer?

b. Based on net revenues of $60 million in the base year and the operating relationships set forth in the previous table, calculate the value of the equity of Highstyle. Use a tax rate of 40% and revenue growth rates as follows.

Revenue	Growth Rate (%)
Year 1	32
Year 2	30
Year 3	28
Year 4	26
Year 5	25
Year n + 1 and on	0

Use a discount rate of 25% for the initial five-year period to reflect the high risk of a relatively young, small, privately held firm not publicly traded. Use a 10% discount factor for the terminal period.

c. If the discount varied by +/− 5% and the operating income percentage varied by +/− 5%, calculate a range of plausible values the buyer could pay for Highstyle.

d. The buyer valued Highstyle at $150 million net of debt of $20 million. This represented a multiple of 2.5 of the base year revenues. Multiples for similar companies were only 1.5 times base year revenues. The buyer gave the owners $150 million of its own stock (20% of total), which was publicly traded. Evaluate the price paid for Highstyle.

part 5

Financial Policy

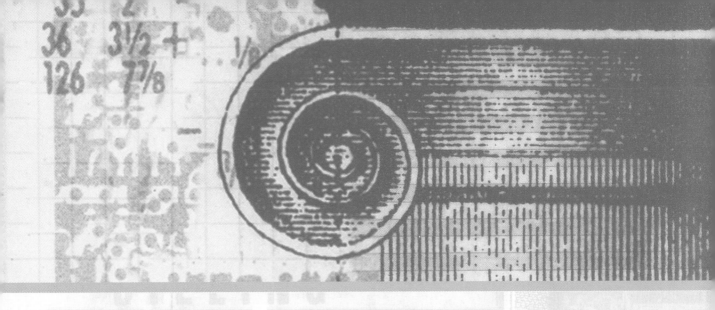

CONTENTS

Cost of Capital and Financial Structure

13

In Chapter 10, we presented numerous capital investment analysis techniques, and in Chapter 11 we discussed how to determine cash flows through the use of numerous project examples. Paramount to the investment evaluation is the discount rate (the cost of capital). The cost of capital is the opportunity cost of funds invested in the firm. It represents the minimum acceptable rate of return for corporate investments. In the Chapter 11 new-product example, we saw that a one-percentage-point change in the cost of capital (from 11 to 12%) had a significant impact on the NPV. The NPV fell by $2.8 million (or 76%).

Learning Outcomes

After completing this chapter, you should be able to:

1 Understand the importance and the concept behind the cost of capital

2 Estimate the cost of the various components of capital

3 Determine appropriate weights for those components

4 Compute the cost of capital

5 Comprehend the financial structure of a firm and the decisions that drive a firm to a particular capital structure

6 Define the concept of a hurdle rate

TABLE 13.5	Hershey's Cost of Debt Alternative (Historical) Technique

$MILLIONS	BALANCE 12/31/05	WEIGHT %	INTEREST RATE %	WEIGHTED COST %
Short-term debt	$819.1	46.49	4.30	2.00
Debentures				
Due 2021	100.0	5.68	8.80	0.50
Due 2027	250.0	14.19	7.20	1.02
Notes				
Due 2007	151.2	8.58	6.95	0.60
Due 2012	150.0	8.51	6.95	0.59
Due 2015	250.0	14.19	4.85	0.69
Other	41.6	2.36	6.70	0.16
	$1,761.9	100.00		5.55
			× (1 − Tax Rate)	63.8
			After-tax Cost of Debt	3.54

Table 13.5 and adds a line to it for new debt to be issued, dollar amount, and estimated interest rate. That new debt is combined with the current debt, weights are recalculated, and a modified cost of debt is calculated. In this way, limited current market conditions are introduced into the calculation.

In summary, the recommended technique (the current market cost of debt) estimates Hershey's after-tax cost of debt at 4.01% (the previously noted market cost of debt for a high-quality borrower). This is 0.47% (47 basis points) higher than Hershey's historical cost of debt (calculated in Table 13.5). To reflect the opportunity cost of debt, we remain steadfast in our recommendation of using the current market cost of debt (4.01%).

COST OF PREFERRED STOCK

Preferred stock is a hybrid security. It is a hybrid in the sense that although it is classified as equity, preferred stockholders do not participate in the successful growth of the corporation like a common stockholder. A preferred stockholder receives a contractually set dividend. A limited amount of adjustable-rate preferred stock is also available (a topic outside the scope of this text).

This dividend does not change (fixed rate) over time like a common stock dividend (because the dividend does not change, the cost of preferred stock behaves similarly to the cost of debt). Because preferred stock has no maturity date, the cost also behaves as a perpetual bond or a perpetuity (with no growth in the cash flow). The cost of preferred stock is calculated as in Equation 13.4.

$$K_{ps} = D_{ps}/P_{ps} \qquad (13.4)$$

Where:

$$K_{ps} = \text{Cost of preferred stock}$$

$$D_{ps} = \text{Preferred stock dividend}$$

$$P_{ps} = \text{Price of preferred stock}$$

For example, if a company has preferred stock with a dividend of $4.00 and the current price of that stock is $48.00, the cost of the preferred stock is 8.33% (calculated via Equation 13.5).

$$K_{ps} = D_{ps}/P_{ps}$$
$$K_{ps} = \$4.00/\$48.00 \qquad\qquad (13.5)$$
$$K_{ps} = 8.33\%$$

Figure 13.2 outlines the cash flows to a preferred stockholder. Each year the preferred stockholder receives $4.00. Although Figure 13.2 stops at year 100, preferred stock dividends are perpetual. By equating that stream of dividends to the $48.00 cost of the preferred stock, the resulting return on the investment is 8.33%. Said differently, by discounting the perpetual stream of dividends at an investor's required rate of return (i.e., 8.33%) that investor would be willing to pay $48.00 for the preferred stock. Once again, this technique incorporates the current stock price and the current opportunity cost of preferred stocks. The current market cost is our recommended approach to calculating the cost of preferred stock.

Note that there are no related tax deductions for the firm that has outstanding preferred stock and pays preferred stock dividends. Because dividends are not tax deductible in the United States, the after-tax cost of preferred stock is the same cost as the pre-tax cost of preferred stock. Consequently, most manufacturing firms have little to no preferred stock outstanding.

On the other hand, utilities make broad use of preferred stock because it bolsters the equity base of the utility without diluting the common stock ownership. This larger equity base allows a utility to take on additional borrowing. The cost of the preferred stock is passed on to consumers of the utility's services in the rate base.

COST OF PREFERRED STOCK: ALTERNATIVE TECHNIQUE

Similar to the historical cost of debt discussed previously, some firms consider a historical cost of preferred stock. When preferred stock is issued, it is issued with a dividend rate tied to the stated par value of the stock. This rate is the historical cost of preferred stock. In this example, if the preferred stock sold for $50 and had a $50 par value the resulting historical cost of preferred stock would be 8.00% (calculated per Equation 13.6).

$$K_{ps} = D_{ps} / P_{ps}$$
$$K_{ps} = \$4.00 / \$50.00$$
$$K_{ps} = 8.00\% \qquad\qquad (13.6)$$

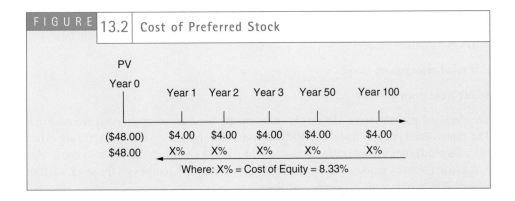

FIGURE 13.2 | Cost of Preferred Stock

Over time, the market price of the stock fluctuates and the resulting cost rises or falls in reaction to the underlying preferred stock price movement. By using today's stock price of $48, a more current cost of preferred stock of 8.33% is attained and reflects the opportunity cost of preferred stock funds. Although preferred stock is not a common form of financing for most non-utility firms, common stock or common equity generally provides the largest form of financing for most corporations.

COST OF COMMON EQUITY

Common equity represents the major component of a corporation's balance sheet. The most common equity items from a balance sheet include the following.

- Common stock at par value

- Additional capital paid in excess of par

- Treasury stock

- Retained earnings

- Numerous accounting adjustments

The first two items, *common stock at par* and *additional capital paid in excess of par*, represent the original amounts for which the common stock was issued. *Treasury stock* reflects amounts paid to repurchase shares of stock that are no longer outstanding but remain available for issuance. *Retained earnings* include cumulative earnings in the corporation that were retained (i.e., not paid out as dividends) in the corporation.

The numerous accounting adjustments include such things as cumulative foreign translation adjustments, certain employee compensation involving shares of stock, and other more recently adopted accounting conventions that recognize the equity impact of certain quasi-income or expense items without requiring those items to be recorded through net income. The cost of equity encompasses all aspects of the common equity section.

CALCULATING THE COST OF COMMON EQUITY

When calculating the cost of debt (or the interest), the contractual obligations of interest and the repayment of principal make determining the cost of debt a straightforward and explicit exercise. Common equity has no explicit return obligations. Instead, implicit investor expectations determine stock prices, which in turn drive the cost of common equity. The cost of equity represents the opportunity cost of equity capital. To accomplish this estimate, we attempt to understand what a reasonable investor should expect when they make an investment in the equity of a particular firm.

The following three approaches to calculating the cost of common equity are reviewed in subsequent material.

- Dividend growth model

- Capital asset pricing model

- Arbitrage pricing theory

The dividend growth model (DGM) is an internally focused, company-specific measure. The capital asset pricing model (CAPM) and the arbitrage pricing theory (APT) are externally focused, company-specific measures. The CAPM considers the stock's return relationship to the stock market's return as a whole, whereas APT focuses on the stock's return relationship to numerous economic variables.

All three techniques are discussed in the following section. The strengths and weaknesses of all three are highlighted. Although carrying its own shortcomings, the CAPM is the recommended approach for estimating the cost of common equity.

Dividend Growth Model

Most corporations have little activity in the common equity market. Their activity is limited to issuing (selling) common stock and repurchasing stock if the corporation has an ongoing share repurchase program. The stock market's primary purpose is to facilitate secondary trading or trading between individuals (or between their financial institutions, such as mutual funds, insurance companies, and banks).

If a company chooses to pay dividends, those dividends are generally the only ongoing cash flow contact a company has with its common equity holder. As a common equity stockholder, the investor also participates in the growth of the corporation into perpetuity. The growth in increased sales, profits, and cash flow is forwarded to the common equity investor through higher dividends (which result in higher share prices). The DGM is an application of the perpetuity notion discussed in Chapter 3, where we solved for the value of a perpetuity with a stream of steadily growing cash flows (calculated per Equation 13.7).

$$P_{cs} = D_{cs1}/(K_{cs} - G)\qquad\qquad\text{(13.7)}$$

Where:

$$P_{cs} = \text{Price of common stock}$$
$$D_{cs1} = \text{Common stock dividend for year 1}$$
$$K_s = \text{Cost of common stock}$$
$$G = \text{Growth rate}$$

Rearranging terms, we arrive at Equation 13.8.

$$P_{cs}(K_{cs} - G) = D_{cs1}$$
$$(K_{cs} - G) = D_{cs1}/P_{cs}\qquad\qquad\text{(13.8)}$$
$$K_{cs} = (D_{cs1}/P_{cs}) + G$$

The DGM approach to estimating the cost of equity compares today's stock price with the anticipated level of dividend payments. To apply this to Hershey's specific case, Hershey raised its dividend to $0.93 for the coming year. The stock price as of December 2005 was $55.25, and our estimated growth rate is 7.1%. Hershey's cost of common equity capital is 8.8%, calculated per Equation 13.9.

$$K_s = (\$0.93/\$55.25) + 7.1\%$$
$$= 1.7\% + 7.1\%\qquad\qquad\text{(13.9)}$$
$$= 8.8\%$$

The 8.8% cost of equity is comprised of a 1.7% dividend yield and 7.1% expected growth (see material following). The dividend, stock price, and resulting dividend yield can be observed, whereas the growth rate must be estimated.

Figure 13.3 points out the concept behind the DGM. The share of stock pays a $0.93 dividend at the end of year 1. After the assumed 7.1% growth, the year 2 dividend is $1.00 and the year 3 is $1.07. By year 50, the dividend per share has grown to $26.80, assuming

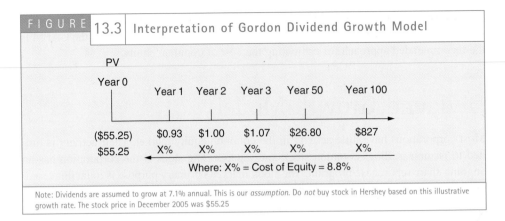

Note: Dividends are assumed to grow at 7.1% annual. This is our *assumption*. Do *not* buy stock in Hershey based on this illustrative growth rate. The stock price in December 2005 was $55.25

a 7.1% growth rate. By year 100, the dividend has grown to more than $827 per share and is still growing into perpetuity.

The DGM finds the discount rate that equates the future projected dividends (which are projected to infinity) to today's stock price. This process is similar to finding an internal rate of return. Although it sounds as if the mathematics should be more complicated, Equation 13.8 provides the discount rate.

The estimated growth rate is a major component when applying the DGM. The estimated growth rate represents the future growth in dividends. However, the future growth in dividends is a function of the underlying growth of the business. That is, the dividend growth rate is tied to the growth exhibited in sales, income, cash flow, and so on.

There are at least three different approaches to estimating the long-term growth rate. This growth rate can be estimated by calculating an internal growth rate, calculating historical growth rates, or observing management's stated growth objective if it is publicly disclosed via the annual report or other public statements.

The *internal growth rate* is a financial ratio that is an extension of return on retained earnings. The *return on retained earnings* is similar to the return on equity except for the distortional effects of stock issuance and repurchases and the fact that the effects of accounting adjustments have been eliminated. The internal growth rate considers a firm's profitability, tax rate, asset efficiency, capital structure, and dividend policy. The internal growth rate assumes that all of the underlying relationships (profitability, and so on) remain constant or have minimal fluctuation. The internal growth rate is calculated per Equation 13.10.

$$G = RORE \times (1 - DPR) \tag{13.10}$$

Where:

$$G = \text{Internal growth rate}$$
$$RORE = \text{Return on retained earnings}$$
$$= (\text{normalized income}_t / \text{retained earnings}_{(t-1)})$$
$$DPR = \text{Dividend payout ratio}$$
$$= (\text{dividends per share}_t / EPS_t)$$

Return on retained earnings is calculated as 2005 normalized income divided by the 2004 retained earnings. The *dividend payout ratio* is calculated as 2005 dividends paid per common share divided by 2005 basic normalized earnings per common share.

In Hershey's case, the 2005 internal growth rate is calculated per Equation 13.11 ($ millions, except per-share values).

$$G = RORE \times (1 - DPR)$$
$$G = (\$567/\$4,836) \times (1 - (\$0.93/\$2.38))$$
$$G = 11.7\% \times (1 - 0.391)$$
$$G = 7.1\%$$

(13.11)

Based on a tax-rate-adjusted 2005 net (normalized) income, the internal growth rate appears to be in the mid-range of the historical growth rate of sales, of the normalized income per share (Table 7.5 from Chapter 7), and of the dividends per share (DPS) for both short-term and long-term growth rates (see table following).

	GROWTH RATES	
	2004/2005 (%)	2000–2005 (%)
Sales	9.2	4.8
Normalized income per share	14.4	14.3
Dividends per share	11.4	11.5

The internal growth rate (7.1%) is bracketed by long-term and short-term sales growth. Finally, the third technique is to observe statements made by senior executives. However, Hershey's management team has been silent regarding the targeted growth rate in dividends. Consequently, after we consider all of the information cited previously and apply our best judgment (led by the concern over the limited sales growth) we use the 7.1% internal growth rate as our dividend growth rate.

The DGM approach to estimating the cost of equity has some appeal to management because it directly links the strategic plan, goals, and objectives to the cost of capital (in addition to being easy to calculate). However, if a company does not pay a dividend or has an erratic growth rate the DGM becomes less useful in estimating the cost of equity. Alternative approaches must be employed in these cases.

Capital Asset Pricing Model

The CAPM approach to estimating the cost of equity, as discussed in Chapter 6, compares the shareholder return (stock price appreciation plus dividends) to the return of the market (i.e., S&P 500). From the Cost of Capital survey, 81% of the companies use CAPM to estimate their cost of equity. It is our recommended approach as well. The cost of common stock (K_{cs}), or the cost of equity, via the CAPM approach can be represented as in Equation 13.12.

$$K_{cs} = R_f + \beta (K_m - R_f)$$

(13.12)

Where:

R_f = Risk-free rate of return

β = Beta (statistical relationship, discussed in material following)

$(K_m - R_f)$ = Market's return in excess of the risk-free rate

By using the CAPM, the cost of equity is estimated from a "risk-free" base level and adjusted for risk relative to the stock market. It provides a relative stock return, which is aligned to the overall return of the market.

Since 1926, the market has had on average an excess return of 4.89% more than the risk-free long-term government bond rate. To illustrate the use of the CAPM for Hershey Foods Corporation, we have Equation 13.13.

$$K_{cs} = R_f + \beta (K_m - R_f) \tag{13.13}$$

Where:

$$R_f = 5.35\% \text{ (15 May 2006, from previous)}$$
$$\beta = 0.70 \text{ (Value Line, December of 2005)}$$
$$(K_m - R_f) = 4.89\% \text{ (trend since 1926)}$$
$$K_{cs} = 5.35\% + 0.70 (4.89\%)$$
$$K_{cs} = 8.77\%$$

From the CAPM, the cost of equity capital is estimated at 8.77%.

Issues Related to the Capital Asset Pricing Model

Estimating the cost of equity via the CAPM has some appeal because it employs an independent statistical relationship between the individual stock and the stock market. CAPM alleviates the need to estimate a long-term growth rate for the firm. Companies can use CAPM whether or not they have a dividend or a steady stable growth in that dividend. However, CAPM entails issues related to the following.

- Risk-free rate
- Beta calculation
- Excess return of the market
- Correlation between one stock and the market
- Conceptual matters

Each of these areas is discussed in the sections following. Although the CAPM approach remains the recommended estimation technique, anyone employing CAPM should be aware of these issues.

RISK-FREE RATE

You face many choices when selecting the risk-free rate. Should the rate be based on short-term U.S. Treasury bills (T-bills), long-term U.S. Treasury bonds (T-bonds), or some other measure of risk-free return? We advocate that the risk-free rate should be measured via the long-term U.S. T-bonds. Long-term government bonds incorporate the market's expectations about short-term (T-bill) interest rates and are more indicative of a risk-free rate of return (with a similar "long-term maturity" time frame as a share of stock, or the underlying life of the investment). Consequently, our recommendation is to use the long-term U.S. T-bond rate as the risk-free rate.

The Cost of Capital survey found a wide dispersion of the risk-free rate. A third of the companies base the risk-free rate on 10-year U.S. T-bonds, another third use 10- to 30-year U.S. T-bonds, and the last third use a number of other measures. The 30-year U.S. T-bond risk-free rate was the most commonly (40%) used basis by financial advisors.

BETA CALCULATION

Numerous variations are used to calculate the specific returns that underlie the beta calculation. For example, the number of years (three years versus five years), the period of return (weekly versus monthly), and the style of return (annual versus annualized) all affect the specific value of beta. In the Cost of Capital survey, the authors compared betas from Value Line, Bloomberg, and S&P. All three services calculate betas slightly differently. The Cost of Capital survey found that the range of estimated betas over these three sources differed by 0.42 on average for the 29 corporations included in their study.

EXCESS RETURN OF THE MARKET

Excess return measures the amount the market's return exceeds the risk-free rate of return. In the CAPM, it is intended to be a forward-looking measure based on an expected excess return. However, many companies approximate an expected excess return by looking at the historical excess returns. Again, it matters whether the risk-free rate is a short-term U.S. T-bill, long-term U.S. T-bond, or some other rate. It also matters if the return is the average of annual returns or whether it is a compound annual growth rate (CAGR, as calculated in Chapter 3). Finally, it also depends on the time period used to develop historical excess returns.

Repeating the data that we used in Chapter 6, you will recall that from 1925 to 2005,

The following table represents the 1925-to-2005 CAGR for each investment and the resulting excess returns.

INVESTMENT	CAGR (%)	EXCESS RETURN (%)
Large company stocks	10.36	N/A
Long-term Treasury bonds	5.47	4.89
U.S. Treasury bills	3.71	6.65

The excess returns were calculated by subtracting the CAGRs of the bonds and bills from the CAGR of the stocks.

Some argue that the period of 1925 to 2005 is irrelevant today. Those same people advocate a shorter time frame. Examining a variety of time periods over the more recent past 30 years, indicates the following:

- The average annual excess returns tend to be higher than a CAGR excess return for either U.S. treasury bills or bonds.

- The annual excess returns are higher when using U.S. treasury bills than bonds due to the liquidity premium.

- Over the past 30 years, the excess return has decreased when using U.S. treasury bonds, but has fluctuated when using U.S. treasury bills.

Historical excess returns vary between 1.48% and 8.55%, depending on the specific viewpoint of the best way to derive the historical excess returns.

Our recommendation for the excess return premium is based on the CAGR of large company stocks and long-term U.S. T-bonds from 1925 to the most recent year. The CAGR of the long-term government bonds is subtracted from the CAGR of large company stocks to yield an excess return of 4.89%. This return is an appropriate proxy for future expectations of an excess return. The market's excess return based on a shorter time period becomes arbitrary.

The past 80 years have seen many different economic events, from the depression to booms, stagnation, and the 2000 "bubble burst" and through to general recovery. For consistency with our prior recommendation, long-term government bonds should be used as the risk-free rate. Extending the "maturity" time frame argument, excess returns as measured by the CAGR provides long-term growth rates to match the long-term aspects of stocks. This technique/ assumption of choice will greatly impact the resulting cost of equity and cost of capital.

Correlation Between One Stock and the Market   A graphical representation of the CAPM as shown in Figure 13.4 illustrates a relationship between the excess return of a stock and the excess return of the market. Figure 13.4 was first introduced in Chapter 6. We have plotted market returns on the x-axis (independent variable) and the returns of The Hershey Company on the y-axis (dependent variable). We calculated the regression of the returns of Hershey on the market returns. The slope of the regression calculated in Figure 13.4 is the beta of the equity returns of Hershey. For the time period 2001 through 2005 (the time of the new CEO), using monthly returns, the beta of Hershey was 0.46 – relatively low. As previously discussed in Chapter 6, the higher the stock's beta the more sensitive the stock's excess return is to market's excess return.

Another statistical relationship is measured by correlation (R), also known as the "goodness of fit" between the two variables. The coefficient of determination (R^2) ranges between 0.00 and 1.00, with a measure of 1.00 indicating an exact relationship between the two variables.

Figure 13.4 presents actual data between the excess returns of Hershey and the excess returns of the stock market as measured by the S&P 500. Figure 13.4 was constructed by comparing weekly excess returns over a three-year period. Because the returns were calculated on a weekly basis, some observations produced small (positive and negative) weekly returns.

Figure 13.4 shows a positive relationship between the excess return of Hershey's stock and the stock market. The relationship is dispersed, and the graph in Figure 13.4 has a weak R^2 of 0.22. This is not unique to Hershey. Few individual stocks have an R^2 greater than 0.30. There are other variables that effect a stock's value and returns. The general movement of the stock market is only a portion of that relationship.

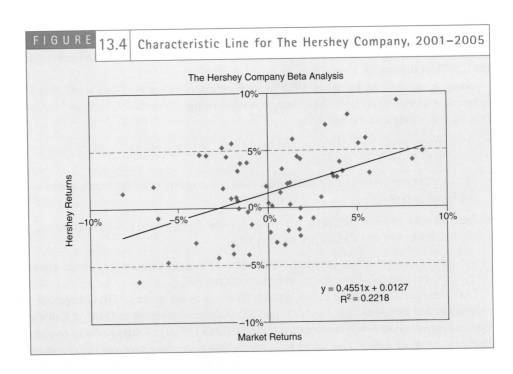

FIGURE 13.4   Characteristic Line for The Hershey Company, 2001–2005

The Hershey Company Beta Analysis

y = 0.4551x + 0.0127
R^2 = 0.2218

Conceptual Issues The CAPM remains a conceptually useful framework and an approach that is easy to apply when estimating the cost of equity. There are some additional conceptual issues with CAPM. CAPM assumes (1) that all markets are efficient, with all investors having access to the same information with the same expectations, (2) that all investors are risk adverse, rational, and view securities the same way, and (3) that there are no transaction costs or taxes and that there are no restrictions on securities.

Numerous studies have called into question the validity of CAPM. Two issues have been forwarded that from a theoretical view may invalidate CAPM. First, for CAPM to be true the regression line must always pass through the origin. That implies that when the market's excess return is zero so is the stock's excess return. Studies have found that the intercept term is significantly different from zero, which invalidates CAPM.

Second, for CAPM to be true no other factors can explain a security's return. Evidence shows that firm size, dividend yield, price/earnings ratios, and seasonality can explain much of the security's return that is unexplained by CAPM. This also invalidates CAPM.

In June of 1992, Eugene Fama and Kenneth R. French published "The Cross-Section of Expected Stock Returns" (*Journal of Finance*, pp. 427-465). The study tested more than 2,000 stocks and failed to find a significant relationship between the historic betas and historic returns during the period 1963 to 1990. Although this study called into question the historical results of CAPM, it did not comment on the validity of CAPM as an expectational model. APT is an approach that has been more recently popularized in the financial literature and may some day replace CAPM as the recommended approach to estimating the cost of equity.

Arbitrage Pricing Theory

APT was first presented in December of 1976 by Stephen Ross in "The Arbitrage Theory of Capital Asset Pricing" (*Journal of Economic Theory*, pp. 341-360). The theory suggests that a stock's return is a function of many economic factors. In general terms, the cost of equity (K_{cs}) via the APT approach can be expressed as in Equation 13.14.

$$K_{cs} = R_f + \beta_1 F_1 + \beta_2 F_2 + \dots + \beta_n F_n \qquad (13.14)$$

Where:

$$R_f = \text{Risk-free rate of return}$$
$$\beta_{1,\,2,\,n} = \text{Betas (statistical relationships)}$$
$$F_{1,\,2,\,n} = \text{Economic factors}$$

Economic factors to be used in APT are currently a topic of research. Although work is ongoing, the following economic factors are leading candidates for inclusion in the APT.

- Unanticipated changes in inflation

- Unanticipated changes in industrial production

- Unanticipated changes in risk premiums

- Unanticipated changes in the difference between interest rates for short-term and long-term securities

Additional research needs to be conducted on the APT. After the research and simplification, APT may be the recommended tool for estimating the cost of equity. However, until then the recommended approach for calculating the cost of equity remains CAPM.

Cost of Equity: Summary

The cost of debt is an explicit cost (interest expense), whereas the cost of equity is implicit. In the previous sections, we reviewed three common techniques for estimating the cost of common stock or equity capital. Each technique has certain limitations and interpretations of required assumptions, which render each technique less than perfectly applicable. These are summarized as follows.

- *Dividend growth model (DGM):* Most applicable to firms that pay dividends with a steady, stable growth rate underlying those dividends. Subject to wide variations in expected growth rate assumptions.

- *Capital asset pricing model (CAPM):* Subject to wide interpretations and calculation of major components such as the risk-free rate, beta, and market risk premium.

- *Arbitrage pricing model:* Requires additional research, refinement, and simplification before meriting wide application.

Our recommendation remains: Estimate the cost of equity via the CAPM.

Cost of New Debt and Equity

For new bonds, preferred stock, and common stock, issuance costs must be considered and will slightly increase the cost of each capital source. For debt, new bonds are typically issued close to or at par value or the maturity value of $1,000. The stated interest rate is the pre-tax cost of debt. For example, a 10-year bond issued at $1,000 and paying $100 of interest each year before returning its $1,000 of principal costs 10% pre-tax and 6% after tax (assuming a 40% tax rate). If there is a 3% issuance fee, the proceeds are only $970 (instead of $1,000). The cost of debt is recalculated based on this lower initial value, resulting in a pre-tax cost of debt of 10.50% and 6.30% after tax (assuming a 40% tax rate).

For preferred stock and common stock, the price per share is reduced by the issuance cost per share. Equation 13.4 (for preferred stock) and Equation 13.9 (for common stock) are adjusted to reflect the price of a share of stock less the issuance cost per share, calculated per Equation 13.15 for preferred stock and Equation 13.16 for common stock.

$$\text{Preferred Stock } K_{ps} = D_{ps}/(P_{ps} - C_{ps}) \qquad (13.15)$$

Where:

K_{ps} = Cost of preferred stock
D_{ps} = Dividend
P_{ps} = Price of preferred stock
C_{ps} = Cost per share to issue preferred stock

$$\text{Common Stock } K_{cs} = (D_{cs1}/(Pcs - C_{cs})) + G \qquad (13.16)$$

Where:

K_{cs} = Cost of common stock
D_{cs1} = Dividend for year 1
P_{cs} = Price of common stock
C_{cs} = Cost per share to issue common stock
G = Growth rate

To illustrate using preferred stock, if a company issues four million preferred shares to raise approximately $200 million, the company may pay 2- to 3% issuance costs. The final specific issuance fee would be a negotiation point. At a 3% issuance cost, this would be $6.0 million of issuance costs ($1.50 per share). The adjusted cost of the preferred stock would be as calculated in Equation 13.17.

$$K_{ps} = D_{ps}/(P_{ps} - C_{ps})$$
$$K_{ps} = \$4.00/(\$50.00 - \$1.50) \qquad (13.17)$$
$$K_{ps} = 8.25\%$$

This refinement provides a better estimate of newly issued preferred stock and is applicable when the DGM is employed to estimate the cost of common equity. If CAPM is the preferred approach for measuring the cost of newly issued equity, the issuance cost (as a percentage of proceeds) should be tacked on to the newly issued equity.

Capital Component Costs: Summary

In the preceding pages, we discussed the cost of debt, preferred stock, and common stock. We also discussed common alternatives used in practice. The following summarize our recommendations.

- *Cost of debt:* Current market cost of debt after tax.

- *Preferred stock:* Cost based on current market value of preferred stock.

- *Common stock:* CAPM using the long-term U.S. T-bond (Treasury bond) rate as the risk-free rate and a market risk premium based on the large company stock historical relationship with U.S. T-bonds.

The next section discusses the appropriate weights to use in finding the WACC.

Weighting the Capital Components

At this point, the costs of each capital component (debt, preferred stock, and common stock) were addressed individually. The final step in estimating the cost of capital is to weight each component and calculate the WACC. Two customary methods are book-value weights and market-value weights.

Book-value weights are based on the capital structure represented by the balance sheet. For Hershey Foods as of December 31, 2005, the balance sheet included debt of $1,762 million (short-term debt, current portion of long-term debt, and long-term debt) and equity of $1,021 million for a total capital pool of $2,783 million. Hershey has no outstanding preferred stock. Consequently, debt represents 63.3% of the capital structure and equity represents 36.7%.

Book-value equity is an accounting concept that primarily keeps track of earnings retained in the business over the years, along with the original level of equity capital injected into the firm net of any stock repurchase. Most of Hershey's equity capital was injected in the 1920s, with a small issue in 1984. However, from the early 1990s Hershey bought back almost $4 billion of its stock on the open market. As we saw, Hershey's stockholders' equity section actually decreased in 2005 due to the stock repurchases offset by the additional earnings retained in the business. The book value of equity is subject to numerous accounting adjustments.

The basis for *market-value weights*, the market value of debt and equity, is not subject to the mechanics of accounting. The market value of equity is determined by the total capitalization of the outstanding shares of stock. In this case, Hershey has 240.5 million shares of stock outstanding at $55.25 per share for a market value of $13,288 million (compared to its book value of $1,021 million).

A current stockholder of Hershey Foods demands that Hershey earn the cost of equity 8.77% (as calculated by CAPM) on the current investment value of $55.25, not on the $4.25 book value per share ($1,021 million book value of equity divided by 240.5 million shares outstanding). The major difference between book- and market-based weights is the value of equity. In the case of Hershey Foods, capital structure weights ($ millions) are as follows.

	BOOK WEIGHTS		MARKET WEIGHTS	
	Amount	%	Amount	%
Debt	$1,762	63.3	$1,762	11.7
Equity	1,021	36.7	13,288	88.3
Total	$2,783	100.0	$15,050	100.0

In this example, the market value of the debt is similar to the book value of debt. The majority of Hershey's debt is privately held. Obtaining current market value of that debt would be almost impossible. The impact of using market or book values for the debt is inconsequential. Therefore, two simplifying approaches may be reasonable and not materially distorting: (1) extrapolate market value to book value relationships of traded debt to the privately placed debt or (2) simply assume that the market value of private debt is similar to the book value of the private debt (as we did here). Our recommendation remains to use current market values where available.

In addition, most corporations have a long-term strategic plan that includes projected financial statements (as advocated in Chapter 9). A corporation may also have as a part of its strategic plan (or separate from it) a long-term financing plan that may include debt issuance, debt repayment, equity issuance, equity repurchase, and so on. A corporation may establish some long-term goals or objectives surrounding its capital structure. This is called a *target capital structure*, which should be based on the future market values.

However, often when a firm has a targeted capital structure it is "book based" and not market based. That is, a corporation such as Hershey may set an internal objective of establishing a capital structure of 40% debt and 60% equity because it can better control the book weights. It is always better to consider market weights rather than book weights.

In this regard, current market-based weights are better than current or targeted book weights. However, if a market-based capital structure is a firm's objective and it is diligently working toward that objective this target market-based capital structure should be used as the appropriate weighting structure. (Note: This target capital structure is hypothetical for illustrative purposes and does not reflect an objective that Hershey may or may not have.) The four potential weighting structures indicate the following capital structures.

	CURRENT		TARGET	
	Book (%)	Market (%)	Book (%)	Market (%)
Debt	63.3	11.7	40.0	12.0(?)
Equity	36.7	88.3	60.0	88.0(?)

Our recommendation is to use a target capital structure if that target is based on targeted market values. If the target capital structure is based on book weights (as most objectives are) or does not exist, the current market-based capital structure weights should be used.

Cost of Capital Application

The WACC (or simply, cost of capital) brings together the individual costs of each capital source. The individual costs are weighted by the capital structure techniques discussed in the previous section.

Table 13.6 outlines Hershey's capital structure on a current market-weight basis (i.e., a total capital structure of $15,050 million, with 11.7% in debt and 88.3% in equity). Hershey's debt on an after-tax basis costs 4.01% (current market), whereas equity (using the CAPM) costs 8.77%. The resulting cost of capital is 8.21%. If Hershey had preferred stock, that would be inserted and considered in a similar fashion. The following table summarizes and compares other weightings in practice and the resulting cost of capital.

	CURRENT WEIGHTS		TARGET WEIGHTS	
	Book (%)	Market (%)	Book (%)	Market (%)
Debt (4.01%)	63.3	11.7	40.0	12.0(?)
Equity (8.77%)	36.7	88.3	60.0	88.0(?)
Cost of Capital	5.76	8.21	6.87	8.20

Hershey's recommended cost of capital is 8.21% (or simply 8%). In calculating the cost of capital, it is easy to get carried away with a false sense of precision. Given all of the assumptions about the capital structure, future growth rates, beta, the market's excess return, and so on (as well as the ever-changing nature of the precise capital structure and stock price), the degree of precision must be carefully balanced. Once again, judgment must enter into the final recommendation.

Financial Structure

This section develops an overview of financial structure. *Financial structure* indicates the amount of debt and equity used in financing a firm. For any financial structure, debt is always a less expensive form of capital than equity because the cost of debt is tax deductible and because in the case of bankruptcy debt holders have priority over equity holders. However, debt also comes with fixed explicit costs. Every dollar of debt increases the risk of the firm and the cost of all financing. With too much debt and wavering business conditions, a firm may be forced into bankruptcy.

Without going into many of the theoretical details underlying financial structure theory, we represent the traditional financial structure in Table 13.7 and Figure 13.5. The X axis shows debt as a pecentage of the capital (debt + equity) structure. The Y axis lists the after-tax cost as a percentage. The graph itself contains three lines: the cost of debt (the lowest

TABLE 13.6	Hershey's Cost of Capital Market Basis Weights		
	% OF TOTAL	AFTER-TAX COST(%)	WEIGHTED COST(%)
Debt[a] $1,762	11.70	4.01	0.47
Equity[b] $13,288	88.30	8.77	7.74
Total	100.00		8.21

[a]The market value of the debt is assumed to be the same as the book value of the debt.
[b]The market value of the equity is calculated as $55.25 (price per share as of 31 December, 2005) times 240.5 million shares outstanding.

TABLE 13.7	Capital Structure Theory: Three Structures		
	% OF TOTAL	AFTER-TAX COST %	WEIGHTED COST %
Structure 1			
Debt	0	4.0	0.0
Equity	100	11.0	11.0
Capital	100		11.0
Structure 2			
Debt	35	4.5	1.6
Equity	65	13.0	8.4
Capital	100		10.0
Structure 3			
Debt	50	6.0	3.0
Equity	50	18.0	9.0
Capital	100		12.0

line), the cost of equity (the highest line), and the resulting cost of capital (the middle line). Each is discussed below.

The cost of debt for a corporation is similar to the cost of personal debt. The more debt you have the riskier you are and the higher the cost of debt. For an individual, the least expensive form of debt is a mortgage. It is a form of secured debt collateralized by your house, and it is tax deductible. However, a mortgage can only be used to borrow a limited percentage of your house's fair market value. Personally, it is your least expensive financing source.

After your mortgage, the next least expensive debt financing is available through a home equity loan. The home equity loan is collateralized by additional fair market value of equity left in your house beyond the primary mortgage. Once again, a home equity loan has a significant advantage because the interest payments are generally tax deductible. After the home equity loan, educational loans may provide the next least costly form of debt financing. Automobile loans secured by your automobile, unsecured personal loans, and credit card loans are additional sources of personal borrowing (all with increasing costs and no tax deductions). If an individual needs to borrow beyond this level, a visit may be necessary to secondary and tertiary lenders at dramatically higher interest costs.

These same parameters apply in concept to a corporation (represented by the cost-of-debt line in Figure 13.5). However, any interest expense is generally tax deductible for a

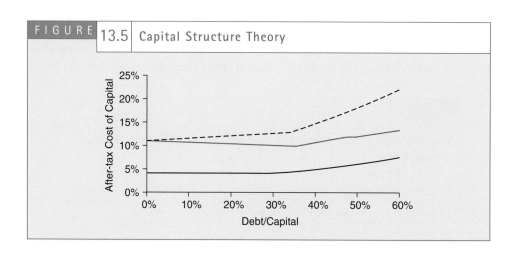

FIGURE 13.5	Capital Structure Theory

corporation. Up to some point, the cost of debt is relatively flat for a corporation. As represented in Figure 13.5, somewhere between 25% and 30% debt begins to cost slightly more. As the corporation takes on more debt, its marginal cost continues to increase.

The cost of equity begins with a slight upward trend. The first dollar of debt and each subsequent dollar make the corporation a bit riskier. This added risk is reflected as a higher cost of equity. Note that for all capital structures the cost of debt is always less than the cost of equity for any given financial structure.

The cost-of-capital line is a mathematical representation of the individual cost of debt and cost of equity appropriately weighted for the total capital structure. To illustrate the cost-of-capital line, we review the three financial structures found on Table 13.7 in the sections that follow.

FINANCIAL STRUCTURE 1

The first financial structure is for an all-equity firm. This firm uses no debt and consequently its cost of capital is equal to the cost of equity (11.0%). The cost of debt is at its lowest level, but there is no debt outstanding.

FINANCIAL STRUCTURE 2

At the second financial structure, the firm has 35% debt and 65% equity. Note that the debt and equity both cost more under this structure than under the first structure. However, by moving to this financial structure from the first financial structure the corporation substitutes less expensive debt (4.5%,in this structure) for more expensive equity (11.0%, in the first structure). Weighting the individual cost results in a 10.0% cost of capital. The second capital structure takes advantage of the less expensive cost of debt and results in a lower cost of capital.

FINANCIAL STRUCTURE 3

At the third financial structure, the firm's financial structure is evenly split as 50% debt and 50% equity. Note that the debt and equity both cost more under this structure than under the second structure. Unfortunately, due to the higher cost of both debt and equity the resulting cost of capital is 12.0% (which is higher than either of the two previous structures).

NOTES ON FINANCIAL STRUCTURE

This analysis of the structures suggests that there is an optimum financial structure that minimizes the cost of capital. In today's cost reduction environment, businesses press to do more with less. Most organizations have implemented cost reduction programs. Everyone is striving to wring the costs out of every step in the supply chain and the support functions. Contracts with suppliers are renegotiated to reduce costs. We "beat up" other suppliers and play off relationships to save one-quarter of one cent on envelopes or other office supplies.

Employees are asked to take lower pay raises or to forego raises or even to take pay cuts. The cost of benefit packages and health insurance is now shared with employees. All of this is done in the name of cost reduction. Although reducing all explicit costs within a firm is important, the most widely used commodity in any organization is capital. The chief financial officer's responsibility is to minimize the cost of capital (structure 2 in this case). The impact is major in the valuation of the firm!

General Theories of Capital Structure

There are two general theories related to capital structure: trade-off theory and pecking order theory. *Trade-off theory* considers the tax deductibility of interest from debt financing a strong motivator for increasing leverage. However, the increasing present value of the cost of financial distress (bankruptcy) motivates the manager to limit the amount of debt financing. The "trade-off" is what the manager needs to constantly balance. In Table 13.7, trade-off theory leads the manager to carefully balance the tax deductibility of the cost of debt against the likelihood of bankruptcy. In Figure 13.5, 35% provides an optimum trade-off.

In general, firms with high growth opportunities use less debt because financial distress could destroy the realization of those potentials. Similarly, firms in the pharmaceutical industry have low debt ratios even though their book profit ratios appear to be above average. However, risks of unsuccessful efforts at creating new profitable drugs and risks of suits resulting from adverse drug effects after years of use are substantial.

In general, intangible assets are subject to erosion in financial distress, and therefore debt is avoided by firms with a high ratio of intangible assets to physical assets. *Pecking order theory* says that companies will first use sources of internally generated funds to finance their activities, then net debt financing (net of repayments), and finally new equity financing. Pecking order theory is strongly supported by historical data on the sources and uses of funds by nonfinancial corporations in the United States.

We compiled data for the years 1985 through 2005 from the Federal Reserve Flow of Funds publications. We present the last five years of these data in Table 13.8. We found that internal financing generally accounted for 86% of total sources and uses of funds on

TABLE	13.8	Sources and Uses of Funds Non–farm, Nonfinancial Corporate Business ($ Billions)				
		2001	2002	2003	2004	2005
Line						
36	Net funds raised in markets	$173.3	$(16.6)	$ 26.9	$ 33.4	$ (76.7)
58	– Financing gap	156.5	18.4	(0.8)	47.0	(102.3)
	Net working capital and other	16.8	(35.0)	27.7	(13.6)	25.6
11	+ Capital expenditures	800.4	737.1	751.5	861.0	925.3
	Total uses	**$817.2**	**$702.1**	**$779.2**	**$847.4**	**$ 950.9**
5	U.S. Internal funds, book	$632.5	$720.9	$765.5	$853.7	$1,051.3
7	+ Inventory valuation adjustment	11.3	(2.2)	(13.3)	(39.6)	(23.7)
	Internal financing	643.8	718.7	752.2	814.1	1,027.6
37	Net new equity issues	(48.1)	(41.6)	(57.8)	(141.1)	(366.0)
38	+ Credit market instruments	221.4	25.0	84.7	174.5	289.3
	External financing	173.3	(16.6)	26.9	33.4	(76.7)
	Total sources	**$817.1**	**$702.1**	**$779.1**	**$847.5**	**$ 950.9**
	Uses of funds					
	Capital expenditure	97.9%	105.0%	96.4%	101.6%	97.3%
	Net working capital and other	2.1%	–5.0%	3.6%	–1.6%	2.7%
	Sources					
	Internal financing	78.8%	102.4%	96.5%	96.1%	108.1%
	External financing	21.2%	–2.4%	3.5%	3.9%	–8.1%
	New equity	–5.9%	–5.9%	–7.4%	–16.6%	–38.5%
	New debt	27.1%	3.6%	10.9%	20.6%	30.4%

Source: Federal Reserve, "Flow of Funds Accounts of the United States," 9 March 2006, Table F.102.

average over the past 21 years. However, most recently internal financing accounted for at least 96% of the funds used in business.

Note that in 2005 net new equity issues actually saw a decline of $366 billion. This is because gross equity issuance was more than offset by stock repurchases and the reduction in equities resulting from mergers. In most years, financing from new equity was negative.

Our view is that trade-off theory and pecking order theory both help explain financial structure decision processes. Pecking order theory might be thought of as "a dynamic adjustment of capital structures to changing economic conditions and to the changing circumstances of individual firms." Internal financing accounts for a high percentage of the investment needs of firms. Internal financing in growing firms makes sense because investment requirements are high. As equity grows, a basis is established for obtaining debt financing under favorable terms. For more details, see Myers (1984).

Factors Affecting Financial Structure

The factors influencing capital structure decisions can be grouped under three major categories: economic environments, industry characteristics, and firm characteristics. These are discussed in the sections that follow.

ECONOMIC ENVIRONMENTS

The state of the economy is a major influence on financing decisions. In an economic expansion, the growth rates of gross domestic product (GDP) are positive and increasing. Corporate profits are also rising. Optimism is high and the spread between interest rates on low-rated versus higher-rated debt instruments narrows. Firms increase their investment outlays, and rising stock prices provide a favorable environment for merger activity.

The financial environment may perform a counterbalancing role. As noted previously, as the economy boomed in the late 1990s the interest rate policy of the Federal Reserve system was in the direction of raising rates to dampen speculative excesses. When the economy turned down in the year 2000, the Fed reversed its course. Although the recession was officially over by the end of 2001, its perceived fragility led to a continuation of low interest rates.

Financial economists generally hold that econometric attempts to forecast turning points in the economy or interest rates do not succeed. Nevertheless, the persistence of the federal funds rate at 1% as GDP growth continued led to changes in business financial policies. The following table shows that corporate bonds on the balance sheets of non-farm nonfinancial corporations between 2001 and 2005 grew from $2,578 billion to $3,007 billion, an increase of 3.9% (CAGR).

($ BILLIONS)	2001	2005	CAGR (%)
Corporate bonds	$2,578	$3,007	3.9
Bank loans	744	635	(3.9)

Source: Federal Reserve, "Flow of Funds Accounts of the United States," March 9, 2006, Table B.102.

In contrast, bank loans during the same period declined from $744 billion to $635 billion (a decrease of 3.9%). Financial officers of firms were shifting from the relatively shorter-term bank loans to the relatively longer-term bond issues. Financial managers were forecasting that interest rates would inevitably rise. This example demonstrates how the economic and financial environments influence financial structure decisions.

INDUSTRY CHARACTERISTICS

The sales of durable goods industries are subject to greater volatility than those of non-durable manufacturing industries. Hence, we will expect debt ratios for non-durable manufacturing to be higher than for all manufacturing. This is confirmed by the data. The ratio of long-term debt to stockholders' equity is 65% for non-durable manufacturing, whereas for all manufacturing the ratio is only 54%. (U.S. Census Bureau, April of 2004, pp. 4–5).

Traditionally, utility industries had high debt ratios. The products they sold were necessities, and as population and income grew the revenues of utilities could be forecast with a relatively high degree of accuracy. In recent years, the introduction of competition into regulated industries and investments by utilities outside their traditional businesses have decreased debt ratios. The telecommunications industry was deregulated by the act of 1996. In the booming economy, many new entries were made into the telecommunications industry financed considerably by debt. But overcapacity developed and debt ratios involuntarily increased with the erosion of both book and market values of telecom equities.

Table 13.9 presents a list of the highest and lowest industry rankings based on the ratios of debt to the book value of equity using the Ibbotson compilations. The highest ratios included utilities and amusement parks. We have already explained why the debt ratios for utility firms are high. The high ratio for amusement parks may be related to the consolidations that took place in the ownership of theme parks in the late 1990s, which were

TABLE 13.9	Highest and Lowest Industry Rankings (Debt-to-Book Value of Equity)			
SIC CODE	Sector	Industry	DEBT BV Equity(%)	DEBT MV Equity(%)
	Highest			
79	S	Amusement and Recreation Services	150.47	111.46
49	U	Electric, Gas, and Sanitary Utilities	144.33	103.09
22	M	Textile Mill Products	119.69	159.58
15	N	Building Construction	118.56	111.85
70	S	Hotels, Rooming Houses, and Other Lodging	117.19	127.38
26	M	Paper and Allied Products	115.36	107.81
	Lowest			
56	R	Apparel and Accessory Stores	9.42	5.61
47	T	Transportation Services	12.50	3.19
57	R	Home Furniture, Furnishings, and Equipment Stores	12.80	6.37
38	M	Measuring, Analyzing, and Controlling Equipment	14.91	7.24
87	S	Engineering and Related Services	17.99	10.28
73	S	Business Services	19.43	8.27
31	M	Leather and Leather Products	21.24	23.34

Source: Ibbotson Associates, *Cost of Capital 2003 Yearbook.*
Abbreviations: (M) manufacturing, (N) natural resources, (R) retail, (S) services, (T) transportation, (U) utilities.

financed with debt based on optimistic expectations of high growth in future revenues. Other high ratios may also be explained by the erosion of book equity values.

The lowest ratios of debt to equity in Table 13.9 are found in the service industries, which have relatively small investments in tangible assets. Apparel retail is highly competitive, with easy entry and considerable use of facilities and fixtures rental. Predictably, the ratios of debt to the market value of equities are generally lower than the ratios with the book value of equities in the denominator. This reflects market-to-book ratios of equity greater than 1. The highest and lowest industry rankings appear to be similar whether the book or market values of equities are employed.

These statistics on high- and low-debt-structure industries suggest some generalizations. Industries whose firms have large investments in tangible assets can obtain financing that can be secured by the assets. If financial distress should occur, tangible assets may have resale markets that provide substantial recoveries. Firms with intangible assets are likely to use less debt financing. The pharmaceutical industry has large investments in their scientific staff. These scientists can move to other firms with more favorable prospects. If the intangible assets are patent rights, they have limited protection periods. Firms whose intangible assets are based on competitive superiorities may find them eroded by industry changes or the competitive reactions of rivals.

In general, firms in service industries depend on individuals with specialized expertise. These assets have relatively high mobility and may move to other firms. Firms in wholesale and retail trade have relatively more of their assets in inventories and receivables. They rely more on short-term financing because their peak investment requirements may be seasonal and provide the basis for repayment as inventories and receivables decline. On the other hand, one of the classic cases in finance involves growing firms with increasing investments in inventories and receivables. As the sales of such firms grow, their required investments in working capital become permanent and hence these should be financed from equity (balanced with some long-term financing).

Another principle set forth by Titman (1984) and Titman and Wessels (1988) is that firms that sell durable goods have a need to provide assurance that the firm will be able to continue to service and provide replacement products. This limits their ability to incur debt, which can jeopardize their continuity.

INDIVIDUAL FIRM CHARACTERISTICS

Life cycle influences are strong. In the early stages, firms need to establish a foundation of equity financing. Growth generally requires some form of venture capital financing. If a firm succeeds and grows with profitability, financing from internal sources may predominate. Table 13.10 presents growth rates in revenues, net profits, and market capitalization for six leading firms: Cisco, Dell, Intel, Merck, Microsoft, and Wal-Mart. Merck is at the bottom of the list, reflecting the relative maturity of the pharmaceutical industry and its high risks of keeping the pipeline filled with successful new products. The performance of Wal-Mart is remarkable because it emerged as a leader in the very old industry of retail trade, using an innovative business model.

Table 13.11 also presents capital structure relationships for the six companies. In every case, the market value of their equity exceeds their book total assets. For all but Wal-Mart, their holdings of cash and equivalents far exceed their long-term debt. As a consequence, their net debt-to-equity ratios are negative (as shown in column 8). Four of the six make little use of supplier credit. The accounts payable of Dell represents 117% of shareholders' equity. For Wal-Mart, the ratio is 43%. The following section provides a cost of capital case study of the U.S. food industry.

TABLE 13.10	Compound Annual Growth Rates for Six Large Corporations ($ Millions)		
	1994	2003	CAGR[a](%)
Revenues			
Cisco Systems	$1,243	$18,878	35.3
Dell	3,475	41,444	31.7
Intel	11,521	30,141	11.3
Merck & Co.	14,970	22,486	4.6
Microsoft	3,753	32,187	27.0
Wal-Mart Stores	82,494	256,329	13.4
Net Profits			
Cisco Systems	315	4,287	33.7
Dell	149	2,645	37.6
Intel	2,563	5,641	9.2
Merck & Co	2,997	6,590	9.1
Microsoft	953	10,526	30.6
Wal-Mart Stores	2,681	8,861	14.2
Market Capitalization			
Cisco Systems	7,654	129,113	36.9
Dell	1,270	76,245	57.6
Intel	26,762	160,229	22.0
Merck & Co.	42,302	115,645	11.8
Microsoft	23,914	281,348	31.5
Wal-Mart Stores	57,884	229,561	16.5

[a]CAGR = Compound Annual Growth Rate = $(X_{2003}/X_{1994})^{(1/9)} - 1$
Source: Value Line.

Industry Group Analysis Application: Food Industry

The food industry is characterized by moderate sales growth, stable cash flows, and balanced investment in current and long-term assets. The industry is viewed favorably by lenders, but managers have varying impressions of leverage. There is a wide dispersion of the use of leverage within the industry. Table 13.12 presents the market-based capital structure for 12 food companies in the food processing industry. Four companies (Dean Foods, Kellogg, International Multifood, and Conagra) use a significant proportion of debt in their capital

TABLE 13.11	Capital Structure Relationships for Six Large Companies ($ Billions)								
	(1) TOTAL ASSETS	(2) MARKET CAP	(3) RATIO (2)/(1)	(4) CASH + EQUIV.	(5) LONG-TERM DEBT	(6) NET DEBT (5)-(4)	(7) STOCKHOLDERS' EQUITY	(8) DEBT/EQUITY (6)/(7)	(9) ACCTS. PAYABLE
Cisco Systems	$37	$129	3.49	$8	$0	$-8	$28	-29%	$1
Dell	19	76	4.01	5	1	-4	6	-67%	7
Intel	47	160	3.41	8	1	-7	38	-18%	2
Merck & Co.	41	116	2.82	4	5	1	16	6%	1
Microsoft	80	281	3.52	49	0	-49	61	-80%	2
Wal-Mart Stores	105	230	2.19	5	20[a]	15	44	34%	19

Source: Annual Reports and Value Line.

TABLE 13.12	Food Processing Industry Estimated Cost of Capital				
CURRENT MARKET	DEBT Weight%	Cost%	EQUITY Weight%	Cost%	COST OF CAPITAL%
Campbell Soup Co.	8.5	3.8	91.5	10.3	9.7
Conagra Foods	27.6	4.9	72.4	10.3	8.8
Dean Foods Company	43.6	5.4	56.4	9.7	7.8
General Mills	17.8	5.6	82.2	9.4	8.7
Heinz (HJ) Co.	12.8	5.6	87.2	9.7	9.2
Hershey Foods Corp.	9.8	4.5	90.2	9.4	8.9
International Multifoods	28.9	3.4	71.1	10.3	8.3
Kellogg Co.	34.3	7.5	65.7	9.7	9.0
McCormick & Co.	7.3	5.5	92.7	9.1	8.9
Sara Lee Corp.	15.7	5.0	84.3	10.0	9.2
Tootsie Roll Industries Inc.	0.3	4.3	99.7	9.4	9.4
Wrigley (Wm) Jr. Co.	0.0	0.0	100.0	10.8	10.8

Sources: Samuel C. Weaver, "Using Value Line to Estimate the Cost of Capital and Industry Capital Structure," *Journal of Financial Education*, Fall 2003, Volume 29, pp. 55–71.

structure, whereas companies (term inclusive of company divisions) such as Wrigley and Tootsie Roll use almost no debt.

Table 13.12 estimates the after-tax cost of debt for these companies, as well as their costs of equity. Finally, the cost of capital is estimated for each of these 12 firms. The graphs in Figure 13.6 illustrate the underlying capital structure and cost of capital components. The top graph shows the cost of debt (triangles), the estimated cost of equity using CAPM (diamonds), and resulting cost of capital (black squares).

The lower graph focuses on only the cost of capital, by narrowing the Y-axis range. From the lower graph, a downward slope in the cost of capital is casually noted (which suggests that there is still room for the industry to become more leveraged and to reduce its cost of capital further). Clearly, the food industry as a whole is "to the left" of the minimum cost of capital and has room to take on more debt to reduce the overall cost of capital.

Divisional/Project Hurdle Rates

Most corporations are complex entities comprised of numerous divisions or separate businesses. For example, General Electric lists the following segment operations in its 2005 annual report.

2005 Revenues	$Millions
Infrastructure	$41,803
Industrial	32,631
Healthcare	15,153
NBC Universal	14,689
Commercial finance	20,646
Consumer finance	19,416
Corporate items and eliminations	5,364
Consolidated Revenues	$149,702

Divisional hurdle rates are determined for each division as if it were a standalone business. For example, industry betas (as in Chapter 6) and industry financial structures are estimated for the

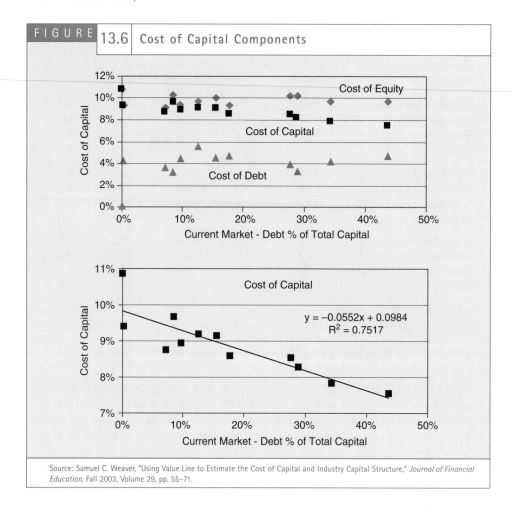

FIGURE 13.6 Cost of Capital Components

Source: Samuel C. Weaver, "Using Value Line to Estimate the Cost of Capital and Industry Capital Structure," *Journal of Financial Education*, Fall 2003, Volume 29, pp. 55–71.

various industry segments (infrastructure, industrial, healthcare, commercial finance, and so on). After estimating the industry betas and financial structure, a cost of capital can be calculated (as discussed previously) for each division. Each division will have its own estimated cost of capital, which is the minimal acceptable rate of return for that division. Consequently, a 10% returning project may be acceptable in one division but not in another [just as a 10% returning project might be acceptable in one industry (company) and not another].

Some companies take the divisional cost of capital concept to a deeper level; that is, to strategic business unit, project category type, or project cost of capital. Although there is limited financial theory directly applicable in practice, the conceptual attraction of project hurdle rates is well founded in theory (i.e., added risk requires added return). Companies identify their own project categories, such as cost reduction, cost avoidance, capacity expansion, new product/line extension, and new product/brand. Often the project categories include regulatory (or environmental) capital, R&D capital, and administrative capital. Although most companies limit their project categories to three to seven, one major Fortune 50 company used 26 individual project categories.

Although a company may not be able to exactly quantify the cost of capital requirement for a new product, the management recognizes that a new product is riskier than capacity expansion for existing products (which is riskier than investment in a cost savings project). Some companies arbitrarily extend this argument and require higher returns for capacity expansion projects than for cost savings projects, and even higher returns for new products than capacity expansion projects.

Survey OF PRACTICE

A recent survey of 29 corporations and 10 financial advisors found that most:

- Use a market based cost of debt, although many use a current or historical cost of debt
- CAPM is the tool of choice for estimating the cost of equity
- Within CAPM, the long term Treasury bond is the usual risk free rate
- The equity risk premium varies widely
- Weights are based on market values using a targeted capital structure

Results follow:

Percent of respondents in using each approach.

	Corporations	Financial Advisors
Cost of Debt		
Market	52	60
Current (or historical)	37	30
Other	11	10
Cost of Equity		
CAPM	81	80
Other	19	20
Risk free rate		
90-day T-bill	4	10
3 to 7-year Treasury	7	10
10 to 30-year Treasury	70	70
Other	23	10
Equity risk premium		
Fixed rate of 4% to 5%	11	10
Fixed rate of 5% to 6%	37	0
Fixed rate of 7% to 7.4%	0	50
Other (9 techniques)	52	40
Weights		
Market	59	90
Book	15	10
Other	23	10
Weights		
Target	52	90
Current	15	10
Other	23	10

"Best Practices in Estimating the Cost of Capital: Survey and Synthesis," Bruner, Robert F., Kenneth M. Eades, Robert S. Harris, and Robert C. Higgins, *Financial Practice and Education*, Volume 8, Number 1, Spring/Summer 1998.

summary

The cost of capital is the opportunity cost of funds required to compensate investors for their investment in the organization. Because investors generally dislike risk, the required rate of return is higher on riskier securities. As a class, bonds are less risky than preferred stocks. Preferred stocks, in turn, are less risky than common stocks. The result is that the required rate of return is lowest for bonds, higher for preferred stocks, and highest for common stocks. Within each of these security classes are variations among the issuing firms' risks. Hence, required rates of return vary among firms.

The cost of debt is defined as the required yield to maturity on new increments of debt capital, K_d, multiplied by 1 minus the tax rate. Financing costs must represent current opportunity costs, and therefore actual historical financing costs (reflected on the books) are not relevant. The cost of preferred stock with no maturity date is the required yield. It is found as the annual expected preferred dividend divided by the preferred stock price. The cost of common equity is the return required by a reasonable investor. The cost of common equity may be calculated by at least three methods. The recommended approach is the CAPM (the risk-free rate plus the product of the market risk premium and the firm's beta).

The first step in calculating the weighted cost of capital, K, is to determine the cost of the individual capital components. The next step is to establish the proper set of weights to be used in the averaging process. The basic issues are whether to use book or market value in calculating the weights of each source of financing and as of what time period, current or targeted (projected). With regard to market or book weights, the theory and practice is quite clear: use market weights. With regard to timing, target is preferred if that target is stated as market-based weights. Most targets are not; most targets are stated as book weights. In these cases, current market weights are preferable to target book weights.

Increasing the leverage ratio in a firm will make the debt and equity riskier because it increases the probability of bankruptcy. If bankruptcy costs are substantial, with increasing leverage the cost of capital will fall, reach a minimum, and then rise. The minimum region on this curve indicates an optimal cost of capital and the optimal amount of debt or leverage ratio.

Questions

13.1 How could the cost of capital structure influence a product's price or quality?

13.2 Explain why there is a cost of equity. Should the cost of equity be recognized on the income statement, much as the cost of debt is recognized?

13.3   Should the cost of equity be tax deductible, just like the cost of debt? Should dividends paid be a tax deduction for the paying firm? Do these tax differences distort the use of debt and equity?

13.4   If Hershey were going to make an acquisition outside the food processing industry (let's say in the computer industry), whose cost of capital should be used? That is, if Hershey were going to acquire a computer company should Hershey use (1) its cost of capital, (2) the computer company's cost of capital, or (3) a weighted average of both companies' cost of capital.

13.5   Assume that Hershey Foods has a policy that cost savings projects must earn a 16% hurdle rate and that new products must earn a 25% hurdle rate. The hurdle rate is a result of historical analysis and the perceived risk associated with both project types. You have funding requests for two projects: project A (a cost savings project with a 16.5% rate of return) and project B (a higher-returning new product with a 22% rate of return). If you can only fund one of them, which project should you recommend and why?

13.6   Evaluate the following statement: "Sometimes equity is cheaper than debt! For example, suppose you were the chief financial officer of a corporation. Based on your company's strategic plan, you believe your company's current market price is overvalued. You decided to sell two million shares at $50 per share. Three years later, your premonitions unfold and the stock price drops to $25 per share. You decide to repurchase two million shares of your stock at $25 per share. Your equity was free! In fact, you made money from the equity, so equity can be cheaper (in fact, significantly cheaper) than debt!"

13.7   Evaluate the following statement: "Equity is our least expensive form of capital! Our dividend yield is less than 1%, so our cost of equity is also less than 1%."

13.8   Why is it difficult to pinpoint the optimum cost of capital?

13.9   How does the cost of capital curve (Figure 13.1) influence a stock's value?

13.10   Explain why equity is more expensive than debt.

13.11   When is leverage a good position for a firm?

13.12   How can a company have a capital structure that is 90% (or more) debt on their books and still be considered a reasonable investment?

Problems

13.1

Current cost of debt: Tasha's Toys sold a 30-year bond issue five years ago. It pays a 9% annual coupon and has a $1,000 face value. If the current price is $868.91 and the tax rate is 34%, what is the current after-tax cost of debt?

13.2

Cost of debt: An outstanding bond has a $1,000 face value, a 9.5% annual coupon, and 10 more years until it matures. The bond currently sells for $1,153. What is the *historical after-tax cost of debt* and the *current after-tax cost of debt*? Assume a 40% tax rate.

13.3

Dividend growth model: Cornerstone, Inc. just paid a dividend of $3.00 per share. This dividend, along with sales, earnings, aseets, and so on is expected to grow at a rate of 6% forever. The current market price for a share of Cornerstone is $63.75. What is the cost of Cornerstone's equity?

13.4

Dividend growth model: The treasurer of Iowa Corn, Inc. is analyzing the company's cost of equity using the DGM. She estimates that the following dividends will be paid per share, including an $11.00 extraordinary dividend in year 2.

YEAR	AMOUNT
1	$0.75
2	12.00
3	1.00
4	1.25
5	1.65
6	2.15
Thereafter	2.50

Currently, the stock trades at $23.54. What is the cost of equity using the DGM?

13.5

Capital asset pricing model: What is the expected return on asset X if it has a beta of 0.85, the expected market return is 11.50%, and the risk-free rate is 5.75%?

13.6

Capital asset pricing model: What is the expected return on asset X if it has a beta of 1.55, the risk-free rate is 5.38%, and the expected market premium is 4.80%?

13.7

Current market value: Given the following information, what is the current market value of Abbott Corporation?

Common stock:

- 73.5 million shares outstanding
- $27.50 per share
- Total stockholders' equity of $350 million
- Bond issue 1:
- $625 million total face value
- Selling for 98% of face value
- Bond issue 2:
- $200 million total face value
- Selling for $975 per bond

What are the current market values of debt and equity?

13.8

Cost of capital.

a. Per the following table, calculate the cost of each financing source for Keyboard, Inc. The tax rate is 40%.

FINANCIAL	SOURCE	COST
Debt	Twelve-year bond, 6.75% annual coupon, current price of $960.81	
Preferred Stock	Dividend of $5.50, current price of $63.75	
Common Stock	Beta of 1.45, excess market return of 5.63%, risk-free rate of 6.05%	

b. Currently, there are 121 million shares of common stock outstanding at $48 per share and four million shares of preferred stock outstanding. There is also currently $956 million of debt outstanding. Calculate the WACC using current market weights.

c. The company is targeting a capital structure of 25% debt, 5 preferred stock, and 70% common equity. Recalculate the cost of capital based on target weights. Compare your answer to problem 13.8b.

13.9

Cost of capital: You have obtained the following information about a company:

- Interest income of $19.6 million on a year-end cash position of $425 million (average cash position $350 million).

- Gross interest expense is $28.5 million on an average balance of $325 million of long-term debt.

- A dividend yield of 2.5% currently exists, with expectations of the dividend increasing 11.5% each year.

- No preferred stock is outstanding.

- Stockholder equity totals $1,565 million.

- The tax rate is 40%.

Calculate the cost of capital.

13.10.

NPV and cost of capital: HT, Inc. is considering a new process to speed production and reduce costs. The project will last seven years and have an initial investment of $1,400,000. The after-tax cash flows are estimated at $315,000 per year. The firm has a targeted debt-to-equity ratio of 1.5. Its pre-tax cost of equity is 14%, and its pre-tax cost of debt is 8%. The tax rate is 40%. What is the NPV of this project?

Financing Sources and Strategies

This chapter discusses long-term financing: sources, specific forms, and procedures for obtaining long-term financing. The chapter begins with a review of the financing alternatives in the early stage of a firm's existence, from private placement of debt and equity to the initial public offering phase in which the organization decides to go public for the first time. The common forms of long-term financing include long-term debt, preferred stock, and common stock. Each is examined in this chapter.

The chief financial officer or the treasurer of an organization is responsible for making recommendations to the board of directors and chief executive officer. These recommendations carefully weigh the advantages and disadvantages of each financial instrument. Once the decision is made, the chief financial officer or the treasurer is responsible for obtaining the long-term financing for the organization.

For other executives of the corporation, a basic understanding of the process and available financing alternatives acquaints the executive with specific terms and concepts, broadens the executive's understanding of financial markets, and enhances knowledge of why specific financing decisions are made within the organization.

Initial Sources of Long-term Financing

Through the stages of a firm's development, an organization deals with various sources of available financing (Figure 14.1). During the first phase (start-up), a firm avails itself of financing from personal savings, personal loans, and government agencies such as the Small Business Administration (SBA) or Small Business Investment Corporation (SBIC). The SBA and SBIC are federal agencies. State governments may also have "incubator" funds available to encourage rural or inner-city development or to attract various start-up businesses.

During rapid growth, the second phase, a firm finances itself through internal sources or direct financing. The firm can obtain direct financing in the form of a loan from a commercial bank, insurance company, or pension fund. In addition, a firm can obtain funds from private equity placement with venture capitalists. These sources are discussed in detail in material following. The third phase, growth to maturity, is financed by going public and through money and capital markets. An investment bank is generally involved in this process. Investment banking is discussed in material following, along with the common forms of long-term financing: long-term debt (including lease alternatives), preferred stock, and common stock. During the firm's final phase, maturity and industry decline, a firm finances through internal sources while repaying its debt or repurchasing its shares.

Direct Financing: Term Loans and Private Placements

Venture capital (VC) financing is a form of direct financing (discussed later in the chapter). This section concentrates on obtaining direct debt financing (loans). Direct long-term financing includes (1) term lending by commercial banks and insurance companies and (2) private

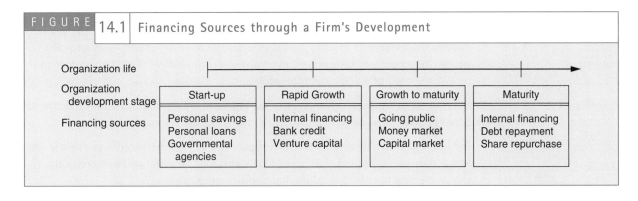

FIGURE 14.1   Financing Sources through a Firm's Development

Organization life				
Organization development stage	Start-up	Rapid Growth	Growth to maturity	Maturity
Financing sources	Personal savings Personal loans Governmental agencies	Internal financing Bank credit Venture capital	Going public Money market Capital market	Internal financing Debt repayment Share repurchase

placement of securities with insurance companies and pension funds. *Term loans* are direct business loans with a maturity of more than one year but less than 15 years, with provisions for systematic repayment (amortization during the life of the loan).

Private placements are direct business loans with a maturity of more than 15 years. The distinction is, of course, arbitrary. Private placement differs from the term loan only in its arbitrary maturity length. This distinction becomes even fuzzier when we discover that some private placements call for repayment of a substantial portion of the principal within five to ten years. Thus, term loans and private placements represent about the same type of direct financing arrangement.

Evaluation of Direct Financing

From the standpoint of the borrower, the advantages of direct financing are as follows.

- Much seasonal short-term borrowing can be dispensed with, thereby reducing the danger of nonrenewal of loans or substantially higher interest rates.

- The borrower avoids the expenses of Securities and Exchange Commission (SEC) registration and investment bankers' distribution.

- Less time is required for obtaining a loan than is involved in a bond issue.

- Because only one lender is involved, rather than many bond holders, the borrower may have the flexibility to modify the loan agreement (indenture).

The disadvantages to a borrower of direct financing are as follows.

- The interest rate may be higher on a term loan than on a short-term loan because the lender is tying up money for a longer period and therefore does not have the opportunity to review the borrower's status periodically (as is done whenever short-term loans are renewed).

- The cash drain is large. Because the loans provide for regular *amortization (payment of interest and principal)* or *sinking fund* payments, the company experiences a continuous cash drain. From this standpoint, direct loans are less advantageous than equity funds (which never have to be repaid), a preferred stock without maturity, or even a bond issue without a sinking fund requirement.

- Because the loan is a long-term commitment, the lender employs high credit standards, insisting that the borrower be in a strong financial position and have a good current ratio, a low debt-to-equity ratio, good activity ratios, and good profitability ratios.

- The longer-term loan agreement has restrictions that are not found in a 90-day note.

- Investigation costs may be high. The lender stays with the company for a longer period. Therefore, the longer-term outlook for the company must be reviewed, and the lender makes a more elaborate investigation than would be done for a short-term note. For this reason, the lender may set a minimum on any loan (for example, $50,000) in order to recover the costs of investigating the applicant.

In addition, there are some advantages to the public distribution of securities that are not achieved by term loans or private placement, including the following.

- The firm establishes its credit and achieves publicity by having its securities publicly and widely distributed. This initial offering, along with solid financial performance, will enable the firm to engage in future financing at lower rates.

- The wide distribution of debt or equity may enable its repurchase on favorable terms at some subsequent date if the market price of the securities falls.

It is apparent that direct long-term debt financing has both advantages and limitations. Its use continues through the rapid growth stage and into the growth-to-maturity stage as a firm assesses and makes trade-offs with other forms of financing.

Venture Capitalists

Firms that have growth potential face greater risks than almost any other type of business, and their higher risks require special types of financing. This led to the development of the *private equity placement* and *specialized VC financing* sources. Some VC companies are organized as partnerships. Others are more formal corporations termed *investment development companies*. Some companies are formed for a single investment opportunity, whereas others manage a very active portfolio of properties. Typical sources of VC financing include the following.

- Many investment banks and commercial banks have established VC subsidiaries.

- VC firms (VC specialists) are firms whose owners typically have had prior investment banking or commercial banking experience.

- Some VC investment activity is conducted by wealthy individuals. This type of VC financing is categorized as "angel" financing.

- Another longtime source of VC is represented by large, well-established business firms. A number of large corporations, many in the pharmaceutical or computer technology area, have invested both money and various types of know-how to start or to help develop small business firms. The owner of the small firm is usually a specialist, frequently a technically oriented person who needs both money and help in such administrative services as accounting, finance, production, and marketing. The small firm's owner contributes entrepreneurship, special talents, a taste for risk taking, and a passion to see the successful development and commercialization of their idea. Some major corporations have found that there is a mutual advantage for this form of VC investment. In fact, this is how many pharmaceutical companies gain breakthrough compounds and technology.

Some venture capitalists are purely financial investors. These investors provide capital in the hope of a commensurate rate of return for the risk being undertaken. Other VC investors are strategic investors, who also want to earn a commensurate rate of return but who are keenly interested in the company's products or services.

When a new business makes an application for financial assistance from a VC firm, it receives a rigorous examination. Some development companies use their own staffs for this investigation, whereas others depend on a board of advisers acting in a consultative capacity. A high percentage of applications are rejected, but if the application is approved funds are provided. VC companies generally take an equity position in the firms they finance, but they may also extend debt capital. However, when loans are made they generally involve convertibles or *warrants* or are tied in with the purchase of stock by the investment company.

Often the VC firm will take *convertible preferred stock* for its investment. This avoids burdening the new capital-hungry firm with a requirement to pay interest on debt or technically be in default. The convertible preferred stock also provides the VC firm with a priority position in liquidation and the opportunity to obtain a substantial equity position if the venture turns out well.

Another technique is the use of a *staged capital commitment (SCC)*. In SCC, the venture capitalist agrees to provide capital in various stages in the venture as opposed to providing all expected capital requirements up front. The venture capitalist also typically reserves the option to abandon, revalue, or increase his or her capital commitment to the project at each future round of financing.

SCC reduces the perceived risk to the venture capitalist because the venture capitalist receives a wealth of information about the company (e.g., how the company has performed relative to its initial business plan, if the management team works well together, whether the market research reveals adequate demand, and if new competition has surfaced) before the next round of financing arrives. This new information reduces the uncertainty of the value of the company and aids in the venture capitalist's decision as to how to proceed. The knowledge that the company is scheduled to run out of cash is a powerful motivator for management to focus its energies on creating value from its limited resources.

Investment Banking

In the U.S. economy, saving is done by one group of persons and investing by another. (The term *investing* is used here in the sense of actually putting money into plant, equipment, and inventory and not in the sense of purchasing securities.) Savings are placed with financial intermediaries, who in turn make the funds available to firms wishing to acquire plants and equipment and to hold inventories.

One of the major institutions performing this channeling role is the investment banking institution. The term *investment banker* is somewhat misleading because investment bankers are neither investors nor bankers. That is, they do not invest their own funds permanently and they are not repositories for individuals' funds (as are commercial banks or savings banks). What, then, is the nature of investment banking?

The many activities of investment bankers can be described first in general terms and then with respect to specific functions. The traditional function of the investment banker has been to act as the middleman in channeling individuals' savings and funds into the purchase of business securities. The investment banker does this by purchasing and distributing the new securities of individual companies.

Functions of the Investment Banker

The major functions of the investment banker include underwriting, distribution of securities, and advice and counsel. These functions are examined in the sections that follow.

UNDERWRITING

Underwriting is the insurance function of bearing the risks of adverse price fluctuations during the period in which a new issue of securities is being distributed. The nature of the investment banker's underwriting function can best be conveyed by example. A business firm needs $500 million. It selects an investment banker, holds conferences, and decides to issue $500 million of bonds. An underwriting agreement is drawn up. On a specific day, the investment banker presents the company with a check for $500 million (less commission). In return, the investment banker receives bonds in denominations of $1,000 each to sell to the public.

The company receives the $500 million before the investment banker has sold the bonds. Between the time the firm is paid the $500 million and the time the bonds are sold, the investment banker bears all the risk of market price fluctuations in the bonds. Selling bonds can conceivably take the investment banker days, months, or longer to sell bonds. If the bond market deteriorates in the interim, the investment banker carries the risk of loss on the sale of the bonds.

One fundamental economic function of the investment banker, then, is to underwrite the risk of a decline in the market price between the time the money is transmitted to the firm and the time the bonds are placed in the hands of their ultimate buyers. For this reason, investment bankers are often called underwriters; that is, they underwrite risk during the distribution period.

DISTRIBUTION

The second function of the investment banker is marketing new issues of securities. The investment banker is a specialist, with a staff and organization to distribute securities. The investment banker therefore has the capacity to perform the physical distribution function more efficiently and more economically than an individual corporation. A single corporation that wants to sell or issue its securities would need to establish a securities marketing and selling organization, which would be a very expensive and ineffective method of selling securities.

The investment banker has a permanent trained staff and dealer organization available to distribute securities. In addition, the investment banker's reputation for selecting good companies and pricing securities fairly builds up a broad clientele over time, and this increases the efficiency with which securities can be sold.

ADVICE AND COUNSEL

Through experience, the investment banker engaged in the origination and sale of securities becomes an expert adviser about terms and characteristics of securities that will appeal to investors. This advice and guidance is valuable. Furthermore, the firm's reputation as a seller of securities depends on the subsequent performance of the securities. Therefore, investment bankers often sit on the boards of firms whose securities they have sold. In this way, they can provide continuing financial counsel.

CERTIFICATION FUNCTION

A number of factors give rise to the certification function of investment bankers. Information asymmetry exists when the managers know more about the company than the prospective buyers of its securities. Because investment bankers conduct continuing in-depth studies of the companies, they are in a position to reduce information asymmetry. In addition, they are likely to provide monitoring of the company's performance.

The ability of the underwriter to maintain the confidence of a syndicate of other underwriters and selling firms depends on his reputation for both knowledge and unquestionable integrity. Thus, the reputation of the investment banker depends on his being informed and honest. The investment banker has the ability to perform as a guarantor of issue quality and fair pricing.

Investment Banking Operations

Probably the best way to gain a clear understanding of the investment banking function is to trace the history of a new issue of securities. This section describes those steps.

PRE-UNDERWRITING CONFERENCES

First, the members of the issuing firm and the investment banker hold a pre-underwriting conference, at which they discuss the amount of capital to be raised, the type of security to be issued, and the terms of the agreement. At some point, the issuer and the investment banker enter an agreement that an *issuance (or flotation)* will take place. The investment banker then begins to conduct an underwriting investigation. A public accounting firm is called upon to make an audit of the issuing firm's financial situation and to help prepare registration statements in connection with these issues for the SEC.

A firm of lawyers is called in to interpret and judge the legal aspects of the flotation. In addition, the originating underwriter (who is the manager of the subsequent underwriting syndicate) makes an exhaustive investigation of the company's prospects. When the investigations are completed, but before registration with the SEC is made, an underwriting agreement is drawn up by the investment banker. Terms of the tentative agreement may be modified through discussions between the underwriter and the issuing company, but the final agreement will cover all underwriting terms except the price of the securities.

REGISTRATION STATEMENT AND PROSPECTUS

A *registration statement* containing all relevant financial and business information on the firm is filed with the SEC. The statutes set a 20-day waiting period (which in practice may be shortened or lengthened by the SEC), during which the SEC staff analyzes the registration statement to determine whether there are any omissions or misrepresentations of fact. During the examination period, the SEC can file exceptions to the registration statement or can ask for additional information from the issuing company or the underwriters. Also during this period, the investment bankers are not permitted to offer the securities for sale, although they can print a *preliminary prospectus* (known as a *red herring*) with all the customary information except the offering price.

The *prospectus* summarizes the content of the SEC registration statement for the general public. The document provides an overview of the company, along with historical financial information; discusses the specific uses of the funds; and specifies the underlying business risks. The prospectus also lists the costs of raising the funds. "Road shows" are often scheduled at this time. The "*road show*" is a presentation by the company (and often with the investment banker) used to market the stock to potential investors before it is actually available for sale.

A *shelf registration* is a process that quickens the registration process, but it is only available to large firms (more than $150 million in assets). This process allows the issuing company to file the general background SEC registration material (company's history and historical financials) well in advance of a potential issue of securities. The shelf registration remains available for a two-year period. Specific use of the funds is often left open for if and when the firm decides to issue new securities. At that time, the company specifies the use of the funds.

PRICING SECURITIES

The actual price the underwriter pays the issuer is not generally determined until the end of the registration period. There is no universally followed practice, but one common arrangement for a new issue of stock calls for the investment banker to purchase the securities at a prescribed number of points below the closing price on the last day of registration. Typically, such agreements have an escape clause that provides for the contract to be voided if the price of the securities falls below some predetermined figure.

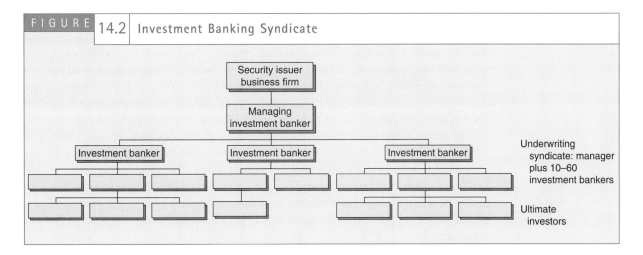

FIGURE 14.2 | Investment Banking Syndicate

The investment banker has an easier job if the issue is priced relatively low, but the issuer of the securities naturally wants as high a price as possible. Some conflict on price, therefore, arises between the investment banker and the issuer. If the issuer is financially sophisticated and makes comparisons with similar security issues, the investment banker is forced to price close to the market. On seasoned issues with a good historical record of prices, pricing is related to recent patterns. The problem is more difficult on initial public offerings with no prior public trading.

UNDERWRITING SYNDICATE

The investment banker with whom the issuing firm has conducted its discussions does not typically handle the purchase and distribution of the issue alone, unless the issue is a very small one. If the sums of money involved are large and the risks or price fluctuations are substantial, the investment banker forms a syndicate in an effort to minimize the amount of personal risk. A *syndicate* is a temporary association for the purpose of carrying out a specific objective. The nature of the arrangements for a syndicate in the underwriting and sale of a security through an investment banker can best be understood with the aid of Figure 14.2.

The managing underwriter invites other investment bankers to participate in the transaction on the basis of their knowledge of the particular type of offering to be made and their strength and dealer contacts in selling securities of this type. Each investment banker has business relationships with other investment bankers and dealers and thus has a *selling group* composed of these people.

Each level commits to underwriting certain amounts of the total offering. A dealer purchases securities outright, holds them in inventory, and sells them at whatever price can be obtained. The dealer may benefit from price appreciation or may suffer a loss on declines, as any merchandiser does. A broker, on the other hand, takes orders for purchases and transmits them to the proper exchange. The gain to the broker is the commission charged for the service.

Going Public and Initial Public Offerings

We have described how firms may be aided during the early stages of their growth by sources such as VC. We have also described the nature of investment banking in bringing seasoned issues of debt and equity to the market. We can draw on this background to discuss going public and initial public offerings (IPOs).

Going public represents a fundamental change in lifestyle in at least four respects: (1) the firm moves from informal, personal control to a system of formal controls, (2) information must be reported on a timely basis to outside investors, even though the founders may continue to have majority control, (3) the firm must have breadth of management in all business functions to operate its expanded business effectively, and (4) the publicly owned firm typically draws on a board of directors (which should include representatives of the public owners and other external interest groups) to help formulate sound plans and policies.

The timing of the decision to go public is also especially important, because small firms are more affected by variations in money market conditions than larger companies. During periods of tight money and high interest rates, financial institutions (especially commercial banks) raise credit standards and require a stronger balance sheet record and a longer and more stable record of profitability in order to qualify for bank credit. Because financial ratios for small and growing firms tend to be less strong, such firms bear the brunt of credit restraint.

In a *firm-commitment cash offer,* the investment banker agrees to underwrite and distribute the issue at an agreed-upon price for a specified number of shares to be bought by the underwriters. The issuer still bears some risk with regard to both price and number of shares sold. These are subject to revision by the investment banker between the date a preliminary agreement is signed and the actual issue date after SEC clearance and other procedures have been completed. Typically, a day before the actual issue date in a conference between the investment banker, lawyers, accountants, and the issuer the number of shares to be sold may be adjusted downward (depending on the strength of the market) and an issue price is set.

A *best-efforts offering* is subject to the additional risk that if a minimum number of shares is not sold the investment banker withdraws the offering. Best-efforts offerings generally involve smaller issuers and smaller size of issue. The investment banker may find it difficult to make a good estimate of the potential market. In a best-efforts offering, the issuer has no assurance the offer will succeed.

THE DECISION TO GO PUBLIC

In order to list their stock, firms must meet exchange requirements relating to such factors as size of company, number of years in business, earnings record, the number of shares outstanding, and the market value of shares. In the United States, requirements become more stringent as viewed on a spectrum ranging from the regional exchanges toward the New York Stock Exchange (NYSE).

The firm itself makes the decision whether to seek to list its securities on an exchange. Typically, the stock of a new and small company is traded over the counter (there is simply not enough activity to justify the use of an auction market for such stocks). As the company grows and establishes an earnings record, expands its number of shares outstanding, and increases its list of stockholders, it may decide to apply for listing on one of the regional exchanges. For example, a West Coast company may list on the Pacific Stock Exchange.

As the company grows still more, and its stock becomes distributed throughout the country, it may seek a listing on the American Stock Exchange (the smaller of the two national exchanges). Finally, as it matures it may if it qualifies switch to the "Big Board," the NYSE. With all of the foregoing as background, what are the pros and cons for a firm going public? A number of advantages can be stated.

- Obviously, funds are raised.

- The disclosure and external monitoring may make it easier to raise additional funds.

- Listing may lead to lowering the required return, cost of capital, as the exchanges contend. Although some studies have concluded that the key is the information, availability is the underlying key.

- A public price is established. Its subsequent behavior is a test of the performance of the firm.

- Public prices are often useful to have for estate and tax purposes.

- Increased liquidity is provided because of the market that may develop in the stock.

- Listed companies receive a certain amount of free advertising and publicity.

- There is some added prestige of being a listed firm.

A number of potential disadvantages of going public must be considered.

- Some loss of control is involved in sharing ownership.

- The initial cost of an IPO can be 10% or more of the amount of funds raised. You have direct expenses such as the underwriter's fee (or the difference between the proceeds received by the company and the agreed-upon price of the securities), attorney's fees, accountant's fees, expenses for filing the registration, printing costs related to the prospectus, and "road show" travel costs. You also have the indirect expense of management's time and the distraction from the business. Finally, there are other "costs" involved, such as underpricing, where the securities sell for more than the anticipated price and the investment banker earns the difference (as well as a "green shoe" option). The "*green shoe*" *option* allows the investment banker to purchase additional securities at the anticipated price. The investment banker only enacts the option when shares are earning more than the anticipated price. Thus, this option "costs" the issuing company lost funds from properly priced initial securities.

- The activities of the firm are now more fully disclosed.

- More formal reporting to public agencies is required, which can be costly.

- If the firm's shares do not attract a following, the market for them may be relatively inactive and thereby lose the potential benefits of performance evaluation and aligning incentives.

- Outside investors may push for short-term performance results to an excessive degree.

- A public firm must publish information that may disclose vital and competitively sensitive information to rival firms.

- Stockholders' servicing costs and other related expenses may also be a consideration for smaller firms.

- An advantage of not going public is that major programs do not have to be justified by detailed studies and reports to the board of directors. Action can be taken more speedily, and sometimes getting a new investment program under way early is critical for its success.

Generalization is not possible. The going-public decision depends on the circumstances of the firm and the preferences of its major owners. The advantages and disadvantages of going public may be so closely balanced that the decision may be reversed as time, circumstances, and preferences change. The following sections discuss concepts related to debt, preferred stock, and common stock. Each discussion concludes with advantages/ disadvantages to issuers of each form of capital.

Long-term Debt Financing

In Chapter 5, we discussed much of the economic background that influences and determines interest rates. We also discussed bond valuation. This section reviews debt (specifically long-term debt) as a form of financing.

TYPES OF DEBT

A *note* is typically a debt with a maturity of less than 10 years. A bond is a longer-term promissory note. A *mortgage* represents a pledge of designated property for a loan. Under a *mortgage bond*, a corporation pledges certain real assets as security for the bond. The pledge is a condition of the loan. A mortgage bond, therefore, is secured by real property. *Real property* is defined as real estate—land and buildings. A *chattel mortgage* is secured by personal property (such as an automobile or manufacturing equipment), but this is generally an intermediate-term instrument.

Secured Debt   Secured debt can be classified according to (1) the priority of claims, (2) the right to issue additional securities, and (3) the scope of the lien.

- *Priority of claims:* A senior mortgage has prior claims on assets and earnings. Senior railroad mortgages, for example, have been called the "mortgages next to the rail" (implying that they have the first claim on the land and assets of the railroad corporations). A *junior mortgage* is a subordinate lien, such as a second or third mortgage. It is a lien or claim junior to others.

- *Right to issue additional securities:* Mortgage bonds can also be classified with respect to the right to issue additional obligations, pledging already encumbered property.

- *Scope of the lien:* Bonds can also be classified with respect to the scope of their lien. A lien is granted on certain specified property. When a *specific lien* exists, the security for a first or second mortgage is a specifically designated property. On the other hand, a *blanket mortgage* pledges all real property currently owned by the company. Real property includes only land and those things affixed thereto. Thus, a blanket mortgage is not a mortgage on cash, accounts receivable, or inventories (which are items of personal property).

Unsecured Bonds   The reasons for a firm's use of unsecured debt are diverse. Paradoxically, the extremes of financial strength and weakness may give rise to its use. In addition, tax considerations and great uncertainty about the level of the firm's future earnings have given rise to special forms of unsecured financing.

- *Debentures:* A *debenture* is an unsecured bond, and as such provides no lien on specific property as security for the obligation. Debenture holders, therefore, are general creditors whose claim is protected by property not otherwise pledged. The advantage of debentures from the issuer's standpoint is that the property is left unencumbered for subsequent financing. However, in practice the use of debentures depends on the nature of the firm's assets and its general credit strength.

- *Subordinated debentures:* The term *subordinate* means below or inferior. Thus, *subordinated debt* has claims on assets after unsubordinated debt in the event of liquidation. Debentures can be subordinated to designated notes payable—usually bank loans—or to any or all other debt. In the event of liquidation or reorganization, the debentures cannot be paid until senior debt *as named in the indenture* has been paid. Senior debt, typically, does not include trade accounts payable.

In comparison to subordinated debt, preferred stock suffers from the disadvantage that its dividends are not tax deductible. Subordinated debentures have been referred to as a special type of preferred stock, the dividends of which *are* tax deductible. Subordinated debt has therefore become an increasingly important source of corporate capital.

DEBT CHARACTERISTICS

Debt characteristics may take many forms. Some are common to most instruments, whereas others vary with individual firms and financial circumstances.

Par Value   *Par value* is the maturity value or the stated face value of the debt. Bonds generally have a par value of $1,000. However, for calculation purposes often $100 is used. For example, the formulas in Excel are based on $100. However, the results are easily converted to a $1,000 basis.

Periodic Payments   Traditionally, debt instruments carry specified *periodic payments*. Bond debt historically carried detachable dated *coupons*. Owners would "clip the coupons" and send them to the paying agent of the issuer. In recent years, new bonds are simply registered by a "book entry." The new procedure reduces transaction costs.

A fixed periodic payment divided by the par value gives an interest rate. For example, Wal-Mart in 2003 filed a prospectus with the SEC to issue five-year maturity notes with interest accruing from October 2, 2003 and maturing on October 1, 2008. The notes were to be registered in denominations of $1,000 carrying semiannual payments representing an annual interest rate of 3.375% of their $1,000 par value. The total interest paid each year would be $33.75, representing a "coupon rate" of 3.375%. Hence, the dollar amount of interest paid by Wal-Mart on each $1,000 bond would be $16.875 (to be paid each April 1 and October 1 beginning on April 1, 2004. The periodic interest rates need not be fixed. Firms may also issue *floating-rate debt*. The interest rate may be adjusted based on some benchmark market rate. For example, the rate on a U.S. Treasury note (T-note) or bond of comparable maturity could be used as the benchmark. The adjustment factor could be some percentage of the change in the T-note or bond. In addition, *zero coupon bonds* *("zeros")* may be used. Such debt may be issued at a discount from their maturity value to yield a percentage rate comparable to debt with specified interest rates. Another variation is to issue debt with interest rates below those on comparable instruments, requiring that the offer price be below their maturity or redemption price. These forms are referred to as *original issue discount (OID)* debt.

Sinking Funds   Some debt may have a *sinking fund provision*. One form is to have the firm deposit funds with a trustee, who accumulates the funds and their earnings to retire the debt at maturity. More generally, a sinking fund is used to purchase a specified amount of the issue periodically. This has the advantage of reducing the supply of those instruments in the market, supporting their price to some degree. The Wal-Mart bonds made no provision for any sinking fund.

Redeemable (Call) Provisions   A prospectus may specify that the bonds or other debt instruments may be *redeemable* or *callable*. A *call provision* enables the issuer to redeem the debt before its maturity date. Sometimes a premium above maturity price is paid, but not always. The Wal-Mart bonds "will not be redeemable prior to maturity."

Convertible Debt may carry a provision that its instruments be *convertible* into common stock at a specified price at the option of the holder. *Convertibles* generally carry a lower interest rate than nonconvertible debt because they grant the holder an option to take capital gains. *Debt with warrants* is similar to convertibles except that this can be detached from the debt instrument. The Wal-Mart bonds were not convertible and did not carry warrants.

Indexed Bonds *Indexed bonds (purchasing-power bonds)* protect against inflation risks. They carry interest rates that are a specified amount plus the rate of some measure of inflation during the previous period.

Protection of Creditors

Before the rise of large aggregations of savings through insurance companies or pension funds, no single buyer was able to purchase an issue of such size. Bonds, therefore, were issued in denominations of $1,000 each and were sold to a large number of purchasers. To facilitate communication between the issuer and the numerous bond holders, a trustee was appointed to represent the bond holders.

TRUSTEES

A *trustee* is presumed to act at all times for the protection of the bond holders and on their behalf. Any legal entity is considered competent to act as a trustee. Typically, however, the duties of the trustee are handled by a department of a commercial bank. Trustees have three main responsibilities.

- They certify the issue of bonds. This duty involves making certain that all legal requirements for drawing up the bond contract and the indenture have been carried out.

- They police the behavior of the corporation in its performance of the responsibilities set forth in the indenture provisions.

- They are responsible for taking appropriate action on behalf of the bond holders if the corporation defaults on payment of interest or principal.

INDENTURE

The long-term relationship between the borrower and the lender of a long-term promissory note is established in a document called an *indenture*. In the case of an ordinary 60- or 90-day promissory note, few developments that will endanger repayment are likely to occur in the life or affairs of the borrower. The lender looks closely at the borrower's current position because current assets are the main source of repayment. A bond, however, is a long-term contractual relationship between the bond issuer and the bond holder. Over this extended period, the bond holder has cause to worry that the issuing firm's position may change materially.

The bond indenture can be a document of several hundred pages that discusses a large number of factors important to the contracting parties, including (1) the form of the bond

TABLE 14.1	Key Long-term Debt Concepts

- Secured debt: Mortgage.
- Unsecured debt: Debenture and subordinated debentures (junior to other debentures).
- Call provision: Allows debt to be prematurely retired.
- Sinking fund: Requires deposits throughout bond's term to a fund for repayment of the principal.
- Other features: Convertible, indexed, floating-rate, debt ratings.
- Indenture: Formal bond agreement.
- Covenants: Protection for bond holders, including priority of claims, right to issue additional securities, and scope of lien (secured debt).

and the instrument, (2) a complete description of property pledged, (3) the authorized amount of the bond issue, (4) detailed protective clauses, or *covenants*, (5) a minimum current ratio requirement, and (6) provisions for redemption or call privileges. *Bond covenants* can be divided into four broad categories: (1) those restricting the issuance of new debt, (2) those with restrictions on dividend payments, (3) those with restrictions on merger activity, and (4) those with restrictions on the disposition of the firm's assets.

Bond covenants that restrict dividend payments are necessary if for no other reason than to prohibit the extreme case of shareholders voting to pay themselves a liquidating dividend that would leave the bond holders holding an empty corporate shell. Restrictions on dividend policy are relatively easy to monitor, and they protect debt holders against the unwarranted payout of the assets that serve as collateral. Appropriately, most indentures refer not only to cash dividends but to all distributions in respect to capital stock (whether dividends, redemptions, purchases, retirements, partial liquidations, or capital reductions and whether in cash, in kind, or in the form of debt obligations to the company).

During the merger movement of the 1980s, acquiring companies often financed their acquisitions by selling additional long-term debt. The resulting large debt increases diluted the position of pre-merger bond holders. As a result of the additional debt taken on to finance mergers, the prices of bonds held by the earlier bond holders suffered declines. As a result, during the 1980s "put provisions" were increasingly included in the indentures of new bond issues. These new covenants enabled bond holders to "put" (sell) the bonds to the issuing companies at their original face values. The "puts" protected bond holders from the dilution resulting from the sale of substantial amounts of additional bonds. Table 14.1 summarizes the noted long-term debt concepts.

Bond Rating Criteria

Chapter 5 also introduced the broad concept of bond ratings (AAA, AA, A, BBB, BB, and so on). In this section, we want to focus on the individual company that uses long-term debt as a source of financing. A rating may be initiated by the agency or by the company. The reviews may be on an annual cycle, although specific reviews can be more or less frequent as business conditions warrant. The process often begins with contact between the company and the agency and may include a meeting between members of the company's senior management team and representatives of the agency. The review includes a qualitative

T A B L E 14.2	Key Financial Ratios (Industrials) Three-year (2002–2004) Medians						
	AAA	AA	A	BBB	BB	B	CCC
1. EBIT/interest (times)	23.8	19.5	8.0	4.7	2.5	1.2	0.4
2. EBITDA/interest (times)	25.5	24.6	10.2	6.5	3.5	1.9	0.9
3. Cash from operations/ total debt (%)	203.3	79.9	48.0	35.9	22.4	11.5	5.0
4. Free operating cash flow/ total debt (%)	127.6	44.5	25.0	17.3	8.3	2.8	−2.1
5. Total debt/EBITDA	0.4	0.9	1.6	2.2	3.5	5.3	7.9
6. Return on capital (%)	27.6	27.0	17.5	13.4	11.3	8.7	3.2
7. Total debt/capital (%)	12.4	28.3	37.5	42.5	53.7	75.9	113.5

Source: Standard & Poor's 2006 Corporate Rating Criteria, p. 43.

assessment of the company, a quantitative financial analysis, and a review of the various aspects of the specific indenture.

The qualitative assessment reviews the company and its industry with a general and specific eye to the impact of current events and long-term direction of the U.S. economy and the international economy (including specific companies wherein the issuer does business) with regard to general business and macroeconomic conditions. The company is also assessed with regard to its market share trends, labor (i.e., union) situations, competitive threats, and the like. Even the current management team is assessed for indications of its credibility and knowledge of the industry.

The quantitative analysis involves a review of the company's growth, profitability (and ability to control costs), activity, liquidity, and above all its leverage similar to the financial ratio analysis discussed in Chapter 7. Illustrative are the calculations presented in *Standard & Poor's 2006 Corporate Rating Criteria*. Table 14.2 relates selected financial ratios to bond ratings. Row 1 presents a times-interest-earnings multiple.

As the ability to pay the interest expense falls, so does the debt rating. As debt ratios rise, ratings fall. When earnings or cash coverage ratios decline (lines 3 through 5), ratings decline. When profitability measures deteriorate (line 6), ratings are lower. Finally, line 7 presents the ratio of total interest-bearing debt to capital (interest-bearing debt plus book shareholder equity).

Many studies have sought to test whether it is possible to predict bond ratings. An early article used a factor analysis and multiple-discriminant model (Pinches and Mingo, 1973). The *multiple-discriminant analysis (MDA)* was able to correctly predict only two-thirds of the actual ratings. They conclude that bond ratings "rely fairly heavily on qualitative factors" (p. 15). Many subsequent studies further tested quantitative aspects of the determination of bond ratings, with similar results. Quantitative factors are unable to replicate ratings for individual bonds.

Bond Refinancing

With the start of the new century, many individuals took advantage of low interest rates and refinanced home mortgages, home equity loans, consumer credit loans, and the like. Many companies also took advantage of low interest rates to refinance outstanding debt obligations. Some other companies, after careful review, decided not to refinance. This section discusses the evaluation process for a refinancing. Although this particular discussion is centered on corporate refinancing, the same principles apply to evaluting a personal refinancing decision.

The analysis of this decision is very similar to the analysis of a capital investment, as we saw in Chapter 11. We need to examine the net-of-tax investment and the annual (ongoing) cash savings. Our illustration revolves around a company that issued a $200 million 15-year bond five years ago, when interest rates were 8.00%. The cost of issuing that bond was $6.0 million, along with a discount of $0.3 million, for a total issuance cost of $6.3 million.

A sizeable decline in interest rates currently allows the company to borrow $200.0 million at 6.50% for 10 years (matching the remaining term of the original bond). Once again, the total cost of issuing the bond is estimated to be $6.0 million (assuming no discount). However, the company needs to pay a call premium of 5.0% ($10 million) to call the existing bonds from their holders. Intuitively, the question is whether the company should incur the $16.0 million of cost to reduce its interest expense by $3.0 million each year.

The analysis can best be framed by comparing the present value of the savings versus the present value of the cost. If savings exceed the cost, the original bond should be called and refinanced. But as with any analysis important details need to be examined and after-tax cash flow amounts considered. Let's further assume that this company has a 40% tax rate. Panel A of Table 14.3 lists the initial costs, and panel B details the annual savings. Table 14.4 combines both analyses to determine the NPV of the transaction.

INITIAL COST

Panel A of Table 14.3 examines the initial year's cost (or benefit) on an after-tax basis. The first item, the $6.0 million cost of issuing (or floating) the new bond, is the same before and after taxes. There are no tax savings in the initial year related to the cost of floating the bond or the bond discounts incurred. This floatation cost will be amortized on a straight-line basis over the 10-year life of the bond. The second item in panel A represents the $10.0 million of the call premium. That is an immediately recognized expense and is fully tax deductible. This results in a net after-tax cash outflow of $6.0 million.

Finally, we need to consider the impact of the existing bond's unamortized issuance (or floatation) costs and its unamortized discount. The initial floatation costs and bond discount on the existing bond were $6.0 million and $0.3 million, respectively. These amounts have been amortized for five of the existing bond's 15 years.

If a new bond is issued, the company will be able to immediately deduct the unamortized portion of these expenses and receive an immediate tax benefit. These expenses were actually paid for five years ago, when the existing bond was originally issued. Consequently, this is a non-cash expense at this time. However, it does provide a tax savings, which is properly recognized in panel A of Table 14.3. In total, the initial investment amount is $10.32 million after tax.

ONGOING BENEFITS

Panel B of Table 14.3 presents the benefits (or costs) that occur throughout the 10-year life of the new bond. First, the new bond saves the company $3.0 million of interest expense each year. Of course, this reduction in interest expense causes the company to pay more taxes. After considering the taxes, the company will save $1.8 million each year.

Although both the existing bond and the new bond cost $6.0 million to issue, the company amortized the existing bond's cost over a 15-year period ($0.4 million per annum).

| TABLE | 14.3 | Bond Refinancing Analysis ($000's) |

A. Initial Cost (or Benefit)—Year 0

NEW OR EXISTING BOND	ITEM	Pre-Tax Cost (Savings)	Tax Consequence	YEAR 0 IMPACT After-Tax Cost (Savings)	After-Tax Calculation (40% Tax Rate)
1. New	Refinancing or floatation cost	$6,000.0	Tax savings over bond's life.	$6,000.0	No immediate tax impact
2. Existing	Call premium	10,000.0	Immediately tax deductible.	6,000.0	$10,000 (1-tax rate)
3. Existing	Tax savings on existing bond's: Floatation cost: Unamortized portion: $4,000 ($6,000 × 2/3)		Immediate tax savings.	(1,600.0)	$4,000 (tax rate)
	Existing bond price discount: Unamortized portion: $200 ($300 × 2/3)		Immediate tax savings.	(80.0)	$200 (tax rate)
Total after-tax year 0 investment amount				$ 10,320.0	

B. Ongoing Benefit (or Cost)—Years 1–10

NEW OR EXISTING BOND	ITEM	Pre-Tax Cost (Savings)	Tax Consequence	YEARS 1–10 IMPACT After-Tax Cost (Savings)	After-Tax Calculation (40% Tax Rate)
1. Existing New	Interest payments 8.00% Interest on $200,000.0	$ 16,000.0	Deductible when paid.	$9,600.0	$16,000 (1-tax rate)
	6.50% Interest on $200,000.0 Net Savings	(13,000.0) 3,000.0	Deductible when paid.	(7,800.0) 1,800.0	$13,000 (1-tax rate)
2. Existing New	Tax shield from refinancing costs paid in initial year Amortization of $6,000 over 15 years = $400/yr Amortization of $6,000 over 10 years = $600/yr			(160.0) 240.0 80.0	$400 (tax rate) $600 (tax rate)
3. Existing New	Tax shield from bond discount incurred in initial year Amortization of $300 over 15 years = $20/yr None anticipated so no amortization expense			(8.0) — (8.0)	$20 (tax rate) $0 (tax rate)
Total after-tax savings—years 1–10				$1,872.0	

| TABLE | 14.4 | Net Present Value of Bond Refinancing ($000s) |

PERIOD	AFTER-TAX IMPACT	VALUE (TABLE 14.3)	PRESENT VALUE[a]
Years 1–10	Annual after-tax impact (cash flow savings)	$1,872.0	$15,259.5
Year 0	Initial year after-tax investment (cash cost)	(10,320.0)	(10,320.0)
	Net present value of bond refinancing		$4,939.5

[a]The present value is calculated at the after-tax cost of the new debt, or 3.9% (6.5% * 0.60).

The new bond has a shorter time frame and hence more amortization occurs each year ($0.6 million). This additional ($0.2 million) non-cash expense results in a tax savings of $0.08 million per year.

Finally, the existing bond was issued at a discount of $0.3 million, which is amortizable over the life of the bond (15 years).

The new bond is not expected to be issued at a discount. Consequently, there is no amortization of the new bond discount and the company will lose a tax savings of $8 thousand. In total, the company will have almost $1.9 million in after-tax savings each year for the next 10 years if the new bond is issued.

NET PRESENT VALUE OF REFINANCING

By comparing the present value of the savings to the present value of the cost, we can decide to refinance the existing bond or wait for more opportunistic circumstances. Table 14.4 shows this final step. The present value of the annual after-tax savings for each of the next 10 years is $15.3 million. When compared to the initial after-tax cost of $10.3 million, there is a clear indication to refinance (e.g., a positive NPV of refinancing of almost $5.0 million).

Note that the annual savings were discounted at the after-tax cost of the new debt (3.9%) and not at the company's cost of capital (10.5%).

Because we are substituting new debt for an already existing debt issue, we do not consider the cost of equity or the cost of capital. We are looking for the lowest cost of debt and we are comparing similar debt instruments. We therefore use only the cost of debt when discounting future after-tax savings. Note: If the cost of capital would have mistakenly been used, our NPV would have been $(0.2) million and we would not have refinanced! However, in this example, the company should complete the refinancing.

Evaluation of Debt as a Source of Long-term Financing

From the viewpoint of long-term debt holders, debt is less risky than preferred or common stock, has limited advantages in regard to income, and is weak in regard to control. Considerations include the following.

- Debt is less risky compared to preferred or common stock because it gives the holder priority both in earnings and in liquidation. Debt also has a definite maturity and is protected by the covenants of the indenture.

- In the area of income, the bond holder has a fixed return (except in the case of income bonds or floating-rate notes). Interest payments are not contingent on the company's level of earnings or current market rates of interest. However, debt does not participate in any superior earnings of the company, and gains are limited in magnitude.

- In the area of control, the bond holder usually does not have the right to vote. However, if the bonds go into default bond holders in effect take control of the company.

From the viewpoint of long-term debt issuers, there are several advantages and disadvantages to bonds. The advantages are as follows.

- The cash cost of debt is limited. Bond holders do not participate in superior profits, if earned.

- Not only is the cost limited but the required return is lower than that of equity.

- The owners of the corporation do not share their control when debt financing is used.

- The interest payment on debt is deductible as a tax expense.

- Flexibility in the financial structure of the corporation can be achieved by inserting a call provision (which allows for the early retirement of debt) in the bond indenture.

The disadvantages are as follows.

- Debt has committed charges whose nonpayment is default.

- As seen in Chapter 13, higher financial leverage brings higher required rates of return on equity earnings. Thus, even though leverage may be favorable and may raise earnings per share the higher required rates attributable to leverage may drive the common stock value down. An indirect cost of using more debt is a higher cost of equity.

- Debt usually has a fixed maturity date, and the financial officer must make provision for repayment of the debt.

- Because long-term debt is a commitment for a long period, it involves risk. The expectations and plans on which the debt was issued may change, and the debt may prove to be a burden. For example, if income, employment, the price level, and interest rates all fall greatly the prior assumption of a large amount of long-term debt may have been an unwise financial policy.

  The railroads are sometimes given as an example in this regard. They were able to meet their ordinary operating expenses during the 1930s but were unable to meet the heavy financial charges they had undertaken earlier, when their prospects looked more favorable than they turned out to be.

- In a long-term contractual relationship, the indenture provisions are likely to be much more stringent than they are in a short-term credit agreement.

- The firm may be subject to much more limiting restrictions than if it had borrowed on a short-term basis or had issued common stock. There is a limit on the extent to which funds can be raised through long-term debt. Generally accepted standards of financial policy dictate that the debt ratio shall not exceed certain limits. When debt goes beyond these limits, its cost rises rapidly.

Leasing is a form of debt and is reviewed in Chapter 15.

Preferred Stock Financing

Preferred stock has claims and rights ahead of common stock but behind all bonds. The preference may be a prior claim on earnings, a prior claim on assets in the event of liquidation, and/or a preferential position with regard to both earnings and assets. The hybrid nature of preferred stock becomes apparent when we try to classify it in relation to bonds and common stock. The priority feature and the (generally) fixed dividend indicate that preferred stock is similar to bonds. Payments to preferred stockholders are limited in amount, so that common stockholders receive the advantages (or disadvantages) of leverage. However, if the preferred dividends are not earned failure to pay the stipulated dividend does not cause default of the obligation (as does failure to pay bond interest). In this characteristic, preferred stock is similar to common stock.

Major Provisions of Preferred Stock

Preferred stock can be found in many forms. The following sections examine the main terms and characteristics in each case, as well as the possible variations in relation to the circumstances in which they could occur.

PRIORITY IN ASSETS AND EARNINGS

Many provisions in a preferred stock certificate are designed to reduce the purchaser's risk in relation to the risk carried by the holder of common stock. Preferred stock usually has priority with regard to earnings and assets. Two provisions designed to prevent undermining this priority are often found. The first states that without the consent of the preferred stockholders there can be no subsequent sale of securities having a prior or equal claim on earnings. The second seeks to keep earnings in the firm. It requires a minimum level of retained earnings before common stock dividends are permitted. To ensure the availability of liquid assets, the maintenance of a minimum current ratio may also be required.

CUMULATIVE DIVIDENDS

A high percentage of preferred stock issues provide for *cumulative dividends*; that is, all past preferred dividends must be paid before common dividends can be paid. The cumulative feature is a protective device. If the preferred stock were not cumulative, preferred and common stock dividends could be suspended for a number of years. The company could then vote a large common stock dividend but only the stipulated payment to preferred stock. Obviously, without the cumulative dividend provision management could evade the preferred position that the holders of preferred stock have tried to obtain. The cumulative feature prevents such evasion.

CONVERTIBILITY

A substantial portion of preferred stock issued is convertible into common stock. For example, one share of preferred stock might be convertible into two shares of the firm's common stock at the option of the preferred stock shareholder. The *convertibility provision* remains a "sweetener" that reduces the initial cost of both debt and preferred stock. We may note at this point that VC firms frequently use convertible preferred stock. The main reasons are that the VC firm receives income if earned by the firm, has priority in liquidation, and if the firm does well can convert to an equity position and participate in the position.

OTHER PROVISIONS

Other provisions encountered in preferred stocks include the following.

- *Voting rights:* Sometimes preferred stockholders are given the *right to vote* for directors. When this feature is present, it generally permits the preferred stockholders to elect a minority of the board (say, three out of nine directors). The voting privilege becomes operative only if the company has not paid the preferred dividend for a specified period (say, six, eight, or ten quarters).

- *Participating:* A rare type of preferred stock is one that participates with the common stock in sharing the firm's earnings. The following factors generally relate to participating preferred stocks: (1) the stated preferred dividend is paid first (e.g., $5 a share), (2) income is allocated to common stock dividends up to an amount equal to the preferred dividend (in this case, $5), and (3) any remaining income is shared between common and preferred stockholders.

- *Sinking fund:* Some preferred issues have a *sinking fund requirement*, which ordinarily calls for the purchase and retirement of a given percentage of the preferred stock each year.

- *Maturity:* Preferred stocks almost never have *maturity dates* on which they must be retired. However, if the issue has a sinking fund this effectively creates maturity dates. Convertibility may also shorten the life of preferred stock.

- *Call provision:* A *call provision* gives the issuing corporation the right to call in the preferred stock for redemption, as for bonds. If it is used, the call provision states that the company must pay an amount greater than the par value of the preferred stock, the additional sum being defined as the call premium. For example, a $100 par value preferred stock might be callable at the option of the corporation at $108 a share.

- *Adjustable-rate preferred stock (ARPS):* Under unexpected inflation, preferred stock with fixed dividend rates becomes undesirable from the investor's point of view because of the risk that the market value of the preferred will fall. In order to share the risk and to make preferred issues more attractive to investors, many companies (particularly utilities) have begun to issue preferred stock with dividends tied to rates on various U.S. government obligations.

- *Auction-rate preferred stock:* Both ARPS and *auction-rate preferred stock* have a floating dividend rate and tax advantages. They differ in that whereas the dividend rate on the ARPS is typically tied to a government obligation the auction-rate preferred stock is set and reset by Dutch auctions. In the *Dutch auction process*, the bidder submits to the seller in charge of the auction the number of shares desired and a specified dividend level. The lowest dividend that will allow all of the available shares to be completely sold will be the dividend for the next 49 days, at which point a new auction resets the dividend.

Evaluation of Preferred Stock as a Source of Long-term Financing

There are advantages and disadvantages to selling preferred stock. The following are among the advantages.

- In contrast to bonds, the obligation to make committed interest payments is avoided.

- A firm wishing to expand can obtain higher earnings for the original owners by selling preferred stock with a limited return rather than by selling common stock.

- By selling preferred stock, the financial manager avoids the provision of equal participation in earnings the sale of additional common stock would require.

- Preferred stock also permits a company to avoid sharing control through voting participation.

- In contrast to bonds, it enables the firm to conserve mortgageable assets.

- Because preferred stock typically has no maturity or sinking fund, it is more flexible than a bond.

The following are among the disadvantages.

- Characteristically, preferred stock must be sold on a higher yield basis than that for bonds.

- Preferred stock dividends are not deductible as a tax expense, which is a characteristic that makes their cost differential very great in comparison to that of bonds.

- As explored in Chapter 13, the after-tax cost of debt is approximately 60 to 65% of the stated coupon rate for profitable firms. The after-tax cost of preferred stock, however, is generally the full percentage amount of the preferred dividend.

In fashioning securities, the financial manager needs to consider the investor's point of view. Frequently, it is asserted that preferred stocks have so many disadvantages for both the issuer and the investor that they should never be issued. Nevertheless, preferred stock provides the following advantages to the investor.

- It provides reasonably steady income.

- Preferred stockholders have a preference over common stockholders in liquidation.

- Many corporations (for example, insurance companies) like to hold preferred stocks as investments because 70 or 80% of the dividends received on these shares are not taxable.

Preferred stock also has the following disadvantages for investors.

- Although the holders of preferred stock bear a substantial risk, their returns are limited.

- Price fluctuations in preferred stock may be greater than those in bonds.

- The stockholders have no legally enforceable right to dividends.

- Accrued dividend arrearages are seldom settled in cash comparable to the amount of the obligation incurred.

Basically, preferred stock enables a firm to use leverage without fixed charges. For corporate investors, at least 70% of the dividends can be excluded from taxable income (so that the 35% tax rate becomes only 10.5%). Generally, preferred stocks have been sold largely by utility companies (for whom the nondeductibility of dividends as an expense for tax purposes is less of a disadvantage). This is because of the nature of the regulatory rate-making process, which essentially treats taxes paid as an expense to be considered in setting allowable rates of return.

Common Stock Financing

Two important positive considerations are involved in owning equity: income and control. The right to income carries the risk of loss. Control also involves responsibility and liability. Through the right to vote, holders of common stock have legal control of the corporation. As a practical matter, however, in many corporations the principal officers constitute all or a majority of the members of the board of directors. In this circumstance, the board may be controlled by the management rather than by the owners. However, numerous examples demonstrate that stockholders can reassert their control if they are dissatisfied with the corporation's policies.

In recent years, proxy battles with the aim of altering corporate policies have occurred with increasing frequency, and firms whose managers are unresponsive to stockholders' desires are subject to takeover bids by other firms. Another consideration involved in equity ownership is risk. Upon liquidation, holders of common stock are last in the priority of claims. Therefore, the portion of capital they contribute provides a cushion for creditors, if losses occur upon dissolution. The equity-to-total-assets ratio indicates the percentage by which assets may shrink in value upon liquidation before creditors will incur losses.

MAJOR PROVISIONS OF COMMON STOCK

The rights of holders of common stock in a business corporation are established by the laws of the state in which the corporation is chartered and by the terms of the charter granted by the state. Charters are relatively uniform on many matters, including collective and specific rights. Certain collective rights are usually given to the holders of common stock: (1) the right to amend the charter with the approval of the appropriate officials in the state of incorporation, (2) the right to adopt and amend bylaws, (3) the right to elect the directors of the corporation, (4) the right to authorize the sale of fixed assets, (5) the right to enter into mergers, (6) the right to change the amount of authorized common stock, and (7) the right to issue preferred stock, bonds, and other securities.

Holders of common stock also have specific rights as individual owners: (1) the right to vote in the manner prescribed by the corporate charter, (2) the right to sell their stock certificates (their evidence of ownership) and in this way to transfer their ownership interest to other persons, (3) the right to inspect the corporate books, and (4) the right to share residual assets of the corporation upon dissolution. (However, the holders of common stock are last among the claimants to the assets of the corporation.)

NATURE OF VOTING RIGHTS AND PROXY CONTESTS

For each share of common stock owned, the holder has the right to cast one vote at the annual meeting of stockholders or at such special meetings as may be called. Provision is made for the temporary transfer of the right to vote by an instrument known as a *proxy*. The transfer is limited in its duration. Typically, it applies only to a specific occasion, such as the annual meeting of stockholders. The SEC supervises the use of the proxy machinery and frequently issues rules and regulations to improve its administration.

A method of voting that has come into increased prominence is cumulative voting. Cumulative voting for directors is required in 22 states, including California, Illinois, Michigan, Ohio, and Pennsylvania. It is permissible in 18 states, including Delaware, New Jersey, and New York. Ten states make no provision for it.

Cumulative voting permits multiple votes for a single director. For example, suppose six directors are to be elected. Without cumulative voting, the owner of 100 shares can cast 100 votes for each of the six openings. When cumulative voting is permitted, the stockholder can accumulate the votes and cast all of them for one director instead of 100 each for six directors. Cumulative voting is designed to enable a minority group of stockholders to obtain some voice in the control of the company by electing at least one director to the board.

PREEMPTIVE RIGHT

The *preemptive right* gives holders of common stock the first option to purchase additional issues of common stock. In some states, the right is made part of every corporate charter. In others, the right must be specifically inserted in the charter. The purpose of the preemptive right is twofold. First, it protects the power of control for present stockholders. If it were not for this safeguard, the management of a corporation could issue new common stock to new stockholders in an attempt to wrest control from current stockholders.

The second, and by far the more important, protection the preemptive right affords stockholders concerns dilution of value. Selling new common stock at below market value enables new shareholders to purchase stock on terms more favorable than those that had been extended to the old shareholders. The preemptive right prevents such occurrences.

Evaluation of Common Stock as a Source of Long-term Financing

The advantages of financing with common stock include the following.

- Common stock does not entail fixed charges. If the company generates the earnings, it can pay common stock dividends. Unlike interest, there is no legal obligation to pay dividends.

- Common stock carries no fixed maturity date.

- Because common stock provides a cushion against losses to creditors, the sale of common stock increases the creditworthiness of the firm.

- Common stock can at times be sold more easily than debt. It appeals to certain investor groups because (1) it typically carries a higher expected return than preferred stock or debt and (2) in that it represents the ownership of the firm it provides the investor with a better hedge against inflation than straight preferred stock or bonds. Ordinarily, common stock increases in value when the value of real assets rises during an inflationary period.

- Returns from common stock in the form of capital gains may be subject to a lower personal income tax rate on capital gains. The effective personal income tax rates on common stock returns may be lower than the effective tax rates on the interest or preferred stock dividends.

- Employee stock participation programs can be an effective tool used by the company to align the financial interests of its general employee population, its management group, and its owners (the stockholders). Specific employee programs include the following.

  - Employee purchase plans in which the employer encourages the purchase of the company's stock through payroll deductions by absorbing the individual transaction fees or by even allowing the employee to purchase the stock at a slight discount to the current market price.

  - Executive and employee stock option plans whose value is tied to the underlying performance of the stock market.

  - *Employee stock ownership plans (ESOPs)*, which the company establishes to supplement or replace its employee retirement program while continuing to purchase stock on behalf of the ESOP trustee. An additional benefit of using equity as an employee motivator is that a high concentration of stock in employees' hands may limit an unwanted or hostile acquisition.

Disadvantages to the issuer of common stock include the following.

- The sale of common stock may extend voting rights or control to the additional stock owners. For this reason, among others, additional equity financing is often avoided by small and new firms (whose owner-managers may be unwilling to share control of their companies with outsiders).

- The use of debt may enable the firm to utilize funds at a fixed low cost, whereas common stock gives equal rights to new stockholders to share in the future net profits of the firm.

- The costs of underwriting and distributing common stock are usually higher than those for underwriting and distributing preferred stock or debt.

- As we saw in Chapter 13, if the firm has more equity or less debt than is called for in the optimum capital structure the average cost of capital will be higher than necessary.

- Common stock dividends are not deductible as an expense for calculating the corporation's income subject to the federal income tax, but bond interest is deductible. The impact of this factor is reflected in the relative cost of equity capital in regard to debt capital.

summary

This chapter discussed many aspects of long-term financing, including sources of long-term financing, procedures for obtaining that financing, and a review of the unique characteristics and advantages/disadvantages of each form. We also considered financing for the new firm in its initial stages of start-up and rapid growth through to its more mature stages.

Three major forms of direct financing are (1) term lending by commercial banks, (2) the private placement of securities with insurance companies and pension funds, and (3) private equity placement (also called VC financing). Term loans and private placements represent similar financing arrangements. VC financing has taken on increased importance in recent years. Sources of VC financing include commercial banks, investment banks, VC firms, wealthy individuals (also called "angel" financing), and corporate-sponsored venture capitalists. VC firms typically use convertible preferred stock in staged financing as the good performance of the recipient firm is demonstrated.

The investment banker provides middleman services to both the seller and the buyer of new securities, helping to plan the issue, underwriting the issue, and handling the job of selling the issue to the ultimate investor. The investment banker must also look to the interests of the brokerage customers. If these investors are not satisfied with the banker's products, they will deal elsewhere. Thus, the investment banker performs a certification role for the issuer.

Going public and initial public offerings represent a fundamental change in the lifestyle of business firms. Costs of flotation are higher for initial public offerings than for seasoned issues. Flotation costs are higher for best-efforts offerings than for firm commitments. Best-efforts offerings typically involve smaller firms whose share prices exhibit greater volatility in the after-market.

Debt can take many forms, such as secured or unsecured debt and short-term or long-term debt. We discussed the various common attributes of debt and presented an appropriate analysis in which a company considers refinancing an existing debt instrument. Although the characteristics of preferred stock vary, some patterns persist.

Preferred stocks usually have priority over common stocks with respect to earnings and claims on assets in liquidation. Preferred stocks are perpetual (no maturity) but are sometimes callable. They are typically nonparticipating and offer only contingent voting rights. Preferred stock dividends are usually cumulative. Common stock involves the balancing of risk, income, and control. We analyzed various dimensions of the rights of common stockholders.

Questions

14.1   What is the difference between a VC firm and an investment banking firm?

14.2   Why are convertible preferred stock (preferred stock that is convertible into common stock) and a staged capital commitment employed by VC firms?

14.3   Define these terms: *brokerage firm*, *underwriting*, *selling group*, and *investment banking*.

14.4   Discuss the steps an entrepreneur might follow to raise capital to invest in a business.

14.5   Before entering a formal agreement, investment bankers carefully investigate the companies whose securities they underwrite. This is especially true of the issues of firms going public for the first time. Because investment bankers do not themselves plan to hold the securities but intend to sell them to others as soon as possible, why are they so concerned about making careful investigations? Does your answer to the question have any bearing on the fact that investment banking is a very difficult field to enter? Explain.

14.6   If competitive bidding were required on all security offerings, would flotation costs be higher or lower? Would the size of the issuing firm be material in determining the effects of required competitive bidding?

14.7   Each month, the SEC publishes a report of the transactions made by the officers and directors of listed firms in their own companies' equity securities. Why do you suppose the SEC makes this report?

14.8   Prior to 1933, investment banking and commercial banking were both carried on by the same firm. In that year, however, the Banking Act required that these functions be separated. Discuss the pros and cons of this forced separation.

14.9   Suppose two similar firms are each selling $10 million of common stock. The firms are of the same size, are in the same industry, have the same leverage, and so on. One is publicly owned and the other is closely held. Will their costs of flotation be the same? If the issue were $10 million of bonds, would your answer be the same?

14.10 Evaluate the following statement: The fundamental purpose of the federal security laws dealing with new issues is to prevent investors, principally small ones, from sustaining losses on the purchase of stocks.

14.11   What issues are raised by the increasing purchase of equities by institutional investors?

14.12   What are the reasons for not letting officers and directors of a corporation make short sales in their company's stock?

14.13   It is frequently stated that the primary purpose of the preemptive right is to allow individuals to maintain their proportionate share of the ownership and control of a corporation. Just how important do you suppose this consideration is for the average stockholder of a firm whose shares are traded on the NYSE or the American Stock Exchange?

14.14   Is the preemptive right likely to be of more importance to stockholders of closely held firms? Explain.

14.15   Does it matter who owns a corporation's stock; that is, institutions versus individuals (also called retail stockholders)? To what type of firm could it matter?

14.16   Hershey holds about a 37% market share in the United States, whereas M&M Mars (Masterfoods) has about a 28% market share. Mars is a privately held family business and Hershey is publicly traded. What advantages and disadvantages does Hershey face? What advantages and disadvantages does Masterfoods face?

Leases

No matter the industry or specific business, all firms are generally interested in using buildings and equipment. One way of obtaining their use is to purchase them, but an alternative is to lease them. Originally, leasing was most often associated with real estate (land and buildings) but today virtually any type of fixed asset can be leased. We estimate that from 15 to 20% of all new capital equipment put in use by business each year is leased. In many cases, our analysis will show that leasing is a perfect substitute for borrowing. Hence, managers should think of the lease/borrow decision rather than the lease/purchase decision.

Learning Outcomes

After completing this chapter, you should be able to:

1 Ascertain the differences between different types of leases: operating and capital

2 Compare the accounting results for both operating and capital leases

3 Conduct a lease versus borrow analysis

4 Compute the net advantage of leasing an asset

5 Discuss when leasing may provide systematic benefits

Leasing simultaneously provides for the use of assets and their financing. One advantage over debt is that the lessor has a better position than a creditor if the user firm experiences financial difficulties. If the lessee does not meet the lease obligations, the lessor has a stronger legal right to take back the asset because the lessor still legally owns it. A creditor, even a secured creditor, encounters costs and delays in recovering assets that have been directly or indirectly financed.

Because the lessor has less risk than other financing sources used in acquiring assets, the riskier the firm seeking financing the greater the reason for the supplier of financing to formulate a leasing arrangement rather than a loan. The relative tax positions of lessors and users of assets may also affect the lease versus borrow decision. In this chapter, we discuss the various types of leases, accounting for leases, and the evaluation of the lease/borrow decision.

Types of Leases

Leases take several different forms, the most important of which are operating leases, financial leases, and a sale and leaseback. A lease can extend from a day to 30 years or longer. Before addressing the types of leases, let's clarify the terms *lessor* and *lessee*. The *lessor* is the party (individual, corporation, partnership, and so on) that owns the asset. In a building example, we would call the landlord the lessor. The *lessee* is the one who is using the asset. Continuing the building example, the lessee is the renter or tenant. The lessor is the one selling the use of the property or equipment, whereas the lessee is the one purchasing the use of the property or equipment. These three major types of leases are described in the sections that follow.

OPERATING LEASES

An *operating lease* is a contractual arrangement wherein the lessor agrees to provide an asset to the lessee for a specified period of time. The lessee agrees to make periodic payments to the lessor for use of the asset. The length of the lease can be a day, a week, a month, a year, or even longer, but usually less than five years.

Frequently, an operating lease may contain a cancellation clause, giving the lessee the right to cancel the lease and return the equipment before the expiration of the basic agreement. This cancellation clause usually contains a negotiated cancellation penalty that is payable by the lessee. In effect, the cancellation clause is a put option that allows return of the equipment if technological developments render it obsolete or if it simply is no longer needed, which is an important consideration for the lessee.

Another important characteristic of the operating lease is that frequently it is not fully amortized. That is, the leasing period is shorter than the useful life of the underlying asset, and the payments required under the lease contract may not be sufficient to recover the full cost of the equipment. Obviously, the lessor expects to recover the cost either in subsequent renewal payments or upon disposal of the equipment. In some cases, there may be another option that allows the lessee to purchase the asset at a predetermined price upon termination. In any case, at the end of the lease the asset is returned to the lessor (who can lease the asset again or sell it).

There may be additional clauses within a lease that among other things restrict the use of the asset. In a shopping mall, the lessor may try to attract a greeting card store to complement the other stores in the mall. To make this a more attractive location to a greeting card store, the lessor may specifically identify in leases with the other tenants that their stores can only have a limited amount of shelf space devoted to greeting cards.

Other examples are found every day in the classified section of the local newspaper. New-car dealers often offer attractive leasing rates. You may be able to secure the use of a $20,000 vehicle for $2,000 down and $239 per month for 36 months. The lessee only recovers $10,604 [$2,000 + 36($239)]. Even without considering the time value of money, total payments are far short of the original value of the vehicle. In this case, the lessor is also factoring in the anticipated resale value of the vehicle in three years. To further enhance resaleability, the lease limits mileage to 10,000 or 12,000 miles per year before a significant per-mile charge is imposed. The lease may even include a predetermined special buyout provision at termination. Payments on an operating lease are often considered as rent expense by the lessee.

A variation of the operating lease is an operating lease that includes maintenance services in addition to financing. This lease is referred to as an *operating service lease*. IBM is one of the pioneers of the service lease contract. Computers and office copying machines, together with automobiles and trucks, are the primary types of equipment covered by operating leases. These leases ordinarily call for the lessor to maintain and service the leased equipment, and the costs of this maintenance are either built into the lease payments or contracted for separately.

FINANCIAL LEASES

A strict *financial lease* is one that does not provide for maintenance services, is not cancelable, and is fully amortized (that is, the lessor contracts for rental payments equal to the full price of the leased equipment). The typical arrangement involves the following steps.

1. The firm that will use the equipment prepares a capital expenditure analysis (see Chapters 10 and 11) that indicates a positive NPV for the project.

2. This firm then selects the specific items it requires and negotiates the price and delivery terms with the manufacturer or distributor. If the specific terms are significantly different than in the capital evaluation, the NPV must be reexamined and verified.

3. Next, the user firm arranges with a bank or leasing company for the latter to purchase the equipment from the manufacturer or distributor, simultaneously executing an agreement to lease the equipment from the financial institution. The terms call for full amortization of the financial institution's cost, plus a return on the lessor's investment. The lessee generally has the option to renew the lease at a reduced rental upon expiration of the basic lease but does not have the right to cancel the basic lease without completely paying off the financial institution.

A special type of the financial lease is a leveraged lease. In a *leveraged lease*, the lessor will be an equity partner in the asset. In this case, the lessee will provide say 20% of the funds to the lessor in order to purchase the asset. Financial leases are almost the same as sale and leaseback. The main difference is that the leased equipment is new and the lessor purchases it from a manufacturer or a distributor instead of from the user-lessee. A sale and leaseback can thus be thought of as a special type of financial lease.

SALE AND LEASEBACK

Under a *sale and leaseback arrangement*, a firm owning land, buildings, or equipment sells the property to a financial institution and simultaneously executes an agreement to lease the property back for a certain period under specific terms. Note that the seller, or lessee, immediately receives the purchase price put up by the purchaser (lessor). At the same time, the seller-lessee retains the use of the property. This parallel is carried over to the lease payment schedule.

Under a mortgage loan arrangement, the financial institution receives a series of equal payments just sufficient to amortize the loan and to provide the lender with a specified rate of return on investment. Under a sale and leaseback arrangement, the lease payments are set up in the same manner. The payments are sufficient to return the full purchase price to the financial institution in addition to providing it with some return on its investment.

This type of arrangement is often used to finance new buildings or major pieces of equipment. The initial benefit is that the construction of the facility or equipment is completely the responsibility of the user of the asset. In that way, the lessee designs and builds exactly what they need. There is no financial intermediary acting as project manager. The project manager is the lessee and the one with expert knowledge about the business needs.

Accounting for Leases

Consistent reporting of the same economic event is a tenant of US GAAP. Leasing is an area in which wide variations in financial performance could be obtained by the lessee if there were no specific rules governing the reporting of leases. We begin with an illustration.

COMPARISON OF FINANCIAL STATEMENTS

Let's say that at the end of last year the engineering group at Turnberry Corporation proposed a cost savings project. A capital authorization request indicated a strong positive NPV, and management approved the project. At the beginning of this year, further analysis examines the accounting ramifications of three options for acquiring the use of this asset: (1) purchase and borrow, (2) operating lease, and (3) financial (capital) lease. At the beginning of the year, Turnberry had the assets, liabilities, and stockholders' equity outlined in the following table.

Table 15.1 reflects the projected accounting performance and position under the three alternative financing approaches.

ASSETS		LIABILITIES AND EQUITY	
Current assets	$1,400	Current liabilities	$500
		Long-term debt	700
Gross, PP&E	1,000	Total liabilities	1,200
Accumulated depreciated	(400)		
Net, PPE	600	Equity	800
Total assets	$2,000	Total liability & equity	$2,000

ACCOUNTING PERFORMANCE WITH AN ASSET PURCHASE

Assume that at the beginning of the current year Turnberry enters into an agreement to purchase this asset for $1,000 as well as to finance this asset with long-term debt. The asset is expected to have a life of 10 years and no salvage value at the end of that period. In addition, the asset will be financed with a 10-year amortizable loan at 8.0% interest.

The first column of Table 15.1 illustrates the financial performance and position of Turnberry at the end of the year, assuming the purchase of this asset and borrowing of funds. The income statement reflects sales less other operating expenses and $180 of expenses related to the purchasing and borrowing, which leads to a net income of $192. The expense

TABLE 15.1	Accounting Examples—Year 1		
INCOME STATEMENT	**ASSET PURCHASE**	**OPERATING LEASE**	**CAPITAL LEASE**
Sales	$5,000	$5,000	$5,000
Expenses:			
Other operating expense	4,500	4,500	4,500
New equipment depreciation	100	180[a]	100
Interest expense	80	n/a	80
Total expense	4,680	4,680	4,680
Pre-tax income	320	320	320
Taxes (40%)	128	128	128
Net Income	$192	$192	$192
ASSETS			
Current assets	$1,703	$1,672	$1,703
Prior gross, plant, prop. & equip.	1,000	1,000	1,000
Prior accumulated depreciation	(480)	(480)	(480)
Prior net, PPE	520	520	520
New plant, property & equipment	1,000	n/a	1,000
New accumulated depreciation	(100)	n/a	(100)
New net, PPE	900	n/a	900
Total assets	$3,123	$2,192	$3,123
LIABILITIES & EQUITY			
Current liabilities	$500	$500	$500
Prior, long-term liabilities	700	700	700
New borrowings	931	n/a	931
Total liabilities	2,131	1,200	2,131
Stockholders' equity	992	992	992
Total liab. & equity	$3,123	$2,192	$3,123
FINANCIAL METRICS			
Net margin	3.8%	3.8%	3.8%
Asset turnover	1.60	2.28	1.60
Return on assets	6.1%	8.8%	6.1%
Financial leverage	3.15	2.21	3.15
Return on equity	19.4%	19.4%	19.4%

[a] Under the Operating Lease scenario, the $180 expense represents the operating lease.

of $180 is comprised of two items: depreciation expense ($100) and interest expense ($80, first-year loan amortization schedule). The balance sheet includes a net amount of $900 for this new asset ($1,000 purchase price less one year's depreciation) and a net amount of $931 of liabilities for the new loan ($1,000 amount borrowed less a one-year amortizable loan). Note the performance metrics at the bottom of Table 15.1.

ACCOUNTING PERFORMANCE WITH AN OPERATING LEASE

The second column in Table 15.1 shows what could happen if Turnberry enters into a 10-year operating lease. The terms of the lease agreement require Turnberry to pay $180 a year, which covers the financing cost, administrative cost (say $11), and reasonable profit (say $20) for the lessor.

Reviewing the financial performance, net income continues to be reported as $192 for the projected year because the operating lease payment is equal to the total of depreciation and interest expense in the asset purchase scenario. Consequently, the net margin is the same as in the asset purchase scenario. However, the structural effects of an operating lease are clearly evident on the balance sheet when compared to the asset purchase scenario. Assets and liabilities are underreported. As a result, asset turnover is stronger and financial leverage is stronger than when the asset is purchased. The asset turnover shows greater strength (2.28 versus 1.60) because the new asset is not recorded on the books. Likewise, financial leverage shows a stronger position (2.21 versus 3.15) because the ongoing liability is not recorded on the books either.

Although the economics and realities of the situation (a 10-year use of the underlying asset) are the same under either scenario, the reporting and analytical results differ. Under the operating lease scenario as presented in Table 15.1, the company has effectively gained *"off balance sheet" financing*. That is, they entered into a long-term lease, gained the long-term use of the asset, and never recognized this additional commitment (or liability). The accounting profession recognized this inconsistency and addressed it.

ACCOUNTING FOR LEASES: US GAAP

In November of 1976, the Financial Accounting Standards Board (FASB) issued its Statement of Financial Accounting Standards No. 13, Accounting for Leases. Like other FASB statements, the standards set forth must be followed by business firms if their financial statements are to receive certification by auditors. FASB Statement No. 13 has implications both for the utilization of leases and for their accounting treatment. The elements of FASB Statement No. 13 most relevant for financial analysis of leases are summarized in material following. For some types of leases, this FASB statement requires that the obligation be capitalized on the asset side of the balance sheet, with a reduced lease obligation on the liability side. The accounting treatment depends on the type of lease.

1. Capital Leases
2. Operating Leases

From the standpoint of the lessee, if a lease is not a capital lease it is classified as an operating lease. A lease is classified in Statement No. 13 as a capital lease if it meets *one or more* of four Paragraph 7 criteria.

1. The lease transfers ownership of the property to the lessee by the end of its term.
2. The lease gives the lessee the option to purchase the property at a price sufficiently below the expected fair value of the property that the exercise of the option is highly probable.
3. The lease term is equal to 75% or more of the estimated economic life of the property.
4. The present value of the minimum lease payments exceeds 90% of the fair value of the property at the inception of the lease. The discount factor to be used in calculating the present value is the implicit rate used by the lessor or the lessee's incremental borrowing rate, whichever is lower. (Note that the lower discount factor results in a higher calculated present value for a given pattern of lease payments. It thus increases the likelihood that the 90% test will be met and that the lease will be classified as a capital lease.)

The classification of capital lease is more detailed than the two categories of operating and financial leases described previously for the lessor.

- Sales-type leases

- Direct financing leases

- Leveraged leases

- Operating leases (all leases other than the first three)

The first three types are financing leases (capital leases) for accounting purposes. Sales-type leases and direct financing leases meet one or more of the four Paragraph 7 criteria and both of the Paragraph 8 criteria, which are (1) collectibility of the minimum lease payments is reasonably predictable and (2) no important uncertainties surround the amount of unreimbursable costs yet to be incurred by the lessor under the lease.

Sales-type leases normally arise when manufacturers or dealers use leasing in marketing their products. *Direct financing leases* are leases (other than leveraged leases) for which the *cost-of-carrying* amount* is equal to the fair value of the leased property at the inception of the lease. *Leveraged leases* are direct financing leases in which substantial financing is provided by a long-term creditor on a non-recourse basis with respect to the general credit of the lessor.

ACCOUNTING BY LESSEES

For operating leases, rentals must be charged to expense over the lease term. Thus, clearly a one-week car rental while on a business trip, a three-month rental of additional office space, or a six-month rental of a billboard are examples of operating leases. The associated fees are properly charged to rental expense and handled as in the second column (Operating Lease) in Table 15.1. Footnotes detail future rental obligations for each of the next five years and in total.

A lease that meets any one of the four criteria noted previously is considered a *capital lease*. For lessees, capital leases are to be capitalized and shown on the balance sheet both as a fixed asset and a non-current obligation. This is similar to how the purchase of the asset would be recorded. Capitalization represents the present value of the minimum lease payments minus that portion of lease payments representing executory costs such as insurance, maintenance, and taxes to be paid by the lessor (including any profit return in such charges). The discount factor is as described in Paragraph 7(4): the lower of the implicit rates used by the lessor and the incremental borrowing rate of the lessee.

For example, the lease in column 2 of Table 15.1 would have been classified as a capital lease because it meets at least the third test of Paragraph 7 [lease term is equal to 75% or more of the estimated economic life of the property]. Recall that the operating lease payment was $180 per year. That payment included $11 of administrative expense and $20 of profit for the lessor. Therefore, the net lease payment was $149 per annum. Capitalizing this lease payment at an 8% incremental borrowing rate for the lessee yields a present value of $1,000 (or the cost of the equipment).

The asset must be amortized in a manner consistent with the lessee's normal depreciation policy for owned assets. During the lease term, each lease payment is to be allocated between a reduction of the obligation and the interest expense to produce a constant rate of interest on the remaining balance of the obligation. Thus, for capital leases the balance sheet includes the items in the final column of Table 15.1. The accounting for the capital lease is the same as for the purchase and borrow scenario (column 1 of Table 15.1). Both the asset and liability are recognized on the balance sheet. "Off balance sheet" financing is gone!

For the year, Turnberry recognizes $100 of depreciation expense and $80 in interest. At the end of the first year, the leased asset has a book value of $900 and the lease obligation has a value of $931. The value of the lease obligation reflects the first year's lease payment of $149, with $80 assigned to interest expense and a $69 principal repayment. The results of a capitalized lease or an outright purchase and borrow are identical. Thus, through FASB Statement No. 13 capitalized leases have eliminated the common distortions between leasing and borrowing.

---

*The cost of carry is the asset value that gets reflected on the balance sheet of the lessee.

In addition to the balance sheet capitalization of capital leases, substantial additional footnote disclosures are required for both capital and operating leases. These include a description of leasing arrangements, an analysis of leased property under capital leases by major classes of property, a schedule by years of future minimum lease payments (with executory and interest costs broken out for capital leases), and contingent rentals for operating leases.

FASB Statement No. 13 sets forth requirements for capitalizing leases and for standardizing disclosures by lessees for both capital leases and operating leases. Lease commitments, therefore, do not represent "off balance sheet" financing for capital assets, and standard disclosure requirements make general the footnote reporting of information on operating leases. Hence, the argument that leasing represents a form of off-balance-sheet financing that lenders may not take into account in their analysis of the financial position of firms seeking financing is simply invalid. Sophisticated lenders have never been fooled by most off-balance-sheet leasing obligations. However, the capitalization of capital leases and the standard disclosure requirements for operating leases will make it easier for general users of financial reports to obtain additional information on firms' leasing obligations. Hence, the requirements of FASB Statement No. 13 are useful. Probably, the extent or use of leasing will remain substantially unaltered because the particular circumstances that have provided a basis for its use in the past are not likely to be greatly affected by the increased disclosure requirements.

Internal Revenue Service Requirements for a Lease

The full amount of the annual lease payments is deductible for income tax purposes, provided the Internal Revenue Service (IRS) agrees that a particular contract is a genuine lease and not simply an installment loan called a lease. This makes it important that the lease contract be written in a form acceptable to the IRS. Following are the major requirements for bona fide lease transactions from the standpoint of the IRS.

- The term must be less than 30 years. Otherwise, the lease is considered a sale.

- The rent must represent a reasonable return to the lessor (in the range of 7 to 12% on the investment).

- The renewal option must be bona fide, and this requirement can best be met by giving the lessee the first option to meet an equal bona fide outside offer.

- There must be no repurchase option. If there is, the lessee should merely be given parity with an equal outside offer.

The IRS wants to be sure that the business arrangement is truly a lease and not a mask for a sale.

The Investment Decision

The first step before making the lease or borrow decision is to make the investment decision. Before going any further, we must turn to the central issue; namely, whether the investment should be undertaken in the first place. If the project has a large negative NPV, it will not make any difference how we finance it. Any value added by financing can be easily outweighed by unfavorable operating cash flows from the project itself. In addition, remember that the strict financial leases are not cancelable except via bankruptcy.

Owning an asset exposes one to more risk than simply taking a lending or a lease position. Owning and operating a project involves the total risk of its cash flows, not merely the relatively secure risk of a debt position. For our example, using the tools of Chapter 13 we estimate that the appropriate cost of capital for this project is 10%. After discussing the potential investment with marketing, production, engineering, and accounting, let's assume the following about the investment.

- I_0 = Investment in year 0 = $80,000

- n   = Project life   = 5 years

- R   = Incremental revenue = $60,000

- C   = Cost of sales   = $25,200 (or 42.0% of Sales), excluding Dep_t

- M   = Marketing expense   = $6,000 (or 7.5% of sales), excluding Dep_t

- T   = Tax rate   = 37.5%

- Dep_t = Depreciation   = $16,000 per year (I/n)

- k   = Cost of capital   = 10%

Using the capital budgeting techniques of Chapters 10 and 11, the NPV of the project is calculated per Equation 15.1.

$$NPV = -I_0 + \sum_{t=1}^{n} \frac{(R_t - C_t - M_t)(1-T) + TDep_t}{[1+k]^t}$$

$= -80,000 + \text{PVIFA} (10\%, 5 \text{ yrs.}) [(60,000 - 25,200 - 6,000)(1 - 0.375) + 0.375(16,000)]$

$= -80,000 + 3.7908 [(28,800) (0.625) + 0.375 (16,000)]$

$= -80,000 + 3.7908 [(18,000) + (6,000)]$ (15.1)

$= -80,000 + 3.7908 [24,000] = \$10,979$

Where:

Increase in Cash Operating Income = (R – C – M)

Increase in Cash After-tax Operating Income = (R – C – M) (1 – T)

Increase in Operating Cash Flow = [(R – C– M) (1 – T)] + T (Dep)

Under our assumptions, the project generates an incremental cash flow* of $24,000 per year and should be accepted because it has a positive NPV at the company's (or this project's) cost of capital. Note that because this project is an average risk project for this company and this industry we assume that the cost of capital is the same for the project as it is for the company.

---

*For simplicity we chose to present the cash flow per above [(R-C-M) (1-T) + T(Dep)] this is identical to computing after-tax operating income ($8,000) and adding back depreciation, as follows:

[After Tax Operating Income] + (Depreciation) = Incremental Cash Flow

[(R-C-M-Dep) (1-T) + (Dep)]

[($60,000-$25,200-$6,000-$16,000)(1-.0375)+($16,000)]

[($12,800)(0.625)+$16,000]=$8,000+$16,000=$24,000.

The project is a "Go"! The question now shifts to how we are going to finance the project. Will we use all equity? Will we use some equity? How large of a role does debt play? These were the issues considered in Chapter 13. If we conclude that we will not issue any additional equity and that we

will raise the funds through the debt market, we need to seek the lowest cost of debt. Leasing is merely an alternative debt form. We are now ready to make the next decision: lease versus borrow!

The Financing Decision: Lease Versus Borrow

We next consider the framework for the analysis of the cost of owning versus the cost of leasing. The form of leasing to be analyzed initially will be a pure financial lease that is fully amortized, noncancelable, and without provision for maintenance services. As before, we assume the asset's salvage value is zero.

THE LESSOR'S POINT OF VIEW

To lay a foundation for the leasing versus owning cost comparison, the lessor's point of view will first be considered. The leasing company (lessor) could be a commercial bank, a subsidiary of a commercial bank, or an independent leasing company. These various types of lessors are considered to be providing financial intermediation services of essentially the same type. Each form of financial intermediary is considered to be providing a product, which represents a form of senior debt financing to the company that uses the equipment.

Because the product being sold by the financial intermediary is a debt instrument, the income to that intermediary is considered a return on debt that earns the intermediary's cost of capital. This is equivalent to the judgment that the financial intermediary's cost of capital, composed of both debt and equity capital, is approximately equal to the rate charged on the debt (or equivalent) instruments that comprise its assets (the assets of the lessor in our analysis).

We can then proceed to calculate the required lease-rental charge that must be made by the lessor to obtain a fair rate of return for a lending position. We combine the facts about the asset described previously with the following.

- k_b = before-tax cost of debt = 8%

- T = lessor's corporate tax rate = 37.5%

- NPV_{LOR} = NPV of the lease-rental income from the assets to the lessor

With these facts, the equilibrium lease-rental rate in a competitive market of lessors can be calculated. What has been posed is a standard capital budgeting question: What cash flow return from the use of an asset will earn the applicable cost of capital? Previously, we looked at the investment decision for the user of the asset. Does the investment provide enough cash to make it economically viable and to yield a positive NPV?

The lessor needs to address a similar question before offering to lease the asset: At what minimum lease payment will the lessor be willing to enter into the lease? The investment in the capital budgeting project is $-I_0$. The return is composed of two elements: the cash inflow from the lease rental and the tax shelter from depreciation.

The discount factor is the lessor's opportunity cost of funds for these types of investments (i.e., weighted cost of capital), which as we have indicated will be equal to the applicable rate on debt instruments of the risk of the cash flows involved. The after-tax weighted cost of capital to the lessor is 5%. In other words, the bank or leasing company has to earn at least 5% after taxes in order for the lease to have a positive NPV. Note that the after-tax rate of return is equal to:

$$\text{Lessor's Cost of Capital} = k_{LOR} = k_b (1 - T) = 0.08 (1 - 0.375) = 0.05$$

Next, we can compute the minimum competitive lease fee that would be charged by the lessor. Equation 15.2 discounts the lease cash flows at the lessor's after-tax cost of capital (5%). The cash flows are the after-tax lease payments received plus the depreciation tax shield provided because the lessor owns the asset. The NPV of the lease to the lessor is:

$$NPV_{LOR} = -I_0 + \sum_{t=1}^{n} \frac{L_t(1-T) + TDep_t}{(1+k_{LOR})^t}$$

$$= -I_0 + PVIFA\ (5\%, 5\ \text{yrs.})[L_t(1-T) + TDep_t] \qquad (15.2)$$

Where:

L_t = periodic lease payment (assumed to be paid at the end of each period)

We can now solve for the equilibrium lease-rental rate required by the lessor by utilizing the data inputs we have provided. The NPV of the lease is set equal to zero so that we can compute the minimum lease payment required by the lessor. The minimum fee will also be the competitive fee if the leasing industry is perfectly competitive.

- $0 = -\$80,000 + (4.3295)[0.625L_t + 0.375(\$16,000)]$
- $0 = -\$80,000 + 2.7059L_t + \$25,977$
- $L_t = \$19,965$

The tax shield on the depreciation provides the lessor with a $25,977 benefit in present value terms. The tax shield reduces the net investment amount and results in a minimum lease payment of $19,965 per year.

THE LESSEE'S POINT OF VIEW

Presented with a lease-rental rate of $19,965, the user firm takes the lease fee as an input in making a comparison of the cost of leasing with the cost of borrowing. The analysis of the possible benefits of leasing compared to borrowing involves the analysis of the following cash flows.

- *Net cost of borrowing:* (1) a cash savings equal to the dollar amount of the investment outlay, I_0, which the firm does not have to incur if it leases and (2) the present value of the opportunity cost of the lost depreciation tax shield, $PV(TDep_t)$.

- *Net cost of leasing:* A cash outflow amounting to the present value of the after-tax lease dollars that must be paid out, $PV[L_t (1 - T)]$.

These three terms are presented in Equation 15.3, which gives the net advantage of leasing (NAL) compared to borrowing in present value terms.

$$NAL = \text{Cost of Borrowing} - \text{Cost of Leasing}$$
$$NAL = [I_0 - PV(T * Dep_t)] - PV[L_t(1 - T)] \qquad (15.3)$$

The cost of borrowing is the investment outlay (I_0) offset by the present value of the depreciation tax shield ($T*Dep_t$.) The cost of leasing is the present value of the after-tax cost of the annual lease payment. We assume that from the standpoint of the user firm debt and lease financing are perfect substitutes. This is certainly true for strict financial leases. We can write the NAL of the lease from the lessee's point of view as expressed by Equation 15.4.

$$NAL = \left[I_0 - \sum_{t=1}^{n} \frac{T*Dep_t}{[1+(1-T)k_b]^t} \right] - \sum_{t=1}^{n} \frac{L_t(1-T)}{[1+(1-T)k_b]} \tag{15.4}$$

Note that Equation 15.4 is exactly the same as Equation 15.2, the value of the lease from the lessor's point of view, if two conditions are met: (1) the lessee and the lessor have the same tax rate, T, and (2) the after-tax weighted average cost of capital to the lessor, k_{LOR}, is equal to the after-tax cost of borrowing to the lessee. For the time being, we have assumed that the tax rates of the lessee and lessor are equal, but they need not be. The discount rates have to be the same because the cash flows in the numerators of Equations 15.2 and 15.4 are identical and have the same risk. The rate earned by the lessor is the rate paid by the lessee. Substituting the numbers from our example into Equation 15.4, we have:

$$NAL = \{I_0 - PVIFA(5\%, 5yrs.)[T * Dep_t]\} - PVIFA(5\%, 5yrs.)[L_t(1 - T)]$$
$$= [80,000 - 4.3295(0.375)(16,000)] - [4.3295(19,965)(1 - 0.375)]$$
$$= (80,000 - 25,976) - 54,024$$
$$= 54,024 - 54,024 = \$0$$

The cost of ownership and borrowing is $54,024, net of the depreciation tax shield. This is the same as the cost of leasing in present value terms. The NAL is zero and the firm is indifferent between the two methods of financing the project, leasing or borrowing. In our example, the cost of borrowing equals the cost of leasing. Consequently, there is equilibrium between the lessor market and the user market. The lessor earns its cost of capital, which determines the lease-rental charge it must make. At this lease-rental rate, and given that the lessee and lessor have identical tax rates, the lessee is indifferent between borrowing to own the asset or leasing it.

THE EFFECT OF TAXES

Whenever the lessor (owner of the asset) has a higher tax rate than the lessee (user of the asset), there is a possibility (but not necessity) of a financial advantage of leasing over borrowing in order to finance a project. To illustrate this result, assume that the numbers from the lessor's point of view are unchanged. With a 37.5% tax rate, the lessor would require a lease fee of $L_t = \$19,965$ in order to earn 5% after taxes.

However, suppose the lessee's tax rate is 0 rather than 37.5% (as assumed earlier). This may be the case for a corporation with large net operating losses (NOLs), a university, church, or other non-profit entity. If so, the after-tax cost of debt to the lessee increases from 5% to 8%, which is the same as the pre-tax cost of borrowing. Substituting the lease fee and depreciation opportunity costs into Equation 15.4, along with the 0% tax rate and the higher after-tax borrowing rate (8%), we have:

$$NAL = \{I_0 - PVIFA(8\%, 5yrs.)[T * Dep_t]\} - PVIFA(8\%, 5yrs.)[L_t(1 - T)]$$
$$= [80,000 - 3.9927(0.000)(16,000)] - [3.9927(19,965)(1 - 0.000)]$$
$$= (80,000 - 0) - 79,714$$
$$= 80,000 - 79,714 = \$286$$

Now the net advantage of leasing is positive because the cost of borrowing is greater than the cost of leasing. The lease has a positive NPV when compared to borrowing. Therefore, from the lessee's point of view leasing is preferred to borrowing as a means of financing the project. The increased value to the lessee results from the fact that the lessor can take better advantage of the tax shelters (depreciation and interest expenses) because of the lessor's higher tax rate.

Alternative Computation Procedures in the Leasing Analysis

Thus far, we have made the leasing versus owning analysis using compact equations. The same results can be obtained when the flows are tabulated by years in a spreadsheet. As we saw in Chapters 10 and 11, spreadsheets provide a convenient tool for illustration and discussion. In practice, spreadsheets would be the tool of choice for analyzing the lease versus borrow decision.

To introduce the leasing model via spreadsheets, we begin by using the previous example. The cost of the asset is $80,000, and the required lease-rental rate is calculated to be $19,965 under straight-line depreciation. The earlier analysis treated leasing and borrowing as substitutes. Thus, under the ownership scenario the $80,000 is assumed to be borrowed at an 8% before-tax cost of debt by the user of the asset. Once again, we will derive the net advantage of leasing by comparing the net present cost of purchasing and borrowing versus the net present cost of leasing. The lower cost provides the advantage and should be pursued.

We assume that the loan of $80,000 is paid off at a level annual amount that covers annual interest charges plus amortization of the principal. Just as we did in Chapter 3, we can calculate the annual payments on this loan. The amount is an annuity that can be determined by the use of a financial calculator (PV = $80,000, i% = 8%, N = 5) or the present value of an annuity formula, given by Equation 15.5.

$$\$80,000 = \sum_{t=1}^{n} \frac{a_t}{(1+k_b)^t}$$

$$a_t = \frac{\$80,000}{(PVIFA)(8\%, 5yrs.)} \tag{15.5}$$

$$= \frac{\$80,000}{3.9927} = \$20,037$$

Solving Equation 15.5 for the annual loan payments results in $20,037, which represents the principal plus interest payments listed in column 3 of Table 15.2. Note that the present value of five years of $20,037 payments at 8% is $80,000 (the original amount of the investment). The sum of these five annual payments (including a final year reduced payment) is $100,182, which represents repayment of the principal of $80,000 plus the sum of the annual interest payments.

The interest payments of each year are determined by multiplying column 2 (the balance of principal owed at the end of the year) by 8%, the assumed cost of borrowing. The sum of the annual interest payments does, in fact, equal the total interest of $20,182 obtained by deducting the principal of $80,000 from the total of the five annual payments shown in

TABLE	15.2	Loan Amortization Table

YEAR (1)	BEGINNING BALANCE (2)	PAYMENT (3)	8.0% INTEREST (2)*0.08 (4)	PRINCIPAL (3)–(4) (5)	ENDING BALANCE (2)–(5) (6)
1	$80,000	$ 20,037	$ 6,400	$13,637	$66,363
2	66,363	20,037	5,309	14,728	51,635
3	51,635	20,037	4,131	15,906	35,729
4	35,729	20,037	2,858	17,179	18,550
5	18,550	20,034	1,484	18,550	0
	Total	$100,182	$20,182	$80,000	
	PV of the payment = $80,000				

column 3. A schedule of cash outflows for the borrow-own alternative is then developed to determine the present value of the after-tax cash flows. This is illustrated in Table 15.3.

The analysis of cash outflows begins with a listing of the loan payments, as shown in column 2. Next, the annual interest payments from Table 15.2 are listed in column 3. Because straight-line depreciation is assumed, the annual depreciation charges are $16,000 per year (as shown in column 4). The tax shelter to the owner of the equipment is the sum of the annual interest plus depreciation multiplied by the tax rate. Although interest is a tax-deductible expense, we are already capturing the interest component within the annual loan payment (as in Table 15.2). Consequently, we only need to explicitly include the tax savings that results from paying interest. Likewise, depreciation is a non-cash expense that does provide a tax shelter or tax reduction. The amounts of the total annual tax shield are shown in column 5. Column 6 is cash flow after taxes, obtained by deducting column 5 from column 2.

Because the cost of borrowing is 8%, its after-tax cost with a 37.5% tax rate is 5%. The present-value factors at 5% are listed in column 7. They are multiplied by the after-tax cash flows to obtain column 8, the present value of the after-tax costs of owning the asset. As before, the total cost of borrowing is $54,024.

The costs of leasing the asset can be obtained in a similar manner, as shown in Table 15.4. The annual lease payments are shown in column 2. By multiplying 0.625 (or 1-tax rate) times column 2 figures, the after-tax cost of leasing is obtained and shown in column 3. The present-value factors (5%) are listed in column 4 and multiplied times the figures in column 3. Column 5 presents the after-tax costs of leasing by year, which total $54,024 (as we saw before).

TABLE	15.3	Cost of Borrowing

YEAR (1)	LOAN PAYMENT (2)	INTEREST (3)	DEPREC. (4)	TAX SHIELD [(3)+(4)]*0.375 (5)	AFTER–TAX CASH FLOW (2)–(5) (6)	0.08*(1–0.375) PVIF 5.0% (7)	PRESENT VALUE (6)*(7) (8)
1	$ 20,037	$ 6,400	$16,000	$ 8,400	$11,637	0.9524	$11,083
2	20,037	5,309	16,000	7,991	12,046	0.9070	10,926
3	20,037	4,131	16,000	7,549	12,488	0.8638	10,788
4	20,037	2,858	16,000	7,072	12,965	0.8227	10,666
5	20,034	1,484	16,000	6,557	13,478	0.7835	10,561
Total	$100,182	$20,182	$80,000	$37,568	$62,615	4.3295	$54,024

TABLE 15.4	Cost of Leasing			
YEAR (1)	LEASE PAYMENT (2)	AFTER-TAX CASH FLOW (2)*(1-0.375) (3)	0.08*(1-0.375) PVIF 5.0% (4)	PRESENT VALUE (3)*(4) (5)
1	$19,965	$12,478	0.9524	$11,884
2	19,965	12,478	0.9070	11,318
3	19,965	12,478	0.8638	10,779
4	19,965	12,478	0.8227	10,266
5	19,965	12,478	0.7835	9,777
Total	$99,825	$62,391	4.3295	$54,024

Indifference between the costs of borrowing and the costs of leasing is obtained once again. A number of factors could change this result: differences in costs of capital, differences in applicable tax rates or usability of tax subsidies, differences in patterns of payments required under leasing versus owning, and so on. This equality relationship is a helpful starting point and is useful in understanding and measuring the effects of structural factors that may cause a favorable cost of leasing. In the previous discussion, we considered the impact of tax differences (specifically, that the lessee pays no income taxes and the lessor pays a 37.5% tax rate).

Table 15.5 combines the cost of borrowing and the cost of leasing into one analysis. As we saw before, there is a $286 advantage to leasing under this scenario. If an acquirer of an asset has some special tax circumstances (e.g., large NOLs that will be used to offset

TABLE 15.5	Net Advantage of Leasing: Tax-free Lessee						

COST OF BORROWING

YEAR (1)	LOAN PAYMENT (2)	INTEREST (3)	DEPREC. (4)	TAX SHIELD [(3)+(4)]*0.00 (5)	AFTER-TAX CASH FLOW (2)-(5) (6)	0.08*(1-0.00) PVIF 8.0% (7)	PRESENT VALUE (6)*(7) (8)
1	$20,037	$6,400	$16,000	—	$20,037	0.9259	$18,553
2	20,037	5,309	16,000	—	20,037	0.8573	17,178
3	20,037	4,131	16,000	—	20,037	0.7938	15,906
4	20,037	2,858	16,000	—	20,037	0.7350	14,728
5	20,035	1,484	16,000	—	20,035	0.6806	13,635
Total	$100,183	$20,182	$80,000	—	$100,183	3.9927	

Cost of borrowing $80,000

COST OF LEASING

YEAR (1)	LEASE PAYMENT (2)	AFTER-TAX CASH FLOW (2)*(1-0.00) (3)	0.08*(1-0.00) PVIF 8.0% (4)	PRESENT VALUE (3)*(4) (5)
1	$19,965	$19,965	0.9259	$18,486
2	19,965	19,965	0.8573	17,117
3	19,965	19,965	0.7938	15,849
4	19,965	19,965	0.7350	14,675
5	20,034	19,965	0.6806	13,588
Total	$100,182	$99,825	3.9927	$79,714

Cost of leasing $79,714
Net advantage of leasing $286

any taxable income for the foreseeable future) or the entity is a tax-free entity (e.g., a university), leasing should be considered. Although it is impossible to say that leasing will always be more advantageous for an organization with a lower tax rate, it is a sure sign that additional analysis should be conducted.

This example started by assuming equivalent tax rates for the lessor and lessee. Lease payments were established on that premise. The lessor is made whole at lease rates of $19,965 per year. From the tax-free lessor perspective, even if the lease payments rose to $20,000 there is an advantage to leasing of $146. In fact, it is only when annual lease payments reach the same level as annual loan payments ($20,037) that the user of the asset becomes indifferent to leasing. In practice, the actual annual lease payments may be somewhere between $19,965 and $20,037 (depending on competitive forces and the negotiating skills of the lessor and lessee).

In recent years, railroads and airlines have been large users of leasing because they could not utilize the tax shield, as have industrial companies faced with similar situations (i.e., NOLs). The analytical framework established in Table 15.5 will be useful as we consider other differences that may arise between lessee and lessor.

Additional Influences on the Leasing Versus Owning Decision

Although a tax rate differential is potentially one important distinctive and advantageous difference in the lessor and lessee's analysis, a number of other "operational" ownership factors can influence the user firm's costs of leasing versus owning capital assets. These include the following.

- Differences in asset purchase price

- Differences in maintenance costs

- Benefits of residual values to the owner of the assets

- Possibility of reducing obsolescence costs

These four operational differences are discussed in the sections that follow.

DIFFERENCES IN ASSET PURCHASE PRICE

Assuming a competitive economic situation, asset purchase prices should generally be equal for anyone purchasing the same asset. A piece of manufacturing equipment should cost the same amount regardless of whether the lessor or the lessee is purchasing it. This was the assumption previously, where the asset cost $80,000 for both the lessor and user lessee.

However, there may be situations involving specific assets in which the lessor has a distinct purchase price advantage. For example, some automobile leasing companies get preferential pricing of $1,000 or more below invoice because they are one of the top 10 automobile purchasers in the world. In this case, the leasing company (lessor) can price the lease with this preferential pricing in mind and pass some (or all) of these savings along to the lessee.

Another example, with similar circumstances, would be the technology and computer hardware area. Land and/or buildings provide a final example. It may ultimately be less expensive for a lessor to purchase a 50-acre tract of land than for 10 possible users to purchase 10 5-acre tracts of land. It may be less expensive for the lessor to build one distribution center complex than for 10 different users to build 10 different facilities. If for no other reason than the shared infrastructure (roadways, permits, initial security installation, and so on), a pricing advantage may be in favor of the lessor and may be passed along in whole (or in part) to the lessee in the form of a reduced lease payment.

DIFFERENCES IN MAINTENANCE COSTS

Maintenance costs are included in the lease-rental rate in some cases. For this to be an operating structural advantage, the key question is whether the maintenance can be performed at a lower cost by the lessor or by the lessee. In our previous examples, a lessor may or may not be able to provide less expensive maintenance in a timely manner on vehicles or computer hardware. Certainly such activities would be contracted for by the leasing company, and the question remains: Can the lessor supply the maintenance at a lower price than for which the user-lessee can separately contract?

If the lessor is large, maybe some economies of scale would result that could be passed on as lower lease payments. Depending on the background (industry, size, and so on) of the lessee and criticality of the asset to the user, it may be more cost effective (with better and more timely performance) for the lessee to have a separately contracted maintenance department. In the example of the distribution center, the lessor may be able to more efficiently (with less cost) be able to provide ongoing building maintenance, area maintenance, security, and so on to 10 lessees than each individual lessee could do for themselves on a separate tract of land. On the other hand, for specific manufacturing equipment the maintenance advantage probably goes to the user-lessee rather than to the financing company.

RESIDUAL VALUES

When a user-lessee leases an asset, the lessor owns the property at the expiration of the lease. The value of the property at the end of the lease is called the *residual value*. On the surface, it would appear that where residual values are large owning is less expensive than leasing. Once again, these benefits can be passed on to the user-lessee in reduced lease payments that consider an estimated residual value. Alternatively, the lessee can be given an opportunity to purchase the asset at the expiration of the lease. Consequently, the existence of a residual value by itself is unlikely to result in materially lower costs of owning.

For the most part, it is difficult to generalize about whether residual value considerations are likely to make the effective cost of leasing higher or lower than the cost of owning. In a limited number of cases, such as vehicles and computer hardware, the lessor may once again have a systematic advantage related to residual or resale value. In the automobile leasing example, not only does the leasing company have access to vehicles at a lower price but better access to the resale market and commands a slightly higher price in the residual value. This difference can be passed on in the form of a lower lease payment.

OBSOLESCENCE COSTS

Another popular notion is that leasing costs will be lower because of the rapid obsolescence of some types of equipment. If the obsolescence rate on equipment is high, leasing rates must reflect that rate. Thus, in general terms it can be argued that neither residual values nor obsolescence rates can basically affect the relative cost of owning versus leasing unless the lessor has some operating advantage that increases residual value or lessens the effects of obsolescence.

Certain leasing companies may be well equipped to handle the obsolescence problem. For example, some large equipment manufacturers are also reconditioners of their products and specialists in the tasks their products perform. Clark Equipment Company has expertise in materials handling equipment and has its own sales organization and system of distributors. This may enable Clark to write favorable leases for equipment. If the equipment becomes obsolete to one user, it may be satisfactory for other users with different materials handling requirements (and Clark is well situated to locate the other users).

The situation is similar in computer leasing. This illustration indicates how a leasing company, by combining lending with other specialized services, may reduce the social costs of obsolescence and increase effective residual values. By such operations, the total cost of obtaining the use of such equipment is reduced. Possibly other institutions that do not combine financing and specialist functions (such as manufacturing, reconditioning, servicing, and sales) may in conjunction with financing institutions perform the overall functions as efficiently and at as low a cost as integrated leasing companies. However, this is a factual matter depending on the relative efficiency of the competing firms in different lines of business and different types of equipment.

Table 15.6 summarizes these additional influences on leasing, highlights the specific item of influence, and for those potential influences indicates when the potential influence is effective. For example, when the purchase price is lower for the lessor (or higher from the lessee's perspective) it may imply a benefit to leasing.

OTHER INFLUENCES

The following benefits are on occasion cited as reasons to lease or to own an asset. We are not convinced that these distinctions exist except in very specific cases over short time periods.

- More favorable tax treatment, such as more rapid write-off

- Possible differences in the ability to utilize tax reduction opportunities

- Different costs of capital for the lessor versus the user firm

- Financing costs higher in leasing

- Possibility of increased credit availability under leasing

The first two items derive their benefit from the tax structure, whereas the last three items are financing related.

Favorable Tax Treatment Unless the lessor has some special treatment for depreciation, the lessor and lessee would be subject to the same depreciation schedule and neither would have an advantage. Similarly, some suggest that leasing is a method for the user-lessee to depreciate land that is otherwise non-depreciable. Once again, the tax rules

TABLE 15.6	Additional Influences: Leasing Versus Owning Decision			
			WHEN IS LEASING ADVANTAGEOUS TO LESSEE	
ADDITIONAL INFLUENCES		SPECIFIC ITEM	Lessor	Lessee
1. Differences in asset purchase price.		Purchase price	Lower	Higher
2. Differences in maintenance costs.		Maintenance costs	Lower	Higher
3. Unique benefits of residual values to the owner of the assets.		Residual value	Higher	Lower
4. Possibility of reducing obsolescence costs by the leasing firms.		Obsolescence costs	Lower	Higher

apply to the lessor and lessee in a similar fashion. So the lessor would not be able to depreciate land and so they would not be able to pass along any tax savings.

In our example of the $80,000 asset, if $20,000 would have been land related and could not be depreciated the neutral lease payments (Equation 15.2) would have reflected the loss of that tax shield and would have been higher. Thus, making the decision between leasing and financing in this case is a neutral decision. Finally, we should note that although we are representing depreciation as straight-line depreciation both the lessor and lessee would be subject to MACRS depreciation for tax purposes. We show straight-line simply for the ease of illustration.

Differences in Tax Rates or Tax Subsidies

An advantage to leasing or to purchasing may occur when the tax rates of lessors and user firms are different (as we saw previously). But even here unambiguous estimates of tax rates and taxable income are not always possible. The effects of differential taxes depend on the relationships among earnings from the capital assets (capital gains and losses versus ordinary income) and their interactions with differential tax rates and tax subsidies. Further tax-specific discussion is beyond the scope of this book, but suffice it to say that that if a firm has unusual tax arrangements it should consult a tax attorney to determine if unique benefits are available.

Different Costs of Capital for the Lessor Versus the User Firm

If the lessor has a lower cost of capital than the user, the user-lessee's cost of leasing is likely to be lower than the cost of owning to the user. But is it realistic to assume that the cost of capital would be different? To answer this question, the basic risks involved in using capital assets must be considered. Under the standard "price equals marginal cost" condition of competitive markets, it is the project's cost of capital that is the relevant discount rate. Hence, it is difficult to visualize why the risk in use of a capital asset will be different whether the asset is owned by a leasing company or by the user firm.

This risk is borne by the leasing company if the lease contract is cancelable at any time with no penalty, borne by the user firm if the lease contract is non-cancelable over the life of the asset, and shared by them under any contractual arrangement between these two extremes. However, competitive capital markets will ensure that the implicit discount rate in the leasing arrangement as negotiated will reflect the allocation of the risks under the particular sharing arrangement.

Another possibility is that the user firm may have a lower cost of capital than the leasing company. If this were true, the user firm should consider exiting its primary business and should consider entering the leasing business!

Under competitive market conditions, it is unlikely that the disequilibrium conditions implied by the different costs of capital will persist. The supply of lessors will either increase or decrease to restore equilibrium in the benefits to a user firm from leasing versus owning an asset. Without this competitive condition, a "cost of capital advantage" could exist.

Financing Costs Higher in Leasing

A familiar view is that leasing always involves higher implicit financing costs. This argument is also of doubtful validity. First, when the nature of the lessee as a credit risk is considered there may be no difference. A leasing company generally evaluates its clients just as a financing company would evaluate a loan applicant. Second, it is difficult to separate the money costs of leasing from the other services embodied in a leasing contract.

If because of its specialized operations the leasing company can perform nonfinancial services such as maintenance of the equipment at a lower cost than the lessee or some other institution can perform them the effective net (net of maintenance) cost of leasing may be lower than the cost of funds obtained from borrowing or other sources. The efficiencies of performing specialized services may thus enable the leasing company to operate by charging a lower total cost than the lessee would have to pay for the package of money plus services on any other basis.

Increased Credit Availability Sometimes it is said that firms wishing to purchase a specific piece of equipment can obtain more money for longer terms under a lease arrangement than under a secured loan agreement, and that leasing may not have as much of an impact on future borrowing capacity as does borrowing to purchase the equipment. As we saw when we compared asset purchase (column 1) with a capital lease (column 3) in Table 15.1, the capital lease requirements of FAS 13 have gone a long way toward neutralizing this point. Under FAS 13, capital leases are formally recognized as debt and both the asset and debt amounts are reflected on the balance sheet.

However, this may still be an issue if the user firm acquires assets via operating leases (Table 15.1, second column). When the restrictive criteria of a capital lease are not met, no additional debt is reflected on the balance sheet. This form of off-balance-sheet financing has become a popular target of analysis in recent years. Certainly, any professional investor should consider the impact of operating lease obligations (albeit many analysts may still give less weight to an operating lease than to a capital lease or outright loan).

INCLUDING THE ADDITIONAL INFLUENCES IN THE ANALYSIS

From operations, differences in purchase price, maintenance costs, residual value, and obsolescence costs may provide the large lessor with economies of scale an opportunity to pass some of these cost reductions on in the form of lower lease payments. As we saw previously, tax rate advantages can be claimed by the lessor and passed along to the user lessee in the form of lower lease payments.

In the example discussed previously, we assumed that the lessor and lessee had the same $80,000 purchase price and that the maintenance costs, residual value, and obsolescence costs were the same. Although we were silent as to these last three influences (indicating that their values were zero), we could have assumed that maintenance costs were $1,000 per annum for both the lessor and lessee. With the same tax rate and discount rate, the present value cost is the same for the lease or own-borrow scenarios and consequently does not need to be considered. To illustrate, let's make the following changes for both the lessor and lessee.

	LESSOR/LESSEE
Maintenance costs (per year)	1,000
Residual (salvage or terminal) value	$10,000

We will assume the same tax rate (37.5%) and borrowing rate (8% pre-tax, 5% post-tax). As we did before, let's examine the lessor's view and determine the minimum lease payment under this scenario by employing Equation 15.6.

$$NPV_{LOR} = -I_0 + \sum_{t=1}^{n} \frac{L_t(1-T) + TDep_t}{(1+k_{LOR})^t}$$

$$= -I_0 + PVIFA\ (5\%,\ 5\ yrs.)[L_t(1-T) + TDep_t]$$

(15.6)

We assume that the asset is completely depreciated. That is, we ignore the residual value when calculating annual straight-line depreciation. We do that in order to better isolate the impact of the residual value assumption. This equation must be expanded (Equation 15.7) to consider the annual maintenance costs and the residual value.

$$NPV_{LOR} = -I_0 + \sum_{t=1}^{n} \frac{L_t(1-T) + TDep_t - M_t(1-T)}{(1+k_{LOR})^t} + \frac{RV(1-T)}{(1+k_{LOR})^n}$$

$$= -Io + PVIFA\ (5\%,\ 5\ yrs.)[L_t\ (1-T) + TDep_t - M_t\ (1-T)]$$
$$+ PVIF\ (5\%,\ yr.\ 5)[RV(1-T)]$$

(15.7)

Where:

$$M_t = \text{Periodic maintenance costs}$$
$$RV = \text{Residual value (end of the period, year } n)$$

As we did before, we can solve this equation for the minimum lease payments (or the point where the NPV_{LOR} is equal to zero).

$$\$0 = -\$80,000 + (4.3295)[0.625\ L_t + 0.375(\$16,000) - \$1,000(0.625)]$$
$$+ (0.7835)[\$10,000(0.625)]$$
$$\$0 = -\$80,000 + 2.7059\ L_t + \$25,977 - \$2,706 + \$4,897$$
$$L_t = \$19,155$$

The minimum lease payment is $19,155 (compared to $19,965 from the previous example). In this scenario and in present value terms, the lessor now has a $4,897 residual value offset by a maintenance expense of $2,706. Compared to the earlier example, this investment costs the lessor $2,191 less than before. These savings can be passed along to find the minimum lease payment of $19,155.

Table 15.7 shows the neutral situation in which the lessor's operating effects are the same for the user-lessee. Note that the net advantage of leasing is $0. What if the lessor enjoys operating advantage over the lessee? We would now like to examine the situation in which the lessor has purchase price, maintenance cost, and residual value/obsolescence cost advantages. These are as follows.

	LESSOR	USER-LESSEE
Purchase price	$80,000	$82,000
Maintenance costs (per year)	1,000	1,500
Residual value	$10,000	$ 9,000

Table 15.8 presents the cost of purchasing and borrowing versus the cost of leasing at the lessor's minimum lease payment. In this case, the leasing option has a $3,194 advantage and the user should enter into the lease arrangement. Note that the cost of leasing is still (as in Table 15.7) $51,832 and the cost of ownership has increased. However, chances are that the lessor would not offer leasing terms as favorable and would probably negotiate a higher lease payment. As long as the lease payment is less than $20,335,* there is an advantage to leasing! The present value of a lease payment of $20,335 or $12,709 after tax at 5 years and 5% equals $55,026 or the cost of purchase.

_____

*Taxes are the first of the few structural factors that may cause leasing to be advantageous.

TABLE 15.7 Net Advantage of Leasing: Neutral Operating Benefits

A. LOAN AMORTIZATION TABLE

YEAR (1)	BEGINNING BALANCE (2)	PAYMENT (3)	8.0% INTEREST (2)*0.08 (4)	PRINCIPAL (3)−(4) (5)	ENDING BALANCE (2)−(5) (6)
1	$80,000	$20,037	$ 6,400	$13,637	$66,363
2	66,363	20,037	5,309	14,728	51,635
3	51,635	20,037	4,131	15,906	35,729
4	35,729	20,037	2,858	17,179	18,550
5	18,550	20,034	1,484	18,550	0
Total		$100,182	$20,182	$80,001	

PV of the payment = $80,000

B. COST OF BORROWING

YEAR (1)	LOAN PAYMENT (2)	INTEREST (3)	DEPREC. (4)	TAX SHIELD [(3)+(4)]*0.375 (5)	MAINTENANCE COSTS (6)	AFTER-TAX MAINTENANCE (6)*(1−0.375) (7)	RESIDUAL VALUE (8)	AFTER-TAX RESIDUAL (8)*(1−0.375) (9)	AFTER-TAX CASH FLOW (2)−(5)+(7)−(9) (10)	0.08*(1−0.375) PVIF 5.0% (11)	PRESENT VALUE (10)*(11) (12)
1	$20,037	$ 6,400	$16,000	$ 8,400	$1,000	$ 625	—	—	12,262	0.9524	$11,678
2	20,037	5,309	16,000	7,991	1,000	625	—	—	12,671	0.9070	11,493
3	20,037	4,131	16,000	7,549	1,000	625	—	—	13,113	0.8638	11,327
4	20,037	2,858	16,000	7,072	1,000	625	—	—	13,590	0.8227	11,181
5	20,034	1,484	16,000	6,557	1,000	625	10,000	6,250	7,853	0.7835	6,153
Total	$100,182	$20,182	$80,000	$37,568	$5,000	$3,125	$10,000	$6,250	$59,490	4.3295	

Cost of borrowing $51,832

C. COST OF LEASING

YEAR (1)	LEASE PAYMENT (2)	AFTER-TAX CASH FLOW (2)*(1−0.375) (3)	0.08*(1−0.375) PVIF 5.0% (4)	PRESENT VALUE (3)*(4) (5)
1	$19,155	$11,972	0.9524	$11,402
2	19,155	11,972	0.9070	10,859
3	19,155	11,972	0.8638	10,342
4	19,155	11,972	0.8227	9,849
5	19,155	11,972	0.7835	9,380
Total	$95,775	$59,859	4.3295	

Cost of Leasing $51,832
Net Advantage of Leasing $0

TABLE 15.8   Net Advantage of Leasing: Operating Benefits to Lessor

A. LOAN AMORTIZATION TABLE

YEAR (1)	BEGINNING BALANCE (2)	PAYMENT (3)	INTEREST (2)*0.08 (4)	PRINCIPAL (3)−(4) (5)	ENDING BALANCE (2)−(5) (6)
1	$82,000	$ 20,537	$ 6,560	$13,977	$68,023
2	68,023	20,537	5,442	15,095	52,928
3	52,928	20,537	4,234	16,303	36,625
4	36,625	20,537	2,930	17,607	19,018
5	19,018	20,540	1,521	19,019	0
Total		$102,688	$20,688	$82,000	

PV of the Payment = $82,000

B. COST OF BORROWING

YEAR (1)	LOAN PAYMENT (2)	INTEREST (3)	DEPREC. (4)	TAX SHIELD [(3)+(4)]*0.375 (5)	MAINTENANCE COSTS (6)	AFTER-TAX MAINTENANCE (6)*(1−0.375) (7)	RESIDUAL VALUE (8)	AFTER-TAX RESIDUAL (8)*(1−0.375) (9)	AFTER-TAX CASH FLOW (2)−(5)+(7)−(9) (10)	0.08*(1−0.375) PVIF 5.0% (11)	PRESENT VALUE (10)*(11) (12)
1	$ 20,537	$ 6,560	$16,400	$ 8,610	$1,500	$ 938	–	–	$12,865	0.9524	$12,252
2	20,537	5,442	16,400	8,191	1,500	938	–	–	13,284	0.9070	12,049
3	20,537	4,234	16,400	7,738	1,500	938	–	–	13,737	0.8638	11,866
4	20,537	2,930	16,400	7,249	1,500	938	–	–	14,226	0.8227	11,704
5	20,540	1,521	16,400	6,721	1,500	938	9,000	5,625	9,132	0.7835	7,155
Total	$102,688	$20,688	$82,000	$38,508	$7,500	$4,688	$9,000	$5,625	$63,243	4.3295	

Cost of borrowing $55,026

C. COST OF LEASING

YEAR (1)	LEASE PAYMENT (2)	AFTER-TAX CASH FLOW (2)*(1−0.375) (3)	0.08*(1−0.375) PVIF 5.0% (4)	PRESENT VALUE (3)*(4) (5)
1	$19,155	$11,972	0.9524	$11,402
2	19,155	11,972	0.9070	10,859
3	19,155	11,972	0.8638	10,342
4	19,155	11,972	0.8227	9,849
5	19,155	11,972	0.7835	9,380
Total	$95,775	$59,859	4.3295	

Cost of leasing $51,832

Net advantage of leasing $ 3,194

Cost Comparison for Operating Leases

Under an operating lease, the lessor must bear the risk involved in the use of the asset because the lease is cancelable and therefore may be returned by the lessee. Operating leases are virtually equivalent to having the lessor own the equipment and operate it. In these circumstances, the required rate of return is not the rate on a portfolio of assets of loaned funds. Rather, it is something higher.

The *operating lease*, from the lessor's point of view, has three elements: (1) the cash flows received from the lease contract, (2) the expected market or salvage value of the asset, and (3) the value of an American put option. The put option captures the present value of the lessee's right to cancel the lease and return the asset whenever the value of the economic rent on the asset falls below the lease fee. This may happen if the asset wears out faster than anticipated or if the asset (for example, a computer) becomes obsolete faster than expected. Equation 15.8 shows how the NPV of the lease to the lessor must be adjusted for operating leases.

$$NPV_{LOR} = -I_0 + \sum_{t=1}^{n} \frac{L_t(1-T) + TDep_t}{[1+(1-Tk_b]^t} + \frac{E(MV)}{(1+k_1)^n} - P \qquad (15.8)$$

Where:

NPV_{LOR} = present value to the lessor
L_t = lease rental fee without the cancellation feature
$E(MV)$ = expected after tax market value of the asset
k_1 = the risk-adjusted discount rate for the salvage value
P = the value of the American put implied by the cancellation feature

Because the lessor is giving up something by allowing the lease to be cancelled, it is necessary to charge a higher lease fee. How much higher depends on the value of the American put, P. As the risk of obsolescence increases so does the value of the put option held by the lessee. Because there are no free lunches, the lease fee charged by the lessor will rise to reflect the extra risk being undertaken.

An internal rate of return analysis of a cancelable operating lease that uses only the first three terms of Equation 15.8, thereby leaving out the put option, will show that the lessor sets the lease fee such that a high rate of return is being charged. The lessee would be badly mistaken to compare the rate required on a cancelable operating lease with the rate required on a straight (non-cancellable) financial lease (or comparable debt financing).

summary

L easing has long been used in connection with the acquisition of equipment by railroad companies. In recent years, it has been extended to a wide variety of equipment, such as computers, airplanes, or any type of asset. The lessor leases the asset to a user (lessee). The most important forms of lease financing are (1) operating leases, which are often cancelable and call for payments under the lease contract that may not fully recover the cost of the equipment, (2) financial leases, which do not provide for maintenance services, are not cancelable, and do fully amortize the cost of the leased asset during the basic lease contract period, and (3) sale and leaseback, in which a firm owning land, buildings, or equipment sells the property and simultaneously executes an agreement to lease it for a certain period under specific terms similar to a capital lease.

It is important to remember that lease financing is a substitute for debt. There is no such thing as a company that is 100% lease financed. Lease financing, like debt financing, requires an equity base. Prior to FASB Statement No. 13, all leases were accounted for as operating leases, which is to say that the financing provided by leasing was "off balance sheet." FASB Statement No. 13 dealt with this issue, provided specific criteria, and resulted in capitalization of financing leases both as an asset and as long-term financing.

The first step in a lease versus purchase analysis is the investment decision, which requires the user to discount the cash flows of the project under consideration at the appropriate weighted average cost of capital. Then, if the project makes investment sense the second step is to decide whether it should be financed with a mixture of debt and equity or with a lease.

As shown in Equation 15.4, the NAL is determined by comparing the cost of borrowing (the investment amount offset by the depreciation tax shield discounted at the after-tax cost of debt) and the cost of leasing (lease fees discounted at the lessee's after-tax cost of debt). If the NAL is positive, leasing is preferred to borrowing as a means of financing the project. Always be sure that the NPV of the project plus the NAL of the lease is positive.

In the absence of major tax advantages and other "market imperfections," there should be no advantage to either leasing or owning. A wide range of factors that may influence the indifference result can be introduced. These possible influences include operating differences, tax differences, and financing differences. Whether these other factors will actually give an advantage or disadvantage to leasing depends on the facts and circumstances of each transaction analyzed.

Hershey is a highly creditworthy corporation whose debt is highly rated. They are also a high marginal taxpayer with a very effective purchasing department that vigorously negotiates the best price for its purchases. Consequently, Hershey (or any company in a similar position) is faced with limited structural differences that make leasing advantageous. Two noted areas of opportunity are (1) automobiles and trucks and (2) computer equipment. In these cases, leasing companies have purchasing and disposal advantages they pass on to the lessee.

Questions

15.1   Discuss this statement: "The type of equipment best suited for leasing has a long life in relation to the length of the lease; is a removable, standard product that could be used by many different firms; and is easily identifiable. In short, it is the type of equipment that could be repossessed and sold readily. However, we would be quite happy to write a ten-year lease on paper towels for a firm such as Merck & Co., Incorporated."

15.2   Leasing is often called a hedge against obsolescence. Under what conditions is this actually true?

15.3   Is leasing in any sense a hedge against inflation for the lessee? For the lessor?

15.4   Why might a university be likely to lease equipment?

15.5   What type of equipment might The Hershey Company, a highly creditworthy firm and a high marginal taxpayer, consider leasing? Why?

15.6   One alleged advantage of leasing is that it keeps liabilities off the balance sheet, thus making it possible for a firm to obtain more leverage than it otherwise could. This raises the question of whether both the lease obligation and the asset involved should be capitalized and shown on the balance sheet. Discuss the pros and cons of capitalizing leases and related assets. What is the difference between an operating lease and a capital lease?

15.7   Why is a major portion of retail space in a mall leased and not owned by the retailer occupying the store?

15.8   As an individual you have a choice to lease a new car or purchase it outright and borrow the required cash. Consider the following types of individuals and discuss if they should consider leasing or purchasing their next car.

   a.   Tom usually holds on to his cars for an average of six years.

   b.   Bette likes to be seen in a new car and never drives the same car for more than two years.

   c.   Henry drives his car largely for work and claims any associated expenses as a tax deduction.

   d.   Frank drives 30,000 miles per year.

15.9   What is an operating service lease?

15.10   How does a sale and leaseback arrangement differ from a typical mortgage loan?

15.11   Is it realistic to assume that the cost of capital would be different for the lessor and the user firm?

15.12   Does leasing involve higher financing costs?

Problems

15.1

The Clarkton Company produces industrial machines, which have five-year lives. Clarkton is willing to either sell the machines for $30,000 or lease them at a rental that because of competitive factors yields an after-tax return to Clarkton of 6% (its cost of capital).

   a.   What is the company's competitive lease-rental rate? (Assume straight-line depreciation, zero salvage value, and an effective corporate tax rate of 40%.)

   b.   The Stockton Machine Shop is contemplating the purchase of a machine exactly like those rented by Clarkton. The machine will produce net benefits of $10,000 per year. Stockton can purchase the machine for $30,000 or rent it from

Clarkton at the competitive lease-rental rate. Stockton's cost of capital is 12%, its cost of debt 10%, and T = 40%. Which alternative is better for Stockton?

c. If Clarkton's cost of capital is 9% and competition exists among lessors, solve for the new equilibrium rental rate. Will Stockton's decision be altered?

15.2

The Hastings Company is faced with the decision of whether it should purchase or lease a new forklift truck. The truck can be leased on an eight-year contract for $4,641.44 a year or it can be purchased for $26,000. The salvage value of the truck after eight years is $2,000. The company uses straight-line depreciation. The discount rate applied is its after-tax cost of debt. The company can borrow at 15% and has a 40% marginal tax rate and a 1% cost of capital.

a. Analyze the lease versus purchase decision using the firm's after-tax cost of debt as the discount factor.

b. Discuss your results.

15.3

The McNelis Corporation seeks to acquire the use of a rolling machine at the lowest possible cost. The choice is either to lease one at $21,890 annually or to purchase one for $54,000. The company's cost of capital is 14%, its cost of debt is 10%, and its tax rate is 40%. The machine has an economic life of six years and no salvage value. The company uses straight-line depreciation. The discount rate applied is the after-tax cost of debt. Which is the less costly method of financing?

15.4

The Scott Brothers department store is considering a sale and leaseback of its major property, consisting of land and a building, because it is 30 days late on 80% of its accounts payable. The recent balance sheet of Scott Brothers is as shown in the following table. ($ thousands)

	2007		2007
Cash	$ 288	Accounts payable	$1,440
Accounts receivable	1,440	Bank loans (at 8%)	1,440
Inventory	1,872	Other current liabilities	720
Total current assets	3,600	Total current liabilities	3,600
Land	1,152	Equity	2,160
Building	720		
Fixtures and equipment	288		
Net fixed assets	2160		
Total assets	$5,760	Total liabilities & equity	$5,760

In addition, profit before taxes is $36,000; after taxes, $20,000. Annual depreciation charges are $57,600 on the building and $72,000 on the fixtures and equipment. The land and building could be sold for a total of $2.8 million. The annual net rental will be $240,000.

a. How much capital gains tax will Scott Brothers pay if the land and building are sold? (Assume all capital gains are taxed at a 15% tax rate.)

b. Compare the current ratio before and after the sale and leaseback if the after-tax net proceeds are used to clean up the bank loans and to reduce accounts payable and other current liabilities.

c. If the lease had been in effect during the year shown in the balance sheet, what would Scott Brothers' profit for that year have been?

d. What are the basic financial problems facing Scott Brothers? Will the sale and leaseback solve them?

Dividends and Share Repurchases

A company does not generally have direct contact with its shareholders. Yes, it releases earnings information and other SEC required filings, but those are examples of indirect contact with its shareholders. This chapter discusses a company's direct contact with stockholders through dividends, share repurchases, and other investor relations activities. In brief, the subject is how to return funds to equity investors.

Learning Outcomes

After completing this chapter, you should be able to:

1 Grasp the mechanics of a dividend payment

2 Comprehend the various analytical views that go into a dividend decision

3 Understand related dividend issues, such as a stock split, stock dividend, and investor dividend reinvestment programs

4 Explain the benefits and rationale for a stock repurchase program

5 Address the question of whether dividend policy matters

Dividend Payment Procedures

The technical aspects of dividend payment procedures are relevant to analyzing the impact of dividend payments. Table 16.1 presents the dividend record of The Hershey Company. Five aspects of dividend procedures are covered in Table 16.1. One is the date the board of directors at its quarterly meeting makes a dividend declaration, which is called the "declaration date." The following is the April 2006 dividend press release from The Hershey Company.

HERSHEY, Pa., April 18 — The Board of Directors of The Hershey Company today declared quarterly dividends of $0.245 on the Common Stock. The dividends are payable June 15, 2006, to stockholders of record May 25, 2006. It is the 306th consecutive regular dividend on the Common Stock.

TABLE 16.1   The Hershey Company Dividend Record

(1) DECLARATION	(2) DECLARED AMOUNT	(3) EX-DIVIDEND	(4) HOLDER OF RECORD	(5) PAYABLE	(6) ADJUSTED[a]
04/18/06	$0.2450	05/23/06	05/25/06	06/15/06	$0.24500
02/16/06	0.2450	02/22/06	02/24/06	03/15/06	0.24500
10/04/05	0.2450	11/22/05	11/25/05	12/15/05	0.24500
08/09/05	0.2450	08/23/05	08/25/05	09/15/05	0.24500
04/19/05	0.2200	05/23/05	05/25/05	06/15/05	0.22000
02/15/05	0.2200	02/23/05	02/25/05	03/15/05	0.22000
10/05/04	0.2200	11/22/04	11/24/04	12/15/04	0.22000
07/28/04	0.2200	08/23/04	08/25/04	09/15/04	0.22000
04/21/04	0.3950	05/21/04	05/25/04	06/15/04	0.19750
02/17/04	0.3950	02/23/04	02/25/04	03/15/04	0.19750
10/07/03	0.3950	11/21/03	11/25/03	12/15/03	0.19750
08/05/03	0.3950	08/21/03	08/25/03	09/15/03	0.19750
04/22/03	0.3275	05/21/03	05/23/03	06/13/03	0.16375
02/12/03	0.3275	02/21/03	02/25/03	03/14/03	0.16375
10/01/02	0.3275	11/20/02	11/22/02	12/13/02	0.16375
08/06/02	0.3275	08/21/02	08/23/02	09/13/02	0.16375
04/30/02	0.3025	05/22/02	05/24/02	06/14/02	0.15125
02/13/02	0.3025	02/21/02	02/25/02	03/15/02	0.15125
10/02/01	0.3025	11/20/01	11/23/01	12/14/01	0.15125
08/07/01	0.3025	08/22/01	08/24/01	09/14/01	0.15125
04/24/01	0.2800	05/23/01	05/25/01	06/15/01	0.14000
02/07/01	0.2800	02/21/01	02/23/01	03/15/01	0.14000
11/07/00	0.2800	11/20/00	11/22/00	12/15/00	0.14000
08/01/00	0.2800	08/23/00	08/25/00	09/15/00	0.14000
04/25/00	0.2600	05/23/00	05/25/00	06/15/00	0.13000
02/09/00	0.2600	02/23/00	02/25/00	03/15/00	0.13000

[a]On April 21, 2004 the board declared a two-for-one stock split. To better portray the quarterly dividend trend, declared dividends have been adjusted to reflect the split.

Two is the amount of the dividend $0.245 per share payable to anyone who held Hershey stock as of May 25, 2006 (the "holder of record" date) and payable on June 15, 2006. The "holder of record" date is the date on which the company closes its stock transfer books and makes up a list of the shareholders as of that date. Because the purchaser of a stock has three business days to settle the transaction, the purchase must be made before the ex dividend date (May 23, 2006) to become a holder of record. This is found in Table 16.1, the Ex-Dividend Date (column 3).

Thus, if you were to purchase the stock on Monday, May 22, 2006, you would receive the dividend. If you were to purchase the stock the next morning (May 23, 2006, the ex-dividend date) you would not receive the dividend.

Technically, on the declaration date the dividend payable becomes a current liability of the company. The accounting entry is to debit retained earnings and credit dividend payable. During the period between the declaration date and the payment date, the shareholders are general creditors of the company for the amount of the dividend payable. This is an example of a current non interest-bearing liability previously discussed.

Making the Dividend Decision

As you can tell from the earnings announcement, Hershey has paid a dividend seemingly forever [or at least for 306 quarters (76.5 years)]! Hershey's management and the board of directors generally take a limited amount of time to discuss regular dividend announcements.

However, note in Table 16.1 that every August the dividend increases. The decision to increase the dividend in August was a given. The question ultimately was, "By how much do we increase the dividend?" In the past, this decision required analysis by the financial management team. By the time the dividend increase recommendation reached the board it was well thought out, with only a brief discussion at the board level.

To guide the decision, we completed analysis of the dividends quarterly growth rate, the growth rate for the year, the anticipated dividend payout of net income, and the anticipated dividend payout of cash flow for the current year. The last two items required a latest-year forecast (or outlook) to better understand the implications (the anticipated underlying growth in income and cash flow). In addition, we used a planning model (as in Chapter 9) to anticipate the long-term effects of the different dividend increase alternatives.

We also examined outside and industry perspectives. We analyzed investment analyst reports to see what (if anything) they anticipated for Hershey as a dividend increase. We examined the practices of other food processing companies who announced dividend increases earlier that year. In addition, we took into account any other general economic issues, such as any changes in shareholder tax laws.

Finally, we considered the dividend yield a prospective stockholder would realize.

In the end, the decision came down to fractions of a penny per share. For example, Hershey's current dividend per share is $0.245 (Table 16.1). Therefore, a 10% increase would mean that the dividend per share per quarter would increase by $0.0245 to $0.2695. Perhaps the quarterly dividends indicated in Table 16.2 would then be considered.

First, this continues to be hypothetical for illustration only. Using quarters of a penny, a range of potential dividends would be examined. From this array, management would choose either a more conservative dividend ($0.265) or a more aggressive dividend ($0.275).

TABLE 16.2	Analysis of a Dividend Decision				
QUARTERLY AMOUNT	GROWTH	ANNUAL DIVIDEND[a] Amount	Growth(%)	EXPECTED PAYOUT[b](%)	DIVIDEND YIELD[c](%)
$0.2450	0.00%	$0.980	5.38	41.70	1.78
0.2650	8.16%	1.020	9.68	43.40	1.85
0.2675	9.18%	1.025	10.22	43.62	1.86
0.2700	10.20%	1.030	10.75	43.83	1.87
0.2725	11.22%	1.035	11.29	44.04	1.88
0.2750	12.24%	1.040	11.83	44.26	1.89

[a]The annual dividend includes two quarters at the dividend under analysis and the $0.49 of dividends paid in the first half of 2006.
[b] The expected EPS is for illustration only ($2.35).
[c]The dividend yield uses a price of $55 per share.

Restrictions on Dividend Payments

A number of restrictions influence dividend payment procedures. These include legal rules, tax rules, and indenture restrictions.

LEGAL RULES

Although some statutes and court decisions governing dividend policy are complicated, their essential nature can be stated briefly. The legal rules provide that dividends must be paid from earnings — either from the current year's earnings or from past years' earnings as reflected in the balance sheet account "retained earnings."

State laws emphasize three rules: (1) the net profits rule, (2) the capital impairment rule, and (3) the insolvency rule. The *net profits rule* provides that dividends can be paid from past and present earnings. The *capital impairment rule* protects creditors by forbidding the payment of dividends from capital. Paying dividends from capital would be distributing the investment in a company rather than earnings. It is possible, of course, to return stockholders' capital. When this is done, however, the procedure must be clearly stated as such. A dividend paid out of capital is called a *liquidating dividend*.

The *insolvency rule* provides that corporations cannot pay dividends while insolvent. (Insolvency is defined here, in the bankruptcy sense, as liabilities exceeding assets. To pay dividends under such conditions would mean giving stockholders funds that rightfully belong to creditors.) Legal rules are significant in that they provide the framework within which dividend policies can be formulated. Within their boundaries, however, financial and economic factors have a major influence on policy.

TAX ON IMPROPERLY ACCUMULATED EARNINGS

To prevent wealthy stockholders from using the corporation as an "incorporated pocketbook" by which they can avoid high personal income tax rates, tax regulations applicable to corporations provide for a special surtax on improperly accumulated income. However, Section 531 of the Revenue Act of 1954 places the burden of proof on the Internal Revenue Service (IRS) to justify penalty rates for accumulation of earnings. That is, earnings retention is justified unless the IRS can prove otherwise.

The Tax Act of 2004 reduced the penalty rate on accumulated earnings to 15%. In earlier years, the rates were more punitive, running as high as 37.5%. An accumulation of $250,000 or less is generally regarded within the reasonable needs of most businesses. *Reasonable needs* include "specific, definite, and feasible plans" for the use of the accumulated earnings. A substantial amount of marketable securities on a firm's balance sheet may trigger an IRS investigation of the issue. In mid 2004, Microsoft had liquid assets in excess of $50 billion. To maintain its historical growth rates of revenues and profitability, Microsoft has been trying to offset the slowing growth of revenues from its operating systems. Entry into new product market areas may require large outlays with substantial risks.

INDENTURE RESTRICTIONS

As discussed in Chapter 5 in regard to long-term debt securities, the relationship between borrowers and creditors is governed by a detailed contract called a *bond indenture*. The bond indenture includes legal agreements called covenants, which represent restrictions on the future behavior of borrowers administered by banks or other trustees. Bond covenants frequently restrict a firm's ability to pay cash dividends.

Such restrictions, which are designed to protect the position of the lender, usually state that (1) future dividends can be paid only out of earnings generated after the signing of the loan agreement (that is, they cannot be paid out of previous retained earnings) and (2) that dividends cannot be paid when net working capital (current assets minus current liabilities) is below a specified amount. Similarly, preferred stock agreements generally state that no cash dividends can be paid on the common stock until all accrued preferred dividends have been paid.

STOCK DIVIDENDS AND STOCK SPLITS

Another aspect of dividend payment procedures is the use of stock dividends and stock splits. A *stock dividend* is paid in additional shares of stock instead of in cash and simply involves a bookkeeping transfer from retained earnings to the capital stock account. The transfer from retained earnings to the capital stock account must be based on market value. In other words, if a firm's shares are selling for $100 and it has 1 million shares outstanding, a 10% stock dividend requires the transfer of $10 million (100,000 × $100) from retained earnings to capital stock.

Stock dividends are thus limited by the size of retained earnings. The rule was put into effect to prevent the declaration of stock dividends unless the firm has had earnings. In a stock split there is no change in the capital accounts. Instead, a larger number of shares of common stock is issued. In a *two-for-one split*, stockholders receive two shares for each one previously held. The book value per share is cut in half, and the par (stated) value per share of stock is similarly changed. In the past 25 years, Hershey has completed four different stock splits.

DATE	STOCK SPLIT
6/15/2004	2 for 1
9/13/1996	2 for 1
9/15/1986	3 for 1
9/15/1983	2 for 1

The first three dividend splits were completed in conjunction with a dividend increase. From a practical standpoint, there is little difference between a stock dividend and a stock split. The New York Stock Exchange (NYSE) considers any distribution of stock totaling less than 25% of outstanding stock to be a stock dividend and any distribution of 25% or more a stock split. Because the two are similar, the issues outlined in material following are discussed in connection with both stock splits and stock dividends.

REASONS FOR STOCK SPLIT USE

Many hypotheses have been put forth to explain why corporations have stock splits. Logically, a paper transaction that doubles the number of shares outstanding without changing the firm in any other way should not create shareholder wealth out of thin air. The exact effect of stock splits on shareholder wealth has been studied extensively. The pioneering study by Fama, Fisher, Jensen, and Roll (1969) measured unexpected stock price changes around split ex dates.

Monthly data for 940 splits between 1927 and 1959 revealed no significant changes in shareholder wealth in the split month. However, for a subsample of firms that split and increased their dividends they found an increase in shareholders' wealth in the months following the split. For a dividend decrease subsample, they found a decrease in shareholders' wealth. These results are consistent with the idea that splits are interpreted as messages about current dividend increases and about higher future cash flows. Subsequent studies found similar results.

The evidence suggests that regardless of the effect on the total market value of the firm stock dividends and stock splits increase the number of shareholders. It may also be argued that stock splits and stock dividends are used because there is an "optimal" price range for common stocks. Moving the security price into this range is alleged to make the market for trading in the security "wider" or "deeper," and hence there is more trading liquidity.

Most consumer goods and services companies want to maintain a lower stock price ($25 to $50 per share) so that more people can afford to invest in the company. (Usually stock is traded in round lots of 100 shares.) At a price point of $25 per share, generous grandparents can more easily invest in a round lot of stock than if the stock were priced at $200 per share. This logic increases customer loyalty in the product marketplace as well.

Although this sounds reasonable, there is some doubt on the effectiveness in the period immediately after the stock split. Copeland (1979) reports that market liquidity is actually lower following a stock split. Trading volume is proportionately lower than its pre-split level, brokerage revenues (a major portion of transactions costs) are proportionately higher, and bid/ask spreads are higher as a percentage of the bid price. The *bid price* is the price a potential buyer offers (say $20) and the *ask price* is what the seller requires (such as $20.50). The *bid/ask spread* is the difference (in this case, $0.50). In this example, the brokerage makes 2.5%. At $40 a share (pre-split), this same $0.50 spread would only be 1.25%. Thus, a brokerage firm increases its profitability by trading lower-priced stocks.

TAX ASPECTS OF STOCK DIVIDENDS AND SPLITS

When a shareholder receives a stock dividend, cash is not actually received. Stock dividends are usually not taxable because the economic position of a shareholder is not changed. They still have the same proportion of total shares they owned before the stock dividend. However, the tax basis needs to be recalculated. For example, the shareholder owns 100 shares in company A purchased at $60 per share. The tax basis of these shares is $6,000. Company A declares a 10% stock dividend, and thus 10 more shares are received. The basis in the 110 shares is $6,000 divided by 110, which is $54.54 per share. The tax basis for the total 110 shares remains $6,000. The holding period of all shares is based on the purchase date of the original 100 shares.

Stock splits are treated similarly because the proportional position of shareholders is unchanged. For example, a shareholder owns 100 shares of company B purchased at $50 per share. Company B announces a 2-for-1 stock split, and thus the shareholder now owns 200 shares. The tax basis of the 200 shares remains at $5,000.

Sometimes in a stock dividend or split the shareholder receives a *fractional share*. The shareholder may either pay for an additional half-share or receive the value of the half-share in cash. For example, a shareholder owns 25 shares of company C with an original tax basis of $15 per share for a total of $375. Company C declares a 3-for-2 split when its stock is worth $20 per share. The shareholder receives 12.5 additional shares for a total of 37.5 shares. The new tax basis per share is now $375 divided by 37.5, which equals $10 per share.

The shareholder decides to take cash for the value of the half-share sold on the payment date of the stock split. The half-share sold for $10 has a basis of half of $10 ($5), representing a capital gain of $5 (which would be taxable). The shareholder's basis in the remaining 37 shares multiplied by $10 per share is the original $375 less $5 basis represented by the half-share that was sold (this explanation is based on an example in *www.turbotax.com*).

Direct Investment Plans and Dividend Reinvestment Plans

Direct investment plans (DIPs) and dividend reinvestment plans (DRIPs) are reaching substantial levels. Many companies offer an investment plan that can include online cash purchases of securities and automatic withdrawals from checking/savings accounts. In addition to these investment features, companies also offer direct stock purchase plans that allow purchases through an investment plan, eliminating the need to use a traditional broker. Specialized companies have been established to facilitate such transactions. Equiserve, for example, handles more than 25 million shareholder accounts and 1,300 corporate clients (*www.equiserve.com*).

Dividend reinvestment plans permit shareholders to reinvest dividends paid on their shares in additional shares, again bypassing traditional investment channels such as securities brokers. DeGennaro (2003) studied 906 of the 1,135 companies listed in the *Guide to Dividend Reinvestment Plans* (1999). The 906 companies provided plan terms and were included in the 1999 Compustat database. Their total assets were $12,566 billion, representing average total assets of $13.87 billion per company. The other firms in Compustat without DRIP plans had total assets of only $2.33 billion per firm. Thus, DRIP plans are used most heavily by the largest firms.

DeGennaro (2003) also compares the 906 DRIP companies to a size match sample of non-DRIP companies whose total assets averaged $14.41 billion per firm. Firms with DRIP plans averaged 49,650 common shareholders compared with 23,460 for non-DRIP companies. The average number of shares traded per shareholder in a DRIP company is

2,890 annually compared to about 8,200 for a non-DRIP company. DRIP companies have higher dividends per share and higher payout ratios. They have larger investments in fixed assets, but make smaller annual capital expenditures. Thus, DRIP companies tend to be relatively more mature. The DRIP plans attract a specific clientele of a broad and relatively stable base of shareholders with relatively small positions (DeGennaro, p. 6).

From the standpoint of investors, the use of DRIP plans reduces their transaction costs. However, brokers offer a wider range of investment choices, relatively fast order execution, and the convenience of reporting all transactions on one statement. Analysts' reports and advice by brokers may also have positive value.

Firms offer direct investment plans for several reasons. First, the underwriting costs of raising new equity funds are probably reduced in the 4% to 6% range for these relatively large firms. Second, the announcement returns on public equity offerings are in the range of a negative 3% for industrials and somewhat less than 1% for utilities. Third, investors may regard the DRIP plan as a service that increases their goodwill toward the company. Fourth, if DRIPs increase the number of happy shareholders the firm may increase sales of some of its products. Fifth, regulated firms (such as public utilities, financial institutions, and industries subject to regulation, such as pharmaceutical companies) may benefit from a broad, loyal base of buy-and-hold investors. Sixth, the DRIP plans may attract firms' own employees [as in 401k matching programs and employee stock option plans (ESOPs)].

Financial innovation is a continuing process. The Internet facilitates many types of transaction cost reduction activities. Major brokerage houses have been developing plans similar to DRIPs in that dividends can be reinvested automatically and sometimes with reduced brokerage fees.

Aggregate Patterns of Dividends and Stock Repurchases

To provide financial managers some perspectives on how to make sound decisions on dividend and share repurchase policies, we start with the big picture. Table 16.3 presents data on dividends, share repurchases, and after-tax profits. We found during the 22-year period 1984 through 2005, the compound annual growth rates of after-tax profits was 5.5%, dividends at 7.8%, share repurchases at 11.2%, and GDP at 5.4%. Thus, profits and dividends grew at a slightly higher rate than the economy as a whole, whereas share repurchases grew at a substantially higher rate. As shown in Table 16.3, dividends have been about 60 to 70% of profits, share repurchases about 40 to 45%, and combined largely in the 100- to 110-% range.

An argument can be made that capital consumption (depreciation) should be added to after-tax profits to obtain a measure of corporate cash flows. These results are shown in Table 16.4, in which dividends become about 25% of cash flows, share repurchases about 20%, and the sum about 45%. If depreciation is added to after-tax profits, consideration of capital expenditures might also have to be made.

The relationships can also be presented graphically (as in Figure 16.1, which presents the annual percentage changes for the time series discussed previously). percentage changes in aggregate after-tax profits are shown as a heavy solid line. Dividends are shown as a line and dash, and show the least degree of variability. The greatest volatility is shown by the percentage changes in share repurchases. This suggests that share repurchases have

TABLE 16.3	Dividends Plus Share Repurchase to After-Tax Profits, 1984–2005 (in Billions of Dollars)					

				PERCENTAGE OF AFTER-TAX PROFITS		
YEAR	AFTER-TAX PROFITS	DIVIDENDS	SHARE REPURCHASES	Dividends (%)	Share Repurchases (%)	Dividends + Share Repurchases (%)
1984	172.0	67.2	27.3	39.1	15.9	54.9
1985	175.2	72.0	20.3	41.1	11.6	52.7
1986	145.9	72.9	28.2	50.0	19.3	69.3
1987	165.5	76.3	55.0	46.1	33.2	79.3
1988	202.3	82.2	37.4	40.6	18.5	59.1
1989	181.7	105.4	63.7	58.0	35.1	93.1
1990	175.8	118.3	36.1	67.3	20.5	87.8
1991	172.9	125.5	20.4	72.6	11.8	84.4
1992	194.8	134.1	35.6	68.8	18.3	87.1
1993	231.2	149.1	38.3	64.5	16.6	81.1
1994	283.1	157.9	73.8	55.8	26.1	81.8
1995	311.4	178.0	99.5	57.2	32.0	89.1
1996	370.1	197.5	176.3	53.4	47.6	101.0
1997	411.5	215.9	181.8	52.5	44.2	96.6
1998	379.7	241.0	224.2	63.5	59.0	122.5
1999	366.3	224.6	153.6	61.3	41.9	103.2
2000	306.2	251.3	153.1	82.1	50.0	132.1
2001	245.5	245.4	153.3	100.0	62.4	162.4
2002	332.3	254.8	119.7	76.7	36.0	112.7
2003	356.4	292.7	91.5	82.1	25.7	107.8
2004	467.4	366.9	242.0	78.5	51.8	130.3
2005	512.9	228.5	278.5	44.6	54.3	98.8
	Wtd. Average					
	1984–1988			43.0	19.5	62.6
	1989–1994			63.8	21.6	85.4
	1995–1998			56.5	46.3	102.8
	1999–2005			72.1	46.1	118.1
	2002–2003			79.5	30.7	110.2
	2004–2005			60.7	53.1	113.8

Sources: Share repurchase data are stock buyback allocations from SDC. All others are for nonfinancial corporations from Bureau of Economic Analysis, *National Income and Products Accounts Interactive Data Tables*, Table 1.14 (www.bea.gov).

taken the place of dividend extras, which have virtually disappeared. Adding repurchases to dividends introduces more variability.

The foregoing materials establish that aggregate dividends and stock repurchases are substantial. They have represented from 80 to 97% of after-tax profits. When capital consumption measures (depreciation) are added to after-tax profits to obtain a measure of gross cash flows (Table 16.4), the percentages in recent years have ranged from about 38 to 46%.

TABLE 16.4	Dividends Plus Share Repurchase to Cash Flows, 1984–2005 (in Billions of Dollars)					
				PERCENTAGE OF CASH FLOWS		
YEAR	CASH FLOWS[a]	DIVIDENDS	SHARE REPURCHASES	Dividends (%)	Share Repurchases (%)	Dividends + Share Repurchases (%)
1984	402.7	67.2	27.3	16.7	6.8	23.5
1985	422.6	72.0	20.3	17.0	4.8	21.8
1986	401.2	72.9	28.2	18.2	7.0	25.2
1987	432.0	76.3	55.0	17.7	12.7	30.4
1988	483.9	82.2	37.4	17.0	7.7	24.7
1989	483.3	105.4	63.7	21.8	13.2	35.0
1990	495.0	118.3	36.1	23.9	7.3	31.2
1991	514.3	125.5	20.4	24.4	4.0	28.4
1992	548.4	134.1	35.6	24.5	6.5	30.9
1993	594.6	149.1	38.3	25.1	6.4	31.5
1994	674.6	157.9	73.8	23.4	10.9	34.3
1995	726.4	178.0	99.5	24.5	13.7	38.2
1996	806.6	197.5	176.3	24.5	21.9	46.3
1997	878.6	215.9	181.8	24.6	20.7	45.3
1998	873.0	241.0	224.2	27.6	25.7	53.3
1999	890.1	224.6	153.6	25.2	17.3	42.5
2000	874.0	251.3	153.1	28.8	17.5	46.3
2001	892.3	245.4	153.3	27.5	17.2	44.7
2002	975.9	254.8	119.7	26.1	12.3	38.4
2003	1013.9	292.7	91.5	28.9	9.0	37.9
2004	1153.6	366.9	242.0	31.8	21.0	52.8
2005	1252.6	228.5	278.5	18.2	22.2	40.5
		Wtd. Average				
		1984–1988		17.3	7.9	25.1
		1989–1994		23.9	8.1	32.0
		1995–1998		25.3	20.8	46.1
		1999–2005		26.4	16.9	43.3
		2002–2003		27.5	10.6	38.1
		2004–2005		24.7	21.6	46.1

[a]Cash flows = after-tax profits plus capital consumption (depreciation).

Sources: Share repurchase data are stock buyback allocations from SDC. All others are for nonfinancial corporations from Bureau of Economic Analysis, *National Income and Products Accounts, Interactive Data Tables*, Table 1.14 (www.bea.gov).

Share Repurchases

Share repurchases began to increase rapidly in the 1980s. Grullon and Michaely (2002) explained the growth in repurchases by the adoption of Rule 10b-18 in 1983 by the Securities and Exchange Commission (SEC). This rule provided a safe harbor protecting repurchasing firms against charges of stock price manipulation. It also reduced the likelihood that the IRS would tax repurchases at ordinary income tax rates as cash dividends.

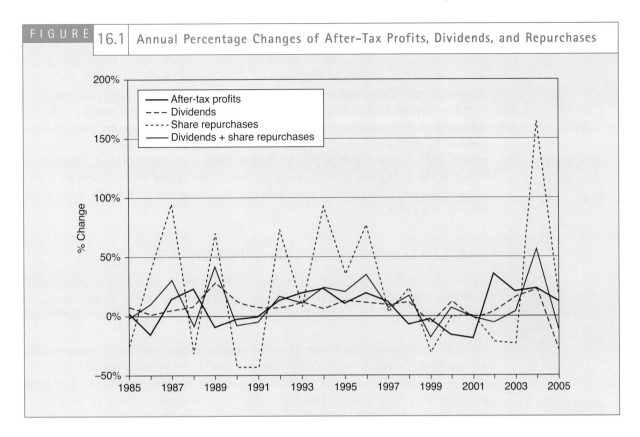

FIGURE 16.1 | Annual Percentage Changes of After-Tax Profits, Dividends, and Repurchases

TYPES OF SHARE REPURCHASES

Three main types of share repurchase activity have been employed. The largest of these three methods is the *open market share repurchase (OMR)*. OMR announcements enable firms to create for themselves options to exchange cash for its shares. These announcements are recitals indicating that a company's board of directors has authorized a market purchase of a total dollar amount or percentage of its shares. The announcement is not an unconditional offer to purchase, nor a fixed commitment. The Hershey Company has used the OMR to repurchase almost $3.5 billion of its shares since 1993.

Fixed-price tender offers (FPTs) grant shareholders an *in-the-money put*. Dutch auctions (DAs) grant shareholders a put at a range of prices, some of which are "in the money."

The relative uses of the three forms of share repurchases have changed over time (Grullon and Ikenberry 2000). FPTs peaked at $13.4 billion in 1985, representing 35.8% of total repurchases. DAs reached $7.7 billion in 1988, at 17% of the total. OMRs reached $215.0 billion in 1998, constituting almost 97% of the total.

The early studies of share repurchases were of FPTs covering the decades of the 1970s and 1980s. The leading studies for this period found large event returns. Dann (1981) calculated for his sample of 143 FPTs during 1962 through 1976 a 17% cumulative abnormal return (CAR) for a three-day window. The initial premium averaged 23% for an average 20% fraction of shares outstanding. At the expiration of the FPT, share prices on average were 13% (the shareholders' wealth effect) above their pre-announcement level. Later studies found similar results.

The dominant explanation for the large positive CARs for this period was undervaluation. The FPT announcements were signals of this undervaluation. Of this period, Warren Buffet was quoted as saying that in the mid 1970s many stocks traded below their intrinsic values and "the wisdom of making these [share repurchases] was virtually screaming at managements" (McGough et al. 2000).

A fundamental difference between fixed-price tender offers and DA repurchases (DARs) is brought out by the description of the first firm to utilize the DA (Bagwell 1992). In 1981, Todd Shipyards was planning a fixed-price tender offer at $28 for about 10% of its 5.5 million shares outstanding. Bear Stearns, the investment banker for Todd, suggested instead a DAR at a range of prices not to exceed $28. The fee paid to Bear Stearns would be 30% of the savings if the clearing price was less than $28. Todd employed the DA. The clearing purchase price was $26.50.

THE REASONS FOR SHARE REPURCHASES

With the foundation of the empirical findings developed in the previous sections, we summarize the reasons for the rise in the use of share repurchases that provide guidance for financial managers.

Tax Aspects One argument for the growth of share repurchases is their tax advantages in substituting capital gain tax rates for the higher personal income tax rates. But the highest dividend payers greatly increased their dollar dividend payments during the period of the highest growth in share repurchases and also accounted for a considerable volume of share repurchases. Hence, their share repurchases did not substitute for dividend payments. If the tax advantages of share repurchases were dominating reasons, the dollar amount of dividends paid would not have increased.

The Jobs and Growth Tax Relief Reconciliation Act of 2003 (enacted into law on May 28, 2003) reduces the tax benefits of share repurchases. Effective retroactively to January 1, 2003 and in force through the end of 2008, the new tax on dividends will be the 15% capital gains rate. For persons in the 10% and 15% tax brackets, the dividend tax rate will be 5% through 2007 and zero % in 2008. Note here that there is a tax clientele structure built into the new tax law on dividends.

However, differences continue on the tax treatment of dividends versus share repurchases. One is the uncertain duration of the new tax law. A second is that although dividends are taxed on the full amount share repurchases will be taxed on the difference between the price received and the tax basis of the stock. A third is that the dividend receivers still have their stock. In the stock repurchase the investor's wealth (less tax) has been converted to liquid form.

Cash Payouts Flexibility A second reason for share repurchases is that they provide firms with flexibility in adjusting cash payouts to temporary fluctuations in net income.

Change in Financial Structure The debt-to-equity ratio is one measure of a firm's financial structure. In Chapter 7, we considered the favorable impact leverage can have on financial returns (specifically the return on equity) by prudently leveraging the company. We saw that leverage magnifies the return on assets, leading to an increased ROE. Using a share repurchase strategy, the leverage ratio can be increased quickly. A firm can issue debt in order to make share repurchases. Thus, debt increases while at the same time stockholders' equity (book value) decreases.

More importantly, in Chapter 13 we examined leverage based on market values and argued that many firms are not in the lower region on the cost-of-capital curve. If the firm has been operating with less than the optimal debt/leverage ratio, the share repurchase will move the firm toward that ratio. If so, it might lower the firm's cost of capital, with a resulting increase in share price and market value.

Offset Dilution from the Exercise of Stock Options   Stock options are being used more frequently by firms in executive compensation programs and extended broadly to recruit or retain target employees. As stock options are exercised, the number of the firm's shares outstanding increases. Conceivably, this could create downward pressure on the firm's stock prices. Share repurchases can be used to offset this potential dilutive effect. Share repurchases have also been used to more than offset the effect of the exercise of stock options and may therefore have had an accretive effect on share prices. The FASB recommendation for expensing stock options may reduce their use. For example, in mid 2003 Microsoft reported a shift from the use of stock options to restricted stock grants.

Management Incentives   Share repurchases increase non-sellers' percentage of ownership in a firm. Because officers and directors might hold a significant percentage of ownership of the firm, their nonparticipation in share repurchases will increase their proportionate ownership by an even greater degree. If the percentages are substantial, the incentives of officers and directors to think like owners of the firm will be strengthened. Agency problems will be reduced.

Takeover Defense   Share repurchases can be used as a takeover defense for two reasons. First, the share repurchase plan might be viewed more favorably than the takeover. Second, when a firm tenders for a percentage of its shares the shareholders who offer their shares for sale are those with the lowest reservation prices. Those who do not tender have the higher reservation prices. Hence, for a takeover bidder to succeed with the remaining higher-reservation-price shareholders the premium offered will have to be higher. The required higher premium might deter some potential acquirers from making bids.

Management Responsibility   When officers and directors return excess cash to shareholders through share repurchase programs they are acting in the best interest of the shareholders (the owners). By not using the funds for unwise diversification or negative NPV investments in the firm's traditional lines of business activity, officers and directors increase the trust and confidence of the shareholders. This will have a positive influence on share prices.

Undervaluation   Throughout this text we have put forth an approach that is common in many corporations throughout the world. The approach we offer includes (1) analysis of a company's most recent financial position and general economic climate (Chapters 2 through 8), (2) projection of the anticipated performance of the company (Chapters 9 through 11), (3) valuation of those strategic financial plans while considering business options (Chapter 12), and (4) striving for the lowest cost of capital (Chapter 13). In Chapter 12, we found that Hershey's stock is fairly valued at about $55 (both the plan valuation and the recent market price as of December 31, 2005).

If this plan (and valuation) would have been developed by Hershey's management team, this relationship would suggest that the other seven motives needed to play a role in Hershey's decision. On the other hand, if Hershey's strategic plan estimated an intrinsic value of $60 per share, the stock would be currently undervalued and a strong catalyst for repurchasing shares would exist.

However, managers of firms may be overly optimistic about the intrinsic value of their companies. For example, as the share price of Sun Microsystems began to decline from its peak price of more than $60 per share Sun embarked on an aggressive share repurchase program in February of 2001. With a share price of $20, Sun announced plans to purchase $1.5 billion of its stock "because the shares were cheap." On April 28, 2006 the stock was $5. Sun had purchased 300 million shares. The loss was substantial (Norris 2006). Many examples of other large losses were reported (McGough 2000). The losses during years 1998 through 2000 and the company names include Hewlett-Packard ($3.2 billion), Intel ($4.6 billion), Microsoft ($2.7 billion), Gillette ($473 million), and McDonald's ($359 million). These examples represent strong evidence that sometimes managers know less than market outsiders.

Officers and directors usually do not tender or sell into share repurchase programs because they might judge that the price of the stock is likely to increase in future years. Their nonparticipation might therefore serve as a signal that the stock is under-valued. A special case of the undervaluation scenario is when a sharp decline in overall stock prices has taken place. When the stock market suffered a sharp decline in October of 1987, many firms initiated substantial share repurchase programs in the subsequent weeks. These share repurchase programs represented a statement by their managements that the overall market decline did not justify the sharp drops in the share prices of their individual firms.

Does Payout Policy Matter?

The Modigliani and Miller (MM) paper on capital structure irrelevance was published in 1958. Their paper on dividend irrelevance was published three years later (Miller and Modigliani 1961). MM argued that with the investment programs of firms fixed and given their cash flows dividend policy cannot affect firm value or the firm's cost of capital.

The recent finance literature argues that dividend irrelevance is based on the assumption that firms distribute 100% of free cash flows (FCFs) in every period (DeAngelo and DeAngelo 2006, and DeAngelo, DeAngelo, and Stulz 2006). When the MM assumptions are relaxed to allow retention of FCF, both payout and investment become policy decisions to be made by financial managers. The new theory of dividend policy includes a trade-off theory and a life cycle theory.

The trade-off theory argues that there are advantages and disadvantages of earnings retention. It is widely emphasized that if a firm would require external financing in the future it is costly to pay cash dividends on which the recipients pay personal taxes.

In addition to the payout taxes, when the firm does raise additional funds in the future flotation costs would be incurred. Another argument for earnings retention is to build up funds to support future investment opportunities. This view is presented in a formal model by Myers and Majluf (1984). Under the assumption of *asymmetric information*, it is advantageous for the firm to retain earnings to build up what Myers and Majluf call finan-cial slack so that investment opportunities can be financed internally.

The finance literature also identifies factors that limit earnings retention. These include (1) the agency costs of mismanagement of FCFs, (2) the utility functions of some investors possibly placing a greater value on earlier consumption rather than tax deferral, (3) behav-ioral biases such as a preference for a bird in hand versus a bird in the bush, (4) tax-exempt entities not being disadvantaged by dividend income, (5) the use of dividends to signal by managers, and (6) penalty taxes for excess earnings retentions (DeAngelo and DeAngelo 2006). We comment briefly on two of the functions of dividend payouts.

TAXATION BACKGROUND

This section summarizes some relevant tax information. The 2003 Tax Act reduced the top dividend tax rate from 38.6 to 15%. Under the new law, the federal tax rate on ordinary personal income ranges from 10 to 35%. It provided that dividends will not be subject to ordinary personal income tax rates but at capital gains rates. The tax on long-term capital gains was reduced from 20 to 15%. The new rules expire after 2008.

In addition, different groups are taxed at different rates. A corporation that owns 20% or more of another does not have to pay taxes on dividends received from that corporation on 80% of the dividends received. If ownership is less than 20%, 70% is the maximum deduction, as discussed in Chapter 4. Tax-free institutions such as pension funds pay zero tax on dividends received.

CLIENTELE EFFECTS

It has been argued that these different tax situations create a clientele effect. Groups that pay high tax rates on dividends would prefer to invest in the stocks of companies that pay low dividends. If different investors' clientele have different dividend preferences, corporations would be expected to adjust their dividend payment patterns to any unsatisfied preferences (representing an incomplete market). In equilibrium, corporate dividend payout patterns would match the preferences of the dividend clienteles. The *clientele effect* is a possible explanation for management reluctance to alter established payout policies because such changes might cause current shareholders to incur unwanted transactions costs.

A variation on the clientele effect is the reputation of institutional investors. Institutional investors have the resources and incentives to be superior monitors of corporate performance (Allen, Bernardo, and Welch 2000). Because they do not pay taxes they prefer dividends in high-quality companies. The joint influence of investments by institutions and the payment of dividends provide a positive signal.

DIVIDENDS AS SIGNALS

Because as insiders they have superior access to information about the firm's cash flows, managers choose to establish unambiguous signals about the firm's future if they have the proper incentive to do so (Ross 1977, Bhattacharya 1979, Miller and Rock 1985). For a signal to be useful, the following four conditions must be met.

- Management must always have the right incentive to send a truthful signal, even if the news is bad.

- The signal of a successful firm cannot be easily mimicked by less successful competitors.

- The signal must be significantly correlated with observable events (for example, higher dividends today must be correlated with higher future cash flows).

- There cannot be a more cost-effective way of sending the same message.

The *incentive-signaling approach* suggests that management might choose real financial payouts such as dividends (or debt payments) as a means of sending unambiguous signals to the public about the future performance of the firm. These signals cannot be mimicked by unsuccessful firms because such firms do not have sufficient cash flow to back them up and because managers have correct incentives to tell the truth.

LIFE CYCLE THEORY OF PAYOUT POLICY

The second part of the new theory of dividend policy is represented by a life cycle theory. The theory and evidence on life cycle influences on payouts are summarized in Table 16.5. The papers that develop the theory and evidence also provide guidance to the formulation of payout policy by financial managers (Fama and French 2001, Grullon, Michaely, and Swaminathan 2002, DeAngelo and DeAngelo 2006, DeAngelo, DeAngelo, and Stulz 2006). In theory, the central guide to financial managers is to retain earnings when such reinvestments develop NPV increases greater in the firm than if paid out to investors (who on average receive market returns). When internal returns are less than market returns, payouts are made.

A related general proposition is that when firms retain cash flows rather than paying them out they can expect to reach a stage at which the cash flows should be payout as dividends or share repurchases in the future. These retained cash flows should ultimately be paid out in a pattern that does not decrease NPVs generated from investments.

The Small, Young, Growing Firm The mortality rate among new firms is high. Those that survive can experience high growth rates and make large expenditures on plant equipment and working capital to support their growth. Whether profitable or not, if future profit prospects are favorable external financing is expected to be available to be added to internal funds retained. Firms at this stage have great need of financing and are unlikely to make cash payouts. Key investors and key employees are likely to be granted stock options or direct payments of equity shares.

Larger Firms with Moderate Growth Rate As firms reach a sales level of more than $200 million, the growth rate in sales is likely to moderate. Needs for external financing are likely to be somewhat reduced. Some dividend payouts may be initiated, but they are likely to be only 20 to 30% of cash flows. It makes sense for firms at this stage to build cushions against temporary reverses or to support new growth opportunities. Favorable spikes of cash inflows or the need to offset the exercise of stock options may make the use of share repurchases desirable.

Firms in Maturity or Decline As firms reach a period in which their sales growth declines to less than the average for the economy (GDP growth between 1996 and 2006 was at a compound annual rate of 5.4%), their need to finance capital expenditures and working capital diminishes and may become negative. The firms begin to have payouts that represent a high percentage of their profits after tax. Share repurchases may exceed cash dividend payouts.

These three major patterns provide guidelines for financial managers. Stages may be more finely divided, but the logic of the patterns remains. We next turn to the broad evidence supporting the life cycle framework for formulating payout policies.

TABLE 16.5	Life Cycle Patterns in Payouts				
STAGE IN LIFE CYCLE		SALES SIZE	GROWTH RATE IN SALES (%)	FINANCING NEEDS	PAYOUTS
I	Young	Under $200 million	10 to 30	High	None
II	Adult	Over $200 million	6 to 10	Moderate	Some
III	Maturity or decline	Over $200 million	+2 to −5	Zero or negative	High

EMPIRICAL EVIDENCE ON THE LIFE CYCLE THEORY

In this section we review the empirical evidence supporting the life cycle theory of dividends.

Stage 1 Evidence Considerable evidence on stage 1 firms is developed by Fama and French (FF) (2001). FF report that in 1973 52.8% of publicly traded nonfinancial non-utility firms paid dividends. This rose to 66.5% in 1978 and then declined to 20.8% in 1999. This dramatic decline in dividend payers is attributable in part to a shift of publicly traded firms toward characteristics of firms that have never paid dividends, but also from a reduced propensity to pay dividends. FF state that the "Lower propensity to pay is quite general" (p. 40). FF define "propensity" as the probability that a firm in a given category of firms will be a dividend payer.

The number of publicly traded firms grew from 3,638 in 1978 to 5,670 in 1997, declining to 5,113 in 1999. The increase in the number of firms was associated with a shift to newer and smaller firms, largely non dividend payers. These firms are characterized by higher rates of investment, higher R&D rates, low earnings, and higher ratios of market value of assets to book value. In addition, their investments exceed pre-interest earnings. Their size is about one-tenth the size of payers. The data developed by FF is the story of the increase in the relative numbers of stage 1 firms during the 1978 to 1999 period.

Behavior of Firms in Stage 2 The behavior of firms in stage 2 can be conveyed by an illustrative case study. Hershey is a modest-growth company whose sales doubled from 1991 on a comparably reported basis. Its dividends per share grew from $0.285 to $0.98. Hershey paid out slightly over 40% of its earnings in the form of dividends.

As shown in Figure 16.2, net income (as reported) increased from more than $219 million to $493 million and FCF (cash from operations less capital expenditures) increased from a three-year average of $112 million in 1991 to a three-year average of almost $418 million in 2005. A considerable cushion between total earnings and earnings per share has been maintained in relation to dividend payments. You can also see that share repurchases represented a much higher percentage of cash flows. Hershey's dividends reflect a steady growth, whereas share repurchases seem somewhat erratic. This was the same message we saw on a macro level for the United States as a whole in Figure 16.1.

Stage 3 Patterns DeAngelo, DeAngelo, and Skinner (DDS) (2004) present data that illustrates the behavior of stage 3 companies. Table 16.6 lists the 25 industrial firms that paid the largest dividends in the year 2000. They represent largely relatively mature companies. The 25 firms account for 54.9% of aggregate dividends for all industrials. Table 16.7 shows that the real dividends paid by the top 25 increased by 77.1% between 1978 and 2000, by all firms by 22.7%, and by all other dividend-paying firms by a decline of 10.7%. Supporting FF (2001), the total number of dividend payers decreased from 2,176 in 1978 to 930 in 2000 (a decline of 57.3%).

DDS sketch broader implications of the high earnings and dividend concentration that prevent the market from providing dividend heterogeneity either across or within industries. From this they observe that it would be unlikely that clientele pressure would have a strong impact on a firm's dividend policy except for circumstances such as a small number of controlling shareholders. Signaling theories are also weakened by the concentration of earnings and dividends in large well-known firms. Analysts and the financial press follow such firms closely and publish much information about them.

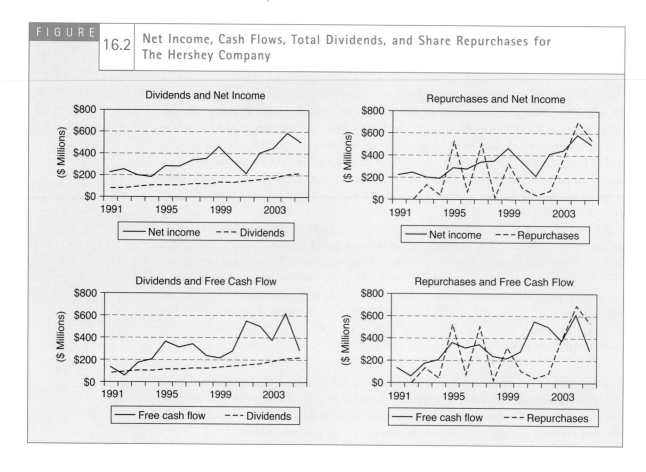

Dividend signaling should occur in lesser-known firms, which account for a small proportion of dividend activity. Because earnings and dividends are highly concentrated, they conjecture that share repurchase activity is also likely to be concentrated in a small number of large firms.

Before the recent finance literature on payout policies, a disconnect between theory and practice existed. The new theories of trade-offs and life cycle patterns provide practical guidelines for financial managers. Payout decisions require balancing the advantages of retentions against the potential disadvantages.

The life cycle theory of payouts warns financial managers in start-up firms that although revenues may be growing and considerable cash is flowing into the firm their current salary withdrawals and consumption patterns will have to be constrained. They will need to plan in advance for outside financing and develop relationships with financing sources.

As firms become larger and more stable, investors will expect payouts to be initiated and grow. But at this stage firms need to maintain a margin of safety between cash inflows and payout levels. The market will expect dividend payouts to grow reinforced by share repurchases that can be adjusted during adverse cyclical developments.

As firms mature into lower growth rates, the financial markets will penalize firms with large buildups of financial assets. The use of such funds for investments into unrelated product market areas risks dissipation of funds that should have been paid out to investors. Adverse effects on enterprise values will result. Increased payouts as firms mature will signal that managements are behaving responsibly to the interests and expectations of investors.

TABLE 16.6	Dividends in 2000 for 25 Firms

FIRM	REAL DIVIDENDS IN 2000 ($ MILLIONS, 1978 BASE)
1. Exxon Mobil	$2,318
2. General Electric	2,138
3. Philip Morris	1,722
4. Verizon	1,672
5. SBC	1,304
6. Merck	1,100
7. Ford	1,036
8. Pfizer	973
9. AT&T	941
10. Bristol Myers Squibb	731
11. Johnson & Johnson	653
12. Chevron	639
13. Coca-Cola	638
14. Procter & Gamble	636
15. Du Pont	551
16. BellSouth	539
17. General Motors	490
18. American Home Products	455
19. Abbott Labs	446
20. Eli Lilly	439
21. Texaco	370
22. 3M	348
23. IBM	344
24. Wal-Mart	337
25. Schering-Plough	304
Total for 25 firms	$21,124
Total as a % of aggregate for all industrials	54.9%

Source: DeAngelo, Harry, Linda DeAngelo and Douglas J. Skinner, "Special Dividend and the Evolution of Dividend Signaling," *Journal of Financial Economics*, 57, September 2000, pp. 309–354.

TABLE 16.7	Changes in Dividend Concentration

| | REAL DIVIDENDS | | |
	1978	2000	% CHANGE
Top 25 dividend payers in 2000	$11,925	$21,124	77.1
All other industrial firms	19,417	17,337	–10.7
Total for all industrials	$31,342	$38,461	22.7

Source: DeAngelo, Harry, Linda DeAngelo and Douglas J. Skinner, "Special Dividend and the Evolution of Dividend Signaling," *Journal of Financial Economics*, 57, September 2000, pp. 309–354.

Survey OF PRACTICE

In 1997, H. Kent Baker and Gary E. Powell surveyed executives at 392 New York Stock Exchange traded companies. Using a 4 point scale (where 0 indicates no importance and 3 indicates high importance), they asked the executives to rate how important twenty particular factors were in arriving at a dividend decision. The top five responses are noted below:

Rank	Factor	Score (0–3 High)
1.	Level of current and expected future earnings	2.72
2.	Pattern or continuity of past dividends	2.33
3.	Concern about maintaining or increasing stock price	2.18
4.	Concern that a dividend change may provide a false signal to investors	1.98
5.	Stability of cash flow	1.94

Source: "Determinants of Corporate Dividend Policy: A Survey of NYSE Firms," Baker, H. Kent and Gary E. Powell, *Financial Practice and Education,* Spring/Summer 2000, Volume 10, Number 1, pp. 29–40.

Some other factors that were rated of low importance include: characteristic of current shareholders such as their tax position (importance scale of 1.04 or number 16 of 20) and the preference to pay dividends instead of undertaking risky reinvestment (importance scale of 0.90 or number 18 out of 20).

summary

A firm's dividend and share repurchase policies are the means by which funds are returned to equity investors. The dividend decision takes into account internal and external considerations. These include dividend growth rates, payout, and yields (as well as general economic and industry conditions). Of course, this analysis is in light of restrictions that govern dividend payments: legal rules, tax rules, and indenture restrictions.

Another aspect of dividend policy is the use of stock dividends and stock splits. A stock dividend is a dividend paid with additional shares of stock instead of with cash, and simply involves a bookkeeping transfer from retained earnings to the capital stock account. In a stock split, more shares of common stock are issued but there is no change in the capital accounts.

Although stock dividends and stock splits are defined differently, the two have essentially the same effects. Stock dividends and splits are paper transactions that change the number of shares outstanding, but otherwise leave the firm unchanged. However, empirical studies show that shareholder wealth increases are associated with split announcements, suggesting that signaling and other financial changes are involved. The following is relevant tax information from the 2003 Tax Act.

* The top dividend tax rate was reduced from 38.6% to 15%.

* The federal tax rate on ordinary personal income ranges from 10% to 35%.

* Dividends will not be subject to ordinary personal income tax rates but at capital gains rates.

* Long-term capital gains were reduced from 20% to 15%.

Such diverse tax situations cause different investors to have different dividend preferences (i.e., the clientele effect). Corporations are expected to adjust their dividend payment patterns.

Share repurchases began a rapid increase in the 1980s, which can be explained in part by the adoption of Rule 10b-18 by the SEC in 1983 not to subject the gains to ordinary income tax rates. Three main types of share repurchase activity have been employed. However, the most common (more than 90%) is the OMR announcement, in which a firm announces a share repurchase program and then repurchases shares in the stock market.

Reasons for the rise and decline in the use of share repurchases include the following.

* Tax aspects

* Cash payouts flexibility

* Change to financial structure

* Offset dilution from the exercise of stock options

* Management incentives

* Takeover defense

* Management responsibility

* Undervaluation

The modern theory of dividend policy assigns important responsibilities to financial managers. Dividend decisions are guided by a trade-off theory and a life cycle theory. The benefits of earnings retention include avoidance of taxes on payouts of dividends and share repurchase, avoidance of the subsequent flotation costs for external financing, and having insufficient financial slack to finance positive NPV investments.

The potential negative effects of earnings retention include (1) agency costs of misuse of free cash flows, (2) the preferences of some investors favoring earlier consumption ahead of tax deferral, (3) creation of other behavior biases, such as the preference for the certainty of receiving cash dividends, (4) tax-exempt entities receiving no benefit from a delay in receiving dividend income, (5) the use of cash dividends and share repurchases to signal favorable future developments, and (6) penalty taxes for excess retention of earnings.

The life cycle theory of dividend and share repurchase cash payouts recognizes the different benefits of retention and payouts for firms at different stages of their development. Small, new, growing firms with substantial financing needs benefit from the use of internal funds and become non dividend payers. In stage 2, firms may retain some earnings to finance continued investment and growth opportunities, but also enhance entity value by demonstrating an increasing flow of cash payouts to investors. As firms mature, growth rates slow and increased dividend payouts demonstrate that free cash flows will not be misused. Thus, over the changing patterns of the life cycle of firms different payout policies will help the realization of the NPV of investments to shareholders.

Questions

16.1   As an investor, would you rather invest in a firm with a policy of maintaining a constant payout ratio, a constant dollar dividend per share, or a constant regular quarterly dividend plus a year-end extra when earnings are sufficiently high or corporate investment needs are sufficiently low? Explain your answer.

16.2   How would each of the following changes probably affect aggregate payout ratios? Explain your answer.

- An increase in the personal income tax rate.
- The asset life used in the MACRS depreciation for federal income tax purposes is extended. For example, the depreciable life of industrial equipment is extended from seven years to ten years.
- A rise in interest rates.
- An increase in corporate profits.
- A decline in investment opportunities.

16.3   Discuss the pros and cons of having the directors formally announce what a firm's dividend policy will be in the future.

16.4   Most firms would like to have their stock selling at a high price/earnings ratio with extensive public ownership (many different shareholders). Explain how stock dividends or stock splits may be compatible with these aims.

16.5   What is the difference between a stock dividend and a stock split? As a stockholder, would you prefer to see your company declare a 100% stock dividend or a two-for-one split?

16.6   In theory, if we had perfect capital markets we would expect investors to be indifferent about whether cash dividends were issued or an equivalent repurchase of stock outstanding were made. What factors might in practice cause investors to value one over the other?

16.7   Discuss this statement: The cost of retained earnings is less than the cost of new outside equity capital. Consequently, it is totally irrational for a firm to sell a new issue of stock and to pay dividends during the same year.

16.8   Would it ever be rational for a firm to borrow money to pay dividends? Explain.

16.9   Unions have presented arguments similar to the following: "Corporations such as Kraft Foods retain about half their profits for financing needs. If they financed by selling stock instead of by retained earnings, they could cut prices substantially and still earn enough to pay the same dividends to their shareholders. Therefore, their profits are too high." Evaluate this statement.

16.10   If executive salaries are tied more to the size of the firm's sales or its total assets rather than to profitability, how might managers' policies be adverse to the interests of stockholders?

Problems

16.1

Target dividend policy: The Bane Engineering Company has $20 million of back-logged orders for its patented solar heating system. Management plans to expand production capacity by 30% with a $60 million investment in plant machinery. The firm wants to maintain a 45% debt-to-total-asset ratio in its capital structure. It also wants to maintain its past dividend policy of distributing 20% of after-tax earnings. In 2006, earnings were $26 million. How much external equity must the firm seek at the beginning of 2007?

16.2

Residual dividend policy: Lifton Company expects next year's after-tax income to be $50 million. The firm's debt/equity ratio is 75%. If Lifton has $40 million of profitable investment opportunities and wishes to maintain its debt/equity ratio, how much shout it pay out in dividends next year?

16.3

Stock split and dividends: After a three-for-one stock split, Novak Company paid a dividend of $0.50. This represents an 8% increase over last year's pre-split dividend. Novak Company's stock sold for $80 prior to the split. What was last year's dividend per share?

16.4

Alternative dividend policies: In 2006 the Odom Company paid dividends totaling $3,375,000. For the past 10 years, earnings have grown at a constant rate of 10%. After-tax income was $11,250,000 for 2006. However, in 2007 earnings are expected to be $20,250,000 and capital investment (including working capital) is expected to be $15,000,000. It is projected that Odom Company will not be able to maintain this higher level of earnings and will return to its previous 10% growth rate. Calculate dividends for 2007 if Odom Company follows each of the following policies.

- Its dividend payment is stable and growing.
- It continues the 2006 dividend payout ratio.
- It uses a pure residual dividend policy (30% of the $15,000,000 investment was financed with debt).
- The investment in 2007 is financed 90% with retained earnings and 10% with debt. Any earnings not invested are paid out as dividends.
- The investment in 2007 is financed 30% with external equity, 30% with debt, and 40% with retained earnings. Any earnings not invested are paid out as dividends.

16.5

Stock split and dividends: Raffer Company stock earns $3 per share, sells for $36, and pays a $1.50 dividend per share. After a two-for-one split, the dividend will be $0.85 per share. By what percentage has the payout increased?

16.6

Effects of stock dividend: Barnes Company has 500,000 shares of common stock outstanding. Its capital stock account is $500,000, and retained earnings are $2 million.

Barnes is currently selling for $10 per share and has declared a 10% stock dividend. After distribution of the stock dividend, what balances will the retained earnings and capital stock accounts show?

16.7

Expected dividends: The following quarterly dividend payment information has been gathered.

	2004	2005	2006
First quarter	$0.1975	$0.2200	$0.2450
Second quarter	0.1975	0.2200	0.2450
Third quarter	0.2200	0.2450	N/A[a]
Fourth quarter	0.2200	0.2450	N/A

[a]N/A = Not available.

a. Calculate the dividend per share growth when the dividend increase was announced. (That is, calculate the change from the second to the third quarter.)

b. Calculate the growth in total annual dividend per share from 2004 to 2005.

c. One analyst estimates a 2006 dividend of $0.98 per share, whereas a second analyst estimates a 2006 dividend of $1.03. Calculate the anticipated third-quarter dividend, the dividend growth rate from the second quarter's dividend, and the growth in the annual dividend.

16.8

Dividend growth rates: The management team at Hershey has narrowed the possible dividends for a third-quarter 2006 dividend increase. Based on the possible range of quarterly dividends and the data from the previous table, complete the following table.

THIRD-QUARTER 2006 DIVIDEND CONSIDERATION	GROWTH FROM 2006 SECOND-QUARTER DIVIDEND	RESULTING 2006 ANNUAL DIVIDEND	GROWTH FROM 2005 ANNUAL DIVIDEND
$0.2450			
0.2650			
0.2675			
0.2700			
0.2725			
0.2750			

16.9

Expected payout: From the information in problem 16.8, examine the 2006 dividend payout per share for the following three third-quarter dividend increases and 2006 outlook of earnings per share. The "normalized" earnings per share for 2005 were $2.29.

THIRD-QUARTER 2006 DIVIDEND CONSIDERATION	RESULTING 2006 ANNUAL DIVIDEND	ESTIMATED 2006 EARNINGS PER SHARE		
		$2.55	$2.65	$2.75
$0.2650				
0.2700				
0.2750				

16.10

Expected dividend yields: From the information in problem 16.8, examine the 2006 dividend yields for the following three third-quarter dividend increases and 2006 year-end estimated stock prices.

THIRD-QUARTER 2006 DIVIDEND CONSIDERATION	RESULTING 2006 ANNUAL DIVIDEND	ESTIMATED 2006 YEAREND STOCK PRICE		
		$50	$55	$60
$0.2650				
0.2700				
0.2750				

16.11

Dividend policy and value: The directors of Northwest Lumber Supply have been comparing the growth of their market price with that of one of their competitors, Parker Panels. Their findings are summarized in the tables following.

NORTHWEST LUMBER SUPPLY					
Year	Earnings	Dividend	Payout (%)	Price	PE
2006	$4.30	$2.58	60	$68	15.8
2005	3.85	2.31	60	60	15.6
2004	3.29	1.97	60	50	15.2
2003	3.09	1.85	60	42	13.6
2002	3.05	1.83	60	38	12.5
2001	2.64	1.58	60	31	11.7
2000	1.98	1.19	60	26	13.1
1999	2.93	1.76	60	31	10.6
1998	3.48	2.09	60	35	10.1
1997	2.95	1.77	60	30	10.2

PARKER PANELS					
Year	Earnings	Dividend	Payout (%)	Price	PE
2006	$3.24	$1.94	60	$70	21.6
2005	2.75	1.79	65	56	20.4
2004	2.94	1.79	61	53	18.0
2003	2.93	1.73	59	48	16.4
2002	2.90	1.65	57	44	15.2
2001	2.86	1.57	55	41	14.3
2000	2.61	1.49	57	35	13.4
1999	1.66	1.50	97	20	12.9
1998	2.24	1.50	67	34	15.2
1997	2.19	1.49	68	30	13.7

Both companies are in the same markets, and both are similarly organized (approximately the same degree of operating and financial leverage). Northwest has been consistently earning more per share, yet for some reason it has not been valued at as high a PE ratio as Parker. What factors would you point out as possible causes for this lower market valuation of Northwest's stock?

16.12

Financing growth requirements and payout policy: Associated Engineers has experienced the sales, profit, and balance sheet patterns found in the table following. Identify the financial problem that has developed, and recommend a solution for it.

Associated Engineers Financial Data, 1997–2006 (Millions of Dollars)

	1997	1998	1999	2000	2001	2002	2003	2004	2005	2006
Income Statements:										
Sales	$100	$140	$180	$200	$240	$400	$360	$440	$480	$680
Profits after tax	10	14	18	20	24	40	36	44	48	68
Dividends	8	10	12	12	14	20	20	28	36	48
Retained earnings	**$2**	**$4**	**$6**	**$8**	**$10**	**$20**	**$16**	**$16**	**$12**	**$20**
Cumulative retained earnings	$2	$6	$12	$20	$30	$50	$66	$82	$94	$114
Balance Sheets:										
Current assets	$20	$30	$40	$50	$60	$100	$80	$110	$120	$160
Net fixed assets	30	40	50	50	60	100	100	110	120	180
Total assets	**$50**	**$70**	**$90**	**$100**	**$120**	**$200**	**$180**	**$220**	**$240**	**$340**
Trade credit	$8	$12	$16	$18	$20	$36	$30	$40	$40	$120
Bank credit	8	12	20	20	26	58	28	40	40	40
Other	2	10	12	12	14	16	16	18	16	16
Total current liabilities	**18**	**34**	**48**	**50**	**60**	**110**	**74**	**98**	**96**	**176**
Long-term debt	0	0	0	0	0	10	10	10	20	20
Total debt	18	34	48	50	60	120	84	108	116	196
Common stock	30	30	30	30	30	30	30	30	30	30
Retained earnings	2	6	12	20	30	50	66	82	94	114
Net worth	**32**	**36**	**42**	**50**	**60**	**80**	**96**	**112**	**124**	**144**
Total liabilities and equity	**$50**	**$70**	**$90**	**$100**	**$120**	**$200**	**$180**	**$220**	**$240**	**$340**

16.13

Dividend policy and value: Consider two firms in a world without taxes. They both initially have $100 of assets and both can earn 10% on assets with certainty. Both are all-equity firms with a 10% cost of equity capital. One pays out all of its earnings in dividends, whereas the other has a 50% dividend payout.

a.   What is the market value of equity for each firm?

b.   What does your answer to problem 16.13a tell you about the effect of dividend policy decisions on the market value of the firm in a world without taxes?

16.14

Payout policy and value: Firms A and B carry no debt, have the same current earnings before interest and taxes (EBIT = $1,000), have the same tax rate ($T = 40\%$), and have the same non-levered cost of capital ($k_u = 10\%$). However, their growth rates and dividend policies are dramatically different. Firm A retains 80% of its net income for future investment and its dividends grow (forever) at 8% per year ($g = .08$). Firm B retains only 20% of its net income and its dividends grow at 4% per year ($g = .04$).

a. Which firm is worth more?

b. Explain the intuition behind your answer to problem 16.14a.

part 6

Growth Strategies for Increasing Value

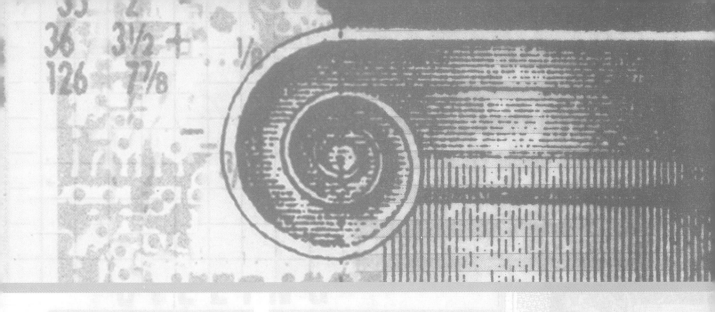

Mergers and Acquisitions

In January of 1979, The Hershey Company ventured into the restaurant business. For the sum of $165 million, Hershey purchased the Friendly Ice Cream (FIC) Corporation (a chain of family restaurants primarily in the Northeast and Florida). As the name implies, one of the Friendly featured items is ice cream. At the time, Hershey paid a 40% premium to FIC stockholders. The rational was simple: diversification. During the 1970s, the price of cocoa whipsawed, and management felt it was time to diversify. The general thought that was held by many was "After all, people have to eat and if they don't eat at home, they'll eat out!"

If diversification were the driving motive and as a stockholder you were concerned about the "evil" cocoa bean, why couldn't you just sell some of your Hershey stock and purchase FIC stock at the current market price? Why did the company need to do that on your behalf and pay a 40% premium? These are fair questions to ask and should be one of the first set of questions to ask in any potential acquisition review. In 1988, Friendly was sold for approximately $365 million. A "post completion" audit showed that Hershey just barely attained a positive return that exceeded the cost of capital.

This chapter begins by setting the stage for the total size of merger and acquisition activities. We discuss the major motives for acquisitions and review some documented results. We then discuss the underlying accounting for an acquisition and illustrate an acquisition valuation (as discussed in Chapter 12). Finally, we conclude this chapter with sound strategies that increase the likelihood of a successful acquisition.

Learning Outcomes

After completing this chapter, you should be able to:

1. Participate actively in corporate merger and acquisition programs

2. Explain the dynamic environment for mergers and acquisitions (M&As)

3. Discern between appropriate M&A rationale and overly aggressive rationale

4. Critically evaluate other alternative partnering arrangements

5. Explain the implications that most acquisitions do not add value to the acquiring firm, whereas the target firm receives an immediate benefit

6. Prepare a valuation of an acquisition target using a discounted cash flow model (as in Chapter 12) and an alternative approach using valuation "comps" (comparables)

7. Detail why acquisitions succeed and why acquisitions fail

Data on Merger Activity

Data on merger activity in the United States since 1975 is presented in Table 17.1.

Before 2004, the peak year in terms of the number of mergers announced was the year 2000. The 1980s had been considered a decade of high merger activity. However, the 9566 announcements in 2000 were nearly three times the previous peak in 1986. With regard to price-adjusted values of merger announcements, the peak took place in 1999 (at $1.457 trillion), representing 4.47 times the previous peak value of the 1980s. The year 2004 represented a strong recovery in merger activity, representing a nearly 50% increase over 2003. By 2005, the number of deals increased to 10,332, the largest ever.

Worldwide merger activity paralleled the U.S. experience (as shown in Table 17.2). The peak was reached in 2000, at $3.445 trillion. The data in Table 17.2 are from the Securities Data Corporation (SDC) and represent merger completions. The data in Table 17.1 are from

TABLE 17.1	Merger Announcements: The Mergerstat Series						
YEAR	TOTAL DOLLAR VALUE PAID ($BILLION)	NUMBER TOTAL	NUMBER OF TRANSACTIONS VALUED AT: $100 Million or More	$1 Billion or More	GDP DEFLATOR (2000 = 100)	2000 CONSTANT DOLLAR CONSIDERATION	PERCENTAGE CHANGE
1975	11.8	2,297	14	0	38.0	31.1	
1976	20.0	2,276	39	0	40.2	49.8	60
1977	21.9	2,224	41	1	42.8	51.2	3
1978	34.2	2,106	80	0	45.8	74.7	46
1979	43.5	2,128	83	3	49.5	87.8	17
1980	44.3	1,889	94	4	54.0	82.0	−7
1981	82.6	2,395	113	12	59.1	139.7	70
1982	53.8	2,346	116	6	62.7	85.8	−39
1983	73.1	2,533	138	11	65.2	112.1	31
1984	122.2	2,543	200	18	67.7	180.6	61
1985	179.8	3,011	270	36	69.7	257.9	43
1986	173.1	3,336	346	27	71.3	242.9	−6
1987	163.7	2,032	301	36	73.2	223.6	−8
1988	246.9	2,258	369	45	75.7	326.2	46
1989	221.1	2,366	328	35	78.6	281.5	−14
1990	108.2	2,074	181	21	81.6	132.6	−53
1991	71.2	1,877	150	13	84.4	84.3	−36
1992	96.7	2,574	200	18	86.4	111.9	33
1993	176.4	2,663	242	27	88.4	199.6	78
1994	226.7	2,997	383	51	90.3	251.2	26
1995	356.0	3,510	462	74	92.1	386.5	54
1996	495.0	5,848	640	94	93.9	527.4	36
1997	657.1	7,800	873	120	95.4	688.7	31
1998	1,191.9	7,809	906	158	96.5	1,235.5	79
1999	1,425.9	9,278	1,097	195	97.9	1,457.0	18
2000	1,325.7	9,566	1,150	206	100.0	1,325.7	−9
2001	699.4	8,290	703	121	102.4	683.0	−48
2002	440.7	7,303	608	72	104.2	422.9	−38
2003	504.6	7,983	654	88	106.3	474.7	12
2004	750.7	9,783	841	134	109.1	688.1	45
2005	1,011.0	10,332	963	170	112.2	901.1	31

Source: *Mergerstat Review* published by Factset Mergerstat, LLC Santa Monica, CA.

TABLE 17.2	Worldwide M&A Activity, 1995–2005 ($Billion)[a]							
YEAR	1998	1999	2000	2001	2002	2003	2004	2005
Non-U.S.	$647	$914	$1,664	$829	$647	$599	$649	$1,062
U.S.	1,374	1,423	1,782	1,156	625	522	857	981
Total	$2,020	$2,337	$3,445	$1,985	$1,272	$1,121	$1,506	$2,043
%U.S.	68.0%	60.9%	51.7%	58.2%	49.1%	46.5%	56.9%	48.0%

[a]In non-U.S. mergers, a U.S. company is neither a buyer nor target. U.S. mergers include those in which a U.S. firm is either a buyer or a target.
[b]Source: SDC data in *Mergers & Acquisitions*, 2006 Almanac, February 2006.

Mergerstat, based on announcements and various selection criteria. Mergerstat provides published data on the United States in greater detail than SDC, but does not present aggregate worldwide tables. Data for the United States differ for the reasons indicated, but the trend patterns convey similar economic implications. Activity after 2000 declined in both the United States and the rest of the world. The economic downturn and the decline in stock prices that began in early 2000 caused a decline in M&A activity through 2003.

The 10 largest mergers in history are presented in Table 17.3. Seven of the 10 occurred during the merger boom of 1998 to 2000. Pfizer accounted for two of the top 10. AOL-Time Warner is widely regarded as one of the most unsuccessful. In contrast, Exxon-Mobil had significant gains within the first year after completion. The price of oil was slightly under $10 per barrel in late 1998 when the merger was announced. By May of 2006, the price of oil had risen to more than $70 a barrel. This illustrates that world economic developments can greatly influence the success or failure of a merger.

M&As represent a key strategy of most management teams. M&As effect our business and personal lives and have just become a fact of life these days. Although it is always interesting to read about one public company purchasing another public company, most acquisitions (85+%) are of one company purchasing a private company (such as a division or even a line of business from another publicly traded company, a "mom & pop" operation, start-up business, or other non publicly traded organization).

Our central proposition of this chapter is that broadly M&A decisions reflect two main forces: adjustments to shocks and enhancing the company's capabilities. The timing of aggregate merger activity (so-called merger waves) is explained by macroeconomic forces: levels of economic activity (GDP), stock price movements, and financing conditions.

TABLE 17.3	100 Largest Announcements in History			
RANK	BUYER	SELLER	PRICE OFFERED (MILLIONS)	YEAR ANNOUNCED
1	Pfizer Inc.	Warner-Lambert Co.	$116,705.4	1999
2	America Online Inc.	Time Warner Inc.	101,002.5	2000
3	Exxon Corp.	Mobil Corp.	81,429.8	1998
4	SBC Communications Inc.	Ameritech Corp.	75,233.5	1998
5	Vodafone Group Plc., UK	Air Touch Communications Inc.	62,768.0	1999
6	Bell Atlantic Corp.	GTE Corp.	60,489.9	1998
7	Pfizer Inc.	Pharmacia Corp.	58,293.8	2002
8	Procter & Gamble Co.	Gillette Co.	57,920.3	2005
9	JPMorgan Chase & Co. Inc.	Bank One Corp.	57,614.9	2004
10	British Petroleum Co. PLC UK	Amoco Corp.	56,482.0	1998

Source: *Mergerstat Review* published by Factset Mergerstat, LLC, Santa Monica, CA.

This chapter is based on a theory of strategic M&As. It describes how managers seek to enhance the long-run value of firms by making positive net present value (NPV) internal and external investments. Firms engage in internal investments, mergers, divestitures, alliances, licensing, and so on in programs over a continuing succession of years to strengthen their managerial capabilities and resources in relation to the product/market areas in which they enter and exit over time.

The Change Forces

M&A activity in recent years has reflected powerful change forces in the world economy. These include the fact that (1) the pace of technological change has accelerated, (2) the costs of communication and transportation have been greatly reduced, (3) markets have become international in scope, (4) the forms, sources, and intensity of competition have expanded, (5) new industries have emerged, and (6) while regulations have increased in some areas deregulation has taken place in other industries.

Overriding all are technological changes, which include biotechnology, personal computers, computer services, software, servers, and the many advances in information systems (including the Internet). Nations have adopted international agreements such as the General Agreement on Tariffs and Trade (GATT), which have resulted in freer trade. The growing forces of competition have produced deregulation in major industries such as financial services, airlines, and medical services (Jensen 1993).

More generally, Mitchell and Mulherin (1996) developed evidence that a wide variety of "shocks" cause changes in industry structures. We extend their industry shock model in Table 17.4, listing 10 sources of change and their impacts on 34 individual industries. We begin with technology change. The computer industry was vertically integrated in the

TABLE 17.4	Change Forces and Motivations for M&As	
CHANGE FORCES	**INDUSTRIES**	
1. Technology change	• Broadcasting, entertainment • Internet • Packaging & containers • Computers	• Telecommunications • Tire & rubber • Retailing • Defense
2. Globalization	• Apparels, textiles • Metals & mining • Financial services	• Packaging & containers • Tire & rubber • Wireless
3. Commoditization 4. Low growth 5. Chronic excess capacity (consolidation)	• Chemical • Food processing • Automobile	• Pharmaceuticals • Toiletries & cosmetics • Integrated steel
6. Fragmentation (roll-ups)	• Staffing services • Rental equipment	• Facility services • Electrical contracting
7. Large capital investment subject to high risks	• Pharmaceuticals	
8. Price volatility	• Coal, uranium, geothermal • Integrated petroleum • Oilfield services	• Petroleum producing
9. Deregulation	• Air transport • Broadcasting, entertainment • Truck & transport leasing	• Medical services • Natural gas • Financial services
10. Augment capabilities	• Pharmaceuticals	• Computers

1970s when mainframes were the major product. IBM produced the chips, the hardware, the operating systems, other application software, the sales and distribution systems, and organization of service and maintenance engineers.

By the 1990s, horizontal value chains had developed with multiple competitors. Chips were produced by Intel, Advanced Micro Devices, Motorola, and other companies. PC producers included IBM, Dell, Compaq, Apple, Hewlett-Packard, and many others. Microsoft dominated operating systems. The computer industry occupied only part of the value chains of the broader information industry. Servers and networks were developed. The Internet developed. Cable and digital satellite systems were created. Wireless telecommunication developed. New companies included Oracle, Sun Microsystems, Cisco, 3Com, Qualcomm, Vodafone, Nokia, and others. Older companies such as Ericsson moved from traditional telephone products to wireless.

Extending Capabilities

The economic theory of mergers is that they help firms adjust to the many change forces, including increased competitive pressures. The business rationale for mergers is that they can be positive NPV investments. Mergers increase value when the value of the combined firm is greater than adding the pre-merger values of the independent entities.

SYNERGISTIC (POSITIVE NET PRESENT VALUE) INVESTMENTS

We can formalize these generalizations in the following relationships.

$$NVI = V_{BT} - (V_B + V_T)$$

Where:

$$NVI = \text{Net value increase}$$
$$V_B = \text{Value of bidder alone}$$
$$V_T = \text{Value of target alone}$$
$$V_{BT} = \text{Value of firms combined}$$

A simple example will illustrate. Company B (the bidder) has a current market value of $40 (it is understood that all numbers are in billions). Company T (the target) has a current market value of $40. The sum of the values as independent firms is therefore $80. Assume that the combined company will have a value of $100 ($V_{BT}$). The amount of value created is $20. That is, the acquisition creates $20 of synergy.

How will the increase in value be divided? Targets usually receive a premium. What about the bidders? If the bidder pays a premium of less than $20, it will share in the value increase. If B pays a premium larger than $20, the value of the bidder will decline. If the bidder pays $50 for the target, a premium of 25% has been paid to T. The value increases are shared equally. If B pays $60 for T, all gains go to the target. B achieves no value increase. If B pays $70 for T, the value of B will decline to $30.

A high percentage of the large transactions beginning in 1992 have been *stock-for-stock transactions*. Some hold the view that this does not represent real money. But this is not valid. Suppose that B exchanges 1.25 of its shares for 1 share of T. Because B is valued at $40, T will receive $1.25 \times \$40$, which equals $50. The premium paid is 25%. Based on their previous $40 values, B and T each owned 50% of the pre-merger combined values.

Post-merger, the percentages of ownership will remain 50/50. But if B exchanges 1.5 of its own shares per share of T, this is equivalent to paying $60 in value for the target. The target shareholders will have 1.5 shares in the new company for every 1.0 share held by the bidder shareholders. Target shareholders will own 60% of the company. The bidder will own only 40%. The value of the target will be $60. The bidder value will be $40, unchanged. Hence, none of the synergy gains will be received by the bidder shareholders.

The situation is even worse if B pays more than $60 for the target. If B pays $70 for the target, the value of the bidder shares must decline to $30 because the combined value is $100. The consequences are terrible. The shares of the bidder will decline in value by $10 (25%). Furthermore, the B shareholders will own only 30% of the combined company. For every share B now owns, the target shareholders will own 2.3 shares. Thus, the exchange ratios in stock-for-stock deals can have major consequences. In addition, in a stock-for-stock transaction the target firm participates in the risks of the future performance of the combined firm.

ENHANCING CAPABILITIES

The sources of positive NPV investments in M&As are listed under nine categories.

A. Economies of scale

B. Economies of scope

C. Extending technological capabilities

D. Industry consolidation strategies

E. Industry roll-ups

F. New capabilities and managerial skills

G. First mover advantages

H. Customer relationships

I. Globalization

Adding capabilities and new managerial skills can take many forms, including the adoption of best practices. Sources of economies of scale and scope are listed in categories A and B. Methods of extending technological capabilities are set forth in category C. Categories D, E, and F represent forms of industry adjustment. First mover advantages (G) include preempting acquisitions by competitors and achieving critical mass before rivals. Customer relationships (H) include improved distribution systems. Particularly important are the potentials of globalization (I) as a method of adding markets and new capabilities. Table 17.5 further expands on these nine capabilities.

More generally, efficiency improvements can result from combining firms of unequal managerial capabilities. A relatively efficient bidder may acquire a relatively inefficient target. Value can be increased by improving the efficiency of the target. Sometimes the combination will achieve a more efficient critical mass. The investments in expensive specialized machinery may be large. Combining firms may achieve better utilization of large fixed investments. Plants that have old or inefficient-sized equipment may be shut down after the merger.

The Q ratio is widely used as a measure of managerial efficiency. The Q ratio is defined as the ratio of the market value of the firm's securities to the replacement costs of its assets. In the late 1970s and early 1980s, the Q ratio had been running between 0.5 and 0.6. If a company wished to add to capacity in producing a particular product, it could acquire the additional capacity more cheaply by purchasing a company that produced the product rather than building brick-and-mortar from scratch.

If firm A sought to add capacity, this implied that its marginal Q ratio was greater than 1. But if other firms in its industry had average Q ratios of less than 1 it was efficient for

TABLE	17.5	Enhancing Capabilities by M&A

A. Economies of scale
   1. Cut production costs due to large volume
   2. Combine R&D operations
   3. Increased R&D at controlled risk
   4. Increased sales force
   5. Cut overhead costs
   6. Strengthen distributions systems
B. Economies of scope
   1. Broaden product line
   2. Provide one-stop shopping for all services
   3. Obtain complementary products
C. Extending technological capabilities
   1. Enter technologically dynamic industries
   2. Seize opportunities in industries with developing technologies
   3. Exploit technological advantage
   4. Add new R&D capabilities
   5. Add key complementary technical capabilities
   6. Add key technological capabilities
   7. Add new key patent or technology
   8. Acquire technology for lagging areas
D. Industry consolidation strategies
   1. Eliminate industry excess capacity
   2. Shift from overcapacity area to area with more favorable sales capacity
   3. Exit a product area that has become commoditized to area of specialty
E. Industry roll-ups: taking fragmented industries and because of improvements in communication and transportation rolling up many individual firms into larger firms obtaining the benefits of strong and experienced management teams over a large number of smaller units
F. New capabilities and managerial skills
   1. Acquire capabilities in new industry
   2. Obtain talent for fast-moving industries
   3. Apply a broad range of capabilities and managerial skills in new areas

G. First mover advantages
   1. Preempt acquisitions by competitor
   2. Achieve critical mass before rivals
H. Customer relationships
   1. Develop new key customer relationships
   2. Follow clients
   3. Combined company can meet customers' demand for a wide range of services
   4. Improve distribution systems
I. Globalization
   1. International competition – to establish presence in foreign markets and to strengthen position in domestic market
   2. Size and economies of scale required for effective global competition
   3. Growth opportunities outside domestic market
   4. Diversification
      a. Product line
      b. Geographically: enlarge market
      c. Reduce systematic risk
      d. Reduce dependence on exports
   5. Favorable product inputs
      a. Obtain assured sources of supply: sources of raw materials
      b. Labor (inexpensive, well-trained, etc.)
      c. Need for local manufacturing
   6. Improve distribution in other countries
   7. Political/regulatory policies
      a. Circumvent protective tariffs, etc.
      b. Political/economic stability
      c. Government policy
      d. Invest in a safe, predictable environment
      e. Take advantage of common markets
   8. Relative exchange rate conditions

firm A to add capacity by purchasing other firms. For example, if the Q ratio were 0.6 and if in a merger the premium paid over market value was even as high as 50%, the bid price would be a Q ratio of 0.9 and still the resulting price would be 10% below the current replacement costs of the assets acquired. There is a valid economic basis for high Q-ratio firms purchasing low Q-ratio firms. This also creates the potential for the high Q-ratio firms to improve the performance of the low Q-ratio firms.

The Legal and Regulatory Environments

Changes in the legal and regulatory environments have increased the probability of a bidding situation in a merger transaction. During the 1960s, the numbers of merger transactions and tender offers grew to levels substantially higher than ever experienced in prior U.S. financial history. Tender offers usually involve a premium. Complaints were made that unsophisticated shareholders rushed to tender their shares for fear that the deal might be completed before they could share in the premium prices. Tender offer deals could be completed in six days and it was argued that investors needed more time to consider their alternatives.

In response, Congress enacted the Williams Act of 1968 (which provided that acquirers must report to the SEC when they had accumulated 5% of the equity shares of a target). Acquiring firms were required to keep the deal open for at least 20 days. Target shareholders could change their votes during the 20-day waiting period. Acquiring firms were also required to explain their future intentions with respect to their 5% investment. The waiting period provided a window during which other firms might become interested and increased the probability of competing bids. Multiple bids for public companies are commonplace (Boone and Mulherin 2005).

In addition, in 1982 Martin Lipton (a leading M&A attorney) developed the first type of poison pill as a takeover defense. The basic "flip-in" poison pill provides for a special dividend of one stock purchase right to each outstanding equity share triggered by the acquisition of a specified percentage of a company's total equity shares. The flip-in provides that when triggered the rights enable holders to purchase additional shares in the issuing company at a substantial discount (except the investors whose actions triggered the rights). Subsequent court rulings held that the poison pills can be put in place by the board of directors or management without approval by shareholders. These changing environments and the institutional setting provide a background for analyzing the alternative theories of mergers described previously.

Alternative Methods for Value Growth

Firms use multiple methods for value growth. Mergers and acquisitions are only one form. These activities are ongoing and take place year after year. Table 17.6 summarizes alternative methods for value growth. We use the term *M&As* to include these multiple activities.

A joint venture is a separate business entity that usually involves only a fraction of the activities of the participating organizations. The participants in a joint venture continue as separate firms, but create a new corporation, partnership, or other business form. Joint ventures are limited in scope and duration.

There are several objectives that may be achieved by a joint venture. Working with other firms reduces the investment costs of entering potentially risky new areas. Even though investment requirements are less than solely internal operations, the joint venture may still enjoy the benefits of economies of scale, critical mass, and the learning curve. In addition,

TABLE 17.6	Alternative Methods for Value Growth

1. Internal projects: Investment expansions developed within the firm.
2. Mergers: Any transaction that forms one economic unit from two or more previous units. The equity or ownership stock of the target is acquired. All of the liabilities of ownership carry over to the acquiring firm.
3. Joint ventures: A combination of subsets of assets contributed by two (or more) business entities for a specific business purpose and a limited duration.
4. Alliances: More informal inter-business relationships.
5. Licensing: Developing proprietary technology for rent to others.
6. Minority investments: A small fraction, usually less than 5%, of the equity of the target is acquired. This gives the acquiring firm increased knowledge of the activities of the relatively new area represented by the investment.
7. Share Repurchase: An announcement of a repurchase of the firm's own shares, generally in the open market.

joint ventures allow firms the opportunity to gain knowledge. Firms may share or exchange technology to accomplish what one firm could not do alone. There is a potential for sharing managerial skills in organization, planning, and control.

Joint ventures have proven to be particularly advantageous in the international setting. In some situations, local governments may not allow an acquisition. A joint venture presents an opportunity to combine some assets without violating such a regulation. International joint ventures usually reduce risks of firms operating in foreign countries. In addition, joint ventures have been used as a means of circumventing certain international trade barriers.

When a firm purchases a segment divested by another firm, it may have a high uncertainty about its future performance under the buyer's management. This uncertainty might make it difficult for the parties to agree on a price. Joint ventures can serve a useful function as an interim step. A common pattern is for the acquirer to pay cash for 40 to 45% of the divested segment it is purchasing as its contribution to the formation of the joint venture. The joint venture may be used as a device for the selling firm to convey knowledge of manufacturing and/or distribution.

The motivations and the incentives are all in the right directions. The better the selling firm does in teaching the acquirer the potentials of the segment the higher the future value of the segment. As a consequence, after a year or two the buyer may complete the purchase of the percentage of the joint venture it does not own. Typically, the price paid for the second segment is substantially higher than for the first segment because the acquirer better understands the potentials of the business. Value is created by minimizing employee turnover and avoiding the impairment of supplier and distribution networks.

Alliances are less formal than joint ventures. A new entity need not be created. A formal contract may not be written. The relative size of participants may be highly unequal. Partner firms pool resources, expertise, and ideas so that the partners will have a continuing need for one another. Evolving relationships require adaptability and change over time. The alliance may involve multiple partners. Because the relationships are less legalistic, mutual trust is required. The speed of change in relationships may be rapid. Firms may modify and move to other alliances as attractive possibilities emerge. Some creative people do not wish to be in the environment of large firms, but large firms may increase their access to creative people by alliances with smaller firms.

Alliances may have some advantages over mergers or joint ventures. They are more informal and provide flexibility. They may provide a firm with access to new markets and technologies with relatively small investments. Alliances provide the ability to create and disband projects with minimal formality. Working with partners possessing multiple skills can create major synergies.

Figure 17.1 portrays the relative strengths of multiple strategies for expansion with regard to achieving 10 benefits that contribute to a successful firm. Alternative growth strategies have different relative strengths. We have coded the strength of the benefit of the alternative strategies. High is the darkest, low is clear, and medium is lightly shaded. Figure 17.1 reveals a mosaic in which alternative strategies have different strengths and weaknesses. Internal growth avoids antitrust problems.

Mergers can add capabilities and markets in a relatively short period of time. Joint ventures add capabilities with limited investment commitments. Alliances add knowledge of new areas in relatively informal arrangements that may be expanded or contracted. Licensing can increase markets and yield high returns on investments already made. Minority investments in companies in new areas provide information on potentially attractive areas, yield high financial returns, and (for companies such as Intel) expand the use of their products.

| FIGURE 17.1 | Multiple Strategies for Growth* | | | | | |

Benefits	Internal	Merger	JV	Alliance	Licensing	Investment
Learn new areas	L	H	H	H	H	H
Combine best practices	L	H	M	M	L	M
Increase demand for products	L	M	M	L	L	H
Add capabilities	L	H	H	M	L	M
Add products	L	H	M	L	L	L
Add markets	L	H	M	M	H	L
Speed	L	H	M	M	H	M
Costs known	L	M	H	M	L	H
Avoid antitrust	H	L	H	H	H	M
Clarity	H	M	L	L	H	M

*Strength of benefit: H = High, M = Medium, L = Low.

LEVERAGED BUYOUTS

The most complete form of ownership change is represented by taking a public company private through a *leveraged buyout (LBO)*. When former managers are the prime movers in the transaction, it is called a *management buyout (MBO)*. The basic idea is to raise the necessary funds to purchase control from the existing public shareholders, using financing with a large percentage debt component and providing management with a high percentage of the remaining small equity base. A turnaround was usually involved in the sense that fundamental operating changes were made to increase profitability and value.

Highly leveraged transactions have been used prior to the 1980s, when LBOs became substantial in dollar volume. But the high degree of diversification activity that took place during the conglomerate merger movement of the 1960s resulted in many firms having segments that did not receive informed guidance by top management. During the 1980s, LBOs were one of the methods for unwinding the diversification of the 1960s.

In both the early 1980s and after 1992, LBOs have earned superior returns to investors in all stages. There are several reasons for this. First, the most important reason is the improvement in operations, reducing cost and increasing cash flows. This is achieved by bringing in management with experience and competence in the operations of the company. Second, the increased percentage of equity ownership by management strengthened management incentives. Third, a higher percentage of equity in financial structures provides greater flexibility in making the additional investments that may be required. Fourth, financial buyers may assist in formulating strategies and providing managerial expertise.

LBOs guided by these principles can achieve returns to investors higher than returns from broad stock indexes such as the S&P 500. A Barron's article of March 14, 2005 (Santoli) reports that in 2004 LBO volume reached $68.3 billion, a level exceeded only by the 1988 total (which included the $28 billion RJR Nabisco deal). The buyout activity of 2004 and into 2005 was characterized by private equity firms that have amassed total funds of $800 billion. Yet some of the deals have been so large that buyout firms have joined in making bids. This enables the individual private equity firms to diversify their investments in this relatively high-risk business.

In addition, the private equity firms have been able to purchase, restructure, recapitalize, and resell their companies (sometimes within a one-year period). Santoli gives one-year flip-over examples for five financial buyers: Bain Capital, Blackstone Group, Kohlberg Kravis Roberts, Madison Dearborn, and Thomas H. Lee. These successes led to the creation of 800 private equity funds by 2005, with the capacity to raise $250 billion. In addition, large cash balances in individual companies and $1 trillion or more in hedge funds could drive up purchase prices, lowering returns in LBO transactions.

PROGRAMS OF M&A ACTIVITIES

Firms employ multiple forms of M&A activities. In addition, M&As are programs conducted over multiple years. Table 17.7 illustrates how these activities are repeated year after year. During the 13-year period 1990 to 2002, the General Electric Company engaged in 1,449 multiple growth activities. This represents an average of 111 transactions per year. This illustrates the dynamism of M&A activities. It also emphasizes that empirical studies of the performance effect of any one of these more than 1,000 transactions are difficult to interpret. The multiple activities year after year are surely anticipated to some degree by the market. These multiple activities over extended time periods provide new perspectives in looking at the effects of M&A activity. The traditional emphasis is to look at individual M&As. But it is clear that General Electric was building up competencies to cover a broader area of related activities. The company also engaged in a large number of divestitures. But our compilations of the acquisition and divestitures of many companies demonstrate the broadening of company capabilities in related activities.

In summary, the theory of strategic mergers emphasizes adjustments to change forces and broadening capabilities to improve performance. This theory emphasizes market forces that cause firms to use multiple methods of growth. These include internal, merger and acquisitions, joint ventures, alliances, licensing, and minority investments. We also include asset restructuring, discussed in the following section.

TABLE 17.7	GE M&A Activity								
				TYPE OF ACTIVITY					
Year	Merger	Asset Acquisition	Minority Investment	Divestiture	Share Repurchase	Alliance	Joint Venture	Major Licensing	Total
1990	5	16	4	5	1	6	17	3	57
1991	4	13	6	7	—	19	28	2	79
1992	0	11	10	10	—	24	28	2	85
1993	4	21	6	7	—	24	24	3	89
1994	4	29	7	10	1	29	28	4	112
1995	3	31	6	11	—	22	22	4	99
1996	8	31	4	6	2	12	25	0	88
1997	14	58	12	9	1	18	34	0	146
1998	9	57	16	18	—	29	36	1	166
1999	5	60	23	20	—	37	25	0	170
2000	7	46	23	7	—	46	30	0	159
2001	9	50	11	15	—	18	9	0	112
2002	8	41	4	16	—	12	6	0	87
	80	464	132	141	5	296	312	19	1449

Source: Securities Data Corporation.

BEHAVIORAL PRICING OF M&As

The three leading behavioral theories of mergers are hubris, market misvaluations, and agency theories. These theories regard mergers as departures from rational decision making.

Hubris and the Winner's Curse Roll (1986) analyzed the "winner's curse" in takeover activity. Postulating strong market efficiency in all markets, the prevailing market price of the target already reflected the full value of the firm. The higher valuation of the bidders (over the target's true economic value), he states, resulted from *hubris*—their excessive self-confidence (pride, arrogance). Hubris is one of the factors that caused the *winner's curse* phenomenon to occur. Even if there were synergies, the actual or potential competition of other bidders could cause the winning bidder to pay too much.

Stock Market Misvaluations Shleifer and Vishny (SV, 2003) present a theory of mergers based on overvaluation of bidders and undervaluation of targets. They argue that firms have a powerful incentive to achieve overvaluation of their equities to make their acquisitions with stock. The benefits of high valuation also stimulate firms to engage in earnings manipulation, "a phenomenon whose prevalence is becoming increasingly apparent" (SV 2003, p. 309).

The main implications of their model are that acquisitions for stock are more likely to occur when (1) market valuations are high and there is a supply of highly overvalued firms (bidders) and less overvalued ones (targets), (2) the market belief that there is synergy that makes the acquisition attractive in the short run and enables the acquirer to pay a premium, and (3) target managers have short horizons or are paid off to accept the merger. In contrast, cash acquisitions are more likely when targets are undervalued firms and the acquisitions are more hostile.

In the Roll model the financial markets are efficient but bidders are irrational. In the Shleifer-Vishny model, financial markets are inefficient but bidders and targets have perfect information. Both the winner's curse theory of Roll and the stock market misvaluations of SV are types of *behavioral finance theories*.

Agency Problems The Tyco story and the personal excesses of its CEO, Dennis Kozlowski, at the expense of Tyco's shareholders is a fitting example of agency problems. An agency problem arises when managers own only a fraction of the ownership shares of the firm (Jensen and Meckling 1976). This partial ownership may cause managers to work less vigorously than otherwise and/or to consume more prerequisites (luxurious offices, expensive art, company jets and cars, lavish private parties, memberships in clubs) because the majority owners bear most of the cost.

Furthermore, the argument goes, in large corporations with widely dispersed ownership there is not sufficient incentive for individual owners to expend the substantial resources required to monitor the behavior of managers. Hence, managers may use mergers to increase firm size to increase their own salaries, bonuses, and perks. In addition, managers may be motivated in some mergers because it enables them to cash in on substantial stock option arrangements.

EMPIRICAL REVIEW OF ACQUISITION RESULTS

A number of approaches to merger performance have been developed. We review this literature to evaluate the alternative theories or explanations of M&As. Many studies have calculated the stock price impact days before the acquisition announcement and days immediately after the acquisition. These approaches are called *"event study methods."* We summarized the pattern of returns with single bidders versus multiple bidders for target firms in Figure 17.2 and for acquiring firms in Figure 17.3.

In Figure 17.2, the returns to target firms begin to rise about 20 days before the announcement date. On the announcement date, a further increase moves the abnormal returns of single-bidder target firms to about 25 to 30%. Shortly after the announcement date, the returns to target firms drift down slightly. In multiple-bidder contest, the event returns to targets continue to rise after the announcement date. As subsequent bids take place, the event returns continue to rise. About 40 days after the announcement date for the first bidder, the event returns to the target firms level off at about 35 to 40%.

In Figure 17.3, we see that the event returns for acquiring firms that are single bidders rise to more than 2% at the announcement date. Subsequently, the event returns drift down, but only slightly. For acquiring firms that are competing in multiple-bidder contests, the event returns are slightly positive. But shortly after the announcement date, as new bidders come onto the scene, the event returns drop to negative levels.

In stock-for-stock mergers, target firms gain on average about 20 to 25%. When the method of payment is cash, the abnormal returns to targets are 25 to 35%. Two reasons have been suggested for the higher event returns to targets in cash acquisitions. One is that when targets receive stock in the acquiring company as payment they share in the future performance and risks of a combined enterprise. A second is that

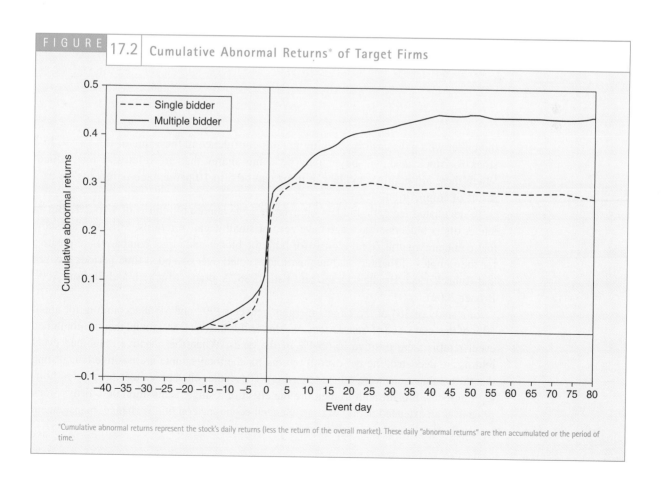

FIGURE 17.2 | Cumulative Abnormal Returns* of Target Firms

*Cumulative abnormal returns represent the stock's daily returns (less the return of the overall market). These daily "abnormal returns" are then accumulated or the period of time.

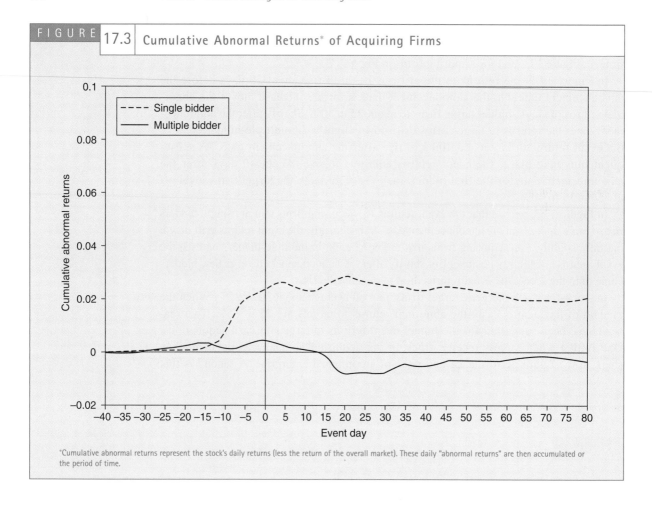

FIGURE 17.3 | Cumulative Abnormal Returns* of Acquiring Firms

*Cumulative abnormal returns represent the stock's daily returns (less the return of the overall market). These daily "abnormal returns" are then accumulated or the period of time.

the buyer who pays cash is showing greater confidence in the value of the target. In a stock-for-stock deal, the buyer may be using shares that are relatively overvalued. When there are multiple bidders, returns can be 5 to 10 percentage points higher as a result of competition.

In negotiated mergers, bidders on average have abnormal returns of 1 to 2%. But in tender offers bidders on average have zero or small negative returns. Most studies show that combined returns (total returns for both the bidder and target company) are positive for the samples of mergers and acquisitions studied over extended time periods (Jensen and Ruback 1983, Bradley, Desai, and Kim 1988, Andrade, Mitchell, and Stafford 2001, Bruner 2002).

In a study of 364 of the largest mergers between 1992 and 1998 accounting for about 50% of the total value of transactions, Weston and Johnson (1999) found that the combined event returns were positive in 65.4% of the deals. When the negative combined event returns are deducted, the net overall returns for the total sample are positive (suggesting that the combinations were value increasing). The studies cited previously have been short-term in focus. It is difficult to measure the effect of a single acquisition on a firm's stock price over an extended period of time. General economic conditions change, management teams change, and other acquisitions occur.

RESULTS OF M&As IN PRACTICE

Fuller, Netter, and Stegemoller (2002) study merger programs and distinguish among public, private, and/or subsidiary targets as well. Regardless of method of payment, multiple acquirers of public firms earn insignificant returns. For private and subsidiary targets, acquirers' returns are significantly positive for all methods of payment. Acquisitions of private companies outperformed acquisitions of public companies in both the short and long run. These results are consistent with Chang's (1998) findings. They also find that small private firms are not as readily marketable as publicly traded firms (*illiquidity effect*). The buyer negotiates a higher discount rate, resulting in a lower valuation.

In their analysis of deals by 1,700 acquirers between 1986 and 2001, Harding and Rovit (2004) found that the number of deals and relative deal size influences results. There exists a positive relation between annual returns and experience, in which firms that have completed the most deals realize the highest annual excess returns. They find that acquirers who completed 20 deals or more during the 15-year period generated average annual excess shareholders' returns approximately twice as high as companies with no acquisitions. For the 15-year period, the most frequent acquirers outperform acquirers with fewer than five deals by a factor of 1.7.

In a study by Hazelkorn, Zenner, and Shivdasani (HZS, 2004), a sample of 1,547 transactions for the 12-year period between 1990 and 2002 was analyzed. They found similar results for short-term periods, but measured over two years one-fifth of the transactions experienced industry-adjusted returns below a negative 40% and another one-fifth achieved returns in excess of 40%. Thus, wide differences between the performance of acquirers in individual transactions are observed. They also present data showing that short-term returns were good indictors of long-run returns.

What is clear from these distributions is that there exist winners and losers, even though the average return may be zero. Thus, mergers and acquisitions do have the potential to create value for acquiring firms if performed effectively. This confirms why M&A activity exists. Even though in the aggregate there are no gains, the potential for creating positive abnormal returns leads to M&A activity.

Accounting Conventions for Mergers

The Financial Accounting Standards Board (FASB) issued two statements in June of 2001 that made fundamental changes in accounting for mergers and acquisitions. Statement of Financial Accounting Standards No. 141 on business combinations abolishes the use of the *pooling-of-interest method (pooling method)*. FASB 141 requires that all business combinations be accounted for by a single method: the *purchase method*. Statement of Financial Accounting Standards No. 142 on goodwill and other intangible assets set forth procedures for accounting for acquired goodwill and other intangible assets, as well as for their impairment.

The basic procedures for purchase accounting have a logic. A simple example will illustrate. Usually the purchase price will be greater than the book value of shareholders' equity of the target. For example, in 1988 Hershey purchased the Dietrich Corporation of Reading, Pennsylvania. The approximate purchase price was $100 million. For their $100 million, Hershey received $65 million of assets such as accounts receivable, inventory, land, buildings, equipment, and so on.

Hershey also assumed $25 million of liabilities (accounts payable, debt, and so on). In total, for the $100 million purchase price Hershey received "net assets" of $40 million. The difference is what is termed "goodwill" or the "extra" value paid for the ongoing business and established products of the Dietrich Corporation. Goodwill is more formally referred to as intangibles resulting from business acquisitions. We can summarize the debits and credits as follows.

- Debit ($ millions):

  - Specific asset accounts purchased: $65.0

  - Goodwill: $60.0

  - Total debit adjustments (purchase price): $125.0

- Credit ($ millions):

  - Specific liabilities assumed: $25.0

  - Cash paid: $100.0

  - Total credit adjustments (purchase price): $125.0

If shares of stock are used to pay for the acquisition instead of cash, additional entries to stockholders' equity are required.

Acquisition Valuation

In Chapter 12, we discussed and presented a valuation model for The Hershey Company. In that model, we saw that Hershey was fairly valued at about $55 per share. The model is repeated here as Table 17.8. If a bidder wanted to acquire Hershey, the premium that would be offered could be about 40% more than the current price. In our example, the "bid" would be $77 per share.

In order to achieve this end, the acquiring company would need to streamline all areas of Hershey, stimulate its growth by perhaps distributing its products outside North America, and gain some additional synergies itself. These are depicted in Table 17.9. In this case, the acquiring company could try to achieve the following.

- Increase sales growth in the first four years as indicated in the following table.

SALES GROWTH	2006	2007	2008	2009
Original	5.0%	5.0%	4.5%	4.0%
Revised	10.0	12.0	8.0	6.0

- Reduce expenses (selling, marketing, and administrative) by 3% points each year.

- Realize $67.2 million of additional synergies annually.

The enterprise value of $20,214.1 million is reduced for the 2005 debt ($1,762.0 million) and augmented by the 2005 cash level ($67.2 million), which results in an equity value of $18,519.3 million or $77 per share (240.5 million shares outstanding). Although these objectives do not seem out of reach, a great deal of care must be exhibited that these objectives can be realized.

TABLE 17.8 — Comprehensive Valuation Model–Base Valuation ($55 per share)

Including Terminal Year ($ Millions)

	YEAR 1 2006	YEAR 2 2007	YEAR 3 2008	YEAR 4 2009	YEAR 5 2010	YEAR 6 2011	YEAR 7 2012	YEAR 8 2013
Panel A: Projected Free Cash Flow								
Net revenue	$5,077.8	$5,331.7	$5,571.6	$5,794.5	$6,026.3	$6,207.1	$6,362.3	$6,521.4
Cost of sales (excluding depreciation)	2,894.3	3,017.7	3,136.8	3,244.9	3,356.6	3,444.9	3,512.0	3,599.8
Selling, marketing, and administrative	949.5	986.4	1,019.6	1,048.8	1,078.7	1,098.7	1,113.4	1,141.2
Depreciation	204.4	218.1	232.6	247.6	263.1	279.1	295.6	312.6
Operating income	1,029.6	1,109.5	1,182.6	1,253.2	1,327.9	1,384.4	1,441.3	1,467.8
Taxes	381.0	410.5	437.6	463.7	491.3	512.2	533.3	543.1
After-tax operating income	648.6	699.0	745.0	789.5	836.6	872.2	908.0	924.7
% of sales	12.8%	13.1%	13.4%	13.6%	13.9%	14.1%	14.3%	14.2%
Depreciation	204.4	218.1	232.6	247.6	263.1	279.1	295.6	312.6
Working capital investment	108.7	44.7	60.0	28.3	24.4	27.8	28.1	20.7
Capital expenditures	(185.0)	(190.0)	(200.0)	(200.0)	(210.0)	(210.0)	(220.0)	(220.0)
Free cash flow	$776.7	$771.8	$837.6	$865.4	$914.1	$969.1	$1,011.7	$1,038.0
% of sales	15.3%	14.5%	15.0%	14.9%	15.2%	15.6%	15.9%	15.9%
Terminal value								$18,665.8
Present value	$717.8	$659.3	$661.2	$631.4	$616.4	$604.0	$582.7	$552.6
								$9,936.5

$5,025.4 8-year total
9,936.5 Terminal value
$14,961.9 Value of the operations

	YEAR 1 2006	YEAR 2 2007	YEAR 3 2008	YEAR 4 2009	YEAR 5 2010	YEAR 6 2011	YEAR 7 2012	YEAR 8 2013
Panel B: Valuation Model Relationships								
Year 0 revenue $4,836.0								
Revenue growth	5.00%	5.00%	4.50%	4.00%	4.00%	3.00%	2.50%	2.50%
Tax rate	37.00%	37.00%	37.00%	37.00%	37.00%	37.00%	37.00%	37.00%
% of sales								
Cost of sales (excluding depreciation)	57.00%	56.60%	56.30%	56.00%	55.70%	55.50%	55.20%	55.20%
Selling, marketing, and administrative	18.70%	18.50%	18.30%	18.10%	17.90%	17.70%	17.50%	17.50%
Expenses excluding depreciation	75.70%	75.10%	74.60%	74.10%	73.60%	73.20%	72.70%	72.70%
Operating margin before depreciation	24.30%	24.90%	25.40%	25.90%	26.40%	26.80%	27.30%	27.30%
Fixed capital investment	3.64%	3.56%	3.59%	3.45%	3.48%	3.38%	3.46%	3.37%
Depreciation (% of sales)	4.03%	4.09%	4.17%	4.27%	4.37%	4.50%	4.65%	4.79%
Net, fixed investment	0.38%	0.53%	0.59%	0.82%	0.88%	1.11%	1.19%	1.42%
Working capital (dis.) investment	-2.14%	-0.84%	-1.08%	-0.49%	-0.40%	-0.45%	-0.44%	-0.32%
Cost of capital	8.20%							

TABLE 17.9 Comprehensive Valuation Model–Acquisition Target Valuation ($77 per share)

Including Terminal Year ($ Millions)

	YEAR 1 2006	YEAR 2 2007	YEAR 3 2008	YEAR 4 2009	YEAR 5 2010	YEAR 6 2011	YEAR 7 2012	YEAR 8 2013
Panel A: Projected Free Cash Flow								
Net revenue	$5,319.6	$5,958.0	$6,434.6	$6,820.7	$7,093.5	$7,306.3	$7,489.0	$7,676.2
Cost of sales (excluding depreciation)	3,032.2	3,372.2	3,622.7	3,819.6	3,951.1	4,055.0	4,133.9	4,237.3
Selling, marketing, and administrative	835.2	923.5	984.5	1,029.9	1,056.9	1,074.0	1,085.9	1,113.0
Depreciation	214.1	243.7	268.6	291.4	309.7	328.5	347.9	368.0
Acquirer's synergies (additional expense reductions)	(67.2)	(67.2)	(67.2)	(67.2)	(67.2)	(67.2)	(67.2)	(67.2)
Operating income	1,305.3	1,485.8	1,626.0	1,747.0	1,843.0	1,916.0	1,988.5	2,025.1
Taxes	483.0	549.7	601.6	646.4	681.9	708.9	735.7	749.3
After-tax operating income	822.3	936.1	1,024.4	1,100.6	1,161.1	1,207.1	1,252.8	1,275.8
% of sales	15.5%	15.7%	15.9%	16.1%	16.4%	16.5%	16.7%	16.6%
Depreciation	214.1	243.7	268.6	291.4	309.7	328.5	347.9	368.0
Working capital investment	113.9	50.0	69.3	33.3	28.7	32.7	33.1	24.4
Capital expenditures	(193.8)	(212.3)	(231.0)	(235.4)	(247.2)	(247.2)	(259.0)	(259.0)
Free cash flow	$956.5	$1,017.5	$1,131.3	$1,189.9	$1,252.3	$1,321.1	$1,374.8	$1,409.2
% of sales	18.0%	17.1%	17.6%	17.4%	17.7%	18.1%	18.4%	18.4%
Terminal value								$25,340.9
Present value	$884.0	$869.1	$893.1	$868.2	$844.4	$823.3	$791.9	$750.2
								$13,490.0

$6,724.1 8-year total
13,490.0 Terminal value
$20,214.1 Value of the operations

Panel B: Valuation Model Relationships								
Year 0 revenue $4,836.0								
Acquirer's synergies	$67.2	$67.2	$67.2	$67.2	$67.2	$67.2	$67.2	$67.2
Revenue growth	10.00%	12.00%	8.00%	6.00%	4.00%	3.00%	2.50%	2.50%
Tax rate	37.00%	37.00%	37.00%	37.00%	37.00%	37.00%	37.00%	37.00%
% of sales								
Cost of sales (excluding depreciation)	57.00%	56.60%	56.30%	56.00%	55.70%	55.50%	55.20%	55.20%
Selling, marketing, and administrative	15.70%	15.50%	15.30%	15.10%	14.90%	14.70%	14.50%	14.50%
Expenses excluding depreciation	72.70%	72.10%	71.60%	71.10%	70.60%	70.20%	69.70%	69.70%
Operating margin before depreciation	24.30%	24.90%	25.40%	25.90%	26.40%	26.80%	27.30%	27.30%
Fixed capital investment	3.64%	3.56%	3.59%	3.45%	3.48%	3.38%	3.46%	3.37%
Depreciation (% of sales)	4.03%	4.09%	4.17%	4.27%	4.37%	4.50%	4.65%	4.79%
Net, fixed investment	0.38%	0.53%	0.59%	0.82%	0.88%	1.11%	1.19%	1.42%
Working capital (dis.) investment	-2.14%	-0.84%	-1.08%	-0.49%	-0.40%	-0.45%	-0.44%	-0.32%
Cost of capital	8.20%							

Survey OF PRACTICE

A survey of 75 CFOs reflects on acquisitions completed during the period 1990 to 2001. Sixty-nine of the 75 respondents suggested that "synergy" played a role in the acquisition. Anticipated synergy came from:

Source	Impact	%
Operations	Economies of scale that increase productivity or decrease costs.	89.9
Financial	Lower transaction costs or tax gains	5.8
Market power	Reduced competition	4.3
	Total	100.0

Discounted cash flow valuation techniques played a major role in deriving at an appropriate valuation:

Valuation Methodology	%
Valuation of publicly traded targets	
Discounted cash flow (DCF) approach	49.3
DCF along with market multiples	33.3
Market multiples only	12.0
Other	5.4
Total	100.0
Valuation of private targets	
Discounted cash flow approach	48.4
Industry price-to-earnings approach	31.3
Industry price-to-book approach	6.3
Other	14.1
Total	100.0

Additional, analysis entailed a review of comparables.

Source: "Merger Motives and Target Valuation: A Survey of Evidence from CFOs," Mukherjee, Tarun K., Halili Kiymaz, and H. Kent Baker, *Journal of Applied Finance*, Fall/Winter 2004, Volume 14, Number 2, pp. 7–24.

Comparable Companies or Comparable Transactions Valuation

In the *comparable companies (comparable transactions) valuation approach*, key relationships are calculated for a group of similar companies or similar transactions as a basis for the valuation of companies involved in a merger or takeover. This approach is used as an approximation valuation technique by investment bankers and in legal cases. The method is not complicated. Marketplace transactions are used. It is a commonsense approach that says that similar companies should sell for similar prices. This straightforward

TABLE 17.10	Comparable Companies Ratios (Company W Is Compared with Companies TA, TB, and TC)			
RATIO	COMPANY TA	COMPANY TB	COMPANY TC	AVERAGE
Enterprise market value/revenues	1.4	1.2	1.0	1.2
Enterprise market value/EBITDA	15.0	14.0	22.0	17.0
Enterprise market value/free cash flows	25.0	20.0	27.0	24.0

approach appeals to businesspersons, to their financial advisors, and to the judges in courts of law called upon to render decisions on the relative values of companies in litigation.

First, a basic idea is illustrated in a simple setting, followed by applications to actual companies in an M&A setting. In Table 17.10, the comparable companies approach is illustrated. We are seeking to place a value on company W. We find three companies that are comparable. To test for comparability we consider size, similarity of products, age of company, growth rates, and recent trends, among other variables.

Assume that the companies TA, TB, and TC meet most of our comparability requirements. We then calculate the ratio of the enterprise market value to revenues, the ratio of the enterprise market value to *EBITDA (earnings before interest, taxes, depreciation and amortization)*, and the ratio of the enterprise market value to free cash flows for the individual companies. Other ratios could be employed. The resulting ratios are given in Table 17.10.

These ratios are then averaged, and the average ratios are applied to the absolute data for company W (Table 17.11). For the averages to be meaningful, it is important that the ratios we calculate for each company be relatively close in value. If they are greatly different, which implies that the dispersion around the average is substantial, the average (a measure of central tendency) would not be very meaningful. In the example given, the ratios for the three comparable companies do not vary widely. Hence, it makes some sense to apply the averages.

We find that recently company W had revenues of $100 million, EBITDA of $7 million, and free cash flows of $5 million, as shown in Table 17.11. We next apply the average market ratios from panel A to obtain the indicated enterprise value for company W. We have three estimates of the indicated enterprise value of W based on the ratio of enterprise market value to revenues, to EBITDA, and to free cash flows. The results are close enough to be meaningful. When we average them, we obtain approximately $120 million for the indicated enterprise market value for company W.

TABLE 17.11	Application of Valuation Ratios to Company W		
ACTUAL RECENT DATA FOR COMPANY W		AVERAGE RATIO	INDICATED ENTERPRISE MARKET VALUE
Revenues	= $100	1.2	$120
EBITDA	= $7	17.0	$119
Free cash flows	= $5	24.0	$120
		Average =	$120

Although this approach is easy to apply, it does not incorporate the anticipated performance of the target company. These techniques can also be used after the discounted cash flow approach to valuation is completed. These "comps" can provide a reasonableness test for the resulting DCF valuation.

Sound Strategies for M&As

The empirical studies provide a basis for the judgment that many mergers that take place in a given year represent adjustments to industry shocks. If management responses are not made, the firms would have increasingly serious problems. Extending capabilities on a continuing basis is required by change forces. This judgment is supported by the data on the use of multiple growth methods by companies and repeated use of many types of M&A activity year after year. A framework for sound strategic M&A decisions includes a number of principles.

- Successful M&As must take place within the framework of a firm's strategic planning processes.

- Alternative techniques (alliances, joint ventures, and so on) should be considered along with M&As.

- Multiple acquisitions can take place simultaneously.

- M&As alone cannot create a strong firm.

- To achieve higher returns to shareholders than its comparison firms requires an effective organization and the development of a strong portfolio of growth opportunities.

- The acquiring firm must have strength in markets in which its core capabilities give it a competitive advantage.

- In each market area, the firm must achieve competitive leadership or divest the segment.

- The combination of internal programs and M&As are required for continued leadership.

- The firm must have a group of officers that develops experience in all forms of M&As and continuously interacts with the top executive.

- All segments of the firm must recognize its multiple strategies and make contributions to overall results based on boundary-less interactions.

- Continuous reviews of managers based on their plans, programs, and executions must be conducted by top executives.

- Managers who do not execute must be replaced.

- Executive compensation must be based on performance meaningfully measured.

- The chairman and/or CEO needs to interact continuously to provide inspiration and executive development.

The moral of all of the foregoing is that M&As cannot do the job alone. But M&As can perform a critical role in developing an organization that delivers superior returns to shareholders. Firms that have completed the most M&A deals achieved the highest annual excess returns. Integration challenges increase exponentially with the size of targets.

Table 17.12 includes traits of unsuccessful acquisitions. They are self-evident.

TABLE 17.12	Why Acquisitions Fail

1. Ineffective integration (poorly planned, poorly executed, too slow, too fast)
2. Culture clashes
3. No business-economic logic to the deal
4. Businesses unrelated (bad fit)
5. Did not understand what they purchased (Internet, high-tech.)
6. Unduly hyped by investment bankers, consulting firms, and/or lawyers
7. Underestimated regulatory delays or prohibitions
8. Hubris of top executives (ambition to run a bigger firm and increase salary)
9. Top executives want to cash out stock options
10. Suppression of effective business systems of target firms, destroying the basis of their prior success
11. Too much debt (future interest payments a burden)
12. Too much short-term debt (repayment before synergies are realized)
13. Power struggles or incompatibility in new boardroom
14. Mergers of equals delays requisite decisions
15. Target resistance (white knights, scorched earth, antitrust)
16. Multiple bidders cause overpayment
17. Hostile takeovers prevent obtaining sufficient information, fail to uncover basic incompatibilities or create resentment and persistent ill will
18. Basic industry problems such as overcapacity (autos, steel, telecoms)
19. Overly optimistic expected synergies
20. Pay too much

Survey OF PRACTICE

In 2002, Robert F. Bruner surveyed 100 scientific studies and 14 informal studies. The studies included event studies primarily stockholder return studies, accounting studies which examined the reported financial results, surveys of executives, and clinical studies where a single acquisition was studied extensively. Through this survey research, Bruner summarized attributes that contribute to the profitability of an acquisition:

1. Diversification destroys value; focus conserves value.
2. Expected synergies are important drivers of value creation.
3. Value acquiring pays; glamour acquiring does not.
4. M&A to build market power (market share) does not pay.
4. Paying with stock is generally costly; while paying with stock is neutral.
5. M&A regulation is costly to investors.
6. Tender offers create value for bidders.
7. When managers have more at stake, more value is created.
8. Initiation of an M&A program creates value for the buyer.

In general, Bruner concludes that M&A activity does pay for the buying firm. However, given that the returns that a buyer earns on average are minimal, he concludes that executives must consider acquisitions with caution.

Source: "Does M&A Pay? A Survey of Evidence for the Decision-Maker," Bruner, Robert F., *Journal of Applied Finance*, Spring/Summer 2002, Volume 12, Number 1, pp. 7–27.

summary

This chapter viewed business finance decisions in a dynamic framework of M&A activities. It described the major change forces behind the worldwide growth in M&A activities. Growth opportunities can be enhanced by both internal and external strategies. Multiple growth strategies include M&As, joint ventures, alliances, partnerships, investments, licensing, and exclusive agreements.

Large companies impacted by external change factors often require large acquisitions to offset substantial declines in their core businesses. But combining two large firms involves difficult problems of cultural and organizational integration. The empirical data we summarize demonstrates that performance is superior when firms engage in a large number of relatively small acquisitions. Cisco Systems made a large number of acquisitions of relatively smaller companies to achieve a strong position in servers and related markets.

We discussed multiple forms of M&A activities. These include mergers, takeovers, alliances, joint ventures, licensing, and minority investments, among others. The data demonstrate planned programs of multiple M&A activities over sustained years of activities to adjust to changes and to augment capabilities. The measurements of market reactions to individual mergers are likely to be confounded by various degrees of anticipation of future activities in the long-term programs observed.

Merger activities reflect increasingly competitive pressures. In response to such pressures, firms seek to adjust to their changing environments by programs to augment their capabilities and resources. Regardless of whether a high percentage of M&A activities succeed or fail economic forces will continue to result in these forms of external investments. In addition, in such turbulent and changing economic and financial environments some elements of behavioral finance will be manifested. Some evidence of winner's curse, hubris, and misvaluations will be observed.

On the positive side, empirical data demonstrate that there are wide distributions of positive and negative returns from M&A activities. M&As alone cannot create a superior firm from a weak one. M&As conducted over long periods effectively related to long-range plans based on strong core capabilities can help managers achieve superior returns to shareholders.

Valuation uses historical data as a starting point to establish first-approximation patterns. Valuations depend on forecasts. The reliability of the forecasts depends heavily on a thorough analysis of the industry, including how it is impacted by evolving changes in the economies of the world and by competitive strategies and tactics. Valuation requires a thorough understanding of the business economics and financial characteristics of the industry.

Precision is not possible, nor is it required. Recognizing that forecasts are subject to revision has positive aspects as well as challenges. It can be a valuable planning framework for guiding the firm to sound strategies and improved efficiencies. Valuation depends on identifying the critical factors that influence the levels of the value drivers. The DCF valuation approach provides a valuable framework to help identify what is really important to the future value of the firm.

Sensitivity analysis helps identify the really critical factors for the future. Such an analysis helps develop a business model for the firm with expectations of continuous reviews based on an effective information feedback system in the firm. It supports a flexible long-range planning process as a basis for short-term and medium-term budgets. It requires in-depth understanding of the industry, its environment, and its competitors to guide strategies, policies, and decisions.

Questions

17.1   How are mergers and acquisitions related to capital budgeting?

17.2   What are some of the major change forces influencing the world economy today, and how have these forces impacted M&A activity in recent years?

17.3   What is the economic rationale for mergers?

17.4   How can mergers improve the efficiency of a firm?

17.5   Explain the significance of the Q ratio in determining whether a company that wishes to add capacity should acquire a company that produces the product or produce the product itself?

17.6   What are some of the advantages of a joint venture (JV) over a merger? What purpose does a JV serve in divestitures?

17.7   What challenges and advantages do alliances bring to partner firms?

17.8   Why do companies engage in a wide range of M&A activities?

17.9   How do winner's curse and hubris play a role in mergers and acquisitions?

17.10   Describe Shleifer and Vishny's (2003) theory of mergers and how they explain the merger waves of the past 40 years.

17.11   What actions do firms take to try to overcome agency problems?

17.12   In an acquisition, a bidder values potential synergy and pays for it up front. Discuss the impact of this on the likely "success" of the acquisition.

17.13   A computer analyst made the comment, "Why didn't management ask us? Our computer systems are not easy to integrate, but they still want it done in three months with no consulting support!" Discuss this comment. Why aren't more people involved in acquisition analysis and discussion before the deal is consummated?

17.14   "The smartest thing you can do sometimes is walk away from an acquisition." Discuss this statement.

17.15   Why should the CEO always be involved with acquisition decisions?

Problems

17.1

In 1996, Hershey purchased Leaf North America, which was a $500 million revenue business that was projected to grow at 3% per year. One the immediate synergies that accrued to Hershey was reduced sales and marketing expense (as a percentage of sales). Leaf had been paying brokers 5% of sales to distribute its products. When Hershey acquired them, Hershey stopped using brokers and instead had its own 1,500-person sales force begin selling 80% of the Leaf product line as well as Hershey's brands.

a. Assuming a 40% tax rate and a 9% cost of capital, what was this synergy worth? Assume a perpetuity growing at 3% per year.

b. What other issues should Hershey consider related to this reorganization?

17.2

Comparable companies valuation: Fill in the blanks in the following, and discuss your results.

Panel A

COMPARABLE COMPANIES RATIOS (COMPANY W IS COMPARED WITH COMPANIES TA, TB, AND TC)

Ratio	Company TA	Company TB	Company TC	Average
Enterprise market value/revenues	2.0	2.5	1.0	_____
Enterprise market value/EBITDA	20	10	5	_____
Enterprise market value/free cash flows	30	20	25	_____

Panel B

APPLICATION OF VALUATION RATIOS TO COMPANY W

Actual Recent Data for Company W		Average Ratio	Indicated Enterprise Market Value
Revenues	= $200	_____	_____
EBITDA	= $10	_____	_____
Free cash flows	= $5	_____	_____
		Average =	_____

17.3

Comparable companies valuation: The Ellis Company is a small jewelry manufacturer. The company has been successful and has grown. Now, Ellis is planning to sell an issue of common stock to the public for the first time, and it faces the problem of setting an appropriate price on its common stock. The company feels that the proper procedure is to select firms similar to it, with publicly traded common stock, and to make relevant comparisons. The company finds several jewelry manufacturers similar to it with respect to product mix, size, asset composition, and debt/equity proportions. Of these, Bonden and Seeger are most similar, with data as shown in the following table.

RELATIONSHIPS	BONDEN (PER SHARE)	SEEGER (PER SHARE)	ELLIS (TOTALS)
Earnings per share	$ 5.00	$ 8.00	$1,500,000
Price per share	48.00	65.00	—
Dividends per share	3.00	4.00	700,000
Book value per share	45.00	70.00	12,000,000

a. Calculate the per-share data for Ellis assuming that 500,000 shares of stock will be sold.

b. Calculate the PE, dividend yield, and market-to-book relations for Bonden and Seeger.

c. Apply the relationships to the Ellis per-share data to establish boundaries for the indicated market price for the Ellis stock.

d. Using the boundaries, and taking trend patterns into account, what is your recommendation for an issuing price for the Ellis stock?

17.4

Valuation of a firm: After six years as vice president of a New York bank, Henry Thorson has decided to simplify his lifestyle and become a small-town shopkeeper. He has found an apparently successful variety store in rural Pennsylvania for sale at a price of $120,000. The most recent balance sheet is given in the following table.

ASSETS		LIABILITIES	
Cash	$18,000	Notes payable, bank	$6,000
Receivables, net	6,000	Accounts payable	12,000
Inventories	39,000	Accruals	3,000
Net fixed assets	42,000	Net worth	84,000
Total assets	$105,000	Total liabilities and net worth	$105,000

Annual pre-tax earnings (after rent, interest, and salaries) have averaged $24,000 for the preceding three years. The store has been in business in the same community for 20 years and has six years remaining on a 10-year lease. The purchase price includes all assets, except for cash, and Thorson would have to assume all debts.

a. Is the price of $120,000 reasonable?

b. What other factors should be considered in arriving at a purchase price?

c. What is the significance, if any, of the lease?

17.5

Comparable companies valuation: Given the following information on the Pink Company and the Red Company, as well as the Blue and Brown companies, use the investment banker comparables method to value the equity of Blue and

Brown. All four firms are roughly similar in size and have similar product/market mix characteristics.

	PINK CO.	RED CO.	BLUE CO.	BROWN CO.
Revenues	$600	$400	$500	$400
EBDIT	40	40	33	40
Depreciation	6	8	7	13
EBIT	34	32	26	27
Interest expense	10	10	8	8
EBT	24	22	18	19
Current taxes	7	6	5	6
Net income	17	16	13	13
Current ratio	2/1	2/1	2/1	2/1
Interest-bearing debt/NW	50%	50%	55%	45%
Fixed-charge coverage	3 times	3 times	3 times	3 times
Revenue growth	25%	30%	24%	31%
EBIT growth	30%	30%	26.5%	26.5%
Net income growth	30%	30%	28%	28%
Marginal free cash flow to total investment capital, net (r)	50%	25%	53%	26.5%
Marginal investment requirements to free cash flow, net (b)	0.6	1.2	0.5	1.0
Market value	$400	$350		
Book value	300	200	150	100
Replacement cost	500	400	300	300

In performing the comparables analysis, use the following ratios.

- Market-to-book value
- Market to replacement cost
- Market to sales
- Price to earnings (PE)
- Market to after-tax operating income; in other words, EBIT $(1 - T)$

17.6

Valuation of a firm: Use the constant growth valuation model developed in Chapter 12 (Equation 12.5). Value a firm with the following characteristics.

Where:

- R_0 = Revenue (or sales) of firm = $10,000
- m = Operating income (EBIT) margin (% of sales) = 20%
- T = Tax Rate = 40%
- d = Depreciation (% of sales) = 4%
- I_{fg} = Capital expend., gross or fixed capital invested (% of sales) = 4%
- I_w = Working capital investment (% of sales) = 6%
- g = Growth = 5%
- k = Cost of capital = 12%

17.7

Valuation of target firm: The Allan Company is very similar to and is in the same industry as the Brock Company. Both Allan Co. and Brock Co. have a cost of equity of 12%, cost of debt of 8%, and 30% debt. If Brock had revenues of $1,000 in the last fiscal year and is expected to have an operating margin (m) of 15%, investment (I) of 8%, growth rate (g) of 18%, 5 years of supernormal growth (n), and 40% tax rate (T), what value should Allan Co. be willing to pay for Brock Co.?

17.8

Valuation of target firm: Suppose Allan Co. is instead interested in the Concord Company, a firm in a completely unrelated (and riskier) industry. Concord Co. has the same parameters as Brock Co. (problem 17.7), except that Concord Co. has a cost of equity of 15%, a cost of debt of 10%, and 20% debt. What value should Allan Co. be willing to pay for Concord Co.?

17.9

Valuation of combined firms: The Kuban Company decides to purchase the Hansco Company. Both firms have the same characteristics as Brock Co. (problem 17.7), except that Kuban Co. has a beta of 1.2 and Hansco Co. has a beta of 1.4. Both firms have 30% debt and a cost of debt of 8%. Because of the nature of the synergies anticipated in the acquisition, the combined firm is expected to have a beta of 1.1.

a. If the risk-free rate is 6% and the equity risk premium is 5%, calculate the cost of capital for the two firms and the combined firm.

b. Assuming the value drivers remain constant (and revenues are simply combined), what would be the value of the combined company?

17.10

Using a model similar to that of Table 17.8, the senior management team is examining the Precious Cosmetics Corporation (PCC) for an acquisition bid. PCC had sales of $834 million last year, and the management team is comfortable with the following set of assumptions:

	YEAR 1 (%)	YEAR 2 (%)	YEAR 3 (%)	YEAR 4 (%)	YEAR 5 (%)	YEAR 6 (%)	YEAR 7 (%)	YEAR 8 (%)
Revenue growth	50.0	40.0	35.0	25.0	15.0	10.0	8.0	6.0
Tax rate	33.0	34.0	35.0	36.0	37.0	38.0	38.0	38.0
% of sales								
Cost of sales (excluding depreciation)	52.0	51.7	51.5	51.2	51.0	50.8	50.5	50.5
Selling, marketing, and administrative	27.7	27.6	27.5	27.4	27.3	27.2	27.1	27.0
Other operating expense, net	2.0	2.0	2.0	2.0	1.0	1.0	1.0	1.0
Expenses excluding depreciation	79.7	79.3	79.0	78.6	78.3	78.0	77.6	77.5
Operating margin before depreciation	20.3	20.7	21.0	21.4	21.7	22.0	22.4	22.5
Fixed capital investment	6.0	5.0	4.0	25.0	5.0	4.0	4.0	4.0
Depreciation (% of sales)	4.0	4.0	4.0	4.3	4.5	4.5	4.0	4.0
Net, fixed investment	2.0	1.0	0.0	20.8	0.5	-0.5	0.0	0.0
Working capital investment	6.5	6.0	5.5	7.0	5.0	5.0	4.0	3.0
Cost of capital 11.5%								

a. What is the value of this explicit eight-year period?

b. Assuming a 4% growth rate, what is the value of the perpetuity in year 8. The perpetuity starts in year 9.

c. What is the present value of that perpetuity today (year 0)?

d. What is the total value of PCC?

e. Assuming cash and marketable securities of $39.4 million and existing debt of $157.1 million, what should the management team be willing to pay for PCC's equity?

f. Repeat problems 17.10a through d using a 10.5% cost of capital. What should the management team be willing to pay for PCC's equity.

17.11

Using a model similar to that of Table 17.8, answer the following questions as you prepare a valuation of the Chester Division of Cedar Crest Corporation. Last year, sales were $285.6 million. Assume the following information:

	YEAR 1 (%)	YEAR 2 (%)	YEAR 3 (%)	YEAR 4 (%)	YEAR 5 (%)
Revenue growth	18.00	15.00	12.00	10.00	8.00
Tax rate	35.50	35.50	36.00	36.00	37.00
% of sales					
Cost of sales (excluding depreciation)	43.60	43.30	43.00	42.70	42.40
Selling, marketing, and administrative	27.70	27.60	27.50	27.40	27.30
Expenses excluding depreciation	71.30	70.90	70.50	70.10	69.70
Operating margin before depreciation	28.70	29.10	29.50	29.90	30.30
Fixed capital investment	6.00	6.00	5.50	5.00	5.00
Depreciation (% of sales)	4.00	4.25	4.50	4.75	5.00
Net, fixed investment	2.00	1.75	1.00	0.25	0.00
Working capital investment	5.00	5.50	6.00	6.00	6.00
Cost of capital 12.70%					

a. What is the value of this explicit five-year period?

b. Assuming a 4% growth rate, what is the value of the perpetuity in year 5. The perpetuity starts in year 6.

c. What is the present value of that perpetuity today (year 0)?

d. What is the total value of the Chester Division?

e. Repeat problems 17.11a through d using a 10.7% and a 14.7% cost of capital. What are the resulting values for the Chester Division?

The following five problems (17.12 to 17.16) are focused case studies of recent mergers.

17.12

A preemptive purchase: Haircare, Inc. is an innovative firm in the consumer products industry. An acquirer was interested in Haircare to defend against aggressive pricing reductions by its distributors. The acquisition would block competitors from gaining access to the Target company's customers and market share.

Analysis revealed operating relationships (as a percentage of revenues) for Haircare as shown in the first table.

	YEAR 0 (%)	YEAR 1 (%)	YEAR 2 (%)	YEAR 3 (%)	YEAR 4 (%)	YEAR 5 (%)	YEAR N + 1 (%)
Operating income	—	16.0	16.0	16.0	16.0	16.0	16.0
After-tax operating income	—	9.6	9.6	9.6	9.6	9.6	9.6
Depreciation	—	4.0	4.0	4.0	4.0	4.0	4.0
Change in working capital	—	2.0	2.0	2.0	2.0	2.0	0.0
Capital expenditures	—	6.0	6.0	6.0	6.0	6.0	4.0
Change in other assets net	—	0.00	0.00	0.00	0.00	0.00	0.00
Free cash flow	—	5.6	5.6	5.6	5.6	5.6	9.6

The second table presents data on transactions ($ millions) involving comparable hair products companies. The base year revenues of Haircare were $100 million.

BUYER	TARGET	TRANSACTION VALUE	EV / SALES	DESCRIPTION
Procter & Gamble Company	Bristol-Myers Squibb Company Clairol, Inc.	$4,950.0	2.6	Hair color and hair care products
Wella AG	Graham Webb International	$78.0	1.5	Professional hair care products
Chromatics Color Sciences International, Inc.	Gordon Laboratories, Inc.	$56.9	1.7	Skin care, cosmetics, nail care, toiletries, and beauty products
Alberto-Culver Company	Pro-Line Corporation	$70.0	1.6	Hair care products for the ethnic market
Dial Corporation	Sarah Michaels, Inc.	$185.0	2.3	Hair care products and related toiletries
Henkel KGaA	Dep Corporation	$90.0	0.8	Hair care and styling products
Estée Lauder	Aveda	$300.0	3.0	Hair care products
		Average	1.97	

EV/sales is enterprise value (or the value of the operations) dividend by sales.

a. Calculate a DCF valuation of Haircare net of its $10 million debt using a five-year DCF spreadsheet model. Assume a tax rate of 40% and a revenue growth rate of 12% for the first five years. Use a discount rate of 20% for the initial five-year period to reflect the high risk of a relatively young, small privately held firm not publicly traded. Use a 10% discount factor for the terminal period.

b. Why was the acquirer willing to pay a premium over the DCF valuation?

17.13

Verizon-MCI merger: Following on other consolidations in the telecommunications industry (SBC's acquisition of AT&T and Sprint's acquisition of Nextel), Verizon Communications announced on February 14, 2005 a deal to acquire MCI for $6.748 billion. Its merger terms are indicated in the following table.

MERGER TERMS	SHARES	VERIZON STOCK PRICE	VALUE PER SHARE	VALUE ($ BILLIONS)
Verizon shares	132.1	$36.31	$14.75[a]	$4.797
Cash			$ 1.50	$0.488
Special dividends			$ 4.50	$1.463
Total value of merger			$20.75	$6.748
MCI stock value (on 11 February 2005)			$20.75	
Premium			0.0%	

[a]Each share of MCI stock was traded for 0.406 shares of Verizon stock (0.406 × $36.31) along with $1.50 cash per share and a $4.50 special dividend per share.

The terms of the deal included shares in the merged firm, cash, and special dividends, which valued each share of MCI at a 0% premium of $20.75. This merger combines the nation's largest regional phone company (Verizon) with the nation's second largest long-distance company (MCI), creating a company that could potentially stand as No. 2 in the market. Ownership ratios between the two companies are indicated in the following table.

	DOLLAR AMOUNTS			PERCENTAGE	
	VERIZON	MCI	TOTAL	VERIZON	MCI
Pre-merger					
Share price[a]	$36.31	$20.75			
Shares outstanding (million)	2780[b]	325[c]			
Total market value (billion)	$100.942	$6.744	$107.686	93.7%	6.3%
Exchange terms		0.406 for 1			
Post-merger					
No. of shares (million)	2780	132.1	2912	95.5%	4.5%

[a]Before merger announcement: February 11, 2005.
[b]Source: Value Line.
[c]$325 = \dfrac{132.1 \text{(Verizon shares)}}{0.406 \text{(Exchange rate)}}$

MCI had made a recovery from a highly publicized $11 billion accounting scandal in 2002, after which they changed their name to WorldCom, followed by Chapter 11 bankruptcy. Nonetheless, a merger was considered essential for the firm to survive among larger competitors. Although it is no longer a leading company, MCI is still valuable to acquirers because it holds a large corporate customer base and has a worldwide telephone and data network. In 2000, MCI's bid for Sprint was rejected by federal antitrust officials on the fear that the merger would create a telecom giant, whose reach would extend worldwide, and have too much control on the Internet's backbone networks (wireless, data communications, and long distance).

Before the Verizon merger announcement, Qwest Communications had been in talks to purchase MCI, making a final bid of $7.3 billion ($0.6 billion above Verizon's purchase price). However, that bid was rejected by MCI's board in favor of Verizon's lower bid for several reasons. Qwest stands as the smallest and weakest of the Bell operating companies, with several problems of its own. Not only does it suffer from its own accounting scandals (paying a $250 million settlement with the SEC) but has $17 billion in debt and a declining landline business of 4% a year.

The company has experienced net losses since 2000, amounting to over $45 billion. It is also a weaker partner than Verizon from a strategic perspective. It does not have its own essential wireless network and serves a rural region with only a few business centers in 14 states. For MCI, Qwest's financial difficulties and their questionable ability to maintain long-term value were significant concerns against choosing the company as its best suitor.

The announcement of a Verizon-MCI merger shortly after SBC's agreement to acquire AT&T has analysts questioning who will be the winners and losers from the rapidly consolidating telecommunications industry. Some of the concerns deal with consequences for customers because the elimination of two long-distance providers (MCI and AT&T) reduces choices and competition. The only opponent left to counter the telecom giants is the cable industry, which is slowly moving into phone services. Antitrust regulators have yet to approve the two telecom deals.

Evident winners of these big mergers have been the debt holders of the acquired firms. The Verizon deal, which includes the assumption of about $4 billion of MCI's debt, is clearly beneficial to MCI bond holders. Previously deemed as riskier junk bonds, the "implicit support" of creditworthy Verizon raises MCI's ratings to investment-grade securities. Similar gains have been noted for AT&T and Nextel on announcement of mergers with SBC and Sprint, respectively. (Source: *Wall Street Journal*.)

a. In the merger terms table, the data show that the total value per share received by MCI in the merger terms approximated its closing market value on February 11, 2005, the Friday before the merger was announced on the following Monday. Why was no premium paid to MCI shareholders?

b. From the data in the problem, why did the ownership share of MCI stockholders decrease from their pre-merger relationship?

c. Do you think this merger creates antitrust problems?

d. From the standpoint of the MCI bond holders, what is an important advantage of Verizon as the acquirer versus Qwest?

17.14

Kmart-Sears merger: Once a giant in the retail industry, Sears, Roebuck & Co. has been struggling in recent years with low profit margins and declining sales. Although the company still stands as the nation's largest appliance provider (holding an enviable 40% share of the appliance market), increasing competition from the top two retailers (Wal-Mart Stores Inc. and Home Depot Inc.) is slowly taking away their advantage. Wal-Mart and Home Depot provide customers with a wider variety of products at lower prices in better locations.

A major disadvantage for the company is that Sears has long been tied to mall locations. Today's increasing popularity and convenience of standalone stores makes this a growing concern. Research by Customer Growth Partners LLC shows that consumers spend more than 80% of their dollars in locations outside malls.

Kmart's acquisition of Sears is an attempt to alleviate this problem. By combining Kmart's 1,500 store locations with Sears' merchandise, management expects to increase consumer reach and potentially create the nation's third largest retail firm. The merger was announced on November 17, 2004 and completed on March 24, 2005, forming Sears Holdings Corporation. The merger terms gave Sears' shareholders a choice between $50 cash or 0.5 shares of the merged firm for each share of Sears (the election was prorated to guarantee 55% conversion into shares and 45% conversion into cash). The total weighted average value per Sears share of $50.34 values this deal at $10.671 billion (see following table).

MERGER TERMS	SHARES	KMART STOCK PRICE	VALUE PER SHARE	TOTAL VALUE ($ BILLIONS)
Kmart shares (55% of Sears shares exchanged at 0.5 to 1)	116.6	$101.22	$50.61	$5.901
Cash (45% of Sears shares)	95.4		$50.00	$4.770
Total	212.0		$50.34	$10.671
Sears stock value (on November 16, 2004)			$45.20	
Premium			11.37%	

After the announcement, Kmart shares rose by $7.78 (7.7%) and Sears shares rose by $7.79 (17%). The market seems optimistic about the possibilities of the new combined retail chain. The ownership ratios between the two companies are indicated in the following table.

	DOLLAR AMOUNTS			PERCENTAGE	
	KMART	SEARS	TOTAL	KMART	SEARS
Pre-merger:					
Share price	$101.22	$45.20			
Shares outstanding (million)	102	212			
Total market value (billion)	$10.324	$9.582	$19.906	51.9%	48.1%
Exchange terms (45% of Sears shares exchanged for cash)					
		0.5 for 1			
Post-merger:					
Number of Shares (million)	102	58[a]	160	63.8%	36.2%

[a] At 212 million pre-merger shares, 55% converted; 0.5 ratio = 212 × 0.55 × 0.50 = 58 million.
Sources: *Wall Street Journal* and *New York Times.*

a.   Sears owns a large share of the nation's appliance market, with its own Kenmore brand commanding 25% of that share. Why would this merger with Kmart be advantageous?

b.   The newly formed Sears Holdings Corporation shows an increase in ownership for Kmart shareholders. If a premium of 11.37% was paid, how is this increase possible?

17.15

IBM-Lenovo joint venture: Amid fears of potential national security risks and criticisms from rival PC manufacturers, IBM's sale of its PC group to China's

Lenovo Group Limited for $1.750 billion was announced on December 8, 2004. This joint venture will make Lenovo one of the largest PC makers worldwide [third, just behind Dell and Hewlett-Packard (HP)], giving them the opportunity to expand globally beyond Chinese markets. In exchange for the use of IBM's brand name for five years and being granted preferred supplier status of PCs to IBM, Lenovo will pay US$650 million in cash, assume US$500 million of IBM's liabilities, and give IBM an 18.9% minority interest in the company.

JOINT VENTURE TERMS	TOTAL VALUE ($ BILLIONS)
Lenovo shares (18.9% minority interest)	$0.600
Cash	0.650
Debt relief	0.500
Total	$1.750

This is a move seen as beneficial to both companies. Although IBM is often credited with leading computer technology, tough competition from major rivals such as Dell and HP has made its PC unit unprofitable. In recent years, IBM has been divesting its personal computer business (sale of PC factories in North Carolina to Sanmina-SCI and sale of its hard drive unit to Hitachi) to focus on the more profitable areas of consulting, services, and corporate networks. Entrance into the rapidly growing Chinese market through this joint venture is also a huge advantage for IBM. Lenovo, as China's largest PC maker, already commands 27% of the market share and will likely give IBM a foot up on the competition.

Chinese companies, though competitive in profitability, have rarely been able to obtain global reach. Lenovo, formerly known as Legend and partly government owned, ranked ninth in PC sales worldwide in 2004. However, its previous attempts to expand into foreign markets were not very successful. Lenovo's purchase of IBM's PC unit combines sales power with a global brand name, giving them the opportunity to become an internationally known company.

Opponents of the merger have cited national security issues as some of the risks of the merger. They argue that the Chinese government is trying to acquire sensitive American technology and obtain facilities to spy on the United States. However, these fears are largely unfounded because IBM's PC operations do not have any real military use. (Sources: Lenovo Group Limited, http://www.lenovogrp.com; Fear of China: I Spy Spies, The Economist, February 5, 2005, p. 60; Kanellos, Michael, IBM Sells PC Group to Lenovo, *http://www.news.com*.)

a. For IBM, the joint venture comes at a time when competition and low margins have made its PC unit unprofitable. Why would the Lenovo Group be willing to take over this business?

b. IBM's announcement of the sale generated many fears and criticisms. What are some of these arguments? Why is it a national concern?

17.16

Procter & Gamble–Gillette merger: The creation of a worldwide consumer products powerhouse was achieved with Procter and Gamble's $54 billion bid to acquire Gillette on January 28, 2005. The deal gives 0.975 shares of P&G for every share of Gillette, valuing Gillette at $54.05 per share (representing a 20% premium using Gillette's stock value before the merger announcement). The combination of the two firms will bring together some of the nation's well-known product lines (P&G's Tide, Pampers, Folgers, Charmin, and Crest, and Gillette's Duracell, Oral B, and Mach 3). The merger terms are indicated in the following table.

MERGER TERMS	SHARES	P&G STOCK PRICE	VALUE PER SHARE	TOTAL VALUE ($ BILLIONS)
P&G shares	965.25	$55.44	$54.05	$53.513
Gillette stock value (on 27 January 2005)			$45.00	
Premium			20%	

Many analysts say that the friendly union between the two companies comes in response to the growing power of giant retailers; namely, Wal-Mart, whose bargaining strength has pushed even large suppliers such as P&G and Gillette to lower prices. Wal-Mart's development of private label brands to compete against national brands has also been troubling to both firms. Consumers today often choose private brands over the more well-known brand names because prices are lower and products are viewed as similar. By combining the power of two consumer products suppliers, P&G hopes to recapture bargaining power against retailers.

This merger may be the first of many for the household products industry. Rival firms (such as Clorox, Kimberly-Clark, Colgate-Palmolive, Alberto-Culver, and Unilever) who wish to be competitive and regain pricing power could begin to seek potential partners. For consumers, the start of these mergers might mean higher prices if the balance of power shifts from retailers to suppliers. However, retailers who wish to stay competitive may swallow the price increase themselves without passing it on to consumers. The ownership ratios between the two companies are indicated in the following table.

	DOLLAR AMOUNTS			PERCENTAGE	
	P&G	Gillette	Total	P&G	Gillette
Pre-merger:					
Share price[a]	$55.44	$45.00			
Shares outstanding (million)[b]	2515	990			
Total market value (billion)	$139.432	$44.550	$183.982	75.8%	24.2%
Exchange terms		0.975 for 1			
Post-merger:					
No. of shares (million)	2515	965.25	3480.25	72.3%	27.7%

[a]Before merger announcement: January 26, 2005.
[b]Sources: Value Line, *Wall Street Journal, New York Times, Businessweek.*

a. Why is the acquisition of Gillette by Procter & Gamble influential for the consumer products industry?

b. How is this union a reaction to change forces in the market, and how will it affect the bargaining power between suppliers and retailers?

International Financial Management

Learning Outcomes

After completing this chapter, you should be able to:

1 Utilize the mechanics of exchange rates

2 Conceptualize the major economic drivers that lead to stable (parity) relationships in:

   ● Exchange rates and commodity prices (purchasing power parity)
   ● Exchange rates and interest rates (interest rate parity)
   ● Interest rates and inflation rates (Fisher relation)
   ● Exchange rates, interest rates, and inflation rates (international Fisher effect)
   ● Current and future exchange rates (forward rate unbiased)

3 Appreciate foreign currency management in a multinational organization

4 Be able to apply this international dimension to capital investment and the cost of capital

One of the major change forces to which firms must adjust has been globalization. This chapter is designed to develop an appreciation of the international economic forces that come into play in the world's currency and interest rate markets. The topic of international financial management is as broad as the first 17 chapters of this text. That is why we designed this chapter to develop the basic economic underpinnings that drive all international transactions.

One measure of the internationalization of firms has been developed by the United Nations Conference on Trade and Development (UNCTAD, 2002). UNCTAD calculated a *transnationality index (TNI)* as the average of three ratios: foreign assets to total assets, foreign sales to total sales, and foreign employment to total employment. The top 100 transnational corporations (TNCs) have an average TNI of 55.7%. Thus, for the top 100 TNCs in 2000 more than half of their activity (whether measured by assets, sales, or employment) is outside the country in which they are domiciled.

The UNCTAD study notes that the ranking of the top 100 is related to the degree of their activity in cross-border M&As. The 20 most active companies in cross-border M&A deals during 1987 through 2001 accounted for 20% of the total. British Petroleum (BP) spent $94 billion for 98 cross-border deals. General Electric spent $25.4 billion for 228 cross-border deals (UNCTAD Study p. 89). The UNCTAD study also observes that of the 50 largest "economies" in 2000 14 were TNCs.

The world's top 20 non-financial TNCs ranked by foreign assets in 2000 are listed in Table 18.1. In addition to the rankings by foreign assets, the associated TNI ranking is also listed. Of the top 20, the United States was the home country for only five. Three of the ten were petroleum companies and three were in the motor vehicle industry. Of the top 20, six were in the petroleum industry and five were in auto manufacturing. The data show how internationalized the world economy has become.

TABLE 18.1 The World's Top 20 Nonfinancial Transnationals Ranked by Foreign Assets, 2000

Foreign Assets	TNI	Corporation	Home Economy	Industry	TNI (%)
1	15	Vodafone	United Kingdom	Telecommunications	81.4
2	73	General Electric	United States	Electrical & electronic	40.3
3	30	ExxonMobil	United States	Petroleum	67.7
4	42	Vivendi Universal	France	Diversified	59.7
5	84	General Motors	United States	Motor vehicles	31.2
6	46	Royal Dutch/Shell	U.K./Netherlansds	Petroleum	57.5
7	24	BP	United Kingdom	Petroleum	76.7
8	80	Toyota Motor	Japan	Motor vehicles	35.1
9	55	Telefonica	Spain	Telecommunications	53.8
10	47	Fiat	Italy	Motor vehicles	57.4
11	57	IBM	United States	Electrical & electronic	53.5
12	44	Volkswagen	Germany	Motor vehicles	59.4
13	64	ChevronTexaco	United States	Petroleum	47.2
14	52	Hutchison Whampoa	Hong Kong, China	Diversified	55.9
15	23	Suez	France	Electricity, gas, and water	77.1
16	93	DaimlerChrysler	Germany	Motor vehicles	24.0
17	11	News Corporation	Australia	Media	84.9
18	4	Nestle	Switzerland	Food & beverages	94.7
19	62	TotalFinaElf	France	Petroleum	47.6
20	87	Repsol YPF	Spain	Petroleum	29.3

Source: United Nations Conference on Trade and Development, *World Investment Report 2002: Transnational Corporations and Export Competitiveness*, Table IV.1.

An interesting example is the 3M Corporation. It is not listed as one of the top 100 measured by foreign assets. 3M was listed number 281 in *Fortune*'s ranking of the Global 500 largest corporations for 2003. Yet of 3M's worldwide sales of $18.2 billion in 2003 international sales were $10.7 billion, representing 58% of the company's total. Of its total 67,000 employees worldwide, 33,329 were U.S. and 33,749 were international (slightly more than 50% abroad).

Analyst reports on 3M suggest a time-phased strategy is used to develop its international activities. For products developed in the United States, plant capacity is built with economies of size that are realized only after foreign sales have been developed. When foreign sales achieve a sufficient volume, plants are then established abroad.

The foregoing background was developed to convey the pervasiveness of international business activities. TNCs or MNCs (multinational corporations) by definition are involved in some form of international operations but they are not all giant firms. The U.S. Department of Commerce reports that more than 50% of all firms that export or import products or services are small firms with less than 100 employees. The relative value of domestic versus foreign currencies has an influence on the prices of goods manufactured and sold domestically in both direct and indirect ways (described in material following).

This chapter the first discusses the high volatility in foreign exchange rates. It then explores international parity relationships, management of foreign exchange risks, and the cost of capital, capital investment, and currency risk.

Volatility in Exchange Rates

International financial management is of importance because of the continued volatility of the relative values of national currencies. Figure 18.1 illustrates that the trade weighted-average index (the base of the index is March of 1973) in relationship to the currency values of a group of major foreign countries has changed significantly over time. Between January of 1973 and January of 1981 this index fluctuated within a relatively narrow range (between 90 and 110). The U.S. dollar strengthened relative to the comparison currencies by more than 50% between 1981 and 1985. The index then declined from 140 to under 80 by 1995. The dollar value in relationship to the other currencies then increased in value to a high of 109 in 2002, declining to 82 in November of 2006.

Fluctuations in individual currencies are even greater based on the Federal Reserve source cited in Figure 18.1. The number of Japanese yen per dollar was as high as 145 in 1998, dropping to almost 100 in late 1999 and then rising to 118 by November of 2006. The number of dollars per British pounds moved from almost 1.39 in 2001 to 1.90 on November 6, 2006. The number of Canadian dollars per U.S. dollar was about 1.42 in 1998, reached a level of 1.60 in early 2002, and dropped to 1.13 by November 2006. The number of dollars per Euro was more than 1.18 in 1998, declined to 0.87 in 2000, and then rose to 1.27 by November 6, 2006 as the Euro strengthened.

Fluctuations in exchange rates cause amounts realized in the home currency to change substantially. For example, suppose a Japanese auto producer needs to receive 2 million yen per car to cover costs plus the required return on capital. When the exchange rate was 265 yen to the dollar, as it was in early 1985, the Japanese producer would have to receive $7,547 per car. At 100 yen to the dollar, the Japanese producer would have to receive $20,000 per car. Thus, when the yen is strong the price charged in dollars by Japanese auto sellers has to be higher or profit margins lower. Conversely,

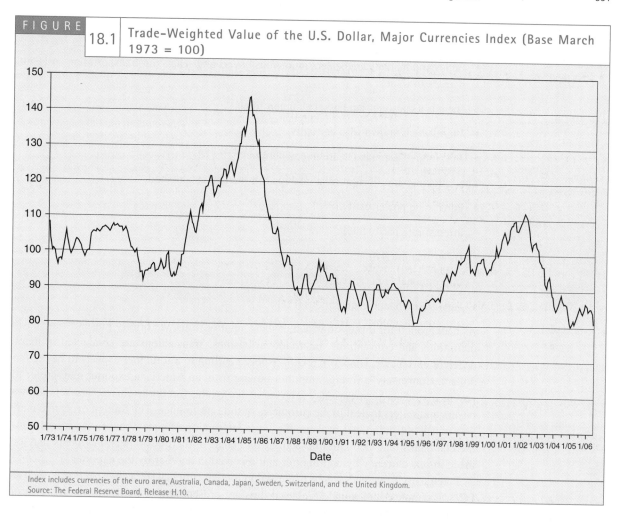

FIGURE 18.1 Trade-Weighted Value of the U.S. Dollar, Major Currencies Index (Base March 1973 = 100)

Index includes currencies of the euro area, Australia, Canada, Japan, Sweden, Switzerland, and the United Kingdom.
Source: The Federal Reserve Board, Release H.10.

at a weak yen of 200 to the dollar the price per car can drop to $10,000 per car while maintaining margins.

The nature of risks in an international financial setting takes on new dimensions. We shall focus on corporate financial policies for managing these risks. In addition to the pattern of cash inflows and cash outflows a firm develops, we shall examine the changes in its balance sheet in terms of monetary versus non-monetary net positions. We shall also examine the use of the forward markets for dealing with foreign exchange fluctuations and analyze the use of money and capital markets for managing foreign exchange risks. Issues here are whether outlays limiting the risks of exchange rate fluctuations are worth the cost.

International Parity Relationships

Sound decision making in managing foreign exchange risks requires an understanding of the key equilibrium relations involving international prices, interest rates, inflation rates, and spot versus forward exchange rates. The analysis begins with assumptions required to establish the fundamental propositions, which can then be modified as applications require. The basic assumptions are those required for perfect markets.

- Financial markets are perfect (numerous buyers and sellers; no taxes, no information or transactions costs, no government controls).

- Goods and markets are perfect (numerous buyers and sellers; no transportation costs, no barriers to trade).

- There is a consumption basket common to all.

- The future is known with certainty.

- The competitive markets are in equilibrium.

The following equilibrium relationships can then be established.

- Purchasing power parity (PPP)

- Interest rate parity (IRP)

- Fisher relation (FR)

- International Fisher effect (IFE)

- Forward exchange expectations (FEE)

As background for discussing each of these relationships, we briefly present some basic definitions and conventions. International business transactions are conducted in many different currencies. However, a U.S. exporter selling to a foreigner expects to be paid in dollars. Conversely, a foreign importer buying from an American exporter may prefer to pay in his or her own currency. The existence of the foreign exchange markets allows buyers and sellers to deal in the currencies of their preference. The foreign exchange markets consist of individual brokers, the large international money banks, and many commercial banks that facilitate transactions on behalf of their customers. Payments may be made in one currency by an importer and received in another by the exporter.

Foreign exchange rates can be expressed in foreign currency (FC) units per dollar, such as FC/$. Examples with rounded relationships are presented. For the Euro we have: Euro/dollar (€/$ or 0.8/$). For the Mexican peso we have mpeso/US dollar (mp/$ or mp10/$). Alternatively, exchange rates can be expressed in dollars per FC units, such as $/FC. The examples with relationships are dollars per euro or dollars/euro or $/€ or $1.25/€. For the Mexican peso: U.S. dollar/mpeso or $/mp or $0.10/mp. A list of illustrative exchange rates and their values is found in Table 18.2. Note that for four of the countries their rates are expressed as $/FC. For all of the others, the relationship is expressed as FC/$. Because the conventions are not consistent in practice, we shall generally use both forms, making explicit the direction of the measurement.

In the foreign exchange rate literature, the symbols S and F are used to refer to spot and future exchange rates. However, it is sometimes ambiguous whether it represents the units of foreign currency per dollar or the dollar value of the foreign currency. We shall always subscript the S and F to make clear the relationships between the currencies involved. Table 18.3 lists the key input items utilized in the following discussion of the parity relationships.

Purchasing Power Parity

ABSOLUTE PURCHASING POWER PARITY

The PPP doctrine is an expression of the *law of one price*. In competitive markets, the exchange-adjusted prices of identical tradable goods and financial assets must be equal

TABLE 18.2	Illustrative Exchange Rates	
COUNTRY	**MONETARY UNIT**	**12 MAY 2006**
Australia*	Dollar	0.7728
Brazil	Real	2.1340
Canada	Dollar	1.1085
China, P.R.	Yuan	8.0056
Denmark	Krone	5.7841
EMU Members*	Euro	1.2888
Hong Kong	Dollar	7.7532
India	Rupee	44.8900
Japan	Yen	110.4900
Malaysia	Ringgit	3.5825
Mexico	Peso	11.0530
New Zealand*	Dollar	0.6291
Norway	Krone	6.0142
Singapore	Dollar	1.5686
South Africa	Rand	6.2375
South Korea	Won	932.7700
Sri Lanka	Rupee	102.6500
Sweden	Krona	7.2632
Switzerland	Franc	1.2020
Taiwan	Dollar	31.3500
Thailand	Baht	37.9000
United Kingdom*	Pound	1.8911
Venezuela	Bolivar	2144.6000

[a.] Rates in foreign currency units per U.S. dollar (X) except as noted by * (E).
Source: Federal Reserve Statistical Release, H.10, 5/12/06.

worldwide (taking into account information and transaction costs). PPP deals with the rates at which domestic goods are exchanged for foreign goods. A formal expression of the absolute version of PPP is Equation 18.1.

$$P_{p,0} = P_{\$,0} \times S_{p/\$,0} \qquad (18.1)$$

An example is expressed in Equation 18.2.

$$\begin{aligned} P_{p,0} &= \$10 \times 10p/\$ \\ &= 100p \end{aligned} \qquad (18.2)$$

TABLE 18.3	Symbol Definitions and Inputs	
SYMBOL	**DEFINITION**	**ILLUSTRATIVE INPUT**
$S_{p/\$,0}$	Spot exchange rate, pesos per dollar	10 p/$
$F_{p/\$,0}$	Forward exchange rate, pesos per dollar	10.381 p/$
$P_{\$,1}/P_{\$,0}$	Rate of price level change in U.S.	1.02547
$P_{p,1}/P_{p,0}$	Rate of price level change in Mexico	1.04
$R_{\$,0}$	U.S. nominal interest rate	5% per annum
$R_{p,0}$	Mexico nominal interest rate	9% per annum
r	Real rate of interest	

Thus, if 10 pesos purchases a quantity of wheat in Mexico and the spot exchange rate is 10 p/$, the same quantity of wheat will sell for $1 in the United States. Expressed equivalently, the PPP doctrine states that people will value currencies for how much those currencies will purchase. If an American dollar purchases the same basket of goods and services as five units of a foreign currency, we would have an exchange rate of five foreign currency units to the dollar (i.e., each foreign currency unit should be worth $0.20).

An attempt to compare price indices to computed PPP assumes that it is possible to compile comparable baskets of goods in different countries. As a practical matter, the parity rate is in general estimated from changes in the purchasing power of two currencies with reference to some past base period when the exchange rate was (theoretically) in equilibrium.

RELATIVE PURCHASING POWER PARITY

In using the PPP, our emphasis is on formulating it as an expression that states that *changes* in exchange rates (from period 0 to period 1) reflect *changes* in the relative prices between two countries. In formal terms, the relative PPP may be stated as in Equation 18.3.

$$\frac{E(S_{p/\$,1})}{S_{p/\$,0}} = \frac{P_{p,1}/P_{p,0}}{P_{\$,1}/P_{\$,0}} \tag{18.3}$$

Here, the terms are as defined in Table 18.3 and E is the expectation operator. An example is given in Equation 18.4.

$$
\begin{aligned}
E(S_{p/\$,1}) &= S_{p/\$,0} \times \frac{P_{p,1}/P_{p,0}}{P_{\$,1}/P_{\$,0}} \\
&= 10\,\text{p/\$} \times \frac{1.04}{1.02547} \\
&= 10.142\,\text{p/\$}
\end{aligned}
\tag{18.4}
$$

For the country with the higher expected inflation rate, the expected future spot exchange rate will fall. More general numerical examples illustrate some of the implications of the PPP doctrine. Assume that for a given time period foreign price levels have risen by 32%, whereas domestic price levels have risen by 20%. If the initial exchange rate is FC 10 to $1, the subsequent new exchange rate will be as follows.

$$E(S_{FC/\$,1}) = S_{FC/\$,0} \times \frac{P_{FC,1}/P_{FC,0}}{P_{\$,1}/P_{\$,0}} = 10 \times \frac{1.32}{1.20} = 11 \text{ FC/\$}$$

It will now take 10% more foreign currency units to equal $1 because the relative inflation rate has been higher in the foreign country. Alternatively, with an exchange rate of FC 10 to $1 assume that foreign prices have risen by 17% and domestic prices have risen by 30%. The expected new exchange rate would be as follows.

$$E(S_{FC/\$,1}) = S_{FC/\$,0} \times \frac{P_{FC,1}/P_{FC,0}}{P_{\$,1}/P_{\$,0}} = 10 \times \frac{1.17}{1.30} = 9 \text{ FC/\$}$$

In the present instance, the number of foreign currency units needed to purchase $1 would drop by 10%. Thus, the value of the foreign currency has increased due to the differential rates of inflation in domestic versus foreign prices.

Empirical studies indicate that although the PPP relationship does not hold perfectly it holds in the long run (Solnik 2000, Levich 2001, Madura 2003). More fundamentally, the doctrine predicts that an equilibrium rate between two currencies will reflect market forces and that random deviations from the central tendency will tend to be self-correcting (i.e., it suggests the existence of some strong equilibrating forces). Furthermore, it argues that the relationships between exchange rates will not be haphazard but will reflect underlying economic conditions and changes in these conditions. The relationships are not precise because of a number of factors, including the following.

- Differences in incomes or other endowments between the two countries

- Differences in tastes and/or market baskets consumed

- Changes in government policies

- Transportation costs

- Lags in market responses

- Differences between two countries in the price ratios of internationally traded goods to domestically traded goods

- The addition of a risk premium influence

- Expectational errors

INTEREST RATE PARITY

IRP holds that the ratio of the forward and spot exchange rates will equal the ratio of foreign and domestic nominal interest rates. The formal statement of the IRP may be expressed as in Equation 18.5.

$$\frac{F_{p/\$,0}}{S_{p/\$,0}} = \frac{1 + R_{p,0}}{1 + R_{\$,0}} \quad (18.5)$$

Here, the terms are as defined in Table 18.3. Adding 1 to the left and right side of Equation 18.5, an equivalent expression for the IRP is 18.6.

$$\frac{F_{p/\$,0} - S_{p/\$,0}}{S_{p/\$,0}} = \frac{R_{p,0} - R_{\$,0}}{1 + R_{\$,0}} \quad (18.6)$$

The general expression for the IRP in Equation 18.6 provides a basis for some illustrative examples. In Table 18.4 we present an example of IRP between the Mexican peso and U.S. dollar. At time 0, $100 can be invested for one year in bonds denominated either in Mexican pesos or U.S. dollars. We use annual rates for simplicity. If the $100 is invested at the U.S. interest rate, its end-of-year value would be $105.

Alternatively, the $100 can be converted into pesos and invested in a peso security (at the same time purchasing a peso forward contract to receive dollars in the future). Converting the $100 into pesos provides 1000 p, invested at the Mexican rate of 9% to obtain an end-of-year 1090 p. The forward contract converts this amount to $105.0. This is a parity relationship in which the forward discount on the peso of 3.81% is equal to the discounted interest rate differential (as shown in Table 18.4).

TABLE 18.4	Example of Interest Rate Parity (A) Equilibrium Mexican Peso and U.S. Dollar, $F_{p/\$,0} = 10.381 p/\$$

$S_{p/\$,0} = 10\ p/\$$
$F_{p/\$,0} = 10.381\ p/\$$
$R_{\$,0} = 5\%$ per annum
$R_{p,0} = 9\%$ per annum

	YEAR 0	YEAR 1
Dollar	$100	$100 \times (1 + R_{\$,0}) = \$100 \times 1.05$ = \$105.0
Peso	$100 \times S_{p/\$,0} =$ $100 \times 10\ p/\$ =$ = 1000 p	In peso: $1000\ p \times (1 + R_{p,0}) =$ $1000\ p \times 1.09 =$ = 1090 p
		In $: $1090\ p \times (1/F_{p/\$,0}) =$ $1090\ p \times (\$1/10.381\ p) =$ = \$105.0

Foreword Peso Discount-Discounted Interest Rate Differential

$$\frac{F_{p/\$,0} - S_{p/\$,0}}{S_{p/\$,0}} = \frac{R_{p,0} - R_{\$,0}}{1 + R_{\$,0}}$$

$$\frac{10.381 - 10}{10} = \frac{0.09 - 0.05}{1.05}$$

$$\frac{0.381}{10} = \frac{0.04}{1.05}$$

$$0.03810 = 0.03810$$

If interest rate parity does not hold, Tables 18.5 and 18.6 demonstrate how covered interest arbitrage will move the market toward parity. In Table 18.5, the peso forward rate requires more pesos per dollar than the parity rate and thus the peso is at a forward discount. This is an example of arbitrage. That is, a 1,000-peso Mexican security is sold short (equivalent to borrowing 1,000 p). At the end of the year, 1,090 p must be repaid.

The 1000 p can be invested in a U.S. security at the spot exchange rate. We purchase a peso forward contract to receive 10.5p/$ at the end of the year. The pesos received and what they earn are outlined in Table 18.4. But now the forward rate at which the pesos are converted into dollars is higher, and thus the 1000 p borrowed can be repaid and yield a profit of 12.5 p per 1,000 p invested (with a present value of 11.905 p). The premium on the dollar in the forward market minus the premium in the investment market, as shown in Table 18.5, sums to the same profit level (1.190%).

The covered arbitrage transaction can be shown graphically as in Figure 18.2. Equilibrium is shown at point A, which plots on the IRP line using the data from Table 18.4. The results from Table 18.5 are plotted as point B, with a premium of 5% on the forward dollar and the premium in the financial markets. With the higher forward rate, the peso is at a discount (investors prefer dollar investments to peso investments). The transactions for the covered arbitrage outflows from pesos to dollars move the relationships toward IRP, eliminating covered interest arbitrage profits.

$$d = \frac{F_{p/\$,0} - S_{p/\$,0}}{S_{p/\$,0}} - \frac{R_{p,0} - R_{\$,0}}{1 + R_{\$,0}}$$

$$= \frac{10.5 - 10}{10} - \frac{0.09 - 0.05}{1.05}$$

$$= \frac{0.5}{10} - \frac{0.04}{1.05}$$

$$= 0.05 - 0.03810$$

$$= 0.01190$$

Purchasing the peso forward causes it to rise. This reduces the dollar premium in the forward market, causing it to decline below the 5% shown in Table 18.5. Thus, covered arbitrage transactions causing capital to flow from pesos to dollars will move point B to A. More generally, the premium in the forward market will decline and the premium in the security market will narrow. In our example, we changed only the forward rate to go toward IRP. The differential in the interest rates was held unchanged.

In Table 18.6, the new forward peso rate is reduced below the IRP rate so that the forward dollar is now at a discount and the peso is at a premium. Hence, we obtain point C in Figure 18.2 (at which capital flows from dollar investments to peso investments). The arbitrage transactions will move the markets toward IRP. Selling the peso forward causes the forward rate to fall (more pesos per dollar, toward 10.381p/$), which represents an increase of the forward premium on the dollar. Selling the dollar security will cause its yield to rise, and purchasing the peso security will cause its yield to fall (decreasing the premium toward the lower premium in the forward dollar market toward the equilibrium depicted in Figure 18.2 and outlined in Table 18.4).

TABLE 18.5	Example Covered Interest Rate Arbitrage (B) Mexican Peso to U.S. Dollar, $F_{p/\$,0}$ = 10.5p/$		

$S_{p/\$,0}$ = 10 p/$
$F_{p/\$,0}$ = 10.5 p/$
$R_{\$,0}$ = 5% per annum
$R_{p,0}$ = 9% per annum

	YEAR 0		YEAR 1
Borrow (short) pesos. Repay at $R_{p,0}$.	−1000 p		$-1000\ p \times (1 + R_{p,0})$ = $-1000\ p \times 1.09$ = = −1090 p
Sell pesos spot. Invest (long) dollars at $R_{\$,0}$. Buy peso forward.	$1000\ p \times (1/S_{p/\$,0})$ = $1000\ p \times (\$1/10\ p)$ = = $100	In $: In peso:	$\$100 \times (1 + R_{\$,0})$ = $\$100 \times 1.05$ = = $105.0 $\$105.0 \times F_{p/\$,0}$ = $\$105.0 \times 10.5\ p/\$$ = = 1102.5 p
Net peso position.	0 p		−1090 p + 1102.5 p = = 12.5 p
PV net peso position at $R_{\$,0}$.	0 p		12.5 p / (1.05) = = 11.905 p

T A B L E 18.6	Example of Covered Interest Arbitrage (C) U.S. Dollar to Mexican Peso, $F_{p/\$,0} = 9.8p/\$$	

$S_{p/\$,0} = 10\ p/\$$
$F_{p/\$,0} = 9.8\ p/\$$
$R_{\$,0} = 5\%$ per annum
$R_{p,0} = 9\%$ per annum

	YEAR 0	YEAR 1
Borrow (short) $100. Repay at $R_{\$,0}$.	−$100	$-\$100 \times (1 + R_{\$,0}) = -\$100 \times 1.05 = $ = −$105.0
Buy peso spot. Invest (long) peso at $R_{p,0}$. Sell peso forward.	$\$100 \times S_{p/\$,0} = $ $\$100 \times 10\ p/\$ = $ = 1000 p	In peso: $1000\ p \times (1 + R_{p,0}) = $ $1000\ p \times 1.09 = $ = 1090 p In $: $1090\ p \times (1/F_{p/\$,0}) = $ $1090\ p \times (\$1/9.8\ p) = $ = $111.225
Net dollar position.	$0	−$105.0 + $111.225= =$6.225
Net peso position.	0 p	$\$6.225 \times F_{p/\$,0} = $ $\$6.225 \times 9.8\ p/\$ = $ = 61.0 p
PV net peso position at $R_{\$,0}$.	0 p	61.0 p / (1.05) = = 58.095 p

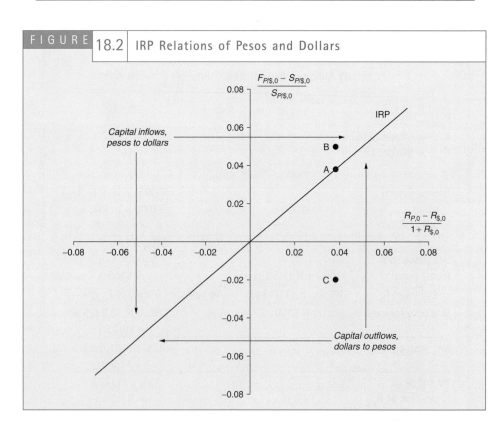

F I G U R E 18.2	IRP Relations of Pesos and Dollars

$$d = \frac{F_{p/\$,0} - S_{p/\$,0}}{S_{p/\$,0}} - \frac{R_{p,0} - R_{\$,0}}{1 + R_{\$,0}}$$

$$= \frac{9.8 - 10}{10} - \frac{0.09 - 0.05}{1.05}$$

$$= \frac{-0.2}{10} - \frac{0.04}{1.05}$$

$$= -0.02 - 0.03810$$

$$= -0.05810$$

FISHER RELATION

The FR describes how price changes in a single country cause a difference between real and nominal interest rates. When pairs of countries are involved, the IFE describes relationships between interest rate differences across countries and expected exchange rate changes. The FR can be stated in a number of forms, as in Equations 18.7 through 18.9.

$$E\left(\frac{P_1}{P_0}\right) = \frac{1 + R}{1 + r} \qquad (18.7)$$

$$R = (1 + r)E\left(\frac{P_1}{P_0}\right) - 1 \qquad (18.8)$$

$$r = (1 + R)\frac{1}{E(P_1 / P_0)} - 1 \qquad (18.9)$$

Here, the terms are as defined in Table 18.3 and E is the expectation operator. Although the FR can be stated in a number of forms, its nature can be conveyed by a simple numerical example. Over a given period of time, if the price index is expected to rise 10% and the real rate of interest is 7% the current nominal rate of interest is as follows.

$$R = [(1.07)(1.10)] - 1 = 17.7\%$$

Similarly, if the nominal rate of interest is 12% and the price index is expected to rise 10% over a given time period the current real rate of interest is as follows.

$$r = [1.12(100/110)] - 1 = 1.018 - 1 = 0.018 = 1.8\%$$

INTERNATIONAL FISHER EFFECT

The domestic version of the FR states that nominal interest rates will reflect both real rates and rates of price changes. The IFE recognizes that differences in nominal interest rate levels will have an impact on expected foreign exchange rates. The derivation of the IFE is based on arbitrage activities under the assumption of perfect capital markets.

The analysis proceeds in a manner similar to that used in Table 18.4 in developing interest rate parity relations. An investor can invest in a U.S. security or a peso security. Using the data from Table 18.4, the investor can invest $100 in a U.S. security that pays 5% per period. His ending wealth will be $100 \times 1.05 = $105. Alternatively, if the $100 is invested in a peso security, the investor would first convert the $100 at the spot exchange rate of 10 pesos per dollar to obtain 1,000 pesos. The ending wealth will be as follows.

$$(\$100 \times 10 \text{ p/\$})(1 + 0.09)[1/E(S_{p/\$,1})]$$

Each investment should produce the same ending wealth. For this to be true, the expected future spot price would have to be 10.381 p/$. In general terms, the expected future spot exchange rate or the expected exchange rate percentage of change must equal the percent interest differential. This gives us Equation 18.10.

$$\frac{E(S_{p/\$,1}) - S_{p/\$,0}}{S_{p/\$,0}} = \frac{R_{p,0} - R_{\$,0}}{1 + R_{\$,0}} \tag{18.10}$$

Equation 18.10 differs from Equation 18.6. The four terms in Equation 18.6 can be observed at the time of the arbitrage investment. However, in Equation 18.10 only three terms can be observed because the expected future spot rate is not realized until the end of the period. Hence, ex post the IFE represents borrowing or investing on an uncovered basis. If the expectations with respect to the future spot rate are not realized, the investor would have gains or losses. Capital does not flow into high-interest-rate countries if the differential reflects high expected inflation and currency depreciation. Similarly, capital does not flow out of low-interest-rate countries with low expected inflation and strong currencies.

FORWARD RATE UNBIASED

Under perfect capital market assumptions, the IFE will hold. The forward exchange premium or discount will equal the expected percentage change in the exchange rates (calculated per Equation 18.11 or Equation 18.12).

$$\frac{F_{p/\$,0} - S_{p/\$,0}}{S_{p/\$,0}} = \frac{E(S_{p/\$,1}) - S_{p/\$,0}}{S_{p/\$,0}} \tag{18.11}$$

or

$$F_{p/\$,0} = E(S_{p/\$,1}) \tag{18.12}$$

Under real-world market conditions, risk premiums and expectational errors are likely to cause inequalities between short-term movements in expected exchange rate changes and percentage changes in the forward premium or discount. If over time these differences between the beginning-period forward rate and the ending-period actual spot exchange rate are small, on average the forward rate is an unbiased predictor of the future spot rate.

Perspectives on Parity Relationships

Under the assumption of perfect market conditions, we have derived the parity relationships in international finance: PPP, IRP, IFE, and the forward rate unbiased (FRU) theory. The relationships are summarized in Table 18.7. PPP represents an equilibrium condition based on the arbitrage of goods sold in different countries and priced in different currencies. IRP results from arbitrage between interest rate differentials on securities and the relation between forward and spot exchange rates. The IFE differs from IRP in that the expected future spot rate substitutes for the current forward rate.

MANAGEMENT OF FOREIGN EXCHANGE RISKS

One issue is whether parity conditions make it unnecessary to deal with foreign exchange risk. Dufey and Srinvasulu (1983) address this question. They point to a number of market

TABLE 18.7	Parity Relationships in International Finance Pesos per Dollar

Purchasing power parity (PPP)

Absolute version
$$P_p = P_\$ \times S_{p/\$,0}$$

Relative version
$$\frac{E(S_{p/\$,1})}{S_{p/\$,0}} = \frac{P_{p,1}/P_{p,0}}{P_{\$,1}/P_{\$,0}}$$

Interest rate parity (IRP)
$$\frac{F_{p/\$,0}}{S_{p/\$,0}} = \frac{1+R_{p,0}}{1+R_{\$,0}}$$

$$\frac{F_{p/\$,0}-S_{p/\$,0}}{S_{p/\$,0}} = \frac{R_{p,0}-R_{\$,0}}{1+R_{\$,0}}$$

Fisher relation (FR)
$$E\left(\frac{P_{p,1}}{P_{p,0}}\right) = \frac{1+R_{p,0}}{1+r}$$

$$R_{p,0} = (1+r) \times E\left(\frac{P_{p,1}}{P_{p,0}}\right) - 1$$

$$r = (1+R_{p,0}) \times \frac{1}{E(P_{p,1}/P_{p,0})} - 1$$

International Fisher Effect (IFE)
$$\frac{E(S_{p/\$,1})-S_{p/\$,0}}{S_{p/\$,0}} = \frac{R_{p,0}-R_{\$,0}}{1+R_{\$,0}}$$

Forward rate unbiased (FRU)
$$\frac{F_{p/\$,0}-S_{p/\$,0}}{S_{p/\$,0}} = \frac{E(S_{p/\$,1})-S_{p/\$,0}}{S_{p/\$,0}}$$

$$F_{p/\$,0} = E(S_{p/\$,1})$$

imperfections that must be taken into account, such as incomplete securities markets, positive transactions and information costs, the deadweight costs of financial distress, and agency costs. Hence, the departures from parity conditions and their slow rates of correction make it desirable for corporate management to cope with exchange risk.

EMPIRICAL STUDIES OF FOREIGN EXCHANGE EXPOSURE

A number of articles have dealt with the issue of how to measure foreign exchange exposure. Hekman (1985) develops a model of *foreign exchange exposure* defined as the sensitivity of an investment's value in a reference currency to changes in exchange rate forecasts. This sensitivity is due to some share of the cash flows from the investment are denominated in foreign currency. A portion of cash flows denominated in a reference currency affected by future exchange rates will also generate sensitivity.

Kaufold and Smirlock (KS, 1986) measure uncertainty about the domestic currency value of a corporation's *net foreign exchange position* as a function of the duration of the cash flows and unanticipated changes in foreign interest and exchange rates. They assert that despite the expanding opportunities for the use of interest rate swaps and currency swaps it is often not possible to completely eliminate net foreign exposures of firms.

It may not always be possible to find firms with exactly offsetting positions, and the forward and futures currency markets may not be operative for the requisite maturities involved. KS therefore develop illustrations of how to hedge a U.S. firm's foreign currency exposure using the domestic interest rate futures contract and the relevant currency futures contract. They observe that complete hedging requires that both domestic and foreign interest rates be related to the domestic risk-free rate without error.

Adler and Dumas (1984) take a market approach to the nature of currency risk exposure. They reason that the exposure to exchange risk is essentially the same as exposure to market risk. They propose that a portfolio's average *exposure to exchange risk* measured on a historical basis can be measured by regressing its total dollar value on a vector of exchange rates. The resulting partial regression coefficients will represent the exposure to each currency. In principle, if the same relationships hold in the future these exposures could be hedged. They recognize that as exposures vary over time it would be necessary to seek to derive multiperiod hedging rules.

NET MONETARY ASSET POSITION EXPOSURE

The exposure of a business firm to foreign exchange risks is determined by the patterns of its cash flow and asset/liability positions, which in turn depend on the patterns of flow of future receipts and payments and the patterns of the firm's net monetary asset position. Monetary assets are those assets denominated in a fixed number of units of money (such as cash, marketable securities, accounts receivable, tax refunds receivable, notes receivable, and prepaid insurance). Monetary liabilities are those liabilities expressed in fixed monetary terms (such as accounts payable, notes payable, tax liability reserves, bonds, and preferred stock). The effects of a *net monetary position exposure* can be formulated as follows.

$$
\begin{aligned}
C_p &= [(MA - ML)/X_0 - (MA - ML)/X_1](1 - t_{u.s}) \\
&= (E_0 - E_1)(MA - ML)(1 - t_{u.s}) \\
&= (E_0 - E_1)(NMP)(1 - t_{u.s})
\end{aligned}
$$

Where:

C_p = cost of net monetary position (NMP) due to exchange rate changes

MA = monetary assets

ML = monetary liabilities

E_0 = exchange rate at the beginning in \$/FC

E_1 = exchange rate a period later in \$/FC

X_0 = exchange rate at the beginning in FC/\$ = $1/E_o$

X_1 = exchange rate a period later in FC/\$ = $1/E_1$

$t_{u.s}$ = tax rate in the United States

The effects of a decline in foreign currency value are that a net FC monetary creditor loses and a net FC monetary debtor gains. To illustrate, postulate:

$$MA = FC200,000 \qquad X_0 = FC4/\$ \qquad E_0 = \$0.25/FC$$
$$ML = FC100,000 \qquad X_1 = FC5/\$ \qquad E_1 = \$0.20/FC$$

We calculate the net monetary loss (ignoring taxes for simplicity) as follows.

$$NMP = MA - ML = FC200,000 - FC100,000 = FC100,000;$$
$$C_p = NMP(E_0 - E_1) = FC100,000(\$0.25/FC - \$0.20/FC)$$
$$= \$5,000$$

Our calculations show a decrease in the dollar value of our asset position (i.e., a loss of $5,000). We now let ML = FC 300,000. Then:

$$NMP = MA - ML = FC200,000 - FC300,000 = -FC100,000;$$
$$= NMP(E_0 - E_1) = -FC100,000(\$0.25/FC - \$0.20/FC)$$
$$= -\$5000$$

The net amount owed is decreased by $5,000, representing a gain. The effects of an increase in FC value are the opposite. The net monetary debtor loses and the net monetary creditor gains.

TRANSACTION EXPOSURE

The impact of an exposed position is similar if the exposure results from an excess of receipts over payments due to be paid in the foreign currency. Unless the FC payments and receipts in relation to the future net monetary position of the firm exactly offset, the firm is exposed to a decline or increase in the value of foreign currencies. If the normal pattern of operations will put the firm in an exposed position, the adjustments required may involve costs. For example, one strategy may be to rearrange the pattern of payments and the pattern of holdings of monetary assets and liabilities in foreign currencies to achieve perfect balance so that the net exposure is zero.

However, changes in the flow of receipts and payments or in the holdings of monetary assets and liabilities may represent departures from the firm's normal operations. Such artificial changes from the firm's normal patterns may involve costs. To determine whether such adjustments are better than alternative methods of limiting exposure requires that management calculate the cost of altering the patterns of cash flows or of its net monetary position. This may be a rather complex undertaking for an individual firm, but is nonetheless necessary if the firm is to make a rational choice among alternatives.

If parity conditions hold, managers can evaluate the variables involved to set prices to reflect expected parity relations. For example, assume the following patterns. The expected price change over the next year in the foreign country is 10%. The expected price change over the next year in the domestic country is 0%. If the current (spot) exchange rate is 10 units per U.S. dollar, the expected foreign exchange rate would be 11 units per U.S. dollar according to the PPP condition.

In Table 18.8, line A assumes no price inflation in the foreign country. So, the exchange rate stays at 100. Column 2 is production units times the exchange rate in column 1. Column 3 is the price to the dealer, which is column 2 times 1.20 (the markup factor). The cost of the dealer is column 3 divided by column 1. So, the cost of the dealer is $12,000. Column 5 is the dealer's price, which is his cost times 1.30 (the markup factor). Column 6 is the dealer's gross profit. It is column 5 less column 4.

T A B L E 18.8	Effective Transaction Exposure Management				
Production (units)	10,000				
Markup by manufacturer	20%				
Markup by dealer	30%				
Current exchange rate (¥/$)	100				
New exchange rate (¥/$)	110				
(1) EXCHANGE RATE YEN/$	(2) MANUFACTURER COST (¥) (1) × UNITS	(3) PRICE TO DEALER (¥) (2) × 1.20	(4) COST TO DEALER ($) (3) ÷ (1)	(5) DEALER'S PRICE ($) (4) × 1.30	(6) DEALER'S GROSS PROFIT ($) (5) − (4)
A.　100	¥ 1,000,000	¥ 1,200,000	$ 12,000.0	$15,600.0	$3,600.0
B.　110	¥ 1,100,000	¥ 1,320,000	$ 12,000.0	$15,600.0	$3,600.0

In line B, an inflation rate in the foreign country of 10% is expected by all parties. So, the manufacturing cost is ¥1,100,000. The price to the dealer is ¥1,320,000. Because the dealer has bought the yen in the futures market for $12,000, that is his cost. Hence, the dealer's price and the dealer's gross profits are the same as in line A because PPP holds.

A firm seeking protection against the foreign exchange risk exposure may employ alternative methods. One is the use of the forward market discussed in the previous example. The other is the use of the money and capital markets. If the IRP relationship holds, it is a matter of indifference as to which of these two methods is employed. For example, if the amount of foreign currency involved is 100,000 FC units the cost of hedging in the foreign market (C_f) is as follows.

$$C_f = (E_0 - E_f)(FC\ Exposure)$$
$$= (\$0.25/FC - \$0.20/FC)(FC100,000)$$
$$= \$5,000$$

The logic here is that if the current forward rate correctly reflects the expected future spot rate, the net exposure loss has already taken place. The economic benefit of the hedge is that the loss is limited (it is like an insurance payment). If the future spot rate turned out to be lower than the current forward, a dollar value of the foreign currency of $0.18 rather than $0.20, the loss from the exposure has been fixed in advance.

An alternative to hedging by purchasing the forward rate is to borrow FC100,000 to eliminate the *net monetary asset positive position*. The cost can be explained by using the IRP conditions. Suppose that interest rates in the foreign market are 32.5%, whereas interest rates in the domestic market are 6%. For our current example, this would be as follows.

$$(X_1 - X_0)/X_0 = (R_{FC} - R_{US})/(1 + R_{US})$$

Using the data from our present example, we have:

$$(5 - 4)/4 = (0.325 - 0.06)/1.06$$

We see that the dollar premium in the forward market is equal to the interest rate premium in the capital markets. The FC100,000 borrowed at 32.5% represents a one-period cost of FC32,500. If the FC funds are used to purchase dollars at $0.25/FC, we obtain $25,000. We earned 6% on the $25,000, which is $1,500. We paid FC32,500 interest on the FC100,000. We translate at $0.20/FC to total $6,500. Net of the $1,500 we earned from the dollar investment, our cost is $5,000. This is equal to the cost of using the forward exchange market.

We next consider the position of a firm in a negative net monetary position or that will be required, at some time in the future, to make net payments in excess of future receipts. The situation is the reverse of a firm in a positive monetary position. Instead of facing the risk of devaluation of FC units, the firm faces the risk of appreciation in the value of FC units. Hence, its protective action in the forward market is to purchase the FC units. If it does not obtain this protection, it will face an uncertain cost if the future spot rate is higher than the current forward rate. If it uses the money and capital markets, it will borrow in the United States and invest in the FC units in which it will have to make future payments.

This analysis demonstrates that if a firm is in an exposed foreign exchange position it will incur some costs to obtain protection against that exposed position. Even rearranging the firm's pattern of payments and receipts or monetary assets and liabilities will represent a departure from normal operations and therefore involve some costs. If the firm uses the forward market or borrows it incurs some costs, but it will know the exact amount of these costs.

We have already discussed the use of forward contracts. The use of currency futures is the same in principle as forward contracts except in contract characteristics. For example, currency futures are traded in standardized lots at exchanges. Forward contracts are tailor-made in over-the-counter transactions (OTCs). The option concepts readily carry over to currency calls and puts. We shall discuss interest rate swaps and currency swaps.

INTEREST RATE SWAPS (INTERNATIONAL SETTING)

An *interest rate swap* is an agreement between two parties for the exchange of a series of cash payments, one on a fixed rate liability and the other on a floating rate liability. For example, a financial institution (FI) has a portfolio of assets consisting of long-term fixed-rate mortgages. Its liabilities are shorter-term deposits and money market certificates. It faces the risk of a rise in interest rates on its shorter-duration liabilities.

An interest rate swap can reduce its risk exposure. The intermediary is a European bank acting on behalf of a corporate customer seeking floating-rate funding in dollars. The FI agrees to make fixed interest payments to the intermediary, which in turn agrees to make variable interest payments to the FI. The interest rates paid to each other are negotiated. Although both parties swap net interest payments on their underlying liabilities, the principal amounts are not exchanged.

Another source of interest rate swaps results from different comparative advantages in generating funds in either the fixed- or floating-rate interest markets. An example would be that a low-rated company seeks fixed-rate long-term credit but has access to variable-interest-rate funds at a margin of 1.5% over the London Interbank offer rate (LIBOR), whereas its direct borrowing costs in a fixed-rate public market would be 13%. A high-rated company may have access to fixed-rate funds in the Eurodollar bond market at 11% and variable-rate funds at LIBOR +.5%. Thus, it has a relatively greater advantage in the fixed-rate market. The high-rated company would borrow fixed-rate funds at 11% in the Eurobond market, whereas the low-rated company would borrow an identical amount of variable-rate funds at 1.5% over LIBOR. They swap the payment streams, negotiating the interest rate savings. A commercial bank or other financial intermediary can act as the counterparty to each side of the transaction, often guaranteeing it and saving both parties interest costs on their preferred debt service flow. For its services, the intermediary would receive compensation.

CURRENCY SWAPS

In *currency swaps*, the two debt service flows are denominated in different currencies, and principle amounts may also be exchanged. A U.S. corporation may seek fixed-rate funds in Euros, whereas a German corporation may desire variable-rate dollar financing. A bank intermediary may arrange a currency swap. The U.S. company borrows variable-rate funds in dollars, whereas the German company borrows fixed-rate funds in Euros.

The two companies swap. Both exchange-rate and interest-rate risks are thereby managed at cost savings to both parties because they borrow initially in the market where they have a comparative advantage and then swap for their preferred liability. Currency swaps illustrate the basic principle of international transactions in that all parties benefit as a result of their differing comparative advantage. They then swap for the preferred liability. It enables firms to manage their portfolios at lowered transaction costs.

THE COST OF CAPITAL, CAPITAL INVESTMENT, AND CURRENCY RISK

The cost of capital is relevant for decisions such as capital budgeting for foreign projects and for valuing foreign subsidiaries and foreign investments such as cross-border mergers. We begin with a simple procedure for estimating the cost of capital in a capital budgeting example and then compare alternative methods of calculating the cost of equity.

COST OF DEBT RELATIONSHIPS

We begin with an example of calculating the cost of debt. We find that the spot price of the Mexican peso is 9.52 pesos per dollar and that the one-year forward rate is 10.75 pesos per dollar. So, it takes more pesos to purchase a dollar in the futures market than in the spot market. We use a U.S. prime rate of 9% as an indication of the borrowing cost to a prime business customer in the United States. We now apply the IRP relation to obtain the current interest rate in Mexico. We have:

$$\frac{F_{p/\$,0}}{S_{p/\$,0}} = \frac{10.75}{9.52} = \frac{1 + R_{p,0}}{1.09}$$

Solving for $R_{p,0}$, we obtain 1.23 (or a Mexican interest rate to a prime borrower in Mexico of 23%). There are many real-world frictions that cause departures from parity conditions in the short run. But these are the relationships toward which international financial markets are always moving. Experience and empirical evidence teach us that the parity conditions provide a useful guide to business executives. For an individual manager to believe that he can outguess the international financial markets, which reflect the judgments of many players, is hubris in the extreme. He puts his company at the peril of severe losses.

COST OF EQUITY AND COST OF CAPITAL

We begin with the basic idea behind the capital asset pricing model (CAPM), widely used to calculate the cost of equity. CAPM states that the cost of equity capital is the risk-free return plus a risk adjustment (which is the product of the return on the market as a whole multiplied by the beta risk measure of the individual firm or project). How the market is defined depends on whether the global capital market is integrated or segmented.

If integrated, investments are made globally and systematic risk is measured relative to a world market index. If capital markets are segmented, investments are predominantly made in a particular segment or country and systematic risk is measured relative to a domestic index. With the rise of large financial institutions investing worldwide and mutual funds that facilitate international or foreign investments, the world is moving toward a globally integrated capital market.

But we are not there yet because of the home bias phenomenon (i.e., investors placing only a relatively small part of their funds abroad). For recent data, see Hulbert (2000). The reasons are not fully understood. One possibility is that there may be extra costs of obtaining and digesting information. Another possibility is the greater uncertainty associated with placing investments under the jurisdiction of another country whose authorities may change the rules of the game. If capital markets are not fully integrated, there are gains from international diversification. An MNC would apply a lower cost of capital to a foreign investment than would a local (foreign) company (Chan, Karolyi, and Stulz 1992; Stulz 1995a, 1995b; Stulz and Wasserfallen 1995; Godfrey and Espinosa 1996).

Let's continue with the Mexico example. A firm domiciled in Mexico would have a beta based on market returns for investments in Mexico. An MNC domiciled outside Mexico will have a cost of equity capital related to its beta measured with respect to the markets in which it operates. A world market index might be a reasonable approximation.

If we calculated the cost of equity for an investment in Mexico in nominal peso terms, it would necessarily reflect a risk differential above the cost of debt borrowing in Mexico. If the cost of debt borrowing in Mexico is about 23% based on our prior analysis, the cost of equity is likely to be four to seven percentage points higher. Assuming a leverage ratio of debt to enterprise market value of 50%, a cost of equity of 30%, and a tax rate of 40%, we can calculate the weighted cost of capital as follows.

$$\text{WACC} = (0.23)(0.6)(0.5) + (0.30)(0.5) = 0.219$$

We could use this discount factor of approximately 22% in calculating the present value of an investment in Mexico. The cash flows expressed in pesos discounted by the peso cost of capital would give us a present value expressed in pesos. This present value converted to dollars at the spot rate should give us the NPV of the investment in dollars.

We should obtain the same result by beginning with the cash flows in pesos, converting them to dollars over time, and discounting them by the WACC of the U.S. firm. We illustrate this second method. The project yields cash flows over a five-year period, at the end of which it can be sold to a local buyer. First, we calculate the expected foreign exchange rate expressed in the number of pesos per dollar.

We start with the spot rate of 9.5 pesos per dollar. From PPP, for each subsequent year t we multiply the 9.5 by $(1.16/1.03)^t$ (the relative rates of price level changes, as indicated in Table 18.9). These are inputs we use in Table 18.10, the calculation of the present value of the firm or project expressed in dollars.

Line 1 represents the preliminary estimates of cash flows from the firm or project expressed in pesos. In line 2 we recognize that these projections are subject to error. We are particularly concerned that the foreign country may change the rules of the game.

TABLE 18.9	Calculation of Expected Future Exchange Rates	
YEAR	RELATIVE RATES OF PRICE LEVEL CHANGES	$E(S_{P/\$,T})$
0	$S_{p/\$,0}$ = pesos per $ =	9.50
1	9.5(1.16/1.03) =	10.70
2	9.5(1.16/1.03)^2 =	12.05
3	9.5(1.16/1.03)^3 =	13.57
4	9.5(1.16/1.03)^4 =	15.28
5	9.5(1.16/1.03)^5 =	17.21

TABLE 18.10	Calculation of Present Value Dollars						
		YEAR					
	0	1	2	3	4	5	5[a]
1. Initial expected cash flows in pesos		1,000	1,100	1,200	1,400	1,600	10,000
2. Probability (risk) factors		0.9	0.9	0.8	0.8	0.6	0.5
3. Risk-adjusted expected peso cash flow		900	990	960	1,120	960	5,000
4. Exchange rate in year t $(S_{p/\$,t})$		10.7	12.05	13.57	15.28	17.21	17.21
5. Expected dollar cash flows		$84	$82	$71	$73	$56	$291
6. Applicable discount factor @10%		1.10	1.21	1.33	1.46	1.61	1.61
7. Discounted dollar cash flows		$76.47	$67.90	$53.15	$50.06	$34.64	$180.40
8. Present value	$462.61						

[a]Sale of assets for 10,000 pesos in year 5.

Political instability might bring a government with an anti-foreign-business philosophy into power. Discriminatory taxes might be imposed. Restrictions on repatriation of funds might be enacted. Militant unions might raise wage costs, reducing net cash flows. We feel it is better to explicitly recognize these risk adjustments in the cash flows, rather than fudge the discount factor. The discount factor should reflect systematic risk and not the idiosyncratic factors described.

Line 3 therefore represents the risk-adjusted expected peso cash flows. In line 4 we list the results from Table 18.10, where the expected future exchange rates were calculated. In line 5 the exchange rates are applied to the expected peso cash flows of line 3 to give us the expected cash flows expressed in dollars.

In line 6 we apply a discount factor. In the discussion of IRP, we assumed a before-tax cost of debt for the U.S. firm of 9%. We postulate further a cost of equity, leverage, and tax rates to yield a WACC of 10%. Because we already covered these procedures in Chapters 10 and 11, we can streamline this discussion to focus on the foreign investment issues. Line 7 presents the discounted dollar cash flows using the data in lines 5 and 6. In line 8 the present values from line 7 are summed to obtain the total present value of the firm or project of $463 million. The U.S. firm could incur investment outlays with a present value of up to $463 million to earn its cost of capital.

We have illustrated a systematic methodology for valuing foreign acquisitions or making direct investments. The numbers used in the example were simplified to facilitate the exposition. The underlying principles and concepts would be the same if we were using a complex sophisticated computer program. The method is similar to the valuation of domestic investments. The complications are mainly foreign exchange risks and foreign country risks. The parity relationships provide useful guidelines for thinking about foreign exchange rates, relative inflation, and relative interest rates.

In Table 18.10 we did not mean to imply that the risk factors applied in line 2 were to be approached passively. A company can use a wide range of strategies to minimize the unfavorable possibilities. A sound project or the purchase of a foreign firm can contribute to increased employment, productivity, and output in the foreign country.

The technological and management practices the parent brings to the subsidiary may make its continued participation indispensable. In addition, the foreign operations can be so organized that it could not function without the unique parts provided by the parents. Another possibility is that the investment is part of an international agency program to develop the infrastructure of the host country. Arbitrary changes in the rules of the game could injure the reputation and reduce future international support of a self-serving government.

Survey OF PRACTICE

A survey of 392 CFOs provided insights on domestic and international capital investments and financing. In brief the survey found overlap in the capital evaluation techniques that are used in practice. The survey indicated that 75.61% of the respondents use internal rate and 74.93% of the respondents use net present value always or almost always when making a capital investment. Additionally, 56.94% use some sort of hurdle rate when evaluating capital investment. While these results are similar to the Ryan and Ryan survey in Chapter 10, this survey also examines international investment and financing.

The companies were asked about the discount rate that they use always or almost always when evaluating international investment opportunities. Multiple responses indicate sensitivity analysis was performed. Accordingly, the following lists the percentage of respondents:

Capital Investment Discount Rate in International Market	%
The discount rate for the entire company	58.79
Risk matched discount rate – both country and project	50.95
International discount rate for specific country	34.52
Divisional discount rate for unit undertaking international project	15.61

The survey also asked if the respondents seriously considered issuing debt in the foreign country. If there was a positive response, the respondent was asked what factors influenced. The following list the percentage of respondents that said these factors were important or very important to them when considering the issuance of foreign debt:

Influential Factors When Issuing Foreign Debt	%
Providing a natural hedge between investment return and interest	85.84
Keeping the source of funds close to the use of funds	63.39
Favorable corporate tax treatment in foreign country	52.25
Lower foreign interest rates	44.25

The principles of this chapter and text are well applied in practice.

Source: "The Theory and Practice of Corporate Finance: Evidence from the Field," Graham, John R., and Campbell R. Harvey, *Journal of Financial Economics*, 60, May/June 2001, pp. 187–243.

summary

The foreign exchange of values of currencies have continued to exhibit high levels of volatility. The Euro was worth $1.18 in late 1998, dropped to $0.85 by mid 2001, and by late 2006 had risen to $1.27 (representing a 49.4% rise in relation to the dollar). The number of yen per dollar had fallen to almost 100 by late 1999, rose to 133 by early 2002, and then fell back to 118 by November 2006.

The fluctuations in exchange rates have greatly affected the terms of trade. The causes and consequences of exchange rate fluctuations continue to be of importance to economies and business firms.

Empirical studies find substantial short-run departures from PPP. The half-life of PPP deviations is three to five years, with correction rates of only 15% per year. With regard to IRP, the forward discount or premium should be an unbiased estimate of subsequent exchange rate changes. Theory predicts that the regression coefficient calculated for the two relationships should be a positive 1. The empirical literature finds the coefficient to be less than 1, with an average coefficient of –0.88 across a large number of published studies.

Because the lags are unpredictable and the movements in currency markets extremely volatile, many retail investors find it difficult to profitably exploit these imbalances (the forward bias). Investment advisors seek to exploit the slow correction by going long in a group of the highest-yielding (higher forward discount) currencies and short in a group of the lowest-yielding (higher forward premium) currencies. The investors obtain the benefits of averaging over a group of securities. This is similar to a value investor going long on a portfolio of low market-to-book securities and going short on high market-to-book securities. In addition, the investor reviews general economic developments and technical factors to be sure that special influences will not result in a prolonged continuation of the disequilibrium relations.

Despite efforts to forecast foreign exchange behavior, a wide range of economic, financial, and speculative instabilities create major uncertainties. Considerable empirical evidence establishes that departures from parity conditions are large and movements toward equilibrium are slow. Hence, business firms face foreign exchange risk.

Monetary assets decrease in value with inflation, and monetary liabilities are reduced with inflation. One method of risk management is to seek balance in monetary assets and liabilities. Real assets rise in monetary units with inflation. Business firms can also seek to balance production and sales patterns in relation to currency risk. If these practices involve substantial departures from normal firm operations, costs are incurred. Hedging activities by the use of forward and futures markets are also costly.

The use of swaps and options has payoffs achieved by incurring costs. This result affects asset pricing models. Multinational enterprises that sell their products globally with shares traded on the U.S. and other major stock exchanges should have similar costs of capital. Valuation methodology employs the general principles discussed in previous chapters. However, for companies in emerging countries valuation presents greater challenges.

Sovereign and political risks must be reflected in cash flows. The cost of equity in dollars considers the company's beta for comparable companies in the United States. In theory, the cost of equity calculation reflects currency risks in the spirit of a multifactor model. The cost of debt in local currency can be converted to the cost of debt in dollars using IRP relations (and vice versa).

Questions

18.1   Many companies hedge their foreign currency exposure. For example, Hershey's strategic plan calls for a new production line to be added in two years. The cost of the new production line is $60 million. The manufacturer of the equipment is a German-based company that demands payment in Euros. Euros currently cost $1.25 per Euro.

   a.   What is the current price in Euros of the $60 million equipment?

   b.   Without hedging, if the price of Euros rises to $1.40 each what is the dollar cost of the asset?

   c.   Without hedging, if the price of Euros falls to $1.10 each what is the dollar cost of the asset?

   d.   If you could purchase a two-year forward contract at $1.30 per Euro, what is the dollar cost of the asset?

18.2   Should Nestle, which produces and sells products all over the world, purchase or sell forward foreign exchange contracts to hedge all transactions that involve foreign currencies?

18.3   Comment on the following statement: "Currency hedging only provides a benefit when you guess right about the directional movement of the currency. Guess wrong and a currency hedge results in added costs." Do you agree with this statement? What is the purpose of hedging?

18.4   Empirical studies find a *forward exchange rate bias*, which means that future spot rates are different from those predicted by current forward rates. For example, if country B has a higher nominal interest rate structure than country A this implies higher expected future inflation in country B than in A so that the forward exchange rate of country A should be at a premium over the current spot rate. The expected future spot rate should also be higher than the current spot rate, by the same percentage as the forward premium. Over a large number of empirical studies, often the actual future spot rate is lower than the current spot rate. What are some possible explanations for the forward rate bias? How could forecasters seek to profit from the bias?

18.5   Because parity conditions do not generally hold in the short run, do they fail to add to our understanding of the behavior of foreign exchange rates?

18.6   You are given the prices of products in two countries, as follows.

	PRODUCT	
	X	Y
Country A	$3	$1
Country B	FC12	FC6

At an exchange rate of 5 foreign currency units per dollar, describe the pattern of exports and imports between countries A and B.

18.7   Country A and country B are each on a full gold standard, with fixed exchange rates. Country A runs an export surplus, whereas country B runs an export balance deficit. Describe the adjustment process that will restore balance to the flow of trade between the two countries.

18.8   Country A and country B are on the gold standard. The currency of country A contains 1 ounce of gold, whereas the currency of country B contains 0.05 ounce of gold. What will be the par exchange rate between the two countries?

18.9   Consider two countries C and D operating in a world with completely flexible exchange rates. Country C runs a substantial export surplus to country D, which experiences a substantial trade deficit. Assuming no initial offsetting capital flows, explain the adjustment process to bring the trade between the two countries into balance.

Problems

18.1

Currency exchange rates: In 1980, the number of Japanese yen required to equal one U.S. dollar was 226.63. In December of 2006, the U.S. dollar was worth 110 yen.

   a.   What is X_0 (1980)? What is X_1 (2006)?

   b.   What is E_0 (1980)? What is E_1 (2006)?

   c.   What was the percentage devaluation or revaluation of the yen in terms of the U.S. dollar?

   d.   What was the percentage devaluation or revaluation of the dollar in terms of the yen?

18.2

Currency exchange rates: In March of 1976, the number of Japanese yen required to equal one U.S. dollar was 300.517. In April of 2002, the U.S. dollar was worth 130.772 yen.

   a.   What is X_0 (1976)? What is X_1 (2002)?

   b.   What is E_0 (1976)? What is E_1 (2002)?

   c.   What was the percentage devaluation or revaluation of the yen in terms of the U.S. dollar?

   d.   What was the percentage devaluation or revaluation of the dollar in terms of the yen?

18.3

Currency exchange rates: If the exchange rate between dollars and Euros is €0.76313 = $1.00, and between dollars and pounds is £1 = $1.86916, what is the exchange rate between Euros and pounds?

18.4

Currency exchange rates: If the exchange rate between dollars and a Korean won is 960 won = $1.00, and between U.S. dollars and Canadian dollars is $1 Canadian = $0.8932 U.S., what is the exchange rate between Canadian dollars and Korean wons?

   c. Does the commission increase or decrease the dollar value of the foreign currency?

   d. What price in foreign currency units can the foreign company establish by using the forward market in dollars?

18.14

Unicorp makes a sale of goods to a foreign firm and will receive FC 400,000 three months later. Unicorp has incurred costs in dollars and wishes to make definite the amount of dollars it will receive in three months. It plans to approach a foreign bank to borrow an amount of local currency such that the principal plus interest will equal the amount Unicorp expects to receive. The interest rate it must pay on its loan is 28%. With the borrowed funds, Unicorp purchases dollars at the current spot rate that are invested in the United States at an interest rate of 8%. When Unicorp receives the FC 400,000 at the end of three months, it uses the funds to liquidate the loan at the foreign bank. The effective tax rate in both countries is 40%.

   a. What is the net amount Unicorp will receive if the current spot rate is FC 2.00 to the dollar?

   b. How much less is this than the amount Unicorp would have received if the remittance had been made immediately instead of three months later?

   c. At what forward rate of exchange would the amount received by Unicorp have been the same as that it would have obtained using the capital markets? Would Unicorp have sold the FC forward short or long to hedge its position?

   d. If a speculator took the opposite position from Unicorp in the forward market for FC, would the speculator sell long or short? If the speculator received a risk premium for holding this position, would this place the current forward rate in FC above or below the expected future spot rate in FC per dollar?

18.15

Multicorp has made a purchase of goods from a foreign firm that will require payment of FC 500,000 six months later. Multicorp wishes to make definite the amount of dollars it will need to pay the FC 500,000 on the due date. The foreign firm is domiciled in a country whose currency has been rising in relation to the dollar in recent years. The tax rate in both countries is 40%. Multicorp plans to borrow an amount in dollars from a U.S. bank to immediately exchange into FCs to purchase securities in the foreign country, which with interest will equal FC 500,000 six months later. The interest rate that will be paid in the United States is 10%. The interest rate that will be earned on the foreign securities is 8%. When at the end of six months Multicorp is required to make the payment in FC it will use the funds from the maturing foreign securities in FC to meet its obligation in FC. At the same time, it will pay off the loan plus interest in the United States in dollars.

   a. What is the net amount Multicorp pays to meet the obligation of FC 500,000 in six months if the current spot rate is FC 2.00 to the dollar?

   b. How much less is this than the amount Multicorp would have paid if payment had been made immediately instead of six months later?

18.5

Implied interest rates and forward exchange rates: In January of 2006, the following information was found about the exchange rates between the dollar and the U.K. pound.

$$X_0 = £\ 0.5350/\$$$
$$E_0 = \$1.8693/£$$
$$X_1\ (90\ \text{days}) = £\ 0.5378/\$$$
$$E_1\ (90\ \text{days}) = \$1.8596/£.$$

The U.S. prime interest rate on that day was 5.75%.

   a. What is implied about the U.K. interest rate?

   b. If the forward exchange rate was $1.87/£, what would be the U.K. interest rate?

   c. If the U.K. interest rate was 6%, what would be the 90-day forward rate on U.K. pounds per dollar?

18.6

Interest rate parity: The treasurer of a company in Mexico borrowed $10,000 in dollars at a 12% interest rate when the exchange rate was 9 pesos to the dollar. His company paid the loan plus interest one year later, when the exchange rate was 11 pesos to the dollar.

   a. What rate of interest was paid based on the pesos received and paid by the treasurer?

   b. Show how your result illustrates the IRP.

18.7

Interest rate parity: The treasurer of a company in Mexico is comparing two borrowing alternatives for a 180-day loan. He can borrow in U.S. dollars from a U.S. bank at a 10% interest rate or from a Mexican bank in pesos at a 30% interest rate. The spot exchange rate is 10 pesos to the dollar. The 180-day forward exchange rate is 11 pesos to the dollar.

   a. What is the effective interest rate in pesos on the U.S. loan?

   b. Verify your answer by use of the IRP relationship.

18.8

International parity relationships: In January of 2006 (when ¥112 = $1), it was expected that by the end of 2006 the price level in the United States would have risen by 2.5% and in Japan by 0%. Assume that the real rate of interest in both countries is 3%.

   a. Use the PPP to project the expected yen per $1 at the end of 2006 (the expected future spot rate of yen per $1).

   b. Use the FR to estimate the nominal interest rates in each country that make it possible for investments in each country to earn their real rate of interest.

   c. Use the IRP to estimate the current one-year forward rate of yen per $1.

   d. Compare your estimate of the current forward rate in problem 18.8c with your estimate of the expected future spot rate in problem 18.8a.

   e. Prove analytically that the FR and the IRP guarantee consistency with the PPP relation when real interest rates in the different countries are equal. (Assume that all fundamental relations hold.)

18.9

Balance of payments: Keep in mind the effects of individual transactions on the balance of payments, which are listed in the following table.

EFFECTS ON BALANCE OF PAYMENTS, COUNTRY A	
Plus (P)	Minus (M)
1. Exports and income receipts	1. Imports and income payments
2. Increase in liabilities to foreigners	2. Decrease liabilities to foreigners
3. Decrease claims on foreigners	3. Increase claims on foreigners
3a. Decrease investments	3a. Increase investments
3b. Sell assets	3b. Purchase assets

Indicate the plus entry and the minus entry for the following transactions. For example, the country exports goods in the amount of $1,000 paid for by the importer by a check on a foreign bank. The entry would be: P1 $1000 M3 $1000.

a. Country A exports $5,000 of goods to country B paid for by the exporter by a check on his account with a bank in country A.

b. Country A imports $8,000 worth of merchandise, paid for by a check on a bank in country A.

c. Direct investment income of $6,000 was received by a firm in country A from a foreign subsidiary, which paid by drawing a check on a bank in its own country F.

d. A multinational firm domiciled in country A made an investment of $10 million on a direct basis to establish a foreign subsidiary in country G. Payment was made by drawing on its bank account in country A.

e. A citizen of country A made a gift of $5,000 to a friend in a foreign country, who deposited the check drawn on a bank in country A in his own bank in country M.

f. A citizen in country A purchased an airline ticket to Europe that he purchased from Lufthansa Airlines by a check for $600 drawn on a bank in country A.

18.10

International parity relationships: In January of 2007 (when FC4 = $1) it was expected that by the end of 2007 the price level in the United States would have risen by 2% and in the foreign currency by 5%. The real rate of interest in both countries is 3%.

a. Use the PPP to project the expected FCs per $1 at the end of 2007 (the expected future spot rate of FCs per $1).

b. Use the FR to estimate the nominal interest rates in each country that make it possible for investments in each country to earn their real rate of interest.

c. Use the IRP to estimate the current one-year forward rate of FCs per $1.

d. Compare your estimate of the current forward rate in problem 18.10c with your estimate of the expected future spot rate in problem 18.10a.

e. Prove analytically that the FR and IRP guarantee consistency with the PPP relation when real interest rates in the different countries are equal. (Assume that all fundamental relations hold.)

18.11

Interest rate parity: A Mexican corporation borrowed $5,000,000 at a 12% interest rate when the exchange rate was 9 pesos per dollar. When the company repaid the loan plus interest one year later, the exchange rate was 10.5 pesos to the dollar.

What was the rate of interest on the loan based on the pesos received and paid back?

Use the IRP to illustrate this result.

18.12

Forward currency market: An American manufacturing company has imported industrial machinery at a price of FC 6 million. The machinery will be delivered and paid for in six months. For planning purposes, the American company wants to establish what the payment (in dollars) will be in six months. It decides to use the forward market to accomplish its objective. The company contracts its New York bank, which provides the quotations given in the following table. The bank states that it will charge a commission of 0.25% on any transaction.

	FC	$
Six-month Euro rates	8%	9%
Spot exchange rates	2.08	—

a. Does the American company enter the forward market to go long or short of forward FC?

b. What is the equilibrium forward rate for the foreign currency expressed as FC/$?

c. Does the commission increase or decrease the number of FC/$ in the transaction?

d. What price in dollars can the American company establish by using the forward market in foreign currency units?

18.13

Forward currency market: A foreign company purchases industrial machinery from a U.S. company at a price of $15 million. The machinery will be delivered and paid for in six months. The foreign company seeks to establish its costs in FCs. It decides to use the forward market to accomplish its objective. The company contacts its bank, which provides the quotations listed in the following table. The bank states that it will charge a commission of 0.25% on any transaction.

	FC	$
Six-month rates	8	9
Spot exchange rates	2.041FC/$	$0.49/FC

a. Does the foreign company enter the forward market to go long or short forward dollars?

b. What is the equilibrium forward rate for the foreign currency expressed $/FC?

c. At what forward rate of exchange would the amount paid by Multicorp have been the same as that it would have paid using the capital markets? Would Multicorp have taken the long position in the forward FC or have sold the FC forward short to hedge its position?

d. If a speculator took the opposite position from Multicorp in the forward market for FCs, would the speculator be long or short? If the speculator received a risk premium for holding this position, would this place the current forward rate in FC above or below the expected future spot rate in FC per dollar?

Time Value of Money Tables

CONTENTS

This appendix includes the following time value of money tables:

TABLE A.1   Future Value of $1 Lump Sum

$$FV_{r,n} = P_o FVIF(r,n) = P_o(1+r)^n$$

n	1%	2%	3%	4%	5%	6%	7%	8%	9%	10%	11%	12%	15%	18%	20%	25%	30%	40%	50%
0	1.0000	1.0000	1.0000	1.0000	1.0000	1.0000	1.0000	1.0000	1.0000	1.0000	1.0000	1.0000	1.0000	1.0000	1.0000	1.0000	1.0000	1.0000	1.0000
1	1.0100	1.0200	1.0300	1.0400	1.0500	1.0600	1.0700	1.0800	1.0900	1.1000	1.1100	1.1200	1.1500	1.1800	1.2000	1.2500	1.3000	1.4000	1.5000
2	1.0201	1.0404	1.0609	1.0816	1.1025	1.1236	1.1449	1.1664	1.1881	1.2100	1.2321	1.2544	1.3225	1.3924	1.4400	1.5625	1.6900	1.9600	2.2500
3	1.0303	1.0612	1.0927	1.1249	1.1576	1.1910	1.2250	1.2597	1.2950	1.3310	1.3676	1.4049	1.5209	1.6430	1.7280	1.9531	2.1970	2.7440	3.3750
4	1.0406	1.0824	1.1255	1.1699	1.2155	1.2625	1.3108	1.3605	1.4116	1.4641	1.5181	1.5735	1.7490	1.9388	2.0736	2.4414	2.8561	3.8416	5.0625
5	1.0510	1.1041	1.1593	1.2167	1.2763	1.3382	1.4026	1.4693	1.5386	1.6105	1.6851	1.7623	2.0114	2.2878	2.4883	3.0518	3.7129	5.3782	7.5938
6	1.0615	1.1262	1.1941	1.2653	1.3401	1.4185	1.5007	1.5869	1.6771	1.7716	1.8704	1.9738	2.3131	2.6996	2.9860	3.8147	4.8268	7.5295	11.3906
7	1.0721	1.1487	1.2299	1.3159	1.4071	1.5036	1.6058	1.7138	1.8280	1.9487	2.0762	2.2107	2.6600	3.1855	3.5832	4.7684	6.2749	10.5414	17.0859
8	1.0829	1.1717	1.2668	1.3686	1.4775	1.5938	1.7182	1.8509	1.9926	2.1436	2.3045	2.4760	3.0590	3.7589	4.2998	5.9605	8.1573	14.7579	25.6289
9	1.0937	1.1951	1.3048	1.4233	1.5513	1.6895	1.8385	1.9990	2.1719	2.3579	2.5580	2.7731	3.5179	4.4355	5.1598	7.4506	10.6045	20.6610	38.4434
10	1.1046	1.2190	1.3439	1.4802	1.6289	1.7908	1.9672	2.1589	2.3674	2.5937	2.8394	3.1058	4.0456	5.2338	6.1917	9.3132	13.7858	28.9255	57.6650
11	1.1157	1.2434	1.3842	1.5395	1.7103	1.8983	2.1049	2.3316	2.5804	2.8531	3.1518	3.4785	4.6524	6.1759	7.4301	11.6415	17.9216	40.4957	86.4976
12	1.1268	1.2682	1.4258	1.6010	1.7959	2.0122	2.2522	2.5182	2.8127	3.1384	3.4985	3.8960	5.3503	7.2876	8.9161	14.5519	23.2981	56.6939	129.7463
13	1.1381	1.2936	1.4685	1.6651	1.8856	2.1329	2.4098	2.7196	3.0658	3.4523	3.8833	4.3635	6.1528	8.5994	10.6993	18.1899	30.2875	79.3715	194.6195
14	1.1495	1.3195	1.5126	1.7317	1.9799	2.2609	2.5782	2.9372	3.3417	3.7975	4.3014	4.8871	7.0757	10.1472	12.8392	22.7374	39.3738	111.1201	291.9293
15	1.1610	1.3459	1.5580	1.8009	2.0789	2.3966	2.7590	3.1722	3.6425	4.1772	4.7846	5.4736	8.1371	11.9737	15.4070	28.4217	51.1859	155.5681	437.8939
16	1.1726	1.3728	1.6047	1.8730	2.1829	2.5404	2.9522	3.4259	3.9703	4.5950	5.3109	6.1304	9.3576	14.1290	18.4884	35.5271	66.5417	217.7953	656.8408
17	1.1843	1.4002	1.6528	1.9479	2.2920	2.6928	3.1588	3.7000	4.3276	5.0545	5.8951	6.8660	10.7613	16.6722	22.1861	44.4098	86.5042	304.9135	985.2613
18	1.1961	1.4282	1.7024	2.0258	2.4066	2.8543	3.3799	3.9960	4.7171	5.5599	6.5436	7.6900	12.3755	19.6733	26.6233	55.5112	112.4554	426.8789	1,477.8919
19	1.2081	1.4568	1.7535	2.1068	2.5270	3.0256	3.6165	4.3157	5.1417	6.1159	7.2633	8.6128	14.2318	23.2144	31.9480	69.3889	146.1920	597.6304	2,216.8378
20	1.2202	1.4859	1.8061	2.1911	2.6533	3.2071	3.8697	4.6610	5.6044	6.7275	8.0623	9.6463	16.3665	27.3930	38.3376	86.7362	190.0496	836.6826	3,325.2567
21	1.2324	1.5157	1.8603	2.2788	2.7860	3.3996	4.1406	5.0338	6.1088	7.4002	8.9492	10.8038	18.8215	32.3238	46.0051	108.4202	247.0645	1,171.3556	4,987.8851
22	1.2447	1.5460	1.9161	2.3699	2.9253	3.6035	4.4304	5.4365	6.6586	8.1403	9.9336	12.1003	21.6447	38.1421	55.2061	135.5253	321.1839	1,639.8978	7,481.8276
23	1.2572	1.5769	1.9736	2.4647	3.0715	3.8197	4.7405	5.8715	7.2579	8.9543	11.0263	13.5523	24.8915	45.0076	66.2474	169.4066	417.5391	2,295.8569	—
24	1.2697	1.6084	2.0328	2.5633	3.2251	4.0489	5.0724	6.3412	7.9111	9.8497	12.2392	15.1786	28.6252	53.1090	79.4968	211.7582	542.8008	3,214.1997	—
25	1.2824	1.6406	2.0938	2.6658	3.3864	4.2919	5.4274	6.8485	8.6231	10.8347	13.5855	17.0001	32.9190	62.6686	95.3962	264.6979	705.6410	4,499.8796	—
30	1.3478	1.8114	2.4273	3.2434	4.3219	5.7435	7.6123	10.0627	13.2677	17.4494	22.8923	29.9599	66.2118	143.3706	237.3763	807.7936	2,619.9956	—	—
35	1.4166	1.9999	2.8139	3.9461	5.5160	7.6861	10.6766	14.7853	20.4140	28.1024	38.5749	52.7996	133.1755	327.9973	590.6682	2,465.1903	9,727.8604	—	—
40	1.4889	2.2080	3.2620	4.8010	7.0400	10.2857	14.9745	21.7245	31.4094	45.2593	65.0009	93.0510	267.8635	750.3783	1,469.7716	7,523.1638	—	—	—
50	1.6446	2.6916	4.3839	7.1067	11.4674	18.4202	29.4570	46.9016	74.3575	117.3909	184.5648	289.0022	1,083.6574	3,927.3569	9,100.4382	—	—	—	—
60	1.8167	3.2810	5.8916	10.5196	18.6792	32.9877	57.9464	101.2571	176.0313	304.4816	524.0572	897.5969	4,383.9987	—	—	—	—	—	—

TABLE A.2   Present Value of $1 Lump Sum

$$PV_{r,n} = FV_{r,n}\,PVIF(r,n) = FV_{r,n}(1+r)^{-n}$$

n	1%	2%	3%	4%	5%	6%	7%	8%	9%	10%	11%	12%	15%	18%	20%	25%	30%	40%	50%
0	1.0000	1.0000	1.0000	1.0000	1.0000	1.0000	1.0000	1.0000	1.0000	1.0000	1.0000	1.0000	1.0000	1.0000	1.0000	1.0000	1.0000	1.0000	1.0000
1	0.9901	0.9804	0.9709	0.9615	0.9524	0.9534	0.9346	0.9259	0.9174	0.9091	0.9009	0.8929	0.8696	0.8475	0.8333	0.8000	0.7692	0.7143	0.6667
2	0.9803	0.9612	0.9426	0.9246	0.9070	0.8900	0.8734	0.8573	0.8417	0.8264	0.8116	0.7972	0.7561	0.7182	0.6944	0.6400	0.5917	0.5102	0.4444
3	0.9706	0.9426	0.9151	0.8890	0.8638	0.8396	0.8163	0.7938	0.7722	0.7513	0.7312	0.7118	0.6575	0.6086	0.5787	0.5120	0.4552	0.3644	0.2963
4	0.9610	0.9238	0.8885	0.8548	0.8227	0.7921	0.7629	0.7350	0.7084	0.6830	0.6587	0.6355	0.5718	0.5158	0.4823	0.4096	0.3501	0.2603	0.1975
5	0.9515	0.9057	0.8626	0.8219	0.7835	0.7473	0.7130	0.6806	0.6499	0.6209	0.5935	0.5674	0.4972	0.4371	0.4019	0.3277	0.2693	0.1859	0.1317
6	0.9420	0.8880	0.8375	0.7903	0.7462	0.7050	0.6663	0.6302	0.5963	0.5645	0.5346	0.5066	0.4323	0.3704	0.3349	0.2621	0.2072	0.1328	0.0878
7	0.9327	0.8706	0.8131	0.7599	0.7107	0.6651	0.6227	0.5835	0.5470	0.5132	0.4817	0.4523	0.3759	0.3139	0.2791	0.2097	0.1594	0.0949	0.0585
8	0.9235	0.8535	0.7894	0.7307	0.6768	0.6274	0.5820	0.5403	0.5019	0.4665	0.4339	0.4039	0.3269	0.2660	0.2326	0.1678	0.1226	0.0678	0.0390
9	0.9143	0.8368	0.7664	0.7026	0.6446	0.5919	0.5439	0.5002	0.4604	0.4241	0.3909	0.3606	0.2843	0.2255	0.1938	0.1342	0.0943	0.0484	0.0260
10	0.9053	0.8203	0.7441	0.6756	0.6139	0.5584	0.5083	0.4632	0.4224	0.3855	0.3522	0.3220	0.2472	0.1911	0.1615	0.1074	0.0725	0.0346	0.0173
11	0.8963	0.8043	0.7224	0.6496	0.5847	0.5268	0.4751	0.4289	0.3875	0.3505	0.3173	0.2875	0.2149	0.1619	0.1346	0.0859	0.0558	0.0247	0.0116
12	0.8874	0.7885	0.7014	0.6246	0.5568	0.4970	0.4440	0.3971	0.3555	0.3186	0.2858	0.2567	0.1869	0.1372	0.1122	0.0687	0.0429	0.0176	0.0077
13	0.8787	0.7730	0.6810	0.6006	0.5303	0.4688	0.4150	0.3677	0.3262	0.2897	0.2575	0.2292	0.1625	0.1163	0.0935	0.0550	0.0330	0.0126	0.0051
14	0.8700	0.7579	0.6611	0.5775	0.5051	0.4423	0.3878	0.3405	0.2992	0.2633	0.2320	0.2046	0.1413	0.0985	0.0779	0.0440	0.0254	0.0090	0.0034
15	0.8613	0.7430	0.6419	0.5553	0.4810	0.4173	0.3624	0.3152	0.2745	0.2394	0.2090	0.1827	0.1229	0.0835	0.0649	0.0352	0.0195	0.0064	0.0023
16	0.8528	0.7284	0.6232	0.5339	0.4581	0.3936	0.3387	0.2919	0.2519	0.2176	0.1883	0.1631	0.1069	0.0708	0.0541	0.0281	0.0150	0.0046	0.0015
17	0.8444	0.7142	0.6050	0.5134	0.4363	0.3714	0.3166	0.2703	0.2311	0.1978	0.1696	0.1456	0.0929	0.0600	0.0451	0.0225	0.0116	0.0033	0.0010
18	0.8360	0.7002	0.5874	0.4936	0.4155	0.3503	0.2959	0.2502	0.2120	0.1799	0.1528	0.1300	0.0808	0.0508	0.0376	0.0180	0.0089	0.0023	0.0007
19	0.8277	0.6864	0.5703	0.4746	0.3957	0.3305	0.2765	0.2317	0.1945	0.1635	0.1377	0.1161	0.0703	0.0431	0.0313	0.0144	0.0068	0.0017	0.0005
20	0.8195	0.6730	0.5537	0.4564	0.3769	0.3118	0.2584	0.2145	0.1784	0.1486	0.1240	0.1037	0.0611	0.0365	0.0261	0.0115	0.0053	0.0012	0.0003
21	0.8114	0.6598	0.5375	0.4388	0.3589	0.2942	0.2415	0.1987	0.1637	0.1351	0.1117	0.0926	0.0531	0.0309	0.0217	0.0092	0.0040	0.0009	0.0002
22	0.8034	0.6468	0.5219	0.4220	0.3418	0.2775	0.2257	0.1839	0.1502	0.1228	0.1007	0.0826	0.0462	0.0262	0.0181	0.0074	0.0031	0.0006	0.0001
23	0.7954	0.6342	0.5067	0.4057	0.3256	0.2618	0.2109	0.1703	0.1378	0.1117	0.0907	0.0738	0.0402	0.0222	0.0151	0.0059	0.0024	0.0004	0.0001
24	0.7876	0.6217	0.4919	0.3901	0.3101	0.2470	0.1971	0.1577	0.1264	0.1015	0.0817	0.0659	0.0349	0.0188	0.0126	0.0047	0.0018	0.0003	0.0001
25	0.7798	0.6095	0.4776	0.3751	0.2953	0.2330	0.1842	0.1460	0.1160	0.0923	0.0736	0.0588	0.0304	0.0160	0.0105	0.0038	0.0014	0.0002	0.0000
30	0.7419	0.5521	0.4120	0.3083	0.2314	0.1741	0.1314	0.0994	0.0754	0.0573	0.0437	0.0334	0.0151	0.0070	0.0042	0.0012	0.0004	0.0000	0.0000
35	0.7059	0.5000	0.3554	0.2534	0.1813	0.1301	0.0937	0.0676	0.0490	0.0356	0.0259	0.0189	0.0075	0.0030	0.0017	0.0004	0.0001	0.0000	0.0000
40	0.6717	0.4529	0.3066	0.2083	0.1420	0.0972	0.0668	0.0460	0.0318	0.0221	0.0154	0.0107	0.0037	0.0013	0.0007	0.0001	0.0000	0.0000	0.0000
50	0.6080	0.3715	0.2281	0.1407	0.0872	0.0543	0.0339	0.0213	0.0134	0.0085	0.0054	0.0035	0.0009	0.0003	0.0001	0.0000	0.0000	0.0000	0.0000
60	0.5504	0.3048	0.1697	0.0951	0.0535	0.0303	0.0173	0.0099	0.0057	0.0033	0.0019	0.0011	0.0002	0.0000	0.0000	0.0000	0.0000	0.0000	0.0000

TABLE A.3 | Future Value of $1 Annuity

$$FVA_{r,t} = a\ FVIFA\ (r,t) \equiv a[(1+r)^n - 1]/r$$

	1%	2%	3%	4%	5%	6%	7%	8%	9%	10%	11%	12%	15%	18%	20%	25%	30%	40%	50%
1	1.0000	1.0000	1.0000	1.0000	1.0000	1.0000	1.0000	1.0000	1.0000	1.0000	1.0000	1.0000	1.0000	1.0000	1.0000	1.0000	1.0000	1.0000	1.0000
2	2.0100	2.0200	2.0300	2.0400	2.0500	2.0600	2.0700	2.0800	2.0900	2.1000	2.1100	2.1200	2.1500	2.1800	2.2000	2.2500	2.3000	2.4000	2.5000
3	3.0301	3.0604	3.0909	3.1216	3.1525	3.1836	3.2149	3.2464	3.2781	3.3100	3.3421	3.3744	3.4725	3.5724	3.6400	3.8125	3.9900	4.3600	4.7500
4	4.0604	4.1216	4.1836	4.2465	4.3101	4.3746	4.4399	4.5061	4.5731	4.6410	4.7097	4.7793	4.9934	5.2154	5.3680	5.7656	6.1870	7.1040	8.1250
5	5.1010	5.2040	5.3091	5.4163	5.5256	5.6371	5.7507	5.8666	5.9847	6.1051	6.2278	6.3528	6.7424	7.1542	7.4416	8.2070	9.0431	10.9456	13.1875
6	6.1520	6.3081	6.4684	6.6330	6.8019	6.9753	7.1533	7.3359	7.5233	7.7156	7.9129	8.1152	8.7537	9.4420	9.9299	11.2588	12.7560	16.3238	20.7813
7	7.2135	7.4343	7.6625	7.8983	8.1420	8.3938	8.6540	8.9228	9.2004	9.4872	9.7833	10.0890	11.0668	12.1415	12.9159	15.0735	17.5828	23.8534	32.1719
8	8.2857	8.5830	8.8923	9.2142	9.5491	9.8975	10.2598	10.6366	11.0285	11.4359	11.8594	12.2997	13.7268	15.3270	16.4991	19.8419	23.8577	34.3947	49.2578
9	9.3685	9.7546	10.1591	10.5828	11.0266	11.4913	11.9780	12.4876	13.0210	13.5795	14.1640	14.7757	16.7858	19.0859	20.7989	25.8023	32.0150	49.1526	74.8867
10	10.4622	10.9497	11.4639	12.0061	12.5779	13.1808	13.8164	14.4866	15.1929	15.9374	16.7220	17.5487	20.3037	23.5213	25.9587	33.2529	42.6195	69.8137	113.3301
11	11.5668	12.1687	12.8078	13.4864	14.2068	14.9716	15.7836	16.6455	17.5603	18.5312	19.5614	20.6546	24.3493	28.7551	32.1504	42.5661	56.4053	98.7391	170.9951
12	12.6825	13.4121	14.1920	15.0258	15.9171	16.8699	17.8885	18.9771	20.1407	21.3843	22.7132	24.1331	29.0017	34.9311	39.5805	54.2077	74.3270	139.2348	257.4927
13	13.8093	14.6803	15.6178	16.6268	17.7130	18.8821	20.1406	21.4953	22.9534	24.5227	26.2116	28.0291	34.3519	42.2187	48.4966	68.7596	97.6250	195.9287	387.2390
14	14.9474	15.9739	17.0863	18.2919	19.5986	21.0151	22.5505	24.2149	26.0192	27.9750	30.0949	32.3926	40.5047	50.8180	59.1959	86.9495	127.9125	275.3002	581.8585
15	16.0969	17.2934	18.5989	20.0236	21.5786	23.2760	25.1290	27.1521	29.3609	31.7725	34.4054	37.2797	47.5804	60.9653	72.0351	109.6868	167.2863	386.4202	873.7878
16	17.2579	18.6393	20.1569	21.8245	23.6575	25.6725	27.8881	30.3243	33.0034	35.9497	39.1899	42.7533	55.7175	72.9390	87.4421	138.1085	218.4722	541.9883	1,311.6817
17	18.4304	20.0121	21.7616	23.6975	25.8404	28.2129	30.8402	33.7502	36.9737	40.5447	44.5008	48.8837	65.0751	87.0680	105.9306	173.6357	285.0139	759.7837	1,968.5225
18	19.6147	21.4123	23.4144	25.6454	28.1324	30.9057	33.9990	37.4502	41.3013	45.5992	50.3959	55.7497	75.8364	103.7403	128.1167	218.0446	371.5180	1,064.6971	2,953.7838
19	20.8109	22.8406	25.1169	27.6712	30.5390	33.7600	37.3790	41.4463	46.0185	51.1591	56.9395	63.4397	88.2118	123.4135	154.7400	273.5558	483.9734	1,491.5760	4,431.6756
20	22.0190	24.2974	26.8704	29.7781	33.0660	36.7856	40.9955	45.7620	51.1601	57.2750	64.2028	72.0524	102.4436	146.6280	186.6880	342.9447	630.1655	2,089.2064	6,648.5135
21	23.2392	25.7833	28.6765	31.9692	35.7193	39.9927	44.8652	50.4229	56.7645	64.0025	72.2651	81.6987	118.8101	174.0210	225.0256	429.6809	820.2151	2,925.8889	9,973.7702
22	24.4716	27.2990	30.5368	34.2480	38.5052	43.3923	49.0057	55.4568	62.8733	71.4027	81.2143	92.5026	137.6316	206.3448	271.0307	538.1011	1,067.2796	4,097.2445	–
23	25.7163	28.8450	32.4529	36.6179	41.4305	46.9958	53.4361	60.8933	69.5319	79.5430	91.1479	104.6029	159.2764	244.4868	326.2369	673.6264	1,388.4635	5,737.1423	–
24	26.9735	30.4219	34.4265	39.0826	44.5020	50.8156	58.1767	66.7648	76.7898	88.4973	102.1742	118.1552	184.1678	289.4945	392.4842	843.0329	1,806.0026	8,032.9993	–
25	28.2432	32.0303	36.4593	41.6459	47.7271	54.8645	63.2490	73.1059	84.7009	98.3471	114.4133	133.3339	212.7930	342.6035	471.9811	1,054.7912	2,348.8033	–	–
30	34.7849	40.5681	47.5754	56.0849	66.4388	79.0582	94.4608	113.2832	136.3075	164.4940	199.0209	241.3327	434.7451	790.9480	1,181.8816	3,227.1743	8,729.9855	–	–
35	41.6603	49.9945	60.4621	73.6522	90.3203	111.4348	138.2369	172.3168	215.7108	271.0244	341.5896	431.6635	881.1702	1,816.6516	2,948.3411	9,856.7613	–	–	–
40	48.8864	60.4020	75.4013	95.0255	120.7998	154.7620	199.6351	259.0565	337.8824	442.5926	581.8261	767.0914	1,779.0903	4,163.2130	7,343.8578	–	–	–	–
50	64.4632	84.5794	112.7969	152.6671	209.3480	290.3359	406.5289	573.7702	815.0836	1,163.9085	1,668.7712	2,400.0182	7,217.7163	–	–	–	–	–	–
60	81.6697	114.0515	163.0534	237.9907	353.5837	533.1282	813.5204	1,253.2133	1,944.7921	3,034.8164	4,755.0658	7,471.6411	–	–	–	–	–	–	–

TABLE A.4   Present Value of $1 Annuity

$$PVA_{r,t} = a\ PVIFA\ (r,t) \equiv a[1 - (1 + r)^{-n}]/r$$

n	1%	2%	3%	4%	5%	6%	7%	8%	9%	10%	11%	12%	15%	18%	20%	25%	30%	40%	50%
1	0.9901	0.9804	0.9709	0.9615	0.9524	0.9434	0.9346	0.9259	0.9174	0.9091	0.9009	0.8929	0.8696	0.8475	0.8333	0.8000	0.7692	0.7143	0.6667
2	1.9704	1.9416	1.9135	1.8861	1.8594	1.8334	1.8080	1.7833	1.7591	1.7355	1.7125	1.6901	1.6257	1.5656	1.5278	1.4400	1.3609	1.2245	1.1111
3	2.9410	2.8839	2.8286	2.7751	2.7232	2.6730	2.6243	2.5771	2.5313	2.4869	2.4437	2.4018	2.2832	2.1743	2.1065	1.9520	1.8161	1.5889	1.4074
4	3.9020	3.8077	3.7171	3.6299	3.5460	3.4651	3.3872	3.3121	3.2397	3.1699	3.1024	3.0373	2.8550	2.6901	2.5887	2.3616	2.1662	1.8492	1.6049
5	4.8534	4.7135	4.5797	4.4518	4.3295	4.2124	4.1002	3.9927	3.8897	3.7908	3.6959	3.6048	3.3522	3.1272	2.9906	2.6893	2.4356	2.0352	1.7366
6	5.7955	5.6014	5.4172	5.2421	5.0757	4.9173	4.7665	4.6229	4.4859	4.3553	4.2305	4.1114	3.7845	3.4976	3.3255	2.9514	2.6427	2.1680	1.8244
7	6.7282	6.4720	6.2303	6.0021	5.7864	5.5824	5.3893	5.2064	5.0330	4.8684	4.7122	4.5638	4.1604	3.8115	3.6046	3.1611	2.8021	2.2628	1.8829
8	7.6517	7.3255	7.0197	6.7327	6.4632	6.2098	5.9713	5.7466	5.5348	5.3349	5.1461	4.9676	4.4873	4.0776	3.8372	3.3289	2.9247	2.3306	1.9220
9	8.5660	8.1622	7.7861	7.4353	7.1078	6.8017	6.5152	6.2469	5.9952	5.7590	5.5370	5.3282	4.7716	4.3030	4.0310	3.4631	3.0190	2.3790	1.9480
10	9.4713	8.9826	8.5302	8.1109	7.7217	7.3601	7.0236	6.7101	6.4177	6.1446	5.8892	5.6502	5.0188	4.4941	4.1925	3.5705	3.0915	2.4136	1.9653
11	10.3676	9.7868	9.2526	8.7605	8.3064	7.8869	7.4987	7.1390	6.8052	6.4951	6.2065	5.9377	5.2337	4.6560	4.3271	3.6564	3.1473	2.4383	1.9769
12	11.2551	10.5753	9.9540	9.3851	8.8633	8.3838	7.9427	7.5361	7.1607	6.8137	6.4924	6.1944	5.4206	4.7932	4.4392	3.7251	3.1903	2.4559	1.9846
13	12.1337	11.3484	10.6350	9.9856	9.3936	8.8527	8.3577	7.9038	7.4869	7.1034	6.7499	6.4235	5.5831	4.9095	4.5327	3.7801	3.2233	2.4685	1.9897
14	13.0037	12.1062	11.2961	10.5631	9.8986	9.2950	8.7455	8.2442	7.7862	7.3667	6.9819	6.6282	5.7245	5.0081	4.6106	3.8241	3.2487	2.4775	1.9931
15	13.8651	12.8493	11.9379	11.1184	10.3797	9.7122	9.1079	8.5595	8.0607	7.6061	7.1909	6.8109	5.8474	5.0916	4.6755	3.8593	3.2682	2.4839	1.9954
16	14.7179	13.5777	12.5611	11.6523	10.8378	10.1059	9.4466	8.8514	8.3126	7.8237	7.3792	6.9740	5.9542	5.1624	4.7296	3.8874	3.2832	2.4885	1.9970
17	15.5623	14.2919	13.1661	12.1657	11.2741	10.4773	9.7632	9.1216	8.5436	8.0216	7.5488	7.1196	6.0472	5.2223	4.7746	3.9099	3.2948	2.4918	1.9980
18	16.3983	14.9920	13.7535	12.6593	11.6896	10.8276	10.0591	9.3719	8.7556	8.2014	7.7016	7.2497	6.1280	5.2732	4.8122	3.9279	3.3037	2.4941	1.9986
19	17.2260	15.6785	14.3238	13.1339	12.0853	11.1581	10.3356	9.6036	8.9501	8.3649	7.8393	7.3658	6.1982	5.3162	4.8435	3.9424	3.3105	2.4958	1.9991
20	18.0456	16.3514	14.8775	13.5903	12.4622	11.4699	10.5940	9.8181	9.1285	8.5136	7.9633	7.4694	6.2593	5.3527	4.8696	3.9539	3.3158	2.4970	1.9994
21	18.8570	17.0112	15.4150	14.0292	12.8212	11.7641	10.8355	10.0168	9.2922	8.6487	8.0751	7.5620	6.3125	5.3837	4.8913	3.9631	3.3198	2.4979	1.9996
22	19.6604	17.6580	15.9369	14.4511	13.1630	12.0416	11.0612	10.2007	9.4424	8.7715	8.1757	7.6446	6.3587	5.4099	4.9094	3.9705	3.3230	2.4985	1.9997
23	20.4558	18.2922	16.4436	14.8568	13.4886	12.3034	11.2722	10.3711	9.5802	8.8832	8.2664	7.7184	6.3988	5.4321	4.9245	3.9764	3.3254	2.4989	1.9998
24	21.2434	18.9139	16.9355	15.2470	13.7986	12.5504	11.4693	10.5288	9.7066	8.9847	8.3481	7.7843	6.4338	5.4509	4.9371	3.9811	3.3272	2.4992	1.9999
25	22.0232	19.5235	17.4131	15.6221	14.0939	12.7834	11.6536	10.6748	9.8226	9.0770	8.4217	7.8431	6.4641	5.4669	4.9476	3.9849	3.3286	2.4994	1.9999
30	25.8077	22.3965	19.6004	17.2920	15.3725	13.7648	12.4090	11.2578	10.2737	9.4269	8.6938	8.0552	6.5660	5.5168	4.9789	3.9950	3.3321	2.4999	2.0000
35	29.4086	24.9986	21.4872	18.6646	16.3742	14.4982	12.9477	11.6546	10.5668	9.6442	8.8552	8.1755	6.6166	5.5386	4.9915	3.9984	3.3330	2.4999	2.0000
40	32.8347	27.3555	23.1148	19.7928	17.1591	15.0463	13.3317	11.9246	10.7574	9.7791	8.9511	8.2438	6.6418	5.5482	4.9966	3.9995	3.3332	2.5000	2.0000
50	39.1961	31.4236	25.7298	21.4822	18.2559	15.7619	13.8007	12.2335	10.9617	9.9148	9.0417	8.3045	6.6605	5.5541	4.9995	3.9999	3.3333	2.5000	2.0000
60	44.9550	34.7609	27.6756	22.6235	18.9293	16.1614	14.0392	12.3766	11.0480	9.9672	9.0736	8.3240	6.6651	5.5553	4.9999	4.0000	3.3333	2.5000	2.0000

Financial Calculators

CONTENTS

This appendix discusses the functionality of two popular, inexpensive financial calculators:

HEWLETT-PACKARD HP-10B

The Hewlett-Packard HP-10B business calculator is a versatile, easy-to-use tool providing both basic and advanced financial functions. Students should have little difficulty using its powerful features to solve numerous problems in the introductory corporate finance course. Before beginning a new problem, users should:

- Clear the display and financial registers by pressing
  [____] {CLEAR ALL}. (Press [C] to clear just the display).

- Set the display format to four decimal places by pressing
  [____] {DISP} 4.

- Set the compounding frequency to 1x per period by pressing
  1 [____] {P/YR}. (The default setting is 12x per period).

- Set payments to occur at the *end* of a period. This is the default setting; pressing
  [____] {BEG/END} toggles between 'Begin' and 'End' mode. The 'BEGIN' annunciator should NOT appear in the display.

The *HP-10B* should remember the latter three settings even after the calculator is turned off. However, random cosmic rays have been known to erase these settings, so check them every once in a while.

Present Value/Future Value of a Single Sum

Katie has $5,000 in an account paying interest at a rate of 3 percent, compounded annually. What will her account balance be at the end of five years?	−5,000.00 [PV]
	3.00 [I/YR]
Katie will have $5,796.37 in her account at the end of five years.	5.00 [N]
	[FV] 5,796.37

This information first appeared in *Financial Practice and Education* (Fall/Winter, 1991, pp. 73–88) as **Hewlett Packard HP-10B** by Mark White. It is used with permission from the Financial Management Association International, College of Business Administration #3331, University of South Florida, Tampa, FL 33620-5500, (813) 974-2084.

HP ISBN 0-07-231872-4

Present Value of an Annuity

-50,000.00	PV
12.00	I/YR
10.00	N
PMT	**8,849.21**

Skye just won first prize in the Colossal Lottery. He can choose between $50,000 in cash *now*, or its equivalent paid out in ten annual payments at an interest rate of 12 percent. What will his annual payments be under the second alternative?

Skye's payments are $8,849.21.

Finding an Unknown Interest Rate

-10,000.00	PV
18.00	N
80,000.00	FV
I/YR	**12.25**

Zachary's parents anticipate that a college education will cost $80,000 when he enters school in 18 years. They presently have $10,000 to invest. What rate of return must they earn to cover the cost of his education?

Zachary's parents will need to earn a 12.25% annual return.

Finding an Unknown Number of Periods

-16,000.00	PV
6.00	I/YR
20,000.00	FV
N	**3.83**

Holly is saving to buy a $20,000 speedboat to take to the lake. She has $16,000 in an account paying 6 percent annual interest. How long will it be before she will have enough to buy the boat?

She will have saved enough to purchase the boat in 3.83 years.

Simple Bond Pricing

30.00	PMT
1,000.00	FV
4.00	I/YR
10.00	N
PV	**-918.89**

How much should a rational investor pay for a 5-year, 6 percent *semiannual* coupon bond? The bond has a $1,000 par value and an 8 percent yield to maturity.

The bond's price is $918.89.

Simple Bond Yields to Maturity

-1,100.00	PV
80.00	PMT
1,000.00	FV
10.00	N
I/YR	**6.60**

What is the yield to maturity (YTM) on a 10-year, 8 percent annual coupon bond currently selling for $1,100?

The bond has a YTM of 6.60%.

Investment Analysis using NPV and IRR

-85,000.00	CF_j
30,000.00	CF_j
25,000.00	CF_j
3.00	N_j
10.00	I/YR
{NPV}	**-1,207.91**
{IRR/YR}	**9.32**

The Reid Group has identified an investment project with the following schedule of cash flows. Use the net present value (NPV) and internal rate of return (IRR) criteria to determine whether to accept or reject this project. Assume a 10% hurdle rate.

Year 0:   -$85,000
Year 1: $30,000
Year 2: $25,000
Year 3: $25,000
Year 4: $25,000

The project should be rejected as its NPV of -$1,207.91 is negative and its IRR of 9.32% is less than the hurdle rate.

TEXAS INSTRUMENTS BA II PLUS

Texas Instrument's *BA II Plus* business calculator boasts many useful features and uses a unique system of worksheets for data entry and problem solution. Students will find its powerful financial functions to be very helpful in solving problems in the introductory corporate finance course. Before beginning a new problem, users should:

- Clear the financial registers by pressing 2nd {CLR TVM}. Press CE/C to clear the display.

- Set the display to four decimals by first pressing 2nd {Format} to enter the format worksheet, then pressing 4 ENTER .

- Set the compounding frequency to 1x per period (the default setting is 12x per period) by first pressing 2nd {P/Y} to enter the payment worksheet, then pressing 1 ENTER ▼ 1 ENTER .

- Set payments to occur at the *end* of a period. This is the default setting. Pressing 2nd {BGN} 2nd {SET} toggles between 'Begin' and 'End' modes. The 'BGN' annunciator should NOT appear in the display.

The *BA II Plus* should remember the latter three settings even after the calculator is turned off. However, random cosmic rays have been known to erase these settings, so check them every once in a while.

Present Value/Future Value of a Single Sum

Katie has $5,000 in an account paying interest at a rate of 3 percent, compounded annually. What will her account balance be at the end of five years?	−5,000.00 PV 3.00 I/YR 5.00 N
Katie will have $5,796.37 in her account at the end of five years.	CPT FV 5,796.37

This information first appeared in *Financial Practice and Education* (Fall, 1993, Vol. 3, No. 2) as **Financial Problem Solving with an Electronic Calculator: Texas Instruments' BAII Plus** by Mark White. It is used with permission from the Financial Management Association International, College of Business Administration #3331, University of South Florida, Tampa, FL 33620-5500, (813) 974-2084.

TI ISBN 0-07-231873-2

Present Value of an Annuity

Skye just won first prize in the Colossal Lottery. He can choose between $50,000 in cash *now*, or its equivalent paid out in ten annual payments at an interest rate of 12 percent. What will his annual payments be under the second alternative?

Skye's payments are $8,849.21.

−50,000.00	PV	
12.00	I/Y	
10.00	N	
CPT	PMT	8,849.21

Finding an Unknown Interest Rate

Zachary's parents anticipate that a college education will cost $80,000 when he enters school in 18 years. They presently have $10,000 to invest. What rate of return must they earn to cover the cost of his education?

Zachary's parents will need to earn a 12.25% annual return.

−10,000.00	PV	
18.00	N	
80,000.00	FV	
CPT	I/Y	12.25

Finding an Unknown Number of Periods

Holly is saving to buy a $20,000 speedboat to take to the lake. She has $16,000 in an account paying 6 percent annual interest. How long will it be before she will have enough to buy the boat?

She will have saved enough to purchase the boat in 3.83 years.

−16,000.00	PV	
6.00	I/Y	
20,000.00	FV	
CPT	N	3.83

Simple Bond Pricing

How much should a rational investor pay for a 5-year, 6 percent *semiannual* coupon bond? The bond has a $1,000 par value and an 8 percent yield to maturity.

The bond's price is $918.89.

30.00	PMT	
1,000.00	FV	
4.00	I/Y	
10.00	N	
CPT	PV	−918.89

Simple Bond Yields to Maturity

What is the yield to maturity (YTM) on a 10-year, 8 percent annual coupon bond currently selling for $1,100?

The bond has a YTM of 6.60%.

−1,100.00	PV	
80.00	PMT	
1,000.00	FV	
10.00	N	
CPT	I/Y	6.60

Investment Analysis using NPV and IRR

The Reid Group has identified an investment project with the following schedule of cash flows. Use the net present value (NPV) and internal rate of return (IRR) criteria to determine whether to accept or reject this project. Assume a 10% hurdle rate.

Year 0:	−$85,000
Year 1:	$30,000
Year 2:	$25,000
Year 3:	$25,000
Year 4:	$25,000

The project should be rejected as its NPV of −$1,207.91 is negative and its IRR of 9.32% is less than the hurdle rate.

CF		
2nd	{CLR Work}	
−85,000.00	ENTER	▶
30,000.00	ENTER	▶
1.00	ENTER	▶
25,000.00	ENTER	▶
3.00	ENTER	▶
NPV		
10.00	ENTER	
▶	CPT	−1,207.91
IRR	CPT	9.32

Common Excel Financial Functions

CONTENTS

This appendix presents seven common financial functions incorporated into Excel. The seven functions correspond to the discussion in Chapter 3, Time and Value. The functions include:

The following pages provide overview descriptions of the financial functions and the process to use the functions. For a more in depth discussion including illustrative examples, please reference the topic within the Excel help function.

FV

Returns the future value of an investment based on periodic constant payments and a constant interest rate.

$$FV(rate,nper,pmt,pv,type)$$

Rate is the interest rate per period.

Nper is the total number of payment periods in an annuity.

Pmt is the payment made each period; it cannot change over the life of the annuity. Typically, pmt contains principal and interest but no other fees or taxes. If pmt is omitted, you must include the pv argument.

Pv is the present value, or the lump sum amount that a series of future payments is worth right now. If pv is omitted, it is assumed to be 0 (zero), and you must include the pmt argument.

Type is the number 0 (end of the period) or 1 (beginning of the period) and indicates when payments are due. If type is omitted, it is assumed to be 0.

PV

Returns the present value of an investment. The present value is the total amount that a series of future payments is worth now. For example, when you borrow money, the loan amount is the present value to the lender.

$$PV(rate,nper,pmt,fv,type)$$

Rate is the interest rate per period. For example, if you obtain an automobile loan at a 10 percent annual interest rate and make monthly payments, your interest rate per month is 10%/12, or 0.83%. You would enter 10%/12, or 0.83%, or 0.0083, into the formula as the rate.

Nper is the total number of payment periods in an annuity. For example, if you get a 4-year car loan and make monthly payments, your loan has 4*12 (or 48) periods. You would enter 48 into the formula for nper.

Pmt is the payment made each period and cannot change over the life of the annuity. Typically, pmt includes principal and interest but no other fees or taxes. For example, the monthly payments on a $10,000, four-year car loan at 12% are $263.33. You would enter -263.33 into the formula as the pmt. If pmt is omitted, you must include the fv argument.

Fv is the future value, or a cash balance you want to attain after the last payment is made. If fv is omitted, it is assumed to be 0 (the future value of a loan, for example, is 0). For example, if you want to save $50,000 to pay for a special project in 18 years, then $50,000 is the future value. You could then make a conservative guess at an interest rate and determine how much you must save each month. If fv is omitted, you must include the pmt argument.

Type is the number 0 (end) or 1 (beginning) and indicates when payments are due.

NPV

Calculates the net present value of an investment by using a discount rate and a series of future payments (negative values) and income (positive values).

$$NPV(rate, value1, value2, ...)$$

Rate is the rate of discount over the length of one period.
Value1, value2, ... are 1 to 29 arguments representing the payments and income.
Caution: NPV assumes that the first cash flow occurs in year 1 not in year 0!

PMT

Calculates the payment for a loan based on constant payments and a constant interest rate.

$$PMT(rate, nper, pv, fv, type)$$

Rate is the interest rate for the loan.
Nper is the total number of payments for the loan.
Pv is the present value, or the total amount that a series of future payments is worth now; also known as the principal.
Fv is the future value, or a cash balance you want to attain after the last payment is made. If fv is omitted, it is assumed to be 0 (zero); that is, the future value of a loan is 0.
Type is the number 0 (end) or 1 (beginning) and indicates when payments are due.

RATE

Returns the interest rate per period of an annuity. RATE is calculated by iteration and can have zero or more solutions. If the successive results of RATE do not converge to within 0.0000001 after 20 iterations, RATE returns the #NUM! error value.

$$RATE(nper, pmt, pv, fv, type, guess)$$

For a complete description of the arguments nper, pmt, pv, fv, and type, see PV.
Nper is the total number of payment periods in an annuity.
Pmt is the payment made each period and cannot change over the life of the annuity. Typically, pmt includes principal and interest but no other fees or taxes. If pmt is omitted, you must include the fv argument.
Pv is the present value – the total amount that a series of future payments is worth now.
Fv is the future value, or a cash balance you want to attain after the last payment is made. If fv is omitted, it is assumed to be 0 (the future value of a loan, for example, is 0).
Type is the number 0 (end) or 1 (beginning) and indicates when payments are due.

NPER

Returns the number of periods for an investment based on periodic, constant payments and a constant interest rate.

$$NPER(rate, pmt, pv, fv, type)$$

For a more complete description of the arguments in NPER and for more information about annuity functions, see PV.

Rate is the interest rate per period.

Pmt is the payment made each period; it cannot change over the life of the annuity. Typically, pmt contains principal and interest but no other fees or taxes.

Pv is the present value, or the lump sum amount that a series of future payments is worth right now.

Fv is the future value, or a cash balance you want to attain after the last payment is made. If fv is omitted, it is assumed to be 0 (the future value of a loan, for example, is 0).

Type is the number 0 (end) or 1 (beginning) and indicates when payments are due.

EFFECT

Returns the effective annual interest rate, given the nominal annual interest rate (also called the annual percentage rate or APR) and the number of compounding periods per year.

$$EFFECT(nominal\_rate, npery)$$

Nominal_rate is the nominal interest rate.

Npery is the number of compounding periods per year.

Common Excel Financial Functions for Bond Valuation

The following discussion provides overview descriptions of the financial functions and the process to use the functions. For a more in depth discussion including illustrative examples, please reference the topic within the Excel help function.

Price

Returns the price per $100 face value of a security that pays periodic interest.

PRICE(settlement,maturity,rate,yld,redemption,frequency,basis)

Important: Dates should be entered by using the DATE function, or as results of other formulas or functions. For example, use DATE(2008,5,23) for the 23rd day of May, 2008. *Problems can occur if dates are entered as text.*
Settlement is the security's settlement date. The security settlement date is the date after the issue date when the security is traded to the buyer.
Maturity is the security's maturity date. The maturity date is the date when the security expires.
Rate is the security's annual coupon rate.
Yld is the security's annual yield.
Redemption is the security's redemption value per $100 face value.
Frequency is the number of coupon payments per year. For annual payments, frequency = 1; for semiannual, frequency = 2; for quarterly, frequency = 4.
Basis is the type of day count basis to use.

Basis	Day count basis
0 or omitted	US (NASD) 30/360
1	Actual/actual
2	Actual/360
3	Actual/365
4	European 30/360

Yield

Returns the yield on a security that pays periodic interest. Use YIELD to calculate bond yield.

YIELD(settlement,maturity,rate,pr,redemption,frequency,basis)

Important: Dates should be entered by using the DATE function, or as results of other formulas or functions. For example, use DATE(2008,5,23) for the 23rd day of May, 2008. *Problems can occur if dates are entered as text.*
Settlement is the security's settlement date. The security settlement date is the date after the issue date when the security is traded to the buyer.
Maturity is the security's maturity date. The maturity date is the date when the security expires.
Rate is the security's annual coupon rate.
Pr is the security's price per $100 face value.
Redemption is the security's redemption value per $100 face value.
Frequency is the number of coupon payments per year. For annual payments, frequency = 1; for semiannual, frequency = 2; for quarterly, frequency = 4.
Basis is the type of day count basis to use (see Price for more details).

Common Excel Financial Functions for Capital Investment Decisions

The following material provides overview descriptions of the financial functions and the processes by which they are used. For a more in-depth discussion (including illustrative examples), research the topic within the Excel help function.

NPV

Calculates the NPV of an investment by using a discount rate and a series of future payments (negative values) and income (positive values).

$$NPV(rate,value1,value2, . . .)$$

Here, *rate* is the rate of discount over the length of one period, and *value1*, *value2*, and so on are 1 to 29 arguments representing the payments and income. The variables *value1*, *value2*, and so on must be equally spaced in time and occur at the end of each period. *NPV* uses the order of *value1*, *value2*, and so on to interpret the order of cash flows. Be sure to enter your payment and income values in the correct sequence.

Arguments that are numbers, empty cells, logical values, or text representations of numbers are counted. Arguments that are error values or text that cannot be translated into numbers are ignored.

If an argument is an array or reference, only numbers in that array or reference are counted. Empty cells, logical values, text, or error values in the array or reference are ignored.

IRR

Returns the IRR for a series of cash flows represented by the numbers. These cash flows do not have to be even, as they would be for an annuity. However, the cash flows must occur at regular intervals, such as monthly or annually. The IRR is the interest rate received for an investment consisting of payments (negative values) and income (positive values) that occur at regular periods.

$$IRR(values,guess)$$

Here, *values* is an array or a reference to cells that contain numbers for which you want to calculate the IRR. The *values* parameter must contain at least one positive value and one negative value to calculate the *IRR*.

IRR uses the order of values to interpret the order of cash flows. Be sure to enter your payment and income values in the sequence you want. If an array or reference argument contains text, logical values, or empty cells, those values are ignored.

The *guess* variable is a number you consider close to the result of *IRR*. Microsoft Excel uses an iterative technique for calculating *IRR*. Starting with *guess*, *IRR* cycles through the calculation until the result is accurate within 0.00001%. If *IRR* cannot find a result that works after 20 tries, the *#NUM!* error value is returned. In most cases you do not need to provide *guess* for the *IRR* calculation. If *guess* is omitted, it is assumed to be 0.1 (10%). If *IRR* gives the *#NUM!* error value, or if the result is not close to what you expected, try again with a different value for *guess*.

MIRR

Returns the MIRR for a series of periodic cash flows. MIRR considers both the cost of the investment and the interest received on reinvestment of cash.

MIRR(values,finance_rate,reinvest_rate)

Here, *values* is an array or a reference to cells that contain numbers. These numbers represent a series of payments (negative values) and income (positive values) occurring at regular periods. The *values* parameter must contain at least one positive value and one negative value to calculate the MIRR. Otherwise, *MIRR* returns the *#DIV/0!* error value.

If an array or reference argument contains text, logical values, or empty cells, those values are ignored. However, cells with the value zero are included. The *finance_rate* parameter is the interest rate you pay on the money used in the cash flows. The *reinvest_rate* parameter is the interest rate you receive on the cash flows as you reinvest them.

references and other readings

2005 IRS Data Book, Internal Revenue Service, 2005.

Adler, Michael, and Bernard Dumas, "Exposure to Currency Risk: Definition and Measurement," *Financial Management*, 13(2), 1984, pp. 41–50.

Aggarwal, Reena, "Stabilization Activities by Underwriters after Initial Public Offers," *Journal of Finance*, 55, June 2000, pp. 1075–1103.

Agrawal, Anup, and Nandu J. Nagarajan, "Corporate Capital Structure, Agency Costs, and Ownership Control: The Case of All-Equity Firms," *Journal of Finance*, 45, September 1990, pp. 1325–1331.

Allen, Frank, Antonio E. Bernardo, and Ivo Welch, "A Theory of Dividends Based on Tax Clienteles," *Journal of Finance*, 55, December 2000, pp. 2499–2536.

Allen, Franklin, and Roni Michaely, "Dividend Policy," in R.A. Jarrow, V. Maksimovic, and W.T. Ziemba (eds.), *Handbooks in Operations Research and Management Science: Finance*, Amsterdam: Elsevier Science, 1995, pp. 793–838.

Altman,Edward I., "Financial Ratios, Discriminant Analysis and the Prediction of Corporate Bankruptcy," *Journal of Finance*, 23, September 1968, pp. 589–609.

Andrade, Gregor, Mark Mitchell, and Erik Stafford, "New Evidence and Perspectives on Mergers," *Journal of Economic Perspectives*, 15, Spring 2001, pp. 103–120.

Anslinger, Patricia L., and Thomas E. Copeland, "Growth through Acquisitions: A Fresh Look," *Harvard Business Review*, 74, January/February 1996, pp. 126–135.

Atkins, Allen B., and Edward A. Dyl, "The Lotto Jackpot: The Lump Sum versus the Annuity," *Financial Practice and Education*, Fall/Winter 1995, pp. 107–111.

Bagwell, Laurie Simon, "Dutch Auction Repurchases: An Analysis of Shareholder Heterogeneity," *Journal of Finance*, 47, March 1992, pp. 71–106.

Baker, H. Kent and Gary E. Powell, "Determinants of Corporate Dividend Policy: A Survey of NYSE Firms," *Financial Practice and Education*, Spring/Summer 2000, Volume 10, Number 1, pp. 29–40.

Berkovitch, Elazar, and M.P. Narayanan, "Motives for Takeovers: An Empirical Investigation," *Journal of Financial and Quantitative Analysis*, 28, September 1993, pp. 347–362.

Bhagat, Sanjai, "The Effect of Pre-emptive Right Amendments on Shareholder Wealth," *Journal of Financial Economics,* November 1983, pp. 289–310.

Bhattacharya, S., "Imperfect Information, Dividend Policy, and 'The Bird in the Hand' Fallacy," *Bell Journal of Economics*, 10, Spring 1979, pp. 259–270.

Black, Fisher, and M. Scholes, "The Pricing of Options and Corporate Liabilities," *Journal of Political Economy,* 81, May-June 1973, pp. 637–654.

Black, P., and M. Scholes, "The Effects of Dividend Yield and Dividend Policy on Common Stock Prices and Returns," *Journal of Financial Economics*, 1, May 1974, pp. 1–22.

Booth, James R., and Richard L. Smith II, "Capital Raising, Underwriting and the Certification Hypothesis," *Journal of Financial Economics,* 15, January-February 1986, pp. 261–281.

Bower, D.H., R.S. Bower, and D. Logue, "A Primer on Arbitrage Pricing Theory," *Midland Corporate Finance Journal*, Fall 1984.

Bruner, Robert F., "Does M&A Pay? A Survey of Evidence for the Decision-Maker," *Journal of Applied Finance,*" 12, Spring/Summer 2002, pp. 7–27.

Bruner, Robert F., Kenneth M. Eades, Robert S. Harris, and Robert C. Higgins, "Best Practices in Estimating the Cost of Capital: Survey and Synthesis," *Financial Practice and Education*, Vol. 8, Number 1, Spring/Summer 1998, pp. 13–28.

Byrne, John, "The Best and Worst Boards," *BusinessWeek*, November 25, 1996, pp. 82–106.

Carpenter, Jennifer, and David Yermack, editors, *Executive Compensation and Shareholder Value*, Boston: Kluwer Academic Publishers, 1999.

Caves, Robert E., Jeffrey A. Frankel, and Ronald W. Jones, *World Trade and Payments: An Introduction*, 9th edition, Boston, MA: Addison Wesley, 2002.

Chan, K.C., G. Andrew Karolyi, and Rene M. Stulz, "Global Financial Markets and the Risk Premium on U.S. Equity," *Journal of Financial Economics*, 32, 1992, pp. 137–168.

Chang, Saeyoung, "Takeovers of Privately Held Targets, Methods of Payment, and Bidder Returns," *Journal of Finance*, 53, April 1998, pp. 773–784.

Chen, Hsuan-Chi and Jay R. Ritter, "The Seven Percent Solution," *Journal of Finance*, 55 June 2000, pp. 1105–1131.

Chen, Kung H. and Thomas A. Shimerda, "An Empirical Analysis Of Useful Financial Ratios," *Financial Management*, 10, Spring 1981, pp. 51–60.

Chinn, Wesley E., "Adjusted Key U.S. Industrial Financial Ratios," *Standard & Poor's CreditWeek*, August 29, 2001.

Comment, Robert, and Gregg A. Jarrell, "The Relative Signalling Power of Dutch-Auction and Fixed-Price Self-Tender Offers and Open-Market Share Repurchase," *Journal of Finance*, 46, September 1991, pp. 1243–1272.

Copeland, Thomas E., "What Do Practitioners Want?," *Journal of Applied Finance*, 12, Spring-Summer 2002, pp. 7–14.

Copeland, Thomas E, J. Fred Weston, and Kuldeep Shastri, *Financial Theory and Corporate Policy,* 4th edition, Boston, MA: Pearson Addison Wesley, 2005.

Cornell, Bradford, "Is the Response of Analysts to Information Consistent with Fundamental Valuation? The Case of Intel," *Financial Management*, 30, Spring 2001, pp. 113–136.

Cornell, Bradford, *The Equity Risk Premium: The Long Term Future of the Stock Market*, New York: John Wiley, 1999.

Cox, John C., Stephen A. Ross, and Mark Rubinstein, "Option Pricing: A Simplified Approach," *Journal of Financial Economics*, 7, September 1979, pp. 229–263.

Dann, Larry Y., "Common Stock Repurchases: An Analysis of Returns to Bondholders and Stockholders," *Journal of Financial Economics*, 9, 1981, pp. 113–138.

DeAngelo, Harry, and Linda DeAngelo, "The Irrelevance of the MM Dividend Irrelevance Theorem," *Journal of Financial Economics*, 79, February 2006, pp. 293–315.

DeAngelo, Harry, Linda DeAngelo, and Douglas J. Skinner, "Special Dividends and the Evolution of Dividend Signaling," *Journal of Financial Economics*, 57, September 2000, pp. 309–354.

DeAngelo, Harry, Linda DeAngelo, and Douglas J. Skinner, "Are Dividends Disappearing? Dividend Concentration and the Consolidation of Earnings," *Journal of Financial Economics*, 72, June 2004, pp. 425–456.

DeAngelo, Harry, Linda DeAngelo, and Rene Stulz, "Dividend Policy and the Earned/Contributed Capital Mix: A Test of the Lifecycle Theory," *Journal of Financial Economics*, forthcoming, Volume 81, Issue 2, August 2006, pp. 227–254.

DeAngelo, H., and R. Masulis, "Optimal Capital Structure under Corporate and Personal Taxation," *Journal of Financial Economics*, 8, March 1980, pp. 3–30.

DeGennaro, Ramon P., "Direct Investments in Securities: A Primer," *Federal Reserve Bank of Atlanta Economic Review*, 2003, pp. 1–14.

Dufey, Gunter, and S.L. Srinivasulu, "The Case for Corporate Management of Foreign Exchange Risk," *Financial Management*, 12(4), 1983, pp. 54–62.

Dun & Bradstreet, *Key Business Ratios*, New York: Updated annually.

Dyer, Jeffrey H., Prashant Kale, and Harbir Singh, "When to Ally and When to Acquire," *Harvard Business Review*, July-August 2004, pp. 109–115.

Ellis, Katrina, Roni Michaely, and Maureen O'Hara, "When The Underwriter Is The Market Maker: An Examination of Trading in The IPO Aftermarket," *Journal of Finance*, 55, June 2000, pp. 1039–1074.

Elton, Edwin J., Martin J. Gruber, Deepak Agrawal, and Christopher Mann. "Explaining the Rate of Spread on Corporate Bonds," *Journal of Finance*, 56, February 2001, pp. 247–277.

Fama, Eugene, "The Behavior of Stock Market Prices," *Journal of Business*, January 1965, pp. 34–105.

Fama, Eugene F., "Short-term Interest Rates as Predictors of Inflation," *American Economic Review*, June 1975, pp. 269–282.

Fama, Eugene F., "Efficient Capital Markets: A Review Of Theory And Empirical Work," *Journal of Finance*, 25, May 1970, pp. 383–417.

Fama, Eugene F., "Efficient Capital Markets: II," *Journal of Finance*, 46, December 1991, pp. 1575–1618.

Fama, Eugene F., "Market Efficiency, Long-Term Returns, and Behavioral Finance," *Journal of Financial Economics*, 49, September 1998, pp. 283–306.

Fama, Eugene F. and Kenneth R. French, "Industry Costs of Equity," *Journal of Financial Economics*, 43, February 1997, pp. 153–193.

Fama, Eugene F. and Kenneth R. French, "Testing Trade-Off and Pecking Order Predictions about Dividends And Debt," *Review of Financial Studies*, 15, March 2002, pp. 1–33.

Fama, Eugene, and Kenneth R. French, "Disappearing Dividends: Changing Firm Characteristics or Lower Propensity to Pay," *Journal of Financial Economics*, 60, April 2001, pp. 3–43.

Fama, Eugene F., and Michael C. Jensen, "Separation of Ownership and Control," *Journal of Law and Economics*, 26, 1983, pp. 301–326.

Financial Accounting Standards Board, *Statement of Financial Accounting Standards No. 142: Goodwill and Other Intangible Assets*, June 2001.

Financial Accounting Standards Board, *Statement of Financial Accounting Standards No. 141: Business Combinations*, June 2001.

Financial Research Associates, *Financial Studies of the Small Business*, Arlington. VA: Updated annually.

Fraser, Lyn M. and Aileen Ormiston, *Understanding Financial Statements*, Eighth Edition, Englewood Cliffs: NJ: Prentice-Hall, 2006.

Froot, Kenneth A., "Short Rates and Expected Asset Returns," NBER Working Paper No. 3247, January 1990.

Froot, Kenneth A., and Richard H. Thaler, "Anomalies: Foreign Exchange," *Journal of Economic Perspectives*, 4, Summer 1990, pp. 179–192.

Fuller, Kathleen, Jeffrey Netter, and Mike Stegemoller, "What Do Returns to Acquiring Firms Tell Us? Evidence from Firms That Make Many Acquisitions," *Journal of Finance*, 57, August 2002, pp. 1763–1793.

Galai, Dan, and R.W. Masulis, "The Option Pricing Model and the Risk Factor of Stock," *Journal of Financial Economics*, 3, January-March 1976, pp. 53–82.

Galai, D., and M. Schneller, "The Pricing of Warrants and the Value of the Firm," *Journal of Finance*, 33, December 1978, pp. 1333–1342.

Gentry, James A., "State of the Art of Short-Run Financial Management," *Financial Management*, 17, Summer 1988, pp. 41–57.

Gentry, James A., R. Vaidyanathan, and Hei Wai Lee, "A Weighted Cash Conversion Cycle," *Financial Management*, 19, Spring 1990, pp. 90–99.

Geske, Robert, "The Valuation of Corporate Liabilities as Compound Options," *Journal of Financial and Quantitative Analysis*, 12, November 1977, pp. 541–552.

Geske, Robert, "The Pricing of Options with Stochastic Dividend Yield," *Journal of Finance*, 33, May 1978, pp. 617–625.

Geske, Robert, and R. Roll, "On Valuing American Call Options with the Black-Scholes European Formula," *Journal of Finance*, June 1984, pp. 443–455.

Godfrey, Stephen, and Ramon Espinosa, "A Practical Approach to Calculating Costs of Equity for Investment in Emerging Markets," *Journal of Applied Corporate Finance*, 9, Fall 1996, pp. 80-89.

Graham, John R., "Taxes And Corporate Finance: A Review," *Review of Financial Studies*, 16, Winter 2003, pp. 1075–1129.

Graham, John R., and Campbell R. Harvey, "The Theory and Practice of Corporate Finance: Evidence from the Field," *Journal of Financial Economics*, 60, May/June 2001, pp. 187–243.

Grinblatt, Mark, and Sheridan Titman, *Financial Markets and Corporate Strategy*, Boston: Irwin/McGraw-Hill, 1998.

Grullon, Gustavo and David L. Ikenberry, "What Do We Know about Stock Repurchases?" *Journal of Applied Corporate Finance*, 13, Spring 2000, pp. 31–51.

Grullon, Gustavo, Roni Michaely, and Bhaskaran Swaminathan, "Are Dividend Changes a Sign of Firm Maturity?" *Journal of Business*, 75, 2002, pp. 387–424.

Habib, Michel, and Bruce Johnsen, "The Private Placement of Debt and Outside Equity as an Information Revelation Mechanism," *Review of Financial Studies,* vol. 13, 2000, pp. 1017–1055.

Harding, David, and Sam Rovit, "Building Deals on Bedrock," *Harvard Business Review*, September 2004, pp. 121–128.

Haugen, R.A., and L.W. Senbet, "New Perspectives on Informational Asymmetry," *Journal of Financial and Quantitative Analysis*, 14, November 1979, pp. 671–694.

Hazelkorn, Todd, Marc Zenner, and Anil Shivdasani, "Creating Value with Mergers and Acquisitions," *Journal of Applied Corporate Finance*, 16, Spring/Summer 2004, pp. 81–90.

Heinkel, Robert, and Eduardo S. Schwartz, "Rights Versus Underwritten Offerings: An Asymmetric Information Approach," *Journal of Finance,* March 1986, pp. 1–18.

Hekman, C.R., "A Model of Foreign Exchange Exposure," *Journal of International Business Studies*, 1985, pp. 85–99.

Hulbert, Mark, "A Plan to Overcome Investors' Home Bias," *New York Times*, January 23, 2000, Sec. 3, p. 9.

Iacocca, Lee with William Novak, *Iacocca: An Autobiography*, New York: Bantam Books, 1984.

Ibbotson Associates, *Cost of Capital: 2003 Yearbook, Data through March 2003*, Chicago, 2003.

Ibbotson Associates, Inc., *Stocks, Bonds, Bills and Inflation 2006 Yearbook: Market Results for 1926–2003,* Chicago: Ibbotson Associates, Inc., 2006.

Ikenberry, David, Josef Lakonishok, and Theo Vermaelen, "Market Underreaction to Open Market Share Repurchases," *Journal of Financial Economics*, 39, October-November, 1995, pp. 181–208.

Ingersoll, Jonathan E., Jr., "A Theoretical and Empirical Investigation of the Dual Purpose Funds: An Application of Contingent-Claims Analysis," *Journal of Financial Economics,* 3, January-March 1976, pp. 83–124.

Ingersoll, Jonathan E., Jr., "A Contingent-Claims Valuation of Convertible Securities," *Journal of Financial Economics,* 4, May 1977, pp. 289–322.

Jacquillat, Bertrand, and Bruno Solnik. "Multinationals are Poor Tools for Diversification," *Journal of Portfolio Management*, 4(2), Winter 1978, pp. 8–12.

Jaffe, Jeffrey F., "Special Information and Insider Trading," *Journal of Business,* 47, July 1974, pp. 410–428.

Jensen, Michael C., "Agency Costs of Free Cash Flow, Corporate Finance, and Takeovers," *American Economic Review*, 76, May 1986, pp. 323–329.

Jensen, Michael C., "Presidential Address: The Modern Industrial Revolution, Exit, and the Failure of Internal Control Systems," *Journal of Finance*, 48, 1993, pp.831–880.

Jensen, Michael C. and William H. Meckling, "Theory of the Firm: Managerial Behavior, Agency Costs and Ownership Structure," *Journal of Financial Economics*, 3, 1976, pp. 11–25, 305–360.

Jorion, Philippe and William N. Goetzmann, "Global Stock Markets in the Twentieth Century," *Journal of Finance*, 54, June 1999, pp. 953–980.

Kahle, Kathleen M., "When a Buyback Isn't a Buyback: Open Market Repurchases and Employee Options," *Journal of Financial Economics*, 63, February 2002, pp. 235–261.

Kallberg, J.G. and K. Parkinson, *Corporate Liquidity: Management and Measurement*, Burr Ridge, IL: Irwin/McGraw Hill, 1996.

Kaplan, Steven, and Richard Ruback, "The Valuation of Cash Flow Forecasts: An Empirical Analysis," *Journal of Applied Corporate Finance*, 8, Winter 1996, pp. 45–60.

Kaufold, Howard, and Michael Smirlock, "Managing Corporate Exchange and Interest Rate Exposure," *Financial Management*, 15(3), Autumn 1986, pp. 64–72.

Koller, Tim, Marc Goedhart, and David Wessels, *Valuation: Measuring and Managing the Value of Companies,* 4th edition by McKinsey & Company Inc., New York, John Wiley, 2005.

Kolb, Robert W. and Ricardo J. Rodriguez, "The Regression Tendencies of Betas: A Reappraisal," *Financial Review*, 24, May 1989, pp. 319–334.

Kolb, Robert W. and Ricardo J. Rodriguez. "Is The Distribution of Betas Stationary?," *Journal of Financial Research*, 13, Winter 1990, pp. 279–284.

La Porta, Rafael, Florencio Lopez-De-Silanes, and Andrei Shleifer, "Corporate Ownership Around The World," *Journal of Finance*, 54, April 1999, pp. 471–517.

Lanchner, David, "Pushing Maturities to 1,000 years," *Global Finance*, November 1, 1997, p. 26.

Leibowitz, M.L., "Specialized Fixed Income Security Strategies," in Edward I. Altman, ed., *Financial Handbook*, 5th edition, New York: John Wiley & Sons, 1981, Section 19.

Leibowitz, M.L., and A. Weinberger, *Contingent Immunization: A New Procedure for Structured Active Management*, New York: Salomon Brothers, 1981.

Leibowitz, M. L., and A. Weinberger, *Risk Control Procedures under Contingent Immunization*, New York: Salomon Brothers, 1982.

Leland, H.E., and D.H. Pyle, "Informational Asymmetries, Financial Structure, and Financial Intermediation," *Journal of Finance*, 32, May 1977, pp. 371–387.

Levich, Richard M., *International Financial Markets: Price and Policies*, 2nd edition, New York: McGraw-Hill Irwin, 2001.

Lindley, James T., "Compounding Issues Revisited," *Financial Practice and Education,* Fall 1993, pp. 127–129.

Livingston, *Miles, Money and Capital Markets*, Cambridge, MA: Blackwell, 1996.

MacBeth, James D., and Larry J. Merville, "An Empirical Examination of the Black-Scholes Call Option Pricing Model," *Journal of Finance,* 34, December 1979, pp. 1173–1186.

Madura, Jeff, *International Financial Management,* 7th edition, Mason, OH: Thomson South-Western, 2003.

Maldonado, Rita, and Anthony Saunders, "Foreign Exchange Futures and the Law of One Price," *Financial Management,* 12(1), Spring 1983, pp. 19–23.

Maldonado, Rita, and Anthony Saunders, "International Portfolio Diversification and the Inter-Temporal Stability of International Stock Market Relationships, 1957–1978," *Financial Management,* 10(3), Autumn 1981, pp. 54–63.

Malkiel, Burton Gordon, *A Random Walk Down Wall Street: The Time-Tested Strategy for Successful Investing*, Completely Revised and Updated, New York: W.W. Norton, 2003.

Manne, Henry G., "Mergers and the Market for Corporate Control," *Journal of Political Economy*, 73, April 1965, pp. 110–120.

Margrabe, William, "The Value of an Option to Exchange One Asset for Another," *Journal of Finance,* 33, March 1978, pp. 177–198.

Markowitz, Harry M, "Portfolio Selection," *Journal of Finance*, 7, March 1952, pp. 77–91.

Markowitz, Harry M, "Foundations Of Portfolio Theory," *Journal of Finance*, 46, June 1991, pp. 469–478.

Markowitz, H., "Travels along the Efficient Frontier," *Dow Jones Asset Management*, May/June 1997.

Martin, John D. and J. William Petty, *Value Based Management: The Corporate Response to the Shareholder Revolution*, Boston: Harvard Business School Press, 2000.

McCauley, Robert N., Judith S. Ruud, and Frank Iacono, *Dodging Bullets: Changing U.S. Corporate Capital Structure in the 1980s and 1990s*, Cambridge, MA: MIT Press, 1999.

McGough, Robert, Suzanne McGee, and Cassell Bryan-Low, "Heard on the Street: Poof! Buyback Binge Now Creates Big Hangover," *The Wall Street Journal*, December 18, 2000, p. C1.

McTaggart, James M., Peter W. Kontes, and Michael C. Mankins, *The Value Imperative*, New York: The Free Press, 1994.

Merton, Robert C., "The Theory of Rational Option Pricing," *Bell Journal of Economics and Management Science,* 4, Spring 1973, pp. 141–183.

Merton, Robert C., "On the Pricing of Corporate Debt: The Risk Structure of Interest Rates," *Journal of Finance,* 29, May 1974, pp. 449–470.

Mian, Shehzad I. and Clifford W. Smith, Jr., "Extending Trade Credit and Financing Receivables," *Journal of Applied Corporate Finance*, 7, Spring 1994, pp. 75–84.

Miller, Merton H., "Debt and Taxes," *Journal of Finance*, 32, May 1977, pp. 261–275.

Miller, Merton H., "Leverage," *Journal of Finance*, 46, June 1991, pp. 479–488.

Miller, Merton, "Is American Corporate Governance Fatally Flawed?," *Journal of Applied Corporate Finance*, 6, Winter 1994, pp. 32–39.

Miller, Merton H. and Franco Modigliani, "Dividend Policy, Growth, and the Valuation of Shares," *Journal of Business*, 34, 1961, pp. 411–433.

Miller, Merton H. and Kevin Rock, "Dividend Policy under Asymmetric Information," *Journal of Finance*, 40, 1985, pp. 1031–1051.

Mitchell, Karlyn, "The Debt Maturity Choice: An Empirical Investigation," *Journal of Financial Research*, 16, Winter 1993, pp. 309–320.

Mitchell, Mark L., and Erik Stafford, "Managerial Decisions and Long-Term Stock Price Performance," *Journal of Business*, 73, July 2000, pp. 289–329.

Mitchell, Mark L., and J. Harold Mulherin, "The Impact of Industry Shocks on Takeover and Restructuring Activity," *Journal of Financial Economics*, 41, June 1996, pp. 193–229.

Monks, Robert A.G., and Nell Minow, *Corporate Governance,* 3rd edition, Malden, MA: Blackwell Publishing, 2003.

Mukherjee, Tarun K., Halili Kiymaz, and H. Kent Baker, "Merger Motives and Target Valuation: A Survey of Evidence from CFOs," *Journal of Applied Finance*, Fall/Winter 2004, Volume 14, Number 2, pp. 7–24.

Myers, Stewart C., "Presidential Address: The Capital Structure Puzzle," *Journal of Finance*, 39, July 1984, pp. 575–592.

Myers, Stewart C., and Nicholas S. Majluf, "Corporate Financing and Investment Decisions When Firms Have Information That Investors Do Not Have," *Journal of Financial Economics*, 13, 1984, pp. 187–221.

Nelson, C., and G. William Schwert, "Short-Term Interest Rates as Predictors of Inflation: On Testing the Hypothesis That the Real Rate is Constant," *American Economic Review,* June 1977, pp. 478–486.

Norris, Floyd, "Why Do Firms Pay Investors Who Sell?" *The New York Times*, April, 28, 2006, p. C1.

O'Brien, Thomas J., "The Global CAPM And A Firm's Cost Of Capital in Different Currencies," *Journal of Applied Corporate Finance*, 12, Fall 1999, pp. 73–79.

Opler, Tim, Lee Pinkowitz, Rene Stulz, and Rohan Williamson, "Corporate Cash Holdings," *Journal of Applied Corporate Finance*, 14, Spring 2001, pp. 55–66.

Peterson, Pamela P. and David R. Peterson, *Company Performance and Measures of Value Added*, The Research Foundation of the Institute of Chartered Financial Analysts, 1996.

Phillips, Susan M., and J. Richard Zecher, "Exchange Listing and the Cost of Equity Capital," U.S. Securities and Exchange Commission, Directorate of Economic and Policy Analysis, Capital Marketing Working Paper No. 8, 1982.

Pinches, George E., and Kent A. Mingo, "A Multivariate Analysis of Industrial Bond Ratings," *Journal of Finance*, 28, March 1973, pp. 1–18.

Pitaro, Regina M., *Deals, Deals and More Deals*, Gabelli University Press, 1998.

Porter, Michael E., *Competitive Advantage*, New York: The Free Press, 1985.

Publication 17, "Tax Guide for Individuals," Internal Revenue Service, 2005.

Publication 334, "Tax Guide for Small Business," Internal Revenue Service, 2005.

Rappaport, Alfred, *Creating Shareholder Value: A Guide for Managers and Investors,* 2nd edition, New York, NY: The Free Press, 1998.

Ritter, Jay R. and Ivo Welch, "A Review Of IPO Activity, Pricing, And Allocations," *Journal of Finance*, 57, August 2002, pp. 1795–1828.

Robert Morris Associates, *Annual Statement Studies*, Philadelphia: Updated annually.

Rogoff, Kenneth, "The Purchasing Power Parity Puzzle," *Journal of Economic Literature*, 34, June 1996, pp. 647–668.

Roll, R., "Style Return Differentials: Illusions, Risk Premia, or Investment Opportunities," in Fabozzi (ed.), *Handbook of Equity Style Management*, New Hope, PA: Frank Fabozzi Associates, 1995.

Roll, Richard and Stephen A. Ross, "The Arbitrage Pricing Theory Approach To Strategic Portfolio Planning," *Financial Analysts Journal*, 40, May/June 1984, pp. 14–26.

Roll, Richard, "An Analytic Valuation Formula for Unprotected American Call Options on Stocks with Known Dividends," *Journal of Financial Economics,* 5, November 1977, pp. 251–258.

Roll, Richard, "The Hubris Hypothesis of Corporate Takeovers," *Journal of Business*, 59, April 1986, pp. 197–216.

Ross, Stephen A., "The Arbitrage Theory of Capital Asset Pricing," *Journal of Economic Theory*, 13, December 1976, pp. 341–360.

Ross, S.A., "The Determination of Financial Structure: The Incentive-Signalling Approach," *Bell Journal of Economics*, 8, Spring 1977, pp. 23–40.

Ruback, Richard S., "Capital Cash Flows: A Simple Approach to Valuing Risky Cash Flows," *Financial Management*, 31, Summer 2002, pp. 5–30, 85–103.

Ryan, Patricia and Glenn P. Ryan, "Capital Budgeting Practices of the Fortune 1000: How Have Things Changed?," *Journal of Business and Management*, Vol. 8, Number 4, Winter 2002.

Santoli, Michael, "LBOs are Back," *Barron's*, March 14, 2005, pp. 21–22.

Schallheim, James S., *Lease or Buy*, Boston, MA: Harvard Business School Press. 1994.

Smith, Clifford W., Jr. and L. MacDonald Wakeman, "Determinants of Corporate Leasing Policy," *Journal of Finance*, 40, July 1985, pp. 895–908.

Scherr, Frederick C., "Optimal Trade Credit Limits," *Financial Management*, 25, Spring 1996, pp. 71–85.

Schipper, Katherine, and Rex Thompson, "Evidence on the Capitalized Value of Merger Activity for Acquiring Firms," *Journal of Financial Economics*, 11, 1983, pp. 85–119.

Scholes, M., and J. Williams, "Estimating Betas from Non-synchronous Data," *Journal of Financial Economics*, December 1977, pp. 309–327.

Schramm, Ronald M. and Henry N. Wang, "Measuring of the Cost of Capital in an International CAPM Framework," *Journal of Applied Corporate Finance*, 12, Fall 1999, pp. 63–72.

Scott, David L., and W. Kent Moore, *Fundameentals of Time Value of Money,* New York: Praeger, 1984.

Scott, J.H., "A Theory of Optimal Capital Structure," *Bell Journal of Economics*, 7, Spring 1976, pp. 33–54.

Shao, Lawrence P., and Stephan P. Shao, *Mathematics for Management and Finance,* Mason, Ohio: South-Western, 8th edition, 1998.

Sharpe, William F., "Capital Asset Prices: A Theory of Market Equilibrium Under Conditions of Risk," *Journal of Finance*, 19, September 1964, pp. 425–442.

Shastri, K., "Valuing Corporate Securities: Some Effects of Mergers by Exchange Offers," University of Pittsburgh, WP-517, revised January 1982.

Shiller, Robert J., *Irrational Exuberance*, Princeton, NJ : Princeton University Press, 2000.

Shleifer, Andrei, *Inefficient Markets: An Introduction to Behavioral Finance*, Oxford, United Kingdom: Oxford University Press, 2000.

Shleifer, Andrei, and Robert W. Vishny, "Stock Market Driven Acquisitions," *Journal of Financial Economics*, 70, December 2003, pp. 295–311.

Siegel, Jeremy J., *Stocks for the Long Run: The Definitive Guide To Financial Market Returns and Long-Term Investment Strategies,* 3rd edition, New York: McGraw-Hill, 2002.

Smith, C., Jr., "Option Pricing: A Review," *Journal of Financial Economics,* January-March 1976, pp. 1–51.

Smith, C.W., "Alternative Methods for Raising Capital: Rights Versus Underwritten Offerings," *Journal of Financial Economics,* 5, December 1977, pp. 273–307.

Smith, C.W., "Investment Banking and the Capital Acquisition Process," *Journal of Financial Economics,* 15, 1986, pp. 3–29.

Smith, Clifford W., and Jerold B. Warner, "On Financial Contracting: An Analysis of Bond Covenants," *Journal of Financial Economics,* 7, June 1979, pp. 117–161.

Solnik, B.H., "Why Not Diversify Internationally Rather than Domestically?" *Financial Analyst Journal*, 30(4), May 1974, pp. 48–54.

Solnik, Bruno, *International Investments,* 4th edition, Reading, MA: Addison-Wesley, 2000.

Stancill, James McNeill, *Entrepreneurial Finance*, Mason, Ohio: Thomson South-Western, 2004.

Stoll, Hans R., "The Relationship Between Put and Call Option Prices," *Journal of Finance,* December 1969, pp. 802–824.

Stulz, Rene M., "Globalization of Capital Markets and the Cost of Capital: The Case of Nestle," *Journal of Applied Corporate Finance*, 8, Fall 1995, pp. 30–38.

Stulz, Rene M., "Globalization, Corporate Finance, and the Cost of Capital," *Journal of Applied Corporate Finance*, 12, Fall 1999, pp. 8–25.

Titman, Sheridan, and Roberto Wessels, "The Determinants of Capital Structure Choice," *Journal of Finance*, 43, March 1988, pp. 1–19.

The Hershey Company, *Annual Report and 10K*, 2004 and 2005.

United Nations Conference on Trade and Development, *World Investment Report 2002: Transnational Corporations and Export Competitiveness*, New York and Geneva: United Nations Publication, 2002.

U.S. Census Bureau, *Quarterly Financial Report for Manufacturing, Mining, and Trade Corporations: Fourth Quarter 2003,* Washington, D.C.: U.S. Government Printing Office, April 2004.

Vermaelen, Theo, "Common Stock Repurchases and Market Signalling: An Empirical Study," *Journal of Financial Economics*, 9, 1981, pp. 138–183.

Wasserstein, Bruce, *Big Deal and Beyond*, Warner Books, 2000.

Weaver, Samuel C., "Using Value Line to Estimate the Cost of Capital and Industry Capital Structure," *Journal of Financial Education*, 29, Fall 2003, pp. 55–71.

Welch, Jack with John A. Byrne, *Jack: Straight from the Gut*, New York, Warner Business Books, 2001.

Welch, Ivo, "Views of Financial Economists on the Equity Premium and on Professional Controversies," *Journal of Business*, 73, October 2000, pp. 501–537.

Weston, J. Fred, and Brian Johnson, "What It Takes for a Deal to Win Stock Market Approval." *Mergers & Acquisitions*, 34, September/October 1999, pp. 43–48.

Weston, J. Fred, Mark Mitchell, and J. Harold Mulherin, *Takeovers, Restructuring, and Corporate Governance,* 4th edition, Upper Saddle River, NJ: Prentice-Hall, 2004.

Whaley, R., "Valuation of American Call Options on Dividend-Paying Stocks: Empirical Tests," *Journal of Financial Economics,* 10, March 1982, pp. 29–58.

White, Mark A., *Financial Analysis with an Electronic Calculator,* Chicago: Irwin, Fourth Edition, 2000.

White, Mark A., "Financial Problem Solving with an Electronic Calculator," *Financial Practice and Education,* Fall 1993, pp. 123–126.

A

Abandonment option The option to abandon (or sell) a project is equivalent to a put option.

Accounting returns Returns determined for discrete single time periods (month, quarter, year, and so on) such as return on assets, return on capital, and return on equity.

Adjustable-rate preferred stock (ARPS) Under unexpected inflation, preferred stock with fixed dividend rates becomes undesirable from the investor's point of view because of the risk that the market value of the preferred will fall. In order to share the risk and to make preferred issues more attractive to investors, many companies (particularly utilities) have begun to issue preferred stock with dividends tied to rates on various U.S. government obligations.

Alliance Less formal agreement than a joint venture. A new entity need not be created. A formal contract may not be written.

Allocated costs Costs allocated on the basis of sales or other measures.

Amortization (payment of interest and principal) Present value of an annuity for n periods is used to calculate payments of interest and principal.

Arbitrage pricing model Uses multiple economic factors in addition to market returns to calculate required returns to investments. Requires additional research, refinement, and simplification before meriting wide application.

Ask (asking) price The price a seller requires.

Asymmetric information Decision makers have different information than the general public.

Auction-rate preferred stock Has a floating dividend rate and tax advantages.

B

Average collection period Measures the length of time that it takes to collect from a customer.

Balance sheet Provides a snapshot of what the firm owns and what the firm owes at a specific moment in time.

Base case (decision case) assumptions Initial assumptions for any analysis. Usually it is the most likely situation under analysis.

Basic principle of investment An investment is acceptable only if it earns at least its opportunity cost.

Behavioral finance theories The winner's curse theory and stock market misvaluations of Schleifer and Vishy (SV) are examples.

Benefit stream Stream of positive cash flows in capital investment analysis.

Best-efforts offering Subject to the additional risk that if a minimum number of shares is not sold the investment banker withdraws the offering.

Bid/ask spread Difference between bid price and ask price.

Bid price The price a potential buyer offers.

Blanket mortgage Pledges all real property currently owned by the company.

Bond A longer-term promissory note.

Bond covenants Can be divided into four broad categories: (1) those restricting the issuance of new debt, (2) those with restrictions on dividend payments, (3) those with restrictions on merger activity, and (4) those with restrictions on the disposition of the firm's assets.

Bond indenture Detailed contract involving long-term debt securities that governs the relationship between borrowers and creditors.

Bond valuation Present value of interest payments and maturity value.

Book-value equity An accounting concept that primarily keeps track of earnings retained in the business over the years, along with the original level of equity capital injected into the firm net of any stock repurchase.

Book-value weights Based on the capital structure represented by the balance sheet.

Budget committee Develops operating budgets, both short-term and long-term.

C

Call option The right to buy an asset at a specified price.

Call provision Gives the issuing corporation the right to call in the preferred stock for redemption, as for bonds. Enables the issuer to redeem the debt before its maturity date.

Capital appropriations committee Responsible primarily for capital budgeting and expenditures.

Capital asset pricing model (CAPM) Used in corporate finance to estimate the cost of equity capital, but it is subject to wide interpretations and calculation of major components such as the risk-free rate, beta, and market risk premium.

Capital in excess of par Amount received in sale of equity above accounting par value.

Capital impairment rule Protects creditors by forbidding the payment of dividends from capital. Paying dividends from capital would be distributing the investment in a company rather than earnings.

Capital investment analysis Part of capital expenditure analysis (referred to by some as "capital budgeting").

Capital lease Financial lease payments over the life of a lease are capitalized and shown as a liability.

Capitalization ratio Calculates the percentage that the interest-bearing debt represents of the total capital pool.

Capitalized in-house engineering expenses An accounting require-ment that captures the costs of all engineer-employees (salary, bonus, benefits, and employee taxes) who work on a specific capital investment. These costs are added to the cost of the project and placed on the balance sheet to be depreciated over the project's life rather than being expensed in the year incurred.

Capitalized interest An accounting requirement that captures an implied interest expense while work on a specific capital invest-ment is underway. These interest cost reduce interest expense for a given period and are added to the cost of the project to be depreciated over the project's life rather than being expensed in the year incurred.

Cash budget A day-to-day opera-tional tool that considers anticipated cash receipts and cash disbursements.

Cash cycle Reduces the operating cycle for the number of days that the firm takes until it pays for the inventory.

Chattel mortgage A mortgage secured by personal property (such as an automobile or manu-facturing equipment), but this is generally an intermediate-term instrument.

Clearing float The time required for a check to clear the bank system.

Clientele effect A possible explana-tion for management reluctance to alter established payout policies because such changes might cause current shareholders to incur unwanted transactions costs.

Commitment of funds Signed con-tracts and commitments to pay that have not been billed by the vendor.

Common stock at par The number of common shares issued times their par value.

Comparable companies or (compa-rable transactions) valuation approach Key relationships are calculated for a group of similar companies or similar transactions as a basis for the valuation of companies involved in a merger or takeover.

Compound annual growth rate (CAGR) The increase in value of an asset expressed as a compound interest rate.

Comp ratio "Comparable" ratio.

Consolidated summary status report Senior management vehi-cle for managing the implementa-tion progress of all projects.

Constant-growth valuation model Determines the sources of operating cash flow by allowing the manager, analyst, entrepre-neur, or other interested investor to appropriately develop each strategic performance objective or assumption.

Controller An accounting profes-sional whose function includes accounting, reporting, and control.

Convertibility provision A "sweetener" that reduces the initial cost of both debt and preferred stock.

Convertible preferred stock (convertibles) Preferred stock that avoids burdening the new capital-hungry firm with a requirement to pay interest on debt or technically be in default. They provide the holder with a current dividend and grant the holder an option to take capital gains by converting to common stock.

Convertible *See* Convertible pre-ferred stock.

Corporate charter Technically con-sists of a certificate of incorpora-tion and, by reference, the general corporate laws of the state.

Corporate secretary A professional whose activities are related to the finance function.

Cost avoidance Occurs whenever a project's implementation reduces expenses from a projected level of expenditures.

Cost-of-carrying amount The cost rate of not taking discounts in trade credit transaction.

Cost of debt Interest expense. The recommended technique for calculating the cost of debt is to tax-effect the current market cost of long-term debt.

Cost savings Occur whenever a project's implementation reduces expenses from the current level of expenditures.

Cost savings project A project that will immediately reduce the pro-duction or operating costs of a product.

Coupon The periodic payment rate or amount on a bond.

Crossover rate Where both projects have the same NPV, can be calculated by taking the difference between the projects' cash flows and calculating the IRR on these differences.

Cumulative dividends All past pre-ferred dividends must be paid before common dividends can be paid.

Cumulative voting Permits multiple votes for a single director.

Currency swap Two debt service flows are denominated in different currencies, and principle amounts may also be exchanged.

Current assets Categories that will be converted to cash in the com-ing accounting cycle or fiscal year.

Current liabilities Items that must be paid in the coming accounting cycle or fiscal year.

Current ratio Calculated as current assets divided by current liabilities.

D

Debenture Unsecured debt, as in an unsecured bond. As such, provides no lien on specific property as security for the obligation.

Debt with warrants Similar to convertibles except that this can be detached from the debt instrument.

Decision case cash flow amounts Relevant net cash flows for calculating values of benefits.

Decision case cash flow assumptions Estimates that produce the relevant net cash flows for calculating the present value of benefits.

Decision case NPV analysis Gross present value less investment costs.

Depreciation Allocating the cost of an asset over its life.

Differentiated estimated inflation rates Different inflation for different entities.

Direct financing lease A lease (other than leveraged leases) for which the cost-of-carrying amount is equal to the fair value of the leased property at the inception of the lease.

Discounted cash flow (DCF) method The most widely accepted valuation method. The DCF methodology values the firm as the sum of the free cash flow of the firm discounted at the appropriately weighted average cost of capital.

Discounted payback period (DPBP) A capital valuation technique similar to the payback approach.

Dividend Payment from "earnings and profits" of a corporation, which is also considered a return of capital.

Dividend growth model (DGM) Most applicable to firms that pay dividends with a steady, stable growth rate underlying those dividends. Subject to wide variations in expected growth rate assumptions.

Dividend payout ratio Calculated, for example, as 2005 dividends paid per common share divided by 2005 basic normalized earnings per common share.

Dividend yield The dividend received over a period of time compared to the initial price of the stock.

Divisional hurdle rates Hurdle rates determined for each division as if it were a standalone business.

Dutch auction process The bidder submits to the seller in charge of the auction the number of shares desired and a specified dividend level. The lowest dividend that will allow all of the available shares to be completely sold will be the dividend for the next 49 days, at which point a new auction resets the dividend.

E

Earnings before interest and taxes (EBIT) Net operating income plus net other income and expense.

EBITDA (earnings before interest, taxes, depreciation, and amortization) Earnings before interest, taxes, depreciation, and amortization.

Economic returns Returns determined for a continuous time frame over multiple periods.

Employee stock ownership plans (ESOPs) A type of employee pension plan. Plans by which companies supplement or replace their employee retirement programs while continuing to purchase stock on behalf of the ESOP trustee.

Equity valuation The discounted present value of net cash flows to equity.

Equivalent annual annuity technique Approach when considering the "unequal" life problem.

Event study methods Studies that calculate the stock price impact days before the acquisition announcement and days immediately after the acquisition.

Exposure to exchange risk Measure of risk by regressing a company's total dollar value on a vector of exchange rates.

F

Facilities plan Identifies any opportunities or shortfall in production capacity or new plant requirements.

Financial intermediaries Specialized business firms whose activities include the creation of financial assets and liabilities. They facilitate a flow of capital from savings surplus units to savings deficit units.

Financial intermediation Brings together, through transactions in the financial markets, the savings surplus units and the savings deficit units so that savings can be redistributed into their most productive uses.

Financial lease A lease that does not provide for maintenance services, is not cancelable, and is fully amortized (that is, the lessor contracts for rental payments equal to the full price of the leased equipment).

Financial leverage Measures the extent to which the shareholders' equity investment is magnified by the use of total debt (or liabilities) in financing its total assets.

Financial structure Indicates the amount of debt and equity used in financing a firm.

Firm-commitment cash offer The investment banker agrees to underwrite and distribute the issue at an agreed-upon price for a specified number of shares to be bought by the underwriters.

Fixed capital investment The total of investments in land, buildings and equipment.

Fixed-price tender offers (FPTs) Grant shareholders an in-the-money put.

Floating-rate debt Debt which carries an interest rate which changes according to some benchmark.

Foreign exchange exposure Model defined as the sensitivity of an investment's value in a reference currency to changes in exchange rate forecasts.

Forward exchange rate bias Future spot rates are different from those predicted by current forward rates.

Fractional share In a stock dividend or split, a shareholder may either pay for an additional half-share or receive the value of the half-share in cash.

Full working capital recovery At the termination of operations the full amount of investment in working capital is liquidated—all inventory is sold, all receivables are collected, and all payables are paid.

Future value The value of an investment at some future date at some specific growth (or interest) rate.

G

Green shoe option Allows the investment banker to purchase additional securities at the anticipated price.

H

Hard capital rationing Capital rationing forced on the organization by the financial markets.

Hurdle rate A reinvestment rate calculated as a risk-adjusted cost of capital.

I

Illiquidity effect Refers to the fact that small private firms are not as readily marketable as publicly traded firms. The buyer negotiates a higher discount rate, resulting in a lower valuation.

Incentive-signaling approach Suggests that management might choose real financial payouts such as dividends (or debt payments) as a means of sending unambiguous signals to the public about the future performance of the firm.

Income statement Shows the activities as measured by revenues (or sales) less expenses of the firm throughout the period.

Incremental cash flow The additional cash flows produce by some action.

Indenture The long-term relationship between the borrower and the lender of a long-term promissory note is established in this document.

Indexed bonds (purchasing-power bonds) Protect against inflation risks. They carry interest rates that are a specified amount plus the rate of some measure of inflation during the previous period.

Insolvency rule Provides that corporations cannot pay dividends while insolvent. (*Insolvency* is defined here, in the bankruptcy sense, as liabilities exceeding assets.)

Installed cost Includes the cost of new assets purchased from vendors, the opportunity cost of equipment absorbed by the project, and all installation costs.

Interest coverage Centers on the income statement and examines how many times the interest could be paid off with operating income.

Interest rate swap An agreement between two parties for the exchange of a series of cash payments; one on a fixed rate liability and the other on a floating rate liability.

Internal growth rate A financial ratio that is an extension of return on retained earnings.

Internal rate of return (IRR) A capital valuation technique. The interest rate that equates the present value of future cash flow to the investment outlay. The IRR method, like the NPV method, discounts cash flows. However, the IRR assumes reinvestment at the IRR.

In-the-money put The current price of the asset is below its put price.

Issuance (flotation) Additional securities are sold.

J

Joint ventures Enterprises owned by two or more participants. Particularly advantageous in the international setting. In some situations, local governments may not allow an acquisition. A joint venture presents an opportunity to combine some assets without violating such a regulation.

Junior mortgage A subordinate lien, such as a second or third mortgage. It is a lien or claim junior to others.

L

Lessee In a building example, we would call the one using the asset the lessee.

Lessor Party (individual, corporation, partnership, and so on) that owns the asset. In a building example, we would call the landlord the lessor.

Leverage metrics Measure the extent to which a firm is financed by debt.

Leveraged buyout (LBO) Form of ownership change represented by taking a public company private.

Leveraged lease Lease in which the lessor will be an equity partner in the asset. Direct financing lease in which substantial financing is provided by a long-term creditor on a non-recourse basis with respect to the general credit of the lessor.

Line of credit An agreement between the bank and the borrower concerning the maximum loan balance the bank will allow the borrower.

Liquidating dividend A dividend paid out of capital.

M

Mail float The time (number of days) that the check is "in the mail."

Management buyout (MBO) Form of ownership change in which former managers are the prime movers in the transaction. The basic idea is to raise the necessary funds to purchase control from the existing public shareholders, using financing with a large percentage debt component, and providing management with a high percentage of the remaining small equity base.

Market capitalization The current value of a company's equity based on the stock market at any point in time.

Market to book ratio Measures the value that financial markets attach to the management and organization of the firm as a going concern.

Market rate of return Return on some market index such as all stocks on the New York Stock Exchange.

Market-value weights The market value of debt and equity.

Maturity date Terminal date of an investment.

Metrics Provide a comparative basis for evaluating suppliers and customers, and can be used for historical analysis as well as projected performance.

Modified Accelerated Cost Recovery System (MACRS) An accelerated depreciation method required by the Internal Revenue Service for tax reporting purposes.

Monte Carlo simulation A statistical technique that allows the analyst the opportunity to describe a range of potential values for various and specific assumptions.

Mortgage (mortgage bond) Represents a pledge of designated property for a loan. Under a mortgage bond, a corporation pledges certain real assets as security for the bond. The pledge is a condition of the loan. A mortgage bond, therefore, is secured by real property.

Mortgage bond *See* Mortgage.

Multiple-discriminant analysis (MDA) A statistical procedure which calculates the relative strength of the independent variables similar to multiple regression analysis.

Multiple-stage valuation equation An equation with more than initial and terminal stages.

Mutually exclusive investment A project competing directly with another project.

N

Net foreign exchange position A function of the duration of the cash flows and unanticipated changes in foreign interest and exchange rates.

Net monetary asset positive position More monetary assets such as receivables than monetary liabilities such as accounts payable.

Net monetary position exposure A positive net monetary asset position.

Net present value (NPV) A capital valuation technique. The present value of future cash flow, discounted at the cost of capital, minus the cost of the investment. The NPV method is the preferred capital evaluation technique.

Net profits rule Provides that dividends can be paid from past and present earnings.

Net sales Indicates that gross sales have been reduced for returned products, discounts taken for prompt payment of invoices, allowances for damaged products, and trade promotions or price reductions.

Net working capital (NWC) Formulated as current assets less current liabilities.

Net working capital (NWC) investment In investment valuation, formulated as investment in inventory plus investment in accounts receivable minus accounts payable spontaneous financing equals net working capital investment.

Nominal estimates Estimates that include inflation.

Nontraditional evaluations For example, information technology and strategic plan evaluation using traditional valuation approaches.

Note Typically a debt with a maturity of less than 10 years.

O

Off-balance-sheet financing Entering into a long-term lease, gaining the long-term use of the asset, and never recognizing this additional commitment (or liability).

Oil-well pump problem When in a calculation of the internal rate of return some intermediate outflows cause multiple solutions.

Open market share repurchase (OMR) OMR announcements enable firms to create for themselves options to exchange cash for its shares.

Operating cash flows Also called free cash flows.

Operating cycle The length of time that it takes from the time raw material is received until cash is collected from its sale.

Operating lease A contractual arrangement wherein the lessor agrees to provide an asset to the lessee for a specified period of time. The lessee agrees to make periodic payments to the lessor for use of the asset. From the lessor's point of view, has three elements: (1) the cash flows received from the lease contract, (2) the expected market or salvage value of the asset, and (3) the value of an American put option.

Operating service lease A variation of the operating lease is an operating lease that includes maintenance services in addition to financing.

Opportunity costs Represent cash flows that could be realized from the best alternative use of a surplus asset that will be engaged in the proposed project. Cost of what the funds could earn on an investment of equal risk.

Opportunity cost of capital All cash flows are discounted at the appropriate market-determined opportunity cost of capital in order to determine their present values.

Optimal decision rule (value additivity principle) Decision-making principle that considers all appropriate (incremental after-tax) cash flows, discounts cash flows at the appropriate market-determined opportunity cost of capital, selects from a group of mutually exclusive projects the one that maximizes shareholders' wealth, and allows managers to consider each project independently from all others. Also known as the *value additivity principle*.

Option to defer development For example, for a restaurant an investment in a piece of land in a developing area without incurring the construction costs of that restaurant until the sight proves more attractive.

Option to expand or grow The option to expand the scale of a project's operation is equivalent to a call option.

Option to shrink The option to shrink the scale of a project's operations is equivalent to a put option.

Original issue discount (OID) debt Debt may be issued at a discount from its maturity value to yield a percentage rate comparable to debt with specified interest rates. The OID variation is to issue debt with interest rates below those on comparable instruments, requiring that the offer price be below their maturity or redemption price.

Over-the-counter security markets The term used for all the buying and selling activity in securities that does not take place on a stock exchange.

P

Partnership The association of two or more persons to conduct a business enterprise.

Par value The maturity value or the stated face value of the debt.

Payback period (PBP) A capital valuation technique. The number of years required to return the original investment. Although the payback method is used frequently as a simple rule of thumb, it has serious conceptual weaknesses because it ignores the fact that (1) some receipts come in beyond the PBP and (2) a dollar received today is more valuable than a dollar received in the future (the time value of money).

Pecking order theory Says that companies will first use sources of internally generated funds to finance their activities, then net debt financing (net of repayments), and finally new equity financing.

Pension committee Invests the funds involved in employee pension plans.

Percentage-of-sales method All positive and negative cash flows are expressed as a percentage of sales in planning or valuation analysis.

Period cost Another term for an expense within a time period.

Perpetual cash flow Cash flows that continue forever.

Perpetual valuation model The present value of cash flows that continue forever.

Perpetuity A special case of an annuity wherein the stream of cash flows goes on forever.

Pooling-of-interests method (pooling method) An accounting method for mergers in which all accounts are simply added; it is no longer permitted.

Preemptive right Gives holders of common stock the first option to purchase additional issues of common stock.

Preferred stock Has claims and rights ahead of common stock but behind all bonds.

Preliminary prospectus Also known as a red herring, an SEC registration statement containing all of the customary information except the offering price.

Present value The current value of a series of cash flows.

Price/earnings (P/E) ratios Compare the market price per share to earnings per share.

Priority of claims A senior mortgage has prior claims on assets and earnings.

Private equity placement Purchase of investments by a privately owned firm.

Private placements Direct business loans with a maturity of more than 15 years.

Probabilistic techniques Applicable to the development of cash flows and capital evaluation. Probabilities are applied to the various cash flows and expected values are estimated. Monte Carlo simulation takes the probabilistic evaluation techniques a step further.

Probability analysis Probabilities under alternative future states of the world as assigned.

Processing float The time required by the seller to process the customer's records.

Profitability index (PI) A capital valuation technique that divides the present value of projected cash flows by the investment amount.

Prospectus Summarizes the content of the SEC registration statement for the general public. The document provides an overview of the company, along with historical financial information; discusses the specific uses of the funds; and specifies the underlying business risks. The prospectus also lists the costs of raising the funds.

Proxy Provision is made for the temporary transfer of the right to vote by this instrument.

Purchase method An approved method of merger accounting in which the excess of the price paid over the value of acquired net assets is assigned to goodwill or other intangibles.

Put option The holder has right but is not required to sell an asset to the issuer at a specified price

R

Real-options analysis Helps systematize the decision process. The analytical frameworks developed in a real-options analysis can uncover new dimensions and provide deeper insights. This type of analysis also provides a common language for communication among various managerial functions (strategy, research, production, marketing, and so on). Real-options analysis may provide insights and intuitions that may sometimes challenge conventional thinking. For example, the higher the volatility of outcomes may increase the value of the investment program.

Real property Real estate (land and buildings).

Reasonable needs Include "specific, definite, and feasible plans" for the use of the accumulated earnings.

Registration statement Statement containing all relevant financial and business information on a firm filed with the SEC.

Reinvestment rate The interest rate used to discount cash flows that are retained in the investment.

Reinvestment rate assumption An inaccurate use of terminology for what should be called the *opportunity cost assumption*. The term *reinvestment rate* is misleading because it causes people to become involved in a debate about whether or not cash flows from the project can be reinvested at the IRR of the project.

Residual value The value of a property at the end of a lease. It also can be more broadly used as the terminal value or salvage value in an investment analysis.

Retained earnings Include cumulative earnings in the corporation that were retained (i.e., not paid out as dividends) in the corporation.

Return on retained earnings Similar to the return on equity except for the distortional effects of stock issuance and repurchases and the fact that the effects of accounting adjustments have been eliminated. Calculated, for example, as 2005 net income divided by the 2004 retained earnings.

Right to issue additional securities Mortgage bonds can also be classified with respect to the right to issue additional obligations, pledging already encumbered property.

Right to vote Feature of a holding agreement that generally permits preferred stockholders to elect a minority of the board (say, three out of nine directors).

Risk-adjusted cost of capital A risk adjustment is made to a risk free rate.

Road show A presentation by a company (and often with the investment banker) used to market its stock to potential investors before it is actually available for sale.

Rollover strategy Annual borrowing and refinancing rather than a multi-period time frame.

Rule of 72 A useful mathematical relationship. Divide 72 by the interest rate to obtain the number of years required for an investment to double or divide 72 by the number of years that it takes a sum to double to obtain the rate of return on that investment.

S

Salary and profit-sharing committee Responsible for salary administration as well as the classification and compensation of top-level executives. Also called the compensation committee.

Sale and leaseback arrangement A firm owning land, buildings, or equipment sells the property to a financial institution and simultaneously executes an agreement to lease the property back for a certain period under specific terms.

Sales-type lease Leasing used by manufacturers or dealers to market their products.

Sandbagging predispositions Operating units whose post-completion reviews indicate that this unit continually exceeds evaluation and authorization projections.

Scope of a lien Bonds can also be classified with respect to the scope of their lien. A lien is granted on certain specified property. When a specific lien exists, the security for a first or second mortgage is a specifically designated property. On the other hand, a blanket mortgage pledges all real property currently owned by the company.

Senior mortgage A superseding lien, such as a primary mortgage. It is a lien or claim senior to others.

Sensitivity analysis Examines the degree to which changes in key assumptions effect the output such as NPV. Sensitivity analysis occurs by varying each assumption individually and observing the resulting change in the output such as NPV.

Scenario analysis Examines various business models or circumstances by combining adjustments to a number of assumptions simultaneously. Varies two or more variables simultaneously and observe the resulting change in the output such as NPV.

Selling group Each investment banker has business relationships with other investment bankers and dealers and thus has a group composed of these people.

Shareholder return Measures what shareholders actually earn over a period of time; defined as the sum of capital appreciation and dividends over a period of time.

Shelf registration A process that quickens the registration process, but it is only available to large firms (more than $150 million in assets). This process allows the issuing company to file the general background SEC registration material (company's history and historical financials) well in advance of a potential issue of securities.

Sinking fund payment Future obligations are deposited to help cover the requirements in the future.

Sinking fund provision One form is to have the firm deposit funds with a trustee, who accumulates the funds and their earnings to retire the debt at maturity. More generally, a sinking fund is used to purchase a specified amount of the issue periodically.

Sinking fund requirement Calls for the purchase and retirement of a given percentage of the preferred stock each year.

Soft capital rationing Capital rationing imposed by a company's management.

Sole proprietorship A business owned by one individual.

Specialized VC financing Financing provided by venture capital firms.

Specific lien When a specific lien exists, the security for a first or second mortgage is a specifically designated property.

Staged capital commitment (SCC) Financing provide by lenders to new firms at benchmark dates when performance has been evaluated.

Stakeholder Anyone who has any interest in the firm.

Statement of cash flows Presents the underlying transactions that cause the cash balance to change between periods of time.

Stock dividend Dividend paid in additional shares of stock instead of in cash and involving a book-keeping transfer from retained earnings to the capital stock account.

Stock-for-stock transaction A merger transaction in which the buyer uses its stock to buy the stock of the seller.

Subordinated debt Has claims on assets after unsubordinated debt in the event of liquidation.

Sunk cost A cost (or cash outlay) that has already been made.

Switching option A general name applied to a few similar types of decisions. Restarting or shutting down options pertain to (as their name suggests) restarting or shutting down plant/line operations. The switching option also relates to flexible manufacturing equipment that may cost more initially but can produce more than one product. Manufacturing flexibility has value captured within a switching option.

Syndicate A temporary association for the purpose of carrying out a specific objective.

T

Target capital structure A corporation may establish some long-term goals or objectives surrounding its capital structure, which should be based on the future market values.

Term loans Direct business loans with a maturity of more than one year but less than 15 years, with provisions for systematic repayment (amortization during the life of the loan).

Term structure The relationship between short-term and long-term interest rates.

Terminal rate of return (TRR) A capital valuation technique that is also called the modified internal rate of return. The interest rate that equates the cost of the investment with the accumulated future value of the intermediate cash flows assumed to be reinvested at an appropriate risk-adjusted cost of capital. The TRR explicitly incorporates an opportunity cost of capital as a reinvestment rate.

Terminal value Accumulated future value within TRR. It also can be more broadly used as the residual value or salvage value in an investment analysis.

Time value of money A dollar today is worth more than a dollar received at some future date.

Total asset turnover Sales divided by total assets.

Trade-off theory Considers the tax deductibility of interest from debt financing a strong motivator for increasing leverage.

Transnationality index (TNI) The percentage of a firm's business activities that are performed in foreign countries.

Treasurer Handles the acquisition and custody of funds.

Treasury stock Reflects amounts paid for repurchase shares of stock that are no longer outstanding but remain available for issuance. This reduces the value of the stockholders' equity account.

Trustee Presumed to act at all times for the protection of the bond holders and on their behalf.

Two-for-one split Stockholders receive two shares for each one previously held.

Two-stage supernormal growth model (TSSGM) Similar to the valuation model in that it derives cash flows from operations on a percentage-of-sales basis.

U

Unlimited funds A financial situation in which a firm is able to accept all independent projects that provide an acceptable rate of return.

V

Value additivity principle See *Optimal decision rule*.

Value maximization Provides criteria for pricing the use of resources such as capital investments in plant and machinery.

W

Warrant *See* Debt with warrants.

Weighted average cost of capital (WACC) The cost of capital is calculated using the percent rate on the portion of financing by debt and equity funds.

Winner's curse Phenomenon in which the actual or potential competition of other bidders causes the winning bidder to pay too much.

Working capital recovery In investment valuation, this represents recovery of all working capital over the life of a project in that project's final year. It assumes that all inventory is sold, all receivables are collected, and all suppliers are paid.

Z

Zero coupon bonds ("zeros") The bonds pay no periodic interest, but their maturity value represents interest earned over the life of the bond.

Zero-growth valuation model A valuation model that assumes constant perpetual cash flows. The numerator is unchanged; the denominator is the discount rate.

Figures and tables are indicated by "f" and "t" following the page number.